385

261335 P

11/20/66

PREFACE
to
DRAMA

An Introduction to
Dramatic Literature and Theater Art

by

CHARLES W. COOPER
WHITTIER COLLEGE

THE RONALD PRESS COMPANY ⁊ NEW YORK

FOREWORD

THIS TEXTBOOK for undergraduates is a systematic introduction to Dramatic Literature within a theatrical context and to Theater Art within a literary context.

It comprises two parts. "Part One: the Preface" consists of five essays on dramatic theory, to which are added five shorter plays as examples, with introductory notes and commentary. The point of view of the essays is psychological, and the drama is observed in its relation to common elements in human behavior. Consideration of it is controlled by the discriminating use of certain literary and theatrical terms. Thoughtful analysis of the content of a play enforces close interpretation of the lines and the patterning of the complex dramatic experience. This, in turn, calls for recognition of the theatrical potential of the playscript and for unusually creative reading. Once fully realized, the play then invites discussion in historical perspective and critical consideration of its form and ideas.

"Part Two: the Plays" is an anthology of eight longer dramas, preceded by introductory notes and followed by pairs of selections from dramatic criticism. The plays in *Preface to Drama,* counting the short ones in Part One, make up a baker's dozen, representative of our Western Civilization. Here are exemplified the short play, the medium, and the long—comedy, tragedy, and other types—classical, romantic, and realistic—ancient, more modern, and contemporary—European, British, and American. A handful of the great historic dramatists are here: Sophocles, Shakespeare, and Molière. So, too, are the several fathers of modern drama: Ibsen, Shaw, and O'Neill. And here, as well, are significant recent dramatists: Tennessee Williams and Arthur Miller. Modern literary playwrights, Laurence Housman and Thornton Wilder, rub elbows with theatrical actor-dramatists, Noel Coward and Howard Lindsay. Even the librettist, W. S. Gilbert, has his niche. But the plays selected for inclusion are not merely representative; they have proved to be evocative of student interest and of class discussion, whether for their enduring values or for their immediate relevancy.

iii

To these two parts is added an Appendix containing a variety of supplementary materials: notes for the essays and introductions, queries to stimulate closer reading or discussion, specially devised outline-worksheets to guide disciplined analysis, and suggestions for study and further reading.

In a variety of ways, *Preface to Drama* will serve both those who approach the Drama as one of the major types of Literature and those who approach it as the enduring expression of the Theater. It will serve as an introduction to the drama—whether as a course in English, Speech and Drama, or the Humanities.

To acknowledge indebtedness can be a pleasure as well as a duty. Helpful indeed have been the critical suggestions made by those persons who have read the manuscript in whole or in part: Dr. Ray Nichols and Mr. George Stoughton, Dr. and Mrs. Arthur C. Berdahl, Dr. James Marshall and Dr. Benjamin G. Whitten, my wife Edris B. Cooper, and the students in my courses who gave me the benefit of their frank comments.

Upon my continuing debt to Dr. I. A. Richards and Dr. Albert W. Upton—too great for payment in full—I make another installment of gratitude.

C. W. C.

Whittier College
January 12, 1955

CONTENTS

Part One
THE PREFACE

I

II

v

Part Two

THE PLAYS

I

II

III

IV

V

VI

VII

VIII

Part One

THE PREFACE

I. PRELIMINARY

Orientation to Drama

Wherever and whenever humans have progressed beyond the mere struggle for physical existence, to gods and recreation and self-expression, there has been theater in some sense. . . . —SHELDON CHENEY, *The Theatre*

IN THE THEATER a musical (overture) serves as a pleasant and useful introduction to the comedy or opera about to be performed. In much the same way this preliminary orientation to Drama will serve as a prelude to the essays and plays that follow in this book.

You have already enjoyed seeing plays, certainly, though most of them have probably been in the form of movies, radio dramas, and TV shows. Except for school productions, you may have seen only a few regular stageplays. And possibly you have read no more than a handful of dramas. With the changing emphasis in education, *Julius Caesar* or some other one of Shakespeare's works is the only play studied in common by the great majority of students in most of our public high schools.

If, then, your theater and drama experiences have been few, this will be your chance to fill a gap, we hope not unpleasantly. If, however, you are an old hand at playreading and playgoing, you will be expected to build further upon what knowledge you have already acquired. Your present store and interests, whatever they are, will be with you now as you take your seat and as this overture begins.

§ 1. DRAMATIC, THEATRIC, AND SEMANTIC ELEMENTS IN LIFE

As a first step in our preliminary orientation, let us consider certain elements, commonly observed in human life, that combine to form the drama. Think of your family and friends, your sports and recreation, your business and politics, your social and cultural activities, your education and religion, your inner life and outer behavior. In

3

all of these aspects of your personal life you may observe tension and conflict, mimicry and display, meaning and value. These we shall call the dramatic, the theatric, and the semantic elements in life.

First, let us turn our thoughts to the dramatic element of tension and conflict.

Every one of us has his own personal will and desires, needs and compulsions. You may say that there is nothing at all dramatic about most of them because they are readily fulfilled. But each of us has, daily, certain wants and wishes, demands or impulses that are denied. We come up against all sorts of obstacles and personal opponents. Other people have wills and desires that run counter to ours—rivals for favors or honors or positions. Impersonal obstacles, also, may confront us—storms, depressions, wars. Or we may be blocked by contrary desires or wills within our own personalities. At any rate, tensions develop.

Situations of opposition are charged with emotion. You have at certain crucial times in life found yourself opposed by parental will or social convention, by unrequited love or temptation to wrongdoing, by poverty or misfortune, by superior athletic skill or inflexible man-made or natural laws, etc. Desperately to want an appointment that is refused; to desire affection that is denied; to long for recognition that is withheld; to yearn for clothes or a convertible or good times you can't afford; to be pitted against better or bitter competitors in sport; to be determined to make something of your life no matter what may stand in the way; to have your personal values attacked or undermined or challenged—such emotionally charged situations of opposition are loaded with dramatic potential.

They are most dramatic, of course, if the tension between desire and opposition really leads to conflict—to scheming and strategy, to strife and struggle, to successes and setbacks, to suffering and suspense. Such conflict ends finally in fulfillment or utter frustration of desire, achievement of will or ultimate defeat.

When the conflict is over, the tension is resolved, and the drama is done. The ending of a human drama is wonderful or terrible or amusing or unexpected or depressing or tragic—but it is no longer dramatic. It is the tension and conflict—conflict or competition or compensation or other combative or adjustive behavior—that we have called the dramatic element in life.

The second element we shall call theatric. It was introduced in terms of mimicry and display.

Mimicry—imitation of speech, actions, and appearance—is more widespread in human and even animal life than you might at first think. Children copy their elders; they make believe and pretend in their play. Adolescents learn and practice the manners, the social behavior, the conversation and dress of those whom they choose as their models. Adults mimic the men of distinction, the women of glamor or fashion—as advertisers well know.

It is not only when you dress up for a masked ball or give an imitation of an eccentric professor that you are engaging in mimicry. Your formal clothes, small talk, and manners—with the help of Emily Post, *Esquire,* and *Vogue*—are imitative. So are your every-day behavior and dress—whether you choose to appear casual or collegiate or conservative. Each of us acts a part and all the world's a stage. This universal element of mimicry gets its name from the theatrical mimes or comic actors of ancient Greece and Rome.

There is a related theatric element in life that we shall call exhibi-tion and display, taking off and putting on. Again, you can see in children this tendency to show off and get attention in a variety of ways. In adolescence such display becomes infused with both sexual and social significance, the desire to be attractive and to be accepted. And so it continues into adult life.

We are all aware of the elaborate pageantry, the outward show of certain public events, a national convention or a coronation. So, too, with lodge rituals, fraternity initiations, and commencements. Ostentatious living and entertaining give evidence of this theatric element in life, as do formal dances and fancy-dress balls. Your grotesque mask and costume for Halloween or Mardi gras—your domino for a masquerade—these also go back through the Renais-sance masques and medieval festivals to ancient mimes and mimicry.

Indeed, you can easily see that many fashions are designed to attract by outward show, to display as much as to conceal, to reveal as much as to clothe. This is as true of formal gowns as it is of beachwear, and only somewhat differently for men than for women. Exhibitionism, always held within certain limits by social restraints, is apparently both normal and universal. Display and decency in costume and conduct have contended through the ages, with the conception of decency changing with the times.

We have called this tendency to display or outward show a theat-ric element in life, remembering the ancient origins of Greek drama in pageantry, the fertility rites and revelry honoring Dionysus, god of sex and wine and the theater.

The third matter to which we shall give our attention is here called the semantic element of meaning and value.

Somewhat less will be said here about this wisdom element—the human inclination to interpret life, to seek its meaning, to philosophize, to reflect upon and judge events and personalities. Everyone engages in some metaphysical speculation. Children ask their elders unanswerable questions about life and death. Adolescents develop their private views of man and the universe, and think through the bases of their religious faith or behave in a way that suggests a personal philosophy. Medicine men and ancient prophets, priests and rabbis and ministers, parents and teachers and grandparents—brothers and sisters, friends and lovers in their intimate counsel—reveal this wisdom element in life. And you will find it in folklore and proverbs as well as in preachments and philosophy—this reading of the meaning of life.

It is not only in religious contexts that this wisdom element is to be seen. Such great documents as our Declaration of Independence, the Constitution of the United States, the Charter of the United Nations—the Law itself—are expressions of political and legal philosophy. The curricula of colleges and universities are based upon thoughtful consideration of what may be meant by the good, the true, and the beautiful—the value of personality—freedom and responsibility—the individual and society—vocational and liberal arts, etc. The Olympic games and intercollegiate sports, service organizations and fraternities, marriage and the home, religion and the church—these are all institutions that reveal, in their different ways, man's concern with the values of life.

The dramatic element, of which we spoke first, is tension and conflict. The theatric element, second, is mimicry and display. The semantic or wisdom element, from which we have just turned, is meaning and value. You will find these separate elements here and there throughout life. But you will also find them joined and together. *The dramatic, the theatric, and the semantic elements of life combine to form the Drama.*

Think, for a moment, of the *Julius Caesar* that you read in school —or of the most recent play you have seen in the theater. You will recall the tensions within Brutus and his conflicts with Caesar and Antony, and with Cassius. These characters and incidents, and the dialogue through which they are revealed, are part of Shakespeare's imitation. But *Julius Caesar,* whether read or performed, is more than the mimicry and display of human tensions and conflicts; it is rich in human understanding—Brutus representing the misled ideal-ist—and evokes in the reader or beholder deep thoughts of the meaning and values of life. So, too, with a contemporary comedy or musical, though doubtless with less significance.

It is in the theater, then, that you may see human tensions and conflicts so imitated and displayed as to reflect the meaning and values of human life. The dramatic, the theatric, and the semantic elements of life unite in the Drama.

§ 2. DRAMA IN THREE DIMENSIONS

As a second step in this preliminary orientation, let us describe the Drama (thus dignified with a capital D) by moving out in three different directions.

We shall, first of all, explore the great *diversity* of the Drama, considering all the different sorts of dramatic activity going on in any one city or college town. Perhaps our town, wherever it may be, is not one of the cities having a season of professional plays com-ing from Broadway, for New York is still the heart of the American theater. But there are certainly performances by community players, church guilds, college or university theaters—and there are high school plays as well. Then, too, there are the movie houses and drive-ins, radio drama, and TV—all of them providing mimetic fare of dramatic interest and of more or less significance.

But you can also see much other dramatic activity related to all of this. Stores are selling books of dramas and recordings of plays. Newsstands and the mails distribute magazines about the drama, such as *Variety, Theatre Arts, Educational Theatre Journal,* and *Shakespeare Quarterly.* Journals and newspapers such as *The New Yorker, Time, The Nation,* and the *Daily News* regularly print dramatic criticism or play reviews. Public, school, college, and uni-versity libraries circulate great numbers of books on the drama and theater.

Now consider the study of drama in courses on your own campus. Masterpieces of the drama are often read in Freshman English or Basic Communications (perhaps *Hamlet* or *Emperor Jones*)—in Sophomore Literature or World Civilization (*Everyman* and *Doctor Faustus* or *Œdipus the King* and *Tartuffe*)—in various courses on the periods of English literature, history of drama and theater, and Shakespeare. Then, too, you will find courses in dramatic inter-pretation, acting, play production—probably also in playwriting, in directing, in scene design—perhaps in stagecraft, stage lighting, costume, make-up. And your town or city will doubtless also have women's clubs with drama sections, and special schools and private teachers of dramatic art. In the public schools you will see the use of creative dramatics by teachers of primary grades. And you will hear of dramatic therapy as used by psychiatrists and in mental institutions.

Such, then, is the diversity of the Drama in your own immediate environment, your college or home town. Let us now strike out to survey the Drama in a second dimension, its geographic *distribution*.

Across the face of our land—from Hollywood to Broadway—you will find the Drama: from the Penthouse and Showboat theaters of the University of Washington in Seattle to the Dallas Little Theater; from the Romona pageant at Hemet, California, to the Roanoke drama off the coast of North Carolina; from the straw-hat summer stock in New England to the Colorado festival at Central City; from the Folger Memorial Library in Washington, D.C., to the old opera house in Virginia City, Nevada; from the American Educational Theater Association meeting in Cincinnati, or elsewhere, to the National Theater Council in New York; from the eighth grade play in Sioux Falls to the Pasadena Playhouse with its College of the Theater! The Drama is by no means concentrated in New York City.

Nor is this extent limited to our own shores. We think at once of England, its London theaters, its Shakespeare Memorial at Stratford, its Malvern Festival, its rich dramatic literature (classics in our tongue), its drama scholars at Oxford and Cambridge. Then we turn to the Continent—to Paris, its theaters and playwrights, its opera and comedies—to the provincial cities and even (in their own ways) the towns—then to the Passion Play in Oberammergau—and on to Central Europe and to Russia, where dramatic culture has become an instrument of the State. And, as we go further—to the Orient, to China and Japan; thence down to Burma, to India; across to Africa; and again jump to South America and up home by way of Central America and Mexico—in every corner of the world today we find, in addition to radio and movies, a certain amount of native drama and theater, whether a part of the religious heritage or the contemporary culture of the people.

Such is the wide distribution of the Drama. But there is yet a third dimension of which you may think—the *development* of the Drama—for it reaches back in time to the very dawn of mankind.

The cultural anthropologist will tell us about the dramatic and theatric and wisdom elements in the lives of primitive peoples, and the archeologist will tell us of his theatrical findings in the rubble of forgotten civilizations. And who among us is not interested in the dramatic activities of our American Indians as we can still see them on western reservations.

What we think of as the main stream of our western Drama, however, has developed reasonably directly from the historic Greek drama and theater of the fifth century B.C.—you will read Sophocles' *Antigone* later in this volume—and from the religious and especially Dionysian worship more dimly seen beyond that. Later there were times of apparent dormancy; then new beginnings in the Church of the Middle Ages. With the Renaissance came a rediscovery of ancient drama; then there were interruptions, new directions, foreign influences—and the modern resurgence of drama—marking the course of the 2500 years of dramatic and theatrical history down to our own times. A further sketch of this history will be given in the last of our five essays.

The great *diversity* of drama today, the world-wide *distribution* of it, the long *development* of it—these may be thought of as the three dimensions of Drama.

§ 3. THE AMBIGUITY OF "DRAMA"

So far we have been considering things of various sorts, but without any serious attempt to control the words used to name them. Now, as a third step in our orientation, we shall take a close look at the word "drama" in its several quite different, if related, senses.

When you hear a person say that he is "majoring in drama," you recognize that his activities are largely different from those of the person who is "studying Elizabethan drama." When you read that *A Doll's House* is "neither tragedy nor comedy, but drama" and then that *King Lear* is "greater as a drama than as a play," you realize that the word is being used in two yet different senses. When you say that *Death of a Salesman* is "full of drama," you mean something other than when you refer to "life's little dramas"—or when you tell an overemotional friend to "cut the drama!"

These various senses of "drama," as you can see, fall into three general categories:

First, sometimes the word "drama" is used to refer to *theater art*. "The Drama" is, in this sense, a rough synonym for theater art and may suggest all of the arts and crafts involved in the making of plays —from playwriting through acting, directing, scene design, etc., to stage management. And sometimes "a drama" refers to the stage-play itself; at other times, to a stageplay of the serious, though not tragic, sort.

Second, the word "drama" is used to refer to one branch of *literature*. "The Drama" is, in this sense, one of the three major types of literature, dramatic literature. "A drama," then, is used to name a playbook when considered as a work of dramatic literature. Sometimes the word "drama" (or the French equivalent, *drame*) is used to name a type of dramatic literature intermediate between tragedy and comedy, and "a drama" may then refer to an example of this type, a serious play.

Third, sometimes the word "drama" is used to refer to incidents and situations, not part of the theater or literature, but part of *life*. The qualities that characterize the Drama and dramas (in the various senses above) may be seen in life itself, as we suggested in the opening of this essay. It may be the tension and conflict element that marks the "drama" you witness on the street or in a courtroom. Or it may be the mimetic and display element that is designated "drama." Or it may be the deep stirring of emotional response, empathy and sympathy—with a feeling of significance and value— that calls the word "drama" into use. But these drama-in-life uses of the word are largely sense developments by analogy or metaphor from the theatrical and literary senses described above.

With the word "drama" commonly used in ten or a dozen different senses, you will have to be alert as listener and reader to avoid misinterpretation, and you should make a special effort when you speak or write to make your own use of the word clear. Ambiguity is inherent in language. It is not necessarily harmful; it simply needs to be controlled.

§ 4. LITERATURE, THEATER ART, AND DRAMA

Theater Art and Literature may be considered—to move forward another step in our orientation—as two quite different ones of the seven fine arts. You can name more than seven arts, of course. Man has engaged in creative art activity of great diversity, expressing his various thoughts and visions and feelings in forms that, for him and others, have had beauty and significance. But certain sorts of art works, the art activities creating them, and the art responses to them, have achieved special status in our culture. So, architecture, sculpture, painting, dance, theater art, literature, and music are time-honored in Western Civilization.

It would be interesting to explore the relations of each of these seven fine arts to all of the others. But it is only with theater and literature and their interconnections with the others that we are here concerned.

Theater art has most obvious relations to all of the fine arts—and to many of the so-called applied, decorative, and practical arts as well. Theater art is characteristically housed in theaters that are works of architecture, and details of architecture are often represented in stage settings by scene designers. Sculpture, whether good or bad, has often (from ancient times) adorned theater buildings. Painting, perhaps since the days of the Greeks, has sometimes, though not always, been used in suggesting the scene of the play—backdrops, wooden wings, box sets, etc. Dancing—not only pantomime but choreography—is a component of today's musical comedy, and it has been a part of the theater in every period since its primitive beginnings. Literature has not only fed the theater with story materials appropriate for dramatization, but has itself fed upon the playscripts of each age. It has considered and preserved the classics of the theater. Music is especially friendly to the theater, providing incidental adornment for stageplays and joining hands in musical comedy and opera.

Literature, too, can be seen in its interrelations with certain of the other fine and applied arts. With some stretch of the imagination you can even see a connection between it and architecture, sculpture, painting, and dance; literature has provided them with themes for treatment and has itself found subject matter in them. The most obvious kinship, however, is between literature and theater art, as we have just seen, and between literature and music—for songs are poems with music, and poetry itself, with its strongly auditory and rhythmic quality, has its own special "music," whether to the ear or the mind's ear.

Now let us take a closer look at these two arts that are the subject of our present interest.

Theater art is that one of the fine arts whose media are human actors and the stage. It consists essentially of dramatic and theatrical productions and of the various sorts of creative activity that call them into being. There are, of course, many kinds of productions in the theater. They range all the way from grand opera to burlesque and include musical comedy, revue, variety show, vaudeville, and circus. There are also pantomimes, dance-dramas, ballets, marionette and puppet plays, motion pictures, etc. All of these various productions belong in one way or another to the theater, and most of them are in some degree works of art. However, theater art as here more narrowly defined is the art of the "legitimate theater," as the old licensed theaters were called in which regular plays were performed. The characteristic unit of theater art, then, is what we shall call "a stageplay."

Literature, on the other hand, is that one of the fine arts whose medium is written (now usually printed) language. Literature, then, consists essentially of books—the good books if not exclusively the great ones, the books that are also works of art. So viewed, literature has three main branches: The first is poetry, which includes literary works that are in verse and that are not in dramatic form—that is, poems. The second is prose literature, which includes literary works that are in prose (not verse) and that are not in dramatic form—that is, novels, short stories, essays, biographies, etc. The third branch is dramatic literature, which includes all literary works, whether in prose or in verse, that are in dramatic form (in dialogue with stage directions)—that is, those playbooks considered to be works of art, or what we shall call "dramas."

The Drama in its most comprehensive sense, then, comprises both theater art and dramatic literature.

With that we are now ready to consider more closely the two principal sorts of art works that characterize the drama as a composite fine art.

§ 5. "A STAGEPLAY" AND "A DRAMA" DEFINED

It will be a simple matter now to conclude our preliminary orientation by defining in sequence a number of terms that we have been using with increasing discrimination.

A stageplay is a story presented directly by actors upon a stage before an audience.

As you reread this one-sentence definition of "stageplay," recall particular plays you have seen in the theater—high school or college plays, community or professional productions. Think again of *Julius Caesar,* particularly if you have seen it on the stage. Or, having heard a recorded performance or having seen the film version, you may imagine how it would be if staged.

What it means to define a stageplay as a kind of *story* will be considered further in the next essay, but it has already been suggested in our discussion of the dramatic, theatric, and semantic elements in life. A story is a narration or representation of people doing things—desiring or willing—with scheming and strategy, with strife and struggle, with successes and setbacks, with suffering and suspense—finally achieving or failing. For example: Noble Brutus, who is deeply disturbed by Caesar's rise to absolute power as a popular dictator, is drawn by selfish Cassius into the conspiracy that assassinates Caesar but spares his favorite, Mark Antony, who pursues the conspirators—and Brutus—to their death. Or a story may simply present people to whom things happen—passive rather than active people—but present them in such a way as to hold our attention and evoke our thoughtful and sympathetic interest.

Unlike the other sorts of story—the novel, epic, ballad, short story, puppet play, motion picture, radio drama, and TV show—the stageplay is essentially a story acted out by living people. It is *presented directly by actors*. And the actors use four different means to do this: (1) stage business or *pantomime*, (2) *dialogue*, (3) *costume*, and (4) *make-up*. The actors impersonate the characters in the story. They act the story out by means of appropriate stage business, gesture, and facial expression—pantomime. They engage in speaking "in character" the lines of the dialogue. They are costumed and made-up (or wear masks) to represent the characters. As you think of any stageplay you have seen, you will recognize that these statements describe the manner of presentation directly by actors.

(Cinema, you will observe in contrast, does *not* present its story directly by actors. Neither does radio or TV. A pantomime play, which uses only mimetic action, and a dramatic reading, which uses only dialogue, are *not* stageplays as we fully expect them to be, though they are stories presented directly by actors. The moving picture of *Julius Caesar* is not, then, a stageplay. Nor is the recording—much like a radio drama—of Orson Welles' famous Mercury production.)

Furthermore, a stageplay is presented by actors *upon a stage*. Though we are accustomed to the performance of plays upon a platform stage, let us extend our use of the word "stage" to mean any place set apart for the use of actors in acting out a story in the presence of an audience. That would include the circular floor (orchestra) of the ancient amphitheater and the central floor of the modern arena theater as well as the medieval pageant or wagon stage, the deal boards set up on trestles in an inn yard, the platform and related stages of Shakespeare's time, and the picture-frame stage of today as it gradually developed.

The stage provides the immediate environment for the actors in acting out the story of the stageplay. Theater artists and craftsmen have usually made use of three or four different means to make the stage appropriate or meaningful as the place of the action: (1) *setting,* (2) *properties,* (3) *light,* and (4) *sound* and *music.* Whether scenery as usually considered is used or not, the stage always provides the physical setting for the action. Usually there are some properties —whether furniture or small objects manipulated or carried—used by the actors in acting out the story. Though stage lighting as we think of it is largely modern, at all times light has been essential in making the actors visible, and it has also had special and symbolic use from early times. Sound effects—and music, too—have always been part of the staging of plays. Your momentary reflection upon any play you have seen—whether *Julius Caesar* or some other—will serve to illustrate the importance of the stage and of the setting, props, lights, and sound in its presentation.

However, a story acted out upon a stage is not fully a stageplay unless it is presented *before an audience.* Anyone who has sat through a dress rehearsal realizes how far such a presentation lacks an essential ingredient of the stageplay. For the responses of the spectators, the interactions of actors and audience, are a very real part of the play itself as a work of theater art. Doubtless you have yourself sensed the audience participation in stageplays you have experienced in the theater: the laughter and tears, the nervous tension and suspense, the group responses of pity and fear, the personal attraction and sympathy for a character as portrayed by an actor, the final applause for the cast and their bowing in return.

To summarize this discussion and definition:

A stageplay is a story presented directly by actors (using pantomime, dialogue, costumes, and make-up) *upon a stage* (using setting, properties, lights, and sound) *before an audience.*

Let us proceed more briefly now to consider two or three related terms.

A playscript is the written dialogue and stage directions used in creating a stageplay.

In the next essay we shall consider further the playscript as the playwright devises or adapts the story, conceives the characters, writes the dialogue, and works out the stage directions. You might imagine the playscript of *Julius Caesar* as Shakespeare wrote it, though no one of his plays has survived in his own handwriting or even in a prompter's copy. But from the printed form—*Caesar* was not published for a quarter of a century after it was first written—you can get some notion of how it looked: verse dialogue with the barest stage directions, hardly more than mere entrances and exits.

It is important here to note *how essentially different the playscript is from the stageplay* created from it—the copy of *Julius Caesar* and the living drama in the theater. The one consists of black marks, words on paper; the other, of living persons moving and speaking upon a stage. Yet the pattern and sequence of words that make up the playscript have an amazing potential. They can evoke in the reader a complex response: a running sequence of thoughts and images that *imply* characters and *suggest* human relations and actions, dramatic tensions and conflicts and significant resolutions. Indeed, these words when translated by actors into speech and action upon a stage have the power to engage the interest of an audience of spectators and to pattern in their minds a meaningful human story. The playscript, then, is not a stageplay but a sort of blueprint from which a stageplay may be constructed and created.

Playscripts were handwritten manuscripts, of course, in earlier times. Today they are ordinarily typescripts. The word "script" serves as a common abbreviation for all three terms. For the rehearsal of a play, however, each actor may be given, not a complete script, but only his own part—his lines (with cues) and stage directions. Earlier written on a roll of paper, the actor's part is still called his rôle or "role." Now typed on one side of half-sheets of paper, the actor's part may be called his "sides"—and the number of these half-sheets is some measure of the length of his role. However, with ease of mimeographing and similar reproduction, complete scripts can now be more widely used by actors than formerly, and that brings us to the next term.

A playbook is the printed form of a playscript. There is, then, no essential difference between the "book," as it may be called, and the script; the terms are relatively synonymous. The playbook, as usually published and sold for use in dramatic production, is often printed from a copy of the playscript that has been somewhat abridged or altered in dialogue and amplified in stage directions during the process of rehearsal and production. Such playbooks are often cheaply printed and paper-bound as they are intended for use in the theater rather than in the library.

A drama is a playbook of literary quality. Some playbooks attract readers other than actors and directors intent upon staging a play. Such was the case with the quarto playbooks of Shakespeare's currently successful plays, though none such was published for *Julius Caesar.* People who have seen an outstanding stageplay sometimes want to read the dialogue for themselves. In this way they can revive or review their theater experience. Others, unable to see a successful stageplay in the theater, buy or borrow the book. Often, of course, readers of playbooks are disappointed—the mere printed dialogue and stage directions may be quite incapable of evoking a rich and meaningful story experience in the reader. It is true that outstanding stageplays—great works of theater art—are not necessarily based upon playscripts of the art quality that characterizes literature. The playbook versions of *Uncle Tom's Cabin* and *Rip Van Winkle* and the libretto of *Oklahoma!* are hardly literature.

On the other hand, the playbooks of many successful stageplays, like those reprinted in this volume, do have literary quality. They are capable of providing readers with meaningful and valuable reading experiences. Such playbooks kindle the imagination with "real" persons and scenes and actions, ring the sound of human speech within the mind's ear, stimulate a flow of interpretative and critical thoughts that engage the attention and maintain interest, create mood, and stir responsive emotions. Playbooks that possess the magic of this evocative quality are works of dramatic literature. We shall call them "dramas."

But now, certainly, it is high time to turn to the reading of a short drama that will serve to illustrate some of the things suggested in this preliminary essay, "Orientation to Drama"—but first, a few paragraphs to set the stage for your more enjoyable reading.

Introductory Note to *"A Good Lesson!"*

T HIS SHORT play is one of fifty-four that Laurence Housman wrote about Victoria, the queen who was England's constitutional monarch for two-thirds of the nineteenth century and gave her name to that era. She had been on the throne for twenty-eight years when Housman was born in 1865. Twenty-five years before this, young Victoria (but three years a queen) had married her cousin Albert, the handsome and irreproachable German princeling. As Housman grew up, he saw the aging Queen on a few public occasions. Of her Golden Jubilee in 1887 he wrote, "I saw the Queen really enjoying herself, laughing and crying with happiness. . . ." By the time she died in 1901, Laurence Housman's elder brother, A. E. Housman, the classics scholar and poet, had already published *The Shropshire Lad*, and Laurence Housman (aged thirty-six) was an established writer. His first success, *An Englishwoman's Love Letters* (1900), was published anonymously—and many readers believed that the letters were written by the beloved Queen herself!

It was from her own diaries and letters, as they became available, that Housman learned to know and understand Victoria as a very human little person. She had been dead only twenty years when, in 1921, his first playlets about her were privately performed and published. Thirty short plays based upon actual episodes in her life were published as *Victoria Regina* in 1934. No production of them was anticipated in the regular commercial theater, for Housman had already run afoul of the English Censor with an earlier play depicting royalty. But the book *Victoria Regina* attracted attention, and ten of the episodes were given at the experimental Gate Theater in London. Then Gilbert Miller staged them in New York with Helen Hayes and Vincent Price as Victoria and Albert and with settings and costumes by Rex Whistler. *Victoria Regina* was a popular success, ran 517 performances during the two seasons 1935-37, followed by long weeks in Chicago, San Francisco, and Los Angeles, and by a return to New York in 1938 for 87 more performances. It was then filmed. The book, too, was successful. *Victoria Regina* (with the subsequent volumes of playlets on the Queen) occupies a special niche in dramatic literature, as does the author's other dramatic biography, the *Little Plays of St. Francis*.

Housman lived to see the great-great-granddaughter of Victoria crowned as Queen Elizabeth II.

"A GOOD LESSON!" *

a short play from *Victoria Regina*
by Laurence Housman

1842

It is ten o'clock, and a bright morning. In THE PRINCE'S *writing-room at Buckingham Palace,* MR. ANSON, *his Private Secretary, stands by the table, sorting correspondence; opened letters he places in one heap, unopened in another. The door opens; one of* THE QUEEN'S GENTLEMEN *enters.*

GENTLEMAN. Her Majesty wishes to know whether the Prince has yet returned?

ANSON [*in a quiet, matter-of-fact tone*]. No. . . . At least, so far as I know, he has not.

GENTLEMAN [*hesitating*]. Oh? . . . Do you know, Mr. Anson, where the Prince *is*?

ANSON [*with studied nonchalance*]. Now? . . . No, I don't.

GENTLEMAN [*with embarrassment*]. You know, I suppose, that His Highness did not return to the Palace, last night?

ANSON [*as before*]. From the Royal Academy Dinner? Oh, indeed . . . didn't he?

GENTLEMAN [*making a plunge*]. Did he go, Mr. Anson?

ANSON. Oh, yes, I think so. The papers *say* that he did. Here is his speech, fully reported, in this morning's *Times;* and a very good one, too.

GENTLEMAN. Very strange, Mr. Anson!

ANSON. Not at all. His speeches generally are.

GENTLEMAN. I meant—his not returning.

ANSON [*coldly*]. Hadn't you better report to Her Majesty that His Highness has *not* yet returned? That, I believe, was all you were sent to find out.

GENTLEMAN [*stiffly*]. Certainly. I will.

[*He goes.* ANSON *continues sorting the letters. There comes a knock at the door; and permission given—in comes* THE PRINCE'S *Valet,* MR. RICHARDS.]

RICHARDS. I beg pardon, Sir. I heard you were alone: so I came to see you, Sir.

ANSON. Yes? What is it, Richards?

---

* Reprinted from *Victoria Regina* by Laurence Housman; used by permission of the publishers, Charles Scribner's Sons.

RICHARDS. His Royal Highness, Sir. . . . He hasn't sent for me this morning, Sir: and didn't last night, either. He doesn't seem to have been in his dressing-room at all, Sir: not since I dressed him last night, for the Dinner.

ANSON. Oh, it's all right, Richards. His Royal Highness was unexpectedly called elsewhere, at a late hour last night, so did not return.

RICHARDS [re-assured]. Oh, very good, Sir.

ANSON. I expect His Royal Highness to be back before long. So you be ready for him.

RICHARDS. Yes, Sir. Very good, Sir.

[*He goes.* ANSON, *left to himself, can no longer conceal his anxiety.*]

ANSON. But is it 'all right,' I wonder? . . . God!

[*Nervously he snatches up the paper, then throws it down again. He moves restlessly to the window, and back again. The door opens; in comes* PRINCE ALBERT, *looking very calm and collected.*]

ALBERT [quietly]. Good morning, Anson.

ANSON. Good morning, Sir.

ALBERT. Is there any news this morning?—anything special?

ANSON. In the papers, Sir? A full report of the Academy Banquet. [*He takes up* The Times, *and offers it.*] Did that go off well, Sir?

ALBERT [not taking it]. Very well.

ANSON. I was just reading your Highness's speech.

ALBERT. Yes, Anson; of which you wrote for me the notes.

ANSON. At your Highness's dictation.

ALBERT. Well, I did not make it too long, I hope?

ANSON. It reads very well, Sir. And it seems to have been well received.

ALBERT. Yes; it was altogether a very well managed affair. And I found the company quite interesting. We were talking of the decorations for the walls of the new Houses of Parliament; and I was proposing that there should be a Competition and a Fine Arts Commission to decide it. They thought it was a good idea.

ANSON. Well, Sir, if a Competition will produce the right artists, it certainly will be. But we have not had much practice of mural art in this country, Sir, I'm afraid; we don't run to it.

ALBERT. We must begin, then, and try.

ANSON. Yes, Sir.

ALBERT. That was Sir Francis Chantrey's objection. But when I said to him—'How would it do, then, to employ foreign Artists?' he said that if they came, their heads would be broken; and that—old as he was—he would himself lend a hand for the purpose.

ANSON. Indeed, Sir?

ALBERT. Yes, indeed! So you see! . . .

[THE PRINCE *seats himself at his writing-table*.]

ALBERT. Letters?

ANSON [*handing some*]. These, Sir, I think, are all that your Highness need see for the present.

ALBERT. Thank you.

[THE QUEEN'S GENTLEMAN *again enters*.]

GENTLEMAN. Her Majesty sent me to inquire if your Royal Highness
was disengaged?

ALBERT. Oh, yes. Tell Her Majesty I am quite free, if she wishes to
see me.

[THE GENTLEMAN *bows, and retires*. THE PRINCE *continues to look
over his correspondence*.]

Now you may go, Anson. Take all those other letters, and leave me
these.

[ANSON *retires*. THE PRINCE *goes on opening his correspondence.
A minute passes; suddenly the door is flung open, and* THE QUEEN
makes a flamboyant entry.]

THE QUEEN. Albert! Where have you been?

ALBERT. To Windsor, Victoria.

THE QUEEN. Windsor? Impossible! Why did you not come back,
last night?

ALBERT. I did not come back last night, Victoria, because of the way
in which you sent for me.

THE QUEEN. I told you before you went, that I wished you to be back
by half-past ten at the latest.

ALBERT. Yes.

THE QUEEN. At half-past ten you had not come; so I sent for you.

ALBERT. Yes, I received from you this note. [*He produces it.*] . . .
'Albert, it is quite time you were back. Please to come at once!'

THE QUEEN. Yes; I wrote it; I sent it; and my orders were that it
should be put into your hand by the Messenger to whom I gave it.

ALBERT. It was put into my hand. I sent back word to say that I
had received it.

THE QUEEN. Yes; but you did not come!

ALBERT. I did not come, because I was not then ready to come.

THE QUEEN. Albert! when you go anywhere without me (as you *had*
to do on this occasion), I do not expect you to be late.

ALBERT. No. But when I do go without you, you must leave it for
me to decide, myself, when I shall return.

THE QUEEN. But this time I had already told you my wishes, and had
decided *for* you. . . . I sent again.

ALBERT. Yes. At eleven o'clock, I received this. [*He produces it.*] 'Albert, I order you to return at once! V.R.'

THE QUEEN. And still you did not!

ALBERT. I did not.

THE QUEEN. So you disobeyed your Queen!

ALBERT [*serenely*]. Yes, my Dear; I disobeyed my Queen. Send me to the Tower for it, and cut off my head.

THE QUEEN. I do not regard this as a subject for amusement and jest, Albert.

ALBERT. No? Then it is lucky that *I* do. For if neither of us thought it amusing, we might have quite a serious quarrel about it. But now— as it is only you who do not think it amusing—the quarrel will not be so serious.

THE QUEEN. Albert, what did you do, after I had ordered you to return? Where did you spend the night?

ALBERT. At Windsor, as I have told you.

THE QUEEN. I don't believe it!

ALBERT. Don't you?

[*Quietly he turns back to his letters.*]

THE QUEEN. Albert, I will not be treated like this! Please to remember that, though I am your Wife, I am also your Queen.

ALBERT [*kindly*]. Sit down, my Dear, sit down! there is nothing to stand up about. . . . Last night there was; so I had to. But now I am ready to sit here and talk it over, quite reasonably and comfortably: just you and me, Weibchen—with the Queen left out. . . . Please! [*With a gesture he gets her seated.*] Listen to me, my Dear. When you married me, you made a promise that was strange for a Queen to make: but you made it. . . . To love, honour, and obey. And because it was so strange —so unlikely—I have never once told you to obey me—except for fun, when you wished it. Now, my Dear, as I have not expected *you* to obey *me* in anything—so there are some things in which you must not expect *me* to obey *you*.

THE QUEEN. When you do things for me in public—officially, that is to say—then I *do* expect you to obey me.

ALBERT. When I do things for you in public, my Dear, I obey you by doing them. But you must trust me to do them in my own way—

THE QUEEN. No, Albert.

ALBERT. —not to interfere with me, while I am doing them, as you did last night. That is why, when I started back—after having received your 'orders'—I told the Coachman to drive—not to Buckingham Palace, but to Windsor.

THE QUEEN. The Coachman! You told him that! What must he have thought?

ALBERT. I will tell you what he thought. . . . At first he thought it was very strange. But when we got to Windsor, he thought that he knew the reason.

THE QUEEN. Why, only then?

ALBERT. It was rather late: almost half-past one. But when we got there, there were lights, and music, and dancing.

THE QUEEN. Music! . . . Dancing! . . . *In* the Castle?

ALBERT. In the Castle. . . . Behind our backs—so sure that we should be away—the servants were having a fancy-dress ball.

THE QUEEN [*her anger quite diverted*]. What an improper liberty! Most extraordinary! And how fortunate that you should have caught them!

ALBERT. Yes; a curious coincidence, was it not? So, of course, the Coachman thought that I had got wind of the affair, and had come there to catch them at it.

THE QUEEN. Where were they dancing, Albert?

ALBERT. In the great Hall.

THE QUEEN. And in fancy-dress, you say?

ALBERT. Yes. Two of them had dressed up to look like you and me.

THE QUEEN. Albert! Did you see who they were?

ALBERT. No. They ran too quick. I went in, and stood. . . . They were all very much surprised to see me.

THE QUEEN. Indeed, I should think so! . . . What happened then?

ALBERT. First, the dancing all stopped; then all the music. . . . I stood there and looked at them. It was very funny: I tried not to laugh.

THE QUEEN. I hope you did not, Albert!

ALBERT. No; I composed myself to look as though I was very angry.

THE QUEEN. I hope you did. And then, what did you do?

ALBERT. I told them that they might go on for just five minutes more; but that it was not to happen again.

THE QUEEN. No, indeed!

ALBERT. And it will not, I am sure.

THE QUEEN. Did you get any explanation, as to why they had *dared* to do such a thing?

ALBERT. Oh, yes; it was explained. You see, they were to have had a ball soon after Christmas; but on the very date the Court had to go into mourning; so it was put off, and forgotten. And as they had got all the dresses, they were naturally disappointed.

THE QUEEN. But, Albert, that such a thing *could* happen without our knowing—well, it means that such a lot of other things may be happening too.

ALBERT. Yes; I am afraid so . . . I think, my Dear, that you had better make me your Manager of Windsor—factotum, you call it? They will not like it, because I have too much of a head for business; but it will be good for them. And for you, a great saving of unnecessary expense.

THE QUEEN. Yes; and if I do it at once, everybody will understand *why*.

ALBERT. It was a good thing, Vicky, was it not, that I was brought up rather poor?

THE QUEEN. So was I.

ALBERT. Yes? But you had not to manage much for yourself, had you? What for are you smiling at?

THE QUEEN. The Coachman, Albert! It *was* funny! I'm so glad you went; for now they will all be thinking how clever it was of you to find out! And what a good lesson it was for them, to be sure!

ALBERT. Yes, my Dear, a good lesson. . . . But Weibchen, you have not kissed me 'Good Morning' yet. . . . Please!

> [*And he says it so simply and sweetly, that, quite forgetting now what she first came about, she kisses him with true wifely affection, very fondly and contentedly.*]

————

Brief Commentary on *"A Good Lesson!"*

You may be one of those persons who feel that works of art are to be experienced and enjoyed, not analyzed and explained. But comments, questions, and discussion do encourage discrimination, and discrimination enriches experience and enhances delight. So, let us take a closer look at *"A Good Lesson!"*

Did you notice the way in which dramatic, theatric, and semantic elements of life unite in this short drama?

Tension is clearly evident in the opening lines of the play. Glance back and see. The Queen's Gentleman and Anson both show it, and we are prepared for Victoria's flamboyant and electrically charged entrance. Here is domestic strife at a high level and at a high pitch—the wife's suspicions and the Queen's demands—Albert's calm but assertive defense. Then, with loving kindness, happily using a curious coincidence and protecting Victoria's self-importance, Albert wins her approval of his independence. He wins the conflict without her realizing that she has lost it, and cements their affection that might have been shattered.

Certain critics charged that his *Victoria Regina* was not really a play at all because it was "not dramatic." To which Housman replied: "Anyone who reads those plays as a whole will see that the plot is not a plot of incident, but of character; and what happens to that character is truly dramatic. A self-willed, obstinate, imperious and passionate little person is taken in hand by the man whom she meant to make her adored puppet, and he, wisely and patiently, tames her, and rules her for her own and for her country's good; and that he manages to do it through a series of every-day incidents—some of them quite trivial on the surface—makes, I maintain, a thoroughly good plot; and I think that in spite of the critics, I have found a public here [in the theater audience he was addressing] which agrees with me."

In *"A Good Lesson!"* the dramatic elements of tension and conflict come from an incident in Victoria's actual life, a trivial enough incident. Housman transformed this into his playscript, devised in terms of the theatric elements of mimicry and display.

It is a curious coincidence, again, that the fancy-dress party at Windsor, with two of the household servants impersonating the Queen and Consort, illustrates a theatric element we find in life itself. And there's something theatric, too, in Victoria's imperious entrance—playing the Queen indeed! But Housman's play itself—as you can imagine its being performed by Helen Hayes and Vincent Price—illustrates the theatric elements of mimicry and display, the acting and also the spectacle, settings and costumes designed by Whistler. That which is imitated and exhibited in this way is, of course, the palace scene of domestic tension, conflict, and resolution.

A further comment on the semantic or wisdom element of life that finds its place in Housman's play. This was an everyday sort of incident in the life of the palace, trivial on the surface, yet for Albert it was charged with significance. For him two important life values, love for his wife and his own self-respect, had to be preserved and reconciled. Perhaps this was "A Good Lesson!" not only to the celebrants at Windsor but to Victoria herself—and to Albert—and to us.

II. THE PLAYSCRIPT

Creation by the Playwright

> Playwriting . . . is . . . also like chess, where a whole series of moves must be made to lead up to the one you want. Each of these moves will lead to other moves. And the ultimate aim of none of them should be apparent.
>
> —JOHN VAN DRUTEN, *Playwright at Work*

AMONG THE ARTS, DRAMA—combining theater art and dramatic literature—is peculiarly dynamic. In a very real sense a play is a process rather than a thing. It takes a lot of steps for a dramatic idea to travel from the imagination and mind of the playwright all the way to the mind and imagination of the playgoer or the playreader.

The creation of the playscript is one of these steps. Another step is the reading and study of the script by the actors, director, designer, etc. Then comes their interpretative creation of the play through rehearsals and production. The performance itself is another step. With it comes the re-creation of the play in the minds of the spectators. Printing and publishing of the playbook are usually steps beyond this. And finally your own reading of the book trails along at the far end of the long process.

It is the playscript, the playwright's creative work, that we shall devote ourselves to in this second essay.

§ 1. THE PLAYWRIGHT AND THE SCRIPT

We defined "stageplay" as a story presented directly by actors upon a stage before an audience. And we defined "playscript" as the written dialogue and stage directions used in creating a stageplay. With an eye to both of these definitions, we might say that a playscript is a story devised or adapted by a playwright for presentation upon a stage to an audience.

The writing and devising of a playscript is called "playwriting." But you will note that the man doing the devising and writing is

25

called a "playwright." The "wright" comes from an older form of "work," of which an archaic past tense is still "wrought," as in the expressions "wrought up" and "wrought iron." A "wright" was a constructive worker—a wheelwright, cartwright, wainwright. So, too, a playwright is a maker of playscripts, with emphasis upon construction of plot, development of character, contriving of stage effects —as well as the writing of dialogue for the actors to speak. As a playwright, he is a craftsman, first of all, then a writer. Often he is a man of the theater before he becomes a man of letters, an author, or a poet—a dramatist.

A "dramatist" is a playwright whose scripts have become recognized as dramas, as literature. All the great dramatists—Sophocles, Shakespeare, Molière, Ibsen, Shaw, O'Neill—have been great playwrights. Most of them learned their craft through long years of acting or directing or theater management, or through long years of close study of plays in the theater. Many distinguished men of letters—poets and novelists such as Browning, Shelley, Stevenson, Dickens—have tried without success to devise and write playscripts of distinction. Only a few modern novelists and writers of short stories—such as Maugham, Galsworthy, Chekhov—have really been successful playwrights. The novelist and poet, accustomed to writing for the reader's eye and ear, find it difficult to devise and write a playscript for production by actors in the theater.

A playscript requires an especially complex form of writing. It is somewhat like the architect's blueprints and specifications from which the master builder or building contractor constructs a house, using a great variety of materials and co-ordinating the work of many artisans. It is something like the composer's score from which the musical conductor directs and co-ordinates the rehearsals and performance of a symphony orchestra.

Just as one needs a certain know-how to read music and house plans, so too you will need some special knowledge of the theater in order to realize the full potential of a drama.

§ 2. Story Elements in a Drama

A stageplay is a story of one special sort: presented directly by actors, etc. A drama is a story of another special sort: suggested by printed dialogue and stage directions. A novel, a short story, a biography; an opera, a musical comedy, a dance drama; a radio drama, a TV play, a movie; a cartoon comedy, a puppet play, a pantomime—all of these are stories of one kind or another. Each of them communicates a story in its own particular way.

What, then, is meant by the word "story"?

Well, to start with, a story is about people; it puts you in mind of people as you have known them. There is really no such thing as an animal story. The Aesopic lion, the three little pigs, Black Beauty, Peter Rabbit, Lassie, and Mickey Mouse are essentially human creatures, though whimsically animal in form.

Furthermore, a story is not merely a description of people, character sketches; it is about people doing things. Usually there are a number of things that happen, a chain of events in sequence, with a beginning and an end.

Then, too, a story usually has some point. The things that the people do are made to seem important to us. Although we are all interested in people and their doings, our attention is caught and our interest really aroused when we see significance in what is happening. As we see the relationship of events to one another, causes and results, conflicts of personality and interests, anticipate things to come and speculate upon things past, ask ourselves what it all means —then we are not merely concerned with people and happenings, but with story.

A story, then, is a representation of human beings in a sequence of significant happenings. It is easy to illustrate this by reference to *"A Good Lesson!"* Obviously, as we read the book, human beings (Albert, Victoria, etc.) come to mind in a succession of related incidents that are brought to a meaningful conclusion.

There are six elements in all stories. Various sorts of storytelling will place emphasis upon different ones of these elements, but all stories will at least suggest all of the elements. The following diagram may help you to fix them in mind.

character	action	dialogue
scene	plot	theme

The *characters* are, of course, the people brought to mind by the story. The *actions* are the things that the characters are represented as doing. The *dialogue* is their conversations, what the characters say to each other in the course of what they do. (Speech, of course, *is* action of one special sort, and at times actions "speak" louder than words. But we shall consider action and dialogue as separate story elements.)

The *scenes* are the places where the actions take place, the settings for the events, the environment of the characters. The *plot*—there may be more than one—is the pattern of the successive actions and character relationships. The *theme*—again there may be more than one—is the over-all meaning, the significance of the plot.

As a story, *"A Good Lesson!"* includes Victoria and Albert as characters. Albert's writing room in Buckingham Palace in 1842 is the scene. The sending for Albert, Albert's morning return, Victoria's entrance, her accusation, etc., comprise the action. The tension between Queen and Consort that leads to the clash of wills, with Albert victorious because he is the stronger and the more understanding—this patterns the incidents and forms the plot. The continuous conversation of the characters constitutes the dialogue. The general idea or theme is that domestic differences may so be resolved with love and understanding that the wrongheaded partner is not hurt by defeat. Such, at any rate, is one reader's interpretation of the story elements of this play.

Of the six elements to be found in every story, it is curious that the only one that can be virtually eliminated is dialogue. Dance dramas, pantomimes, silent films, and grand operas tell their stories without spoken dialogue, though they all use dialogue of a sort through the language of gesture, printed subtitles, music and song—with words not necessarily understood!

A playscript, however, is largely dialogue, and it might seem at first thought that a playwright is essentially a writer of dialogue. But the dialogue that makes up a playscript is not merely a flow of parlor wit or profound discourse. It is conversation that suggests or accompanies action, that reveals character and scene, that patterns the plot, that expounds the theme. The playwright, as we said, is a craftsman who devises and constructs before he writes.

In some playscripts the emphasis is placed upon the characters, with very little action and hardly any plot. Other playscripts are strong on action with merely type characters, rather thin dialogue, and nothing but the most obvious of themes. Certain others, it is true, are brilliant conversation pieces, with characters mere mouthpieces for the playwright's own views, and almost no action or plot.

The playwright, then, while using all of the story elements, will have more interest in some than others. If his script is really weak in action or character or scene, the actors and other theater artists will at least try to make up the deficiency. However, good play-scripts—those that become the great dramas—are usually rich in all six of the story elements.

§ 3. Characters and Dramatic Characterization

A story is, first of all, a representation of human beings. The characters of a story are simply the human beings who inhabit it. They do not live elsewhere. Even when drawn from historical personages—like Victoria and Albert—they are fictions.

While in the process of devising a script, the playwright consciously creates or intuitively conceives these characters. They may come to him as mere suggestions or character ideas to be developed later. But finally each character exists in the playwright's mind as a bundle of human qualities, personality traits, drawn together from his experience of people. Family and friends, neighbors and chance acquaintances, historical persons and legendary folk, characters from fiction and drama—all may have supplied details; but the playwright draws in no small measure upon his knowledge of himself. Laurence Housman drew his characterizing data not alone from official biographies of Victoria and Albert, but from the queen's journals and letters. He also drew upon his wider knowledge of human nature and behavior.

It is the playwright's mind and imagination that will impose pattern and unity upon the assorted human tidbits used in characterization. These he synthesizes and gives a personal name as a character for his story.

There are a number of factors that, in addition to the playwright's observation of people, will determine the characters he creates.

One of these is dramatic necessity. If the playwright has already decided upon the main lines of his plot, for instance, or his theme, then this will call for the development of certain characters. If the playwright begins—as is sometimes the case—with a clear conception of his central characters and then proceeds to work out his action, there will still be much reshaping of these characters as the plot develops. So Housman chose to emphasize in *"A Good Lesson!"* those traits of character in both Victoria and Albert—her petulance and simplicity, for instance—suitable to the incident of domestic strife he had chosen to present in this little play. And the minor characters are always more or less determined by the requirements of scene, action, plot, dialogue, or theme.

Another factor that determines the playwright's characters is his dramaturgy, his theory and practice of playwriting. If he believes that all of the characters must be highly individualized, then he will labor to create character-fictions very different from one another and with personalities quite fully and roundly suggested. It may be the playwright's view, however, that even the main persons of his play should be type characters. Or the playwright may individualize the main characters, perhaps with lavish detail, and otherwise people his play with rather sketchy or typical characters.

Yet a third factor that will shape the playwright's characters is his view of life, his general notions about human nature and the causes of individual personality and behavior. The playwright may believe that human personality is controlled by the stars, or that each man is free in his will to shape his own life. Or he may hold that man is a battleground of vices and virtues—or that, born in sin, man is redeemed by vicarious atonement—or that man is the absolute child of his forebears, inheriting the personality and the sins of his fathers—or that man is the creature of environment, shaped by family and surroundings—or that man is pulled and hauled about by his id and superego, by mother fixations, sexual compulsions, inferiority complexes, frustrations, anxieties, psychoneuroses. The playwright's theory of personality will be an important factor in his shaping of dramatic character.

So, from his experience of people, the playwright draws his character material, which is shaped by his dramatic needs, by his theory of playwriting, and by his philosophy of life. Such fictions grow and shape themselves in his imagination as part of his creative activity in contriving a script. In this way Housman's characters were shaped. He needed Anson, the Queen's gentleman, and Richards to get the play started, to explain the situation, to dramatize the Queen's imperious displeasure, to show the anxiety among the Prince's personal attendants. These characters Housman barely outlines—not even a personal name for the gentleman and only a name for Richards. But he conceives his principals as highly individualized, not merely types. Housman thought of himself as a latter-day Victorian, and his views of life were uncomplex, with heredity and environment held nicely in balance by personal will and integrity and manifest destiny.

Now let us ask: How does the playwright "get" his imagined characters into his playscript? In what possible ways can he do this?

First, he can write a *description of the character*. He may include this in the stage direction upon the character's first appearance as a help to the actor in developing his impersonation. Earlier playwrights provided no such character sketches. In any case, the actor's appearance and outward bearing, his costume and make-up can be counted upon to suggest to the spectator some of the character's personality traits.

Second, the playwright can describe the characters as part of the opening dialogue, the so-called "exposition" of the play. He may plant a formal *character sketch in the dialogue,* a description of the hero by another character. Or he may draw such a portrait through conversation. Or he may divide it up further, introducing the character gradually, one trait at a time. Direct comment will be supplemented by the reactions of other characters, revealing their characterizing attitudes and opinions.

Third, the playwright can have his characters reveal themselves *by their own words*. What a character says in a given situation and how he says it will tell you a lot about his temperament, his past life, his present interests and desires. Dialogue can be personalized with individualizing speech patterns and diction, dialect, and odd turns of thought. This self-revelation can be seen in the give and take, question and answer, sally and rejoinder of conversation—and in those whispered thoughts called "asides." It is often richest in the long speeches or monologues. Sometimes, particularly in earlier drama, such revealing monologues are spoken by the character to himself alone. We listen to such "soliloquies" as though hearing the intimate thoughts of the character. The persons of the play will be characterized, then, by the dialogue and speech directions.

Fourth, the playwright can let his characters reveal themselves *by what they do* and *how they do it*. What people do to achieve their will and desires tells you something about them. So does how they go about it and how they react to what others do. The dramatist knows that at times actions do speak louder than words in revealing personality, past lives, present hopes and fears and tensions. Therefore he will use action and reaction—as specified in the stage directions or implicit in the dialogue—as a means of characterization.

Fifth, the playwright can reveal something of the personality of a character *through environment*. A boy's room—possessions, trophies, junk—tells you a lot about him. A man is known by the company he keeps. A woman is characterized by her control of, or by her being controlled by, her surroundings. The dramatist will often describe the scene in his opening stage direction so as to reveal certain traits of the characters. He may also include minor characters as an important part of the social environment.

These, then, are devices used by the playwright as he tries to get the personality of his fictional characters out of his imagination and into the playscript. It seems hardly necessary to point out how Housman characterizes Prince Albert. There is no description of him either in the stage directions or the dialogue of this playlet. It is in what Albert himself says and how he says it that Housman reveals the man, and in what he does and how he does it—also in how others react toward him. Through the scene, too—the orderly writing room, his conscientious personal staff, the vast correspondence—the playwright suggests many traits of the Prince.

Because even a long play is limited in scope to "the two hours' traffic of our stage," the playwright will have to select those personality traits that he feels are most characteristic, that are essential to understanding the action and the plot, that are helpful in communicating the theme. He will stress by repetition, using several devices to establish those traits that he considers most important.

§ 4. Action, Plot, and Dramatic Construction

We turn now, easily enough, from the characters to what they do. Brander Matthews once wrote, in *A Study of the Drama,* that in a good play, "the characters make the plot, and the story is what it is merely because the characters are what they are." A brief discussion of action will be followed by more extended considerations of plot and dramatic construction.

I. The *action* of a play comprises the actions of the characters, what they are represented as doing, the substance of the story. In its most obvious sense an action is anything that a person does. Speech, then, is action of one kind. But there can also be psychological action, silent and motionless—making a decision, or wordless torment, or refusal to nod assent! However, the playwright will commonly imagine his characters as doing things in the more usual and active sense. He will describe these actions in stage directions or make them implicit in the dialogue, as Shakespeare does with such skill.

Something more will be said about action in the next essay—the actors' gestures and movements, the pantomime. Here we shall concern ourselves with the playwright's development of the action, the plotting of the play, the dramatic construction.

II. The *plot* of a play is the pattern of its action. It is not simply the sum and sequence of the things the characters do, the events depicted. That, in a simple sense, is the action of the story. The plot is the design of the happenings—the causal relationship of the events to each other, to the characters and their motives, to the mood and theme, to the framework of the play. The plot of a play is its structure.

In most plays there is usually a central character from the standpoint of plot. He (or she) is called the "protagonist"—a dramaturgic term from the Greek *protos* (the first or chief) and *agonistes* (actor; one who contests, strives desperately, struggles, suffers, agonizes). He is usually the character whom we as readers or spectators will learn to know best. He is usually, but not always, the character with whom we sympathize, with whom we identify ourselves, the hero. The will and desires of the protagonist usually cause him to act; and his actions—and the counteractions of those who oppose him—are the principal events of the story.

Most plays—but by no means all—have *conflict* plots. The will and desires of the protagonist are opposed. If there were no opposition, there would be no scheming and strategy, striving and struggle, successes and setbacks, suffering and suspense. There would, then, be no story in the usual sense. "The spectacle of a will striving towards a goal" was what Brunetière called the *law of the drama,* in an essay by that name. It was this element of tension and conflict that, in the first essay, we noted in both life and the theater.

Because it is the genius of the theater to tell its story by acting it out, the forces of opposition that block or counter the efforts of the protagonist are likely to be people. The chief *opposing force* is usually one particular person called the "antagonist"—from *anti-* (against) and *agonistes*. But the forces of opposition, as we said earlier, need not be a person or persons. They may be impersonal, natural, or supernatural forces—society or war, storm or flood, devil or fate. Or the protagonist's adversary may lie within his own personality—his own opposing will or desires.

In the design of a conflict drama, there is (in addition to the desire or *will of the protagonist* and the *opposing force*) a third factor, *the deciding factor*—the deciding agent, as Samuel Selden calls it in his *Introduction to Playwriting*. This may be a third person or natural force, but it is often found within either the protagonist or the antagonist. It is this third factor that finally decides the issue, allowing the protagonist to win or causing him to lose the conflict. It may be the protagonist's "tragic flaw" or Achilles' heel—or his courage or perseverance or superior intelligence—that will be the deciding factor. Or it may be that the antagonist, who personifies the opposing force, has within his character peculiar strength or weakness, brilliance or stupidity. Or the deciding factor may be the intervention of the law or justice, fate or nature, society or family.

How does this three-force pattern of the conflict plot work out? Think once again of *Julius Caesar*. Brutus (let us say) is the protagonist who desires to maintain Rome as a republic and who joins Cassius and others in their conspiracy hoping to accomplish his desire. Caesar, you may agree, is the chief opposing force, the antagonist, and, though he is killed, Antony and Octavius and his own ghost carry on for him. The deciding factor, perhaps, is within Brutus himself, his generous nature, sparing Antony's life and allowing him to speak at Caesar's funeral. Or you may judge the deciding factor to be Cassius, who in one way and another misled the noble Brutus. In *"A Good Lesson!"* the conflict plot is even simpler: protagonist—Victoria, desiring to rule the man she loves; opposing force—Albert, determined to maintain his integrity; deciding factor—Albert's superior intelligence and forebearance.

Now let us see how the plot of the story—the pattern of the action—is built into the playscript.

III. *Dramatic construction* is a rather technical part of playwriting. It is here that the playwright is most of all a craftsman—or a crafty chess player, as John van Druten has pointed out. Even a limited view of his problems may increase your understanding and appreciation of the drama. Our discussion of this phase of dramaturgy will be developed under three heads: the components of the whole action, the structure of the enacted drama, and the larger units of construction.

A. What are *the components of the whole action* of a play?

To start with let us ask another question: What is the difference between *the whole action* and *the enacted drama*? When you retell the story of a play, you will sometimes have to start way back before the beginning of the enacted drama. You will then have to narrate important events that occurred prior to the rise of the curtain. The *enacted drama* consists of the events presented directly by the actors.

Its beginning—let us repeat—may come a long time after the start of the whole story. When this is so, the significant past events will have to be communicated to the audience in one way or another—by the dialogue or by flashbacks, of which more will be said shortly. At present we are concerned with the whole action, that is, the story from its very start, without regard to how much of it is enacted and how much narrated.

The components of the whole action, the units of which the story is made up, are *incidents*. An incident is simply a significant action or cluster of actions, an event, a happening, something someone does. It is useful to distinguish incidents from situations. A *situation* is a state of affairs, the status quo at any particular time, the relationship of characters to each other at a given moment, to their environment, to what has already happened or is to come. You can narrate an incident, or you can act it out. But you can only describe a situation, or pose it with live actors and then explain their relationships. An incident can be recorded by a movie camera; a still camera can only catch a situation. Incidents are the building blocks of the whole action of a story.

At the starting point of a story the characters are presumed to be in a certain relationship to each other—*the initial situation*. Then something happens—*the inciting incident*—and the status quo is upset, the situation is changed and different. But not for long. For something else then happens, a second incident, and the situation is again altered. One thing leads to another. One action causes a counteraction, and that in turn is the occasion for another. So it goes: (situation) *incident* (situation) *incident* (situation) *incident* (situation), etc. What one character does is the stimulus to which another character's action is a response, and this in turn is the stimulus for yet another response. The incidents of the whole action therefore form a linked cause-and-effect chain from the start, the inciting incident, to *the final incident,* which results in *the final situation*—a state of affairs, such as marriage or death, which for dramatic purposes is considered permanent.

Such, then, are the components of the whole action of a story. Let us now ask another question:

B. What is meant by *the structure of the enacted drama?*

The enacted drama may begin at or near the very starting point of the whole action of the play, and then proceed by presenting the principal incidents in the entire chain of events from first to last.

This is called "chronological structure." Shakespeare often used it, as in *Julius Caesar*. But many plays begin someplace in the middle of the whole action ("in medias res"), and then proceed from there, after filling in the antecedent events as needed. This is sometimes called "dramatic structure." In fact, the Greek tragedies and Ibsen's dramas often begin near the end of the long chain of events comprising the whole action of the story. This is sometimes called "fifth-act structure," because the play presents directly what would be only the last act of a five-act drama using chronological structure, and all the preceding events are narrated bit by bit. A few plays that begin in the middle or near the end of the whole action make use of the "flashback structure," acting out rather than relating the more important of the earlier incidents, as in *Death of a Salesman*.

It was Aristotle in his famous *Poetics* who spoke of a tragedy as a whole which has a beginning, a middle, and an end. We can say as much either for the whole action or for the enacted drama. But it will be important to note that the two beginnings—that of the whole action and that of the enacted drama—are not usually one and the same thing.

Let us consider *the beginning* of the enacted drama.

Unless the structure is strictly chronological, *the situation at rise*—when the curtain first goes up at the beginning of the play—will not be the same as the initial situation in the whole action. For instance, in Housman's playlet, the curtain rises upon Anson at his desk on a certain morning. However, the story really began the evening before. The initial situation in the whole action was the state of affairs when Albert kissed Victoria good-by before going off to make that speech at the Royal Academy Dinner. It was then that Victoria told him to be back by half-past ten at the very latest! And it was during the night that so much of the whole action took place. But in our other example, Caesar's triumphant return to Rome, stirring up the mob, occurs almost within the framework of the enacted drama. In this case the situation at rise is but one incident removed from the initial situation.

The beginning part of the enacted drama is preparation. It includes what is called the *exposition,* the dialogue that explains the situation at rise—identifying the characters and establishing the time and place of the scene. The exposition is also likely to characterize the protagonist and his chief desires, and it may suggest the opposing forces, etc. As part of the beginning—whether directly enacted or related as part of the exposition—comes the inciting incident already referred to. By this time one or more questions emerge: Will the protagonist succeed in gaining his desire? And if so, how? We shall call these the *dramatic questions*. Suspense will be maintained as long as such questions are kept in view but remain unanswered. They will not be fully answered until the end of the play.

The middle of the enacted drama—obviously enough—follows the beginning and precedes the end.

The body of a play consists of the linked chain of incidents, the principal ones being *incidents of conflict* in which the protagonist strives toward his goal or in which the opposing forces move to block him. In these incidents of conflict we realize the dramatic elements such as we find them in life. Here indeed there will be scheming and strategy, strife and struggle, successes and setbacks, suffering and suspense. In the course of the story conflict there will be all manner of *complications* and successive *crises*. Each crisis will be a head-on clash of the opposing forces, an incident of dramatic conflict. The decisive one of these crises—the climactic incident—will be the *climax* of the play, the turning point in the fortunes of the protagonist. In the climactic incident, it is *the deciding factor* (whoever or whatever) that turns the tide. Thereafter we feel confident that the protagonist will gain his desire, though he is not yet extricated from his difficulties or he is still menaced. Or after the climax we may feel that the continuing struggle of the protagonist is in vain and that he is doomed to lose, though we do not yet know how.

The climax serves to answer the primary dramatic question: Will the protagonist succeed in gaining his desire? After the climax there is no more suspense from that question, but there may be from yet more important questions such as this: How will he succeed or ultimately fail? In certain plays—such as Shakespeare's great tragedies as sometimes analyzed—the climax is about midway in the course of the action. The assassination of Caesar, according to Freytag's *Technique of the Drama,* is the climax of the play. It is preceded by the conspiracy, the rising action, and is followed by the falling action, which includes the counteraction of Antony in arms and the quarrel with Cassius. In Housman's little play the climax comes when Victoria as queen and wife demands an explanation of Albert's conduct, and Albert quietly tells her the truth, refuses to quarrel, and makes her sit down to listen to him. It is more usual, however, for the climax to come much later. It is then the last of the crises, perhaps even the last important incident in the body of the play. Following the climax, in this more usual dramatic construction, comes the ending of the play.

The end of the enacted drama follows the middle with its complications, crises, and climax.

The end as a structural part of the whole may be quite short. The essential conflict has already passed its climax. We expect the end and are prepared for it. In a tragedy the final incident—the *catastrophe*—will often be the death of the protagonist or absolute defeat or realization of crushing failure. In comedy the final incident will often serve as a *dénouement*—the untangling or unknotting of the plot lines, the clearing up of unanswered questions. There may be final surprises—a last glorious effort of the defeated protagonist or a final dirty blow from the defeated antagonist. There may be final *reversals* and *discoveries*. All the dramatic questions will not be answered in the mind of the spectator or reader until the *final curtain,* which either shows or promises the end of the story, the *final situation*.

In *Caesar* the final incident is Brutus' death, and the final situation: Antony and Octavius in possession of the field but honoring dead Brutus as "the noblest Roman of them all." At the end of Housman's play, Victoria accepts Albert's integrity and independent action, makes him manager of Windsor; and happy domestic relations are restored.

There is still a third dramaturgic question to be asked:

C. What are *the larger units of dramatic construction?*

Earlier we said that incidents are the component units of the whole action of the play. They are the smaller units of dramatic construction. There are also the larger units of the enacted drama, three of which will be distinguished: the basic scene, the scene as usually defined, and the act. (The word "scene" has already been used in another sense as one of the six story elements, which will be further considered in the next essay.)

A *basic scene* is that part of a play during which no important characters come in or go out, the group of characters remaining the same. A basic scene, then, begins with the entrance or the exit of an important character or group of characters or of several characters in rapid succession. Basic scenes may be called "rehearsal scenes" because each is a convenient unit to rehearse with one group of actors; and they are sometimes called "French scenes" because in classical French dramas each of these units is marked off as a separately numbered scene.

The basic scene is important in dramatic construction because it is a unit in the playwright's composition. That is, he will contrive to have certain characters together in a situation in order to further the story by certain actions and dialogue, incidents and revelations. He will not usually interrupt the dialogue or action until he has accomplished his present dramatic purpose. Then he will, upon some pretext, dismiss characters he no longer wants on stage or bring on others whom he needs.

A *scene*—as in the usual phrase "Scene One" or "Scene Two"—is that part of a play which is continuous in time and place. We could call it an "English scene" as distinguished from the French, for plays in English usually have such units designated as scenes. Or we could call it a "time-and-place scene," because its action is confined to one place and proceeds continuously. It is marked off by a change in place or a lapse of time. Scenes, in this sense, end with the falling of a curtain or the dimming or black-out of the lights or (as in Shakespeare) the clearing of the stage when all the actors leave it. The rising of a curtain (whether or not it reveals a different setting), the heating up of the lights, or the entrance of characters again upon a bare stage will mark the beginning of a new scene.

The scenes of a play are often the most important of the play's units of construction. They are usually designated and numbered as "scenes" by the playwright, unless the whole act or entire play is in but one scene. But sometimes the playwright will simply indicate some manipulation of the lights or a curtain to mark a lapse of time or a change of place, thus starting a new scene as we have here defined it.

The word *act* is used to mean the main divisions of the usual full-length play. Five acts were the number established by Horace and followed by many Renaissance dramatists. But Shakespeare may not usually have bothered about act divisions in his playwriting —at least his plays as published during his own life time were not divided into acts. About a century ago, the four-act structure developed, giving way fifty years ago to the three-act form. Today many plays are written to be performed in two parts, with a single intermission. And a very few long plays have been written in one continuous scene—with no change of place or lapse of time—the curtain being dropped once or twice perhaps for resting the audience.

The phrase "one-act play," however, is used in a special sense to mean simply a short play, usually in one scene, about the length of one act of a long play—however long "long" may be!

With this let us conclude this extended section on action, plot, and dramatic construction. But not without a warning: Most plays as you read or see them will probably seem to you to have conflict plots —with protagonist, opposing forces, inciting incident, dramatic questions, complications, crises, deciding factor, climax, and catastrophe or dénouement. Your discovery that a particular play—perhaps among those to come in this book—has a design of a different sort will be an important first step in your determining what its particular pattern, for you, really is.

§5. DIALOGUE AND DRAMATIC COMPOSITION

You can see now, from what has been said about plot and dramatic construction, why we insisted upon the proper spelling of "playwright." However, the dramatist is not only a conscious craftsman but also an intuitive artist. Because of his keen observation of life and theater he will, certainly, do much of his creative work without rationalization. He may carry on extended research, develop elaborate character sketches, formulate detailed scenarios, and then proceed systematically to draft, rewrite, revise, and polish his playscript. Or he may mull over his ideas, engage in apparently irrelevant work, and then suddenly dash off a script at white heat.

It is surprising how rapidly some plays have been written, the actual dramatic composition occupying but a few days or weeks. Shakespeare—who, friends proudly boasted, "never blotted a line"— wrote about two plays a year while engaged also in his profession of regular acting. Ibsen, however, usually labored about two years upon a single play.

When it comes to the actual dramatic composition—once the characterization and plotting are somewhat or fully worked out—the playwright is essentially a writer of dialogue.

Stage directions are a comparatively small and less important part of playwriting. The Greeks wrote none. Shakespeare added to his dialogue very little more than entrances and exits. The modern dramatist, however, usually describes the scene in some detail—not only the setting but the principal stage properties (furniture, etc.)— giving the time of day, the season and weather, sometimes giving specific suggestions as regards lighting and sound effects. He may also describe the characters briefly, as we noted, before starting to write dialogue. Here and there, as he proceeds, he will add phrases suggesting voice tones and gestures to the actors, and he will describe certain actions or business in detail, as well as indicating entrances and exits.

But the playwright, once he starts to write, is essentially a writer of *dialogue;* and of his writing only the dialogue ever reaches the ears of the audience. His most elaborate stage directions and side comments will go no further than the actors in the theater, who may find them suggestive or helpful but are more likely to disregard them in whole or in part. Unlike the novelist, the playwright cannot narrate his story and use dialogue only at the high points. He cannot comment upon the course of the action. He cannot even— as is the case two-thirds of the time in the average movie—suspend dialogue and substitute continuous pantomime with a background of sound and music. It is a convention of drama that someone is talking all the time. The pauses and the brief bits of silent business occupy only a very small fraction of the total time. The dialogue is virtually continuous.

Yet a good stageplay—or a good reading drama—does not seem "talky." *Dialogue is conversation with dramatic purpose.* In a well-written play, the speeches may serve two or three purposes at once—revealing character, serving the action, furthering the plot, suggesting the scene or mood, touching the theme, or providing incidental delight or enrichment to the spectator or reader.

Something has already been said about dialogue as it reveals character. Much the same can be said as regards the suggesting of scene and mood. Speeches also accompany and comment on the action. In addition, as earlier noted, speech may serve as one form of action —think of the verbal combats, the quarrels, the imperatives, the curses, the insults, the fighting words, the asking of forgiveness, the wooing, the consenting, etc. But speeches also can narrate past action or off-stage action, reveal motives, interpret and evaluate action. It is through dialogue principally that the plot of the play will emerge—forces of opposition (if such there are) in conflict, moving through complications and crises to climax and conclusion.

It is in the dialogue that the over-all meaning of the play will be specifically touched and the symbols pointed up. The theme, which presumably will be the most general abstraction of the significance of the play, may be given explicit statement in the dialogue.

But dialogue may serve yet another function—incidental to the main business of the play—sheer verbal delight. The language of drama may be poetry. It may be music to the ears of the auditor or reader, stir his fancy with free imagery, quicken his mind with perceptive metaphor, warm his heart and engage his interests. Whether the play is verse or prose, whether the style is rhetorical or colloquial, whether the mood is grave or gray—dramatic dialogue at its best will be more than merely utilitarian talk, it will be language serving its art function. It will be highly charged and evocative.

The question may be asked, in closing this essay, whether the playwright is himself conscious of the separable story elements, whether he is aware of his own processes in creating characters as individuals or as types, whether he does construct his plot with chess-playing shrewdness, whether he actually writes his dialogue and stage directions with an eye to their various functions and desired effects. A simple answer to this complex question would be a qualified "Yes." The successful playwrights have been conscientious craftsmen in the theater. But the great dramatists have also been intuitive artists whose creative processes have transcended the craft in which they were skilled artisans.

———

Introductory Note to *Fumed Oak*

FUMED OAK is one of nine short plays produced and published in 1936 under the title *Tonight at 8:30*. They were written, directed, and acted in by Noel Coward with his lifelong friend Gertrude Lawrence. In groups of three plays to an evening, 118 performances were given in New York, after they had first played in England. The next season another company presented groups of these plays, first in Santa Barbara, then, with Estelle Winwood, for successful engagements in Los Angeles and San Francisco, and again for five weeks in New York. Ten years later, in 1948, two groups of these plays, including *Fumed Oak,* were revived by Noel Coward with Gertrude Lawrence and played in New York for three weeks, with additional months on the West Coast. One of the series, *Still Life,* was filmed by Noel Coward as *Brief Encounter* with great success, and a moving picture was made of *The Astonished Heart.* In 1953 a cinema group of three was released under the title of *Tonight at 8:30,* one of them being *Fumed Oak.*

Noel Coward is one of the outstanding modern examples of the actor-playwright. Born in a London suburb at the end of 1899, in a family with a musical father, Coward began his stage career at the age of 10, played juvenile parts in repertory with Gertrude Lawrence and Estelle Winwood, had his first play produced at 18, was a hugely successful actor-playwright at 24 (*The Vortex*), and became the wealthiest of playwrights while still in his thirties. He has been both prolific and versatile. Coward is best known for his sophisticated comedies such as *Hay Fever* (which he wrote in three days!), *Private Lives, Design for Living, Blithe Spirit.* He also wrote musical revues and the operetta *Bitter Sweet*—the book, lyrics, and music, including the perennial favorite, "I'll See You Again"—and *Cavalcade,* an epic drama of England during the first thirty years of this century. He has made several excursions into cinema, including the highly original film, *The Scoundrel,* and the war picture of the British navy, *In Which We Serve.* His autobiography, *Present Indicative,* is a witty account of his numerous theatrical activities up to 1937, which he continues in *Future Indefinite* (1954).

Perhaps because of his experience in revues, Noel Coward liked the idea "of playing a series of different rôles during an evening instead of only one." He realized that, "during the last quarter of a century, [the one act play] had fallen from favour." But he felt that "A short play, having a great advantage over a long one in that it can sustain a mood without technical creaking or overpadding, deserves a better fate, and if, by careful writing, acting, and producing I can do a little towards reinstating it in its rightful pride, I shall have achieved one of my more sentimental ambitions."

———

FUMED OAK *

An Unpleasant Comedy in Two Scenes
by Noel Coward

THE CHARACTERS

HENRY GOW
DORIS—*his wife*
ELSIE—*his daughter*
MRS. ROCKETT—*his mother-in-law*

SCENE I. *Morning*   SCENE II. *Evening*

The action of the play passes in the sitting-room of the Gows' house in South London.
The time is the present day.

SCENE I

THE GOWS' SITTING-ROOM *is indistinguishable from several thousand other suburban sitting-rooms. The dominant note is refinement. There are French windows at the back opening on to a narrow lane of garden. These are veiled discreetly by lace curtains set off by pieces of rather faded blue casement cloth. There is a tiled fireplace on the* L.; *an upright piano between it and the window; a fumed-oak sideboard on the* R. *and, below it, a door leading to the hall, the stairs and the front door. There is a fumed-oak dining-room set consisting of a table and six chairs; a sofa; an armchair in front of the fire; and a plentiful sprinkling over the entire room of ornaments and framed photographs.*

When the CURTAIN *rises it is about eighty-thirty on a spring morning. Rain is trickling down the windows and breakfast is laid on the table.*
MRS. ROCKETT *is seated in the armchair by the fire; on a small table*

next to her is a workbasket. She is a fattish, grey-looking woman dressed in a blouse and skirt and a pepper-and-salt jumper of artificial silk. Her pince-nez snap in and out of a little clip on her bosom and her feet are bad, which necessitates the wearing of large quilted slippers in the house. DORIS, *aged about thirty-five, is seated* R. *of the table reading a newspaper propped up against the cruet. She is thin and anæmic, and whatever traces of past prettiness she might have are obscured by the pursed-up, rather sour gentility of her expression. She wears a nondescript coat-frock, a slave bangle and a necklace of amber glass beads.* ELSIE, *her daughter, aged about fourteen, is sitting opposite to her, cutting her toast into strips in order to dip them into her boiled egg. She is a straight-haired ordinary-looking girl dressed in a navy blue school dress with a glacé red leather waist-belt.*

There is complete silence broken only by the occasional rattle of a spoon in a cup or a sniffle from ELSIE, *who has a slight head cold.*

HENRY GOW *comes into the room. He is tall and spare, neatly dressed in a blue serge suit. He wears rimless glasses and his hair is going grey at the sides and thin on the top. He sits down at the table, up stage, without a word.* DORIS *automatically rises and goes out, returning in a moment with a plate of haddock, which she places in front of him and resumes her place.* HENRY *pours himself out some tea.* DORIS, *without looking at him, being re-immersed in the paper, passes him the milk and sugar.* HENRY *stretches for toast across the table.*

The silence continues until ELSIE *breaks it.*

ELSIE. Mum?

DORIS. What?

ELSIE. When can I put my hair up?

DORIS [*snappily*]. When you're old enough.

ELSIE. Gladys Pierce is the same age as me and she's got hers up.

DORIS. Never you mind about Gladys Pierce, get on with your breakfast.

ELSIE. I don't see why I can't have it cut. That would be better than nothing.

[*This remark is ignored.*]
Maisie Blake had hers cut last week and it looks lovely.

DORIS. Never you mind about Maisie Blake neither. She's common.

ELSIE. Miss Pritchard doesn't think so. Miss Pritchard likes Maisie Blake a lot, she said it looked ever so nice.

DORIS [*irritably*]. What?

ELSIE. Her hair.

DORIS. Get on with your breakfast. You'll be late.

ELSIE [*petulantly*]. Oh, Mum——

DORIS. And stop sniffling. Sniffle, sniffle, sniffle! Haven't you got a handkerchief?

ELSIE.   Yes, but it's a clean one.

DORIS.   Never mind, use it.

MRS. ROCKETT.   The child can't help having a cold.

DORIS.   She can blow her nose, can't she, even if she has got a cold?

ELSIE [*conversationally*].   Dodie Watson's got a terrible cold, she's had it for weeks.   It went to her chest and then it went back to her head again.

MRS. ROCKETT.   That's the worst of schools, you're always catching something.

ELSIE.   Miss Pritchard's awful mean to Dodie Watson, she said she'd had enough of it.

DORIS.   Enough of what?

ELSIE.   Her cold.

[*There is silence again, which is presently shattered by the wailing of a baby in the house next door.*]

MRS. ROCKETT.   There's that child again.   It kept me awake all night.

DORIS.   I'm very sorry, I'm sure.   [*She picks up the newspaper.*]

MRS. ROCKETT [*fiddling in her work basket*].   I wasn't blaming you.

DORIS.   The night before last it was the hot-water pipes.

MRS. ROCKETT.   You ought to have them seen to.

DORIS.   You know as well as I do you can't stop them making that noise every now and then.

MRS. ROCKETT [*threading a needle*].   I'm sure I don't know why you don't get a plumber in.

DORIS [*grandly*].   Because I do not consider it necessary.

MRS. ROCKETT.   You would if you slept in my room—gurgle gurgle gurgle all night long—it's all very fine for you, you're at the end of the passage.

DORIS [*with meaning.*]   You don't have to sleep there.

MRS. ROCKETT.   What do you mean by that?

DORIS.   You know perfectly well what I mean.

MRS. ROCKETT [*with spirit*].   Listen to me, Doris Gow.   I've got a perfect right to complain if I want to, and well you know it.   It isn't as if I was staying here for nothing.

DORIS.   I really don't know what's the matter with you lately, Mother, you do nothing but grumble.

MRS. ROCKETT.   Me, grumble!   I like that, I'm sure.   That's rich, that is.

DORIS.   Well, you do.   It gives me a headache.

MRS. ROCKETT.   You ought to do something about those headaches of yours.   They seem to pop on and off at the least thing.

DORIS.   And I wish you wouldn't keep passing remarks about not staying here for nothing.

MRS. ROCKETT.   Well, it's true, I don't.

DORIS. Anyone would think we was taking advantage of you, to hear you talk.

MRS. ROCKETT. Well, they wouldn't be far wrong.

DORIS. Mother, how can you! You're not paying a penny more than you can afford.

MRS. ROCKETT. I never said I was. It isn't the money, it's the lack of consideration.

[ELSIE *puts her exercise book away in her satchel.*]

DORIS. Pity you don't go and live with Nora for a change.

MRS. ROCKETT. Nora hasn't got a spare room.

DORIS. Phyllis has, a lovely one, looking out over the railway. I'm sure her hot-water pipes wouldn't keep you awake, there isn't enough hot water in them.

MRS. ROCKETT. Of course, if I'm not wanted here, I can always go to a boarding-house or a private hotel.

DORIS. Catch you!

MRS. ROCKETT. I'm not the sort to outstay my welcome anywhere . . .

DORIS. Oh, for heaven's sake don't start that again . . . [*She bangs the paper down on the table.*]

MRS. ROCKETT [*addressing the air*]. It seems as though some of us had got out of bed the wrong side this morning.

ELSIE. Mum, can I have some more toast?

DORIS. No.

ELSIE. I could make it myself over the kitchen fire.

DORIS. No, I tell you. Can't you understand plain English? You've had quite enough and you'll be late for school.

MRS. ROCKETT. Never mind, Elsie, here's twopence [*taking it out of her purse*]. You can buy yourself a sponge-cake at Barrets.

ELSIE [*rising and taking the twopence*]. Thanks, Grandma.

DORIS. You'll do no such thing, Elsie. I'm not going to have a child of mine stuffing herself with cake in the middle of the High Street.

MRS. ROCKETT [*sweetly*]. Eat it in the shop, dear.

DORIS. Go on, you'll be late.

ELSIE. Oh, Mum, it's only ten to.

DORIS. Do as I tell you.

ELSIE. Oh, all right.

[*She crosses in front of the table and goes sullenly out of the room and can be heard scampering noisily up the stairs.*]

MRS. ROCKETT [*irritatingly*]. Poor little soul.

DORIS. I'll trouble you not to spoil Elsie, Mother.

MRS. ROCKETT. Spoil her! I like that. Better than half-starving her.

DORIS [*hotly*]. Are you insinuating . . .

MRS. ROCKETT. I'm not insinuating anything. Elsie's getting a big girl, she only had one bit of toast for her breakfast and she used that for her egg. I saw her.

DORIS [*rising and putting away the paper in the sideboard drawer*]. It's none of your business, and in future I'd be much obliged if you'd keep your twopences to yourself. [*She returns to her seat at the table.*]

[*Henry rises and fetches the paper out.*]

MRS. ROCKETT [*hurt*]. Very well, of course if I'm to be abused every time I try to bring a little happiness into the child's life . . .

DORIS. Anyone would think I ill-treated her the way you talk.

MRS. ROCKETT. You certainly nag her enough.

DORIS. I don't do any such thing—and I wish you'd leave me to bring up my own child in my own way.

MRS. ROCKETT. That cold's been hanging over her for weeks and a fat lot you care——

DORIS [*rising and getting tray from beside the sideboard*]. I've dosed her for it, haven't I? The whole house stinks of Vapex. What more can I do?

MRS. ROCKETT. She ought to have had Doctor Bristow last Saturday when it was so bad. He'd have cleared it up in no time.

DORIS [*putting tray on her chair and beginning to clear things on to it*]. You and your Doctor Bristow.

MRS. ROCKETT. Nice thing if it turned to bronchitis.

[*DORIS throws scraps into the fire.*]

Mrs. Henderson's Muriel got bronchitis, all through neglecting a cold; the poor child couldn't breathe, they had to have two kettles going night and day——

DORIS. I suppose your precious Doctor Bristow told you that.

MRS. ROCKETT. Yes, he did, and what's more, he saved the girl's life, you ask Mrs. Henderson.

DORIS. Catch me ask Mrs. Henderson anything, stuck up thing. . . .

MRS. ROCKETT. Mrs. Henderson's a very nice ladylike woman, just because she's quiet and a bit reserved you say she's stuck up . . .

DORIS. Who does she think she is, anyway, Lady Mountbatten? [*She takes the cruet to the sideboard.*]

MRS. ROCKETT. Really, Doris, you make me tired sometimes, you do really.

DORIS. If you're so fond of Mrs. Henderson it's a pity you don't see more of her. I notice you don't go there often.

MRS. ROCKETT [*with dignity*]. I go when I am invited.

DORIS [*triumphantly*]. Exactly.

MRS. ROCKETT. She's not the kind of woman that likes people popping in and out all the time. We can't all be Amy Fawcetts.

DORIS. What's the matter with Amy Fawcett? [*She takes the teapot to the sideboard.*]

MRS. ROCKETT. Well, she's common for one thing, she dyes her hair for another, and she's a bit too free and easy all round for my taste.

DORIS. She doesn't put on airs, anyway.

MRS. ROCKETT. I should think not, after the sort of life she's led.

DORIS [*takes bread to sideboard*]. How do you know what sort of a life she's led?

MRS. ROCKETT. Everybody knows, you only have to look at her; I'm a woman of the world, I am, you can't pull the wool over my eyes——

[ELSIE *comes into the room wearing a mackintosh and a tam-o'-shanter.*]

ELSIE. Mum, we want a new roll of toilet paper.

DORIS. How many times have I told you ladies don't talk about such things!

ELSIE [*as she stamps over to the piano and begins to search untidily through a pile of music on it*]. It's right down to the bit of cardboard.

DORIS [*scraping the bottom of her cup on the saucer*]. Don't untidy everything like that, what are you looking for?

ELSIE. "The Pixies' Parade," I had it last night.

DORIS. If it's the one with the blue cover it's at the bottom.

ELSIE. It isn't—oh dear, Miss Pritchard will be mad at me if I can't find it.

MRS. ROCKETT [*rising*]. Perhaps you put it in your satchel, dear. Here, let me look—— [*She opens* ELSIE's *satchel which is hanging over the back of a chair and fumbles in it.*] Is this it?

ELSIE. Oh, yes, thanks, Grandma.

DORIS. Go along now, for heaven's sake, you'll be late.

[MRS. ROCKETT *helps* ELSIE *on with her satchel.*]

ELSIE. Oh, all right, Mum. Good-bye, Grandma, good-bye, Dad.
HENRY. Good-bye.
MRS. ROCKETT. Good-bye, dear, give Grandma a kiss.

[ELSIE *does so.*]

DORIS [*pushing* ELSIE *out of the door*]. Don't dawdle on the way home.

ELSIE. Oh, all right, Mum.

[*She goes out. The slam of the front door shakes the house.*]

DORIS [*irritably*]. There now.

MRS. ROCKETT [*with studied politeness*]. If you are going down to the shops this morning, would it be troubling you too much to get me a reel of white cotton? [*She sits in the armchair.*]

DORIS [*tidying the piano*]. I thought you were coming with me.

MRS. ROCKETT. I really don't feel up to it.

DORIS. I'll put it on my list.

[*She takes a piece of paper out of the sideboard drawer and scribbles on it.*]

MRS. ROCKETT. If it's out of your way, please don't trouble. It'll do another time.

DORIS. Henry, it's past nine.

HENRY [*without looking up*]. I know.

DORIS. You'll be late.

HENRY. Never mind.

DORIS. That's a nice way to talk, I must say.

MRS. ROCKETT. I'm sure if my Robert had ever lazed about like that in the mornings, I'd have thought the world had come to an end.

DORIS. Henry'll do it once too often, mark my words. [*She crosses behind* HENRY.]

MRS. ROCKETT [*biting off her thread*]. Well, that corner's finished. [*She puts away her embroidery and starts to knit.*]

DORIS [*to* HENRY]. You'll have to move now, I've got to clear. [*Taking first his saucer, then his cup, from his hand.*]

[HENRY *rises absently.*]

MRS. ROCKETT. Where's Ethel?

DORIS. Doing the bedroom.

[HENRY *quietly goes out of the room.*]

[*Throwing more scraps on the fire.*] Look at that wicked waste.

MRS. ROCKETT. What's the matter with him?

DORIS. Don't ask me, I'm sure I couldn't tell you.

MRS. ROCKETT. He came in very late last night, I heard him go into the bathroom.

[*There is a pause.*]

That cistern makes a terrible noise.

DORIS [*emptying crumbs from cloth into fire and folding it*]. Does it indeed!

MRS. ROCKETT. Yes, it does.

DORIS [*slamming the teapot on to the tray*]. Very sorry, I'm sure.

MRS. ROCKETT. Where'd he been?

DORIS. How do I know?

MRS. ROCKETT. Didn't you ask him?

DORIS. I wouldn't demean myself.

MRS. ROCKETT. Been drinking?

DORIS. No.

MRS. ROCKETT. Sounded very like it to me, all that banging about.

DORIS. You know Henry never touches a drop.

MRS. ROCKETT. I know he says he doesn't.

DORIS. Oh, do shut up, Mother, we're not all like Father. [*She puts the cloth in the sideboard drawer, then scrapes grease with her nail from the green cloth on the table.*]

MRS. ROCKETT. You watch your tongue, Doris Gow, don't let me hear you saying anything against the memory of your poor father.

DORIS. I wasn't.

MRS. ROCKETT [*belligerently*]. Oh yes, you were, you were insinuating again.

DORIS [*hoisting up the tray*]. Father drank and you know it, everybody knew it. [*She moves* L.]

MRS. ROCKETT. You're a wicked woman.

DORIS. It's true.

MRS. ROCKETT. Your father was a gentleman, which is more than your husband will ever be, with all his night-classes and his book reading—night-classes, indeed!

DORIS [*poking the fire*]. Who's insinuating now?

MRS. ROCKETT [*angrily*]. I am, and I'm not afraid to say so.

DORIS. What of it?

MRS. ROCKETT [*with heavy sarcasm*]. I suppose he was at a night-class last night?

DORIS [*loudly*]. Mind your own business.

[*HENRY comes in, wearing his mackintosh and a bowler hat.*]

HENRY. What's up?

DORIS. Where were you last night?

HENRY. Why?

DORIS. Mother wants to know and so do I.

HENRY. I was kept late at the shop and I had a bit of dinner in town.

DORIS. Who with?

HENRY. Charlie Henderson.

[*He picks up the paper off the table and goes out. The baby next door bursts into fresh wails.*]

MRS. ROCKETT. There goes that child again. It's my belief it's hungry.

DORIS. Wonder you don't go and give it twopence to buy sponge-cake.

[*She pulls the door open with her foot and goes out with the tray as the lights fade on the scene.*]

SCENE II

IT IS ABOUT *seven-thirty in the evening.* ELSIE *is sitting at the piano practising with the loud pedal firmly down all the time.* MRS ROCKETT *is sitting in her chair by the fire, but she is dressed in her street things and wearing a black hat with a veil.* DORIS, *also in street clothes, is trying on paper patterns.*

There is a cloth across the upstage end of the table on which is set a loaf, a plate of cold ham, a saucer with two tomatoes in it, a bottle of A.1 sauce and a teapot, tea-cup, sugar basin and milk jug.

HENRY *comes in, taking off his mackintosh. He gives one look round the room and goes out into the hall again to hang up his things.* ELSIE *stops playing and comes over to* DORIS.

ELSIE.   Mum, can we go now?
DORIS.   In a minute.
ELSIE.   We'll miss the Mickey.
DORIS.   Put on your hat and don't worry.
ELSIE [*grabbing her hat from the sideboard*].   Oh, all right.

[HENRY *re-enters.*]

DORIS.   Your supper's all ready, the kettle's on the gas stove when you want it. [*Folding up paper patterns.*]   We've had ours.
HENRY.   Oh!
DORIS.   And you needn't look injured, either.
HENRY.   Very well. [*He crosses in front of the table.*]
DORIS.   If you managed to get home a bit earlier it'd save a lot of trouble all round.
HENRY [*amiably*].   Sorry, dear. [*He warms his hands at the fire.*]
DORIS.   It's all very fine to be sorry, you've been getting later and later these last few weeks, they can't keep you overtime every night.
HENRY.   All right, dear, I'll tell them.
DORIS.   Here, Elsie, put these away in the cupboard. Mind your fingers with the scissors.

[*She hands her a pile of material and pieces of paper.* ELSIE *obediently takes them and puts them in the left-hand cupboard of the sideboard.*]

HENRY [*sitting at the table*].   Cold ham, what a surprise!
DORIS [*looking at him sharply*].   What's the matter with it? [*She puts on her coat.*]
HENRY.   I don't know, yet.
DORIS.   It's perfectly fresh, if that's what you mean.

[ELSIE *crosses to* L.C.]

HENRY.   Why are you all so dressed up?

ELSIE. We're going to the pictures. [*She picks up her bag and gloves.*]

HENRY. Oh, I see.

DORIS [*putting on her gloves*]. You can put everything on the tray when you've finished and leave it in the kitchen for Ethel.

HENRY. Good old Ethel.

DORIS [*surprised*]. What?

HENRY. I said good old Ethel.

DORIS. Well, it sounded very silly, I'm sure.

MRS. ROCKETT [*scrutinizing him*]. What's the matter with you?

HENRY. Nothing, why?

MRS. ROCKETT. You look funny.

HENRY. I feel funny.

MRS. ROCKETT. Have you been drinking?

HENRY. Yes.

DORIS. Henry!

MRS. ROCKETT. I knew it!

HENRY. I had a whisky and soda in town and another one at the Plough.

DORIS [*astounded*]. What for?

HENRY. Because I felt like it.

DORIS. You ought to be ashamed of yourself.

HENRY. I'm going to have another one too, a bit later on.

DORIS. You'll do no such thing.

HENRY. That hat looks awful.

DORIS [*furiously*]. Don't you speak to me like that.

HENRY. Why not?

DORIS [*slightly non-plussed*]. Because I won't have it—that's why not.

HENRY. It's a common little hat and it looks awful.

DORIS [*with an admirable effort at control*]. Now listen to me, Henry Gow, the next time I catch you drinking and coming home here and insulting me, I'll . . .

HENRY [*interrupting her gently*]. What will you do, Dorrie?

DORIS [*hotly*]. I'll give you a piece of my mind, that's what I'll do.

HENRY [*rising*]. It'll have to be a very little piece. You can't afford much! [*He laughs delightedly at his own joke.*]

DORIS. I'd be very much obliged if you'd kindly tell me what this means?

HENRY. I'm celebrating.

DORIS. Celebrating! What do you mean, celebrating?

HENRY [*up* L.C.]. To-night's our anniversary.

DORIS [R.C.]. Don't talk so soft, our anniversary's not until November.

HENRY. I don't mean that one. To-night's the anniversary of the first time I had an affair with you and you got in the family way.

DORIS [*shrieking*]. Henry! [*She moves down stage.*]

HENRY [*delighted with his carefully calculated effect*]. Hurray!

DORIS [*beside herself*]. How dare you say such a dreadful thing, in front of the child, too.

HENRY [*in romantic tones*]. Three years and a bit after that wonderful night our child was born! [*Lapsing into his normal voice*] Considering all the time you took forming yourself, Elsie, I'm surprised you're not a nicer little girl than you are.

DORIS. Go upstairs, Elsie.

HENRY. Stay here, Elsie.

[ELSIE *dithers.*]

DORIS. Do as I tell you.

ELSIE [L.C.]. But, Mum . . .

DORIS. Mother, take her for God's sake! There's going to be a row.

[MRS. ROCKETT *rises.*]

HENRY [*firmly*]. Leave her alone and sit down. Leave her alone and sit down.

[MRS. ROCKETT *hesitates.* ELSIE *sits on the piano stool.*]

MRS. ROCKETT [*subsiding into the chair*]. Well, I never, I . . .

HENRY [*happily*]. See? It works like a charm.

DORIS. A fine exhibition you're making of yourself, I must say.

HENRY. Not bad, is it? As a matter of fact, I'm rather pleased with it myself.

DORIS. Go to bed!

HENRY. Stop ordering me about, see. [*Crossing* c.] What right have you got to nag at me and boss me? No right at all. I'm the one that pays the rent and works for you and keeps you. What do you give me in return, I'd like to know? Nothing. [*He bangs the table.*] I sit through breakfast while you and Mother wrangle. You're too busy being snappy and bad-tempered even to say good-morning. I come home tired after working all day and ten to one there isn't even a hot dinner for me; here, see this ham? That's what I think of the ham. [*He throws it at her feet.*] And the tomatoes and the A.1 bloody sauce! [*He throws them, too.*]

DORIS [*screaming*]. Henry! All over the carpet. [*Getting plate and knife.*]

HENRY [*throwing the butter-dish face downwards on the floor*]. And that's what I think of the carpet. [*He moves* L.]

DORIS [*scraping up the butter on to the plate*]. That I should live to see this! That I should live to see the man I married make such a beast of himself!

HENRY. Stop working yourself up into a state, you'll need all your control when you've heard what I'm going to say to you.

DORIS [*making a move to him*]. Look here . . .
HENRY. Sit down. And you. And you.

[MRS. ROCKETT *and* ELSIE *sit again.*]

I'm afraid you'll have to miss the pictures for once.
DORIS. Elsie, you come with me.
MRS. ROCKETT. Yes, go on, Ducks.

[DORIS *makes a movement towards the door, but* HENRY *is too quick for her. He locks the door and slips the key into his pocket.*]

HENRY. I've been waiting for this moment for fifteen years, and believe me it's not going to be spoilt for me by you running away.
DORIS [*on the verge of tears*]. Let me out of this room.
HENRY. You'll stay where you are until I've had my say.
DORIS. Let me out of this room. Don't you lay your hands on me. [*Bursting into tears and sinking down at the table.*] Oh! Oh! Oh! . . .

[*She falls into the chair* R. *of the table as he pushes her.*]

ELSIE [*starting to cry too*]. Mum—— Oh, Mum . . .
HENRY. Here you, shut up, go and get the port out of the sideboard and give some to your mother . . . Go on, do as I tell you.

[ELSIE, *terrified and hypnotized into submission, goes to the sideboard cupboard and brings out a bottle of invalid port and some glasses, snivelling as she does so.* DORIS *continues to sob.*]

That's right. [*He crosses up* C.]
MRS. ROCKETT [*quietly*]. You drunken brute, you!
HENRY [*cheerfully*]. Worse than that, Mother, far worse. Just you wait and see.

[ELSIE *sits on the chair* L. *of the table.*]

MRS. ROCKETT [*ignoring him*]. Take some port, Dorrie, it'll do you good.
DORIS. I couldn't touch any—it'd choke me . . .
HENRY [*pouring some out*]. Come on—here . . .
DORIS. Keep away from me.
HENRY. Drink it and stop snivelling.
DORIS. I'll never forgive you for this, never, never, never, as long as I live. [*She gulps down some port.*]
HENRY [*noting her gesture*]. That's better.
MRS. ROCKETT. Pay no attention, Dorrie, he's drunk.
HENRY. I'm not drunk. I've only had two whiskies and sodas, just to give me enough guts to take the first plunge. You'd never believe how scared I was, thinking it over in cold blood. I'm not scared any

more though, it's much easier than I thought it was going to be. My only regret is that I didn't come to the boil a long time ago, and tell you to your face, Dorrie, what I think of you, what I've been thinking of you for years, and this horrid little kid, and that old bitch of a mother of yours.

MRS. ROCKETT [*shrilly*]. Henry Gow!

HENRY. You heard me, old bitch was what I said and old bitch was what I meant.

MRS. ROCKETT. Let me out of this room. [*Rising and crossing to the window.*] I'm not going to stay here and be insulted—I'm not . . .

[*They all rise.*]

HENRY. You're going to stay here just as long as I want you to.

MRS. ROCKETT. Oh, am I? We'll see about that. . . .

[*With astonishing quickness she darts over to the window and manages to drag one open.* HENRY *grabs her by the arm.*]

HENRY. No, you don't.

MRS. ROCKETT. Let go of me.

DORIS. Oh, Mother, don't let the neighbours know all your business.

HENRY. Not on your life!

MRS. ROCKETT [*suddenly screaming powerfully*]. Help! Help! Police! Help! Mrs. Harrison—help! . . .

[HENRY *drags her away from the window, turns her round and gives her a light slap on the face; she staggers against the piano. Meanwhile he shuts the window again, locks it and pockets the key.*]

DORIS [*looking at him in horror—runs to below the table*]. Oh, God! Oh, my God!

ELSIE [*bursting into tears again*]. Oh, Mum, Mum, he hit Grandma! Oh, Mum . . .

[*She runs to* DORIS, *who puts her arm around her protectively.*]

MRS. ROCKETT [*gasping*]. Oh——my heart! I think I'm going to faint—— Oh—my heart—— Oh—— Oh—— Oh, dear——

[MRS. ROCKETT *slides on to the floor, perceptibly breaking her fall by clinging on to the piano stool.*]

DORIS. Mother!

HENRY. Stay where you are.

[HENRY *goes to the sideboard and pours out a glass of water.* DORIS, *disobeying him, runs over to her mother.* ELSIE *wails.*]

Stand out of the way, Doris, we don't all want to get wet.

[*He approaches with the glass of water.* MRS. ROCKETT *sits up weakly.*]

MRS. ROCKETT [*in a far-away voice*]. Where am I?

HENRY. Number Seventeen Cranworth Road, Clapham.

MRS. ROCKETT. Oh—oh, dear!

HENRY. Look here, Mother, I don't want there to be any misunderstanding about this. I liked slapping you just now, see? It was lovely, and if you don't behave yourself and keep quiet I shall slap you again. Go and sit in your chair and remember if you feel faint the water's all ready for you.

[*He helps her up and escorts her to her chair by the fire. She collapses into it and looks at him balefully.*]

Now then. Sit down, Dorrie, you look silly standing about.

DORIS [*with a great effort at control—sits in* HENRY's *chair*]. Henry——

HENRY [*slowly, but very firmly*]. Sit down! And keep her quiet or I'll fetch her one too.

DORIS [*with dignity*]. Come here, Elsie.

[ELSIE *sits on the chair* R. *of the table.*]

[*Banging her back*] Shut up, will you!

HENRY. That's right.

[*He walks round the room slowly and in silence, looking at them with an expression of the greatest satisfaction on his face. Finally he goes over to the fireplace;* MRS. ROCKETT *jumps slightly as he approaches her, but he smiles at her reassuringly. Meanwhile* DORIS, *recovering from her fear, is beginning to simmer with rage; she remains still, however, watching.*]

[*Sitting on the piano stool*] Now then. I'm going to start, quite quietly, explaining a few things to you.

DORIS. Enjoying yourself, aren't you?

[MRS. ROCKETT *wipes her neck with her handkerchief.*]

HENRY. You've said it.

DORIS [*gaining courage*]. You'll grin on the other side of your face before I've done with you.

HENRY [*politely*]. Very likely, Dorrie, very likely indeed!

DORIS. And don't you Dorrie me either! Coming home here, drunk, hitting poor Mother and frightening Elsie out of her wits.

HENRY. Out of her what?—— Do her good, do 'em both good, a little excitement in the home. God knows, it's dull enough as a rule.

DORIS [*with biting sarcasm*]. Very clever, oh, very clever, I'm sure.

HENRY. Sixteen years ago to-night, Dorrie, you and me had a little rough and tumble in your Aunt Daisy's house in Stansfield Road, do you remember?

DORIS. Henry—— [*Pointing to* ELSIE.]

HENRY [*ignoring her*]. We had the house to ourselves, it being a Sunday, your aunt had popped over to the Golden Calf with Mr. Simmonds, the lodger, which, as the writers say, was her wont——

MRS. ROCKETT [*rising*]. This is disgusting, I won't listen to another word.

HENRY [*rising—rounding on her*]. You will! Shut up!

[MRS. ROCKETT *sits.*]

DORIS. Pay no attention, Mother, he's gone mad.

HENRY. Let me see, now, where was I? Oh yes, Stansfield Road. You'd been after me for a long while, Dorrie. I didn't know it then, but I realized it soon after. You had to have a husband, what with Nora married and Phyllis engaged, both of them younger than you, you had to have a husband, and quick, so you fixed on me. You were pretty enough and I fell for it hook, line and sinker; then, a couple of months later you told me you'd clicked, you cried a hell of a lot, I remember, said the disgrace would kill your mother if she ever found out. I didn't know then that it'd take a sight more than that to kill that leathery old mare——

MRS. ROCKETT [*bursting into tears*]. I won't stand it, I won't! I won't!

HENRY [*rising above her sobs*]. I expect you were in on the whole business, in a refined way of course, you knew what was going on all right, you knew that Dorrie was no more in the family way than I was, but we got married; you both saw to that, and I chucked up all the plans I had for getting on, perhaps being a steward in a ship and seeing a bit of the world. Oh yes, all that had to go and we settled down in rooms and I went into Ferguson's Hosiery.

DORIS. I've given you the best years of my life and don't you forget it.

HENRY. You've never given me the best of anything, not even yourself. You didn't even have Elsie willingly.

DORIS [*wildly*]. It's not true—stop up your ears, Elsie, don't listen to him, he's wicked—he's wicked——

[ELSIE *makes to do it.*]

HENRY [*grimly*]. It's true all right, and you know it as well as I do.

DORIS [*shrilly*]. It was only right that you married me. It was only fair! You took advantage of me, didn't you? You took away my innocence. It was only right that you paid for it.

HENRY. Come off it, Dorrie, don't talk so silly. I was the innocent one, not you. I found out you'd cheated me a long long time ago, and when I found out, realized it for certain, I started cheating you. [*He leans on the chair* L. *of the table.*] Prepare yourself, Dorrie, my girl, you're going to be really upset this time. I've been saving! Every week for over ten years I've been earning a little bit more than you thought I was. I've managed, by hook and by crook, to put by five hundred and seventy-two pounds—d'you hear me?—five hundred and seventy-two pounds!

MRS. ROCKETT [*jumping to her feet*]. Henry! You never have—it's not true——

DORIS [*also jumping up*]. You couldn't have—you'd have given it away—I should have found out——

HENRY. I thought that'd rouse you, but don't get excited.

[MRS. ROCKETT *sits again.*]

I haven't got it on me, it's in the bank. And it's not for you, it's for me—all but fifty pounds of it, that much is for you, just fifty pounds, the last you'll ever get from me——

DORIS. Henry! You couldn't be so cruel. You couldn't be so mean!

HENRY. I've done what I think's fair and what I think's fair is a damn sight more than you deserve. To start with I've transferred the freehold of this house into your name so you'll always have a roof over your head—you can take in lodgers at a pinch, though God help the poor bleeders if you do!

DORIS. Five hundred and seventy-two pounds! You've got all that and you're going to leave me to starve! [*She takes off her coat and puts it on the chair down* R.]

HENRY. Cut out the drama, Dorrie, and have a look at your mother's savings bank book—I bet you'll find she's got enough to keep you in comfort till the day you die. She soaked her old man plenty, I'm sure—before he took to soaking himself!

MRS. ROCKETT. It's a lie. [*She rises.*]

HENRY. Now listen to me! Mother Machree—you've 'ad one sock in the jaw this evening and you're not just asking for another, you're sitting up and begging for it.

[DORIS *pulls the curtains back.*]

MRS. ROCKETT. I'll have you up for assault. I'll have the police on you, my fine fellow!

HENRY. They'll have to be pretty nippy—my boat sails first thing in the morning.

DORIS [*horrified*]. Boat! [*At the window.*]

[MRS. ROCKETT *sits.*]

HENRY [*moving up* C.]. I'm going away. I've got my ticket here in my pocket, and my passport. My passport photo's a fair scream, I wish

I could show it to you, but I don't want you to see the nice new name I've got.

DORIS [*crossing to him*]. Henry, you can't do it, I can have you stopped by law. Its desertion.

HENRY. That's right, Dorrie, you've said it. Desertion's just exactly what it is.

DORIS [*breathlessly*]. Where are you going, you've got to tell me. Where are you going?

HENRY. Wouldn't you like to know? Maybe Africa, maybe China, maybe Australia. There are lots of places in the world you know nothing about, Dorrie. You've often laughed at me for reading books, but I've found out a hell of a lot from books.

[DORIS *sits on* HENRY's *chair.*]

There are islands in the South Seas, for instance, with coco palms and turtles and sunshine all the year round—you can live there for practically nothing, then there's Australia or New Zealand; with a little bit of capital I might start in a small way sheep farming. Think of it; miles and miles of open country stretching as far as the eye can see—good food and fresh air—that might be very nice, that might suit me beautifully. Then there's South America. There are coffee plantations there, and sugar plantations, and banana plantations. If I go to South America I'll send you a whole crate. 'Ave a banana, Dorrie! 'Ave a banana!

DORIS. Henry, listen to me, you can't do this dreadful thing, you can't! If you don't love me any more, think of Elsie.

HENRY [*still in his dream*]. Then there's the sea, not the sea we know at Worthing with the tide going in and out regular and the band playing on the pier. The real sea's what I mean. The sea that Joseph Conrad wrote about, and Rudyard Kipling and lots of other people, too, a sea with whacking great waves and water spouts and typhoons and flying-fish and phosphorus making the foam look as if it was lit up.

[DORIS *turns up stage on her chair.*]

Those people knew a thing or two, I can tell you. They knew what life could be like if you give it a chance. They knew there was a bit more to it than refinement and fumed oak and getting old and miserable with nothing to show for it. I'm a middle-aged man, but my health's not too bad, taken all round. There's still time for me to see a little bit of real life before I conk out. I'm still fit enough to do a job of work—real work, mind you—not bowing and scraping and wearing myself out showing fussy old cows the way to the lace and the china ware and the bargain basement. [*He crosses to the fireplace.*]

DORIS [*hysterically*]. God will punish you, you just see if He doesn't, you just see——

HENRY. God's been punishing me for fifteen years, it's high time He laid off me now. He's been punishing me good and proud for being damn fool enough to let you get your claws into me in the first place——

DORIS [*changing her tactics*]. Henry, have pity, for God's sake have pity.

HENRY. And don't start weeping and wailing either, because it won't wash. I know you, Dorrie, I know you through and through. You're frightened now, scared out of your wits, but give you half a chance and you'd be worse than ever you were. You're a bad lot, Dorrie, not what the world would call a bad lot but what I call a bad lot. Mean and cold and respectable.

DORIS [*rising and going to him*]. Listen to me, Henry, you've got to listen—you must. You can't leave us to starve, you can't throw us on to the streets—if I've been a bad wife to you, I'm sorry—I'll try to be better, really I will, I swear to God I will—— You can't do this. If you won't forgive me, think of Elsie, think of poor little Elsie——

HENRY. Poor little Elsie, my eye! I think Elsie's awful, I always have ever since she was little. She's never done anything but whine and snivel and try to get something for nothing——

ELSIE [*wailing*]. Oh, Mum, did you hear what he said? Oh, Dad, oh dear——

MRS. ROCKETT [*crossing and comforting her*]. There, there, dear, don't listen to him—— [*She sits in the chair L. of the table.*]

HENRY. Elsie can go to work in a year or so; in the meantime, Dorrie, you can go to work yourself, you're quite a young woman still and strong as an ox.—Here's your fifty pounds——

[*He takes an envelope out of his pocket and throws it on to the table. Then he goes towards the door.* DORIS *rushes after him and hangs on to his arm.*]

DORIS. Henry, Henry, you shan't go, you shan't——

HENRY [*struggling with her*]. Leave hold of me. [*He goes to the door.*]

DORIS [*following him*]. Mother, Mother—help—help me, don't let him go——

MRS. ROCKETT. Run, Doris, run!

[HENRY *frees himself from her and, taking her by the shoulders, forces her back into a chair, then he unlocks the door and opens it.*]

HENRY. I'm taking my last look at you, Dorrie. I shall never see you again as long as I live—— It's a dream come true.

[DORIS *buries her head in her arms and starts to sob loudly.* MRS. ROCKETT *sits transfixed, staring at him murderously.*]

[*Quietly*] Three generations. Grandmother, Mother and Kid. Made of the same bones and sinews and muscles and glands, millions of you, millions just like you. You're past it now, Mother, you're past the thick of the fray, you're nothing but a music-hall joke, a mother-in-law with a bit of money put by. Dorrie, the next few years will show whether you've got guts or not. Maybe what I'm doing to you will save your immortal soul in the long run. That'd be a bit of all right, wouldn't it? I doubt it, though, your immortal soul's too measly. You're a natural bully and a cheat and I'm sick of the sight of you; I should also like to take this opportunity of saying that I hate that bloody awful slave bangle and I always have. As for you, Elsie, you've got a chance, it's a slim one, I grant you, but still it's a chance. If you learn to work and be independent and, when the time comes, give what you have to give freely and without demanding lifelong payment for it, there's just a bit of hope that you'll turn into a decent human being. At all events, if you'll take one parting piece of advice from your cruel, ungrateful father, you'll spend the first money you ever earn on having your adenoids out. Goodbye, one and all. Nice to have known you!

[*The wails of* DORIS *and* ELSIE *rise in volume as he goes jauntily out, slamming the door behind him.*]

CURTAIN

———

Brief Commentary on *Fumed Oak*

"*A Good Lesson!*" and *Fumed Oak*—each very British in its way—suggest some interesting comparisons. They are both upon domestic themes. Each of them depicts the eternal conflict of the sexes for domestic sovereignty, a theme as old as Chaucer and older. The marriage of Victoria and Albert—whatever the original necessities of state policy—was built upon a very deep and mutual love. The marriage of Doris and Henry—whatever the original compulsions of their union—was built upon deceit and mutual antipathy. Albert wins his domestic tussle with Victoria and wins a loving sovereignty in their personal relations. Henry wins his dramatic tussle with Doris and throws his hard-gained sovereignty in her face as he leaves her.

But let us look more closely at the dramaturgy of *Fumed Oak*. The protagonist is obviously Henry Gow. He wants to escape from his intolerable family. His principal antagonist is, of course, Doris. The deciding factor is, perhaps, his ability to keep his own counsel, bide his time, save and plan secretively. The whole action takes us back to the time when Doris tricked him into marriage (the inciting incident); the enacted drama shows only the morning and evening events of the final day, culminating in his walking out (the final incident). The play, then, makes use of "fifth-act structure."

The situation at rise shows Henry in the midst of a nagging, whining, complaining household. This is revealed through the dialogue and action of Scene I. There is no more than a hint that Henry is up to anything. The dramatic question—Will Henry free himself?—does not emerge until the exposition of Scene II. Now, upon Henry's return, we see his new-found elation and courage. We hear his shocking revelation of the inciting incident, his self-assertion, his telling off both Doris and her mother, the further exposition of his domestic life, his secretive saving, his plan to leave Doris for the venturesome life that she denied him, his declaration of independence. His exit brings down the final curtain upon the deserted family. In viewing the whole action, one can see the scheming and strategy, the strife and struggle, the successes and set-backs, the suffering and suspense—with conflict, complications, crises, and climax—that comprise the plot of this little domestic drama.

III. THE STAGEPLAY

Production for Presentation

The art of drama is the presentation of life in the theater:
the art of theater is the presentation of drama.
> —ELIZABETH DREW, *Discovering Drama*

THE THEATER AND STAGE together comprise a wonderful workshop, a machine, and a showcase. In it and through it a whole company of artists join their several talents in the co-operative creation of a stageplay. This they purvey, as a perishable commodity, directly to their customers, who consume it on the spot.

In the preceding essay we centered our attention upon the play-script—its creation by the playwright. It is hoped that, with some little knowledge of dramaturgy and the art of playwriting, you will read dramas and see plays with greater understanding and appreciation, and that your complex drama experiences will be more clearly structured and more meaningful.

Now, approaching the drama from a different point of view, we shall focus our thoughts upon the stageplay and *its* creation by the artists of the theater. Even this brief survey of play production may increase your understanding and appreciation of the theater and enrich your enjoyment both as a playgoer and as a playreader.

§ 1. THEATER ART AS INTERPRETATIVE CREATIVE ACTIVITY

Earlier we spoke of a playscript as a blueprint for the building of a stageplay. Just now we have said that the playscript is created by the playwright, and that the stageplay is created by various other theater artists. It is high time we distinguish two different sorts of creative art activity carried on by two general sorts of artists. We shall call the one sort "primary" and the other sort "interpretative."

The sculptor carves a statue, the painter designs and executes a picture, the poet writes a poem. We shall in each case call this *primary* creative activity because the artist gets his inspiration and ideas from within himself, from his imagination and his observation

64

of life. In these cases the person who responds to and experiences the work of art—statue, picture, poem—perceives directly the work created by the primary artist.

However, this is not so with all the arts. The architect's plans, the composer's score, and the playwright's script are also the result of primary creative activity, bred in the artist's imagination from all manner of life experiences and given outward expression in complex symbols: architectural drafting, musical notation, and theatrical language. No one of these artists expects his own work of art—sketches, score, or script—to reach the ultimate art consumer directly. Each of these particular primary artists hopes and intends that his architectural plans will be built, that his musical composition will be performed, that his playscript will be produced.

The processes of architectural building, musical performance, and play production are *interpretative* creative activities carried on by interpretative artists. The interpretative artist in each case does not create "out of his head" like the primary artist. The contractor constructs the building from the architect's plans; the instrumentalists play the music from the composer's written score; the actors perform the stageplay from the playwright's script. The interpretative artist is no less creative an artist than the primary artist. His activity is simply different in kind, requiring different skills, creating quite different works of art. The musical composer relies upon the performers; the performers depend upon the composer. So it is with the playwright and the interpretative artists of the theater; they are mutually interdependent.

The artists and artisans of the theater are various: the producer, stage director, art director, technical director (or some combination of these as the *régisseur* or director)—the actors and actresses, sometimes also singers and dancers—the stage managers and prompter—the scene designer, stage carpenter, flyman, stagehands, scene painter—the master electrician, property master, sound technician—the musical director, for some productions, and musicians—the costume designer, seamstress, costumer, wardrobe mistress, dresser, make-up artist—and the man on the curtain! Even a rather simple stageplay with a small cast and no scene changes will call for a considerable team of artists and craftsmen during the period of rehearsal and construction, with a somewhat different team during opening performances and the run of the show.

The director, actors, designers—and only in less degree the master artisans and technicians—are all interpretative creative artists. They all work directly or indirectly from the playwright's script as they cooperate in the creation of the stageplay. As with all interpretative creative activity, there are three phases to this work in the theater: (1) the reading, study, and understanding of the primary work, the playscript; (2) the developing and constructing of an expressive re-creation of the script; and (3) the communication or presentation of that re-creation to others, the audience. For the actors and director this means study, rehearsal, and performance.

Theater artists, then, are middlemen in the distribution of the playwright's stories to the spectators in the audience.

§ 2. ACTORS AS INTERPRETATIVE ARTISTS

A stageplay, as we said, is a story presented directly *by actors.* Before the actors appear in front of an audience to give a performance of the playwright's story, they will already have engaged in a great deal of creative activity—extensive study and rehearsal. To understand what this involves, it may be well to think of the actor as three persons rolled into one.

The actor is, first of all, an *impersonator,* a personal mimic. That is, he takes upon himself the behavior and speech patterns, the costume and make-up, of the fictional character he represents. He is skilled in characterization—getting into and keeping in character— projecting the presence of a personality. The character, of course, is his part in the play, his role.

Second, the actor is also a *pantomimic*—a mime. That is, he directly acts out the principal incidents of the story. He enters and exits, sits and rises, crosses and stands still, approaches and retreats. He turns and twists, points and gestures, salutes and backslaps, strikes and wards blows. He nods and shakes his head, smiles and laughs, frowns and glances, and so on. The actor, like the dancer, is skilled in the expressive use of his body and its members, in the acting out of the business of the dramatic incidents, and in reacting to the actions of others.

Third, the actor is also a *speaker,* an elocutionist (to use a discredited word), an oral interpreter of dramatic dialogue. This speech art is quite different from the arts of oratory, declamation, public address, oral reading, and conversation. The actor will need superior vocal equipment, adequate tone and volume, expressive range and quality. He will use skills in utterance and phrasing, articulation and enunciation, characterizing diction and dialects.

He will develop the power to communicate ideas and project emotions, the ability to engage in the ensemble of dialogue and the extended monologue, the techniques of pointing, building, and topping. He will learn his lines and cues swiftly and accurately, retain them, and recall them without prompting. And he will have to listen appropriately to the speeches of the other actors.

The actor, then, will be an impersonator, a pantomimic, and a speaker at one and the same time. Therefore, when he is engaged in the study of his role, he will be alert to three different sorts of data: character traits, action hints, and oral clues.

The actor's work will begin with a thoughtful *study* of the whole script, whether through individual reading or rehearsals. He will need to know what this story is that he and others will act out together upon the stage. He will also need to know what the director understands its plot and characters and theme to be. Then he will proceed to the close and careful study of his own lines. What, he will ask of each speech, is the sense, tone, feeling, and intention? What is the relation of this line to the situation and to the incidents past and present? What does it tell about the personality of the character? about his traits, his motivation, his actions and reactions? This study is the first phase of the actor's preparatory work.

The second phase of this creative activity will be carried on largely in *rehearsal,* but also in private oral practice. The actor will try out various readings of the lines. He will develop his gestures and business. He will rehearse the ensemble with others in the cast. Together with the director they will develop their expressive re-creation, making a stageplay from the playwright's script.

Let us see how this threefold actor might go at the study and development of a particular role—it might be Henry Gow or Doris.

In his function of impersonator he will be alert to all the clues to characterization. Henry Gow is described in the opening stage direction as "tall and spare, neatly dressed in a blue serge suit . . . rimless glasses . . . hair is going gray at the sides and thin on top." With no formal character sketch in the dialogue of *Fumed Oak,* Henry is characterized primarily by what he himself says and does. And that is hardly anything at all until the end of Scene I, when he answers Doris's charged question—with a bland lie. It is in Scene II that Henry becomes a person. There, one by one, his personality traits emerge—his fear and hatred of Doris, his contempt for her mother and disgust with the child—his realization of how he was trapped—his long patience, abiding his time of escape, his enjoyment in sudden dominance, his clear-sighted appraisal of the three women, his romantic dream. There is nothing heroic about him. He is essentially a small man, though he has gradually accumulated both the means and the courage to declare his independence and to make a break for it.

As an impersonator the actor will—whether systematically or intuitively—gather the characterizing data and synthesize a personality. Then comes the actor's problem of working out the playing of the part. How can he externalize the character of Henry Gow? What posture and bearing, mode of action and gesture will help him to look the part? What voice quality and diction will be "in character" for those few speeches at the end of Scene I? How much change in speech pattern at the beginning of Scene II? When the suppressed and silent Henry Gow at long last finds his courage and tongue to speak, his outward behavior is transformed. But the actor will—consciously or not—study and practice to create a single characterization.

The actor as pantomimic also will study the script and/or his sides, especially the stage directions that specify his particular business: [HENRY *rises and fetches the paper out. . . . He warms his hands at the fire.*] But he will also note, whether in his private study or in rehearsal, the glances and gestures and stage movement implicit for him in his lines: "That hat looks awful. . . . Leave her alone and sit down." Then, too, the actor will be alert to those lines and actions of others in his scenes that suggest his own reactions— glances, attention, turning, and gestures. The actor and director will have to decide how often, during the opening scene, Henry should attract the audience's attention and evoke their thoughts about his place in this household by some business at the breakfast table.

The actor as speaker will study his lines with utmost critical care and creative imagination. The full meaning of some of Henry's lines may not be as obvious to the actor as he at first thinks. He may reflect upon the presumed intention of the character, but also upon the dramatic intention of the playwright. When Mrs. Rockett, for whom this scene is reminiscent, takes charge of the situation after Henry's return, she says (*scrutinizing him*):

What's the matter with you?
HENRY. Nothing, why?
MRS. ROCKETT. You look funny.
HENRY. I feel funny.

MRS. ROCKETT. Have you been drinking?

HENRY. Yes.

The actor must realize that Henry is by no means drunk—he does not feel queasy or lightheaded—but exhilarated and strange in this new defiance. The "Yes," the actor may decide, is cool and smiling, apparently casual yet pointed, a minor crisis or turning point in the long smoldering war with Doris. So, the full meaning of each speech—its special sense, tone, feeling, and intention—will be thought out. Then the actor will study and practice to find and perfect the speech patterns, tones of voice, and gestures that will express and communicate his understanding.

He will have to learn, memorize, his lines and cues, of course. He will rehearse with the others in his scenes to develop the give and take, the alternate speaking and listening, the ensemble of dialogue. He will become conscious of the shifting dominance from one character to another in the scene, the building up of tension toward the crucial speeches and the relaxing of tension so that the following sequence can then develop and build toward its own crisis. So Henry's speech beginning, "I'm not drunk . . ." will climax in his telling off Mrs. Rockett—to be followed by her attempted escape, with shouts and screams, the business culminating in Henry's slapping her face!

The actor will have to create a single pattern of dialogue and business and character in his own understanding and imagination before he can finally perfect them for performance before an audience. So, too, the reader of a drama must, as he interprets the book, create the patterns of dialogue and business and character in *his* understanding and imagination as part of the process of experiencing the play. For in the drama comparatively little is stated; much is implied.

§ 3. THE ART DIRECTOR AS SCENE DESIGNER

Moving forward in our consideration of the stageplay, we shall again recur to our basic definition: A stageplay is a story presented directly *upon a stage*.

First of all, the stage itself is the physical environment of the actors' performance. It is the place where they act out the story. To serve this primary function, a stage must provide sufficient room for the actors to perform their essential business. There must be adequate access to it for their entrances and exits. And the stage must be visible to the assembled audience. That is, there must be enough light to see the players, and all the spectators should be within eyeshot.

In the second place, the stage is the physical environment of the characters portrayed and the incidents enacted. *Scene,* you will recall, is one of the six elements of story. It is the place of the action, the setting in which the events occur. The stageplay as a story has its scene suggested to the imagination of the audience by the stage setting, the properties, the lights, the sound and music. However, the scene will also be suggested to the imagination of the audience by the dialogue and even the pantomime. Some modern plays have used the most realistic of scenery. Others have used evocative language and movement to suggest the scene. The setting for Shakespeare's plays was the relatively unchanging and unpictorial stage of the Globe Theater, with its curtained inner and upper stages and but few properties. Shakespeare therefore relied largely upon poetry and pageantry to paint the scenes of his dramatic stories—the courtroom, castle tower, romantic woods, moonlit garden, or battlefield. The scene designer emerged as an artist in the Renaissance, though not in England for Shakespeare's theater. The history of this branch of theater art is an interesting one, from Inigo Jones to Donald Oenslager and the other distinguished art directors of our own times. Sometimes, indeed, the scenes, spectacle, and special effects have dominated the productions that they should have served. Occasionally an audience even today will applaud a highly realistic or spectacular stage picture, gorgeous costumes, brilliant sunset, or unbelievable waterfall. At times a play written for production with a simple stage setting is quite overpowered by the elaborate efforts of a scenic designer. More often in our day, however, the stage is unobtrusively pleasing and appropriate for the dramatic purpose.

The art director—the scene and costume designer, whether two persons or one—is an interpretative artist. His creative art activity is based upon the primary work of the playwright. The first thing that he will do is to study the script. Like the actor, he will need to understand the story—the characters, the action, the plot, the theme, the special qualities of the dialogue, and the scene. The art director will also need to know how the stage director interprets the story and its elements if the final production is to possess aesthetic unity as a work of art.

In planning such stage settings as are needed for the production, the scene designer will consider the time and place for each scene, the dramatic action that occurs in it, the relation of the setting to the characters and the social situation, to the plot and the theme, to the historic period and style determined upon for the production.

In addition to this there are three factors of special importance in his designing of each stage setting: First, the *floor plan*—a scaled drawing of the stage floor showing the positions of scenic units and stage properties—must be such as to accommodate the actors and serve their needs in acting out the story. The stage director will insist that this be so. All the requisite scenic elements—the doors, windows, fireplace, closet, stairs, tables, chairs, etc., that are actually to be used by the actors—must find a place in the floor plan. Furthermore, their arrangement must allow the actors to move freely and to occupy strong visual positions during their big scenes. The designer must bear in mind the horizontal plane of the stage.

A second factor that will have to be considered by the scenic designer at the same time is the *stage picture*. In our usual modern theater this means the view of the stage in the vertical plane—what the spectator will see within the proscenium arch as framed by the tormentors and teaser (masking curtains to the sides and above the opening). This elevation drawing will include not only the stage setting but also the principal properties, perhaps also groups of costumed actors. The stage picture will be created by the scene designer with all of his skill in handling of line, mass, and color in composition, using his knowledge of the so-called formal art principles—unity, balance, contrast, rhythm. He will try to realize the expressive values of the play and of the particular scene—its mood and meaning, its plot and period, its setting and style. In doing this the artist will be at his most imaginative as a designer.

The third factor important to the scene designer is *practicability*. The stage setting as planned must be possible of execution. It must be so designed that it can be built, taking account of the dimensions of the stage and of any stock pieces of scenery or equipment to be used. Usually the scene designer develops a three-dimensional cardboard model, complete with major properties, in miniature. From this the scenic studio, technical director, or stage carpenter can work most effectively in assembling or constructing the flats and doorframes, step units and platforms. From this the scenic artist can direct the painting of the set and backdrops. For those plays requiring two or more stage settings, the scenic designer will have to consider the technical problems of scene shifting, the time that can be allowed to make the changes, the space available for storing scenery, the special mechanisms that may be available for handling multiple sets—full flies, turntables, wagon stages, elevators. He may design one small setting to be placed within a larger one—or sections of one set to be reversed to form parts of the second—or an arrangement of simple architectural units to be rearranged from scene to scene, with much of the visual design dependent upon light.

The creative art activity of the scene designer is bounded by the requirements of the actors and director, by the requirements of the stage carpenter and electrician, and by the requirements of the play-script itself and the stage director's understanding of it.

Let us illustrate this matter in some detail from *Fumed Oak*. The art director will first study the opening stage direction, which is unusually explicit for this play: "The Gows' sitting room . . . indistinguishable. . . . refinement. . . . French windows at the back. . . . curtains. . . . tiled fireplace . . . upright piano . . . fumed-oak sideboard . . . door leading to the hall. . . . fumed-oak dining-room set . . . armchair . . . ornaments and framed photographs. . . . morning . . . rain . . . fire."

In designing the floor plan the question is asked: Are all of these scenic elements requisite? Which ones are merely symbolic or atmospheric? The designer will study the actual use of each one in the incidents of the play (Is the piano actually used? Yes, though it could be "written out" of the script and a gramophone substituted. But isn't that piano an important symbol of suburban respectability in that period?) The requisite scenic elements, then, and their relationships as actually used will be the basis for trying out a number of quite different floor plans—with various supplementary scenic elements, such as a settee or a closet door or a stairs, as desired. What room sizes and shapes and angles suggest themselves? what possible positions for the table, the fireplace, the piano, the sideboard, the door or doors, the window? From the various possible floor plans, the art director and the stage director will choose what they think will be the most useful, expressive, and effective.

Then comes the designing of the stage picture for *Fumed Oak*. What about the apparent height of the room? Should it appear high-ceilinged? The height of the door, window, fireplace mantle? What about the walls? painted plaster, paneled, papered, patterned? What dominant wall color? shade? brilliance? What color woodwork? curtains? (They need not be blue, of course, but remember the fumed-oak dining-room furniture.) How about the lamp fixtures? the principal pictures? Should there be a patterned rug?

These properties, of course, form part of the stage picture as much as the walls of the set.

A simple interior such as that for *Fumed Oak* presents no technical problems. But, it is well to remember, this one-act play was originally performed as one of nine—three of them being given on each of three different evenings. Therefore, Gladys E. Calthrop, who designed the settings for Noel Coward, had to consider carefully the matters of scene change and storage.

§ 4. Costumes, Properties, Lights, and Sound

The art director of a production, who is principally responsible for the visual aspects of a stageplay, may not only plan the stage settings but also the *costumes*. Sometimes, however, a separate artist designs the costumes and supervises their creation. Even in producing those modern dress plays for which the actors provide their own wardrobe, there will necessarily be a careful planning of styles, colors, and fabrics in relation to other costumes, the season, the color of the stage setting and lights.

The costume designer will create the designs for each character separately, taking into account his personality traits, his dramatic importance and plot function, the setting and dramatic action of the scene, the historic period of the story and general style of the production. And, of course, he will consider the actor's own physical proportions, for the costume will serve as one of the actor's tools. It will aid him in his impersonation of character and in his execution of the business of the play.

Think for a moment of Doris in Noel Coward's comedy and of the problem of designing a costume or costumes for her. From the opening description—and from the dialogue and stage directions that follow—the art director learns about Doris: She is thirty-five, thin, anemic; she has past prettiness, a pursed-up expression of sour gentility; she is hateful, domineering, whining, nagging—the chief antagonist in the plot—her sitting room, a suburban stereotype of middle-class refinement, fumed-oak furniture. Scene I, breakfast time, she wears a nondescript coat-frock [housecoat], a slave bangle [bracelet], and a necklace of amber glass beads. In Scene II, that evening, ready to go to the movies, she wears street clothes, with a coat, bag, and gloves at hand. The period is "the present day"— that is, 1936, when the play was first produced. These are but some of the factors to consider in designing the costumes for Doris.

But costumes are not designed singly. The costumes for a production are designed as a group. The lines and colors and fabrics must appear in appropriate relation to the character dominance, tensions and conflict, of the dramatic scene. The actors, as costumed and grouped in particular scenes, form centers of interest in the succession of stage pictures. The art director will consider how the costumes will look against the stage setting, within the scenic environment. Then, too, the costume designer must draw sketches that can actually be realized in terms of costume fabrics and construction, that can be worn comfortably by the actors, that can be donned and doffed as necessary within the moments allowed for quick changes by the script.

As scenic designer, the art director will be concerned with the visual aspect of the stage properties—the larger pieces of furniture, the drapes and curtains, the pictures on the wall. However, the actual designing of the full properties for a production will doubtless be left to the master of properties.

Properties are those material things other than scenery and costumes used by the actors in the presentation of a play. They are of several sorts.

There are the larger stage props—furniture, rugs, hangings. Then there are the smaller stage props used in dressing the set—pictures, books, nicknacks, dishes. These are all in place upon the stage when the curtain goes up. Their position is indicated on the prop plot, a floor plan of the set, beneath which they can be conveniently listed. They can then be checked by the prop master or stage manager. Some of these are hand props and will be moved about or carried off-stage by the actors during the course of the play.

A second sort of properties are those hand props carried in by the actors as they enter—such as suitcases, packages, overcoats (not worn), canes, dishes with food. Not on the stage at rise and not worn by the actor, such hand props are placed on tables or racks backstage near the appropriate door to the set. These, too, are listed for convenient checking.

The third sort are the personal props, those worn by the actor or carried in his pockets—spectacles, necklace, envelope with letter, wallet or coin purse with money, pocket watch and chain. Some of these are of great importance to the actor in his business. Others may have a symbolic relation to the theme of the play. The prop master will list them and see to it that the actor has them on his person when he is in costume and ready for the performance.

As you think again of *Fumed Oak,* you can well imagine what
its prop plot and lists would look like—not only the table with chairs,
but the cloth, dishes, silver, food; the sideboard with the items *on* it
and those *in* it; the piano with stool and its pile of music and its
nicknacks; Elsie's exercise book and satchel. Then, too, there are
the various hand props off-stage—the plate of haddock that Doris
fetches from the kitchen, the mackintosh and tam Elsie returns
wearing. Then, too, there are the props for the scene change—the
sewing materials for Doris and the cold supper for Henry. And
Henry, who wears glasses, a personal prop, now carries an envelope
with money in his pocket. The manipulation of these various properties is a significant part of the business of the actors.

Let us turn briefly to another phase of the production—the lights.
The art director will be concerned with the *lighting* of the stageplay, though he may not prepare the technical light plots himself.
Without any light at all, the actors and stage setting would be
invisible. The most obvious function of stage lighting, therefore, is
to let the spectators see clearly what is on the stage and what is
happening. Modern lighting can make the actors brilliantly visible
under spotlights of various directions and colors, which model their
features and forms. But light has other functions as well: It should
be so designed as to induce the mood desired for the scene. It should
suggest the time of day or night, the weather, the season. Then,
too, it must provide such special effects as are called for in the script
—moonlight coming in through a window, brilliant and fading
sunset, burning and crackling logs, lightning, shadows, candelabra.

There is nothing elaborate about the lighting that would be called
for in the production of *Fumed Oak*. It is a rainy spring morning
in Scene I. Dull light is seen through the window; a fire burns in
the grate. The room should seem drab, with very little general
illumination, but the actors must be clearly visible in the principal
acting areas. No light comes from the electric light brackets. In
Scene II, that evening, it is dark outside the window, the fire is still
burning. The electric lights are on (very small lamps inside the
shades); general illumination, perhaps a sickly lemon, should be
provided. Again the actors must be made clearly visible, perhaps
warmly spotted in the areas that Henry will use in his big
scenes.

The stage electrician will be able to light *Fumed Oak* easily
enough, with the advice of the art director and stage director.

Nor will the sound effects man encounter any difficulties.

There are but few special effects called for: The wailing baby—perhaps the prompter will make this sound on cue. Elsie's scampering noisily up stairs—the actress herself will doubtless simulate this effect following her exit. The slamming door as Elsie goes off to school and when Henry makes his final exit—this will probably call for a "door slam," a half door in a stout frame. This may be operated on cue as a function of the properties department. The rain at the beginning may need to be established in the minds of the spectators by a sound effect. *"Rain is trickling down the windows."* Water itself may be used, with special sprinkling gutter and trough—always messy—or a tricky light effect plus the sound of driving rain will create the illusion. The sound of rain can be simulated by lead shot rolled about upon a split-grass tray or by beans in a revolving cardboard drum. If one were to choose music as an overture or between-acts music prior to this particular play, Elsie's sort of heavy-pedaled piano music—whether "The Pixie's Parade" or some other—might do, or gramophone discs of outmoded sentiment.

Sometimes, of course, the sound and music will be very important parts of the production as a whole and will call for a master of sound effects or a musical director to design them and direct their execution or performance.

§ 5. The General Director and the Unified Stageplay

In drawing this essay to a close, something further should be said about the director.

It is the director who designs the general interpretation of the play. It is his understanding of the story—its characters and scene, action and plot, dialogue and theme—that will dominate and unify the production. But his principal job is the directing of rehearsals. There are, of course, different schools of thought about how the director should do his job. Certain directors, after study and analysis of the script, work out their interpretations in greatest detail, the reading of lines, the gestures and stage movement. Then they impose this upon the actors. Other directors feel their way along during numerous reading rehearsals, stimulating and guiding the actors in their individual interpretations, coordinating their efforts, coaching them unobtrusively, shaping the ensemble acting through suggestion rather than dictation. Perhaps most stage directors fall somewhere in between these extremes.

The director is actually a comparative newcomer in theatrical production as a separate person. In ancient times the dramatic poet seems to have directed his own plays. Shakespeare may have had a hand in coaching his fellow players. Molière tripled as playwright, leading actor, and director for his troupe. It became a function of the stage manager in the next two centuries to give the actors their entrances and positions, but without fully blocking out the action of the scenes and without in any sense directing the interpretation of the roles. It is largely within the last hundred years that stage directing has developed as a distinctive art of the theater.

The general director of a production, however, assumes a broader responsibility than the stage direction—though he may also undertake this, planning and conducting the rehearsals. From modern European theater practice, especially the development in the Moscow Art Theater under Stanislavsky, comes the term *régisseur* for what we are more likely to call the producer or director in this comprehensive sense. Such a person serves as a single creative intelligence in the production of a stageplay. He will work with and coordinate all aspects of the production—the interpretation or even the reshaping of the playwright's script—the stage direction of the actors, the characterization, pantomime, speech patterns, rhythms, timing, emphases—the art direction, the scene and properties design, the lighting plan, the costume designs and make-up—the technical direction, the scene and property construction and painting, the execution of the costumes, the sound effects—the musical direction.

It is this general director who will weld the cast, craftsmen, and crew into a unified team—who will bring the scene, characters, action, dialogue, and sundry effects into aesthetic unity—who will project to the audience a patterned story and communicate its larger theme and higher values.

Introductory Note to *The Long Voyage Home*

As a young man Eugene O'Neill wrote four short plays of the sea using as characters Driscoll, Yank, Olson, Smitty, Cocky, and other seamen of a British tramp steamer, the *S. S. Glencairn*. Together these plays comprise one of the first masterpieces of modern American drama. In *The Moon of the Carib-*

bees we see drinking, women, and fighting aboard ship anchored off the West Indies. *Bound East for Cardiff* shows us fellowship and home-hunger as Yank dies in the forecastle. *The Long Voyage Home* depicts an ironic incident ashore. And *In the Zone* dramatizes war tensions, suspicions, and shame, again in the forecastle.

Eugene O'Neill was born in 1888. He was the son of a famous actor, but grew up with contempt for the commercial theater of his youth, though he learned valuable lessons from it. As a young man he led an unsettled and irregular life, went to sea as a common seaman for several years before returning to try his hand at journalism, succumbing to an illness that gave him time to think and to decide to become a playwright.

During his convalescence he went to work at it in earnest, writing many scripts. Then he studied briefly with George P. Baker at Harvard. *Bound East for Cardiff* (1914)—which Baker thought "was no play at all"—was his first play to be produced, by the Provincetown Players (1916). His success in the little theater soon moved, with *Beyond the Horizon* (1920), to the commercial theater. He won both critical and popular acclaim. For the next fourteen years he was the outstanding American playwright—with such works as *The Emperor Jones, Anna Christie, The Hairy Ape, Desire Under the Elms, Strange Interlude, Mourning Becomes Electra,* and *Ah Wilderness!* He won the Pulitzer Prize three times and was awarded the Nobel Prize for literature in 1936, the only American dramatist given such international recognition. With varying success, many of his grim dramas have been transferred to the screen. He experimented in dramaturgy (with throbbing tom-toms, masks, multiple sets, asides and soliloquies) and in dramatic style (with naturalism, realism, expressionism) and greatly extended the range of modern drama.

The Long Voyage Home was written during World War I in the winter of 1917 in Provincetown. H. L. Mencken and George Jean Nathan published it in *Smart Set* (October, 1917). The Provincetown Players produced it in New York (November, 1917). As *S. S. Glencairn,* the four short plays of the sea were first performed together in 1924. In 1937 they were produced with an all-Negro cast in Harlem by the Federal Theater Project. During World War II they were filmed by Walter Wanger under the title *The Long Voyage Home* (1940), with John Wayne as Olson, Thomas Mitchell as Driscoll, Barry Fitzgerald as Cocky, and John Ford directing.

THE LONG VOYAGE HOME *

A Play in One Act by Eugene O'Neill

CHARACTERS

FAT JOE—*proprietor of a dive.*
NICK—*a crimp.*
MAG—*a barmaid.*
OLSON
DRISCOLL
COCKY } —*Seamen of the British tramp steamer,*
IVAN   *Glencairn.*
KATE
FREDA
TWO ROUGHS

SCENE—*The bar of a low dive on the London water front—a squalid, dingy room dimly lighted by kerosene lamps placed in brackets on the walls. On the left, the bar. In front of it, a door leading to a side room. On the right, tables with chairs around them. In the rear, a door leading to the street.*

A slovenly barmaid with a stupid face sodden with drink is mopping off the bar. Her arm moves back and forth mechanically and her eyes are half shut as if she were dozing on her feet. At the far end of the bar stands FAT JOE, *the proprietor, a gross bulk of a man with an enormous stomach. His face is red and bloated, his little piggish eyes being almost concealed by rolls of fat. The thick fingers of his big hands are loaded with cheap rings and a gold watch chain of cable-like proportions stretches across his checked waistcoat.*

At one of the tables, front, a round-shouldered young fellow is sitting, smoking a cigarette. His face is pasty, his mouth weak, his eyes shifting and cruel. He is dressed in a shabby suit, which must have once been cheaply flashy, and wears a muffler and cap.

It is about nine o'clock in the evening.

JOE [*yawning*]. Blimey if bizness ain't 'arf slow to-night. I donnow wot's 'appened. The place is like a bleedin' tomb. Where's all the sailor men, I'd like to know? [*Raising his voice*] Ho, you Nick! [NICK *turns around listlessly.*] Wot's the name o' that wessel put in at the dock below jest arter noon?

NICK [*laconically*]. Glencairn—from Bewnezerry. ['*Buenos Aires.*']

JOE. Ain't the crew been paid orf yet?

* Reprinted by permission of Random House, Inc. Copyright 1919, 1946 by Eugene O'Neill.

NICK. Paid orf this arternoon, they tole me. I 'opped on board of 'er an' seen 'em. 'Anded 'em some o' yer cards, I did. They promised faithful they'd 'appen in to-night—them as whose time was done.

JOE. Any two-year men to be paid orf?

NICK. Four—three Britishers an' a square-'ead.

JOE [*indignantly*]. An' yer popped orf an' left 'em? An' me a-payin' yer to 'elp an' bring 'em in 'ere!

NICK [*grumblingly*]. Much you pays me! An' I ain't slingin' me 'ook abaht the 'ole bleedin' town fur now man. See?

JOE. I ain't speakin' on'y fur meself. Down't I always give yer yer share, fair an' square, as man to man?

NICK [*with a sneer*]. Yus—b'cause you 'as to.

JOE. 'As to? Listen to 'im! There's many'd be 'appy to 'ave your berth, me man!

NICK. Yus? Wot wiv the peelers li'ble to put me away in the bloody jail fur crimpin', an' all?

JOE [*indignantly*]. We down't do no crimpin'.

NICK [*sarcastically*]. Ho, now! Not arf!

JOE [*a bit embarrassed*]. Well, on'y a bit now an' agen when there ain't no reg'lar trade. [*To hide his confusion he turns to the barmaid angrily. She is still mopping off the bar, her chin on her breast, half-asleep.*] 'Ere, me gel, we've 'ad enough o' that. You been a-moppin', an' a-moppin', an' a-moppin' the blarsted bar fur a 'ole 'our. 'Op it aht o' this! You'd fair guv a bloke the shakes a-watchin' yer.

MAG [*beginning to sniffle*]. Ow, you do frighten me when you 'oller at me, Joe. I ain't a bad gel, I ain't. Gawd knows I tries to do me best fur you. [*She bursts into a tempest of sobs.*]

JOE [*roughly*]. Stop yer grizzlin'! An' 'op it aht of 'ere!

NICK [*chuckling*]. She's drunk, Joe. Been 'ittin' the gin, eh, Mag?

MAG [*ceases crying at once and turns on him furiously*]. You little crab, you! Orter wear a muzzle, you ort! A-openin' of your ugly mouth to a 'onest woman what ain't never done you no 'arm. [*Commencing to sob again*] H'abusin' me like a dawg cos I'm sick an' orf me oats, an' all.

JOE. Orf yer go, me gel! Go hupstairs and 'ave a sleep. I'll wake yer if I wants yer. An' wake the two gels when yer goes hup. It's 'arpas' nine an' time as some one was a-comin' in, tell 'em. D'yer 'ear me?

MAG [*stumbling around the bar to the door on left—sobbing*]. Yus, yus, I 'ears you. Gawd knows wot's goin' to 'appen to me, I'm that sick. Much you cares if I dies, down't you?   [*She goes out.*]

JOE [*still brooding over* NICK's *lack of diligence—after a pause*]. Four two-year men paid orf wiv their bloody pockets full o' sovereigns—an' yer lorst 'em. [*He shakes his head sorrowfully.*]

NICK [*impatiently*]. Stow it! They promised faithful they'd come, I tells yer. They'll be walkin' in in 'arf a mo'. There's lots o' time yet. [*In a low voice*] 'Ave yer got the drops? We might wanter use 'em.

JOE [*taking a small bottle from behind the bar*]. Yus; 'ere it is.

NICK [*with satisfaction*]. Righto! [*His shifty eyes peer about the room searchingly. Then he beckons to* JOE, *who comes over to the table and sits down.*] Reason I arst yer about the drops was 'cause I seen the capt'n of the Amindra this afternoon.

JOE. The Amindra? Wot ship is that?

NICK. Bloody windjammer—skys'l yarder—full rigged—painted white—been layin' at the dock above 'ere fur a month. You knows 'er.

JOE. Ho, yus. I knows now.

NICK. The capt'n says as 'e wants a man special bad—ter-night. They sails at daybreak termorrer.

JOE. There's plenty o' 'ands lyin' abaht waitin' fur ships, I should fink.

NICK. Not fur this ship, ole buck. The capt'n an' mate are bloody slave-drivers, an' they're bound down round the 'Orn. They 'arf starved the 'ands on the larst trip 'ere, an' no one'll dare ship on 'er. [*After a pause*] I promised the capt'n faithful I'd get 'im one, and ter-night.

JOE [*doubtfully*]. An' 'ow are yer goin' to git 'im?

NICK [*with a wink*]. I was thinkin' as one of 'em from the Glencairn'd do—them as was paid orf an' is comin' 'ere.

JOE [*with a grin*]. It'd be a good 'aul, that's the troof. [*Frowning*] If they comes 'ere.

NICK. They'll come, an' they'll all be rotten drunk, wait an' see.

[*There is the noise of loud, boisterous singing from the street.*]

Sounds like 'em, now. [*He opens the street door and looks out.*] Gawd blimey if it ain't the four of 'em! [*Turning to* JOE *in triumph*] Naw, what d'yer say? They're lookin' for the place. I'll go aht an' tell 'em.
[*He goes out.*]

[JOE *gets into position behind the bar, assuming his most oily smile. A moment later the door is opened, admitting* DRISCOLL, COCKY, IVAN *and* OLSON. DRISCOLL *is a tall, powerful Irishman;* COCKY, *a wizened runt of a man with a straggling gray mustache;* IVAN, *a hulking oaf of a peasant;* OLSON, *a stocky, middle-aged Swede with round, childish blue eyes. The first three are all very drunk, especially* IVAN, *who is managing his legs with difficulty.* OLSON *is perfectly sober. All are dressed in their ill-fitting shore clothes and look very uncomfortable.* DRISCOLL *has unbuttoned his stiff collar and its ends stick out sideways. He has lost his tie.* NICK *slinks into the room after them and sits down at a table in rear. The seamen come to the table, front.*]

JOE [*with affected heartiness*]. Ship ahoy, mates! 'Appy to see yer 'ome safe an' sound.

DRISCOLL [*turns round, swaying a bit, and peers at him across the bar*]. So ut's you, is ut? [*He looks about the place with an air of recognition.*] 'An the same damn rat's-hole, sure enough. I remember foive or six years back 'twas here I was sthripped av me last shillin' whin I was aslape. [*With sudden fury*] God stiffen ye, come none av your dog's thricks on me this trip or I'll— [*He shakes his fist at* JOE.]

JOE [*hastily interrupting*]. Yer must be mistaiken. This is a 'onest place, this is.

COCKY [*derisively*]. Ho, yus! An' you're a bleedin' angel, I s'pose?

IVAN [*vaguely taking off his derby hat and putting it on again—plaintively*]. I don't li-ike dis place.

DRISCOLL [*going over to the bar—as genial as he was furious a moment before*]. Well, no matther, 'tis all past an' gone an' forgot. I'm not the man to be holdin' harrd feelin's on me first night ashore, an' me dhrunk as a lord. [*He holds out his hand, which* JOE *takes very gingerly.*] We'll all be havin' a dhrink, I'm thinkin'. Whiskey for the three av us— *Irish* whiskey!

COCKY [*mockingly*]. An' a glarse o' ginger beer fur our blarsted love-child 'ere. [*He jerks his thumb at* OLSON.]

OLSON [*with a good-natured grin*]. I bane a good boy dis night, for one time.

DRISCOLL [*bellowing, and pointing to* NICK *as* JOE *brings the drinks to the table*]. An' see what that crimpin' son av a crimp'll be wantin'—an' have your own pleasure. [*He pulls a sovereign out of his pocket and slams it on the bar.*]

NICK. Guv me a pint o' beer, Joe.

[JOE *draws the beer and takes it down to the far end of the bar.* NICK *comes over to get it and* JOE *gives him a significant wink and nods toward the door on the left.* NICK *signals back that he understands.*]

COCKY [*drink in hand—impatiently*]. I'm that bloody dry! [*Lifting his glass to* DRISCOLL] Cheero, ole dear, cheero!

DRISCOLL [*pocketing his change without looking at it*]. A toast for ye: Hell roast that divil av a bo'sun! [*He drinks.*]

COCKY. Righto! Gawd strike 'im blind! [*He drains his glass.*]

IVAN [*half-asleep*]. Dot's gude. [*He tosses down his drink in one gulp.*]

[OLSON *sips his ginger ale.* NICK *takes a swallow of his beer and then comes round the bar and goes out the door on left.*]

COCKY [*producing a sovereign*]. Ho there, you Fatty! Guv us another!

JOE. The saime, mates?

COCKY. Yus.

DRISCOLL. No, ye scut! I'll be havin' a pint av beer. I'm dhry as a loime kiln.

IVAN [*suddenly getting to his feet in a befuddled manner and nearly upsetting the table*]. I don' li-ike dis place! I wan' see girls—plenty girls. [*Pathetically*] I don't li-ike dis place. I wan' dance with girl.

DRISCOLL [*pushing him back on his chair with a thud*]. Shut up, ye Rooshan baboon! A foine Romeo you'd make in your condishun.

[IVAN *blubbers some incoherent protest—then suddenly falls asleep.*]

JOE [*bringing the drinks—looks at* OLSON]. An' you, matey?

OLSON [*shaking his head*]. Noting dis time, thank you.

COCKY [*mockingly*]. A-savin' of 'is money, 'e is! Goin' back to 'ome an' mother. Goin' to buy a bloomin' farm an' punch the blarsted dirt, that's wot 'e is! [*Spitting disgustedly*] There's a funny bird of a sailor man for yer, Gawd blimey!

OLSON [*wearing the same good-natured grin*]. Yust what I like, Cocky. I wus on farm long time when I wus kid.

DRISCOLL. Leave him alone, ye bloody insect! 'Tis a foine sight to see a man wid some sense in his head instead av a damn fool the loike av us. I only wisht I'd a mother alive to call me own. I'd not be dhrunk in this divil's hole this minute, maybe.

COCKY [*commencing to weep dolorously*]. Ow, down't talk, Drisc! I can't bear to 'ear you. I ain't never 'ad no mother, I ain't—

DRISCOLL. Shut up, ye ape, an' don't be makin' that squealin'. If ye cud see your ugly face, wid the big red nose av ye all screwed up in a knot, ye'd never shed a tear the rist av your loife. [*Roaring into song*] We ar-re the byes av We-e-exford who fought wid hearrt an' hand! [*Speaking*] To hell wid Ulster! [*He drinks and the others follow his example.*] An' I'll strip to any man in the city av London won't dhrink to that toast. [*He glares truculently at* JOE, *who immediately downs his beer.*]

[NICK *enters again from the door on the left and comes up to* JOE *and whispers in his ear. The latter nods with satisfaction.*]

DRISCOLL [*glowering at them*]. What divil's thrick are ye up to now, the two av ye? [*He flourishes a brawny fist.*] Play fair wid us or ye deal wid me!

JOE [*hastily*]. No trick, shipmate! May Gawd kill me if that ain't troof!

NICK [*indicating* IVAN, *who is snoring*]. On'y your mate there was arskin' fur gels an' I thorght as 'ow yer'd like them to come dawhn and 'ave a wet wiv yer.

JOE [*with a smirking wink*]. Pretty, 'olesome gels they be, ain't they, Nick?

NICK. Yus.

COCKY. Aar! I knows the gels you 'as, not 'arf! They'd fair blind yer, they're that 'omely. None of yer bloomin' gels fur me, ole Fatty. Me an' Drisc knows a place, down't we, Drisc?

DRISCOLL. Divil a lie, we do. An' we'll be afther goin' there in a minute. There's music there an' a bit av a dance to liven a man.

JOE. Nick, 'ere, can play yer a tune, can't yer, Nick?

NICK. Yus.

JOE. An' yer can 'ave a dance in the side room 'ere.

DRISCOLL. Hurroo! Now you're talkin'.

[*The two women,* FREDA *and* KATE, *enter from the left.* FREDA *is a little, sallow-faced blonde.* KATE *is stout and dark.*]

COCKY [*in a loud aside to* DRISCOLL]. Gawd blimey, look at 'em! Ain't they 'orrible?

[*The women come forward to the table, wearing their best set smiles.*]

FREDA [*in a raspy voice*]. 'Ullo, mates.

KATE. 'Ad a good voyage?

DRISCOLL. Rotten; but no matther. Welcome, as the sayin' is, an' sit down, an' what'll ye be takin' for your thirst? [*To* KATE] You'll be sittin' by me, darlin'—what's your name?

KATE [*with a stupid grin*]. Kate. [*She stands by his chair.*]

DRISCOLL [*putting his arm around her*]. A good Irish name, but you're English by the trim av ye, an' be damned to you. But no matther. Ut's fat ye are, Katy dear, an' I never cud endure skinny wimin.

[FREDA *favors him with a viperish glance and sits down by* OLSON.]

What'll ye have?

OLSON. No, Drisc. Dis one bane on me. [*He takes out a roll of notes from his inside pocket and lays one on the table.*]

[JOE, NICK, *and the women look at the money with greedy eyes.* IVAN *gives a particularly violent snore.*]

FREDA. Waike up your fren'. Gawd, 'ow I 'ates to 'ear snorin'.

DRISCOLL [*springing to action, smashes* IVAN'S *derby over his ears*]. D'you hear the lady talkin' to ye, ye Rooshan swab? [*The only reply to this is a snore.* DRISCOLL *pulls the battered remains of the derby off* IVAN'S *head and smashes it back again.*] Arise an' shine, ye dhrunken swine! [*Another snore. The women giggle.* DRISCOLL *throws the beer left in his glass into* IVAN'S *face. The Russian comes to in a flash, spluttering. There is a roar of laughter.*]

IVAN [*indignantly*]. I tell you—dot's someting I don't li-ike!

COCKY. Down't waste good beer, Drisc.

IVAN [*grumblingly*]. I tell you—dot is not ri-ight.

DRISCOLL. Ut's your own doin', Ivan. Ye was moanin' for girrls an' whin they come you sit gruntin' loike a pig in a sty. Have ye no manners?

[IVAN *seems to see the women for the first time and grins foolishly*.]

KATE [*laughing at him*]. Cheero, ole chum, 'ows Russha?

IVAN [*greatly pleased—putting his hand in his pocket*]. I buy a drink.

OLSON. No; dis one bane on me. [*To* JOE] Hey, you faller!

JOE. Wot'll it be, Kate?

KATE. Gin.

FREDA. Brandy.

DRISCOLL. An' Irish whiskey for the rist av us—wid the excipshun av our timperance friend, God pity him!

FREDA [*to* OLSON]. You ain't drinkin'?

OLSON [*half-ashamed*]. No.

FREDA [*with a seductive smile*]. I down't blame yer. You got sense, you 'ave. I on'y tike a nip o' brandy now an' gen fur my 'ealth.

[JOE *brings the drinks and* OLSON's *change*. COCKY *gets unsteadily to his feet and raises his glass in the air*.]

COCKY. 'Ere's a toff toast for yer: The ladies, Gawd— [*He hesitates —then adds in a grudging tone*]—bless 'em.

KATE [*with a silly giggle*]. Oo-er! That wasn't what you was goin' to say, you bad Cocky, you! [*They all drink*.]

DRISCOLL [*to* NICK]. Where's the tune ye was promisin' to give us?

NICK. Come ahn in the side 'ere an' you'll 'ear it.

DRISCOLL [*getting up*]. Come on, all av ye. We'll have a tune an' a dance if I'm not too dhrunk to dance, God help me.

[COCKY *and* IVAN *stagger to their feet*. IVAN *can hardly stand. He is leering at* KATE *and snickering to himself in a maudlin fashion. The three, led by* NICK, *go out the door on the left*. KATE *follows them*. OLSON *and* FREDA *remain seated*.]

COCKY [*calling over his shoulder*]. Come on an' dance, Ollie.

OLSON. Yes, I come. [*He starts to get up*.]

[*From the side room comes the sound of an accordion and a bois- terous whoop from* DRISCOLL, *followed by a heavy stamping of feet*.]

FREDA. Ow, down't go in there. Stay 'ere an' 'ave a talk wiv me. They're all drunk an' you ain't drinkin'. [*With a smile up into his face*] I'll think yer don't like me if yer goes in there.

OLSON [*confused*]. You wus wrong, Miss Freda. I don't—I mean I do like you.

FREDA [*smiling—puts her hand over his on the table*]. An' I likes you. Yer a genelman. You don't get drunk an' hinsult poor gels wot 'as a 'ard an' uneppy life.

OLSON [*pleased but still more confused—wriggling his feet*]. I bane drunk many time, Miss Freda.

FREDA. Then why ain't yer drinkin' now? [*She exchanges a quick, questioning glance with* JOE, *who nods back at her—then she continues persuasively.*] Tell me somethin' abaht yeself.

OLSON [*with a grin*]. There ain't noting to say, Miss Freda. I bane poor devil sailor man, dat's all.

FREDA. Where was you born—Norway? [OLSON *shakes his head.*] Denmark?

OLSON. No. You guess once more.

FREDA. Then it must be Sweden.

OLSON. Yes. I wus born in Stockholm.

FREDA [*pretending great delight*]. Ow, ain't that funny! I was born there, too—in Stockholm.

OLSON [*astonished*]. You wus born in Sweden?

FREDA. Yes; you wouldn't think it, but it's Gawd's troof. [*She claps her hands delightedly.*]

OLSON [*beaming all over*]. You speak Swedish?

FREDA [*trying to smile sadly*]. Now. Y'see my ole man an' woman come 'ere to England when I was on'y a baby an' they was speakin' English b'fore I was old enough to learn. Sow I never knew Swedish. [*Sadly*] Wisht I 'ad! [*With a smile*] We'd 'ave a bloomin' lark of it if I 'ad, wouldn't we?

OLSON. It sound nice to hear the old talk yust once in a time.

FREDA. Righto! No place like yer 'ome, I says. Are ye goin' up to—to Stockholm b'fore yer ships away agen?

OLSON. Yes. I go home from here to Stockholm. [*Proudly*] As passenger!

FREDA. An' you'll git another ship up there arter you've 'ad a vacation?

OLSON. No. I don't never ship on sea no more. I got all sea I want for my life—too much hard work for little money. Yust work, work, work on ship. I don't want more.

FREDA. Ow, I see. That's why you give up drinkin'.

OLSON Yes. [*With a grin*] If I drink I yust get drunk and spend all money.

FREDA. But if you ain't gointer be a sailor no more, what'll yer do? You been a sailor all yer life, ain't yer?

OLSON. No. I work on farm till I am eighteen. I like it, too—it's nice—work on farm.

FREDA. But ain't Stockholm a city same's London? Ain't no farms there, is there?

OLSON. We live—my brother and mother live—my father iss dead— on farm yust a little way from Stockholm. I have plenty money, now. I go back with two years' pay and buy more land yet; work on farm. [*Grinning*] No more sea, no more bum grub, no more storms—yust nice work.

FREDA. Ow, ain't that luv'ly! I s'pose you'll be gittin' married, too?

OLSON [*very much confused*]. I don't know. I like to, if I find nice girl, maybe.

FREDA. Ain't yer got some gel back in Stockholm? I bet yer 'as.

OLSON. No. I got nice girl once before I go on sea. But I go on ship, and I don't come back, and she marry other faller. [*He grins sheepishly.*]

FREDA. Well, it's nice for yer to be goin' 'ome, anyway.

OLSON. Yes. I tank so.

[*There is a crash from the room on left and the music abruptly stops. A moment later* COCKY *and* DRISCOLL *appear, supporting the inert form of* IVAN *between them. He is in the last stage of intoxication, unable to move a muscle.* NICK *follows them and sits down at the table in rear.*]

DRISCOLL [*as they zigzag up to the bar*]. Ut's dead he is, I'm thinkin', for he's as limp as a blarsted corpse.

COCKY [*puffing*]. Gawd, 'e ain't 'arf 'eavy!

DRISCOLL [*slapping* IVAN'S *face with his free hand*]. Wake up, ye divil, ye. Ut's no use. Gabriel's trumpet itself cudn't rouse him. [*To* JOE] Give us a drink for I'm perishing wid the thirst. 'Tis harrd worrk, this.

JOE. Whiskey?

DRISCOLL. *Irish* whiskey, ye swab. [*He puts down a coin on the bar.*]

[*JOE serves* COCKY *and* DRISCOLL. *They drink and then swerve over to* OLSON'S *table.*]

OLSON. Sit down and rest for time, Drisc.

DRISCOLL. No, Ollie, we'll be takin' this lad home to his bed. Ut's late for wan so young to be out in the night. An' I'd not trust him in this hole as dhrunk as he is, an' him wid a full pay day on him. [*Shaking his fist at* JOE] Oho, I know your games, me sonny bye!

JOE [*with an air of grievance*]. There yer goes again—hinsultin' a 'onest man!

COCKY. Ho, listen to 'im! Guv 'im a shove in the marf, Drisc.

OLSON [*anxious to avoid a fight—getting up*]. I help you take Ivan to boarding house.

FREDA [*protestingly*]. Ow, you ain't gointer leave me, are yer? An' we 'avin' sech a nice talk, an' all.

DRISCOLL [*with a wink*]. Ye hear what the lady says, Ollie. Ye'd best stay here, me timperance lady's man. An' we need no help. 'Tis only a bit av a way and we're two strong men if we are dhrunk. Ut's no hard shift to take the remains home. But ye can open the door for us, Ollie.

[OLSON *goes to the door and opens it.*]

Come on, Cocky, an' don't be fallin' aslape yourself. [*They lurch toward the door. As they go out* DRISCOLL *shouts back over his shoulder.*] We'll be comin' back in a short time, surely. So wait here for us, Ollie.
OLSON. All right. I wait here, Drisc. [*He stands in the doorway uncertainly.*]

[JOE *makes violent signs to* FREDA *to bring him back. She goes over and puts her arm around* OLSON'S *shoulder.* JOE *motions to* NICK *to come to the bar. They whisper together excitedly.*]

FREDA [*coaxingly*]. You ain't gointer leave me, are yer, dearie? [*Then irritably*] Fur Gawd's sake, shet that door! I'm fair freezin' to death wiv the fog.

[OLSON *comes to himself with a start and shuts the door.*]

OLSON [*humbly*]. Excuse me, Miss Freda.
FREDA [*leading him back to the table—coughing*]. Buy me a drink o' brandy, will yer? I'm sow cold.
OLSON. All you want, Miss Freda, all you want. [*To* JOE, *who is still whispering instructions to* NICK] Hey, Yoe! Brandy for Miss Freda. [*He lays a coin on the table.*]
JOE. Righto! [*He pours out her drink and brings it to the table.*] 'Avin' somethink yeself, shipmate?
OLSON. No. I don't tank so. [*He points to his glass with a grin.*] Diss iss only belly-wash, no? [*He laughs.*]
JOE [*hopefully*]. 'Ave a man's drink.
OLSON. I would like to—but no. If I drink one I want drink one tousand. [*He laughs again.*]
FREDA [*responding to a vicious nudge from* JOE'S *elbow*]. Ow, tike somethin'. I ain't gointer drink all be meself.
OLSON. Den give me a little yinger beer—small one.

[JOE *goes back of the bar, making a sign to* NICK *to go to their table.* NICK *does so and stands so that the sailor cannot see what* JOE *is doing.*]

NICK [*to make talk*]. Where's yer mates popped orf ter?

[JOE *pours the contents of the little bottle into* OLSON'S *glass of ginger beer.*]

OLSON. Dey take Ivan, dat drunk faller, to bed. They come back.

[JOE *brings* OLSON's *drink to the table and sets it before him.*]

JOE [*to* NICK—*angrily*]. 'Op it, will yer? There ain't no time to be dawdlin'. See? 'Urry!

NICK. Down't worry, ole bird, I'm orf. [*He hurries out the door.* JOE *returns to his place behind the bar.*]

OLSON [*after a pause—worriedly*]. I tank I should go after dem. Cocky iss very drunk, too, and Drisc—

FREDA. Aar! The big Irish is all right. Don't yer 'ear 'im say as 'ow they'd surely come back 'ere, an' fur you to wait fur 'em?

OLSON. Yes; but if dey don't come soon I tank I go see if dey are in boarding house all right.

FREDA. Where is the boardin' 'ouse?

OLSON. Yust little way back from street here.

FREDA. You stayin' there, too?

OLSON. Yes—until steamer sail for Stockholm—in two day.

FREDA [*she is alternately looking at* JOE *and feverishly trying to keep* OLSON *talking so he will forget about going away after the others*]. Yer mother won't be arf glad to see yer agen, will she? [OLSON *smiles.*] Does she know yer comin'?

OLSON. No. I tought I would yust give her surprise. I write to her from Bonos Eres but I don't tell her I come home.

FREDA. Must be old, ain't she, yer ole lady?

OLSON. She iss eighty-two. [*He smiles reminiscently.*] You know, Miss Freda, I don't see my mother or my brother in—let me tank— [*He counts laboriously on his fingers.*] must be more than ten year. I write once in while and she write many time; and my brother he write me, too. My mother say in all letter I should come home right away. My brother he write same ting, too. He want me to help him on farm. I write back always I come soon; and I mean all time to go back home at end of voyage. But I come ashore, I take one drink, I take many drinks, I get drunk, I spend all money, I have to ship away for other voyage. So dis time I say to myself: Don't drink one drink, Ollie, or, sure, you don't get home. And I want go home dis time. I feel homesick for farm and to see my people again. [*He smiles.*] Yust like little boy, I feel homesick. Dat's why I don't drink noting to-night but dis—belly-wash! [*He roars with childish laughter, then suddenly becomes serious.*] You know, Miss Freda, my mother get very old, and I want see her. She might die and I would never——

FREDA [*moved a lot in spite of herself*]. Ow, don't talk like that! I jest 'ates to 'ear any one speakin' abaht dyin'.

[*The door to the street is opened and* NICK *enters, followed by two rough-looking, shabbily-dressed* MEN, *wearing mufflers, with caps*

pulled down over their eyes. They sit at the table nearest to the door.
JOE *brings them three beers, and there is a whispered consultation,*
with many glances in the direction of OLSON.]

OLSON [*starting to get up—worriedly*]. I tank I go round to boarding
house. I tank someting go wrong with Drisc and Cocky.

FREDA. Ow, down't go. They kin take care of theyselves. They
ain't babies. Wait 'arf a mo'. You ain't 'ad yer drink yet.

JOE [*coming hastily over to the table, indicates the men in the rear
with a jerk of his thumb*]. One of them blokes wants yer to 'ave a wet
wiv 'im.

FREDA. Righto! [*To* OLSON]. Let's drink this. [*She raises her glass.
He does the same.*] 'Ere's a toast fur yer: Success to yer bloomin' farm
an' may yer live long an' 'appy on it. Skoal! [*She tosses down her
brandy. He swallows half his glass of ginger beer and makes a wry face.*]

OLSON. Skoal! [*He puts down his glass.*]

FREDA [*with feigned indignation*]. Down't yer like my toast?

OLSON [*grinning*]. Yes. It iss very kind, Miss Freda.

FREDA. Then drink it all like I done.

OLSON. Well—— [*He gulps down the rest.*] Dere! [*He laughs.*]

FREDA. Done like a sport!

ONE OF THE ROUGHS [*with a laugh*]. Amindra, ahoy!

NICK [*warningly*]. Sssshh!

OLSON [*turns around in his chair*]. Amindra? Iss she in port? I
sail on her once long time ago—three mast, full rig, skys'l yarder? Iss
dat ship you mean?

THE ROUGH [*grinning*]. Yus; right you are.

OLSON [*angrily*]. I know dat damn ship—worst ship dat sail to sea.
Rotten grub and dey make you work all time—and the Captain and
Mate wus Bluenose devils. No sailor who know anyting ever ship on
her. Where iss she bound from here?

THE ROUGH. Round Cape 'Orn—sails at daybreak.

OLSON. Py yingo, I pity poor fallers make dat trip round Cape Stiff
dis time year. I bet you some of dem never see port once again. [*He
passes his hand over his eyes in a dazed way. His voice grows weaker.*]
Py golly, I feel dizzy. All the room go round and round like I wus
drunk. [*He gets weakly to his feet.*] Good night, Miss Freda. I bane
feeling sick. Tell Drisc—I go home. [*He takes a step forward and suddenly collapses over a chair, rolls to the floor, and lies there unconscious.*]

JOE [*from behind the bar*]. Quick, nawh!

[NICK *darts forward with* JOE *following.* FREDA *is already beside
the unconscious man and has taken the roll of money from his inside
pocket. She strips off a note furtively and shoves it into her bosom,
trying to conceal her action, but* JOE *sees her. She hands the roll to*

JOE, *who pockets it.* NICK *goes through all the other pockets and lays a handful of change on the table.*]

JOE [*impatiently*]. 'Urry, 'urry, can't yer? The other blokes'll be 'ere in 'arf a mo'.

[*The* TWO ROUGHS *come forward.*]

'Ere, you two, tike 'im in under the arms like 'e was drunk. [*They do so.*] Tike 'im to the Amindra—yer knows that, don't yer—two docks above. Nick'll show yer. An' you, Nick, down't yer leave the bleedin' ship till the capt'n guvs yer this bloke's advance—full month's pay—five quid, d'yer 'ear?

NICK. I knows me bizness, ole bird. [*They support* OLSON *to the door.*]

THE ROUGH [*as they are going out*]. This silly bloke'll 'ave the s'prise of 'is life when 'e wakes up on board of 'er. [*They laugh. The door closes behind them.*]

[FREDA *moves quickly for the door on the left but* JOE *gets in her way and stops her.*]

JOE [*threateningly*]. Guv us what yer took!

FREDA. Took? I guv yer all 'e 'ad.

JOE. Yer a liar! I seen yer a-playin' yer sneakin' tricks, but yer can't fool Joe. I'm too old a 'and. [*Furiously*] Guv it to me, yer bloody cow! [*He grabs her by the arm.*]

FREDA. Lemme alone! I ain't got no——

JOE [*hits her viciously on the side of the jaw. She crumples up on the floor.*] That'll learn yer! [*He stoops down and fumbles in her bosom and pulls out the banknote, which he stuffs into his pocket with a grunt of satisfaction.*]

[KATE *opens the door on the left and looks in—then rushes to* FREDA *and lifts her head up in her arms.*]

KATE [*gently*]. Pore dearie! [*Looking at* JOE *angrily*] Been 'ittin' 'er agen, 'ave yer, yer cowardly swine!

JOE. Yus; an' I'll 'it you, too, if yer don't keep yer marf shut. Tike 'er aht of 'ere!

[KATE *carries* FREDA *into the next room.* JOE *goes behind the bar. A moment later the outer door is opened and* DRISCOLL *and* COCKY *come in.*]

DRISCOLL. Come on, Ollie. [*He suddenly sees that* OLSON *is not there, and turns to* JOE.] Where is ut he's gone to?

JOE [*with a meaning wink*]. 'E an' Freda went aht t'gether 'bout five minutes past. 'E's fair gone on 'er, 'e is.

DRISCOLL [*with a grin*].   Oho, so that's ut, is ut?   Who'd think Ollie'd
be sich a divil wid the wimin?   'Tis lucky he's sober or she'd have him
stripped to his last ha'penny. [*Turning to* COCKY, *who is blinking
sleepily*]   What'll ye have, ye little scut?   [*To* JOE]   Give me whiskey,
Irish whiskey!

THE CURTAIN FALLS

Brief Commentary on *The Long Voyage Home*

In this third short play we have moved from palace and white-collar sub-
urbia to a waterfront dive. The naturalistic details of these lower depths and
common and degraded people come from O'Neill's own observation during
his youthful *Wanderjahre,* when he lived and drank and gambled as a seaman, for a time "on the beach" at Buenos Aires, later living above Jimmie the
Priest's waterfront saloon in New York City. He was himself on one occasion
doped, robbed, and shipped off, coming to entrained for New Orleans.

As you turn back from the end of this play to its title, you realize this story
of Olson shanghaied as dramatic irony. Olson is hungry for farm and folk,
is now about to embark upon the last leg of his long voyage home. But in
the nature of things—fate, chance, coincidence—he will never get back to
Sweden. On the fearful *Amindra,* bound round the Horn under sail and a
driving and starving captain, Olson's long voyage—so it is hinted—will be to
his death, home to his final rest!

Olson, who certainly has our sympathy, if no more, is pitted against forces
both personal and impersonal. His simple desire is merely to go home. He
therefore wills to stay sober—refuses to drink anything but ginger ale—
because he knows that if he drinks at all he drinks too much, spends or loses
his money, and has to ship off again to sea. It is by coincidence that he falls
into the net of Fat Joe and Nick the crimp, for whom any seaman will serve.
Is it chance? or inscrutable destiny? Or is it Olson's own uncomplex character tempting fate? Except for his refusals of liquor, Olson is a passive protagonist. It is Fat Joe and Freda and Nick who are his plotting, conniving,
active antagonists, who separate him from his friends and administer the
knockout drops (the deciding factor) at the climax of the play. There is
hardly a struggle. At once, the catastrophe: Olson is rolled and shanghaied.
It is a final unhappy circumstance that Driscoll and Cocky return too late
and benighted to engage in his behalf.

O'Neill's playscript is rich in theatrical potential. The imaginative reader
will readily see how a director and actors, scene and costume designers,
property men and technicians would produce *The Long Voyage Home* as a
stageplay.

IV. THE PLAY

Re-creation by Spectator or Reader

> True enjoyment of the theatre . . . comes to playgoers who are active, not passive; whose eyes and ears are open, not shut; who are curious not only about the thing done but also about the manner of its doing; who can be susceptible to subject matter at the same time they are alert to treatment . . . who, even while they are surrendering to the illusion of the stage, do not forget the theatre is make-believe raised to the point of art. . . .
>
> —JOHN MASON BROWN, *The Art of Playgoing*

THE PLAY THAT REALLY COUNTS is neither the playbook nor the stageplay but the play in the mind of the spectator or reader. This is the play in its ultimate synthesis.

We have used the term "a play" in the preceding three essays as a loose synonym for a playscript, playbook, stageplay, or drama, and it is widely so used. The word is as ambiguous as "drama" itself. There are books on writing plays, on designing plays, on directing plays, on producing plays—there are also anthologies of plays.

Let us now, however, specialize our use of the term "a play" in this fourth essay to mean the story (sixfold in its scene, characters, action, plot, dialogue, and theme) as it is realized in the mind. The play, then, in this special sense exists first in the mind of the playwright. A slightly different play comes to life in the minds of the director, each actor, and others as they interpret the playscript. And ultimately, in the mind of each playgoer and each playreader, the play is evoked as a unique synthesis in response to seeing the stageplay or reading the playbook.

§ 1. CREATION, RE-CREATION, AND RECREATION

The dramatist creates the play as he writes the playscript. The actors and others in the theater re-create the play on the stage. The spectators and readers re-create the play in their minds for their recreation, whether from the stageplay or from the playbook itself.

In the preceding essay we spoke of the actors as interpretative creative artists. They study the playscript, trying to realize the play in their imaginations as the playwright conceived it. Then they give creative expression to the play as they understand it, trying through their activity to communicate it to the spectators. We called the original playwriting primary creative activity—it comes first in the sequence of events that comprise the theater process. The production and performance by the director, actors, and others is then secondary or interpretative creative activity—it comes second in the sequence of events in the theater process. We might now think of the spectator's experiencing of the play as tertiary creative activity—it comes third and last in the theater process.

But in one sense all three—playwright, actors, playgoer or reader—are interpretative. The original playwright experiences and interprets life and then gives creative expression to his understanding of it in his script. The actors experience and interpret that script, and then give creative expression to their understanding of it in the stageplay. The spectator experiences and interprets the stageplay—and then gives creative expression to his understanding of it in his own life. So, too, does the reader of a drama, though you may never have thought of playreading and playgoing as experiences that are creative of your personality. Yet it is true that your various attitudes will be shaped and reshaped, established and amplified, adjusted and altered by the experiences you have, whether actual or vicarious. And dramatic, emotionally-charged experiences will be unusually creative in this way, whether they come to you through life itself or through reading or radio or TV—or the theater.

It is not just an accident of word history, then, that gives us the two forms *re-creation* and *recreation*. The arts in various of their forms are recreational, refreshing man in body after his toil, renewing his spirit, diverting his mind, creating him anew. So, Sunday painting or photography, whittling or soap carving, improvising at the piano or singing in a choir, writing verse or letters, folk dancing or taking part in a show—these are all recreational as well as creative and re-creative, with due respect to the Latin *creare,* to create.

Even a brief glance at the word "play" in your dictionary will call your attention to its numerous senses. There are fifty-five in the *American College Dictionary* on my desk. Most of them are directly related to the arts of drama and music, to the combative and mimetic elements in life, to sport and recreation. You see a play or read a play; the actors play their parts, they play in Boston; you play the piano or play an étude; you play volley ball or cards, you play against opponents; you play dumb or play the fool, you played house as a child or played policeman, you play fair or play the game; you play around, you make a play for, or play with. There is a wide range in human expressions of the play instinct, and many of them are related to recreation, sports, and the arts.

To say that playgoing and playreading are recreational is not to belittle them. Reading a drama or seeing a stageplay will provide its special form of pleasure even when the play itself is unpleasant or bitter or tragic. Except when the compulsion is a class assignment, the motivation for theater-going or drama-reading will be the desire for recreation—but recreation of a special and enriching sort. It was Horace, the Roman poet and critic, who said that the successful dramatic poet is the one "who joins the instructive with the agreeable . . . by delighting and at the same time admonishing the reader." The reader or playgoer will not usually be content simply to escape for a few hours, to kill an evening—though such diversion may be necessary and desirable; he will expect profit as well as delight.

§ 2. THE PLAY IN THE SPECTATOR'S MIND

A stageplay—so we defined it—is a story presented by actors upon a stage *before an audience*. In the first essay we spoke briefly of the amazing interaction of the performers and the spectators. In the last essay we considered at some length the theatrical synthesis: the development and integration of the interpretative creative activities of the actors, designers, technicians. Now we must think about the play in the spectator's mind, "the ultimate synthesis," as we called it in the opening sentences of this present essay.

The ultimate synthesis is the play as the spectator experiences it. It is what you progressively realize in your mind in the course of your two hours' response to a stageplay. It is the story that you take home with you at the end of the peformance—not scene, characters, action, plot, dialogue, and theme separately, but synthesized and integrated, a unified whole. In addition to the story you, as a playgoer, may also take home and report a variety of miscellaneous observations—who sat two seats ahead of you, the crowded lobby during intermission, the information about the actors in the printed program, the inept acting of a particular role, the interesting speed of the scene changes, the sequined costume of the leading lady. But these discrete items are irrelevant to the play as synthesized in your mind. And, of course, the play as thus realized will be unique for you and significantly different for each playgoer, depending upon his past experience, his personal temperament, his keeness of observation, his skill in interpretation.

What are the separable aspects of a person's total response to the performance of a stageplay?

The first part of your total response is sensory perception—the actual *seeing and hearing* of the stageplay. Of all the arts, theater art is most fully and equally audio-visual. A musical performance is also perceived by eye as well as ear, but you do not hesitate to close your eyes or to say that you "listen" to music. A dance performance also comes through both eye and ear, but you are essentially a spectator. However, when you go to the theater, both eyes and ears will be alert and active. You will be both observer and auditor, a spectator in the audience.

The richness of your theater experience results from this double stream of sensory data. One or another of the actors on the stage is talking virtually all the time—a continuous flow of auditory stimuli demanding close attention. A stageplay usually has three times as much dialogue per hour as a motion picture, whose sound track is largely naturalistic sound effects and music.

Your ears take in this complex stream of sound waves and transmit patterns of neural energy by way of the auditory nerve to your brain, where the actual hearing takes place. It requires close attention on your part as a listener to take in this flow of dramatic dialogue, to perceive the significant word sounds and phrase patterns, to catch the emotional voice tones and speech tunes, to get the verbal and vocal clues to complex interpersonal relations.

These auditory stimuli are not received separately, of course, but together with the visual stimuli.

Your eyes—always jumping, never remaining fixed for more than a second—are constantly taking in light reflected from the actors, costumes, and stage setting. Your eyes then transmit patterns of neural energy by way of the optic nerve to the visual center of the brain, where conscious seeing takes place.

The way the eye is formed and functions allows you to see only a small area clearly enough to make out details. Your attention and gaze are usually upon the actor who is speaking. Then the light reflected from his face is brought into focus upon the hypersensitive center of your eye, the fovea of the retina, and you can see his facial expression. Now, out of the corner of your eye—the periphery is sensitive to motion—a blur catches your attention as another actor raises his hand or turns, and your eyes move to focus for a clearer view of these new details. All the while, of course, you are conscious of a vague view of the entire scene, which becomes richer in perception as the darting eyes gather in more and more details.

Important visual factors are the perception of depth and of form and color. Binocular vision provides depth cues that make for normal three-dimensional perception in the theater. Definition of form and discrimination of color are provided by the two sorts of retinal nerve endings, the rods and the cones.

What you see and hear, however, is not simply the direct result of neural impulses sent up to the brain from your eyes and ears. Perceptions involve the integration of this sense data with contextual data, past experiences. We see and hear, at least in part, what our past experiences lead us to expect to see and hear. But individual differences in perception are not only due to differences in our life experiences, but also to differences in sensory acuity and attention.

Let us assume that you are attending a performance of *The Long Voyage Home*. Your waterfront experience may be limited, so you fail to "see" that Driscoll has a drunken walk and Olson has sober sea legs. You may be so fascinated by Freda's tempting business at the table that your eyes do not jump over to Fat Joe, and you simply do not "see" the drugging of Olson's drink. Your being color-blind may have been the reason you have not "seen" Nick's red shirt as he moves over to whisper to Fat Joe. The same sorts of differences individualize what you hear.

Visual and auditory perceptions take place, not separately, but as an audio-visual unity. The eyes and ears cooperate as a TV antenna to bring in the patterned light and sound waves and to project the stageplay—full fidelity, sound, color, three-dimension, and no commercials—upon the 24-inch screen of your own brain. This sensory perception of the play is the most immediate aspect of your experience as a playgoer.

What happens next?

§ 3. The Playgoer's Naïve and Critical Responses

There are two sorts of response to this stageplay-as-perceived. One we shall call naïve—free imagery, empathy, emotion, and so on. The other we shall call critical—interpretation, analysis and synthesis, evaluation. These are like two currents in a single stream of response, warm feelings and cool thoughts flowing concurrently. We shall, however, deal with them separately.

Let us first consider your *naïve responses* to the stageplay-as-per-ceived—your various spontaneous, uncritical, natural, and affective responses to what you see and hear during the performance.

Although the setting and actors before you require most of your visual attention, you will also "see" in your mind's eye *free imagery* of other scenes that are described or suggested by the actors' words. Nick's description of the *Amindra* early in the play and Olson's few words later may serve to flash a mental picture before you of that "bloody windjammer—skys'l yarder—full rigged—painted white." And you may also catch a glimpse of Olson's family farm near Stockholm, his brother working the land, and his aged mother writing to him. But all such free images evoked by the dialogue are not visual. There may be auditory free images, too—perhaps the shouted commands of the *Amindra's* driving captain in your mind's ear—and other sorts of imagery, thermal and kinesthetic. Freda's "fair freezin' to death wiv the fog" may give you a momentary image of chill. The sounds of accordion and whooping and stamping may bring to your mind, not only a picture of the rowdy dancing couples in the next room, but also the rhythmic and muscular feel of the dancing itself.

This muscle imagery leads us directly to the next sort of naïve response—*empathy*. This is not merely kinesthetic imagery; it is the actual feeling out in your own muscular structure of the posture and actions that you observe. Psychologically you assume the posture and perform the act, and you may evidence muscular tensions as you empathize your response. Thus, empathizing Driscoll's fury as he recognizes this dive as "the same damn rat's-hole" where he was rolled five or six years back, you may feel *yourself* shaking your own fist under Fat Joe's nose. Or, empathizing Olson's dizzy response to the knockout drops, you may feel *yourself* grow weak, stagger to your feet, collapse and fall. It is in this way, psychologically, that the spectator will at times *live the play*.

From empathy as a kind of naïve response it is but another step to *emotion*. It is still convenient to define emotion in terms of "the feeling of bodily states" at times when a basic drive is blocked or frustrated. Emotions—joy, anger, hate, grief, pity, fear, hunger, love—are dynamic. Psychologists in studying them have been concerned with facial and vocal expressions of emotion—the bodily postures and actions—the respiratory, circulatory, visceral, and glandular conditions and changes. But the *feeling* of joy or fear will be, in no small measure, "the feeling of the bodily states"—the postures, tensions, muscle strains, actions—of the emotion.

The skilled actor gives outward *bodily expression* to the emotion of his character in the dramatic situation—the facial cast, the posture, the manner, the movements actually or conventionally associated with the emotion. Take Driscoll's anger, for instance. To the extent that with lively muscular imagery you empathize his sudden fury, shouting, and fist shaking (as the actor pantomimes them), you will experience "the feeling of the bodily states" of his emotion—the throat tensions and aggressive gestures of that anger. And other expressions of that anger may also, then, be experienced psychologically: the flushed face, disturbed breathing, pounding heart. In this way, *emotion is quite directly communicated by the actors to the audience*.

There are yet other sorts of naïve response in addition to free imagery, empathy, and emotion. Of these others only laughter and tears, hisses and applause—outward audience reactions—will be considered here.

Laughter will range from the smile and faint chuckle to the belly laugh and guffaw. In the full expression of laughter, you are in convulsions, your breath comes in short pants, you may grimace and gasp, with shoulders atwitch and body racked, slapping and nudging, even stamping. Laughter is infectious. It may ripple across an audience or break wide open at a single crack. Even those in an audience who do not "see the point" will empathize the laughter response of others and find themselves merrily laughing too, they know not why.

It is unnecessary to say so much about *tears* as an outward naïve response. In our theater today we do not give way but rather inhibit —though not always successfully—the snuffles and sobs that we might give way to in our extreme private grief. It has not been so in some other periods of the drama, when audiences were induced to weep copiously.

In our theater, also, audiences do not *hiss* the villain—except in sport at burlesqued melodrama. Nor do they hiss disapproval at the end of the play or at the playwright's distasteful views or political sentiments during the scenes. For that matter, audiences do not applaud, as they once did, the grand speeches of noble sentiment—though audiences may still applaud a star actress upon her entrance and any really outstanding performer upon his exit. *Applause* is usually expected of an audience, however, at the ends of scenes or acts and, most particularly, at the final curtain. Such applause may be purely conventional and perfunctory, a fingertip courtesy. Or the clapping may raise the roof, a thunderous expression of approval—with shouting and stamping—continuing (with calculated encouragement of curtain calls) until the audience is thoroughly exhausted. Such applause serves a useful purpose for the individual spectator—it releases energies still dammed up and tensions not fully relaxed by empathized participation in the play.

So much, then, for the various naïve responses that the spectator makes to the stageplay. Now let us consider the other current in the double stream of his responses to the stageplay-as-perceived.

The *critical responses* have already been referred to as interpretation, analysis and synthesis, evaluation.

When you watch and listen to a stageplay—as you perceive the play on the TV screen in your head—the mind will be filled with thoughts, your *interpretation* of the dialogue that you hear and the facial expressions, bodily postures, and actions that you see. It is as though your stream of consciousness were a constant colloquy of quick questions and answers: Why does Cocky use that tone as he orders "a glarse o' ginger beer" for Olson? Why will Olson be "a good boy dis night, for one time"? What does "crimp" mean? Such unasked questions you half answer fleetingly as you see and hear the play. They are your running thoughts about the plain sense of the statements; your thoughts about the tone, feeling, and intention of the character speaking; your understanding of the dramatic situations; your reflections upon past incidents and anticipation of things to come. This is the darting, splashing, eddying stream of thoughts that comprises your interpretation of the dialogue and pantomime as an ongoing complex of signs and symbols.

While this interpretative activity continues, you will be making critical responses of another kind. The miscellaneous data of interpretation are subjected to *analysis and synthesis;* they are sorted and patterned. You gradually realize or figure out the story and its component elements. From the actors' dialogue and pantomime within the stage setting, you gradually realize each of the characters as a personality. Their actions become meaningful, the plot is patterned, the theme emerges. This understanding will not come at once, but gradually as the running data of interpretation are classified and then integrated by your critical intelligence. You will not finally remember the details of what you have seen and heard—or all of your naïve responses and the moments you empathically and vicariously lived through—or all of your interpretative thoughts. You may, however, remember the larger patterns—characters, situations, plot, theme—that develop in the process of your experience.

Other sorts of thoughts may also occur to you while you are experiencing a play. You may have fleeting *evaluative thoughts* about the form of the play, its relation to the playwright and his other work, its relation to historical or contemporary works and events, its relation to the established dramatic types, styles, themes, values. However, much or most of this sort of critical and reflective thinking will come after the final curtain and in the days to come. Something will be said in the next essay about certain of these considerations.

To summarize, then: Through the sensory activity of your eyes and ears the stageplay is perceived as an audio-visual complex. To this, "the play in your mind," you respond naïvely with a flow of free imagery, with empathy as you "live" the play, with emotion, with laughter and applause. At the same time you respond critically to "the play in the mind" with a flow of interpretative thoughts of the meanings of the actors' words and actions, with patterning thoughts about the characters, plot, theme, and so on. "The play in your mind" and your naïve and critical responses to it comprise the play-as-experienced, what we have called "the ultimate synthesis."

However, in the theater the playgoer responds, not merely as an individual, but as one of an audience, a crowd. He becomes anonymous and feels a certain loss of personal responsibility. He follows credulously, with "the willing suspension of disbelief." He enjoys the release of certain inhibitions and the unrestrained participation. The playgoer's individual experience is both personal, then, and also social.

§ 4. THE PLAY AS EXPERIENCED BY THE READER

Playreading, some persons will say, is a sorry substitute for playgoing. Who would sit down alone to read a playbook rather than join a carefree crowd—perhaps with an amiable companion—and experience a colorful and animated stageplay? On the other hand, some persons will frankly prefer to read a drama. Who would spend $6.60 for seats, waste two hours in transportation, endure a bouncing crowd, stay up half the night to see a spectacle with mimicry? Why not simply stay home and enjoy a first-rate reading of the play!

The truth is, of course, that literature and theater are two different arts, as we said earlier. A drama is not a mere substitute for a stageplay. Experiencing a drama through reading yields a different sort of pleasure from the experiencing of a stageplay in the theater.

What are some of the differences? What are the reader's advantages?

Playreading brings you into the most direct possible contact with the mind of the playwright—the language symbols he chose and ordered as the expression of his dramatic conception in dialogue and stage directions. No interpretative artists stand in the way. No actors serve as intermediaries to add their flourishes and inflections based upon their own personal understanding or perhaps misunderstanding of the script. When you read it yourself, you get the drama direct from the playwright.

Another difference is that in playreading you control the tempo. You can read swiftly or slowly at your pleasure. You can speed up or even skip along if the going is smooth or unrewarding. You can retard and even linger over speeches that deserve or evoke reflective thought. You can also repeat the reading of a speech or scene, or glance back to reaffirm an earlier impression.

Then, too, you are free to choose both what you will read and when you will read it. All of dramatic literature awaits you upon the library shelves; you are not bound to what may be playing in the available theaters.

Such, then, are some of the differences and, in their own way, advantages in playreading. Now, what *is* a playreading experience? What does it consist of?

The only play that ever really counts, whether to the playreader or the playgoer, is the play that develops in his mind, the play as he realizes and responds to it. It must be reaffirmed that this will be different for each playreader or playgoer. Perhaps only slightly different, perhaps vastly different, depending upon the individual's past experience, his sensory perception, his predispositions and capacities in naïve and critical responses. The play in the reader's mind develops and always remains a private and personal thing— though we can, in a sort of fumbling way, discuss and share such private possessions.

The *sensory* aspect of playreading is radically different from that of playgoing. It is solely visual—not audio-visual—and it is visual in a special and restricted sense. Your eyes perform a rhythmical gymnastics in reading, which might be represented verbally as: *fixation* (saccadic jump) *fixation* (jump) *fix* (jump) *fix*—BACK SWEEP— *fixation* (jump) *fix* (jump) *fix,* etc. The only actual "seeing," in your brain, is the vague image of the page with clear vision of successive groups of black marks—the words. The immediate response to this fleeting succession of phrase perceptions is verbal interpretation, reading, your running thoughts of the meaning of the words and phrases.

The dramatic form of a playbook makes special demands upon you as a reader. At once you note the small caps, the square brackets and italic type, the systematic indentation of speech headings and stage directions. These, and the theatrical terminology, are all special signs, the by-no-means-uniform conventions of dramatic form.

The sensory and semantic process of mere reading is accompanied by the two concurrent streams of response, naïve and critical, like those of the playgoer, but with notable differences.

Among your *naïve* responses, imagery has two additional functions, both of which are of tremendous importance.

First, there is the *auditory tied-imagery* of the dialogue itself. When you read silently, you will "hear" in your mind's ear the voices of the different characters—their voice tones and speech qualities, their inflectional patterns, pauses, emphases. This auditory imagery is directly tied to your aural experience of language. It will be a misfortune for you if all the speeches "sound" alike, if Olson's rich and sober tones are the same as Ivan's slubber and Freda's rasp-voiced advances. Your enjoyment may actually be proportional to the lively dramatic dialogue that you "hear" as you read Driscoll's enraged recognition of Fat Joe and his blarney.

A second function of the imagination in playreading is the *visual free imagery* of the dramatic scene, characters, action—the "seeing" of the play in the mind's eye as you read. The general view of the scene will be established by the initial stage direction. As you read the description of the scene in *The Long Voyage Home,* your running interpretation of the sense of the words will evoke a sequence of fleeting free images of the bar over on the left and the door to a side room, the tables and chairs on the right, and the street door in the rear. For readers who are visual minded, this will build up in a general image of the scene. This setting, in the dreamlike way of imagery, will fade and change as you go on. Against it or within it will be evoked visual images of the characters—Mag, Joe, Nick—as they are described or as their characteristics emerge from the dialogue and stage directions.

The visual stuff of which these images are compounded comes, of course, from your visual past experience. It may be that into your mind's eye will pop scenery from the warehouse of your memory and stock players already costumed from the casting office of your past acquaintance. You may have difficulty in modifying and adjusting these images to your understanding of the play as you interpret it. It's hard, sometimes, to get a brunette actress out of blonde Freda's role. However, some readers will have but little visual imagery, or only vague pictures will come to mind, or vivid scenes and people but quite without respect for the playwright's expressed intent.

Within wide limits of individual temperament and experience, then, *you, the reader, will "see" and "hear" the play upon the stage of your mind in the theater of your imagination.*

You will also "see" the antecedent events that are suggested in the exposition, and you will enjoy the other sorts of free imagery, too, such as the kinesthetic and thermal imagery mentioned earlier. So, when you read a drama, you may identify yourself with one of the characters—perhaps it will be Olson—see the scene through his eyes, hear the speech of the other characters, feel his speeches upon your own mind's tongue, and empathize the grimaces, gestures, bodily tensions, and actions suggested by the stage directions and the dialogue. This "living of the part"—or of each part in turn—will evoke your emotions as a playreader very much as emotion is evoked in the playgoer, though without the freedom induced by being part of a crowd. Neither loud laughter nor tears—and of course neither hissing nor applause—will ordinarily result as a part of your reading response to a drama.

Let us turn now from the reader's various naïve responses to that other current in his response—the *critical.*

We have already spoken of the reader's immediate semantic response to the successive phrases that he perceives in the process of reading. This is comparable to the playgoer's immediate semantic response as he listens to the actors' speeches.

Reading, of course, is an amazingly complex procedure. You have stored up memory traces of millions of language-and-life experiences —*words* and word forms and word relations used in reference to particular *things,* actions, qualities, ideas. You have, by the subconscious process of abstraction, generalized these many millions so that you have in mind perhaps a hundred thousand word and phrase senses for ten or twenty thousand words in various forms and structures.

When you read a drama, the playwright's words and phrases call up generalized senses from your storehouse of language-and-life experience, references to things, actions, qualities, ideas. As you read a drama, then, you are simply reorganizing your own past experience of scenes and people, human desires, relations, tensions, interactions, deeds, conflicts, emotions, satisfactions, failures, sentiments, and expressions. Tidbits of your own life and observation are called up in this way and synthesized as a new experience, patterned by the playwright's language.

For the most part you will find each stage direction a simple and straight-forward statement, "saying what it means." There's no question when Driscoll *glares truculently at* JOE, *who immediately downs his beer,* when NICK *enters,* etc. The dialogue, however, will often be language at its most complex and compressed, charged with implication, "meaning much more than it says." As you interpret each speech, you will not only be alert to the sense of it, but to other phases of meaning—the intent of the character (and also of the dramatist), the tone of voice as suggesting his attitude, the feeling that he may be expressing or suppressing. "Play fair wid us," says Driscoll, "or ye deal wid me!" and you catch not only his statement but suggestions too—and something of O'Neill's ironic comment on the weakness of these strong men. The playwright may supply brief speech directions, phrases suggesting tone of voice or feeling or intention—*glowering; hastily; with a smirking wink.* But for the most part it will be the literary and dramatic context—the surrounding words or situation—that will provide you with clues to these separable but interrelated aspects of the full meaning as you read along.

Besides the sense, tone, feeling, and intention, there is another possible phase to the complex meaning of dramatic dialogue, and that is pantomime. Implicit in many speeches you will find various gestures, facial expressions, body movements. Actors, of course, will be most sensitive to the actions that are implied by the dialogue, but you as a playreader may consciously alert yourself to this pantomime quality in the flow of dramatic language.

It is not necessary to repeat here what was said about the larger structuring in the playgoer's critical interpretation of the play. As a playreader also, you realize gradually the interrelated elements of the story—building up the *characters* as individual personalities or types, patterning the action and the *plot* structure, generalizing the *theme*.

It is the spectator who imposes design upon the phenomena he sees and hears while in the theater. Likewise *the reader imposes design* upon the miscellaneous data resulting from his running interpretation of the dialogue and stage directions. And again it must be said that some readers are more skillful than others in this process of abstraction and synthesis. Some simply will not make the connections and perceive the relations, therefore will not "see" the characters, will not "find" the plot, will not "get" the general meaning. But even equally competent readers—because of their unique temperaments and life experiences—will impose somewhat *different patterns* upon the drama as they read it. From the same playbook you and others, then, will read individualized plays.

This will be especially true in the interpretation of the theme of the play. Sometimes the playwright is most anxious to communicate his general meaning unambiguously. He may give his script a thematic title, such as *The Long Voyage Home*—he may plant his primary idea firmly in the dialogue—he may construct his plot about "a spire of meaning"—he may create a system of dramatic symbols to objectify his theme. You will be alert to all such clues as you read. Sometimes a one-word theme—jealousy or ambition or loyalties—will emerge. Often an old adage or familiar quotation will seem to express the theme: "He who laughs last . . . ," "The sins of the fathers . . . ," "The best laid plans of mice and men . . . ," etc. But it is important to remember that some of the greatest dramas do not readily yield up their deeper significance. They remain enigmatic.

The ultimate synthesis of the play in the mind of the reader will be abstracted from the flow of sensory perceptions, naïve responses, and critical interpretations. From the dialogue imagined as heard, from the scene and actions imagined as seen, from the living "participation" in situations of tension and incidents of conflict, from the emotions and various reactions experienced, from the critical thoughts structuralizing the characters, the plot, and the theme—from all of these emerges the story as a unity in the reader's experience. *This ultimate synthesis,* for you, *is the play.*

§ 5. Suggestions for Creative Playreading

This essay will be concluded with a series of suggestions on pleasureful and profitable playreading. You can, if you wish, increase your skill in reading dramas. You can make your playreading experiences more creative and enjoyable and, at the same time, more critical and meaningful.

1. *Read drama slowly—orally—uninterruptedly—attentively.* (*a*) Although rapid reading is a useful skill for certain sorts of study, keeping up with the news, and much recreational reading, comparatively slower reading may be necessary for drama, the language of which is highly charged with meaning. Allow yourself almost as much *time to read* a play as it would take to *see* it. (*b*) Furthermore, as dramatic dialogue is written for oral delivery and aural perception, you will get more from it if you encourage vivid auditory and articulatory tied-imagery by reading much of it aloud, alone or with one or two others, or by vocalizing or silently whispering the speeches. *Reread part of each drama out loud,* at least the climatic and final scenes. (*c*) While reading a drama you will do well to avoid the interference of radio or TV—unless you have phenomenal gifts of concentration—for your sensory perceptions will be disturbed and distorted, your dramatic scenes interrupted, your illusion destroyed. Go off *by yourself* or wait until your surroundings are relatively quiet. (*d*) The dramatic form of a playbook demands attentive reading and a special pattern of eye movements, or you will slide over phrases or speech or stage directions that may be significant. Use a *pencil as pointer* at first to guide the way and to slow you down if need be.

2. *Read drama with a mind alert in your running interpretation* to the *theatrical* clues—the *dramatic* relations—the *semantic* potential—the *pantomime* implicit. (*a*) It requires alert reading to catch and interpret the theatrical clues in a drama—to keep in mind the floor plan of the scene with important doors, windows, furniture, and to remember what characters are present in each of the scenes and where they are. It may be helpful to draw a quick *diagram of the floor plan* on a scrap of paper. (*b*) It takes an alert mind to keep the characters affixed to their names, particularly in a populous play, to remember their personality traits and personal relations, to "hear" the successive speeches "in character." A penciled *list of characters,* with a few catchwords and groupings on that scrap of

paper can be helpfully carried from page to page as you read. (c) It calls for alert interpretation of the dialogue itself as well as the speech directions to realize the full potential of each speech—not merely the plain sense but the tone of irony or wheedling, the character's feeling of remorse or insecurity, the motive and intention. You may find it helpful to read with a pencil and *underline words and phrases* of special significance. (d) Then, too, it calls for a special alertness to catch the pantomime implicit in the lines as well as explicit in the stage directions, the meaningful gestures and bits of stage business as well as the larger actions. Here, too, underlining of key words in the directions and *penciling an occasional mark or word* in the margins may help.

3. *Read drama with mind and heart open for* uninhibited *enjoyment*—for vivid free *imagery*—for strong *empathy* and participation—for appropriate *emotion*. (a) Approach a drama with the mind and heart free and willing, relaxed yet ready to respond. If you settle down too comfortably, you may not be in this *attitude of anticipation*. (b) It is possible to encourage your free imagery in visualizing the scene, characters, and action by conscious effort. Keep the diagram mentioned above before you as an aid to picturing the scene, and *"cast" the play* with familiar acquaintances and/or actors from the stage and screen. (c) It is possible to induce greater empathy by consciously imagining yourself playing one of the parts. To free your expressive body, *stand up and move about* at times as you read, as even slight gestures and action on your part will encourage greater empathy. (d) You can also enjoy more adequate emotional responses while reading drama, with the aid of empathy and free imagery and that attitude of readiness. By imagining or *assuming* the *outward expressions* and inward tensions of the emotion, the postures and gestures, you will indeed induce the feeling of the bodily states of the emotion appropriate to the character in the scene.

4. *Consider the drama analytically: the characters—the plot—the theme—the total effect.* (a) Not until you have experienced the whole drama creatively, intuitively synthesizing the characters, should you begin to analyze their personalities; then through the process of close reflection you will come to a clearer understanding of them as fictional human beings. Such a *character worksheet* as that suggested in the Appendix may be helpful. (b) Similarly, after a creative reading of the whole drama, you should give conscious thought to the plot structure and dramatic construction. You may

well *divide off the basic scenes* as you read; then you can go back
to them with the *plot worksheet* (see Appendix) in mind and consider the design of the action of the play. (*c*) Then turn your
thought consciously to the consideration of the general meaning of
the story. Try two or three phrasings, *writing down the theme* or
themes as you abstract them. (*d*) Finally, back off yet further for a
view of the total effect of your experience. Again, *phrase it in
words*.

5. *Consider the drama critically:* its place in *dramatic history*—its
relation to *dramatic type*—its relation to *dramatic style*—its relation
to *dramatic criticism*. It is with this that the next essay will deal.

Introductory Note to *The Happy Journey*

WHEN THORNTON WILDER published *The
Happy Journey to Trenton and Camden* (1931), he was thirty-four
years old, had won the Pulitzer Prize for his second and most original novel, *The Bridge of San Luis Rey,* and had begun his lecturing
at the University of Chicago. He had graduated from Yale in 1920
and had begun teaching at Lawrenceville School, between Trenton
and Princeton, New Jersey, in 1921. It was ten years later that *The
Happy Journey* was performed, the joint effort of Yale and Vassar
students directed by Alexander Dean, and it has become a minor
classic in the American educational theater. It was published in
The Long Christmas Dinner and Other Plays in One Act and then
separately in an acting edition.

Unlike O'Neill, the professional dramatist, and Coward, the commercial actor-playwright, Thornton Wilder is essentially a man of
letters who has written occasionally, but almost always successfully,
for the theater. When he returned to Yale after World War I, he
wrote some one-act plays, determined to "write for pleasure rather
than profit." But it was his ambition to become a playwright with
a Broadway reputation. That he has known what he is about is
clearly revealed in "Some Thoughts on Playwriting" in the Princeton symposium *The Intent of the Artist*.

Something of the unique promise of this *Happy Journey* was
fulfilled by Thornton Wilder in *Our Town* (1938)—as deeply mov-

ing as it is unconventional—which won the Pulitzer Prize and was subsequently made into a successful film. His next play, *The Skin of Our Teeth* (1942) was also controversial, successful, and prize-winning. Both of these dramas, which are contemporary in their dramaturgy, owe little either to the realism of modern drama or to the successive revolts against it. In them Thornton Wilder showed both his broad philosophic interests and his literary style. Here the wisdom element of life is seen through the little dramatic elements that other playwrights might overlook and is exhibited in theatrical terms as universal as they are original.

It should be noted that Thornton Wilder spent part of his boyhood in China, and that the classical Chinese drama is distinguished by the ubiquitous stage manager, conventionalized pantomime, form-less story, and ancient wisdom.

THE HAPPY JOURNEY TO TRENTON AND CAMDEN *

A Play in One Act by Thornton Wilder

No scenery is required for this play. Perhaps a few dusty flats may be seen leaning against the brick wall at the back of the stage.

The five members of the Kirby family and the STAGE MANAGER *compose the cast.*

THE STAGE MANAGER *not only moves forward and withdraws the few properties that are required, but he reads from a typescript the lines of all the minor characters. He reads them clearly, but with little attempt at characterization, scarcely troubling himself to alter his voice, even when he responds in the person of a child or a woman.*

As the curtain rises the STAGE MANAGER *is leaning lazily against the proscenium pillar at the audience's left.. He is smoking.*

ARTHUR *is playing marbles in the center of the stage.*

CAROLINE *is at the remote back right talking to some girls who are invisible to us.*

MA KIRBY *is anxiously putting on her hat before an imaginary mirror.*

MA. Where's your pa? Why isn't he here? I declare we'll never get started.

ARTHUR. Ma, where's my hat? I guess I don't go if I can't find my hat.

MA. Go out into the hall and see if it isn't there. Where's Caroline gone to now, the plagued child?

ARTHUR. She's out waitin' in the street talkin' to the Jones girls.—I just looked in the hall a thousand times, ma, and it isn't there. [*He spits for good luck before a difficult shot and mutters*] Come on, baby.

MA. Go and look again, I say. Look carefully.

[ARTHUR *rises, runs to the right, turns around swiftly, returns to his game, flinging himself on the floor with a terrible impact and starts shooting an aggie.*]

ARTHUR. No, ma, it's not there.

MA [*serenely*]. Well, you don't leave Newark without that hat, make up your mind to that. I don't go no journeys with a hoodlum.

ARTHUR. Aw, ma!

[MA *comes down to the footlights and talks toward the audience as through a window.*]

MA. Oh, Mrs. Schwartz!

THE STAGE MANAGER [*consulting his script*]. Here I am, Mrs. Kirby. Are you going yet?

MA. I guess we're going in just a minute. How's the baby?

THE STAGE MANAGER. She's all right now. We slapped her on the back and she spat it up.

MA. Isn't that fine!—Well, now, if you'll be good enough to give the cat a saucer of milk in the morning and the evening, Mrs. Schwartz, I'll be ever so grateful to you—Oh, good afternoon, Mrs. Hobmeyer!

THE STAGE MANAGER. Good afternoon, Mrs. Kirby, I hear you're going away.

MA [*modest*]. Oh, just for three days, Mrs. Hobmeyer, to see my married daughter, Beulah, in Camden. Elmer's got his vacation week from the laundry early this year, and he's just the best driver in the world.

[CAROLINE *comes "into the house" and stands by her mother.*]

THE STAGE MANAGER. Is the whole family going?

MA. Yes, all four of us that's here. The change ought to be good for the children. My married daughter was downright sick a while ago——

THE STAGE MANAGER. Tchk—tchk—tchk! Yes, I remember you tellin' us.

MA. And I just want to go down and see the child. I ain't seen her since then. I just won't rest easy in my mind without I see her. [*To* CAROLINE] Can't you say good afternoon to Mrs. Hobmeyer?

CAROLINE [*blushes and lowers her eyes and says woodenly*]. Good afternoon, Mrs. Hobmeyer.

THE STAGE MANAGER. Good afternoon, dear.—Well, I'll wait and beat these rugs until after you're gone, because I don't want to choke you. I hope you have a good time and find everything all right.

MA. Thank you, Mrs. Hobmeyer, I hope I will.—Well, I guess that milk for the cat is all, Mrs. Schwartz, if you're sure you don't mind. If anything should come up, the key to the back door is hanging by the ice box.

ARTHUR AND CAROLINE. Ma! Not so loud. Everybody can hear yuh.

MA. Stop pullin' my dress, children. [*In a loud whisper*] The key to the back door I'll leave hangin' by the ice box and I'll leave the screen door unhooked.

THE STAGE MANAGER. Now have a good trip, dear, and give my love to Loolie.

MA. I will, and thank you a thousand times. [*She returns "into the room."*] What can be keeping your pa?

ARTHUR. I can't find my hat, ma.

[*Enter* ELMER *holding a hat.*]

ELMER. Here's Arthur's hat. He musta left it in the car Sunday.

MA. That's a mercy. Now we can start.—Caroline Kirby, what you done to your cheeks?

CAROLINE [*defiant-abashed*]. Nothin'.

MA. If you've put anything on 'em, I'll slap you.

CAROLINE. No, ma, of course I haven't. [*Hanging her head*] I just rubbed 'm to make 'm red. All the girls do that at High School when they're goin' places.

MA. Such silliness I never saw. Elmer, what kep' you?

ELMER [*always even-voiced and always looking out a little anxiously through his spectacles*]. I just went to the garage and had Charlie give a last look at it, Kate.

MA. I'm glad you did. I wouldn't like to have no breakdown miles from anywhere. Now we can start. Arthur, put those marbles away. Anybody'd think you didn't want to go on a journey to look at yuh.

[*They go out through the "hall," take the short steps that denote going downstairs, and find themselves in the street.*]

ELMER. Here, you boys, you keep away from that car.

MA. Those Sullivan boys put their heads into everything.

[THE STAGE MANAGER *has moved forward four chairs and a low platform. This is the automobile. It is in the center of the stage and faces the audience. The platform slightly raises the two chairs in the rear.* PA's *hands hold an imaginary steering wheel and con-*

tinually shift gears. CAROLINE *sits beside him.* ARTHUR *is behind him and* MA *behind* CAROLINE.]

CAROLINE [*self-consciously*].   Goodbye, Mildred. Goodbye, Helen.
THE STAGE MANAGER.   Goodbye, Caroline. Goodbye, Mrs. Kirby. I hope y' have a good time.
MA.   Goodbye, girls.
THE STAGE MANAGER.   Goodbye, Kate. The car looks fine.
MA [*looking upward toward a window*].   Oh, goodbye, Emma! [*Modestly*] We think it's the best little Chevrolet in the world.—Oh, goodbye, Mrs. Adler!
THE STAGE MANAGER.   What, are you going away, Mrs. Kirby?
MA.   Just for three days, Mrs. Adler, to see my married daughter in Camden.
THE STAGE MANAGER.   Have a good time.

[*Now* MA, CAROLINE, *and the* STAGE MANAGER *break out into a tremendous chorus of goodbyes. The whole street is saying goodbye.* ARTHUR *takes out his pea shooter and lets fly happily into the air. There is a lurch or two and they are off.*]

ARTHUR [*in sudden fright*].   Pa! Pa! Don't go by the school. Mr. Biedenbach might see us!
MA.   I don't care if he does see us. I guess I can take my children out of school for one day without having to hide down back streets about it.

[ELMER *nods to a passerby.* MA *asks without sharpness.*]

Who was that you spoke to, Elmer?
ELMER.   That was the fellow who arranges our banquets down to the Lodge, Kate.
MA.   Is he the one who had to buy four hundred steaks? [PA *nods.*] I declare, I'm glad I'm not him.
ELMER.   The air's getting better already. Take deep breaths, children.

[*They inhale noisily.*]

ARTHUR.   Gee, it's almost open fields already. "Weber and Heilbronner Suits for Well-dressed Men." Ma, can I have one of them some day?
MA.   If you graduate with good marks perhaps your father'll let you have one for graduation.
CAROLINE [*whining*].   Oh, Pa! do we have to wait while that whole funeral goes by?

[PA *takes off his hat.* MA *cranes forward with absorbed curiosity.*]

MA.   Take off your hat, Arthur. Look at your father.—Why, Elmer, I do believe that's a lodge-brother of yours. See the banner? I suppose this is the Elizabeth branch.

[ELMER *nods.* MA *sighs:* Tchk—tchk—tchk. *They all lean forward and watch the funeral in silence, growing momentarily more solemnized. After a pause,* MA *continues almost dreamily but not sentimentally*]

Well, we haven't forgotten the funeral that we went on, have we? We haven't forgotten our good Harold. He gave his life for his country, we mustn't forget that. [*She passes her finger from the corner of her eye across her cheek. There is another pause.*] Well, we'll all hold up the traffic for a few minutes some day.

THE CHILDREN [*very uncomfortable*]. Ma!

MA [*without self-pity*]. Well, I'm "ready," children. I hope everybody in this car is "ready." [*She puts her hand on* PA's *shoulder.*] And I pray to go first, Elmer. Yes.

[PA *touches her hand.*]

THE CHILDREN. Ma, everybody's looking at you. Everybody's laughing at you.

MA. Oh, hold your tongues! I don't care what a lot of silly people in Elizabeth, New Jersey, think of me.—Now we can go on. That's the last.

[*There is another lurch and the car goes on.*]

CAROLINE. "Fit-Rite Suspenders. The Working Man's Choice." Pa, why do they spell Rite that way?

ELMER. So that it'll make you stop and ask about it, Missy.

CAROLINE. Papa, you're teasing me.—Ma, why do they say "Three Hundred Rooms Three Hundred Baths"?

ARTHUR. "Miller's Spaghetti: The Family's Favorite Dish." Ma, why don't you ever have spaghetti?

MA. Go along, you'd never eat it.

ARTHUR. Ma, I like it now.

CAROLINE [*with gesture*]. Yum-yum. It looked wonderful up there. Ma, make some when we get home?

MA [*dryly*]. "The management is always happy to receive suggestions. We aim to please."

[*The whole family finds this exquisitely funny. The children scream with laughter. Even* ELMER *smiles.* MA *remains modest.*]

ELMER. Well, I guess no one's complaining, Kate. Everybody knows you're a good cook.

MA. I don't know whether I'm a good cook or not, but I know I've had practice. At least I've cooked three meals a day for twenty-five years.

ARTHUR. Aw, ma, you went out to eat once in a while.

MA. Yes. That made it a leap year.

[*This joke is no less successful than its predecessor. When the laughter dies down,* CAROLINE *turns around in an ecstasy of well-being and kneeling on the cushions says:*]

CAROLINE. Ma, I love going out in the country like this. Let's do it often, ma.

MA. Goodness, smell that air, will you! It's got the whole ocean in it. —Elmer, drive careful over that bridge. This must be New Brunswick we're coming to.

ARTHUR [*jealous of his mother's success*]. Ma, when is the next comfort station?

MA [*unruffled*]. You don't want one. You just said that to be awful.

CAROLINE [*shrilly*]. Yes, he did, ma. He's terrible. He says that kind of thing right out in school and I want to sink through the floor, ma. He's terrible.

MA. Oh, don't get so excited about nothing, Miss Proper! I guess we're all yewman-beings in this car, at least as far as I know. And, Arthur, you try and be a gentleman.—Elmer, don't run over that collie dog. [*She follows the dog with her eyes.*] Looked kinda peakèd to me. Needs a good honest bowl of leavings. Pretty dog, too. [*Her eyes fall on a billboard.*] That's a pretty advertisement for Chesterfield cigarettes, isn't it? Looks like Beulah, a little.

ARTHUR. Ma?

MA. Yes.

ARTHUR [*"route" rhymes with "out"*]. Can't I take a paper route with the Newark *Daily Post*?

MA. No, you cannot. No, sir. I hear they make the paper boys get up at four-thirty in the morning. No son of mine is going to get up at four-thirty every morning, not if it's to make a million dollars. Your *Saturday Evening Post* route on Thursday mornings is enough.

ARTHUR. Aw, Ma.

MA. No, sir. No son of mine is going to get up at four-thirty and miss the sleep God meant him to have.

ARTHUR [*sullenly*]. Hhm! Ma's always talking about God. I guess she got a letter from him this morning.

[MA *rises, outraged.*]

MA. Elmer, stop that automobile this minute. I don't go another step with anybody that says things like that. Arthur, you get out of this car. Elmer, you give him another dollar bill. He can go back to Newark, by himself. I don't want him.

ARTHUR. What did I say? There wasn't anything terrible about that.

ELMER. I didn't hear what he said, Kate.

MA. God has done a lot of things for me and I won't have him made fun of by anybody. Go away. Go away from me.

CAROLINE. Aw, ma,—don't spoil the ride.

MA. No.

ELMER. We might as well go on, Kate, since we've got started. I'll talk to the boy tonight.

MA [*slowly conceding*]. All right, if you say so, Elmer. But I won't sit beside him. Caroline, you come, and sit by me.

ARTHUR [*frightened*]. Aw, ma, that wasn't so terrible.

MA. I don't want to talk about it. I hope your father washes your mouth out with soap and water.—Where'd we all be if I started talking about God like that, I'd like to know! We'd be in the speak-easies and night-clubs and places like that, that's where we'd be.—All right, Elmer, you can go on now.

CAROLINE. What did he say, ma? I didn't hear what he said.

MA. I don't want to talk about it.

[*They drive on in silence for a moment, the shocked silence after a scandal.*]

ELMER. I'm going to stop and give the car a little water, I guess.

MA. All right, Elmer. You know best.

ELMER [*to a garage hand*]. Could I have a little water in the radiator —to make sure?

THE STAGE MANAGER [*in this scene alone he lays aside his script and enters into a rôle seriously*]. You sure can. [*He punches the tires.*] Air all right? Do you need any oil or gas?

ELMER. No, I think not. I just got fixed up in Newark.

MA. We're on the right road for Camden, are we?

THE STAGE MANAGER. Yes, keep straight ahead. You can't miss it. You'll be in Trenton in a few minutes.

[*He carefully pours some water into the hood.*]

Camden's a great town, lady, believe me.

MA. My daughter likes it fine,—my married daughter.

THE STAGE MANAGER. Ye'? It's a great burg all right. I guess I think so because I was born near there.

MA. Well, well. Your folks still live there?

THE STAGE MANAGER. No, my old man sold the farm and they built a factory on it. So the folks moved to Philadelphia.

MA. My married daughter Beulah lives there because her husband works in the telephone company.—Stop pokin' me, Caroline!—We're all going down to see her for a few days.

THE STAGE MANAGER. Ye'?

MA. She's been sick, you see, and I just felt I had to go and see her. My husband and my boy are going to stay at the Y. M. C. A. I hear they've got a dormitory on the top floor that's real clean and comfortable. Had you ever been there?

THE STAGE MANAGER. No. I'm Knights of Columbus myself.

MA. Oh.

THE STAGE MANAGER. I used to play basketball at the Y though. It looked all right to me.

[*He has been standing with one foot on the rung of* MA's *chair. They have taken a great fancy to one another. He reluctantly shakes himself out of it and pretends to examine the car again, whistling.*]

Well, I guess you're all set now, lady. I hope you have a good trip; you can't miss it.

EVERYBODY. Thanks. Thanks a lot. Good luck to you.

[*Jolts and lurches.*]

MA [*with a sigh*]. The world's full of nice people.—That's what I call a nice young man.

CAROLINE [*earnestly*]. Ma, you oughtn't to tell 'm all everything about yourself.

MA. Well, Caroline, you do your way and I'll do mine.—He looked kinda thin to me. I'd like to feed him up for a few days. His mother lives in Philadelphia and I expect he eats at those dreadful Greek places.

CAROLINE. I'm hungry. Pa, there's a hot dog stand. K'n I have one?

ELMER. We'll all have one, eh, Kate? We had such an early lunch.

MA. Just as you think best, Elmer.

ELMER. Arthur, here's half a dollar.—Run over and see what they have. Not too much mustard either.

[ARTHUR *descends from the car and goes off stage right.* MA *and* CAROLINE *get out and walk a bit.*]

MA. What's that flower over there?—I'll take some of those to Beulah.

CAROLINE. It's just a weed, ma.

MA. I like it—My, look at the sky, wouldya! I'm glad I was born in New Jersey. I've always said it was the best state in the Union. Every state has something no other state has got.

[*They stroll about humming. Presently* ARTHUR *returns with his hands full of imaginary hot dogs which he distributes. He is still very much cast down by the recent scandal. He finally approaches his mother and says falteringly:*]

ARTHUR. Ma, I'm sorry. I'm sorry for what I said.

[*He bursts into tears and puts his forehead against her elbow.*]

MA. There. There. We all say wicked things at times. I know you didn't mean it like it sounded.

[*He weeps still more violently than before.*]

Why, now, now! I forgive you, Arthur, and tonight before you go to bed you . . . [*She whispers*] You're a good boy at heart, Arthur, and we all know it.

[CAROLINE *starts to cry too.* MA *is suddenly joyously alive and happy.*]

Sakes alive, it's too nice a day for us all to be cryin'. Come now, get in. You go up in front with your father, Caroline. Ma wants to sit with her beau. I never saw such children. Your hot dogs are all getting wet. Now chew them fine, everybody.—All right, Elmer, forward march.— Caroline, whatever are you doing?

CAROLINE. I'm spitting out the leather, ma.

MA. Then say: Excuse me.

CAROLINE. Excuse me, please.

MA. What's this place? Arthur, did you see the post office?

ARTHUR. It said Lawrenceville.

MA. Hhn. School kinda. Nice. I wonder what that big yellow house set back was.—Now it's beginning to be Trenton.

CAROLINE. Papa, it was near here that George Washington crossed the Delaware. It was near Trenton, mama. He was first in war and first in peace, and first in the hearts of his countrymen.

MA [*surveying the passing world, serene and didactic*]. Well, the thing I like about him best was that he never told a lie.

[*The children are duly cast down. There is a pause.*]

There's a sunset for you. There's nothing like a good sunset.

ARTHUR. There's an Ohio license in front of us. Ma, have you ever been to Ohio?

MA. No.

[*A dreamy silence descends upon them.* CAROLINE *sits closer to her father.* MA *puts her arm around* ARTHUR.]

ARTHUR. Ma, what a lotta people there are in the world, ma. There must be thousands and thousands in the United States. Ma, how many are there?

MA. I don't know. Ask your father.

ARTHUR. Pa, how many are there?

ELMER. There are a hundred and twenty-six million, Kate.

MA [*giving a pressure about* ARTHUR'S *shoulder*]. And they all like to drive out in the evening with their children beside 'm.

[*Another pause.*]

Why doesn't somebody sing something? Arthur, you're always singing something; what's the matter with you?

ARTHUR. All right. What'll we sing? [*He sketches*]
"In the Blue Ridge Mountains of Virginia,
On the trail of the lonesome pine . . ."
No, I don't like that any more. Let's do:
"I been workin' on de railroad
All de liblong day.
I been workin' on de railroad
Just to pass de time away."

[CAROLINE *joins in at once. Finally even* MA *is singing. Even* PA *is singing.*]

[MA *suddenly jumps up with a wild cry:*]

MA. Elmer, that signpost said Camden. I saw it.
ELMER. All right, Kate, if you're sure.

[*Much shifting of gears, backing, and jolting.*]

MA. Yes, there it is. Camden—five miles. Dear old Beulah.—Now, children, you be good and quiet during dinner. She's just got out of bed after a big sorta operation, and we must all move around kinda quiet. First you drop me and Caroline at the door and just say hello, and then you men-folk go over to the Y. M. C. A. and come back for dinner in about an hour.

CAROLINE [*shutting her eyes and pressing her fists passionately against her nose*]. I see the first star. Everybody make a wish.
Star light, star bright,
First star I seen to-night.
I wish I may, I wish I might
Have the wish I wish to-night.
[*Then solemnly*]. Pins. Mama, you say "needles."

[*She interlocks little fingers with her mother.*]

MA. Needles.
CAROLINE. Shakespeare. Ma, you say "Longfellow."
MA. Longfellow.
CAROLINE. Now it's a secret and I can't tell it to anybody. Ma, you make a wish.
MA [*with almost grim humor*]. No, I can make wishes without wait-ing for no star. And I can tell my wishes right out loud too. Do you want to hear them?
CAROLINE [*resignedly*]. No, ma, we know 'm already. We've heard 'm. [*She hangs her head affectedly on her left shoulder and says with*

unmalicious mimicry] You want me to be a good girl and you want Arthur to be honest-in-word-and-deed.

MA [*majestically*]. Yes. So mind yourself.

ELMER. Caroline, take out that letter from Beulah in my coat pocket by you and read aloud the places I marked with red pencil.

CAROLINE [*working*]. "A few blocks after you pass the two big oil tanks on your left . . ."

EVERYBODY [*pointing backward*]. There they are!

CAROLINE. ". . . you come to a corner where there's an A and P store on the left and a firehouse kittycorner to it . . ."

[*They all jubilantly identify these landmarks.*]

". . . turn right, go two blocks, and our house is Weyerhauser St. Number 471."

MA. It's an even nicer street than they used to live in. And right handy to an A and P.

CAROLINE [*whispering*]. Ma, it's better than our street. It's richer than our street.—Ma, isn't Beulah richer than we are?

MA [*looking at her with a firm and glassy eye*]. Mind yourself, missy. I don't want to hear anybody talking about rich or not rich when I'm around. If people aren't nice I don't care how rich they are. I live in the best street in the world because my husband and children live there.

[*She glares impressively at* CAROLINE *a moment to let this lesson sink in, then looks up, sees* BEULAH *and waves.*]

There's Beulah standing on the steps lookin' for us.

[BEULAH *has appeared and is waving. They all call out:* Hello, Beulah—hello. *Presently they are all getting out of the car.* BEULAH *kisses her father long and affectionately.*]

BEULAH. Hello, papa. Good old papa. You look tired, pa.—Hello, mama.—Lookit how Arthur and Caroline are growing!

MA. They're bursting all their clothes!—Yes, your pa needs a rest. Thank Heaven, his vacation has come just now. We'll feed him up and let him sleep late. Pa has a present for you, Loolie. He would go and buy it.

BEULAH. Why, pa, you're terrible to go and buy anything for me. Isn't he terrible?

MA. Well, it's a secret. You can open it at dinner.

ELMER. Where's Horace, Loolie?

BEULAH. He was kep' over a little at the office. He'll be here any minute. He's crazy to see you all.

MA. All right. You men go over to the Y and come back in about an hour.

BEULAH [*as her father returns to the wheel, stands out in the street beside him*]. Go straight along, pa, you can't miss it. It just stares at yuh. [*Puts her arm around his neck and rubs her nose against his temple*] Crazy old pa, goin' buyin' things! It's me that ought to be buyin' things for you, pa.

ELMER. Oh, no! There's only one Loolie in the world.

BEULAH [*whispering, as her eyes fill with tears*]. Are you glad I'm still alive, pa? [*She kisses him abruptly and goes back to the house steps.*]

[THE STAGE MANAGER *removes the automobile with the help of* ELMER *and* ARTHUR *who go off waving their goodbyes.*]

Well, come on upstairs, ma, and take your things. Caroline, there's a surprise for you in the back yard.

CAROLINE. Rabbits?

BEULAH. No.

CAROLINE. Chickens?

BEULAH. No. Go and see.

[CAROLINE *runs off stage.* BEULAH *and* MA *gradually go upstairs.*]

There are two new puppies. You be thinking over whether you can keep one in Newark.

MA. I guess we can. It's a nice house, Beulah. You just got a *lovely* home.

BEULAH. When I got back from the hospital, Horace had moved everything into it, and there wasn't anything for me to do.

[THE STAGE MANAGER *pushes out a bed from the left. Its foot is toward the right.* BEULAH *sits on it, testing the springs.*]

BEULAH. I think you'll find this comfortable, ma.

MA [*taking off her hat*]. Oh, I could sleep on a heapa shoes, Loolie! I don't have no trouble sleepin'. [*She sits down beside her.*] Now let me look at my girl. Well, well, when I last saw you, you didn't know me. You kep' saying: "When's mama comin'? When's mama comin'?" But the doctor sent me away.

BEULAH [*puts her head on her mother's shoulder and weeps*]. It was awful, mama. It was awful. She didn't even live a few minutes, mama. It was awful.

MA [*looking far away*]. God thought best, dear. God thought best. We don't understand why. We just go on, honey, doin' our business. [*Then almost abruptly—passing the back of her hand across her cheek*] Well, now, what are we giving the men to eat tonight?

BEULAH. There's a chicken in the oven.

MA. What time didya put it in?

BEULAH [*restraining her*]. Aw, ma, don't go yet. I like to sit here with you this way. You always get the fidgets when we try and pet yuh, mama.

MA [*ruefully, laughing*]. Yes, it's kinda foolish. I'm just an old Newark bag-a-bones. [*She glances at the backs of her hands.*]

BEULAH [*indignantly*]. Why, ma, you're good-lookin'! We always said you were good-lookin'.—And besides, you're the best ma we could ever have.

MA [*uncomfortable*]. Well, I hope you like me. There's nothin' like bein' liked by your family.—Now I'm going downstairs to look at the chicken. You stretch out here for a minute and shut your eyes.—Have you got everything laid in for breakfast before the shops close?

BEULAH. Oh, you know! Ham and eggs.

[*They both laugh.*]

MA. I declare I never could understand what men see in ham and eggs. I think they're horrible.—What time did you put the chicken in?

BEULAH. Five o'clock.

MA. Well, now, you shut your eyes for ten minutes.

[BEULAH *stretches out and shuts her eyes.* MA *descends the stairs absent-mindedly singing:*]

"There were ninety and nine that safely lay
In the shelter of the fold,
But one was out on the hills away,
Far off from the gates of gold. . . ."

AND THE CURTAIN FALLS

Brief Commentary on *The Happy Journey*

Here it is, then, *The Happy Journey to Trenton and Camden*—without scenery, without props, without plot, without theme in any obvious sense. Whether you see it as presented upon a bare stage or read it here in the book, this *Happy Journey* is essentially a play for the imagination. Its reality as a human drama is in your mind and nowhere else. It is there that Ma Kirby and Pa—their children Arthur and Caroline and their married daughter Beulah—come alive. There, the scenes—the home and neighborhood in Newark, the Chevvy on the road and at the garage, Beulah's house in Camden —are clearly visible.

With realistic dramaturgy and staging it would be possible in a one-act play to show a room of the Newark home or the front of the garage or the Camden bedroom—one only—but not the happy journey! The journey itself, however, is the sort of thing that can be filmed with utmost realism, and of course it can be suggested through the medium of prose fiction. The form that Wilder chose, however, was not short story and not cinema, but theater— with a greater reliance upon the imagination than usual. The special problems that arose in the adaptation of *Our Town* to the screen—Wilder's correspondence with Sol Lesser, the producer, was published—indicate the imaginative quality of Wilder's dramaturgy.

In "Some Thoughts on Playwriting" Wilder points out that "The history of the theater shows us that in its greatest ages the stage employed the greatest number of conventions. The stage is fundamental pretense and it thrives on the acceptance of that fact." He cites examples from Greek, Elizabethan, French classical, and Chinese drama, in which "a whip in a hand and a jogging motion of the body indicated that a man was on horseback." He says, "The devices did not spring from naïveté, however, but from the vitality of the public imagination in those days." So, too, the jogging and lurching of the family in unison, and Mr. Kirby's pantomimic business of driving, delight spectator and reader alike because they are surprised how vivid the details of *The Happy Journey* are in their imaginations.

Thoughtful reflection upon this little drama will provide an occasion for reconsideration of the various interrelated aspects of the drama-reading experience.

V. THE DRAMA

History, Types, Styles, Criticism

> The arts are fragments of the time and place which produced them and cannot be comprehended either conceptually or imaginatively, outwardly or inwardly, without a knowledge and imaginative understanding of their context.
>
> —ERIC BENTLEY, *The Playwright as Thinker*

AFTER A DRAMA HAS BEEN INTERPRETED and experienced fully, with a rich structuring of its dramatic story, then—as we said at the end of the last essay—it is time to ask the critical questions: What is the relation of this play to theatrical and dramatic history? to the major dramatic types? to the dramatic styles? to dramatic and theatrical criticism?

This fifth and last essay will provide a basis, necessarily limited, for answering these questions, which apply not alone to dramas but quite as much to stageplays.

§ 1. GENERALIZATION AND DISCUSSION OF DRAMA

Let us glance back in brief summary of what we have so far considered: *First,* the "Preliminary: Orientation to Drama"—the dramatic and theatric and semantic elements in life that combine in the theater; the Drama, explored in its three dimensions; the interrelation of theater art and dramatic literature; the key terms "stageplay" and "drama" defined. *Second,* "The Playscript: Creation by the Playwright"—with particular emphasis upon the story elements of character, plot, and dialogue. *Third,* "The Stageplay: Production for Presentation"—considering the creative activity of the actors and other interpretative artists of the theater. *Fourth,* "The Play: Recreation by Spectator and Reader"—exploring in some detail the complex psychological responses of the playgoer to a stageplay and of the playreader to a drama.

All of this has involved us in generalizations and discussions of the drama—with illustrative remarks, it is true, about the particular plays so far read. We have generalized about the playwright, the actor, the playgoer, and the playreader. We have discussed the playscript, the stageplay, and the play as experienced in the mind of spectator and reader.

But we have not yet talked about the historian of the theater and drama, about the scholar, about the critic. We have only incidentally suggested the 2500-year history of Western drama and the theatrical history of the particular plays here included as illustrations. We have hardly referred to the major dramatic types and styles. We have only casually referred to works of dramatic criticism and theory. This willful omission has not been neglect but postponement on principle.

You cannot intelligently talk about a play as a work of art until after you have adequately experienced it. You cannot talk about the characters or plot or theme until you have seen or heard or read the entire stageplay or drama—interpreting the dialogue and action, gathering and classifying the various sorts of data, building up the characters, structuralizing the plot, generalizing the meaning. Similarly you cannot talk about the play in relation to dramatic history, types, styles, and criticism until you have adequately experienced it. Therefore we have postponed consideration of dramatic history and criticism.

But there is another principle that has argued against this postponement:

You cannot adequately experience a play as a work of art without interpreting it in its historical context. You cannot consider the characters, plot, and theme without integrating the extrinsic data from theatrical, dramatic, social, and intellectual history with the intrinsic data from the dialogue and action. You cannot help doing this within the limits of your current knowledge. What you know about the theater and drama, about the playwright and his times, *will be* contextual data whether you wish it or not! The conscious enrichment of such background data will make your experiencing of a play more meaningful. Therefore each of the plays has been preceded by an Introductory Note.

Yet another pair of principles are relevant:

You cannot discuss theatrical and dramatic history or generalize the major dramatic types and styles without reference to plays already experienced. You cannot yourself discuss meaningfully Greek drama unless you have yourself experienced the plays of Sophocles and Aristophanes. You cannot talk intelligently about tragedy unless you have read and thought about particular dramas of this type. Yet: *You cannot adequately experience a play of a particular historic period, type, or style without some previous generalization and discussion of it.* Therefore this general introduction to dramatic history and criticism will precede the dramas of the farther past, but further generalization and discussion of the particular problems in dramatic history and criticism will accompany and follow the dramas as they are presented for your reading and enjoyment.

In violation of the first principle above—that you cannot talk about a play until after you have read or seen it—the following section will refer by name to dozens of plays most of which you quite certainly have not read. However, it will refer to these plays out of respect to the second and fourth principles—that you cannot adequately experience plays except in their historical and critical contexts. It is hoped, however, that you may know something about some of the dramas named, and that they will thus add some substance to the generalizations.

You cannot lift yourself by your own bootstraps, it may be true, but the only way you can climb stairs is alternate feet on alternate steps.

§ 2. An Historical Sketch of the Drama and Theater

In this particular brief history of Western theater and drama, seven periods will be distinguished.

The ancient Greek and then Roman drama extends from about 500 B.C. until about 100 A.D., but it lingered on much longer. Greek drama grew out of various religious rites and festivals—as we earlier observed—dance and recitation by a chorus and its leader in outdoor celebration of Dionysus and legendary heroes. Thespis (so it is said) added an actor (the "hypocrite") to the leader of the chorus and thus made possible dramatic dialogue. The Greek theater was a vast hillside amphitheater—as large as the semicircular end section of a modern athletic stadium—with a circular area (the "orchestra") for the chorus and perhaps a slightly elevated stage, behind which was the "skene," a background building with columns and doors not unlike the façade of a palace, used as dressing room. The two or three male actors (who doubled to play all the parts) wore large masks, built-up shoes, and high-waisted costumes to increase their apparent height. In March at the great Dionysian festival, the vast audience assembled at dawn on successive days to see a series of three tragedies plus a satyr play on each day in a state-sponsored competition. Comedies, also, were presented, particularly during the January festival when fewer strangers were present in Athens.

Plays of five Greek dramatists survive. Three of them wrote tragedies: Aeschylus, *Agamemnon, Prometheus Bound,* and others; Sophocles, *Œdipus the King* and *Antigone;* Euripides, *Medea* and *Electra.* Their works were all written in the fifth century B.C. (about 490 to 406 B.C.). There were two writers of Greek comedy some of whose works have come down to us: Aristophanes wrote "old comedy" about 400 B.C., a sort of musical comedy, topical, satirical, and personal—*Lysistrata, The Frogs,* and *The Clouds;* Menander wrote "new comedy" about 300 B.C., the forerunner of modern social comedy, with domestic plots and type characters—long fragments, but no complete plays, surviving. Aristotle's *Poetics* (about 350 B.C.), which analyzes Greek tragedy, is the fountainhead of dramatic criticism.

The Romans took over both the theater and drama of the Greeks. To their outdoor amphitheaters—built in all parts of the Roman Empire—they added a well-raised stage and more elaborate scenic façade. Their playwrights adapted the new comedies of Menander and others: Plautus wrote *The Menaechmi Twins, The Pot of Gold,* and others, about 200 B.C.; and Terence, a freed slave from Carthage, wrote *The Lady of Andros, The Eunuch,* and other comedies of more refined style, about 150 B.C. The only tragedies to survive from Roman times were written (with one exception) by Seneca—Spanish-born tutor of Nero—about 50 A.D. His *Oedipus, Medea,* and *Phaedra* were sensationalized adaptations of Greek originals, and perhaps were not intended for the stage.

For centuries the Roman comedians continued to play, and spectacular shows were given in the theaters. Even after the Christianization of the Empire, strolling players, performing in castle and market town, kept alive the dramatic and theatrical traditions. And the manuscripts of the Roman and Greek dramatists survived at Alexandria, Constantinople, and elsewhere. Some Latin comedies written by the nun Hroswitha about 1000 A.D., in decorous imitation of Terence, suggest a transition from the long-lingering classical tradition to the medieval drama.

The *second* of our seven periods is the Middle Ages, extending roughly from 1000 A.D. until about 1500 A.D. This marked a new and fresh beginning of the drama in western Europe and the British

Isles, again from religious roots, this time Christian and more dimly pagan. From the church liturgy developed the dramatization of brief Biblical scenes, which were moved from the altar to the church porch. Then, undertaken by the medieval trade guilds, cycles of mystery or miracle plays were performed annually in certain of the cities, using "pageants," or wagon stages, moving from place to place in the cathedral or market town like floats in a modern parade. There were as many as forty-two playlets in a series (such as the Coventry cycle), depicting the Christian drama of the fall and redemption, from the creation through doomsday, including *Noah's Flood, Abraham's Sacrifice,* and the Nativity scenes. There were other religious dramas—the saints' plays and morality plays, dramatic allegories like *Everyman (ca.* 1490). In addition to this stream of Christian and Church drama, there was also in the Middle Ages a stream of native folk dance and drama, partly pagan in its origins— May Day games, Robin Hood plays, and the Christmas mummery of *St. George and the Dragon* that continued until the end of this last century. And then, of course, there were medieval strollers who performed farces in market place and innyard—*Master Pierre Patelin (ca.* 1450) being a lively French survival. Such, then, was medieval drama—no theater buildings or amphitheaters, no names of individual playwrights, new beginnings of the drama, wide variety of church and folk dramatic types, no dramatic criticism.

The *third* period, that of Renaissance drama, let us fix rather arbitrarily within the dates 1500-1650 A.D. This period is marked by a flourishing of the theater and drama in western Europe—Italy, France, Spain, and especially England. The theater itself, both in England and in Spain, was developed from medieval origins. The Elizabethan theaters, such as Shakespeare's Globe, were essentially innyards (specially built without inns) with surrounding galleries and a permanent platform stage. They were excellent of their kind. The Spanish corral was essentially a similar development from an outdoor backyard court. It was in Italy that, inspired by the new interest in Roman antiquities, the modern theater was born—a small roofed amphitheater with a platform stage and proscenium. The medieval types of drama pretty well died out by 1550 (though Shakespeare as a boy might have seen the last of the Coventry miracle plays), but the native farce and the morality play both left their mark on English comedy and tragedy.

The rediscovery of the classic drama, particularly Seneca and Plautus, inspired Italian and French tragedy and comedy—and to some degree English, though not Spanish, drama. This was the time of Shakespeare, whose comedies (among them *The Comedy of Errors, As You Like It,* and *The Tempest*), tragedies (*Julius Caesar, Hamlet,* and *Macbeth*), and histories (*Richard III, Henry IV, Part 1,* and *Henry V*) were all written within the twenty years 1590-1610. He was not alone great among the dramatists during the reigns of Elizabeth I (d. 1603) and her Scotch kinsman-successor, James I. Christopher Marlowe is famous for his *Doctor Faustus* and *Edward II,* Ben Jonson for *Volpone* and *The Alchemist,* Beaumont and Fletcher for *Philaster, The Maid's Tragedy,* and others. During this same time Lope de Vega and later Calderon were among the prolific dramatists whose plays of many types made this the "Golden Age" of Spanish drama. In Italy and in France, imitation of classical tragedy and dramatic theory were already establishing the "unities" of neoclassical drama. In French drama, however, Corneille is best remembered for his *Le Cid* (1637), a controversial romantic drama on a Spanish theme.

The *fourth* of these seven periods, the period of neoclassical drama, 1600-1800, overlaps the Renaissance of which it was a direct development. In England—where Ben Jonson in *The Silent Woman* and *Sejanus* showed himself an early neoclassicist—the Puritan Parliament closed the theaters in 1642. With the Restoration of Charles II in 1660, new indoor theaters were soon built along somewhat more modern lines, using scenery and actresses for the first time. In France it was the time of the highest flowering of neoclassic drama, continuing from Corneille's *Medea,* and *The Liar,* into the next generation, with Molière's *Tartuffe, The Misanthrope,* and *The Would-Be Gentleman,* the most famous neoclassic comedies and farces, and Racine's *Phèdre* and *Athalie,* neoclassic tragedies on ancient and biblical themes. In England it was the poet Dryden who wrote in the characteristic forms of social comedy (*Marriage-à-la-mode*), heroic play (*The Conquest of Granada*), and neoclassic tragedy (*All for Love*). But the most brilliant comedies of manners —showing the influence of Molière—*Love for Love* and *The Way of the World,* were written by Congreve about 1700. These were followed in the 1770's by Goldsmith's *She Stoops to Conquer* and by Sheridan's *The Rivals* and *The School for Scandal.* The influence of Molière in comedy was strongly felt throughout the eighteenth century, not only in England and in France (by Beaumarchais, in *The Barber of Seville* and *The Marriage of Figaro*), but also in Denmark by Holberg, in Italy by Goldoni, and in Germany by

Lessing. This neoclassical period was a time of famous actors, such as Betterton and Nell Gwyn and later Garrick and Mrs. Siddons in England, and of notable dramatic criticism, such as Dryden's famous *Essay,* Boileau's *Art of Poetry,* and Lessing's *Hamburg Dramaturgy.*

The *fifth* period, that of romantic drama, 1750-1900, again overlaps the neoclassic period. The physical theater and stage developed, but without radical change. It continued to be the time of great actors, such as Edwin Booth and Henry Irving, Ellen Terry and Sarah Bernhardt. The plays of this time were characterized by sentiment, sonorous speeches, and spectacle, rather than by wit, repartee, and social satire. Shakespeare was the dominant influence rather than Molière. It was a time of a few great dramas in Germany: Schiller's *William Tell,* Goethe's *Faust,* and Hebbel's *Mary Magdalena;* and also in France: Victor Hugo's *Hernani* and the younger Dumas' *Camille.* But no English dramas are memorable until at the end of the period when—with W. S. Gilbert's librettos for *H.M.S. Pinafore* and *The Mikado,* and Oscar Wilde's *Lady Windermere's Fan* and *Salomé*—the "New Drama" was already coming into being. To this nineteenth century belong the American melodramas, such as *Uncle Tom's Cabin* and *The Drunkard,* and the later English farces, such as *Charley's Aunt* and Wilde's *The Importance of Being Earnest.* During this romantic period most of the great English poets (Wordsworth, Coleridge, Byron, Shelley, Keats; Tennyson, Browning, Swinburne) tried their hands at playwriting, but with almost uniform lack of success. However, it was a flourishing time in dramatic criticism—with such works as Freytag's *Technique of the Drama* and the numerous romantic essayists and critics of Shakespeare and the theater, such as Coleridge, Lamb, and Hazlitt—and marked the beginnings of dramatic and theatrical history and scholarship by Malone, Furness, Mantzius.

The *sixth* period, that of modern drama, 1879-1942, overlaps the nineteenth century and may be considered as ending with World War II. The physical theater changed only gradually. Electricity made possible modern stage lighting. Within this period the *régisseur,* stage director, and art director developed, with Max Reinhardt, Stanislavsky, and Gordon Craig among the leaders. The noncommercial theater—the art, "free," little, community, university, and college theaters—came into being, making major contributions to theater art. Among them were the Moscow Art Theater, the Abbey Theater, the Theater Guild, the Pasadena Playhouse, and drama at Harvard and Yale Universities, then North Carolina and Iowa.

This was the time, too, of the birth and growth of the cinema, from silent film to sound and color, a world-wide entertainment syndicate. And then, too, radio drama. In its style of scenic design and production and playwriting, modern drama was dominantly realistic —but with antirealistic styles of great variety characteristic of many of its outstanding plays and productions. So we find expressionism, naturalism, constructivism, surrealism, romanticism—and individualism—warring with realism, the norm for this time.

Modern drama divides itself conveniently into three twenty-one-year generations. The first (1879-1900) is marked by the flowering of modern European dramatists: Ibsen of Norway, "the father of Modern Drama" (*A Doll's House* [1879], *Ghosts, An Enemy of the People, Hedda Gabler*), Hauptmann of Germany (*The Weavers, The Sunken Bell*), Chekhov of Russia (*The Cherry Orchard*), Rostand of France (*Cyrano de Bergerac*), Schnitzler of Austria (*Anatol*), and other significant playwrights from these countries and from Sweden, Hungary, Czechoslovakia, Spain, and Belgium. The second part (1900-1921) is marked by the dominance of the modern British dramatists: G. B. Shaw, the Irish-born critic who turned playwright (*Candida, Caesar and Cleopatra, Pygmalion, Man and Superman,* including "Don Juan in Hell"), J. M. Barrie, the whimsical Scot (*Peter Pan, What Every Woman Knows, Dear Brutus*), Galsworthy, the proper Englishman (*Strife, Justice, Loyalties*), and many other playwrights of more or less distinction, from Pinero and Jones through Milne and Maugham, Synge and O'Casey, and Housman and Priestley, to Emlyn Williams and Coward. The third part of the period (1921-42) is marked by the rather sudden rise of modern American dramatists to world importance for the first time: Eugene O'Neill (*The Emperor Jones, Anna Christie, The Hairy Ape, Stange Interlude*), Maxwell Anderson (*What Price Glory* [with Laurence Stallings], *Elizabeth the Queen, Winterset*), Sidney Howard (*They Knew What They Wanted*), Marc Connelly (*The Green Pastures*), Kaufman and Hart (*You Can't Take It With You*), Philip Barry (*The Philadelphia Story*), Robert Sherwood (*Abe Lincoln in Illinois*), Lillian Hellman (*The Little Foxes*), and a good many others.

Modern drama, which we described as dominantly realistic, has been distinguished by its interest in both normal and abnormal psychology, individual and social, and in heredity and environment as determining human personality. It reflects the strong influence of the new behavioral sciences and of their various schools, particularly

Freud, psychoanalysis, and psychiatry. It depicted not only urban and industrial society, but also the farm and more primitive folk. It concerned itself not only with individual but social problems— the thesis and problem plays—and at times was doctrinaire and proletarian. It saw an experiment in state-supported Federal Theater in America and the state domination of theater in Russia. It was a time of unparalleled scholarship in dramatic history (Chambers, Nicoll, Odell, Mantle, Clark, Freedley, and Gassner) and in dramatic theory and criticism (Brunetière, Shaw, Archer, Matthews, Baker, and Nathan). With the destruction of so much of modern Europe and the disruption of Western culture by World War II, what was called "Modern Drama" seems to have come to an end.

The *seventh* period, of contemporary or postwar drama, may be thought of as beginning in 1942. It has not as yet fully revealed itself, of course, nor do we quite know what direction it will finally take. The chief "modern" dramatists had, for the most part, died or completed their best work before World War II. All the leading European dramatists, the British Shaw, Barrie, Galsworthy, the American O'Neill, Howard, Barry, Connelly, Kaufman and a number of others were either dead, or their work was apparently finished. Only a handful of prewar British and American playwrights such as Coward and Anderson were still active. Realism and certain of the revolts against it seemed to have run their course. But new directions in the theater and drama in America were anticipated even before the war by Saroyan (*The Time of Your Life*) and Thornton Wilder (*Our Town, The Skin of Our Teeth*). After the war came Tennessee Williams (*The Glass Menagerie, A Streetcar Named Desire*) and Arthur Miller (*All My Sons, Death of a Salesman*). A similar stirring of contemporary drama is seen in France by Jean Anouilh (*Antigone*), Giraudoux (*The Madwoman of Chaillot*), Jean Paul Sartre (*The Flies, The Red Gloves*), and in England by T. S. Eliot (*The Cocktail Party*) and Christopher Fry (*The Lady's Not for Burning*). Special characteristics of contemporary drama have been the element of fantasy, as in Mary Chase's *Harvey,* and the new development of musical comedy, such as Hammerstein's librettos for *Oklahoma!* and *South Pacific*. Among the interesting experiments have been central staging of plays in arena theaters, individual stylization using narrators, flashbacks, modern costume, absence of scenery, and mere suggestion of multiple sets as dramaturgic devices. This new period is also marked by the addition of a third dimension to cinema and the advent of television, which brings cinema and its own form of drama into the home.

In the 2500 years of Western drama, the names of the greatest dramatists stand out: Sophocles, Shakespeare, Molière, Ibsen, Shaw, and O'Neill. There is no great name from the medieval drama or from the romantic drama of the nineteenth century or (as yet) in contemporary drama.

§ 3. THE MAJOR DRAMATIC TYPES: TRAGEDY AND COMEDY

We turn from this brief history of the theater and drama to some consideration of the two major types and a brief survey of the many minor types of drama already mentioned in sketching that history. The two major types of drama, of course, are tragedy and comedy. We shall begin with the former.

Tragedy was the first type to develop. It came into being at the very dawn of Greek drama and has been a major type in every period except the medieval. It was first defined in the *Poetics* of Aristotle—who generalized upon his analysis of the great Greek tragedies written half a century before his time. In the medieval period the word "tragedy" was used to name, not drama, but a minor type of poetry recounting the misfortunes of the great and famous, the overturning of people of high place, the falls of princes. The word carried something of this tradition into Shakespeare's time. However, the Renaissance, particularly in France, gave new attention to Aristotle. The rules of neoclassical tragedy, including "the three unities" of time, place, and action, were based upon Aristotle's *Poetics* as then understood. All later writers on tragedy—down to Maxwell Anderson in our time—have been influenced by Aristotle.

The genius of Aristotle's theory is that it defines tragedy in terms of its effect upon the audience. Thus, a tragedy is a dramatic spectacle that arouses the tragic emotions of pity and fear and then purges the spectator of these same emotions. This is "the tragic catharsis," as Aristotle called it. Therefore, a drama is not generally considered tragic merely because it evokes sympathy, pathos, pity, sorrow—tears. It also evokes terror in the audience—"There but for the grace of God stand I!"—the fear that life may yet deal me such devastating blows or entangle me in a web of my own spinning or tempt me at the point of my own weakness! But the final effect—reported by many theatergoers and playreaders alike—is not just

pity for the unfortunate hero and fear for oneself, but pity purged
and replaced (perhaps by admiration) and fear purged and replaced
(perhaps by understanding or faith or courage).

It is only certain sorts of drama that will affect the spectator or
reader in this way. Various theories of tragedy are largely attempts
to define the sorts of drama that achieve the tragic effect. They try
to answer the question: What kind of character, plot, theme, and
style are found in such plays?

As to plot, tragic dramas are most obviously characterized by the
death-ending or comparable misfortune to the tragic hero. This
final defeat or destruction does not come by chance or sudden accident, but follows a losing struggle. Usually there is a personal
antagonist. But the opposing force or the deciding factor may be
fate or nature or society—or something within the tragic hero himself, "the tragic flaw," some fault or weakness of character. As we
identify ourselves with the character of the tragic hero and with his
will and desires, we realize the personal and impersonal forces opposing him and engage our own interests in the scheming and strategy,
strife and struggle, successes and setbacks, suffering and suspense,
through crises and climax to the catastrophic end. With this identification and empathy—as we saw in the fourth essay—comes the
evocation of emotion comparable to that of the protagonist. In this
way, self-pity and pity for the hero merge, and fear for the hero and
personal fear are actually one.

The tragic heroes of Greek tragedy were kings, queens, princes,
warriors of high birth and stature, better and stronger than average
men. So, too, the tragic heroes of the Renaissance, neoclassic, and
romantic periods—with certain exceptions. But the tragic hero,
though noble and strong, is not perfect. In his imperfection lies his
humanity. Thus the spectator or reader is pleased to imagine himself better than he is, while gratified to realize that his betters are as
frail and faulty as himself. There were a few tragedies from the
Renaissance on—domestic tragedy and *tragédie bourgeoise*—that
dramatize the misfortunes of middle-class heroes and heroines. But
it was not until modern drama that many of the protagonists of tragedy were city and country folk, middle class or proletarian.

The style of tragedy—from ancient times up through the romantic
period—was characteristically elevated language and verse. The
dialogue included rhetorical monologues and soliloquies, with
various poetic embellishments, and made use of poetic diction.
Although prose began to be used for comedy during the Renaissance,

verse held its place in the style of tragedy until late in the nineteenth century. Modern tragedy, from Ibsen on, has been in prose, but efforts have been made to re-establish verse tragedy, notably by Maxwell Anderson and T. S. Eliot.

The themes of tragedy are, of course, as various as the plays themselves, and reflect the philosophies of life of the dramatists and their times. Though the general meaning of certain tragedies can be labeled with a word—thus the theme of *Macbeth* is often said to be "ambition"—such simplifications are usually misleading. The great tragedies are often enigmatic—the spectator or reader will puzzle their significance and find it difficult to phrase to his satisfaction—or to the satisfaction of others. Yet, the great tragedies— *Œdipus the King, Hamlet, Phèdre, Faust, Hedda Gabler, Mourning Becomes Electra, Death of a Salesman*—do stir the most profound of human responses, evoking reflective thought upon the value and meaning of life, thoughts that often lie too deep for tears and are too personal for expression in words.

Several subtypes of tragedy—classic, romantic, neoclassic, domestic and romantic (again), realistic, and stylized—are distinguished by the dramatic styles which will be considered in the next section and are characteristic of the historic periods summarized above.

From Tragedy let us turn to Comedy.

Comedy also stems from Greek drama. Again, with the exception of the Middle Ages (when there were comic interludes and farces, it is true, as well as comic incidents in the serious plays), comedy has been a major type of drama in all succeeding periods. If Aristotle did analyze Greek comedy as he did tragedy, that treatise or part of the *Poetics* is lost, though some of his pertinent observations survive. Of the two sorts of Greek comedy already mentioned, it was the "new comedy" of Menander that in Plautus and Terence continued through Roman times and was revived in the Renaissance, developed in Molière and the many playwrights he influenced down to our own time. The "old comedy" of Aristophanes, however, was the ancestor of certain elements in neoclassic comedy (Molière's comedy ballets, Gay's *The Beggar's Opera*), but was not again realized until the end of the romantic period in Gilbert and Sullivan (*H.M.S. Pinafore, The Mikado*) and, in the modern period, George S. Kaufman (*Of Thee I Sing* [with Morris Ryskind], *I'd Rather Be Right* [with Moss Hart]).

In the Middle Ages the word "comedy" was used (as in Dante's *Divine Comedy*) to refer to a serious work with a happy ending.

Something of this meaning carried over into the Renaissance, for many of Shakespeare's "comedies" are serious plays with happy endings, and by no means part of the main stream of comedy.

Comedy, like tragedy, may best be defined in terms of its characteristic effect upon the audience—laughter. There are several related sorts of laughter that may be distinguished: Thoughtless laughter is evoked by the purely comic element of buffoonery and horseplay, extravagant characterization and slapstick, wisecracks and puns. Critical laughter is evoked by the satirical element, the ridiculing of individual and social faults and foibles, personal jibes and pointed retorts, sarcasm and wit. Sympathetic laughter is evoked by the humorous element, high-spirited and good-natured, raillery and pleasantry, humane and earthy.

The comic response will range from the thoughtless horselaugh to a quick smile *without regard to* the persons involved. The satiric response will range from bitter or sardonic laughter to a sneer *at* the persons involved. The humorous response will range from hearty and backslapping guffaws to a warm chuckle *with* the persons involved.

Laughter itself is an amazingly complex response arising from apparently two factors: He who laughs has (1) a sudden perception of some incongruity and (2) a realization that he is not involved in the situation, or that he is superior to it. The feeling of physical well-being and the release of inhibitions heighten the propensity to laughter, and there is a strong thread of sexual suggestion common to a certain amount of laughter. In the belly laugh there is the sudden or startled moment of perception—breathless attention while you "get the point" and "clear yourself"—then comes the ejaculation of breath with diaphragmatic and abdominal spasms, facial contortions, and all sorts of bodily activity, as earlier described. It is fun—all the way from such convulsive laughter—paroxysms that will have you "in stitches"—through the various chuckling and chortling stages to the faint smile of amusement.

What in a comedy causes this laughter response?

For one thing, the situations and incidents. In comedy the plot itself may not cause laughter, but upon the plot-line will be strung along (or hung out) the comic, satiric, or humorous situations and incidents. The chief characteristic of the plot in comedy is the happy ending, and just as death is expected as the final catastrophe in tragedy, so marriage is expected as the final consummation in comedy. The ending may even be happy for the antagonist, who usually gets something less in the way of punishment or defeat than we may think he deserves. A second characteristic of comic plot is the love element or sexual angle. It is almost always there, though not always the main interest, going back through new comedy and even old comedy to the fertility origins of the drama. Third, as characteristic of comic plots, are the numerous complications that may beset the protagonist. We must have many moments of apprehension and growing anxiety to build up tensions so that laughter may come as a happy release. Comic plots involve complications, sexual love, the happy ending.

Laughter is evoked not only by the comic situations and incidents, but also by the characters themselves. It is not usual for the characters in comedy to be highly individualized, though they may be. They are more likely to be the stock characters of ancient comedy, or type characters, sometimes mere caricatures. Yet usually the protagonist or the lovers will be attractive stereotypes. Our identification with them—and antipathy for the antagonist—will point the direction of our laughter. We will want to laugh *with* the hero and heroine and *at* the villain, menace, or rival.

The style of comedy is usually rich in verbal provocations for laughter—wit and the wisecrack, *double-entendre* and puns, whimsy and plays on words, Irish bulls and malapropisms, felicity of expression and vulgar tongue. Comedies were written in verse for the most part up through the Renaissance, though certain ones of Shakespeare's so-called romantic comedies, such as *As You Like It* and *Twelfth Night,* are more prose than verse. Molière's more celebrated comedies are in verse, but his lighter comedies are in prose. The neoclassic and later English comedies were all in prose, which has been the rule for comedy until, interestingly enough, T. S. Eliot and Christopher Fry in our time.

Comedy is more likely than tragedy to have a simply expressible theme. Though it will usually not be hard to phrase—and may be quite obvious—the surface meaning of comedy is likely to be based upon profound assumptions and convictions. Look closely at any one of the great writers of comedy and you will find a philosopher expressing his view of life, concerned with social values, intent often upon human betterment.

Many subtypes of comedy are to be distinguished—classic, romantic, and neoclassic comedy, the comedy of manners and sentimental comedy, serious comedy and farce, folk comedy and social comedy, musical comedy and fantasy.

So much, then, for comedy and tragedy as the two major types of drama. One might say that there is a third major type, however, already referred to in the opening essay as "drama" or "serious drama" or *"drame."*

This third great category comprises all the plays that are neither comedies nor tragedies as above considered. Some of them would be comedies if they were funnier—for they end happily for the protagonist. Some would be tragedies if only they *did not* end happily —for, during the course of their action, they may evoke emotions characteristic of tragedy.

The satyr play of Greek drama and the various dramatic forms of the medieval period (miracle and morality plays, folk plays and interludes) belong in this third category, drama. Some of the "comedies" of Shakespeare—such as *As You Like It, The Merchant of Venice,* and *The Tempest*—are variously called "romantic comedies," "tragicomedies," and "dramatic romances" and are hardly comedies in the usual sense, for, though they end happily, they are not as laughter-provoking as one might expect. Some of the chronicle-history plays are in every sense tragedies—such as Shakespeare's *Richard II*—but others, such as *Henry V,* are heroic dramas. The English "heroic play" of the early neoclassic period, the French *drame* later in the same period, and the "melodrama" of the romantic period are also special subtypes of drama. But the major subtype of serious drama is the problem play—the later *drame,* the thesis play, the drama of ideas, the social drama—that developed in the nineteenth century and that dominated modern drama.

§ 4. CLASSIC, ROMANTIC, REALISTIC, AND RECENT STYLES

We have already used the terms "classic," "romantic," and "realistic" in describing the styles characteristic of the dramas and productions of the various historic periods. Thus we spoke of the classic drama of ancient Greece and Rome—and of the neoclassic period. We spoke of the romantic dramas of the Elizabethan period and the Renaissance—and of what we called the romantic period, principally the nineteenth century. We also characterized as dominantly realistic much of modern drama. Then, too, we have used these adjectives to distinguish some of the subtypes of drama—classical tragedy, romantic comedy, realistic drama.

It is time now to ask more particularly what is meant by these terms, and to ask whether there are more than three of them useful to the student of drama.

The classic style in drama is the style exemplified by the tragedies and new comedies of ancient Greece and by their Roman imitations. All later drama that has consciously copied these models, or that has followed the dramaturgic rules generalized (often falsely) from them, is also called classic or neoclassic (or pseudoclassic).

Both classical tragedy and classical comedy are usually quite formal in their dramatic construction. They often use the fifth-act structure and a single plot, and usually adhere to the unities of time, place, and action. They are relatively short. Classical dramas have comparatively few characters, and these are somewhat formalized. Stock characters people the classical comedies. There is also a rational and formal quality to the dialogue, which in ancient times was always in verse. Stichomythia (verbal combat in alternating verses), choral odes in strophic structure, fully developed and polished rhetoric in the formal speeches—these are special features of the dialogue of the classical tragedies. Their stories were dramatizations of the legends of ancient Greek gods and heroes— Prometheus, Agamemnon, Medea, Œdipus. Their themes were the relations of man and the State, retribution and fate. The stories of new comedy, however, were contemporary domestic and urban relations. So, classic as a style in drama is imitative of ancient models, with somewhat different characteristics in tragedy and comedy.

The romantic style in drama derives from the tragedies and comedies of the Elizabethan and Spanish Renaissance, and we think at once of Shakespeare. This romantic style was consciously imitated in certain dramas of the neoclassic period in conscious revolt against the classic style and the neoclassic rules. The romantic style prevailed in the romantic period of the nineteenth century.

Romantic tragedy, tragicomedy, dramatic romance, and romantic comedy are characteristically loose in their construction. They use chronological structure. They usually do not exhibit the three unities of time, place, and action. They are free in their use of elapsed time, shifts in place, and multiple plots. Though they are usually written or printed in five acts, they are often composed of very many scenes and are characteristically long. Romantic dramas often are peopled by an abundance of characters. The protagonists are likely to be complex in characterization, and minor characters may be individualized out of proportion to their dramatic importance. There is an imaginative and orotund quality to the dialogue, which is characteristically free-moving blank verse in English romantic drama. Poetic diction, flights of fancy, soliloquies and asides, rhetorical set pieces of poetic reflection—these are common features of romantic dialogue. The stories of romantic dramas are often derived from medieval legend and history or from the French or Italian romances. Their themes concern tragic heroes who are slaves of passion—ambition, jealousy, melancholy, avarice, lust. In romantic comedy the themes are often amorous—the course of true love never does run smooth until the happy ending. So, romantic as a style in drama is characterized by Elizabethan and principally (for us) Shakespearean tragedy, dramatic romance, and romantic comedy—*Othello, The Tempest, Twelfth Night.*

The realistic style in drama is largely of more recent development, although there are realistic elements in Plautus, realistic scenes in Shakespeare (such as Falstaff in the Boar's Head Tavern) and in Ben Jonson (*Bartholomew Fair*). The growth of the realistic style— in dramaturgy, in scene design, in acting—developed during the later nineteenth century and (as we have said) dominated modern drama. Realism as a style developed hand in hand with serious drama as a type, and they both owe much to Ibsen.

Realistic drama—realistic comedy as well as tragedy—is characterized by the dramaturgy of the well-made play, which Ibsen got from his French predecessors and early contemporaries. It is characterized by careful construction, exposition, and motivation. It often uses the fifth-act structure. Realistic drama sometimes adheres pretty closely to the three unities, for it is likely to be economical in its shifts of time and place and to use a single plot. It was regularly written in four acts and later in three, and is usually of moderate length. Realistic dramatists used as many characters as needed, and their characters were often individualized with psychological insight. Realistic dialogue is always in prose and usually functional, with individualizing speech patterns and dialects, personalizing details of human interest. It is often highly colloquial and pungent, sometimes vulgar and intentionally shocking. The stories of realistic drama are drawn, not from national legend and foreign romance, but from contemporary life. And that means the life of the rich and the middle-class as well as the poor—the country estates and suburbs as well as commercial and industrial cities and farms. The themes of realistic drama: the personal and social problems of people, big and little. So, realistic as a dramatic style is characteristic of modern drama, and we think of certain dramas of Ibsen, Chekhov, Hauptmann, Shaw, O'Neill, and so many others of the time.

To summarize these three dramatic styles: Classicism is formalized and rational; romanticism is flamboyant and imaginative; realism is familiar and perceptive.

But there are a number of dramatic styles in addition to these three that should be mentioned briefly. In modern drama, realism—the dominant and characteristic style—was constantly under attack, as we earlier observed; and playwrights self-consciously developed a number of antirealistic styles. Romanticism was revived (Rostand's *Cyrano,* Anderson's *Elizabeth the Queen*), and so, in a sense, was neoclassicism (Anouilh's *Antigone,* Jeffers' *Medea*). Expressionism —a style using various sorts of distortion in an effort to give outward expression to inner realities—developed first in central Europe (Capek's *R.U.R.*) and then in America (O'Neill's *Emperor Jones,* Rice's *Adding Machine*). O'Neill, in particular, experimented with many expressionistic devices: tom-toms, masks, multiple sets, asides, soliloquies, double actors. Naturalism—a "slice of life" style that went realism one better in its apparently plotless depiction of sometimes rather sordid life—also developed first in Europe (Hauptmann's *The Weavers,* Gorky's *The Lower Depths,* Chekhov's *The Cherry Orchard*) and then in America (Rice's *Street Scene,* Kingsley's *Dead End*). Yet other styles were symbolism and fantasy (Maeterlinck's *The Blue Bird,* Hauptmann's *The Sunken Bell*), constructivism (a Soviet style exploiting mechanics, structural scenic elements, industrial workers, etc.), and theatricalism (the showy use of extravagance, exaggeration, and scenic distortion as in American musical comedy). All of these antirealistic styles were developed and had at least brief vogue during the period of the realistic modern drama.

§ 5. Dramatic Criticism: a Concluding Word

This essay will be concluded by a few brief paragraphs upon dramatic and theatrical criticism.

Criticism may here be defined as the art and/or science of the interpretation and/or generalization and/or evaluation of dramas and/or stageplays. With all its awkward alternatives this definition is probably ambiguous enough to catch within its maximum scope all the various sorts of activity that have gone under the name of dramatic criticism.

Dramatic criticism has been either frankly intuitive and impressionistic or judicial and rational—something of an art or of a science. It has sometimes been concerned with interpreting the meanings of dramas—or with generalizing statements of dramatic theory—or with judging the worth of particular plays. One stream of dramatic criticism has been devoted to the great dramas and dramatists of the past and present. Another stream has reviewed and considered stageplays of the current or historic theater.

Dramatic criticism has taken the form of scholarly volumes and elaborate treatises, magazine reviews and informal essays, occasional articles and controversial pamphlets, prologues and prefaces, lectures and recorded conversations. The critics have included learned professors, literary critics and historians, playwrights and directors, magazine and newspaper columnists, reviewers and reporters. It is hardly to be wondered at that the criticism they have contributed is so various both in value and in point of view.

We shall not here call the roll of the great and numerous dramatic critics from Aristotle to our own time. A number of them have already been mentioned or will be quoted and referred to in connection with the dramas that follow. Rather, we shall bring this essay—and the series of five—to a close with a more general statement about the dramatic history, dramatic theory, and dramatic criticism that have here been so summarily reviewed.

"The play's the thing"—as, out of context, one so often hears the quotation from Hamlet—for the reader or the spectator. Let history, theory, and criticism serve to enrich the pleasurable and rewarding hours spent in the theater or study—hours spent in experiencing and enjoying stageplays or dramas.

Dramatic and theatrical history may seem no more than a dull recital of factual information, the names of playwrights and productions, synopses and commentary—but, on the other hand, it will provide you with the essential context for the interpretation of a great drama, illuminate and enliven it, so that as reader or beholder you can enter into its spirit, experience its emotion, realize its significance.

Dramatic and theatrical theory may seem no more than dry intellectual generalization, definitions, and formulae of critics, playwrights, and directors regarding dramatic structure, types, and styles—but, on the other hand, some introduction to such things will help you as a playreader to realize a drama as a living play in your imagination and to structuralize your experience in a more meaningful way; it will help you as an actor to realize both the dramatic and theatrical potential of a playbook; it will help you as a playgoer to perceive design and pattern and value in what you hear and behold.

Dramatic and theatrical criticism may seem no more than the unprofitable opinions, personal judgments, subjective appreciations of scholars, essayists, reviewers—but it will often open the door for your fuller and richer understanding, stimulating your independent interpretation, providing you with a basis for comparison and correction of your personal views and evaluation.

Among the fine arts, the drama—in its twofold nature, theater art and dramatic literature—is perhaps the most universal and various. Combining as it does the dramatic elements of tension and conflict with the theatrical elements of mimicry and display to express the wisdom elements of significance and value—which are everywhere present in human life—the drama has changed through the centuries, and it will always change, but it will never die.

The popular plays no less than the great dramas are a record of what man has dreamed and desired, what he has struggled to achieve, what forces have blocked his way, what successes and failures have crowned his efforts. No other art has so fully caught life on the wing and fixed it in enduring amber for man's delight and enrichment.

———

Introductory Note to *H.M.S. Pinafore*

THE LIBRETTO BY W. S. GILBERT for *H.M.S. Pinafore* is hardly longer than the short plays so far included with these essays, yet with its music by Arthur Sullivan it is a full-length operetta.

William S. Gilbert was born in London, the son of a navy surgeon and novelist, in 1836. He was trained as a lawyer, but the year he became a barrister (1866), he also produced his first play, and he had already contributed light verse to *Fun!* He practiced law, but loved the sea and the Navy, wrote more plays, and published his *Bab Ballads* in 1869. One of these, a Navy ballad called "Joe Golightly," includes the main story thread of *Pinafore*. The next year he met Arthur Sullivan, six years his junior but already an established composer. Soon they produced their first operetta, *Thespis* (1871). Some twenty-five years and fourteen musical comedies later, their stormy and quarrelsome collaboration came to an end. After a few more years, Sullivan (Sir Arthur by then) died. Another decade later, in 1911, Gilbert (finally knighted by King Edward VII) died tragically of heart failure while attempting the rescue of a girl from drowning.

Perhaps *H.M.S. Pinafore* is their best work, but many Savoyards (as the devotees of these tuneful comedies are called) uphold the merit of *The Pirates of Penzance* or *The Mikado* or *The Yeomen of the Guard*—or of *Patience* or *Trial by Jury*. Though Gilbert wrote other plays and librettos for other composers, only his *Pygmalion and Galatea* is barely remembered. Sullivan wrote "Onward Christian Soldiers" and "The Lost Chord," but his concert music and other dramatic scores are now forgotten. But their names together will live eternally paired as the creators of the Savoy operas—so called because most of them were produced at the Savoy Theater under the management of Richard D'Oyly Carte. They are still presented annually by the original D'Oyly Carte Company, with the same business and spirit if not the same performers.

H.M.S. Pinafore was first produced in London at the Opera Comique on May 25, 1878. It had a phenomenal run of 700 performances. It was at once pirated for presentation in New York City, where it was a smash hit. Eight different companies were playing it simultaneously in that city—forty-two altogether in the United States—when Gilbert and Sullivan opened with their own authorized version at the Fifth Avenue Theater, the first in America to use Sullivan's full orchestration. There was a breathtaking ovation for Gilbert and Sullivan, whose tunes were now being whistled by everyone and Gilbert responded in a curtain call: "It has been our purpose to produce something that should be innocent but not imbecile." There seemed to be general agreement that they had done so.

H.M.S. PINAFORE

or

THE LASS THAT LOVED A SAILOR

Libretto by William S. Gilbert
Music by Arthur Sullivan

DRAMATIS PERSONÆ

The Rt. Hon. Sir Joseph Porter, K.C.B.—*First Lord of the Admiralty.*
Captain Corcoran—*commanding H.M.S. Pinafore.*
Tom Tucker—*midshipmite.*
Ralph Rackstraw—*able seaman.*
Dick Deadeye—*able seaman.*
Bill Bobstay—*boatswain's mate.*
Bob Becket—*carpenter's mate.*
Josephine—*the Captain's daughter.*
Hebe—*Sir Joseph's first cousin.*
Mrs. Cripps (little buttercup)—*a Portsmouth bumboat woman.*
First Lord's sisters, his cousins, his aunts; Sailors, Marines, etc.

Scene: Quarter-deck of *H.M.S. Pinafore*, off Portsmouth.

ACT I. *Noon.*
ACT II. *Night.*

ACT I

Scene.—*Quarter-deck of H.M.S. Pinafore.* sailors, *led by* boatswain, *discovered cleaning brasswork, splicing rope, etc.*

CHORUS—SAILORS

We sail the ocean blue,
And our saucy ship's a beauty;
We're sober men and true,
And attentive to our duty.
When the balls whistle free
O'er the bright blue sea,

We stand to our guns all day;
When at anchor we ride
On the Portsmouth tide,
We have plenty of time to play.

[*Enter* LITTLE BUTTERCUP, *with large basket on her arm.*]

RECITATIVE—BUTTERCUP

Hail, men-o'-war's men—safeguards of your nation,
Here is an end, at last, of all privation;
You've got your pay—spare all you can afford
To welcome Little Buttercup on board.

ARIA—BUTTERCUP

For I'm called Little Buttercup—dear Little Buttercup,
    Though I could never tell why,
But still I'm called Buttercup—poor Little Buttercup,
    Sweet Little Buttercup I!

I've snuff and tobaccy, and excellent jacky,
    I've scissors, and watches, and knives;
I've ribbons and laces to set off the faces
    Of pretty young sweethearts and wives.

I've treacle and toffee, I've tea and I've coffee,
    Soft tommy and succulent chops;
I've chickens and conies, and pretty polonies,
    And excellent peppermint drops.

Then buy of your Buttercup—dear Little Buttercup;
    Sailors should never be shy;
So, buy of your Buttercup—poor Little Buttercup;
    Come, of your Buttercup buy!

BOATSWAIN. Aye, Little Buttercup—and well called—for you're the rosiest, the roundest, and the reddest beauty in all Spithead.

BUTTERCUP. Red, am I? and round—and rosy! Maybe, for I have dissembled well! But hark ye, my merry friend—hast ever thought that beneath a gay and frivolous exterior there may lurk a canker-worm which is slowly but surely eating its way into one's very heart?

BOATSWAIN. No, my lass, I can't say I've ever thought that.

[*Enter* DICK DEADEYE. *He pushes through sailors, and comes down.*]

DICK. *I have thought it often.*

[All recoil from him.]

BUTTERCUP. Yes, you look like it! What's the matter with the man? Isn't he well?

BOATSWAIN. Don't take no heed of *him;* that's only poor Dick Deadeye.

DICK. I say—it's a beast of a name, ain't it—Dick Deadeye?

BUTTERCUP. It's not a nice name.

DICK. I'm ugly too, ain't I?

BUTTERCUP. You are certainly plain.

DICK. And I'm three-cornered too, ain't I?

BUTTERCUP. You are rather triangular.

DICK. Ha! ha! That's it. I'm ugly, and they hate me for it; for you all hate me, don't you?

ALL. We do!

DICK. There!

BOATSWAIN. Well, Dick, we wouldn't go for to hurt any fellow-creature's feelings, but you can't expect a chap with such a name as Dick Deadeye to be a popular character—now can you?

DICK. No.

BOATSWAIN. It's asking too much, ain't it?

DICK. It is. From such a face and form as mine the noblest sentiments sound like the black utterances of a depraved imagination. It is human nature—I am resigned.

RECITATIVE

BUTTERCUP *[looking down hatchway]*.
    But, tell me—who's the youth whose faltering feet
        With difficulty bear him on his course?
BOATSWAIN. That is the smartest lad in all the fleet—
                Ralph Rackstraw!
BUTTERCUP. Ha! That name! Remorse! remorse!

[Enter RALPH from hatchway.]

MADRIGAL—RALPH

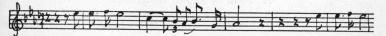

RALPH.   The Nightingale
                Sighed for the moon's bright ray,
                    And told his tale
                In his own melodious way!
                He sang "Ah, well-a-day!"

ALL.   He sang "Ah, well-a-day!"

RALPH.   The lowly vale
For the mountain vainly sighed,
To his humble wail
The echoing hills replied.
They sang "Ah, well-a-day!"

ALL.   They sang "Ah, well-a-day!"

RECITATIVE—RALPH

I know the value of a kindly chorus,
But choruses yield little consolation
When we have pain and sorrow too before us!
I love—and love, alas, above my station!

BUTTERCUP [*aside*].   He loves—and loves a lass above his station!
ALL [*aside*].   Yes, yes, the lass is much above his station!

[*Exit* LITTLE BUTTERCUP.]

BALLAD—RALPH

RALPH.   A maiden fair to see,
The pearl of minstrelsy,
    A bud of blushing beauty;
For whom proud nobles sigh,
And with each other vie
    To do her menial's duty.

ALL.   To do her menial's duty.

RALPH.   A suitor, lowly born,
With hopeless passion torn,
    And poor beyond denying,
Has dared for her to pine
At whose exalted shrine
    A world of wealth is sighing.

ALL.   A world of wealth is sighing.

RALPH.   Unlearned he in aught
Save that which love has taught
    (For love had been his tutor);
Oh, pity, pity me—
Our captain's daughter she,
    And I that lowly suitor!

ALL.   And he that lowly suitor!

BOATSWAIN. Ah, my poor lad, you've climbed too high: our worthy captain's child won't have nothin' to say to a poor chap like you. Will she, lads?

ALL. No, no.

DICK. No, no, captains' daughters don't marry foremast hands.

ALL [*recoiling from him*]. Shame! shame!

BOATSWAIN. Dick Deadeye, them sentiments o' yourn are a disgrace to our common natur'.

RALPH. But it's a strange anomaly, that the daughter of a man who hails from the quarter-deck may not love another who lays out on the fore-yard arm. For a man is but a man, whether he hoists his flag at the main-truck or his slacks on the main-deck.

DICK. Ah, it's a queer world!

RALPH. Dick Deadeye, I have no desire to press hardly on you, but such a revolutionary sentiment is enough to make an honest sailor shudder.

BOATSWAIN. My lads, our gallant captain has come on deck; let us greet him as so brave an officer and so gallant a seaman deserves.

[*Enter* CAPTAIN CORCORAN.]

RECITATIVE

CAPTAIN. My gallant crew, good morning.

ALL [*saluting*]. Sir, good morning!

CAPTAIN. I hope you're all quite well.

ALL [*as before*]. Quite well; and you, sir?

CAPTAIN. I am in reasonable health, and happy
To meet you all once more.

ALL [*as before*]. You do us proud, sir!

SONG—CAPTAIN

CAPTAIN. I am the Captain of the *Pinafore;*

ALL. And a right good captain, too!

CAPTAIN. You're very, very good,
And be it understood,
I command a right good crew,

ALL. We're very, very good,
And be it understood,
He commands a right good crew.

CAPTAIN. Though related to a peer,
I can hand, reef, and steer,
And ship a selvagee;

I am never known to quail
At the fury of a gale,
And I'm never, never sick at sea!

ALL.   What, never?
CAPTAIN.   No, never!
ALL.   What, *never*?
CAPTAIN.   Hardly ever!
ALL.   He's hardly ever sick at sea!
Then give three cheers, and one cheer more,
For the hardy Captain of the *Pinafore*!

CAPTAIN.   I do my best to satisfy you all—
ALL.   And with you we're quite content.
CAPTAIN.   You're exceedingly polite,
And I think it only right
To return the compliment.
ALL.   We're exceedingly polite,
And he thinks it's only right
To return the compliment.
CAPTAIN.   Bad language or abuse,
I never, never use,
Whatever the emergency;
Though "Bother it" I may
Occasionally say,
I never use a big, big D—
ALL.   What, never?
CAPTAIN.   No, never!
ALL.   What, *never*?
CAPTAIN.   Hardly ever!
ALL.   Hardly ever swears a big, big D—
Then give three cheers, and one cheer more,
For the well-bred Captain of the *Pinafore*!

         [*After song exeunt all but* CAPTAIN.]

[*Enter* LITTLE BUTTERCUP.]

RECITATIVE

BUTTERCUP.   Sir, you are sad! The silent eloquence
Of yonder tear that trembles on your eyelash
Proclaims a sorrow far more deep than common;
Confide in me—fear not—I am a mother!
CAPTAIN.   Yes, Little Buttercup, I'm sad and sorry—
My daughter, Josephine, the fairest flower
That ever blossomed on ancestral timber,
Is sought in marriage by Sir Joseph Porter,

Our Admiralty's First Lord, but for some reason
She does not seem to tackle kindly to it.

BUTTERCUP [*with emotion*]. Ah, poor Sir Joseph! Ah, I know too well
The anguish of a heart that loves but vainly!
But see, here comes your most attractive daughter.
I go—Farewell!   [*Exit.*]

CAPTAIN [*looking after her*]. A plump and pleasing person!   [*Exit.*]

[*Enter* JOSEPHINE, *twining some flowers which she carries in a small basket.*]

BALLAD—JOSEPHINE

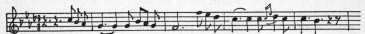

Sorry her lot who loves too well,
    Heavy the heart that hopes but vainly,
Sad are the sighs that own the spell,
    Uttered by eyes that speak too plainly;
        Heavy the sorrow that bows the head
        When love is alive and hope is dead!
Sad is the hour when sets the sun—
    Dark is the night to earth's poor daughters,
When to the ark the wearied one
    Flies from the empty waste of waters!
        Heavy the sorrow that bows the head
        When love is alive and hope is dead!

[*Enter* CAPTAIN.]

CAPTAIN. My child, I grieve to see that you are a prey to melancholy.
You should look your best to-day, for Sir Joseph Porter, K.C.B., will be
here this afternoon to claim your promised hand.

JOSEPHINE. Ah, father, your words cut me to the quick. I can esteem
—reverence—venerate Sir Joseph, for he is a great and good man; but
oh, I cannot love him! My heart is already given.

CAPTAIN [*aside*]. It is then as I feared. [*Aloud*] Given? And to
whom? Not to some gilded lordling?

JOSEPHINE. No, father—the object of my love is no lordling. Oh,
pity me, for he is but a humble sailor on board your own ship!

CAPTAIN. Impossible!

JOSEPHINE. Yes, it is true—too true.

CAPTAIN. A common sailor? Oh fie!

JOSEPHINE. I blush for the weakness that allows me to cherish such
a passion. I hate myself when I think of the depth to which I have
stooped in permitting myself to think tenderly of one so ignobly born,
but I love him! I love him! I love him! [*Weeps.*]

CAPTAIN.　Come, my child, let us talk this over.　In a matter of the heart I would not coerce my daughter—I attach but little value to rank or wealth, but the line must be drawn somewhere.　A man in that station may be brave and worthy, but at every step he would commit solecisms that society would never pardon.

JOSEPHINE.　Oh, I have thought of this night and day.　But fear not, father, I have a heart, and therefore I love; but I am your daughter and therefore I am proud.　Though I carry my love with me to the tomb, he shall never, never know it.

CAPTAIN.　You *are* my daughter after all.　But see, Sir Joseph's barge approaches, manned by twelve trusty oarsmen and accompanied by the admiring crowd of sisters, cousins, and aunts that attend him wherever he goes.　Retire, my daughter, to your cabin—take this, his photograph, with you—it may help to bring you to a more reasonable frame of mind.

JOSEPHINE.　My own thoughtful father!

[*Exit* JOSEPHINE.]

[CAPTAIN *remains and ascends the poop-deck.*]

BARCAROLLE—CHORUS OF WOMEN [*off-stage*]

Over the bright blue sea
Comes Sir Joseph Porter, K.C.B.,
　Wherever he may go
Bang-bang the loud nine-pounders go!
　Shout o'er the bright blue sea
For Sir Joseph Porter, K.C.B.

[*During this the* CREW *have entered on tiptoe, listening attentively to the song.*]

CHORUS OF SAILORS

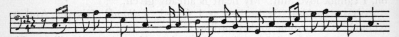

Sir Joseph's barge is seen,
　And its crowd of blushing beauties,
We hope he'll find us clean,
　And attentive to our duties.
We sail, we sail the ocean blue,
　And our saucy ship's a beauty.
We're sober, sober men and true
　And attentive to our duty.

We're smart and sober men,
  And quite devoid of fe-ar,
In all the Royal N.
  None are so smart as we are.

[*Enter* SIR JOSEPH'S FEMALE RELATIVES. *They dance round stage.*]

RELATIVES.   Gaily tripping,
           Lightly skipping,
           Flock the maidens to the shipping.

SAILORS.   Flags and guns and pennants dipping!
           All the ladies love the shipping.

RELATIVES.   Sailors sprightly
           Always rightly
           Welcome ladies so politely.

SAILORS.   Ladies who can smile so brightly,
           Sailors welcome most politely.

CAPTAIN [*from poop*]. Now give three cheers, I'll lead the way

ALL.   Hurrah! hurrah! hurrah! hurray!

[*Enter* SIR JOSEPH *with* COUSIN HEBE.]

SONG—SIR JOSEPH

SIR JOSEPH.   I am the monarch of the sea,
             The ruler of the Queen's Navee,
              Whose praise Great Britain loudly chants.

COUSIN HEBE.   And we are his sisters, and his cousins
              and his aunts!

RELATIVES.   And we are his sisters, and his cousins,
               and his aunts!

SIR JOSEPH.   When at anchor here I ride,
             My bosom swells with pride,
              And I snap my fingers at a foeman's taunts;

COUSIN HEBE.   And so do his sisters, and his cousins, and
               his aunts!

ALL.   And so do his sisters, and his cousins, and
               his aunts!

SIR JOSEPH.   But when the breezes blow,
             I generally go below,
              And seek the seclusion that a cabin grants;

COUSIN HEBE.   And so do his sisters, and his cousins, and
               his aunts!

ALL.   And so do his sisters, and his cousins, and
                        his aunts!
              His sisters and his cousins,
              Whom he reckons up by dozens,
                  And his aunts!

SONG—SIR JOSEPH

SIR JOSEPH.   When I was a lad I served a term
              As office boy to an Attorney's firm.
              I cleaned the windows and I swept the floor,
              And I polished up the handle of the big front door.
                  I polished up that handle so carefullee
                  That now I am the Ruler of the Queen's Navee!

CHORUS.   He polished up that handle so carefullee
              That now he is the Ruler of the Queen's Navee!

SIR JOSEPH.   As office boy I made such a mark
              That they gave me the post of a junior clerk.
              I served the writs with a smile so bland,
              And I copied all the letters in a big round hand—
                  I copied all the letters in a hand so free,
                  That now I am the Ruler of the Queen's Navee!

          CHORUS.—He copied, etc.

              In serving writs I made such a name
              That an articled clerk I soon became;
              I wore clean collars and a brand-new suit
              For the pass examination at the Institute,
                  And that pass examination did so well for me,
                  That now I am the Ruler of the Queen's Navee!

          CHORUS.—And that pass examination, etc.

              Of legal knowledge I acquired such a grip
              That they took me into the partnership.
              And that junior partnership, I ween,
              Was the only ship that I ever had seen.
                  But that kind of ship so suited me,
                  That now I am the Ruler of the Queen's Navee!

CHORUS.—But that kind, etc.

I grew so rich that I was sent
By a pocket borough into Parliament.
I always voted at my party's call,
And I never thought of thinking for myself at all.
 I thought so little, they rewarded me
 By making me the Ruler of the Queen's Navee!

CHORUS.—He thought so little, etc.

Now landsmen all, whoever you may be,
If you want to rise to the top of the tree,
If your soul isn't fettered to an office stool,
Be careful to be guided by this golden rule—
 Stick close to your desks and never go to sea,
 And you all may be Rulers of the Queen's Navee!

CHORUS.—Stick close, etc.

SIR JOSEPH. You've a remarkably fine crew, Captain Corcoran.

CAPTAIN. It *is* a fine crew, Sir Joseph.

SIR JOSEPH [*examining a very small midshipman*]. A British sailor is a splendid fellow, Captain Corcoran.

CAPTAIN. A splendid fellow indeed, Sir Joseph.

SIR JOSEPH. I hope you treat your crew kindly, Captain Corcoran.

CAPTAIN. Indeed I hope so, Sir Joseph.

SIR JOSEPH. Never forget that they are the bulwarks of England's greatness, Captain Corcoran.

CAPTAIN. So I have always considered them, Sir Joseph.

SIR JOSEPH. No bullying, I trust—no strong language of any kind, eh?

CAPTAIN. Oh, never, Sir Joseph.

SIR JOSEPH. What, *never*?

CAPTAIN. Hardly ever, Sir Joseph. They are an excellent crew, and do their work thoroughly without it.

SIR JOSEPH. Don't patronise them, sir—pray, don't patronise them.

CAPTAIN. Certainly not, Sir Joseph.

SIR JOSEPH. That you are their captain is an accident of birth. I cannot permit these noble fellows to be patronised because an accident of birth has placed you above them and them below you.

CAPTAIN. I am the last person to insult a British sailor, Sir Joseph.

SIR JOSEPH. You are the last person who did, Captain Corcoran. Desire that splendid seamen to step forward.

[DICK *comes forward.*]

SIR JOSEPH. No, no, the other splendid seaman.

CAPTAIN. Ralph Rackstraw, three paces to the front—march!

SIR JOSEPH [*sternly*]. If what?

CAPTAIN. I beg your pardon—I don't think I understand you.

SIR JOSEPH. If you *please*.

CAPTAIN. Oh, yes, of course. If you please.

[RALPH *steps forward.*]

SIR JOSEPH. You're a remarkably fine fellow.

RALPH. Yes, your honour.

SIR JOSEPH. And a first-rate seaman, I'll be bound.

RALPH. There's not a smarter topman in the Navy, your honour, though I say it who shouldn't.

SIR JOSEPH. Not at all. Proper self-respect, nothing more. Can you dance a hornpipe?

RALPH. No, your honour.

SIR JOSEPH. That's a pity: all sailors should dance hornpipes. I will teach you one this evening, after dinner. Now tell me—don't be afraid —how does your captain treat you, eh?

RALPH. A better captain don't walk the deck, your honour.

ALL. Aye; aye!

SIR JOSEPH. Good. I like to hear you speak well of your commanding officer; I daresay he don't deserve it, but still it does you credit. Can you sing?

RALPH. I can hum a little, your honour.

SIR JOSEPH. Then hum this at your leisure. [*Giving him MS. music.*] It is a song that I have composed for the use of the Royal Navy. It is designed to encourage independence of thought and action in the lower branches of the service, and to teach the principle that a British sailor is any man's equal, excepting mine. Now, Captain Corcoran, a word with you in your cabin, on a tender and sentimental subject.

CAPTAIN. Aye, aye, Sir Joseph. [*Crossing*] Boatswain, in commemoration of this joyous occasion, see that extra grog is served out to the ship's company at seven bells.

BOATSWAIN. Beg pardon. If what, your honour?

CAPTAIN. If what? I don't think I understand you.

BOATSWAIN. If you *please,* your honour.

CAPTAIN. What!

SIR JOSEPH. The gentleman is quite right. If you *please*.

CAPTAIN [*stamping his foot impatiently*]. If you *please!*   [*Exit.*]

CHORUS FOR EXIT

SIR JOSEPH.   For I hold that on the seas
     The expression, "if you please,"
     A particularly gentlemanly tone implants.

COUSIN HEBE.   And so do his sisters, and his cousins, and
          his aunts!

ALL.   And so do his sisters, and his cousins, and
        his aunts!

         [*Exeunt* SIR JOSEPH *and* RELATIVES.]

BOATSWAIN. Ah! Sir Joseph's a true gentleman; courteous and considerate to the very humblest.

RALPH. True, Boatswain, but we are not the very humblest. Sir Joseph has explained our true position to us. As he says, a British seaman is any man's equal excepting his, and if Sir Joseph says that, is it not our duty to believe him?

ALL. Well spoke! well spoke!

DICK. You're on a wrong tack, and so is he. He means well, but he don't know. When people have to obey other people's orders, equality's out of the question.

ALL [*recoiling*]. Horrible! horrible!

BOATSWAIN. Dick Deadeye, if you go for to infuriate this here ship's company too far, I won't answer for being able to hold 'em in. I'm shocked! that's what I am—shocked!

RALPH. Messmates, my mind's made up. I'll speak to the captain's daughter, and tell her, like an honest man, of the honest love I have for her.

ALL. Aye, aye!

RALPH. Is not my love as good as another's? Is not my heart as true as another's? Have I not hands and eyes and ears and limbs like another?

ALL. Aye; aye!

RALPH. True, I lack birth——

BOATSWAIN. You've a berth on board this very ship.

RALPH. Well said—I had forgotten that. Messmates—what do you say? Do you approve my determination?

ALL. We do.

DICK. *I* don't.

BOATSWAIN. What is to be done with this here hopeless chap? Let us sing him the song that Sir Joseph has kindly composed for us. Perhaps it will bring this here miserable creetur to a proper state of mind.

GLEE—RALPH, BOATSWAIN, BOATSWAIN'S MATE, *and* CHORUS

TRIO.   A British tar is a soaring soul,
              As free as a mountain bird,
          His energetic fist should be ready to resist
              A dictatorial word.
          His nose should pant and his lip should curl,
          His cheeks should flame and his brow should furl,
          His bosom should heave and his heart should glow,
          And his fist be ever ready for a knock-down blow.

CHORUS.—His nose should pant, etc.

TRIO.   His eyes should flash with an inborn fire,
              His brow with scorn be wrung;
          He never should bow down to a domineering frown,
              Or the tang of a tyrant tongue.
          His foot should stamp and his throat should growl,
          His hair should twirl and his face should scowl;
          His eyes should flash and his breast protrude,
          And this should be his customary attitude—(*pose*).

CHORUS.—His foot should stamp, etc.

[*All dance off excepting* RALPH, *who remains, leaning pensively against bulwark.*]

[*Enter* JOSEPHINE *from cabin.*]

JOSEPHINE.   It is useless—Sir Joseph's attentions nauseate me. I know that he is a truly great and good man, for he told me so himself, but to me he seems tedious, fretful, and dictatorial. Yet his must be a mind of no common order, or he would not dare to teach my dear father to dance a hornpipe on the cabin table. [*Sees* RALPH] Ralph Rackstraw! [*Overcome by emotion.*]

RALPH.   Aye, lady—no other than poor Ralph Rackstraw!

JOSEPHINE [*aside*].   How my heart beats! [*Aloud*] And why poor, Ralph?

RALPH.   I am poor in the essence of happiness, lady—rich only in never-ending unrest. In me there meet a combination of antithetical elements which are at eternal war with one another. Driven hither by objective influences—thither by subjective emotions—wafted one moment into blazing day, by mocking hope—plunged the next into the Cimmerian darkness of tangible despair, I am but a living ganglion of irreconcilable antagonisms. I hope I make myself clear, lady?

JOSEPHINE.   Perfectly. [*Aside*] His simple eloquence goes to my heart. Oh, if I dared—but no, the thought is madness! [*Aloud*] Dismiss these foolish fancies, they torture you but needlessly. Come, make one effort.

RALPH [*aside*]. I will—one. [*Aloud*] Josephine!

JOSEPHINE [*indignantly*]. Sir!

RALPH.   Aye, even though Jove's armoury were launched at the head of the audacious mortal whose lips, unhallowed by relationship, dared to breathe that precious word, yet would I breathe it once, and then perchance be silent evermore. Josephine, in one brief breath I will concentrate the hopes, the doubts, the anxious fears of six weary months. Josephine, I am a British sailor, and I love you!

JOSEPHINE.   Sir, this audacity! [*Aside*] Oh, my heart, my beating heart! [*Aloud*] This unwarrantable presumption on the part of a common sailor! [*Aside*] Common! oh, the irony of the word! [*Crossing, aloud*] Oh, sir, you forget the disparity in our ranks.

RALPH.   I forget nothing, haughty lady. I love you desperately, my life is in your hand—I lay it at your feet! Give me hope, and what I lack in education and polite accomplishments, that I will endeavour to acquire. Drive me to despair, and in death alone I shall look for consolation. I am proud and cannot stoop to implore. I have spoken and I wait your word.

JOSEPHINE.   You shall not wait long. Your proffered love I haughtily reject. Go, sir, and learn to cast your eyes on some village maiden in your own poor rank—they should be lowered before your captain's daughter.

DUET—JOSEPHINE and RALPH

JOSEPHINE.
　　　　Refrain, audacious tar,
　　　　　　Your suit from pressing,
　　　　Remember what you are,
　　　　　　And whom addressing!

[*Aside*]
　　　　I'd laugh my rank to scorn
　　　　　　In union holy,
　　　　Were he more highly born
　　　　　　Or I more lowly!

RALPH.
　　　　Proud lady, have your way,
　　　　　　Unfeeling beauty!
　　　　You speak and I obey,
　　　　　　It is my duty!
　　　　I am the lowliest tar
　　　　　　That sails the water,
　　　　And you, proud maiden, are
　　　　　　My captain's daughter!

[*Aside*]　　My heart with anguish torn
　　　　　　Bows down before her,
　　　　　　She laughs my love to scorn,
　　　　　　Yet I adore her!

[*Repeat refrain, ensemble, then exit* JOSEPHINE *into cabin.*]

RECITATIVE

RALPH.　　　Can I survive this overbearing
　　　　　　Or live a life of mad despairing,
　　　　　　My proffered love despised, rejected?
　　　　　　No, no, it's not to be expected!

[*Calling off*]　　Messmates, ahoy!
　　　　　　Come here! Come here!

[*Enter* SAILORS, HEBE, *and* RELATIVES]

ALL.　　　　Aye, aye, my boy,
　　　　　　What cheer, what cheer?
　　　　　　Now tell us, pray,
　　　　　　Without delay,
　　　　　　What does she say—
　　　　　　What cheer, what cheer?

FINALE

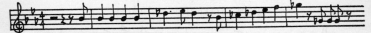

RALPH [*to* COUSIN HEBE].
　　　　　　The maiden treats my suit with scorn,
　　　　　　　Rejects my humble gift, my lady;
　　　　　　She says I am ignobly born,
　　　　　　　And cuts my hopes adrift, my lady.

ALL.　　　　　　Oh, cruel one.

DICK.　　　She spurns your suit? Oho! Oho!
　　　　　　I told you so, I told you so.

SAILORS *and* RELATIVES.
　　　　　Shall { we / they } submit? Are { we / they } but slaves?
　　　　　Love comes alike to high and low—
　　　　　Britannia's sailors rule the waves,
　　　　　　And shall they stoop to insult? No!

DICK.　　　You must submit, you are but slaves;
　　　　　　A lady she! Oho! Oho!
　　　　　You lowly toilers of the waves,
　　　　　　She spurns you all—I told you so!

RALPH.   My friends, my leave of life I'm taking,
              For oh, my heart, my heart is breaking.
              When I am gone, oh, prithee tell
              The maid that, as I died, I loved her well!

ALL [*turning away, weeping*].
              Of life, alas! his leave he's taking,
              For ah! his faithful heart is breaking;
              When he is gone we'll surely tell
              The maid that, as he died, he loved her well.

[*During Chorus* BOATSWAIN *has loaded pistol, which he hands to*
RALPH.]

RALPH.   Be warned, my messmates all
                        Who love in rank above you—
                      For Josephine I fall!

[*Puts pistol to his head. All the sailors stop their ears.*]

[*Enter* JOSEPHINE *on deck.*]

JOSEPHINE.   Ah! stay your hand! I love you!
ALL.   Ah! stay your hand—she loves you!
RALPH [*incredulously*]. Loves me?
JOSEPHINE.   Loves you!
ALL.   Yes, yes—ah, yes,—she loves you!

ENSEMBLE
SAILORS *and* RELATIVES *and* JOSEPHINE

              Oh joy, oh rapture unforeseen,
              For now the sky is all serene;
              The god of day—the orb of love—
              Has hung his ensign high above,
                      The sky is all ablaze.

              With wooing words and loving song,
              We'll chase the lagging hours along,
              And if { I find / we find } the maiden coy,
              I'll / We'll } murmur forth decorous joy
                  In dreamy roundelays!

DICK DEADEYE

He thinks he's won his Josephine,
But though the sky is now serene,
A frowning thunderbolt above
May end their ill-assorted love
      Which now is all ablaze.

Our captain, ere the day is gone,
Will be extremely down upon
The wicked men who art employ
To make his Josephine less coy
      In many various ways.

[Exit DICK.]

JOSEPHINE.	This very night,
HEBE.	With bated breath
RALPH.	And muffled oar—
JOSEPHINE.	Without a light,
HEBE.	As still as death,
RALPH.	We'll steal ashore
JOSEPHINE.	A clergyman
RALPH.	Shall make us one
BOATSWAIN.	At half-past ten,
JOSEPHINE.	And then we can
RALPH.	Return, for none
BOATSWAIN.	Can part them then!
ALL.	This very night, etc.

[DICK *appears at hatchway.*]

RECITATIVE

DICK.   Forbear, nor carry out the scheme you've planned;
          She is a lady—you a foremast hand!
          Remember, she's your gallant captain's daughter,
          And you the meanest slave that crawls the water!

ALL.   Back, vermin, back,
                      Nor mock us!
                   Back, vermin, back,
                      You shock us!

[Exit DICK.]

CHORUS

ALL.
Let's give three cheers for the sailor's bride
Who casts all thought of rank aside—
Who gives up home and fortune too
For the honest love of a sailor true!
For a British tar is a soaring soul
As free as a mountain bird!
His energetic fist should be ready to resist
A dictatorial word!

His foot should stamp and his throat should growl,
His hair should twirl and his face should scowl,
His eyes should flash and his breast protrude,
And this should be his customary attitude—(*pose*).

GENERAL DANCE

END OF ACT I

ACT II

SAME SCENE.—*Night. Awning removed. Moonlight.* CAPTAIN *discovered singing on poop-deck, and accompanying himself on a mandolin.* LITTLE BUTTERCUP *seated on quarter-deck, gazing sentimentally at him.*

SONG—CAPTAIN

Fair moon, to thee I sing,
Bright regent of the heavens,
Say, why is everything
Either at sixes or at sevens?
I have lived hitherto
Free from breath of slander,
Beloved by all my crew—
A really popular commander.
But now my kindly crew rebel,
My daughter to a tar is partial,
Sir Joseph storms, and, sad to tell,
He threatens a court martial!
Fair moon, to thee I sing,
Bright regent of the heavens,
Say, why is everything
Either at sixes or at sevens?

BUTTERCUP. How sweetly he carols forth his melody to the unconscious moon! Of whom is he thinking? Of some high-born beauty? It may be! Who is poor Little Buttercup that she should expect his glance to fall on one so lowly! And yet if he knew—if he only knew!

CAPTAIN [*coming down*]. Ah! Little Buttercup, still on board? That is not quite right, little one. It would have been more respectable to have gone on shore at dusk.

BUTTERCUP. True, dear Captain—but the recollection of your sad pale face seemed to chain me to the ship. I would fain see you smile before I go.

CAPTAIN. Ah! Little Buttercup, I fear it will be long before I recover my accustomed cheerfulness, for misfortunes crowd upon me, and all my old friends seem to have turned against me!

BUTTERCUP. Oh no—do not say "all," dear Captain. That were unjust to one, at least.

CAPTAIN. True, for you are staunch to me. [*Aside*] If ever I gave my heart again, methinks it would be to such a one as this! [*Aloud*] I am touched to the heart by your innocent regard for me, and were we differently situated, I think I could have returned it. But as it is, I fear I can never be more to you than a friend.

BUTTERCUP. I understand! You hold aloof from me because you are rich and lofty—and I poor and lowly. But take care! The poor bumboat woman has gipsy blood in her veins, and she can read destinies.

CAPTAIN. Destinies?

BUTTERCUP. There is a change in store for you!

CAPTAIN. A change?

BUTTERCUP. Aye—be prepared!

DUET—LITTLE BUTTERCUP and CAPTAIN

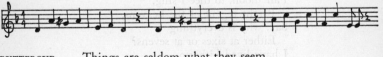

BUTTERCUP.   Things are seldom what they seem,
Skim milk masquerades as cream;
Highlows pass as patent leathers;
Jackdaws strut in peacock's feathers.

CAPTAIN [*puzzled*].   Very true,
So they do.

BUTTERCUP.   Black sheep dwell in every fold;
All that glitters is not gold;
Storks turn out to be but logs;
Bulls are but inflated frogs.

CAPTAIN [*puzzled*].   So they be,
Frequentlee.

BUTTERCUP.	Drops the wind and stops the mill;
	Turbot is ambitious brill;
	Gild the farthing if you will,
	Yet it is a farthing still.
CAPTAIN [*puzzled*].	Yes, I know.
	That is so.
	Though to catch your drift I'm striving,
	It is shady—it is shady;
	I don't see at what you're driving,
	Mystic lady—mystic lady.
[*Aside*]	Stern conviction's o'er me stealing,
	That the mystic lady's dealing
	In oracular revealing.
BUTTERCUP [*aside*].	Stern conviction's o'er him stealing,
	That the mystic lady's dealing
	In oracular revealing.
BOTH.	Yes, I know—
	That is so!
CAPTAIN.	Though I'm anything but clever,
	I could talk like that for ever:
	Once a cat was killed by care;
	Only brave deserve the fair.
BUTTERCUP.	Very true,
	So they do.
CAPTAIN.	Wink is often good as nod;
	Spoils the child who spares the rod;
	Thirsty lambs run foxy dangers;
	Dogs are found in many mangers.
BUTTERCUP.	Frequentlee,
	I agree.
CAPTAIN.	Paw of cat the chestnut snatches;
	Worn-out garments show new patches;
	Only count the chick that hatches;
	Men are grown-up catchy-catchies.
BUTTERCUP.	Yes, I know,
	That is so.
[*Aside*]	Though to catch my drift he's striving,
	I'll dissemble—I'll dissemble;
	When he sees at what I'm driving,
	Let him tremble—let him tremble!

ENSEMBLE

Though a mystic tone $\left\{ \begin{matrix} I \\ you \end{matrix} \right\}$ borrow,

You will ⎫
I shall ⎬ learn the truth with sorrow,

Here to-day and gone to-morrow;
        Yes, I know—
        That is so!

[*At the end exit* LITTLE BUTTERCUP *melodramatically.*]

CAPTAIN. Incomprehensible as her utterances are, I nevertheless feel that they are dictated by a sincere regard for me. But to what new misery is she referring? Time alone can tell!

[*Enter* SIR JOSEPH.]

SIR JOSEPH. Captain Corcoran, I am much disappointed with your daughter. In fact, I don't think she will do.

CAPTAIN. She won't do, Sir Joseph!

SIR JOSEPH. I'm afraid not. The fact is, that although I have urged my suit with as much eloquence as is consistent with an official utterance, I have done so hitherto without success. How do you account for this?

CAPTAIN. Really, Sir Joseph, I hardly know. Josephine is of course sensible of your condescension.

SIR JOSEPH. She naturally would be.

CAPTAIN. But perhaps your exalted rank dazzles her.

SIR JOSEPH. You think it does?

CAPTAIN. I can hardly say; but she is a modest girl, and her social position is far below your own. It may be that she feels she is not worthy of you.

SIR JOSEPH. That is really a very sensible suggestion, and displays more knowledge of human nature than I had given you credit for.

CAPTAIN. See, she comes. If your lordship would kindly reason with her and assure her officially that it is a standing rule at the Admiralty that love levels all ranks, her respect for an official utterance might induce her to look upon your offer in its proper light.

SIR JOSEPH. It is not unlikely. I will adopt your suggestion. But soft, she is here. Let us withdraw, and watch our opportunity.

[*Enter* JOSEPHINE *from cabin.* FIRST LORD *and* CAPTAIN *retire.*]

SCENA—JOSEPHINE

The hours creep on apace,
    My guilty heart is quaking!
Oh, that I might retrace
    The step that I am taking!
Its folly it were easy to be showing,
What I am giving up and whither going.
On the one hand, papa's luxurious home,

Hung with ancestral armour and old brasses,
Carved oak and tapestry from distant Rome,
 Rare "blue and white" Venetian finger-glasses,
Rich oriental rugs, luxurious sofa pillows,
And everything that isn't old, from Gillow's.
And on the other, a dark and dingy room,
 In some back street with stuffy children crying,
Where organs yell, and clacking housewives fume.
 And clothes are hanging out all day a-drying.
With one cracked looking-glass to see your face in,
And dinner served up in a pudding basin!

A simple sailor, lowly born,
 Unlettered and unknown,
Who toils for bread from early morn
 Till half the night has flown!
No golden rank can he impart—
 No wealth of house or land—
No fortune save his trusty heart
 And honest brown right hand!
And yet he is so wondrous fair
That love for one so passing rare,
So peerless in his manly beauty,
Were little else than solemn duty!
 Oh, god of love, and god of reason, say,
 Which of you twain shall my poor heart obey!

[SIR JOSEPH *and* CAPTAIN *enter.*]

SIR JOSEPH. Madam, it has been represented to me that you are appalled by my exalted rank. I desire to convey to you officially my assurance that if your hesitation is attributable to that circumstance, it is uncalled for.

JOSEPHINE. Oh! then your lordship is of opinion that married happiness is *not* inconsistent with discrepancy in rank?

SIR JOSEPH. I am officially of that opinion.

JOSEPHINE. That the high and the lowly may be truly happy together, provided that they truly love one another?

SIR JOSEPH. Madam, I desire to convey to you officially my opinion that love is a platform upon which all ranks meet.

JOSEPHINE. I thank you, Sir Joseph. I *did* hesitate, but I will hesitate no longer. [*Aside*] He little thinks how eloquently he has pleaded his rival's cause!

TRIO

FIRST LORD, CAPTAIN, *and* JOSEPHINE

CAPTAIN.	Never mind the why and wherefore,
	Love can level ranks, and therefore,
	Though his lordship's station's mighty,
	Though stupendous be his brain,
	Though your tastes are mean and flighty
	And your fortune poor and plain,
CAPTAIN *and*	Ring the merry bells on board-ship,
SIR JOSEPH.	Rend the air with warbling wild,

For the union of $\left\{ \begin{array}{c} \text{his} \\ \text{my} \end{array} \right\}$ lordship

With a humble captain's child!

CAPTAIN.	For a humble captain's daughter—
JOSEPHINE.	For a gallant captain's daughter—
SIR JOSEPH.	And a lord who rules the water—
JOSEPHINE [*aside*].	And a *tar* who ploughs the water!
ALL.	Let the air with joy be laden,
	Rend with songs the air above,
	For the union of a maiden
	With the man who owns her love!

SIR JOSEPH.	Never mind the why and wherefore,
	Love can level ranks, and therefore,
	Though your nautical relation [*alluding to* CAPTAIN]
	In my set could scarcely pass—
	Though you occupy a station
	In the lower middle class—
CAPTAIN *and*	Ring the merry bells on board-ship,
SIR JOSEPH.	Rend the air with warbling wild,

For the union of $\left\{ \begin{array}{c} \text{my} \\ \text{his} \end{array} \right\}$ lordship

With a humble captain's child!

CAPTAIN.	For a humble captain's daughter—
JOSEPHINE.	For a gallant captain's daughter—
SIR JOSEPH.	And a lord who rules the water—
JOSEPHINE [*aside*].	And a *tar* who ploughs the water!
ALL.	Let the air with joy be laden,
	Rend with songs the air above,
	For the union of a maiden
	With the man who owns her love!

JOSEPHINE.   Never mind the why and wherefore,
                    Love can level ranks, and therefore
                    I admit the jurisdiction;
                        Ably have you played your part;
                    You have carried firm conviction
                        To my hesitating heart.
CAPTAIN *and*   Ring the merry bells on board-ship,
SIR JOSEPH.   Rend the air with warbling wild,

For the union of $\left\{ \begin{array}{c} \text{my} \\ \text{his} \end{array} \right\}$ lordship

                    With a humble captain's child!
CAPTAIN.   For a humble captain's daughter—
JOSEPHINE.   For a gallant captain's daughter—
SIR JOSEPH.   And a lord who rules the water—
JOSEPHINE [*aside*].   And a *tar* who ploughs the water!
    [*Aloud.*] Let the air with joy be laden.
CAPT. *and* SIR JOSEPH.   Ring the merry bells on board-ship—
JOSEPHINE.   For the union of a maiden—
CAPT. *and* SIR JOSEPH.   For her union with his lordship.
ALL.   Rend with songs the air above
                    For the man who owns her love!

[*Exit* JOSEPHINE.]

CAPTAIN.   Sir Joseph, I cannot express to you my delight at the happy result of your eloquence. Your argument was unanswerable.

SIR JOSEPH.   Captain Corcoran, it is one of the happiest characteristics of this glorious country that official utterances are invariably regarded as unanswerable.

[*Exit* SIR JOSEPH.]

CAPTAIN.   At last my fond hopes are to be crowned. My only daughter is to be the bride of a Cabinet Minister. The prospect is Elysian.

[*During this speech* DICK DEADEYE *has entered.*]

DICK.   Captain.
CAPTAIN.   Deadeye! You here? Don't! [*Recoiling from him.*]
DICK.   Ah, don't shrink from me, Captain. I'm unpleasant to look at, and my name's agin me, but I ain't as bad as I seem.
CAPTAIN.   What would you with me?
DICK [*mysteriously*].   I'm come to give you warning.
CAPTAIN.   Indeed! do you propose to leave the Navy then?
DICK.   No, no, you misunderstand me; listen!

DUET

CAPTAIN *and* DICK DEADEYE

DICK.   Kind Captain, I've important information,
       Sing hey, the kind commander that you are,
     About a certain intimate relation,
       Sing hey, the merry maiden and the tar.

BOTH.   The merry maiden and the tar.

CAPTAIN.   Good fellow, in conundrums you are speaking,
       Sing hey, the mystic sailor that you are;
     The answer to them vainly I am seeking;
       Sing hey, the merry maiden and the tar.

BOTH.   The merry maiden and the tar.

DICK.   Kind Captain, your young lady is a-sighing,
       Sing hey, the simple captain that you are,
     This very night with Rackstraw to be flying;
       Sing hey, the merry maiden and the tar.

BOTH.   The merry maiden and the tar.

CAPTAIN.   Good fellow, you have given timely warning,
       Sing hey, the thoughtful sailor that you are,
     I'll talk to Master Rackstraw in the morning:
       Sing hey, the cat-o'-nine-tails and the tar.

                                   [*Producing a "cat."*]

BOTH.   The merry cat-o'-nine-tails and the tar!

     CAPTAIN.   Dick Deadeye—I thank you for your warning—I will at once take means to arrest their flight. This boat cloak will afford me ample disguise—So! [*Envelops himself in a mysterious cloak, holding it before his face.*]

     DICK.   Ha, ha! They are foiled—foiled—foiled!

[*Enter* CREW *on tiptoe, with* RALPH *and* BOATSWAIN *meeting* JOSEPHINE, *who enters from cabin on tiptoe, with bundle of necessaries, and accompanied by* LITTLE BUTTERCUP.]

ENSEMBLE

CREW.
> Carefully on tiptoe stealing,
> Breathing gently as we may,
> Every step with caution feeling,
> We will softly steal away.

[CAPTAIN *stamps.—Chord.*]

ALL [*much alarmed*]. Goodness me—
> Why, what was that?

DICK.
> Silent be,
> It was the cat!

ALL [*reassured*].
> It was—it was the cat!

CAPTAIN [*producing cat-o'-nine-tails*]. They're right—it was
> the cat!

ALL.
> Pull ashore, in fashion steady,
> Hymen will defray the fare,
> For a clergyman is ready
> To unite the happy pair!

[*Stamp as before, and Chord.*]

ALL.
> Goodness me,
> Why, what was that?

DICK.
> Silent be,
> Again the cat!

ALL.
> It was again that cat!

CAPTAIN [*aside*].
> They're right, it was the cat!

SOLO, DUET *and* CHORUS

CAPTAIN [*throwing off cloak*]. Hold!

[ALL *start.*]

> Pretty daughter of mine,
> I insist upon knowing
> Where you may be going
> With these sons of the brine,
> For my excellent crew,
> Though foes they could thump any,
> Are scarcely fit company,
> My daughter, for you.

CREW.
> Now, hark at that, do!
> Though foes we could thump any,
> We are scarcely fit company
> For a lady like you!

RALPH.   Proud officer, that haughty lip uncurl!
              Vain man, suppress that supercilious sneer,
              For I have dared to love your matchless girl,
              A fact well known to all my messmates here!

CAPTAIN.   Oh, horror!

RALPH *and*   { I, } humble, poor, and lowly born,
JOSEPHINE.   { He, }
              The meanest in the port division—
              The butt of epauletted scorn—
              The mark of quarter-deck derision—
              Have }   { my }
              Has } dared to raise { his } wormy eyes

              Above the dust to which you'd mould { me
                                                  { him

              In manhood's glorious pride to rise,
              I am }   { me!
              He is } an Englishman—behold { him!

ALL.   He is an Englishman!
BOATSWAIN.   He is an Englishman!

BOATSWAIN.   For he himself has said it,
                  And it's greatly to his credit,
                  That he is an Englishman!

ALL.   That he is an Englishman!
BOATSWAIN.   For he might have been a Roosian,
              A French, or Turk, or Proosian,
              Or perhaps Itali-an!

ALL.   Or perhaps Itali-an!
BOATSWAIN.   But in spite of all temptations
              To belong to other nations,
                  He remains an Englishman!

ALL.   For in spite of all temptations, etc.

CAPTAIN [*trying to repress his anger*].
                  In uttering a reprobation
                  To any British tar,
                  I try to speak with moderation,
                  But you have gone too far.

> I'm very sorry to disparage
> A humble foremast lad,
> But to seek your captain's child in marriage,
> Why damme, it's too bad!

[*During this,* COUSIN HEBE *and* FEMALE RELATIVES *have entered.*]

ALL [*shocked*]. Oh!
CAPTAIN. Yes, damme, it's too bad!
ALL. Oh!
CAPTAIN *and* DICK DEADEYE. Yes, damme, it's too bad.

[*During this,* SIR JOSEPH *has appeared on poop-deck.. He is horrified at the bad language.*]

HEBE. Did you hear him—did you hear him?
> Oh, the monster overbearing!
> Don't go near him—don't go near him—
> He is swearing—he is swearing!

SIR JOSEPH. My pain and my distress,
> I find it is not easy to express;
> My amazement—my surprise—
> You may learn from the expression of my eyes!

CAPTAIN. My lord—one word—the facts are not before you
> The word was injudicious, I allow—
> But hear my explanation, I implore you,
> And you will be indignant too, I vow!

SIR JOSEPH. I will hear of no defence,
> Attempt none if you're sensible.
> That word of evil sense
> Is wholly indefensible.
> Go, ribald, get you hence
> To your cabin with celerity.
> This is the consequence
> Of ill-advised asperity!

[*Exit* CAPTAIN, *disgraced, followed by* JOSEPHINE.]

ALL. This is the consequence,
> Of ill-advised asperity!

SIR JOSEPH. For I'll teach you all, ere long,
> To refrain from language strong
> For I haven't any sympathy for ill-bred taunts!

HEBE. No more have his sisters, nor his cousins, nor
> his aunts.

ALL. For he is an Englishman, etc.

SIR JOSEPH. Now, tell me, my fine fellow—for you *are* a fine fellow—

RALPH. Yes, your honour.

SIR JOSEPH. How came your captain so far to forget himself? I am quite sure you had given him no cause for annoyance.

RALPH. Please your honour, it was thus-wise. You see I'm only a topman—a mere foremast hand—

SIR JOSEPH. Don't be ashamed of that. Your position as a topman is a very exalted one.

RALPH. Well, your honour, love burns as brightly in the fo'c'sle as it does on the quarter-deck, and Josephine is the fairest bud that ever blossomed upon the tree of a poor fellow's wildest hopes.

[*Enter* JOSEPHINE; *she rushes to* RALPH's *arms.*]

JOSEPHINE. Darling!

[SIR JOSEPH *horrified.*]

RALPH. She is the figurehead of my ship of life—the bright beacon that guides me into my port of happiness—that the rarest, the purest gem that ever sparkled on a poor but worthy fellow's trusting brow!

ALL. Very pretty, very pretty!

SIR JOSEPH. Insolent sailor, you shall repent this outrage. Seize him!

[TWO MARINES *seize him and handcuff him.*]

JOSEPHINE. Oh, Sir Joseph, spare him, for I love him tenderly.

SIR JOSEPH. Pray, don't. I will teach this presumptuous mariner to discipline his affections. Have you such a thing as a dungeon on board?

ALL. We have!

DICK. They have!

SIR JOSEPH. Then load him with chains and take him there at once!

OCTET

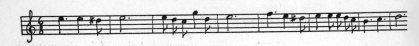

RALPH.
    Farewell, my own,
        Light of my life, farewell!
    For crime unknown
        I go to a dungeon cell.

JOSEPHINE.
    I will atone.
        In the meantime farewell!
    And all alone
        Rejoice in your dungeon cell!

SIR JOSEPH.
A bone, a bone
I'll pick with this sailor fell;
Let him be shown
At once to his dungeon cell.

BOATSWAIN, DICK DEADEYE, *and* COUSIN HEBE.
He'll hear no tone
Of the maiden he loves so well!
No telephone
Communicates with his cell!

BUTTERCUP [*mysteriously*].
But when is known
The secret I have to tell,
Wide will be thrown
The door of his dungeon cell.

ALL.
For crime unknown
He goes to a dungeon cell!

[RALPH *is led off in custody*.]

SIR JOSEPH.
My pain and my distress
Again it is not easy to express.
My amazement, my surprise,
Again you may discover from my eyes.

ALL.
How terrible the aspect of his eyes!

BUTTERCUP.
Hold! Ere upon your loss
You lay much stress,
A long-concealèd crime
I would confess.

SONG—BUTTERCUP *and* CHORUS

BUTTERCUP.
A many years ago,
When I was young and charming,
As some of you may know,
I practised baby-farming.

ALL.
Now this is most alarming!
When she was young and charming,
She practised baby-farming,
A many years ago.

BUTTERCUP.   Two tender babes I nussed:
                   One was of low condition,
              The other, upper crust,
                   A regular patrician.

ALL [*explaining to each other*].
                   Now, this is the position:
              One was of low condition,
              The other a patrician,
                   A many years ago.

BUTTERCUP.   Oh, bitter is my cup!
                   However could I do it?
              I mixed those children up,
                   And not a creature knew it!

ALL.   However could you do it?
              Some day, no doubt, you'll rue it,
              Although no creature knew it,
                   So many years ago.

BUTTERCUP.   In time each little waif
                   Forsook his foster-mother,
              The well-born babe was Ralph—
                   Your captain was the other!!!

ALL.   They left their foster-mother,
              The one was Ralph, our brother,
              Our captain was the other,
                   A many years ago.

  SIR JOSEPH.   Then I am to understand that Captain Corcoran and
Ralph were exchanged in childhood's happy hour—that Ralph is really
the Captain, and the Captain is Ralph?
  BUTTERCUP.   That is the idea I intended to convey, officially!
  SIR JOSEPH.   And very well you have conveyed it.
  BUTTERCUP.   Aye! aye! yer 'onour.
  SIR JOSEPH.   Dear me! Let them appear before me, at once!

  [RALPH *enters as* CAPTAIN; CAPTAIN *as a common sailor.* JOSEPHINE
rushes to his arms.]

  JOSEPHINE.   My father—a common sailor!
  CAPTAIN.   It is hard, is it not, my dear?
  SIR JOSEPH.   This is a very singular occurrence; I congratulate you
both. [*To* RALPH] Desire that remarkably fine seaman to step forward
  RALPH.   Corcoran. Three paces to the front—march!
  CAPTAIN.   If what?

RALPH. If what? I don't think I understand you.

CAPTAIN. If you please.

SIR JOSEPH. The gentleman is quite right. If you *please*.

RALPH. Oh! If you *please*. [CAPTAIN *steps forward*.]

SIR JOSEPH [*to* CAPTAIN]. You are an extremely fine fellow.

CAPTAIN. Yes, your honour.

SIR JOSEPH. So it seems that you were Ralph, and Ralph was you.

CAPTAIN. So it seems, your honour.

SIR JOSEPH. Well, I need not tell you that after this change in your condition, a marriage with your daughter will be out of the question.

CAPTAIN. Don't say that, your honour—love levels all ranks.

SIR JOSEPH. It does to a considerable extent, but it does not level them as much as that. [*Handing* JOSEPHINE *to* RALPH] Here—take her, sir, and mind you treat her kindly.

RALPH *and* JOSEPHINE. Oh bliss, oh rapture!

CAPT. *and* BUTTERCUP. Oh rapture, oh bliss!

SIR JOSEPH. Sad my lot and sorry,
What shall I do? I cannot live alone!

HEBE. Fear nothing—while I live I'll not desert you.
I'll soothe and comfort your declining days.

SIR JOSEPH. No, don't do that.

HEBE. Yes, but indeed I'd rather—

SIR JOSEPH [*resigned*]. To-morrow morn our vows shall all be plighted,
Three loving pairs on the same day united!

QUARTET

JOSEPHINE, HEBE, RALPH, *and* DEADEYE

QUARTET. Oh joy, oh rapture unforeseen,
The clouded sky is now serene,
The god of day—the orb of love,
Has hung his ensign high above,
The sky is all ablaze.

With wooing words and loving song,
We'll chase the lagging hours along,
And if { he finds / I find } the maiden coy,
We'll murmur forth decorous joy,
In dreamy roundelay.

CAPTAIN. For he's the Captain of the *Pinafore*.

ALL. And a right good captain too!

CAPTAIN.   And though before my fall
                   I was captain of you all,
                   I'm a member of the crew.

ALL.   Although before his fall, etc.

CAPTAIN.   I shall marry with a wife,
                   In my humble rank of life!

      [*Turning to* BUTTERCUP]

                   And you, my own, are she—
                   I must wander to and fro;
                   But wherever I may go,
                   I shall never be untrue to thee!
ALL.   What, never?
CAPTAIN.   No, never!
ALL.   What, *never?*
CAPTAIN.   Hardly ever!
ALL.   Hardly ever be untrue to thee.
                   Then give three cheers, and one cheer more
                   For the former Captain of the *Pinafore.*

BUTTERCUP. For he loves Little Buttercup, dear Little Buttercup,
                   Though I could never tell why;
                   But still he loves Buttercup, poor Little Buttercup,
                   Sweet Little Buttercup, aye!

ALL.   For he loves, etc.

SIR JOSEPH. I'm the monarch of the sea,
                   And when I've married thee [*to* HEBE],
                   I'll be true to the devotion that my love implants,
HEBE.   Then good-bye to his sisters, and his cousins, and
                                     his aunts!
                   Especially his cousins,
                   Whom he reckons up by dozens,
                   His sisters, and his cousins, and his aunts!

ALL.   For he is an Englishman,
                       And he himself hath said it,
                       And it's greatly to his credit
                   That he is an Englishman!

                          CURTAIN

Brief Commentary on *H.M.S. Pinafore*

H.M.S. Pinafore is Victorian in its substance and dramaturgy; it is a comedy, satiric and musical; it is romantic in style.

When this libretto was written, Victoria Regina was nearly sixty, the Widow of Windsor, her loving Albert long dead. This was the mid-Victorian era of social respectability. There was a certain comfortable stability in the marked social classes. Officers of the navy, drawn from the upper class, and seamen drawn from the lower, prided themselves on knowing their place. The Tory prime minister, Disraeli, was something of a dandy and had won a reputation as a novelist. Though contemptuous of the middle class, he appointed W. H. Smith, a publisher, to be First Lord of the Admiralty. Disraeli, a shrewd politician, had pushed his program of British imperialism in the Mediterranean (with the Suez Canal), in Africa, in the Pacific, and he crowned Victoria Empress of India! Indeed it was a brilliant libretto, with score for bosun pipes and carronade. English nationalism was intense, and Britannia ruled the waves.

Gilbert's amusing libretto for *Pinafore,* with its witty as well as sentimental lyrics, is as Victorian in its dramaturgy as it is in its substance. The artificial dialogue (asides and soliloquies, purple rhetoric and noble sentiments), the contrived plot (love vs. duty, the final discovery of true identity, the triple couples at the final curtain)—these are hallmarks of the melodramas, sentimental comedies, and farces of the period. Yet with all its silly coincidences and anachronisms, it is no more ridiculous, be it said, than Aristophanes at one end of the history of comedy or Kaufman and Hammerstein at the other.

The plot line, almost but not quite imbecile, has good things strung along it. These are, for the most part, as fresh today as three-quarters of a century ago. For this is comedy, not alone because of its happy ending, but because it continues to be laughter provoking: the plot and action, perhaps more ridiculous to us than intended—the comic characterizations of Little Buttercup, Dick Deadeye, Sir Joseph—the witty and jingling lyrics filled with pointed barbs of satire—the lively and happy tunes, graceful ensembles, and rousing choruses.

To sense the romantic character of its style, it is only necessary to think in contrast of *The Long Voyage Home,* with its realistic depiction of the seamen of the next generation.

Part Two

THE PLAYS

THE INTRODUCTORY NOTE preceding each of these longer dramas is somewhat fuller than those for the short plays in Part One. It will, however, not tell you what to look for in your reading, or what the play "really" means. It will not tell you the story in advance, or analyze the characters, or prequote the choice lines, or discuss in anticipation the symbols and the themes. Were it to do so, rendering almost superfluous the reading of the drama itself, you would be deprived of the pleasure of your own first-hand playreading experience.

The purpose of the Introductory Note—beyond tying each of the eight dramas into the pageant of Western drama as sketched in the fifth essay in Part One—is to provide you with such information as you may almost unconsciously put to use in making your own interpretation of the drama, producing the play in the theater of your own imagination, reflecting upon its pattern and meaning and values. Some facts about the playwright as a man, about certain of his activities and works, about the drama and its production in the theater will serve to enrich your background and supply contextual data useful in your reading of the dramatist's intention and your re-creation of his work of art.

The eight plays that follow are presented chronologically and will, therefore, serve to exemplify the history of our drama and theater. But you may prefer to read them in some other order to illustrate the several dramatic types or styles, or to consider the development of dramaturgy from the less to the more complex.

It is a pleasure to present Sophocles' *Antigone* in one of the very few modern and readable verse translations. The text of *Othello* has been freshly edited, with renewed reference to Folio and Quarto readings and with some slight modernization of spelling (*blessed* for *bless'd* unless it is to be pronounced *blessèd*) and of punctuation (avoiding the Elizabethan colon and Victorian semicolon) and of stage directions, as is not unusual. The numerous glosses have been placed in the margins, where it is hoped they may be used most helpfully or left alone. The translation of Molière's little comedy is here called *The Ridiculous Précieuses,* since no English can catch both the meaning and spirit of its title. There has seemed to be no good reason to depart from the standard version of Ibsen's *Hedda Gabler.* It is fortunate that now Shaw's *Candida* can be presented in a book of this kind, and that permission was given to include *Life with Father.* Tennessee Williams' long production notes, of very real interest to the reader of *The Glass Menagerie,* will be found in the Appendix; also a selection from the prose documentation and discussion that Arthur Miller included here and there in the published form of *The Crucible.*

Two commentaries are printed following each play. They are, for the most part, excerpted from longer reviews and works of dramatic criticism. It is hoped that in their present form, with the excisions clearly indicated, they do no injustice to the opinions of the scholars and critics—among the most notable of our time—who have kindly permitted their inclusion. By no means do the two critics always agree with each other, nor do they at all times speak the mind of the author of this *Preface to Drama.* However, it is expected that, in reading them, you will learn much, disagree often, and be driven back to a closer rereading of the play upon which they are ultimately based.

Materials of another kind—notes and queries, suggestions for reading and study, outline worksheets—will be found in the Appendix.

I. ANTIGONE

A Classical Tragedy by Sophocles

Introductory Note to Sophocles and *Antigone*

THE ULTIMATE GREATNESS of a drama lies in its ability to speak clearly to the condition of successive ages. Among the tragedies surviving from the Greek dawn of the drama, none has more to say to us today than *Antigone,* written by Sophocles some 2400 years ago.

Fortune seems to have favored Sophocles. Born at Colonus near Athens in 496 B.C., the son of a well-to-do manufacturer of armor, he was given the best of physical and intellectual educations. A handsome youth of sixteen, he was chosen to lead the chorus, naked and playing the lyre, celebrating the Athenian victory over the Persian fleet off Salamis. While still in his twenties, he won his first triumph over Aeschylus as a dramatist. He was already a fine-looking man, a talented musician, a charming personality, a respected citizen, a rare genius in the theater. Though without military or political gifts, he was twice elected a commander and later a general commissioner. When he died in 406 B.C. at the age of ninety, Sophocles was honored as a poet and worshipped as a hero.

He wrote about one hundred twenty plays in all and won first prize some twenty times, never falling below second place. He made significant contributions to the art of the theater and drama: added the use of a third actor, introduced painted scenery, developed the separate-play form as distinct from the trilogy, increased the size of the chorus and decreased its importance. Seven of his tragedies survive, including an *Electra* and an *Ajax,* together with a long fragment of a satyr play. Of these, three, written at different periods of his life, deal with incidents in the legendary Thebes story: *Œdipus the King* (ca. 429 B.C.), considered by many the most powerful of the Greek tragedies, tells of Œdipus' fearful discovery of his identity and fate. *Œdipus at Colonus,* written perhaps during

Sophocles' last year (406 B.C.) and produced posthumously by his grandson, depicts the death of the old, blind king in the sacred grove near Sophocles' birthplace. *Antigone,* first of the three to be written (442 B.C.), brings to their tragic end the unhappily begotten children of Œdipus.

The success of *Antigone* won Sophocles the prize and (so it is said) a military command, and the play continued to be popular in ancient times. In modern times, too, there have been many translations and productions. One in German by Hasenclever was staged by Max Reinhardt (1919). Jean Anouilh's version was produced in Paris during the German occupation (1943), heartening the French underground. Translated by Lewis Galantiere, it was played with critical success in America (1946) by Katharine Cornell and Sir Cedric Hardwicke. A recent translation in verse by E. F. Watling (1947) is published in the Penguin Classics. The Fitts and Fitzgerald translation (1939) was successful in a C.B.S. broadcast, and in an Omnibus telecast in 1954 with Beatrice Straight as Antigone.

For the Greek audience, of course, the Thebes story was familiar legend, at least in its main outlines. They had all heard of Œdipus, born to King Laius and his queen, Jocasta, under the dire prophecy that he would grow up to kill his father and marry his mother. To forestall this calamity, they pierced and tied the infant's heels, and ordered a servant to abandon it in the hills. Instead, the tender servant gave it to a royal shepherd from distant Corinth, and the baby was secretly adopted by the childless king and queen of that land to be brought up as their own son and heir. They called the boy Œdipus, little "swell-foot."

When grown to powerful and hot-tempered young manhood, Œdipus heard a dire prophecy—that he would kill his father and marry his mother. To forestall this calamity he abruptly left Corinth and struck out to the north on his own. There were incidents in store for him. He clashed with a small party on the way, an arrogant charioteer who struck at him and crowded him off the road. Œdipus, enraged, killed him and all but one of his companions. Presently he came to a city—it was Thebes—suffering under the spell of a dread Sphinx, whose riddle no man could guess. But Œdipus guessed it, and thus saved the city. The grateful Thebans chose him king—for their ruler Laius was recently dead— and Œdipus married the widowed queen, Jocasta. She bore her young husband four children, and all went well for some fifteen years until a plague descended upon Thebes.

Œdipus, desperate to drive off the pestilence, then sent for advice. Within the city, so he was told, remained the slayer of Laius, who had to be discovered and removed. Œdipus set himself relentlessly to the task. Through his efforts it was gradually revealed to him and to Jocasta—by the old servant who had failed to abandon the infant and who was also the one servant escaping from the roadside brawl, and by the royal shepherd of Corinth (who came to report the death of the King of Corinth)—that Œdipus himself was the slayer of Laius, the evil thing to be cast out. The dire prophecy had been fulfilled: Œdipus had killed his father and married his mother. He went within, discovered Jocasta's suicide, and blinded himself—he could not look upon the fruits of his incest. Leaving Creon (Jocasta's brother) as ruler, he sought banishment.

But blinded Œdipus was not allowed to leave Thebes at once. It was not until his two sons, Eteocles and Polyneices, and his two daughters, Ismene and Antigone, were grown that Œdipus was banished. He then wandered off, accompanied by Antigone, finding refuge in a woods at Colonus. Ismene followed to report strife between her two brothers and against Creon. Then Creon himself came to seize Œdipus and his daughters, who were saved by the intervention of Theseus, king of Athens. Polyneices' approach to secure his father's blessing on his struggle with Eteocles led to the father's curse upon the sons. And, then, Œdipus blessed his daughters and died.

The brothers, in one version of the legend, had agreed to rule alternately, a year at a time. While Eteocles ruled, Polyneices went off to Argos and married the Argive princess. When Eteocles refused to give way in turn to Polyneices, the latter came with an Argive army, headed by seven champions including Polyneices himself and his father-in-law. They attacked the seven gates of Thebes, which were defended by Eteocles and six other worthy leaders. The defenders triumphed. But Œdipus's curse prevailed against his sons, and Eteocles and Polyneices died at each other's hands before the seventh gate. Creon, again, was named king. He ordered the body of Eteocles buried with due ceremony, but the body of Polyneices was to remain unburied, desecrated, a prey to bird and beast.

The story of *Antigone*—the particular incidents of which seem to be original with Sophocles—begins at this point.

ANTIGONE
by Sophocles

AN ENGLISH VERSION BY DUDLEY FITTS AND ROBERT FITZGERALD *

THE CHARACTERS

ANTIGONE—*daughter of Œdipus, former banished king.*
ISMENE—*her elder sister.*

CREON—*their maternal uncle, now King of Thebes.*
HAIMON—*Creon's son, beloved of Antigone.*
EURYDICE—*the Queen, his mother, whose other son has just been killed defending Thebes from attack.*

TEIRESIAS—*the old and blind seer or prophet.*
A SENTRY *and* A MESSENGER

THE CHORUS *of fifteen Thebans, elder citizens, among whom the* CHORAGOS *is the leader.*

Time: *the legendery past of Ancient Greece.*

Place: *the walled city of Thebes with its seven gates.*

SCENE: BEFORE THE PALACE *of Creon, King of Thebes. A central double door, and two lateral doors. A platform extends the length of the façade, and from this platform three steps lead down into the 'orchestra,' or chorus-ground. Time: dawn of the day after the repulse of the Argive army from the assault on Thebes.*

PROLOGUE

[ANTIGONE *and* ISMENE *enter from the central door of the Palace.*]

ANTIGONE. Ismenê, dear sister,
  You would think that we had already suffered enough
  For the curse on Œdipus:
  I cannot imagine any grief
  That you and I have not gone through. And now—

---

* *The Antigone of Sophocles:* An English Version by Dudley Fitts and Robert Fitzgerald, copyright, 1939, by Harcourt, Brace and Company, Inc. Reprinted by permission.

Have they told you of the new decree of our King Creon?
ISMENE. I have heard nothing: I know
That two sisters lost two brothers, a double death
In a single hour; and I know that the Argive army
Fled in the night; but beyond this, nothing.
ANTIGONE. I thought so. And that is why I wanted you
To come out here with me. There is something we must do.
ISMENE. Why do you speak so strangely?
ANTIGONE. Listen, Ismenê:
Creon buried our brother Eteoclês
With military honours, gave him a soldier's funeral,
And it was right that he should; but Polyneicês,
Who fought as bravely and died as miserably,—
They say that Creon has sworn
No one shall bury him, no one mourn for him,
But his body must lie in the fields, a sweet treasure
For carrion birds to find as they search for food.
That is what they say, and our good Creon is coming here
To announce it publicly; and the penalty—
Stoning to death in the public square!
                              There it is,
And now you can prove what you are:
A true sister, or a traitor to your family.
ISMENE. Antigonê, you are mad! What could I possibly do?
ANTIGONE. You must decide whether you will help me or not.
ISMENE. I do not understand you. Help you in what?
ANTIGONE. Ismenê, I am going to bury him. Will you come?
ISMENE. Bury him! You have just said the new law forbids it.
ANTIGONE. He is my brother. And he is your brother, too.
ISMENE. But think of the danger! Think what Creon will do!
ANTIGONE. Creon is not strong enough to stand in my way.
ISMENE. Ah sister!
Œdipus died, everyone hating him
For what his own search brought to light, his eyes
Ripped out by his own hand; and Iocastê died,
His mother and wife at once: she twisted the cords
That strangled her life; and our two brothers died,
Each killed by the other's sword. And we are left:
But oh, Antigonê,
Think how much more terrible than these
Our own death would be if we should go against Creon
And do what he has forbidden! We are only women,
We cannot fight with men, Antigonê!
The law is strong, we must give in to the law
In this thing, and in worse. I beg the Dead

To forgive me, but I am helpless: I must yield
To those in authority. And I think it is dangerous business
To be always meddling.
ANTIGONE.   If that is what you think,
I should not want you, even if you asked to come.
You have made your choice, you can be what you want to be.
But I will bury him; and if I must die,
I say that this crime is holy: I shall lie down
With him in death, and I shall be as dear
To him as he to me.
                    It is the dead,
Not the living, who make the longest demands:
We die for ever. . .
                    You may do as you like,
Since apparently the laws of the gods mean nothing to you.
ISMENE.   They mean a great deal to me; but I have no strength
To break laws that were made for the public good.
ANTIGONE.   That must be your excuse, I suppose. But as for me,
I will bury the brother I love.
ISMENE.   Antigonê,
I am so afraid for you!
ANTIGONE.   You need not be:
You have yourself to consider, after all.
ISMENE.   But no one must hear of this, you must tell no one!
I will keep it a secret, I promise!
ANTIGONE.   Oh tell it! Tell everyone!
Think how they'll hate you when it all comes out
If they learn that you knew about it all the time!
ISMENE.   So fiery! You should be cold with fear.
ANTIGONE.   Perhaps. But I am doing only what I must.
ISMENE.   But can you do it? I say that you cannot.
ANTIGONE.   Very well: when my strength gives out, I shall do no more.
ISMENE.   Impossible things should not be tried at all.
ANTIGONE.   Go away, Ismenê:
I shall be hating you soon, and the dead will too,
For your words are hateful. Leave me my foolish plan:
I am not afraid of the danger; if it means death,
It will not be the worst of deaths—death without honour.
ISMENE.   Go then, if you feel that you must.
You are unwise,
But a loyal friend indeed to those who love you.
                         [*Exit into the Palace.* ANTIGONE *goes off, L.*]

[*Enter the* CHORUS.]

PÁRODOS

CHORUS.   [*strophe 1*

   Now the long blade of the sun, lying
   Level east to west, touches with glory
   Thebes of the Seven Gates. Open, unlidded
   Eye of golden day! O marching light
   Across the eddy and rush of Dircê's stream,
   Striking the white shields of the enemy
   Thrown headlong backward from the blaze of morning!

CHORAGOS.   Polyneicês their commander
   Roused them with windy phrases,
   He the wild eagle screaming
   Insults above our land,
   His wings their shields of snow,
   His crest their marshalled helms.

CHORUS.   [*antistrophe 1*

   Against our seven gates in a yawning ring
   The famished spears came onward in the night;
   But before his jaws were sated with our blood,
   Or pinefire took the garland of our towers,
   He was thrown back; and as he turned, great Thebes—
   No tender victim for his noisy power—
   Rose like a dragon behind him, shouting war.

CHORAGOS.   For God hates utterly
   The bray of bragging tongues;
   And when he beheld their smiling,
   Their swagger of golden helms,
   The frown of his thunder blasted
   Their first man from our walls.

CHORUS.   [*strophe 2*

   We heard his shout of triumph high in the air
   Turn to a scream; far out in a flaming arc
   He fell with his windy torch, and the earth struck him.
   And others storming in fury no less than his
   Found shock of death in the dusty joy of battle.

CHORAGOS.   Seven captains at seven gates
   Yielded their clanging arms to the god
   That bends the battle-line and breaks it.
   These two only, brothers in blood,
   Face to face in matchless rage,

Mirroring each the other's death,
Clashed in long combat.

CHORUS.   [antistrophe 2
   But now in the beautiful morning of victory
   Let Thebes of the many chariots sing for joy!
   With hearts for dancing we'll take leave of war:
   Our temples shall be sweet with hymns of praise,
   And the long night shall echo with our chorus.

                           SCENE I

CHORAGOS.   But now at last our new King is coming:
   Creon of Thebes, Menoiceus' son.
   In this auspicious dawn of his reign
   What are the new complexities
   That shifting Fate has woven for him?
   What is his counsel? Why has he summoned
   The old men to hear him?

   [Enter CREON from the Palace, C. He addresses the CHORUS from
   the top step.]

CREON.   Gentlemen: I have the honour to inform you that our Ship
of State, which recent storms have threatened to destroy, has come safely
to harbour at last, guided by the merciful wisdom of Heaven. I have
summoned you here this morning because I know that I can depend upon
you: your devotion to King Laïos was absolute; you never hesitated in
your duty to our late ruler Œdipus; and when Œdipus died, your loyalty
was transferred to his children. Unfortunately, as you know, his two
sons, the princes Eteoclês and Polyneicês, have killed each other in battle;
and I, as the next in blood, have succeeded to the full power of the
throne.
   I am aware, of course, that no Ruler can expect complete loyalty from
his subjects until he has been tested in office. Nevertheless, I say to you
at the very outset that I have nothing but contempt for the kind of
Governor who is afraid, for whatever reason, to follow the course that
he knows is best for the State; and as for the man who sets private
friendship above the public welfare,—I have no use for him, either. I
call God to witness that if I saw my country headed for ruin, I should
not be afraid to speak out plainly; and I need hardly remind you that
I would never have any dealings with an enemy of the people. No one
values friendship more highly than I; but we must remember that
friends made at the risk of wrecking our Ship are not real friends at all.
   These are my principles, at any rate, and that is why I have made
the following decision concerning the sons of Œdipus: Eteoclês, who

died as a man should die, fighting for his country, is to be buried with full military honours, with all the ceremony that is usual when the greatest heroes die; but his brother Polyneicês, who broke his exile to come back with fire and sword against his native city and the shrines of his fathers' gods, whose one idea was to spill the blood of his blood and sell his own people into slavery—Polyneicês, I say, is to have no burial: no man is to touch him or say the least prayer for him; he shall lie on the plain, unburied; and the birds and the scavenging dogs can do with him whatever they like.

This is my command, and you can see the wisdom behind it. As long as I am King, no traitor is going to be honoured with the loyal man. But whoever shows by word and deed that he is on the side of the State,— he shall have my respect while he is living, and my reverence when he is dead.

CHORAGOS. If that is your will, Creon son of Menoiceus,
  You have the right to enforce it: we are yours.
CREON. That is my will. Take care that you do your part.
CHORAGOS. We are old men: let the younger ones carry it out.
CREON. I do not mean that: the sentries have been appointed.
CHORAGOS. Then what is it that you would have us do?
CREON. You will give no support to whoever breaks this law.
CHORAGOS. Only a crazy man is in love with death!
CREON. And death it is; yet money talks, and the wisest
  Have sometimes been known to count a few coins too many.

[*Enter* SENTRY *from L.*]

SENTRY. I'll not say that I'm out of breath from running, King, because every time I stopped to think about what I have to tell you, I felt like going back. And all the time a voice kept saying, 'You fool, don't you know you're walking straight into trouble?'; and then another voice: 'Yes, but if you let somebody else get the news to Creon first, it will be even worse than that for you!' But good sense won out, at least I hope it was good sense, and here I am with a story that makes no sense at all; but I'll tell it anyhow, because, as they say, what's going to happen's going to happen, and—

CREON. Come to the point. What have you to say?
SENTRY. I did not do it. I did not see who did it. You must not punish
  me for what someone else has done.
CREON. A comprehensive defence! More effective, perhaps,
  If I knew its purpose. Come: what is it?
SENTRY. A dreadful thing . . . I don't know how to put it—
CREON. Out with it!
SENTRY.   Well, then;

The dead man—
                    Polyneicês—

 [*Pause. The* SENTRY *is overcome, fumbles for words.* CREON *waits impassively.*]

         out there—
             someone,—
New dust on the slimy flesh!

 [*Pause. No sign from* CREON.]

Someone has given it burial that way, and
Gone . . .

 [*Long pause.* CREON *finally speaks with deadly control.*]

CREON. And the man who dared do this?
SENTRY.   I swear I
Do not know! You must believe me!
             Listen:
The ground was dry, not a sign of digging, no,
Not a wheeltrack in the dust, no trace of anyone.
It was when they relieved us this morning: and one of them,
The corporal, pointed to it.
         There it was,
The strangest—
    Look:
The body, just mounded over with light dust: you see?
Not buried really, but as if they'd covered it
Just enough for the ghost's peace. And no sign
Of dogs or any wild animal that had been there.

And then what a scene there was! Every man of us
Accusing the other: we all proved the other man did it,
We all had proof that we could not have done it.
We were ready to take hot iron in our hands,
Walk through fire, swear by all the gods,
It was not I!
I do not know who it was, but it was not I!

 [CREON's *rage has been mounting steadily, but the* SENTRY *is too intent upon his story to notice it.*]

And then, when this came to nothing, someone said
A thing that silenced us and made us stare
Down at the ground: you had to be told the news,
And one of us had to do it! We threw the dice,

And the bad luck fell to me. So here I am,
No happier to be here than you are to have me:
Nobody likes the man who brings bad news.
CHORAGOS. I have been wondering, King: can it be that the gods have
    done this?
CREON [*furiously*]. Stop!
    Must you doddering wrecks
Go out of your heads entirely? 'The gods!'
Intolerable!
The gods favour this corpse? Why? How had he served them?
Tried to loot their temples, burn their images,
Yes, and the whole State, and its laws with it!
Is it your senile opinion that the gods love to honour bad men?
A pious thought!—
               No, from the very beginning
There have been those who have whispered together,
Stiff-necked anarchists, putting their heads together,
Scheming against me in alleys. These are the men,
And they have bribed my own guard to do this thing.
    [*Sententiously*] Money!
There's nothing in the world so demoralising as money.
Down go your cities,
Homes gone, men gone, honest hearts corrupted,
Crookedness of all kinds, and all for money!
    [*To* SENTRY]
                    But you—!
I swear by God and by the throne of God,
The man who has done this thing shall pay for it!
Find that man, bring him here to me, or your death
Will be the least of your problems: I'll string you up
Alive, and there will be certain ways to make you
Discover your employer before you die;
And the process may teach you a lesson you seem to have missed:
The dearest profit is sometimes all too dear:
That depends on the source. Do you understand me?
A fortune won is often misfortune.
SENTRY. King, may I speak?
CREON.   Your very voice distresses me.
SENTRY. Are you sure that it is my voice, and not your conscience?
CREON. By God, he wants to analyse me now!
SENTRY. It is not what I say, but what has been done, that hurts you.
CREON. You talk too much.
SENTRY.   Maybe; but I've done nothing.
CREON. Sold your soul for some silver: that's all you've done.
SENTRY. How dreadful it is when the right judge judges wrong!
CREON. Your figures of speech

May entertain you now; but unless you bring me the man,
You will get little profit from them in the end.

[*Exit* CREON *into the Palace.*]

SENTRY. 'Bring me the man'—!
I'd like nothing better than bringing him the man!
But bring him or not, you have seen the last of me here.
At any rate, I am safe!

[*Exit* SENTRY.]

Ode I

CHORUS.   [*strophe* 1
Numberless are the world's wonders, but none
More wonderful than man; the stormgray sea
Yields to his prows, the huge crests bear him high;
Earth, holy and inexhaustible, is graven
With shining furrows where his plows have gone
Year after year, the timeless labour of stallions.

                                                          [*antistrophe* 1
The lightboned birds and beasts that cling to cover,
The lithe fish lighting their reaches of dim water,
All are taken, tamed in the net of his mind;
The lion on the hill, the wild horse windy-maned,
Resign to him; and his blunt yoke has broken
The sultry shoulders of the mountain bull.

                                                          [*strophe* 2
Words also, and thought as rapid as air,
He fashions to his good use; statecraft is his,
And his the skill that deflects the arrows of snow,
The spears of winter rain: from every wind
He has made himself secure—from all but one:
In the late wind of death he cannot stand.

                                                          [*antistrophe* 2
O clear intelligence, force beyond all measure!
O fate of man, working both good and evil!
When the laws are kept, how proudly his city stands!
When the laws are broken, what of his city then?
Never may the anárchic man find rest at my hearth,
Never be it said that my thoughts are his thoughts.

Scene II

[*Re-enter* SENTRY *leading* ANTIGONE.]

CHORAGOS. What does this mean? Surely this captive woman
Is the Princess, Antigonê. Why should she be taken?
SENTRY. Here is the one who did it! We caught her
In the very act of burying him.—Where is Creon?
CHORAGOS. Just coming from the house.

[*Enter* CREON, *C.*]

CREON.   What has happened?
Why have you come back so soon?
SENTRY [*expansively*].   O King,
A man should never be too sure of anything:
I would have sworn
That you'd not see me here again: your anger
Frightened me so, and the things you threatened me with;
But how could I tell then
That I'd be able to solve the case so soon?

No dice-throwing this time: I was only too glad to come!

Here is this woman. She is the guilty one:
We found her trying to bury him.

Take her, then; question her; judge her as you will.
I am through with the whole thing now, and glád óf it.
CREON. But this is Antigonê! Why have you brought her here?
SENTRY. She was burying him, I tell you!
CREON [*severely*].   Is this the truth?
SENTRY. I saw her with my own eyes. Can I say more?
CREON. The details: come, tell me quickly!
SENTRY.   It was like this:
After those terrible threats of yours, King,
We went back and brushed the dust away from the body.
The flesh was soft by now, and stinking,
So we sat on a hill to windward and kept guard.
No napping this time! We kept each other awake.
But nothing happened until the white round sun
Whirled in the centre of the round sky over us:
Then, suddenly,
A storm of dust roared up from the earth, and the sky
Went out, the plain vanished with all its trees
In the stinging dark. We closed our eyes and endured it.
The whirlwind lasted a long time, but it passed;
And then we looked, and there was Antigonê!

I have seen
A mother bird come back to a stripped nest, heard
Her crying bitterly a broken note or two
For the young ones stolen. Just so, when this girl
Found the bare corpse, and all her love's work wasted,
She wept, and cried on heaven to damn the hands
That had done this thing.
                              And then she brought more dust
And sprinkled wine three times for her brother's ghost.

We ran and took her at once. She was not afraid,
Not even when we charged her with what she had done.
She denied nothing.
                        And this was a comfort to me,
And some uneasiness: for it is a good thing
To escape from death, but it is no great pleasure
To bring death to a friend.
                              Yet I always say
There is nothing so comfortable as your own safe skin!
CREON [slowly, dangerously]. And you, Antigonê,
    You with your head hanging,—do you confess this thing?
ANTIGONE. I do. I deny nothing.
CREON [to SENTRY].   You may go.

                                            [Exit SENTRY.]

[To ANTIGONE] Tell me, tell me briefly:
Had you heard my proclamation touching this matter?
ANTIGONE. It was public. Could I help hearing it?
CREON. And yet you dared defy the law.
ANTIGONE.   I dared.
    It was not God's proclamation. That final Justice
    That rules the world below makes no such laws.

Your edict, King, was strong,
But all your strength is weakness itself against
The immortal unrecorded laws of God.
They are not merely now: they were, and shall be,
Operative for ever, beyond man utterly.

I knew I must die, even without your decree:
I am only mortal. And if I must die
Now, before it is my time to die,
Surely this is no hardship: can anyone
Living, as I live, with evil all about me,
Think Death less than a friend? This death of mine
Is of no importance; but if I had left my brother
Lying in death unburied, I should have suffered.

Now I do not.
                    You smile at me. Ah Creon,
Think me a fool, if you like; but it may well be
That a fool convicts me of folly.

CHORAGOS. Like father, like daughter: both headstrong, deaf to reason!
She has never learned to yield.

CREON.   She has much to learn.
The inflexible heart breaks first, the toughest iron
Cracks first, and the wildest horses bend their necks
At the pull of the smallest curb.
                                Pride? In a slave?
This girl is guilty of a double insolence,
Breaking the given laws and boasting of it.
Who is the man here,
She or I, if this crime goes unpunished?
Sister's child, or more than sister's child,
Or closer yet in blood—she and her sister
Win bitter death for this!

    [*To servants*]   Go, some of you,
Arrest Ismenê. I accuse her equally.
Bring her: you will find her sniffling in the house there.

Her mind's a traitor: crimes kept in the dark
Cry for light, and the guardian brain shudders;
But how much worse than this
Is brazen boasting of barefaced anarchy!

ANTIGONE. Creon, what more do you want than my death?
CREON.   Nothing.
That gives me everything.
ANTIGONE.   Then I beg you: kill me.
This talking is a great weariness: your words
Are distasteful to me, and I am sure that mine
Seem so to you. And yet they should not seem so:
I should have praise and honour for what I have done.
All these men here would praise me
Were their lips not frozen shut with fear of you.

    [*Bitterly*] Ah the good fortune of kings,
Licensed to say and do whatever they please!
CREON. You are alone here in that opinion.
ANTIGONE. No, they are with me. But they keep their tongues in leash.
CREON. Maybe. But you are guilty, and they are not.
ANTIGONE. There is no guilt in reverence for the dead.
CREON. But Eteoclês—was he not your brother too?
ANTIGONE. My brother too.

CREON.   And you insult his memory?

ANTIGONE [*softly*].   The dead man would not say that I insult it.

CREON.   He would: for you honour a traitor as much as him.

ANTIGONE.   His own brother, traitor or not, and equal in blood.

CREON.   He made war on his country. Eteoclês defended it.

ANTIGONE.   Nevertheless, there are honours due all the dead.

CREON.   But not the same for the wicked as for the just.

ANTIGONE.   Ah Creon, Creon,
    Which of us can say what the gods hold wicked?

CREON.   An enemy is an enemy, even dead.

ANTIGONE.   It is my nature to join in love, not hate.

CREON [*finally losing patience*].
    Go join them, then; if you must have your love,
    Find it in hell!

CHORAGOS.   But see, Ismenê comes:

[*Enter* ISMENE, *guarded*.]

    Those tears are sisterly, the cloud
    That shadows her eyes rains down gentle sorrow.

CREON.   You too, Ismenê,
    Snake in my ordered house, sucking my blood
    Stealthily—and all the time I never knew
    That these two sisters were aiming at my throne!
                                             Ismenê,
    Do you confess your share in this crime, or deny it?
    Answer me.

ISMENE.   Yes, if she will let me say so. I am guilty.

ANTIGONE [*coldly*].   No, Ismenê. You have no right to say so.
    You would not help me, and I will not have you help me.

ISMENE.   But now I know what you meant; and I am here
    To join you, to take my share of punishment.

ANTIGONE.   The dead man and the gods who rule the dead
    Know whose act this was. Words are not friends.

ISMENE.   Do you refuse me, Antigonê? I want to die with you:
    I too have a duty that I must discharge to the dead.

ANTIGONE.   You shall not lessen my death by sharing it.

ISMENE.   What do I care for life when you are dead?

ANTIGONE.   Ask Creon. You're always hanging on his opinions.

ISMENE.   You are laughing at me. Why, Antigonê?

ANTIGONE.   It's a joyless laughter, Ismenê.

ISMENE.   But can I do nothing?

ANTIGONE.   Yes. Save yourself. I shall not envy you.
    There are those who will praise you; I shall have honour, too.

ISMENE.   But we are equally guilty!

ANTIGONE.   No more, Ismenê.

You are alive, but I belong to Death.

CREON [*to the* CHORUS]. Gentlemen, I beg you to observe these girls:
One has just now lost her mind; the other,
It seems, has never had a mind at all.

ISMENE. Grief teaches the steadiest minds to waver, King.

CREON. Yours certainly did, when you assumed guilt with the guilty!

ISMENE. But how could I go on living without her?

CREON.   You are.
  She is already dead.

ISMENE.   But your own son's bride!

CREON. There are places enough for him to push his plow.
  I want no wicked women for my sons!

ANTIGONE. O dearest Haimon, how your father wrongs you!

CREON. I've had enough of your childish talk of marriage!

CHORAGOS. Do you really intend to steal this girl from your son?

CREON. No; Death will do that for me.

CHORAGOS.   Then she must die?

CREON [*ironically*]. You dazzle me.

                    —But enough of this talk!
  [*To* GUARDS] You, there, take them away and guard them well:
For they are but women, and even brave men run
When they see Death coming.

                                    [*Exeunt* ISMENE, ANTIGONE, *and* GUARDS]

Ode II

CHORUS.   [*strophe 1*
  Fortunate is the man who has never tasted God's vengeance!
  Where once the anger of heaven has struck, that house is shaken
  For ever: damnation rises behind each child
  Like a wave cresting out of the black northeast,
  When the long darkness under sea roars up
  And bursts drumming death upon the windwhipped sand.

                                                    [*antistrophe 1*
  I have seen this gathering sorrow from time long past
  Loom upon Œdipus' children: generation from generation
  Takes the compulsive rage of the enemy god.
  So lately this last flower of Œdipus' line
  Drank the sunlight! but now a passionate word
  And a handful of dust have closed up all its beauty.

                                                    [*strophe 2*
    What mortal arrogance
    Transcends the wrath of Zeus?

Sleep cannot lull him, nor the effortless long months
Of the timeless gods: but he is young for ever,
And his house is the shining day of high Olympos.
   All that is and shall be,
   And all the past, is his.
No pride on earth is free of the curse of heaven.

                                                    [*antistrophe* 2

   The straying dreams of men
   May bring them ghosts of joy:
But as they drowse, the waking embers burn them;
Or they walk with fíxed éyes, as blind men walk.
But the ancient wisdom speaks for our own time:
   Fate works most for woe
   With Folly's fairest show.
Man's little pleasure is the spring of sorrow.

Scene III

CHORAGOS.   But here is Haimon, King, the last of all your sons.
Is it grief for Antigonê that brings him here,
And bitterness at being robbed of his bride?

   [*Enter* HAIMON.]

CREON.   We shall soon see, and no need of diviners.

                                                    —Son,

You have heard my final judgment on that girl:
Have you come here hating me, or have you come
With deference and with love, whatever I do?
HAIMON.   I am your son, father. You are my guide.
You make things clear for me, and I obey you.
No marriage means more to me than your continuing wisdom.
CREON.   Good. That is the way to behave: subordinate
Everything else, my son, to your father's will.
This is what a man prays for, that he may get
Sons attentive and dutiful in his house,
Each one hating his father's enemies,
Honouring his father's friends. But if his sons
Fail him, if they turn out unprofitably,
What has he fathered but trouble for himself
And amusement for the malicious?
                                   So you are right
Not to lose your head over this woman.
Your pleasure with her would soon grow cold, Haimon,
And then you'd have a hellcat in bed and elsewhere.

Let her find her husband in Hell!
Of all the people in this city, only she
Has had contempt for my law and broken it.

Do you want me to show myself weak before the people?
Or to break my sworn word? No, and I will not.
The woman dies.

I suppose she'll plead 'family ties.' Well, let her.
If I permit my own family to rebel,
How shall I earn the world's obedience?
Show me the man who keeps his house in hand,
He's fit for public authority.

       I'll have no dealings
With law-breakers, critics of the government:
Whoever is chosen to govern should be obeyed—
Must be obeyed, in all things, great and small,
Just and unjust! O Haimon,
The man who knows how to obey, and that man only,
Knows how to give commands when the time comes.
You can depend on him, no matter how fast
The spears come: he's a good soldier, he'll stick it out.

Anarchy, anarchy! Show me a greater evil!
This is why cities tumble and the great houses rain down,
This is what scatters armies!

No, no: good lives are made so by discipline.
We keep the laws then, and the lawmakers,
And no woman shall seduce us. If we must lose,
Let's lose to a man, at least! Is a woman stronger than we?

CHORAGOS. Unless time has rusted my wits,
 What you say, King, is said with point and dignity.

HAIMON [*boyishly earnest*]. Father:
 Reason is God's crowning gift to man, and you are right
 To warn me against losing mine. I cannot say—
 I hope that I shall never want to say—that you
 Have reasoned badly. Yet there are other men
 Who can reason, too; and their opinions might be helpful.
 You are not in a position to know everything
 That people say or do, or what they feel:
 Your temper terrifies them—everyone
 Will tell you only what you like to hear.
 But I, at any rate, can listen; and I have heard them
 Muttering and whispering in the dark about this girl.
 They say no woman has ever, so unreasonably,

Died so shameful a death for a generous act:
'She covered her brother's body. Is this indecent?
'She kept him from dogs and vultures. Is this a crime?
'Death?—She should have all the honour that we can give her!'

This is the way they talk out there in the city.

You must believe me:
Nothing is closer to me than your happiness.
What could be closer?　Must not any son
Value his father's fortune as his father does his?
I beg you, do not be unchangeable:
Do not believe that you alone can be right.
The man who thinks that,
The man who maintains that only he has the power
To reason correctly, the gift to speak, the soul—
A man like that, when you know him, turns out empty.

It is not reason never to yield to reason!

In flood time you can see how some trees bend,
And because they bend, even their twigs are safe,
While stubborn trees are torn up, roots and all.
And the same thing happens in sailing:
Make your sheet fast, never slacken,—and over you go,
Head over heels and under: and there's your voyage.

Forget you are angry!　Let yourself be moved!
I know I am young; but please let me say this:
The ideal condition
Would be, I admit, that men should be right by instinct;
But since we are all too likely to go astray,
The reasonable thing is to learn from those who can teach.

CHORAGOS.　You will do well to listen to him, King,
　　If what he says is sensible.　And you, Haimon,
　　Must listen to your father.—Both speak well.
CREON.　You consider it right for a man of my years and experience
　　To go to school to a boy?
HAIMON.　　　　　　　　　　　　It is not right
　　If I am wrong.　But if I am young, and right,
　　What does my age matter?
CREON.　You think it right to stand up for an anarchist?
HAIMON.　Not at all.　I pay no respect to criminals.
CREON.　Then she is not a criminal?
HAIMON.　The City would deny it, to a man.
CREON.　And the City proposes to teach me how to rule?
HAIMON.　Ah.　Who is it that's talking like a boy now?

CREON. My voice is the one voice giving orders in this City!

HAIMON. It is no City if it takes orders from one voice.

CREON. The State is the King!

HAIMON. Yes, if the State is a desert.

[*Pause.*]

CREON. This boy, it seems, has sold out to a woman.

HAIMON. If you are a woman: my concern is only for you.

CREON. So? Your 'concern'! In a public brawl with your father!

HAIMON. How about you, in a public brawl with justice?

CREON. With justice, when all that I do is within my rights?

HAIMON. You have no right to trample on God's right.

CREON [*completely out of control*]. Fool, adolescent fool! Taken in by a woman!

HAIMON. You'll never see me taken in by anything vile.

CREON. Every word you say is for her!

HAIMON [*quietly, darkly*]. And for you.
And for me. And for the gods under the earth.

CREON. You'll never marry her while she lives.

HAIMON. Then she must die.—But her death will cause another.

CREON. Another?
Have you lost your senses? Is this an open threat?

HAIMON. There is no threat in speaking to emptiness.

CREON. I swear you'll regret this superior tone of yours!
You are the empty one!

HAIMON. If you were not my father,
I'd say you were perverse.

CREON. You girlstruck fool, don't play at words with me!

HAIMON. I am sorry. You prefer silence.

CREON. Now, by God—!
I swear, by all the gods in heaven above us,
You'll watch it, I swear you shall!

[*To the* SERVANTS] Bring her out!
Bring the woman out! Let her die before his eyes!
Here, this instant, with her bridegroom beside her!

HAIMON. Not here, no; she will not die here, King.
And you will never see my face again.
Go on raving as long as you've a friend to endure you.

[*Exit* HAIMON.]

CHORAGOS. Gone, gone.
Creon, a young man in a rage is dangerous!

CREON. Let him do, or dream to do, more than a man can.
He shall not save these girls from death.

CHORAGOS. These girls?

You have sentenced them both?

CREON. No, you are right.
I will not kill the one whose hands are clean.

CHORAGOS. But Antigonê?

CREON [*somberly*]. I will carry her far away
Out there in the wilderness, and lock her
Living in a vault of stone. She shall have food,
As the custom is, to absolve the State of her death.
And there let her pray to the gods of hell:
They are her only gods:
Perhaps they will show her an escape from death,
Or she may learn,
                                though late,
That piety shown the dead is pity in vain.

[*Exit* CREON.]

Ode III

CHORUS. [*strophe*
Love, unconquerable
Waster of rich men, keeper
Of warm lights and all-night vigil
In the soft face of a girl:
Sea-wanderer, forest-visitor!
Even the pure Immortals cannot escape you,
And mortal man, in his one day's dusk,
Trembles before your glory.

[*antistrophe*
Surely you swerve upon ruin
The just man's consenting heart,
As here you have made bright anger
Strike between father and son—
And none has conquered but Love!
A girl's glánce wórking the will of heaven:
Pleasure to her alone who mocks us,
Merciless Aphroditê.

Scene IV

CHORAGOS [*as* ANTIGONE *enters guarded*].
But I can no longer stand in awe of this,
Nor, seeing what I see, keep back my tears.
Here is Antigonê, passing to that chamber
Where all find sleep at last.

ANTIGONE.   [*strophe* 1

    Look upon me, friends, and pity me
    Turning back at the night's edge to say
    Goodbye to the sun that shines for me no longer;
    Now sleepy Death
    Summons me down to Acheron, that cold shore:
    There is no bridesong there, nor any music.

CHORUS.   Yet not unpraised, not without a kind of honour,
    You walk at last into the underworld;
    Untouched by sickness, broken by no sword.
    What woman has ever found your way to death?

ANTIGONE.   [*antistrophe* 1

    How often I have heard the story of Niobê,
    Tantalos' wretched daughter, how the stone
    Clung fast about her, ivy-close: and they say
    The rain falls endlessly
    And sifting soft snow; her tears are never done.
    I feel the loneliness of her death in mine.

CHORUS.   But she was born of heaven, and you
    Are woman, woman-born. If her death is yours,
    A mortal woman's, is this not for you
    Glory in our world and in the world beyond?

ANTIGONE.   [*strophe* 2

    You laugh at me. Ah, friends, friends,
    Can you not wait until I am dead? O Thebes,
    O men many-charioted, in love with Fortune,
    Dear springs of Dircê, sacred Theban grove,
    Be witnesses for me, denied all pity,
    Unjustly judged! and think a word of love
    For her whose path turns
    Under dark earth, where there are no more tears.

CHORUS.   You have passed beyond human daring and come at last
    Into a place of stone where Justice sits.
    I cannot tell
    What shape of your father's guilt appears in this.

ANTIGONE.   [*antistrophe* 2

    You have touched it at last: that bridal bed
    Unspeakable, horror of son and mother mingling:
    Their crime, infection of all our family!
    O Œdipus, father and brother!
    Your marriage strikes from the grave to murder mine.

I have been a stranger here in my own land:
All my life
The blasphemy of my birth has followed me.

CHORUS. Reverence is a virtue, but strength
Lives in established law: that must prevail.
You have made your choice,
Your death is the doing of your conscious hand.

ANTIGONE.   [*epode*
Then let me go, since all your words are bitter,
And the very light of the sun is cold to me.
Lead me to my vigil, where I must have
Neither love nor lamentation; no song, but silence.

[CREON *interrupts impatiently.*]

CREON. If dirges and planned lamentations could put off death,
Men would be singing for ever.
[*To the* SERVANTS]   Take her, go!
You know your orders: take her to the vault
And leave her alone there. And if she lives or dies,
That's her affair, not ours: our hands are clean.
ANTIGONE. O tomb, vaulted bride-bed in eternal rock,
Soon I shall be with my own again
Where Persephonê welcomes the thin ghosts underground:
And I shall see my father again, and you, mother,
And dearest Polyneicês—
                                        dearest indeed
To me, since it was my hand
That washed him clean and poured the ritual wine:
And my reward is death before my time!

And yet, as men's hearts know, I have done no wrong,
I have not sinned before God. Or if I have,
I shall know the truth in death. But if the guilt
Lies upon Creon who judged me, then, I pray,
May his punishment equal my own.
CHORAGOS.   O passionate heart,
Unyielding, tormented still by the same winds!
CREON. Her guards shall have good cause to regret their delaying.
ANTIGONE. Ah! That voice is like the voice of death!
CREON. I can give you no reason to think you are mistaken.
ANTIGONE. Thebes, and you my fathers' gods,
And rulers of Thebes, you see me now, the last
Unhappy daughter of a line of kings,
Your kings, led away to death. You will remember

What things I suffer, and at what men's hands,
Because I would not transgress the laws of heaven.
[*To the* GUARDS, *simply*]   Come: let us wait no longer.
[*Exit* ANTIGONE, L., *guarded.*]

Ode IV

CHORUS.   [*strophe 1*

All Danaê's beauty was locked away
In a brazen cell where the sunlight could not come:
A small room, still as any grave, enclosed her.
Yet she was a princess too,
And Zeus in a rain of gold poured love upon her.
O child, child,
No power in wealth or war
Or tough sea-blackened ships
Can prevail against untiring Destiny!

[*antistrophe 1*

And Dryas' son also, that furious king,
Bore the god's prisoning anger for his bride:
Sealed up by Dionysos in deaf stone,
His madness died among echoes.
So at the last he learned what dreadful power
His tongue had mocked:
For he had profaned the revels,
And fired the wrath of the nine
Implacable Sisters that love the sound of the flute.

[*strophe 2*

And old men tell a half-remembered tale
Of horror done where a dark ledge splits the sea
And a double surf beats on the gréy shóres:
How a king's new woman, sick
With hatred for the queen he had imprisoned,
Ripped out his two sons' eyes with her bloody hands
While grinning Arês watched the shuttle plunge
Four times: four blind wounds crying for revenge,

[*antistrophe 2*

Crying, tears and blood mingled.—Piteously born,
Those sons whose mother was of heavenly birth!
Her father was the god of the North Wind
And she was cradled by gales,
She raced with young colts on the glittering hills
And walked untrammeled in the open light:

But in her marriage deathless Fate found means
To build a tomb like yours for all her joy.

[*To the chorus, sharply.*] Come: let us wait no longer.

[*Exit* ANTIGONE *L., guarded.*]

Scene V

[*Enter blind* TEIRESIAS, *led by a boy. The opening speeches of* TEIRESIAS *should be in singsong contrast to the realistic lines of* CREON.]

TEIRESIAS. This is the way the blind man comes, Princes, Princes,
Lock-step, two heads lit by the eyes of one.

CREON. What new thing have you to tell us, old Teiresias?

TEIRESIAS. I have much to tell you: listen to the prophet, Creon.

CREON. I am not aware that I have ever failed to listen.

TEIRESIAS. Then you have done wisely, King, and ruled well.

CREON. I admit my debt to you. But what have you to say?

TEIRESIAS. This, Creon: you stand once more on the edge of fate.

CREON. What do you mean? Your words are a kind of dread.

TEIRESIAS. Listen, Creon:
I was sitting in my chair of augury, at the place
Where the birds gather about me. They were all a-chatter,
As is their habit, when suddenly I heard
A strange note in their jangling, a scream, a
Whirring fury; I knew that they were fighting,
Tearing each other, dying
In a whirlwind of wings clashing. And I was afraid.
I began the rites of burnt-offering at the altar,
But Hephaistos failed me: instead of bright flame,
There was only the sputtering slime of the fat thigh-flesh
Melting: the entrails dissolved in grey smoke,
The bare bone burst from the welter. And no blaze!

This was a sign from heaven. My boy described it,
Seeing for me as I see for others.

I tell you, Creon, you yourself have brought
This new calamity upon us. Our hearths and altars
Are stained with the corruption of dogs and carrion birds
That glut themselves on the corpse of Œdipus' son.
The gods are deaf when we pray to them, their fire
Recoils from our offering, their birds of omen
Have no cry of comfort, for they are gorged
With the thick blood of the dead.

O my son,
These are no trifles! Think: all men make mistakes,
But a good man yields when he knows his course is wrong,
And repairs the evil. The only crime is pride.

Give in to the dead man, then: do not fight with a corpse—
What glory is it to kill a man who is dead?
Think, I beg you:
It is for your own good that I speak as I do.
You should be able to yield for your own good.

CREON.   It seems that prophets have made me their especial province.
All my life long
I have been a kind of butt for the dull arrows
Of doddering fortune-tellers!
                          No, Teiresias:
If your birds—if the great eagles of God himself
Should carry him stinking bit by bit to heaven,
I would not yield. I am not afraid of pollution:
No man can defile the gods.
                          Do what you will,
Go into business, make money, speculate
In India gold or that synthetic gold from Sardis,
Get rich otherwise than by my consent to bury him.
Teiresias, it is a sorry thing when a wise man
Sells his wisdom, lets out his words for hire!

TEIRESIAS.   Ah Creon! Is there no man left in the world—

CREON.   To do what—Come, let's have the aphorism!

TEIRESIAS.   No man who knows that wisdom outweighs any wealth?

CREON.   As surely as bribes are baser than any baseness.

TEIRESIAS.   You are sick, Creon! You are deathly sick!

CREON.   As you say: it is not my place to challenge a prophet.

TEIRESIAS.   Yet you have said my prophecy is for sale.

CREON.   The generation of prophets has always loved gold.

TEIRESIAS.   The generation of kings has always loved brass.

CREON.   You forget yourself! You are speaking to your King.

TEIRESIAS.   I know it. You are a king because of me.

CREON.   You have a certain skill; but you have sold out.

TEIRESIAS.   King, you will drive me to words that—

CREON.   Say them, say them!
Only remember: I will not pay you for them.

TEIRESIAS.   No, you will find them too costly.

CREON.   No doubt. Speak:
Whatever you say, you will not change my will.

TEIRESIAS.   Then take this, and take it to heart!
The time is not far off when you shall pay back
Corpse for corpse, flesh of your own flesh.
You have thrust the child of this world into living night,
You have kept from the gods below the child that is theirs:
The one in a grave before her death, the other,
Dead, denied the grave. This is your crime:

And the Furies and the dark gods of Hell
Are swift with terrible punishment for you.

Do you want to buy me now, Creon?
                                              Not many days,
And your house will be full of men and women weeping,
And curses will be hurled at you from far
Cities grieving for sons unburied, left to rot
Before the walls of Thebes.

These are my arrows, Creon: they are all for you.

   [*To* BOY]   But come, child: lead me home
Let him waste his fine anger upon younger men.
Maybe he will learn at last
To control a wiser tongue in a better head.

                                         [*Exit* TEIRESIAS.]

CHORAGOS.   The old man has gone, King, but his words
   Remain to plague us. I am old, too,
   But I cannot remember that he was ever false.
CREON.   That is true. . . . It troubles me.
   Oh it is hard to give in! but it is worse
   To risk everything for stubborn pride.
CHORAGOS.   Creon: take my advice.
CREON.   What shall I do?
CHORAGOS.   Go quickly: free Antigonê from her vault
   And build a tomb for the body of Polyneicês.
CREON.   You would have me do this?
CHORAGOS.   Creon, yes!
   And it must be done at once: God moves
   Swiftly to cancel the folly of stubborn men.
CREON.   It is hard to deny the heart! But I
   Will do it: I will not fight with destiny.
CHORAGOS.   You must go yourself, you cannot leave it to others.
CREON.   I will go.
                     —Bring axes, servants:
   Come with me to the tomb. I buried her, I
   Will set her free.
                        Oh quickly!
   My mind misgives—
   The laws of the gods are mighty, and a man must serve them
   To the last day of his life!

                                              [*Exit* CREON.]

Pæan

[*strophe 1*

CHORAGOS.   God of many names

CHORUS.   O Iacchos
                                          son
of Cadmeian Sémelê
                      O born of the Thunder!
Guardian of the West
                              Regent
of Eleusis' plain
                      O Prince of mænad Thebes
and the Dragon Field by rippling Ismenos:

[*antistrophe 1*

CHORAGOS.   God of many names

CHORUS.   the flame of torches
flares on our hills
                          the nymphs of Iacchos
dance at the spring of Castalia:

from the vine-close mountain
                                  come ah come in ivy:
Evohé evohé! sings through the streets of Thebes

[*strophe 2*

CHORAGOS.   God of many names

CHORUS.   Iacchos of Thebes
heavenly Child
                  of Sémelê bride of the Thunderer!
The shadow of plague is upon us:
                                          come
with clement feet
                      oh come from Parnasos
down the long slopes
                          across the lamenting water

[*antistrophe 2*

CHORAGOS.   Iô Fire! Chorister of the throbbing stars!
O purest among the voices of the night!
Thou son of God, blaze for us!

CHORUS.   Come with choric rapture of circling Mænads
Who cry *Iô Iacche!*
              God of many names!

ÉXODOS

[*Enter* MESSENGER, *L.*]

MESSENGER.   Men of the line of Cadmos, you who live
  Near Amphion's citadel:
                              I cannot say
  Of any condition of human life 'This is fixed,
  This is clearly good, or bad'. Fate raises up,
  And Fate casts down the happy and unhappy alike:
  No man can foretell his Fate.
                              Take the case of Creon:
  Creon was happy once, as I count happiness:
  Victorious in battle, sole governor of the land,
  Fortunate father of children nobly born.
  And now it has all gone from him! Who can say
  That a man is still alive when his life's joy fails?
  He is a walking dead man. Grant him rich,
  Let him live like a king in his great house:
  If his pleasure is gone, I would not give
  So much as the shadow of smoke for all he owns.
CHORAGOS.   Your words hint at sorrow: what is your news for us?
MESSENGER.   They are dead. The living are guilty of their death.
CHORAGOS.   Who is guilty? Who is dead? Speak!
MESSENGER.   Haimon.
  Haimon is dead; and the hand that killed him
  Is his own hand.
CHORAGOS.   His father's? or his own?
MESSENGER.   His own, driven mad by the murder his father had done.
CHORAGOS.   Teiresias, how clearly you saw it all!
MESSENGER.   This is my news: you must draw what conclusions you
  can from it.
CHORAGOS.   But look: Eurydicê, our Queen:
  Has she overheard us?

[*Enter* EURYDICE *from the Palace, C.*]

EURYDICE.   I have heard something, friends:
  As I was unlocking the gate of Pallas' shrine,
  For I needed her help today, I heard a voice
  Telling of some new sorrow. And I fainted
  There at the temple with all my maidens about me.
  But speak again: whatever it is, I can bear it:
  Grief and I are no strangers.
MESSENGER.   Dearest Lady,
  I will tell you plainly all that I have seen.

I shall not try to comfort you: what is the use,
Since comfort could lie only in what is not true?
The truth is always best.
                              I went with Creon
To the outer plain where Polyneicês was lying,
No friend to pity him, his body shredded by dogs.
We made our prayers in that place to Hecatê
And Pluto, that they would be merciful. And we bathed
The corpse with holy water, and we brought
Fresh-broken branches to burn what was left of it,
And upon the urn we heaped up a towering barrow
Of the earth of his own land.
                              When we were done, we ran
To the vault where Antigonê lay on her couch of stone.
One of the servants had gone ahead,
And while he was yet far off he heard a voice
Grieving within the chamber, and he came back
And told Creon. And as the King went closer,
The air was full of wailing, the words lost,
And he begged us to make all haste. 'Am I a prophet?'
He said, weeping, 'And must I walk this road,
'The saddest of all that I have gone before?
'My son's voice calls me on. Oh quickly, quickly!
'Look through the crevice there, and tell me
'If it is Haimon, or some deception of the gods!'

We obeyed; and in the cavern's farthest corner
We saw her lying:
She had made a noose of her fine linen veil
And hanged herself. Haimon lay beside her,
His arms about her waist, lamenting her,
His love lost under ground, crying out
That his father had stolen her away from him.
When Creon saw him the tears rushed to his eyes
And he called to him: 'What have you done, child? Speak to me.
'What are you thinking that makes your eyes so strange?
'O my son, my son, I come to you on my knees!'
But Haimon spat in his face. He said not a word,
Staring—
            And suddenly drew his sword
And lunged. Creon shrank back, the blade missed; and the boy,
Desperate against himself, drove it half its length
Into his own side, and fell. And as he died
He gathered Antigonê close in his arms again,
Choking, his blood bright red on her white cheek.

And now he lies dead with the dead, and she is his
At last, his bride in the houses of the dead.

> [*Exit* EURYDICE *into the Palace.*]

CHORAGOS.   She has left us without a word. What can this mean?
MESSENGER.   It troubles me, too; yet she knows what is best,
Her grief is too great for public lamentation,
And doubtless she has gone to her chamber to weep
For her dead son, leading her maidens in his dirge.
CHORAGOS.   It may be so: but I fear this deep silence.

> [*Pause.*]

MESSENGER.   I will see what she is doing. I will go in.

> [*Exit* MESSENGER *into the Palace.*]

> [*Enter* CREON *with attendants, bearing* HAIMON's *body.*]

CHORAGOS.   But here is the King himself: oh look at him,
Bearing his own damnation in his arms.
CREON.   Nothing you say can touch me any more.
My own blind heart has brought me
From darkness to final darkness. Here you see
The father murdering, the murdered son—
And all my civic wisdom!

Haimon my son, so young, so young to die,
I was the fool, not you; and you died for me.
CHORAGOS.   That is the truth; but you were late in learning it.
CREON.   This truth is hard to bear. Surely a god
Has crushed me beneath the hugest weight of heaven,
And driven me headlong a barbaric way
To trample out the thing I held most dear.

The pains that men will take to come to pain!

> [*Enter* MESSENGER *from the Palace.*]

MESSENGER.   The burden you carry in your hands is heavy,
But it is not all: you will find more in your house.
CREON.   What burden worse than this shall I find there?
MESSENGER.   The Queen is dead.
CREON.   O port of death, deaf world,
Is there no pity for me? And you, Angel of evil,
I was dead, and your words are death again.
Is it true, boy? Can it be true?
Is my life dead? Has death bred death?

MESSENGER.   You can see for yourself.

[*The doors are opened, and the body of* EURYDICE *is disclosed within.*]

CREON.   Oh pity!
All true, all true, and more than I can bear!
O my wife, my son!
MESSENGER.   She stood before the altar, and her heart
Welcomed the knife her own hand guided,
And a great cry burst from her lips for Megareus dead,
And for Haimon dead, her sons; and her last breath
Was a curse for their father, the murderer of her sons.
And she fell, and the dark flowed in through her closing eyes.
CREON.   O God, I am sick with fear.
Are there no swords here? Has no one a blow for me?
MESSENGER.   Her curse is upon you for the deaths of both.
CREON.   It is right that it should be. I alone am guilty.
I know it, and I say it. Lead me in,
Quickly, friends.
I have neither life nor substance. Lead me in.
CHORAGOS.   You are right, if there can be right in so much wrong.
The briefest way is best in a world of sorrow.
CREON.   Let it come,
Let death come quickly, and be kind to me.
I would not ever see the sun again.
CHORAGOS.   All that will come when it will; but we, meanwhile,
Have much to do. Leave the future to itself.
CREON.   All my heart was in that prayer!
CHORAGOS.   Then do not pray any more: the sky is deaf.
CREON.   Lead me away. I have been rash and foolish.
I have killed my son and my wife.
I look for comfort; my comfort lies here dead.
Whatever my hands have touched has come to nothing.
Fate has brought all my pride to a thought of dust.

[*As* CREON *is being led into the house, the* CHORAGOS *advances and speaks directly to the audience.*]

CHORAGOS.   There is no happiness where there is no wisdom;
No wisdom but in submission to the gods.
Big words are always punished,
And proud men in old age learn to be wise.

———

Two Critical Commentaries on Sophocles' *Antigone*

Commentary by Whitney J. Oates, from his Introduction to *Antigone* in *The Complete Greek Drama,* edited by Whitney J. Oates and Eugene O'Neill, Jr. (New York, Random House, 1938).*

The central conflict of the play between Antigone and Creon is presented in simple terms, and derives, on the surface, from the conventional Greek attitude towards burial ritual. Creon has inflicted upon the dead Polyneices a punishment which the Greeks looked upon with peculiar terror, namely that his body should not receive the requisite funeral rites. In fact, the problem is precisely that which preoccupied Sophocles in the closing scenes of his *Ajax.* However, in the *Antigone,* the poet has universalized the conflict which arises from this particular situation, until it becomes basically a question whether man-made and tyrannically enforced law should take precedence over what any individual conceives in his heart to be divine law. Creon endeavours to impose his human law on Antigone, who disobeys out of respect for a higher law.

Creon is distinctly a tragic figure, who holds firmly to what he believes to be right and who has no doubts as to the absolute validity of his beliefs. Nothing shakes him, not even the criticism and open opposition of his son, Haemon, with whom Creon is sharply contrasted, until it is too late and the catastrophe has already occurred. Creon gains in stature at the conclusion because he realizes his guilt and assumes responsibility for it. In many respects he is not unlike Pentheus, in Euripides' *Bacchae.* As for Antigone, critics are divided in their interpretations. Some hold that she is guilty of pride, *hybris,* and that she is suffering from an absurd and stubborn desire to become a martyr. Others insist that she is unswervingly and magnificently devoted to her ideals for which she is willing to sacrifice her life, that she does not possess any 'tragic flaw' in any sense of the word, and that her fate is completely undeserved. Whatever may be a satisfactory interpretation of her character, at least it is certain that Sophocles has created a living and a vital figure in Antigone. Her devotion to her ideals may perhaps lead her to a somewhat uncompromising harshness towards her sister, but Sophocles makes it clear that she has within her a warmth and gentleness of spirit which she has suppressed but which are revealed, now in her love for Haemon, and now when she asks pathetically, as she is led away to death, why it is that she suffers.

One is tempted to formulate clearly the major issues of the play and forget that they are fused with other varied elements in such a way that the resultant work of art possesses great richness. To cite examples of this richness, one need only mention the brilliant choral ode on the wonders of man, the realistic and somewhat comic treatment of the Guard, or the scene between Haemon and Creon which contains political implications of great significance. As a result, though the *Antigone* may not be the equal of *Oedipus the King,* either in point of technique or of universal meaning, yet it remains one of the most satisfying of all the Greek tragedies. (Vol. I, pp. 421-22)

* Reprinted by permission of Random House, Inc., copyright 1938.

Commentary by Cedric H. Whitman, from *Sophocles, a Study of Heroic Humanism* (Cambridge, Harvard University Press, 1951).*

It was precisely this doubt about the moral trustworthiness of their gods, together with the peculiar willingness of the Athenians to face and argue that doubt, which stimulated a hundred years of tragic poetry. . . . Emphasis has been laid on the relation between the cult of Dionysus and the nature of tragedy itself; tragedy seeks the inner springs of life, whatever they be, and Dionysus well symbolizes them, in their evil as well as in their good. But be it observed that Dionysus was never a god bound by moral responsibility, as Apollo was; and the question of moral responsibility was as fundamental to tragedy as was the cult of Dionysus. . . .

With the world developing around him, and new religious ideas constantly springing to life, Sophocles could not help meeting the challenge of the times and raising the old tragic questions anew, to answer them as he could in his own terms: what justice is there for man? where is the moral balance of life to be found? to whom is man responsible? We have been too prone to think that Sophocles resisted all the novel forces of his day, and to put him in the conservative camp, as if he foresaw in the Sophists the breakdown of Athenian morale, or in the growing power of Athens the as yet untraceable seeds of decay. . . .

The gods of Olympus were slowly becoming mere public figureheads, and so we may assume they were for Sophocles as well. Divinity was elsewhere— a conclusion which logically followed from the realization of man's moral responsibility. The more we look closely for a satisfying justice in the world, the more inevitably we are driven to disillusion and to the admission that justice is with man, not the gods; that man is more responsible than he dreamed, though in a different way; and that perhaps this very quality in man is a kind of divinity. Some such change seems to have taken place in the fifth century. . . .   (pp. 19-21)

If any conceptual contrast fits the *Antigone,* it is the contrast between true and false authority, between the ideal citizen and the lawless ruler.

Antigone's nature has done much damage to her, even as Creon's specious talk has done much to give him dignity, in the eyes of readers. Given a situation in which a high-minded young girl buries her brother in defiance of a royal decree, it would have been easy for Sophocles to make her pathetic. But Antigone is not pathetic. Sharp-tongued, contemptuous, almost ferocious in her declarations of her right, she fights fire with fire. She is at war from the minute the play opens until her death. Such a challenging piece of ungentle womanhood may have been more immediately intelligible to antiquity in the context of an heroic past; to modern minds it has presented a puzzle. Antigone is a woman in serious danger, and yet she talks like an empress. She must be wrong, or at least improper. She ought to have realized her place and urged the tender weakness of her sex; instead, she calls King Creon a fool to his face. Her very harshness has tended to throw

* Reprinted by permission of the publishers from Cedric H. Whitman, *Sophocles, a Study of Heroic Humanism,* Cambridge, Mass.: Harvard University Press, Copyright, 1951, by the President and Fellows of Harvard College.

some sympathy on Creon's side and raise the presumption that the king had a right to decree what he would regarding the burial of traitors. If Antigone denied that right, Creon at least was the king, not she, and he must enforce obedience. But at once we are plunged into the question of the justice of the law, the legality of authority. It is Antigone's claim that a higher law delimits the temporal authority of a king, and that if there is conflict, the king's law must yield. . . . (p. 85)

The character of Creon has been admirably summed up as that of the typical tyrant. His quickness to wrath, his rejection of criticism, his suspicion of corruption among the people, his resentment of women, and his demand for utter servitude all find their parallels in the familiar habits of the great Greek tyrants. But it should be added that he is a tyrant who cloaks himself in the oligarchic watchwords of 'good order' and 'obedience to law.' There can be no talk of a conflict of two rights. No Athenian, in the zenith of the Periclean Age, could grant a point to a man who behaved like a tyrant, and talked like an oligarch, however he sometimes prefaced his real sentiments with fine-sounding doctrines about the stability of the state. The famous stability of the Spartan government meant repression, control from above, and suspicion; and in this kind of stability Creon is fully versed. No wonder that he and Antigone speak constantly at cross purposes and mean different things by 'love' and 'hate.'

It is therefore clear that Antigone's famous stubbornness, the fault for which she has been so roundly reproved, is really moral fortitude. She does not go 'too far.' How far should one go in resisting the tyranny of evil? . . . (p. 90)

As to the little pietism at the end [of the choral ode on Man], it refers neither to Antigone nor Creon, but is typical of the chorus itself. The chorus, in contrast to the heroic individual, ordinarily chooses safety. Its members have no moral position. They may sympathize with Antigone, but they blame her as Creon does. They bow to Creon's will, albeit coolly. Theirs is a detachment without judgment, a moral receptivity without moral will. True, when Creon consults them, they advise him to yield to Teiresias, as the safer course. But not until Creon is crushed do they decide that he was morally wrong. One suspects the chorus in Sophocles of being an intentional symbol of the inadequacy of everyday morality to judge the ultimate questions. (pp. 91-92)

The *Antigone* unquestionably reflects one of the earliest phases of the rift between city and citizen; Creon, drawn in tyrannical or oligarchic colors, embodies the moral atrophy of civic institutions, while the heroine herself presents the ideal of individual moral perception. Her tragedy is a tragedy which Sophocles, writing at the peak of Athenian greatness, could envision as a possibility. Yet, though he may foreshadow the problems, he does not reject the assumption of the city-state; the whole drama is cast in terms of it. The *Antigone* is 'political' through and through, in the broad Greek sense of 'pertaining to the polis.' For the religious adherences of Sophocles are profoundly interwoven with the whole concept of the city-state, and neither could exist without the other. (p. 233)

II. OTHELLO

A Romantic Tragedy by William Shakespeare

Introductory Note to William Shakespeare and *Othello*

ONSIDERING THE 2050 YEARS that separated Greek drama from Elizabethan, the 350 since Shakespeare wrote *Othello* pale to insignificance—a mere dozen to fifteen generations! But the Renaissance in England is close to us in many ways: Drake and Raleigh, the King James Bible and Puritanism, Virginia and Jamestown. With our contemporary interests in psychology, in questions of race, in the resurgence of Machiavellian cunning and Inquisitional cruelty, *Othello* may seem especially close to our own times.

Of William Shakespeare the man we know much less than we might wish. Yet a hard core of relevant facts about him has been determined by patient scholarship. He was born in 1564 in Stratford-on-Avon, a town of two thousand, less than a hundred miles from London. His father was a prominent villager, his mother of the landed gentry. William Shakespeare married at the age of eighteen a woman, Anne Hathaway, perhaps eight years his senior. Six months thereafter a daughter was baptized; and twenty months later a twin son and daughter. Shakespeare, about whose education and early vocation we can do no more than make intelligent guesses, went up to London in his middle twenties. Before he turned thirty he had become an acceptable actor, an established playwright, and a recognized poet. He became a shareholder in the Lord Chamberlain's Company (later renamed the King's Company) of players, and part owner of first one and then another theater. During the twenty years of his principal activities in London (1590-1610) he wrote some thirty-eight playscripts to be produced by his fellow actors. Many of these were published by enterprising booksellers, some of them in a number of editions. His various undertakings made him well-to-do. He secured for his father (and therefore himself) a coat-of-arms. He bought the second-largest house in his home town. He was able to provide well for his daughters. He retired at about forty-six years of age to live in Stratford, and died there on April 23, 1616, on or about his fifty-second birthday.

It is through his works, rather than through the scattered facts about him, that Shakespeare the man may be glimpsed. Thirty-six of his dramas were collected and published in an expensive volume as a memorial to him by two of his fellow actors in 1623, seven years after his death. This is the famous First Folio, of which a good many copies still exist. These plays—plus two long poems, a sonnet sequence, and some miscellaneous verse—provide the evidence of Shakespeare's undoubted genius. The dramas themselves are of great variety: His comedies range from farce and fantasy (*The Comedy of Errors* and *A Midsummer-Night's Dream*), through romantic comedies of character (*The Merchant of Venice* and *As You Like It*) and so-called "dark" comedies (*All's Well That Ends Well* and *Measure for Measure*), to the final dramatic romances (*A Winter's Tale* and *The Tempest*). The histories that he wrote include drum-and-trumpet chronicle plays (three parts of *Henry VI*), bloody melodrama (*Richard III*), poetic tragedy (*Richard II*), character drama (the two parts of *Henry IV*), and heroic drama (*Henry V*). The tragedies of Shakespeare are a rich assortment: those based upon classical history (*Julius Caesar, Antony and Cleopatra, Coriolanus*) and upon classical legend (the bloody *Titus Andronicus* and the enigmatic *Troilus and Cressida*), those based upon Danish and British chronicles (*Hamlet, King Lear, Macbeth*), those based upon romantic tales (*Romeo and Juliet* and *Othello*).

The Tragedy of Othello, the Moor of Venice, was written by Shakespeare some time before November 1, 1604, when it was performed at Court, presumably after successful production at the Globe Theater. We do not know through what channel Shakespeare came by Cinthio's short story that is certainly his source for *Othello*. All of Shakespeare's chief characters are to be found in the Italian novella, though only Desdemona has a name in the original. Most of the situations and incidents are similar in the two. It is interesting to note what Shakespeare did with the virtuous Venetian lady who married the valiant Moor, with the captain (Cassio) belied by the wicked ensign (Iago), with the planting of seeds of suspicion and jealousy, with the false confirmation by mistaken overhearing and the handkerchief, and so on. From many details scattered throughout the story Shakespeare took hints and suggestions that he made his own and worked into the tragedy. But the dramatist's invention supplied the events of the first act and the compression of the tragic finale.

Shakespeare's *Othello* remained unpublished until after his death. In 1622 one version of his manuscript was printed as a quarto booklet. A somewhat longer and revised version was included the next year in the First Folio. The text here presented makes use of various readings from both the Folio and the Quarto, as is usual today.

Generally considered one of Shakespeare's four greatest dramas, *Othello* has been the subject of a vast body of dramatic criticism, from Thomas Rymer's animadversions in his *Short View of Tragedy* (1692), through the eighteenth and nineteenth century British and continental critics (Johnson and Malone, Coleridge and Hazlitt, Maginn and Dowden, Schlegel and Victor Hugo) to the critics and scholars of the twentieth century (A. C. Bradley, Lily B. Campbell, G. Wilson Knight, and others too numerous to mention).

In the theater, *Othello* was revived when the English theaters were reopened after the Restoration. Pepys saw Shakespeare's grand-nephew, Charles Hart, play Othello, with Mrs. Hughes as Desdemona, the first role ever played by a woman on the English public stage. Later in that century Betterton and Mrs. Bracegirdle played the parts. Most of the famous actors and actresses of the eighteenth and nineteenth centuries appeared in *Othello*. The first Negro to portray the Moor of Venice was an American, Ira Aldridge, who, as valet to Edmund Kean, learned the part and then starred in performances both in the United States and abroad. Edwin Booth alternated with Henry Irving in the roles of Othello and Iago in England and with Lawrence Barrett in this country, and he played Iago to the passionate Othello of the great Italian tragedian, Tomaso Salvini, whose son played Cassio in the company, both speaking their parts in Italian! In 1943 Margaret Webster directed a production of *Othello* for the Theatre Guild, with Paul Robeson as the Moor, José Ferrer as Iago, Uta Hagen as Desdemona. After a year in New York (296 performances), this outstanding production—a recording of which is available—played most successfully in Chicago, San Francisco, Los Angeles, and elsewhere to large audiences. The opera *Otello* by Verdi (1887) is frequently performed. The most recent film version is that made by Orson Welles (1954).

OTHELLO

by William Shakespeare

THE CHARACTERS

OTHELLO—*the Moor of Venice, captain (general) of the Venetian army.*

DESDEMONA—*the well-born Venetian lady just married to Othello.*
BRABANTIO—*her father, as yet unaware of the match.*
GRATIANO and LODOVICO—*uncle and kinsman to Desdemona.*

IAGO—*a professional soldier, Othello's ensign, third in command.*
RODERIGO—*a Venetian gentleman, in love with Desdemona.*
EMILIA—*Iago's wife, who serves as Desdemona's maid.*

CASSIO—*a trained officer, chosen to be Othello's lieutenant.*
BIANCA—*a courtesan, Cassio's mistress.*

The DUKE OF VENICE, *and* SENATORS.

MONTANO—*Othello's predecessor as governor of Cyprus.*

SERVANTS, ATTENDANTS, MESSENGERS, SAILORS, GENTLEMEN, *a* HERALD, *a* CLOWN, MUSICIANS, *etc.*

Time: *in the Renaissance period of Venetian power.*

Place: *Various scenes in Venice and then in Cyprus.*

ACT ONE

SCENE I. *Venice. A Street.*

[*Enter* RODERIGO *and* IAGO.]

RODERIGO. Tush! Never tell me! I take it much un-
    kindly
That thou, Iago, who hast had my purse
As if the strings were thine, shouldst know of this.   *the elopement*
  IAGO. 'Sblood, but you will not hear me!   *an oath: by*
If ever I did dream of such a matter,   *God's blood*
Ahbor me.
  RODERIGO. Thou told'st me thou didst hold him in thy   *Othello*
    hate.
  IAGO. Despise me if I do not. Three great ones of
    the city,
In personal suit to make me his lieutenant,   *request*

Off-capped to him; and, by the faith of man— *bowed caps off*
I know my price—I am worth no worse a place.
But he, as loving his own pride and purposes,
Evades them with a bombast circumstance *cottony excuses*
Horribly stuffed with epithets of war,
And, in conclusion,
Nonsuits my mediators, for, 'Certes,' says he, *rejects*
'I have already chosen my officer.' *In truth*
And what was he?
Forsooth, a great arithmetician,
One Michael Cassio, a Florentine
(A fellow almost damned in a fair wife), *his mistress*
That never set a squadron in the field,
Nor the division of a battle knows *except . . .*
More than a spinster—unless the bookish theoric, *theory*
Wherein the togèd consuls can propose *councilors . . .*
As masterly as he. Mere prattle, without practice, *discuss*
Is all his soldiership. But he, sir, had the election,
And I (of whom his eyes had seen the proof *Othello's*
At Rhodes, at Cyprus, and on other grounds
Christian and heathen) must be be-leed and calmed *overcome*
By debitor-and-creditor. This counter-caster, *a bookkeeper*
He, in good time, must his lieutenant be,
And I—God bless the mark!—his Moorship's ancient. *ensign*
    RODERIGO. By heaven, I rather would have been his
        hangman.
    IAGO. But there's no remedy. 'Tis the curse of service.
Preferment goes by letter and affection, *recommenda-*
And not by old gradation, where each second *tions*
Stood heir to the first. Now, sir, be judge yourself, *seniority*
Whether I in any just term am affined *bound*
To love the Moor.
    RODERIGO.   I would not follow him then.
    IAGO. O sir, content you.
I follow him to serve my turn upon him;
We cannot be all masters, nor all masters
Cannot be truly followed. You shall mark
Many a duteous and knee-crooking knave,
That doting on his own obsequious bondage
Wears out his time, much like his master's ass,
For nought but provender, and when he's old,—cashiered! *dismissed*
Whip me such honest knaves. Others there are
Who, trimmed in forms and visages of duty, *appearances*
Keep yet their hearts attending on themselves,
And throwing but shows of service on their lords, *externals*

Do well thrive by 'em, and when they have lined their
    coats
Do themselves homage. Those fellows have some soul,   *service*
And such a one do I profess myself. For, sir,
It is as sure as you are Roderigo,
Were I the Moor, I would not be Iago.
In following him, I follow but myself.
Heaven is my judge, not I for love and duty,
But seeming so for my peculiar end.   *personal*
For when my outward action does demonstrate
The native act and figure of my heart   *true feelings*
In complement extern, 'tis not long after   *outward acts*
But I will wear my heart upon my sleeve
For daws to peck at. I am not what I am.   *birds, fools*

    RODERIGO. What a full fortune does the thick-lips owe,   *Othello . . .*
If he can carry 't thus?   *own*

    IAGO.   Call up her father.
Rouse him, make after him, poison his delight,   *Othello*
Proclaim him in the street, incense her kinsmen,
And though he in a fertile climate dwell,
Plague him with flies. Though that his joy be joy,
Yet throw such changes of vexation on 't
As it may lose some color.   *tarnish*

    RODERIGO. Here is her father's house. I'll call aloud.

    IAGO. Do, with like timorous accent and dire yell   *terrifying*
As when, by night and negligence, the fire
Is spied in populous cities.

    RODERIGO. What, ho, Brabantio! Signior Brabantio,
    ho!

    IAGO. Awake! what, ho, Brabantio! thieves! thieves!
    thieves!
Look to your house, your daughter, and your bags!
Thieves! thieves!

    [BRABANTIO *appears at a window, above.*]

    BRABANTIO. What is the reason of this terrible sum-
    mons?
What is the matter there?

    RODERIGO. Signior, is all your family within?

    IAGO. Are all doors locked?

    BRABANTIO.   Why, wherefore ask you this?

    IAGO. 'Zounds, sir, you're robbed!—for shame, put on   *an oath; by*
      your gown!—   *God's wounds*
                                                   robe
Your heart is burst, you have lost half your soul.
Even now, now, very now, an old black ram

Is tupping your white ewe. Arise, arise! *covering*
Awake the snorting citizens with the bell, *snoring*
Or else the Devil will make a grandsire of you. *considered black*
Arise, I say.

BRABANTIO. What! have you lost your wits?

RODERIGO. Most reverend signior, do you know my
    voice?

BRABANTIO. Not I. What are you?

RODERIGO. My name is Roderigo.

BRABANTIO.   The worser welcome!
I have charged thee not to haunt about my doors.
In honest plainness thou hast heard me say
My daughter is not for thee. And now, in madness,
Being full of supper and distempering draughts, *intoxicating*
Upon malicious bravery dost thou come *bravado*
To start my quiet. *startle*

RODERIGO.   Sir, sir, sir!

BRABANTIO.   But thou must needs be sure,
My spirit and my place have in them power
To make this bitter to thee.

RODERIGO.   Patience, good sir.

BRABANTIO. What tell'st thou me of robbing? This is
    Venice.
My house is not a grange. *farmhouse*

RODERIGO.   Most grave Brabantio,
In simple and pure soul I come to you.

IAGO. 'Zounds, sir, you are one of those that will not
serve God if the Devil bid you. Because we come to do
you service and you think we are ruffians, you'll have your
daughter covered with a Barbary horse, you'll have your *Moorish*
nephews neigh to you, you'll have coursers for cousins *grandsons*
and jennets for germans. *small horse . . .*
    kinsmen

BRABANTIO. What profane wretch art thou?

IAGO. I am one, sir, that come to tell you, your daughter and the Moor are now making the beast with two
backs. *copulating*

BRABANTIO. Thou art a villain.

IAGO.   You are—a senator.

BRABANTIO. This thou shalt answer. I know thee,
    Roderigo.

RODERIGO. Sir, I will answer anything. But, I beseech
    you,
If 't be your pleasure and most wise consent,
As partly I find it is, that your fair daughter
At this odd-even and dull watch o' th' night, *midnight*

Transported with no worse nor better guard
But with a knave of common hire, a gondolier,
To the gross clasps of a lascivious Moor—
If this be known to you, and your allowanc*e*,   *with permission*
We then have done you bold and saucy wrongs.
But if you know not this, my manners tell me
We have your wrong rebuke. Do not believe
That, fro*m* the sense of all civility,   *contrary to*
I thus would play and trifle with your reverence.
Your daughter—if you have not given her leave,
I say again—hath made a gross revolt,
Tying her duty, beauty, wit and fortunes
I*n* an extravagan*t* and wheelin*g* stranger   *To a vagabond*
Of here and everywhere. Straight satisfy yourself.   *. . . roving*
If she be in her chamber or your house,
Let loose on me the justice of the state
For thus deluding you.
    BRABANTIO.   Strike on the tinder, ho!
Give me a taper! Call up all my people!
This accident is not unlike my dream.
Belief of it oppresses me already.
Light, I say! Light!
                                          [Exit.]

    IAGO.   Farewell, for I must leave you.
It seems not meet nor wholesome to my plac*e*   *in my position*
To be produce*d*—as, if I stay, I shall—   *as a witness*
Against the Moor. For I do know the state,
However this may gall him with some chec*k*,   *rebuke*
Cannot with safety cas*t* him, for he's embarked   *dismiss*
With such lou*d* reason to the Cyprus wars,   *strong*
Which even now stand in ac*t*, that, for their souls,   *under way*
Another of his fatho*m* they have not   *depth, capacity*
To lead their business. In which regard,
Though I do hate him as I do Hell's pains,
Yet for necessity of present life,
I must show out a flag and sign of love,
Which is indeed but sign. That you shall surely find him,
Lead to the Sagittar*y* the raisèd search,   *an inn*
And there will I be with him. So, farewell.
                                          [Exit.]

    [Enter, below, BRABANTIO in his dressing gown, and
    SERVANTS *with torches.]*

    BRABANTIO.   It is too true an evil. Gone she is,
And what's to come of my despisèd tim*e*   *life*

Is nought but bitterness. Now, Roderigo,
Where didst thou see her? O unhappy girl!
With the Moor, sayst thou? Who would be a father!
How didst thou know 'twas she? Oh, she deceives me
Past thought. What said she to you? Get more tapers!
Raise all my kindred! Are they married, think you?

RODERIGO. Truly, I think they are.

BRABANTIO. O Heaven! How got she out? Oh, treason of the blood!

Fathers, from hence trust not your daughters' minds
By what you see them act. Is there not charm*s*   *magic*
By which the proper*t*y of youth and maidhood   *nature*
May be abus*ed*? Have you not read, Roderigo,   *deceived*
Of some such thing?

RODERIGO.   Yes, sir, I have indeed.

BRABANTIO. Call up my brother. Oh, would *you* had
      had her!

Some one way, some another! Do you know
Where we may apprehend her and the Moor?

RODERIGO. I think I can discover him, if you please
To get good guard and go along with me.

BRABANTIO. Pray, lead me on. At every house I'll call,
I may comman*d* at most. Get weapons, ho!   *get help*
And raise some special officers of night.
On, good Roderigo. I'll deser*v*e your pains.   *reward*

                                   [*Exeunt.*]

SCENE II. *Another Street. Before the Inn.*

[*Enter* OTHELLO, IAGO, *and* ATTENDANTS *with torches.*]

IAGO. Though in the trade of war I have slain men,
Yet do I hold it very stuff o' th' conscience
To do no contriv*ed* murder. I lack iniquity   *deliberate*
Sometimes to do me service. Nine or ten times
I had thought t' have yerk*ed* hi*m* here under the ribs.   *stabbed*
                                        Brabantio

OTHELLO. 'Tis better as it is.

IAGO.   Nay, but he prated,
And spoke such scurvy and provoking terms
Against your Honor
That with the little godliness I have
I did full hard forbear him. But, I pray, sir,
Are you fast married? Be assured of this,
That the magnifi*c*o is much beloved,   *noble* Brabantio
And hath in his effe*c*t a voice potential   *actually*
As double as the Duke's. He will divorce you,

Or put upon you what restraint and grievance
The law, with all his might to enforce it on,
Will give him cable.   *rope, power*

    OTHELLO.   Let him do his spite.
My services which I have done the Signory   *State of Venice*
Shall out-tongue his complaints. 'Tis yet to know—   *to be known*
Which when I know that boasting is an honor
I shall promulgate—I fetch my life and being   *proclaim*
                                       rank . . .
From men of royal siege, and my demerits   *merits*
May speak unbonneted to as proud a fortune   *as an equal*
As this that I have reached. For know, Iago,
But that I love the gentle Desdemona,
I would not my unhousèd free condition   *unmarried*
Put into circumscription and confine
For the sea's worth. But, look! What lights come
       yonder?

    IAGO.   Those are the raisèd father and his friends.
You were best go in.

    OTHELLO.   Not I. I must be found.
My parts, my title, and my perfect soul   *abilities . . .*
Shall manifest me rightly. Is it they?   *ready*

    IAGO.   By Janus, I think no.   *a euphemized*
                                         oath

    [*Enter* CASSIO *with lights,* OFFICERS *and torches.*]

    OTHELLO.   The servants of the Duke, and my lieutenant.
The goodness of the night upon you, friends!
What is the news?

    CASSIO.   ·The Duke does greet you, General,
And he requires your haste-post-haste appearance,
Even on the instant.

    OTHELLO.   What's the matter, think you?

    CASSIO.   Something from Cyprus, as I may divine.   *surmise*
It is a business of some heat. The galleys
Have sent a dozen sequent messengers   *in sequence*
This very night at one another's heels,
And many of the consuls, raised and met,
Are at the Duke's already. You have been hotly called
       for,
When being not at your lodging to be found,
The Senate sent about three several quests   *separate*
To search you out.

    OTHELLO.   'Tis well I'm found by you.
I will but spend a word here in the house,
And go with you.

                                                [*Exit into the inn.*]

CASSIO.   Ancient, what makes he here?

IAGO.   Faith, he tonight hath boarded a land carrack.   *rich ship*
If it prove lawful prize, he's made for ever.

CASSIO.   I do not understand.

IAGO.   He's married.

CASSIO.   To who?

IAGO.   Marry, to—   *an oath and pun: Mary*

[*Re-enter* OTHELLO.]

                    Come, captain, will you go?

OTHELLO.   Have with you.

CASSIO.   Here comes another troop to seek for you.

IAGO.   It is Brabantio. General, be advised,   *careful*
He comes to bad intent.

[*Enter* BRABANTIO, RODERIGO, *and others, with torches and weapons.*]

OTHELLO.   Holla! Stand there!

RODERIGO.   Signior, it is the Moor.

BRABANTIO.   Down with him! Thief!

[*They draw on both sides.*]

IAGO.   You, Roderigo! Come, sir, I am for you.

OTHELLO.   Keep up your bright swords, for the dew   *sheathe*
   will rust 'em.
Good signior, you shall more command with years
Than with your weapons.

BRABANTIO.   Oh, thou foul thief! Where hast thou
   stowed my daughter?
Damned as thou art, thou hast enchanted her;
For I'll refer me to all things of sense,   *rational*
If she in chains of magic were not bound,
Whether a maid so tender, fair, and happy,
So opposite to marriage that she shunned   *averse*
The wealthy curlèd darlings of our nation,
Would ever have, t' incur a general mock,
Run from her guardage to the sooty bosom   *guardian*
Of such a thing as thou—to fear, not to delight.
Judge me the world, if 'tis is not gross in sense   *obvious*
That thou hast practised on her with foul charms,
Abused her delicate youth with drugs or minerals   *corrupted*
That weaken motion. I'll have 't disputed on.   *will power . . . argued in court*
'Tis probable, and palpable to thinking.
I therefore apprehend and do attach thee   *arrest*
For an abuser of the world, a practiser

Of arts inhibited and out of warrant.   *magic*
Lay hold upon him. If he do resist,   *forbidden*
Subdue him at his peril.
    OTHELLO.   Hold your hands,
Both you of my inclining and the rest.
Were it my cue to fight, I should have known it
Without a prompter. Where will you that I go
To answer this your charge?
    BRABANTIO.   To prison, till fit time
Of law and course of direct session   *general court*
Call thee to answer.
    OTHELLO.   What if I do obey?
How may the Duke be therewith satisfied,
Whose messengers are here about my side
Upon some present business of the state   *immediate*
To bring me to him?
    OFFICER.   'Tis true, most worthy signior.
The Duke's in council, and your noble self,
I am sure, is sent for.
    BRABANTIO.   How? The Duke in council!
In this time of the night! Bring him away.
Mine's not an idle cause. The Duke himself,   *trivial*
Or any of my brothers of the state,
Cannot but feel this wrong as 'twere their own.
For if such actions may have passage free,   *be allowed*
Bondslaves and pagans shall our statesmen be.
                                    [*Exeunt.*]

SCENE III. *The Council Chamber.*

[*The* DUKE *and* SENATORS *are sitting at a table with lights and* ATTENDANTS.]

    DUKE. There is no composition in these news   *agreement*
That gives them credit.
    FIRST SENATOR.   Indeed, they are disproportioned.
My letters say a hundred and seven galleys.
    DUKE. And mine, a hundred forty.
    SECOND SENATOR.   And mine, two hundred.
But though they jump not on a just account—   *agree . . .*
As in these cases, where they aimed reports,   *exact*
'Tis oft with difference—yet do they all confirm   *estimated*
A Turkish fleet, and bearing up to Cyprus.   *making for*
    DUKE. Nay, it is possible enough to judgment.
I do not so secure me in the error.   *feel safe*

But the main article I do approve | believe
In fearful sense. | to be feared
    SAILOR [*within*]. What, ho! What, ho! What, ho!
    OFFICER. A messenger from the galleys.

      [*Enter* SAILOR.]

    DUKE.   Now! What's the business?
    SAILOR. The Turkish preparation makes for Rhodes.
So was I bid report here to the state
By Signior Angelo.
    DUKE. How say you by this change? | What
    FIRST SENATOR.   This cannot be,
By no assay of reason. 'Tis a pageant | reasonable test
To keep us in false gaze. When we consider | looking away
Th' importancy of Cyprus to the Turk,
And let ourselves again but understand
That as it more concerns the Turk than Rhodes,
So may he with more facile question bear it, | easily take it
For that it stands not in such warlike brace | defense
But altogether lacks th' abilities
That Rhodes is dressed in—if we make thought of this, | prepared with
We must not think the Turk is so unskillful
To leave that latest which concerns him first, | to the last
Neglecting an attempt of ease and gain
To wake and wage a danger profitless. | risk
    DUKE. Nay, in all confidence, he's not for Rhodes.
    OFFICER. Here is more news.

      [*Enter a* MESSENGER.]

    MESSENGER. The Ottomites, reverend and gracious, | Turks . . . signiors
Steering with due course toward the isle of Rhodes,
Have there injointed them with an after fleet— | joined . . . second
    FIRST SENATOR. Ay, so I thought. How many, as you
        guess?
    MESSENGER. Of thirty sail, and now they do re-stem | retrace
Their backward course, bearing with frank appearance
Their purposes toward Cyprus. Signior Montano,
Your trusty and most valiant servitor,
With his free duty recommends you thus, | dutifully informs
And prays you to believe him.
    DUKE. 'Tis certain then for Cyprus.
Marcus Luccicos, is not he in town?
    FIRST SENATOR. He's now in Florence.

DUKE. Write from us to him post-post-haste dispatch.
FIRST SENATOR. Here comes Brabantio and the valiant
    Moor.

[*Enter* BRABANTIO, OTHELLO, CASSIO, IAGO, RODERIGO,
and OFFICERS.]

DUKE. Valiant Othello, we must straight employ you
Against the general enemy Ottoman.
[*To* BRABANTIO] I did not see you. Welcome, gentle
    signior,
We lacked your counsel and your help tonight.
    BRABANTIO. So did I yours. Good your Grace, pardon
    me.
Neither my place nor aught I heard of business
Hath raised me from my bed, nor doth the general care
Take hold on me, for my particular grief   *personal*
Is of so floodgate and o'erbearing nature   *overflowing*
That it englut*s* and swallows other sorrows   *swallows*
And it is still itself.
    DUKE.   Why, what's the matter?
    BRABANTIO. My daughter! O my daughter!
    ALL.   Dead?
    BRABANTIO.   Ay, to me.
She is abuse*d*, stol'n from me, and corrupted   *dishonored*
By spells and medicines bought of mountebank*s*.   *quacks*
For nature so preposterously to err
Being not deficient, blind, or lame of sense,
San*s* witchcraft could not.   *without*
    DUKE. Whoe'er he be that in this foul proceeding
Hath thus beguile*d* your daughter of hersel*f*   *cheated . . .*
And you of her, the bloody book of law   *of her senses*
You shall yourself read in the bitter letter
After your own sense—yea, though our proper son   *own*
Stood in your actio*n*.   *accusation*
    BRABANTIO.   Humbly I thank your Grace.
Here is the man, this Moor, whom now, it seems,
Your special mandate for the state affairs
Hath hither brought.
    ALL.   We are very sorry for 't.
    DUKE [*to* OTHELLO]. What, in your own part, can you
    say to this?
    BRABANTIO. Nothing but 'This is so.'
    OTHELLO. Most potent, grave, and reverend signiors,
My very noble and approve*d* good masters: *well-proved*

That I have ta'en away this old man's daughter,
It is most true—true, I have married her.
The very head and front of my offending   *forehead*
Hath this extent, no more. Rude am I in my speech,   *rough*
And little blessed with the soft phrase of peace,
For since these arms of mine had seven years' pith   *marrow*
Till now some nine moons wasted, they have used   *nine months ago*
Their dearest action in the tented field.   *most intense*
And little of this great world can I speak
More than pertains to feats of broil and battle,
And therefore little shall I grace my cause
In speaking for myself. Yet, by your gracious patience
I will a round unvarnished tale deliver   *plain-spoken*
Of my whole course of love—what drugs, what charms,
What conjuration, and what mighty magic—
For such proceedings am I charged withal—
I won his daughter.

    BRABANTIO.   A maiden never bold,
Of spirit so still and quiet that her motion   *inner desire*
Blushed at herself! And she, in spite of nature,
Of years, of country, credit, everything,   *reputation*
To fall in love with what she feared to look on!
It is a judgment maimed and most imperfect
That will confess perfection so could err   *believe*
Against all rules of nature, and must be driven
To find out practices of cunning hell   *plots*
Why this should be. I therefore vouch again
That with some mixtures powerful o'er the blood,
Or with some dram conjured to this effect,
He wrought upon her.   *worked*

    DUKE.   To vouch this is no proof,
Without more certain and more overt test   *open*
Than these thin habits and poor likelihoods   *evidences*
Of modern seeming do prefer against him.   *suspicion*

    FIRST SENATOR.   But, Othello, speak.
Did you by indirect and forcèd courses   *unnatural*
Subdue and poison this young maid's affections?
Or came it by request and such fair question
As soul to soul affordeth?

    OTHELLO.   I do beseech you,
Send for the lady to the Sagittary,
And let her speak of me before her father.
If you do find me foul in her report,
The trust, the office I do hold of you
Not only take away, but let your sentence

Even fall upon my life.

DUKE.   Fetch Desdemona hither.

[Exeunt two or three.]

OTHELLO.   Ancient, conduct them. You best know the
place.

[Exit IAGO.*]*

And till she come, as truly as to heaven
I do confess the vices of my blood,
So justly to your grave ears I'll present
How I did thrive in this fair lady's love,
And she in mine.

DUKE.   Say it, Othello.

OTHELLO.   Her father loved me, oft invited me,
Still questioned me the story of my life   *always . . .*
From year to year, the battles, sieges, fortunes   *about*
That I have passed.
I ran it through, even from my boyish days
To th' very moment that he bade me tell it.
Wherein I spake of most disastrous chances,
Of moving accidents by flood and field,
Of hair-breadth 'scapes i' th' imminent deadly breach,   *threatening*
Of being taken by the insolent foe   *assault*
And sold to slavery, of my redemption thence
And portance in my traveller's history.   *my conduct*
Wherein of antres vast and deserts idle,   *caves . . .*
Rough quarries, rocks and hills whose heads touch   *barren*
heaven,
It was my hint to speak—such was the process—   *occasion*
And of the cannibals that each other eat,   *story*
The Anthropophagi, and men whose heads   *cannibals*
Do grow beneath their shoulders. This to hear
Would Desdemona seriously incline.
But still the house-affairs would draw her thence,
Which ever as she could with haste dispatch
She'd come again, and with a greedy ear
Devour up my discourse. Which I observing,
Took once a pliant hour and found good means   *suitable*
To draw from her a prayer of earnest heart
That I would all my pilgrimage dilate,   *relate fully*
Whereof by parcels she had something heard,   *portions*
But not intentively. I did consent,   *in full design*
And often did beguile her of her tears   *draw from her*
When I did speak of some distressful stroke

That my youth suffered. My story being done,
She gave me for my pains a world of sighs.
She swore, in faith, 'twas strange, 'twas passing strange,
'Twas pitiful, 'twas wondrous pitiful.
She wished she had not heard it, yet she wished
That Heaven had made her such a man. She thanked me, *for her*
And bade me, if I had a friend that loved her,
I should but teach him how to tell my story,
And that would woo her. Upon this hint I spake.
She loved me for the dangers I had passed,
And I loved her that she did pity them.
This only is the witchcraft I have used.
Here comes the lady. Let her witness it.

[*Enter* DESDEMONA, IAGO, *and the rest.*]

DUKE. I think this tale would win my daughter too.
Good Brabantio,
Take up this mangled matter at the best. *as best you*
Men do their broken weapons rather use   *may*
Than their bare hands.

BRABANTIO.   I pray you, hear her speak.
If she confess that she was half the wooer,
Destruction on my head if my bad blame
Light on the man! Come hither, gentle mistress.
Do you perceive in all this noble company
Where most you owe obedience?

DESDEMONA.   My noble father,
I do perceive here a divided duty.
To you I am bound for life and education.
My life and education both do learn me   *teach*
How to respect you—you're lord of all my duty,
I am hitherto your daughter. But here's my husband, *until now*
And so much duty as my mother showed
To you, preferring you before her father,
So much I challenge that I may profess   *claim, declare*
Due to the Moor my lord.

BRABANTIO.   God bu 'y! I have done. *goodbye*
Please it your Grace, on to the state affairs.
I had rather to adopt a child than get it.   *beget*
Come hither, Moor.
I here do give thee that with all my heart
Which, but thou hast already, with all my heart
I would keep from thee. For your sake, jewel,
I am glad at soul I have no other child,
For thy escape would teach me tyranny,

To hang clog*s* on 'em. I have done, my lord.

    DUKE. Let me speak like yourself and la*y* a sentenc*e*, *to hobble them*
Which, as a gris*e* or step, may help these lovers   *utter a maxim*
Into your favor: *degree, step*
'When remedies are past, the griefs are ended
By seeing the worst, which late on hopes depended.'
'To mourn a mischie*f* that is past and gone   *misfortune*
Is the nex*t* way to draw more mischief on.'   *nearest*
'What cannot be preserved when Fortune takes,
Patience he*r* injury a mockery makes.'   *Fortune's*
'The robbed that smiles steals something from the thief;
He robs himself that spends a bootles*s* grief.'   *useless*

    BRABANTIO. So let the Turk of Cyprus us beguil*e*,   *cheat*
We lose it not so long as we can smile.
'He bears the sentence well that nothing bears
But the free comfort which from thence he hears;
But he bears both the sentence and the sorrow
That, to pay grief, must of poor patience borrow.'
These sentences, to sugar or to gall,
Being strong on both sides, are equivoca*l*.   *ambiguous*
But words are words. I never yet did hear
That the bruised heart was pierc*è*d through the ear.
Beseech you, now to the affairs of state.

    DUKE. The Turk with a most mighty preparation
makes for Cyprus. Othello, the fortitud*e* of the place is   *defenses*
best known to you; and though we have there a substitut*e*   *deputy*
of most allowe*d* sufficiency, yet opinion, a sovereign mis-   *admitted*
                                                                 leadership
tress of effect*s*, throws a more safer voice on you. You   *results*
must therefore be content to slubbe*r* the gloss of your new   *tarnish*
fortunes with this more stubborn and boisterous ex-
pedition.

    OTHELLO. The tyrant custom, most grave senators,
Hath made the flinty and steel coach of war
My thrice-driven bed of down. I do agniz*e*   *confess*
A natural and prompt alacrit*y*   *briskness*
I find in hardnes*s* and would undertake   *hardship*
These present wars against the Ottomites.
Most humbly therefore bending to your state,
I crave fit disposition for my wife,
Due referenc*e* of place and exhibitio*n*,   *assignment allowance*
With such accommodation and besor*t*   *attendance*
As level*s* with her breeding.   *suits*

    DUKE.   If you please,
Be 't at her father's.

    BRABANTIO.   I'll not have it so.

OTHELLO. Nor I.

DESDEMONA.   Nor I. I would not there reside,
To put my father in impatient thoughts
By being in his eye. Most gracious Duke,
To my unfolding lend your prosperous ear,   *plan . . .*
And let me find a charter in your voice   *favorable*
T' assist my simpleness.   *sanction*

DUKE.   What would you? Speak.

DESDEMONA. That I did love the Moor to live with him,
My downright violence and storm of fortunes   *actions*
May trumpet to the world. My heart's subdued
Even to the very quality of my lord.   *profession*
I saw Othello's visage in his mind,
And to his honors and his valiant parts
Did I my soul and fortunes consecrate.
So that, dear lords, if I be left behind,
A moth of peace, and he go to the war,
The rites for which I love him are bereft me,
And I a heavy interim shall support
By his dear absence. Let me go with him.   *deeply felt*

OTHELLO. Your voices, lords! Beseech you, let her will   *assent*
Have a free way. I therefore beg it not
To please the palate of my appetite,
Nor to comply with heat—the young affects   *satisfy desire*
In me defunct—and proper satisfaction,   *my own*
But to be free and bounteous to her mind.
And heaven defend your good souls that you think   *forbid*
I will your serious and great business scant
For she is with me. No, when light-wing'd toys   *because . . .*
Of feathered Cupid seel with wanton dulness   *trifles*
My speculative and active instruments,   *close up*
That my disports corrupt and taint my business,   *faculties*
Let housewives make a skillet of my helm,   *amusements*
And all indign and base adversities
Make head against my reputation!   *unworthy*
     overcome

DUKE. Be it as you shall privately determine,
Either for her stay or going. Th' affair cries haste,
And speed must answer. You must hence tonight.

DESDEMONA. Tonight, my lord?

DUKE.   This night.

OTHELLO.   With all my heart.

DUKE. At ten i' the morning here we'll meet again.
Othello, leave some officer behind,
And he shall our commission bring to you,
With such things else of quality or respect   *import or*
     concern

As doth concern you.

OTHELLO. Please your Grace, my ancient—
A man he is of honesty and trust—
To his conveyance I assign my wife,
With what else needful your good Grace shall think
To be sent after me.

DUKE. Let it be so.
Good night to every one. [*To* BRABANTIO] And, noble
    signior,
If virtue no delighte*d* beauty lack,   *delightful*
Your son-in-law is far more fair than black.

FIRST SENATOR. Adieu, brave Moor! Use Desdemona
    well.

BRABANTIO. Look to her, Moor, if thou hast eyes to
    see—
She has deceived her father, and may thee.

OTHELLO. My life upon her faith!
[*Exeunt* DUKE, SENATORS, OFFICERS, *etc.*]

                  Honest Iago,
My Desdemona must I leave to thee.
I prithee, let thy wife attend on her,
And bring her after in the best advantag*e*.   *opportunity*
Come, Desdemona, I have but an hour
Of love, of worldly matters, and direction
To spend with thee. We must obey the time.
[*Exeunt* OTHELLO *and* DESDEMONA.]

RODERIGO. Iago!
IAGO. What sayst thou, noble heart?
RODERIGO. What will I do, think'st thou?
IAGO. Why, go to bed, and sleep.
RODERIGO. I will incontinent*ly* drown myself.   *immediately*
IAGO. Well, if thou dost, I shall never love thee after it.
Why, thou silly gentleman?
RODERIGO. It is silliness to live when to live is a tor-
ment, and then have we a prescription to die when death
is our physician.
IAGO. Oh, villainous! I have looked upon the world
for four times seven years, and since I could distinguish
between a benefit and an injury, I never found a man that
knew how to love himself. Ere I would say I would
drown myself for the love of a guinea-hen, I would
change my humanity with a baboon.
RODERIGO. What should I do? I confess it is my shame
to be so fon*d*, but it is not in my virtu*e* to amend it.   *foolishly in love*
                                                 manhood

IAGO. Virtue? A fig! 'Tis in ourselves that we are thus or thus. Our bodies are our gardens, to the which our wills are gardeners; so that if we will plant nettles or sow lettuce, set hyssop and weed up thyme, supply it with one gender of herbs or distract it with many, either to have it sterile with idleness or manured with industry, why, the power and corrigible authority of this lies in our wills. If the balance of our lives had not one scale of reason to poise another of sensuality, the blood and baseness of our natures would conduct us to most preposterous conclusions. But we have reason to cool our raging motions, our carnal stings, our unbitted lusts, whereof I take this that you call love to be a sect or scion.

RODERIGO. It cannot be.

IAGO. It is merely a lust of the blood and a permission of the will. Come, be a man. Drown thyself? Drown cats and blind puppies. I profess me thy friend, and I confess me knit to thy deserving with cables of perdurable toughness. I could never better stead thee than now. Put money in thy purse, follow these wars, defeat thy favor with an usurped beard. I say, put money in thy purse. It cannot be that Desdemona should long continue her love unto the Moor—put money in thy purse—nor he his to her. It was a violent commencement, and thou shalt see an answerable sequestration. Put but money in thy purse. These Moors are changeable in their wills. Fill thy purse with money. The food that to him now is as luscious as locusts shall be to him shortly as bitter as the coloquintida. She must change for youth. When she is sated with his body, she will find the error of her choice. She must have change, she must. Therefore put money in thy purse. If thou wilt needs damn thyself, do it a more delicate way than drowning. Make all the money thou canst. If sanctimony and a frail vow betwixt an erring barbarian and a super-subtle Venetian be not too hard for my wits and all the tribe of Hell, thou shalt enjoy her—therefore make money. A pox o' drowning thyself! It is clean out of the way. Seek thou rather to be hanged in compassing thy joy than to be drowned and go without her.

RODERIGO. Wilt thou be fast to my hopes if I depend on the issue?

IAGO. Thou art sure of me. Go, make money. I have told thee often, and I tell thee again and again, I hate the Moor. My cause is hearted: thine hath no less reason.

Margin glosses:
- *or: desire*
- *kind*
- *corrective*
- *counterbalance*
- *impulses, desires / unbridled / cutting or shoot*
- *hardest*
- *help*
- *disguise . . . face*
- *corresponding separation*
- *St. John's bread*
- *bitter purge*
- *raise . . . cash*
- *wandering*
- *an oath: disease*
- *achieving*
- *outcome*
- *heart-felt*

Let us be conjunctive in our revenge against him. If
thou canst cuckold him, thou dost thyself a pleasure, me
a sport. There are many events in the womb of time
which will be delivered. Traverse, go!—provide thy
money. We will have more of this tomorrow. Adieu.

    RODERIGO. Where shall we meet i' th' morning?

    IAGO. At my lodging.

    RODERIGO. I'll be with thee betimes.

    IAGO. Go to, farewell. Do you hear, Roderigo?

    RODERIGO. What say you?

    IAGO. No more of drowning, do you hear?

    RODERIGO. I am changed. I'll sell all my land.

    IAGO. Go to, farewell. Put money enough in your
purse.

[Exit RODERIGO.*]*

Thus do I ever make my fool my purse,
For I mine own gained knowledge should profane
If I would time expend with such a snipe
But for my sport and profit. I hate the Moor,
And it is thought abroad that 'twixt my sheets
He's done my office. I know not if 't be true,
But I, for mere suspicion in that kind,
Will do as if for surety. He holds me well.
The better shall my purpose work on him.
Cassio's a proper man. Let me see now.—
To get his place, and to plume up my will
In double knavery—How? how? Let's see.—
After some time t' abuse Othello's ear
That he is too familiar with his wife.
He has a person and a smooth dispose
To be suspected, framed to make women false.
The Moor is of a free and open nature
That thinks men honest that but seem to be so,
And will as tenderly be led by th' nose
As asses are.
I have 't! It is engendered! Hell and night
Must bring this monstrous birth to the world's light.

[Exit]

united

seduce his wife

forward

early

come now

woodcock, fool

it were so

handsome

gratify

deceive

Cassio

disposition

conceived

ACT TWO

SCENE I. *A seaport in Cyprus. An open place
near the wharf.*

[Enter MONTANO, *Governor of Cyprus, with two
other* GENTLEMEN.*]*

MONTANO.   What from the cape can you discern at sea?

FIRST GENTLEMAN.   Nothing at all. It is a high-wrought *heavy sea*
flood;
I cannot 'twixt the heaven and the main
Descry a sail.

MONTANO.   Methinks the wind does speak aloud at
land,
A fuller blast ne'er shook our battlements.
If it hath ruffianed so upon the sea,
What ribs of oak, when mountains melt on them,
Can hold the mortise? What shall we hear of this?   *their joints*

SECOND GENTLEMAN.   A segregation of the Turkish   *dispersal*
fleet.
For do but stand upon the foaming shore,
The chidden billow seems to pelt the clouds,
The wind-shaked surge, with high and monstrous mane,
Seems to cast water on the burning Bear   *the constellation*
And quench the guards of th' ever-fixèd pole.   *Little Bear stars*
I never did like molestation view   *disturbance*
On the enchafèd flood.   *angry sea*

MONTANO.   If that the Turkish fleet
Be not ensheltered and embayed, they are drowned.
It is impossible they bear it out.

[*Enter a third* GENTLEMAN.]

THIRD GENTLEMAN.   News, lads! Our wars are done.
The desperate tempest hath so banged the Turks
That their designment halts. A noble ship of Venice   *enterprise*
Hath seen a grievous wrack and sufferance   *disaster*
On most part of their fleet.

MONTANO.   How! Is this true?

THIRD GENTLEMAN.   The ship is here put in,
A Veronesa, Michael Cassio,
Lieutenant to the warlike Moor Othello,
Is come on shore, the Moor himself at sea,
And is in full commission here for Cyprus.   *is coming with*
                                             full powers

MONTANO.   I am glad on't. 'Tis a worthy governor.

THIRD GENTLEMAN.   But this same Cassio, though he
speak of comfort
Touching the Turkish loss, yet he looks sadly
And prays the Moor be safe, for they were parted
With foul and violent tempest.

MONTANO.   Pray Heaven he be;
For I have served him, and the man commands
Like a full soldier. Let's to the seaside, ho!   *thorough*

As well to see the vessel that's come in
As to throw out our eyes for brave Othello,
Even till we make the main and th' aerial blue   *view*
An indistinct regard.
    THIRD GENTLEMAN.   Come, let's do so;
For every minute is expectancy
Of more arrivance.   *arrivals*

    [*Enter* CASSIO.]

    CASSIO.   Thanks to the valiant of this warlike isle
That so approve the Moor! And let the heavens
Give him defence against the elements,
For I have lost him on a dangerous sea.
    MONTANO.   Is he well shipped?   *in a good ship*
    CASSIO.   His bark is stoutly timbered, and his pilot
Of very expert and approved allowance.   *tested skill*
Therefore my hopes, not surfeited to death,   *sickened*
Stand in bold cure.   *can be cured*
    MESSENGER [*within*].   A sail!—a sail!—a sail!

    [*Enter a* MESSENGER.]

    CASSIO.   What noise?
    MESSENGER.   The town is empty. On the brow o' th' sea
Stand ranks of people, and they cry, 'A sail!'
    CASSIO.   My hopes do shape him for the governor.   *imagine*

    [*A shot is heard.*]

    SECOND GENTLEMAN.   They do discharge the shot of
        courtesy.
Our friends, at least.
    CASSIO.   I pray you, sir, go forth,
And give us truth who 'tis that is arrived.
    SECOND GENTLEMAN.   I shall.
                    [*Exit.*]

    MONTANO.   But, good Lieutenant, is your general
        wived?
    CASSIO.   Most fortunately. He hath achieved a maid   *won*
That paragons description and wild fame,   *surpasses*
One that excels the quirks of blazoning pens,   *phrases . . . praising*
And in th' essential vesture of creation   *perfection*
Does tire the ingener.   *inventor*

    [*Enter* SECOND GENTLEMAN.]

How now! Who has put in?

SECOND GENTLEMAN. 'Tis one Iago, ancient to the
general.

CASSIO. He's had most favorable and happy speed.
Tempests themselves, high seas, and howling winds,
The guttered rocks, and congregated sands,   *jagged*
Traitors ensteeped to clog the guiltless keel,   *submerged*
As having sense of beauty, do omit   *forebear*
Their mortal natures, letting go safely by   *deadly*
The divine Desdemona.

MONTANO.   What is she?

CASSIO. She that I spoke of, our great captain's captain,
Left in the conduct of the bold Iago,
Whose footing here anticipates our thoughts   *escort*
A sennight's speed. Great Jove, Othello guard,   *arrival*
And swell his sail with thine own powerful breath, *week's*
That he may bless this bay with his tall ship,
Make love's quick pants in Desdemona's arms,
Give renewed fire to our extincted spirits,   *extinguished*
And bring all Cyprus comfort!

[*Enter* DESDEMONA, IAGO, EMILIA, *and* RODERIGO, *with*
ATTENDANTS.]

                    Oh! behold,
The riches of the ship is come ashore.
Ye men of Cyprus, let her have your knees.
Hail to thee, lady! And the grace of Heaven,
Before, behind thee, and on every hand,
Enwheel thee round!   *encompass*

DESDEMONA.   I thank you, valiant Cassio.
What tidings can you tell me of my lord?

CASSIO. He is not yet arrived, nor know I aught
But that he's well, and will be shortly here.

DESDEMONA. Oh, but I fear! How lost you company?

[*Cry within.* 'A sail!—a sail!']

CASSIO. The great contention of the sea and skies
Parted our fellowship. But hark! a sail.

[*Within.* 'A sail!—a sail!' *Guns heard.*]

SECOND GENTLEMAN. They give their greeting to the
citadel.
This likewise is a friend.

CASSIO.   See for the news!
                    [*Exit* SECOND GENTLEMAN.]

Good Ancient, you are welcome. [*Kisses* EMILIA] Wel-
    come, mistress.
Let it not gall your patience, good Iago,
That I extend my manners. 'Tis my breeding
That gives me this bold show of courtesy.
    IAGO.   Sir, would she give you so much of her lips
As of her tongue she oft bestows on me,
You'd have enough.
    DESDEMONA.   Alas, she has no speech.
    IAGO.   In faith, too much.
I find it still when I have list to sleep.   *always . . .*
Marry, before your ladyship, I grant,   *desire*
She puts her tongue a little in her heart,
And chides with thinking.
    EMILIA.   You have little cause to say so.
    IAGO.   Come on, come on! You are pictures out o'   *painted & dumb*
        doors,
Bells in your parlors, wildcats in your kitchens,   *ever-clanging*
Saints in your injuries, devils being offended,   *injury to others*
Players in your housewifery, and housewives in your beds.   *triflers . . .*
                                                               hussies
    DESDEMONA.   O fie upon thee, slanderer!
    IAGO.   Nay, it is true, or else I am a Turk.   *heathen*
You rise to play and go to bed to work.
    EMILIA.   You shall not write my praise.
    IAGO.   No, let me not.
    DESDEMONA.   What wouldst thou write of me, if thou
        shouldst praise me?
    IAGO.   O gentle lady, do not put me to 't,
For I am nothing if not critical.   *censorious*
    DESDEMONA.   Come on, assay. There's one gone to the   *try*
        harbor?
    IAGO.   Ay, madam.
    DESDEMONA.   I am not merry, but I do beguile   *disguise*
The thing I am by seeming otherwise.
Come, how wouldst thou praise me?
    IAGO.   I am about it, but indeed my invention comes
from my pate as birdlime does from frieze. It plucks out   *rough cloth*
brains and all. But my muse labors, and thus she is
delivered:
        If she be fair and wise—fairness and wit:
        The one's for use, the other useth it.
    DESDEMONA.   Well praised! How if she be black and   *brunette*
        witty?
    IAGO.
        If she be black, and thereto have a wit,

She'll find a white that shall her blackness fit. *pun: wight, man*

DESDEMONA. Worse and worse.

EMILIA. How if fair and foolish?

IAGO.

She never yet was foolish that was fair,
For even her folly helped her to an heir.

DESDEMONA. These are old fond paradoxes to make *foolish*
fools laugh i' th' alehouse. What miserable praise hast
thou for her that's foul and foolish? *ugly*

IAGO.

There's none so foul and foolish thereunto *besides*
But does foul pranks which fair and wise ones do.

DESDEMONA. O heavy ignorance, that praises the worst
best! But what praise couldst thou bestow on a deserving
woman indeed? one that, in the authority of her merits,
did justly put on the vouch of very malice itself? *win approval*

IAGO.

She that was ever fair and never proud,
Had tongue at will and yet was never loud, *was talkative*
Never lacked gold and yet went never gay,
Fled from her wish and yet said 'Now I may.'
She that being angered, her revenge being nigh,
Bade her wrong stay and her displeasure fly.
She that in wisdom never was so frail
To change the cod's head for the salmon's tail. *gross puns*
She that could think and ne'er disclose her mind,
See suitors following and not look behind,
She was a wight, if ever such wights were—

DESDEMONA. To do what?

IAGO.

To suckle fools and chronicle small beer. *keep family books*

DESDEMONA. O most lame and impotent conclusion!
Do not learn of him, Emilia, though he be thy husband.
How say you, Cassio? Is he not a most profane and liberal *licentious*
counsellor?

CASSIO. He speaks home, madam. You may relish *to the point*
him more in the soldier than in the scholar. *as a*

IAGO [aside]. He takes her by the palm. Ay, well
said, whisper! With as little a web as this will I ensnare *done*
as great a fly as Cassio. Ay, smile upon her, do! I will
gyve thee in thine own courtship. *fetter courtesy*

[CASSIO *speaks to* DESDEMONA *in pantomime.*]
You say true, 'tis so, indeed. If such tricks as these strip
you out of your lieutenantry, it had been better you had
not kissed your three fingers so oft, which now again you *in gallantry*

are most apt to play the *sir* in. Very good! Well kissed!   *gentleman*
An excellent courtesy! 'Tis so, indeed. Yet again your
fingers to your lips? Would they were clysterpipe*s* for   *syringes*
your sake!

[*Trumpets within.*]

The Moor! I know his trumpet.
    CASSIO.   'Tis truly so.
    DESDEMONA.   Let's meet him and receive him.
    CASSIO.   Lo, where he comes!

[*Enter* OTHELLO *and* ATTENDANTS.]

    OTHELLO.   O my fair warrio*r*!   *a soldier's wife*
    DESDEMONA.   My dear Othello!
    OTHELLO.   It gives me wonder great as my content
To see you here before me. O my soul's joy,
If after every tempest come such calms,
May the winds blow till they have wakened death!
And let the laboring bark climb hills of seas
Olympus-high, and duck again as low
As hell's from heaven! If it were now to die,
'Twere now to be most happy, for I fear
My soul hath her content so absolute
That not another comfort like to this
Succeeds in unknown fate.
    DESDEMONA.   The Heavens forbid
But that our loves and comforts should increase
Even as our days do grow.
    OTHELLO.   Amen to that, sweet powers!
I cannot speak enough of this content.
It stops me her*e*. It is too much of joy.   *in my heart*
And this, and this, the greatest discords be   [*They kiss.*]
That e'er our hearts shall make!
    IAGO [*aside*].   Oh! you are well tuned now,   *untune the*
But I'll se*t* down the peg*s* that make this music,   *strings*
As honest as I am.
    OTHELLO.   Come, let us to the castle.
News, friends! Our wars are done. The Turks are
    drowned.
How does my old acquaintance of this isle?——
Honey, you shall be well desire*d* in Cyprus,   *loved*
I have found great love amongst them. Oh, my sweet,
I prattl*e* out of fashion, and I dote   *talk idly*
In mine own comforts. I prithee, good Iago,

Go to the bay and disembark my coffers.   *trunks*
Bring thou the master to the citadel.   *ship's captain*
He is a good one, and his worthiness
Does challenge much respect. Come, Desdemona!   *claim*
Once more, well met at Cyprus!

       [*Exeunt all except* IAGO *and* RODERIGO.]

IAGO. Do thou meet me presently at the harbor. Come   *at once*
hither. If thou be'st valiant—as they say base men being
in love have then a nobility in their natures more than is
native to them—list me. The Lieutenant tonight watches   *hear*
on the court of guard. First, I must tell thee this—Des-   *guard duty*
demona is directly in love with him.
   RODERIGO. With him? Why, 'tis not possible.
   IAGO. Lay thy finger thus, and let thy soul be in-   *on your lips*
structed. Mark me with what violence she first loved the
Moor but for bragging and telling her fantastical lies.   *only*
And will she love him still for prating? Let not thy
discreet heart think it. Her eye must be fed, and what
delight shall she have to look on the devil? When the
blood is made dull with the act of sport, there should be, *lust*
again to inflame it and to give satiety a fresh appetite,
loveliness in favor, sympathy in years, manners, and   *face*
beauties—all which the Moor is defective in. Now, for
want of these required conveniences, her delicate tenderness will find itself abused, begin to heave the gorge,   *be sick of*
disrelish and abhor the Moor. Very nature will instruct
her in it, and compel her to some second choice. Now,
sir, this granted—as it is a most pregnant and unforced   *evident*
position—who stands so eminently in the degree of this
fortune as Cassio does? A knave very voluble, no further   *with no more
conscionable than in putting on the mere form of civil   conscience*
and humane seeming for the better compassing of his salt   *appearance
and hidden affections? Why, none, why, none. A subtle,   lewd*
slippery knave, a finder-out of occasions, that has an eye
can stamp and counterfeit advantages, though true ad-   *make opportuni-
vantage never present itself. A devilish knave! Besides,   ties*
the knave is handsome, young, and hath all those
requisites in him that folly and green minds look after. A *inexperienced*
pestilent complete knave! and the woman has found him
already.
   RODERIGO. I cannot believe that in her. She's full of
most blessed condition.
   IAGO. Blessed fig's end! The wine she drinks is made
of grapes. If she had been blessed, she would never have

loved the Moor. Blessed pudding! Didst thou not see
her paddle with the palm of his hand? Didst not mark   *play*
that?

RODERIGO. Yes, that I did, but that was but courtesy.

IAGO. Lechery, by this hand! an index and obscure
prologue to the history of lust and foul thoughts. They
met so near with their lips that their breaths embraced
together. Villainous thoughts, Roderigo! When these
mutualities so marshal the way, hard at hand comes the   *intimacies*
master and main exercise, the incorporate conclusion.   *carnal*
Pish! But, sir, be you ruled by me. I have brought you
from Venice. Watch you tonight. For your command,
I'll lay 't upon you. Cassio knows you not. I'll not be
far from you. Do you find some occasion to anger Cassio,
either by speaking too loud, or tainting his discipline, or *disparaging*
from what other cause you please which the time shall
more favorably minister.   *provide*

RODERIGO. Well.

IAGO. Sir, he is rash and very sudden in choler, and   *anger*
haply with his truncheon may strike at you. Provoke him   *perhaps*
that he may, for even out of that will I cause these of
Cyprus to mutiny, whose qualification shall come into no   *appeasement*
true taste again but by the displanting of Cassio. So shall *satisfaction*
you have a shorter journey to your desires by the means
I shall then have to prefer them, and the impediment   *promote*
most profitably removed without the which there were
no expectation of our prosperity.

RODERIGO. I will do this, if you can bring it to any
opportunity.

IAGO. I warrant thee. Meet me by and by at the
citadel. I must fetch his necessaries ashore. Farewell.

RODERIGO. Adieu.

[*Exit.*]

IAGO. That Cassio loves her, I do well believe it.   *likely . . .*
That she loves him, 'tis apt and of great credit.   *believable*
The Moor, howbeit that I endure him not,   *although I can*
Is of a constant, noble, loving nature,
And I dare think he'll prove to Desdemona
A most dear husband. Now, I do love her too,
Not out of absolute lust (though peradventure
I stand accountant for as great a sin),   *accountable*
But partly led to diet my revenge,   *feed*
For that I do suspect the lusty Moor
Hath leaped into my seat, the thought whereof

Doth like a poisonous mineral gnaw my inwards. *corrosive poison*
And nothing can nor shall content my soul
Till I am evened with him, wife for wife,
Or failing so, yet that I put the Moor
At least into a jealousy so strong
That judgment cannot cure. Which thing to do, *reason*
If this poor trash of Venice, whom I thrash
For his quick hunting, stand the putting-on, *inciting*
I'll have our Michael Cassio on the hip, *in my power*
Abuse him to the Moor in the rank garb— *coarse fashion, as his wife's lover*
For I fear Cassio with my night-cap too—
Make the Moor thank me, love me, and reward me
For making him egregiously an ass *notably*
And practising upon his peace and quiet *plotting against*
Even to madness. 'Tis here, but yet confused.
Knavery's plain face is never seen till used.

             [*Exit.*]

Scene II. *A Street.*

[*Enter* OTHELLO'S HERALD, *with a proclamation,* PEOPLE *following.*]

 HERALD. It is Othello's pleasure, our noble and valiant
general, that, upon certain tidings now arrived, importing
the mere perdition of the Turkish fleet, every man put *utter loss*
himself into triumph—some to dance, some to make bon- *celebrate*
fires, each man to what sport and revels his addiction *inclination*
leads him. For, besides these beneficial news, it is the
celebration of his nuptial. So much was his pleasure
should be proclaimed. All offices are open, and there is *with free drinks*
full liberty of feasting from this present hour of five till
the bell have tolled eleven. Heaven bless the isle of
Cyprus and our noble general Othello!

            [*Exeunt.*]

Scene III. *A hall in the Citadel.*

[*Enter* OTHELLO, DESDEMONA, CASSIO, *and* ATTENDANTS.]

 OTHELLO. Good Michael, look you to the guard to-
  night.
Let's teach ourselves that honorable stop,
Not to outsport discretion.
 CASSIO. Iago hath direction what to do,

But, notwithstanding, with my personal eye
Will I look to 't.

OTHELLO. Iago is most honest.
Michael, good night. Tomorrow wit*h* your earliest   *when you're up*
Let me have speech with you.

   [*To* DESDEMONA] Come, my dear love.
The purchase made, the fruits are to ensue—
The profit's yet to come 'twixt me and you.
Good night.

   [*Exeunt* OTHELLO *and* DESDEMONA *and* ATTENDANTS.]

  [*Enter* IAGO.]

CASSIO. Welcome, Iago. We must to the watch.

IAGO. Not this hour, Lieutenant, 'tis not yet ten o'clock.
Our general cas*t* us thus early for the love of his Des-   *dismissed*
demona, who let us not therefore blame. He hath not
yet made wanton the night with her, and she is sport for
Jove.

CASSIO. She's a most exquisite lady.

IAGO. And, I'll warrant her, full of game.

CASSIO. Indeed, she is a most fresh and delicate
creature.

IAGO. What an eye she has! Methinks it sound*s* a   *invites love-*
parley to provocatio*n*.   *making*

CASSIO. An inviting eye, and yet methinks right
modest.

IAGO. And when she speaks, is it not an alaru*m* to   *call to arms*
love?

CASSIO. She is indeed perfection.

IAGO. Well, happiness to their sheets! Come, Lieu-
tenant, I have a stou*p* of wine, and here without are a   *half gallon*
brace of Cyprus gallants that would fai*n* have a measure   *gladly*
to the health of black Othello.

CASSIO. Not tonight, good Iago. I have very poor
and unhappy brains for drinking. I could well wish
courtesy would invent some other custom of entertainment.

IAGO. Oh, they are our friends. But one cup. I'll
drink for you.

CASSIO. I have drunk but one cup tonight, and that   *diluted*
was craftily qualifie*d* too, and, behold, what innovatio*n*   *disturbance*
it makes her*e*. I am unfortunate in the infirmity, and   *in his head*
dare not tas*k* my weakness with any more.   *burden*

IAGO. What, man! 'tis a night of revels. The gallants
desire it.

CASSIO. Where are they?

IAGO. Here at the door. I pray you, call them in.

CASSIO. I'll do 't, but it dislikes me.   *displeases*

[*Exit.*]

IAGO. If I can fasten but one cup upon him,
With that which he hath drunk tonight already,
He'll be as full of quarrel and offense
As my young mistress' dog. Now, my sick fool Roderigo,
Whom love hath turned almost the wrong side out,
To Desdemona hath tonight caroused   *drunk healths*
Potations pottle-deep—and he's to watch.   *holding two qts.*
Three lads of Cyprus, noble swelling spirits   *full of pride*
That hold their honors in a wary distance,   *sensitively*
The very elements of this warlike isle,   *typical*
                                                           specimens
Have I tonight flustered with flowing cups,
And they watch too. Now, 'mongst this flock of   *are 'on watch'*
    drunkards,
Am I to put our Cassio in some action
That may offend the isle. But here they come.
If consequence do but approve my dream,   *scheme*
My boat sails freely, both with wind and stream.

[*Re-enter* CASSIO, *with* MONTANO *and* GENTLEMEN,
SERVANTS *following with wine.*]

CASSIO. 'Fore God, they have given me a rouse already.   *deep drink*

MONTANO. Good faith, a little one—not past a pint, as
    I am a soldier.

IAGO. Some wine, ho!   [*Sings*]
        And let me the canikin clink, clink,   *drinking pot*
        And let me the canikin clink.
            A soldier's a man,
            Oh, man's life's but a span;   *short*
        Why then let a soldier drink.
Some wine, boys!

CASSIO. 'Fore God, an excellent song.

IAGO. I learned it in England, where indeed they are
most potent in potting. Your Dane, your German, and   *drinking*
your swag-bellied Hollander—Drink, ho!— are nothing   *paunch*
to your English.

CASSIO. Is your Englishman so exquisite in his drinking?

IAGO. Why, he drinks you with facility your Dane
dead drunk. He sweats not to overthrow your Almain.   *has easy work*
                                                           German

He gives your Hollander a vomit ere the next pottle can
be filled.

CASSIO. To the health of our general!

MONTANO. I am for it, Lieutenant, and I'll do you
justice. *keep up with you*

IAGO. O sweet England! [*Sings*]
   King Stephen was a worthy peer,
     His breeches cost him but a crown.
   He held them sixpence all to dear,
     With that he called the tailor lown. *lout, clown*

   He was a wight of high renown,
     And thou art but of low degree.
   'Tis pride that pulls the country down,
     Then take thine auld cloak about thee.
Some wine, ho!

CASSIO. 'Fore God, this is a more exquisite song than
the other.

IAGO. Will you hear 't again?

CASSIO. No, for I hold him to be unworthy of his place
that does those things. Well, God's above all, and there
be souls must be saved, and there be souls must not be
saved.

IAGO. It's true, good Lieutenant.

CASSIO. For mine own part—no offence to the General,
nor any man of quality—I hope to be saved. *of rank*

IAGO. And so do I too, Lieutenant.

CASSIO. Ay, but, by your leave, not before me. The
lieutenant is to be saved before the ancient. Let's have
no more of this, let's to our affairs. God forgive us our
sins! Gentlemen, let's look to our business. Do not
think, gentlemen, I am drunk. This is my ancient, this
is my right hand, and this is my left hand. I am not
drunk now. I can stand well enough, and I speak well
enough.

GENTLEMEN. Excellent well.

CASSIO. Why, very well, then. You must not think
then that I am drunk.

                        [*Exit.*]

MONTANO. To the platform, masters. Come, let's set
watch. *ramparts / mount guard*

IAGO. You see this fellow that is gone before.
He is a soldier fit to stand by Cæsar
And give direction. And do but see his vice.
'Tis to his virtue a just equinox, *exact equal*

The one as long as th' other. 'Tis pity of him.
I fear the trust Othello puts him in
On some odd time of his infirmity
Will shake this island.

MONTANO.   But is he often thus?

IAGO.   'Tis evermore the prologue to his sleep.
He'll watch the horologe a double set,
If drink rock not his cradle.

clock twice round

MONTANO.   It were well
The General were put in mind of it.
Perhaps he sees it not, or his good nature
Prizes the virtue that appears in Cassio
And looks not on his evils. Is not this true?

[*Enter* RODERIGO.]

IAGO [*aside to him*]. How now, Roderigo? I pray
you, after the Lieutenant. Go!

[*Exit* RODERIGO.]

MONTANO. And 'tis great pity that the noble Moor
Should hazard such a place as his own second
With one of an ingraft infirmity.
It were an honest action to say
So to the Moor.

firmly fixed

IAGO.   Not I, for this fair island.
I do love Cassio well, and would do much
        [*Cry* 'Help! Help!' *within.*]
To cure him of this evil—But hark! what noise?

[*Re-enter* CASSIO, *driving in* RODERIGO.]

CASSIO. Zounds! You rogue, you rascal!

MONTANO. What's the matter, Lieutenant?

CASSIO. A knave teach me my duty! I'll beat the knave
into a wicker bottle.

RODERIGO. Beat me?

CASSIO. Dost thou prate, rogue? [*Striking* RODERIGO.]

MONTANO [*staying him*]. Nay, good Lieutenant. I
pray you, sir, hold your hand.

CASSIO. Let me go, sir, or I'll knock you o'er the
mazzard.

slang: head

MONTANO. Come, come, you're drunk.

CASSIO. Drunk!

[*They fight.*]

IAGO [*aside to* RODERIGO]. Away, I say! Go out, and
cry 'A mutiny!'   *a riot, revolt*

[*Exit* RODERIGO.]

Nay, good Lieutenant! God's will, gentlemen!
Help, ho! Lieutenant! Sir Montano! sir!
Help, masters! Here's a goodly watch indeed!
[*A bell rings.*]
Who's that that rings the bell? Diablo, ho!   *the Devil*
The town will rise. God's will! Lieutenant, hold!
You will be shamed for ever.

[*Enter* OTHELLO *and* GENTLEMEN *with weapons.*]

OTHELLO.   What is the matter here?
MONTANO. Zounds! I bleed still. I am hurt to the
death.

[*He faints.*]

OTHELLO. Hold, for your lives!
IAGO. Hold, hold, Lieutenant! Sir Montano! gentle-
men!
Have you forgot all sense of place and duty?
Hold! the General speaks to you. Hold, hold for shame!
OTHELLO. Why, how now, ho! From whence arises
this?
Are we turned Turks, and to ourselves do that
Which Heaven has forbid the Ottomites?
For Christian shame put by this barbarous brawl.
He that stirs next to carve for his own rage   *satisfy himself*
Holds his soul light, he dies upon his motion.   *making a move*
Silence that dreadful bell! It frights the isle
From her propriety. What's the matter, masters?   *out of her senses*
Honest Iago, that looks dead with grieving,
Speak, who began this? On thy love, I charge thee.
IAGO. I do not know. Friends all, but now, even now,
In quarter and in terms like bride and groom   *at peace*
Devesting them for bed—and then, but now,   *undressing*
As if some planet had unwitted men,   *made men mad*
Swords out, and tilting one at other's breast,   *thrusting*
In opposition bloody. I cannot speak
Any beginning to this peevish odds,   *silly quarrel*
And would in action glorious I had lost
These legs that brought me to a part of it!
OTHELLO. How came it, Michael, you were thus
forgot?   *forgot yourself*
CASSIO. I pray you, pardon me, I cannot speak.

OTHELLO. Worthy Montano, you were wont be civi*l*.   *well behaved*
The gravity and stillnes*s* of your youth   *quiet manner*
The world hath noted, and your name is great
In mouths of wisest censur*e*. What's the matter,   *judgment*
That you unlac*e* your reputation thus   *undo, disgrace*
And spend your rich opinio*n* for the name   *reputation*
Of a night-brawler? Give me answer to it.

MONTANO. Worthy Othello, I am hurt to danger.
Your officer, Iago, can inform you—
While I spare speech, which something now offend*s* me—   *hurts*
Of all that I do know. Nor know I aught
By me that's said or done amiss this night,
Unless self-charity be sometimes a vice,   *love of self*
And to defend ourselves it be a sin
When violence assails us.

OTHELLO.   Now, by Heaven,
My blood begins my safer guides to rule,
And passion, having my best judgment collie*d*,   *blackened*
Assays to lead the way. Zounds! If I stir,
Or do but lift this arm, the best of you
Shall sink in my rebuke. Give me to know
How this foul rou*t* began, who set it on,   *riot*
And he that is approve*d* in this offense,   *proved guilty*
Though he had twinned with me, both at a birth,
Shall lose me. What! In a town of war,
Yet wild, the people's hearts brimful of fear,
To manag*e* private and domestic quarrels   *carry on*
In night, and on the cour*t* and guar*d* of safety!   *on guard duty*
'Tis monstrous. Iago, who began 't?

MONTANO. If partially affine*d*, or leagued in office,   *tied by affection*
Thou dost deliver more or less than truth,
Thou art no soldier.

IAGO.   Touch me not so near.
I had rather have this tongue cut from my mouth
Than it should do offense to Michael Cassio.
Yet I persuade myself, to speak the truth
Shall nothing wrong him. Thus it is, General.
Montano and myself being in speech,
There comes a fellow crying out for help,
And Cassio following him with determined sword
To execute upon him. Sir, this gentleman
Steps in to Cassio, and entreats hi*s* pause.   *him to pause*
Myself the crying fellow did pursue,
Lest by his clamor—as it so fell out—
The town might fall in fright. He, swift of foot,

Outran my purpose, and I returned the rather   *the sooner*
For that I heard the clink and fall of swords
And Cassio high in oath, which till tonight
I ne'er might say before. When I came back—
For this was brief—I found them close together,
At blow and thrust, even as again they were
When you yourself did part them.
More of this matter can I not report,
But men are men, the best sometimes forget.
Though Cassio did some little wrong to him,   *to Montano*
As men in rage strike those that wish them best,
Yet surely Cassio, I believe, received
From him that fled some strange indignity,
Which patience could not pass.
    OTHELLO.   I know, Iago,
Thy honesty and love doth mince this matter,
Making it light to Cassio. Cassio, I love thee,
But never more be officer of mine—

    [*Enter* DESDEMONA, *with others.*]

Look, if my gentle love be not raised up!—
[*To* CASSIO] I'll make thee an example.
    DESDEMONA.   What's the matter?
    OTHELLO. All's well now, sweeting. Come away to   *sweetheart*
    bed.—
Sir, for your hurts, myself will be your surgeon.
Lead him off.
                      [MONTANO *is led off.*]

Iago, look with care about the town,
And silence those whom this vile brawl distracted.
Come, Desdemona. 'Tis the soldiers' life
To have their balmy slumbers waked with strife.
               [*Exeunt all but* IAGO *and* CASSIO.]

    IAGO. What, are you hurt, Lieutenant?
    CASSIO. Ay, past all surgery.
    IAGO. Marry, God forbid!
    CASSIO. Reputation, reputation, reputation! Oh, I have
lost my reputation. I have lost the immortal part of myself, and what remains is bestial. My reputation, Iago,
my reputation!
    IAGO. As I am an honest man, I thought you had re-
ceived some bodily wound. There is more sense in that
than in reputation. Reputation is an idle and most false

imposition, oft got without merit and lost without deserving. You have lost no reputation at all unless you repute yourself such a loser. What, man! There are ways to recover the General again. You are but now cast in his mood, a punishment more in policy than in malice—even so as one would beat his offenseless dog to affright an imperious lion. Sue to him again, and he's yours.

imposed by others

regain favor dismissed

plead with

CASSIO. I will rather sue to be despised than to deceive so good a commander with so slight, so drunken, and so indiscreet an officer. Drunk! and speak parrot! and squabble, swagger, swear, and discourse fustian with one's own shadow! O thou invisible spirit of wine, if thou hast no name to be known by, let us call thee devil!

babble nonsense

IAGO. What was he that you followed with your sword? What had he done to you?

CASSIO. I know not.

IAGO. Is 't possible?

CASSIO. I remember a mass of things, but nothing distinctly—a quarrel, but nothing wherefore. O God, that men should put an enemy in their mouths to steal away their brains! That we should, with joy, revel, pleasure, and applause, transform ourselves into beasts!

IAGO. Why, but you are now well enough. How came you thus recovered?

CASSIO. It hath pleased the devil drunkenness to give place to the devil wrath. One unperfectness shows me another, to make me frankly despise myself.

IAGO. Come, you are too severe a moraler. As the time, the place, and the condition of this country stands, I could heartily wish this had not so befallen. But since it is as it is, mend it for your own good.

moralizer

CASSIO. I will ask him for my place again—he shall tell me I am a drunkard! Had I as many mouths as Hydra, such an answer would stop them all. To be now a sensible man, by and by a fool, and presently a beast! Oh, strange! Every inordinate cup is unblessed and the ingredient is a devil.

hundred-headed

excessive

IAGO. Come, come. Good wine is a good familiar creature if it be well used. Exclaim no more against it. And, good Lieutenant, I think you think I love you.

hope, believe

CASSIO. I have well approved it, sir. I drunk!

IAGO. You or any man living may be drunk at some time. I'll tell you what you shall do. Our General's wife is now the general. I may say so in this respect, for that he has devoted and given up himself to the contemplation,

mark, and denotement of her parts and graces. Confess *observation*
yourself freely to her, importune her help to put you in
your place again. She is of so free, so kind, so apt, so *ready*
blessed a disposition, that she holds it a vice in her goodness not to do more than she is requested. This broken
joint between you and her husband entreat her to splinter, *put in splints*
and my fortunes against any lay worth naming, this crack *bet*
of your love shall grow stronger than it was before.

CASSIO. You advise me well.

IAGO. I protest, in the sincerity of love and honest
kindness.

CASSIO. I think it freely, and betimes in the morning
will I beseech the virtuous Desdemona to undertake for
me. I am desperate of my fortunes if they check me here. *future*

IAGO. You are in the right. Good night, Lieutenant,
I must to the watch.

CASSIO. Good night, honest Iago.

[*Exit* CASSIO.]

IAGO. And what's he, then, that says I play the villain,
When this advice is free I give and honest,
Probal to thinking and indeed the course *probable*
To win the Moor again? For 'tis most easy
Th' inclining Desdemona to subdue
In any honest suit. She's framed as fruitful *made bountiful*
As the free elements. And then for her *the air*
To win the Moor—were 't to renounce his baptism,
All seals and symbols of redeemèd sin—
His soul is so enfettered to her love,
That she may make, unmake, do what she list,
Even as her appetite shall play the god
With his weak function. How am I, then, a villain *qualities*
To counsel Cassio to this parallel course
Directly to his good? Divinity of Hell!
When devils will their blackest sins put on, *instigate*
They do suggest at first with heavenly shows, *seduce*
As I do now. For while this honest fool
Plies Desdemona to repair his fortunes, *urges*
And she for him pleads strongly to the Moor,
I'll pour this pestilence into his ear *Othello's*
That she repeals him for her body's lust. *wants his recall*
And, by how much she strives to do him good,
She shall undo her credit with the Moor.
So will I turn her virtue into pitch,
And out of her own goodness make the net

That shall enmesh them all.

    [*Enter* RODERIGO.]

                How now, Roderigo?

    RODERIGO. I do follow here in the chase, not like a
hound that hunts, but one that fill*s* up the cr*y*. My   *for his bark only*
money is almost spent. I have been tonight exceedingly
well cudgelled. And I think the issue will be, I shall have
so much experience for my pains, and so, with no money
at all and a little more wit, return again to Venice.

    IAGO. How poor are they that have not patience!
What wound did ever heal but by degrees?
Thou know'st we work by wit and not by witchcraft,
And wit depends on dilatory Time.
Does't not go well? Cassio has beaten thee,
And thou by that small hurt hast cashier*ed* Cassio.   *had discharged*
Though other things grow fair against the sun,
Yet fruits that blossom first will first be ripe.
Content thyself awhile. By the mass, 'tis morning.
Pleasure and action make the hours seem short.
Retire thee, go where thou art billeted.
Away, I say. Thou shalt know more hereafter.
Nay, get thee gone.

                     [*Exit* RODERIGO.]

        Two things are to be done:
My wife must mov*e* for Cassio to her mistress—   *urge support*
I'll set her on—
Myself the while to draw the Moor apart,
And bring him jum*p* when he may Cassio find   *suddenly just*
Soliciting his wife. Ay, that's the way.
Dull not devi*ce* by coldness and delay.   *the plan*

                       [*Exit.*]

ACT THREE

SCENE I. *Before the Citadel*.

    [*Enter* CASSIO *with* MUSICIANS.]

    CASSIO. Masters, play here, I will conten*t* your pains.   *pay you for*
Something that's brief, and bid 'Good morrow, General.'

    [*They play. Enter the* CLOWN.]

    CLOWN. Why, masters, have your instruments been in
Naple*s*, that they speak i' th' nose thus?   *notably venereal*

MUSICIAN. How, sir, how?

CLOWN. Are these, I pray, called wind instruments?

MUSICIAN. Ay, marry, are they, sir.

CLOWN. Oh, thereby hangs a tail.

MUSICIAN. Whereby hangs a tale, sir?

CLOWN. Marry, sir, by many a wind instrument that I know. But, masters, here's money for you. And the General so likes your music that he desires you, for love's sake, to make no more noise with it.

MUSICIAN. Well, sir, we will not.

CLOWN. If you have any music that may not be heard, to 't again. But, as they say, to hear music the General does not greatly care.

MUSICIAN. We have none such, sir.

CLOWN. Then put up your pipes in your bag, for I'll away. Go, vanish into air, away!

                              [*Exeunt* MUSICIANS.]

CASSIO. Dost thou hear, my honest friend?

CLOWN. No, I hear not your honest friend, I hear you.

CASSIO. Prithee, kee*p* up thy quillet*s*. There's a poor piece of gold for thee. If the gentlewoman that attends the General's wife be stirring, tell her there's one Cassio entreats her a little favor of speech. Wilt thou do this?

stop your gags

CLOWN. She is stirring, sir. If she will stir hither, I shall seem to notify unto her.

CASSIO. Do, good my friend.

                              [*Exit* CLOWN.]

[*Enter* IAGO.]

                    In happy tim*e*, Iago.   *well met*

IAGO. You have not been a-bed, then?

CASSIO. Why, no. The day had broke
Before we parted. I have made bold, Iago,
To send in to your wife. My suit to her
Is that she will to virtuous Desdemona
Procure me some access.

IAGO.   I'll send her to you presentl*y*,   *at once*
And I'll devise a mean to draw the Moor
Out of the way, that your converse and business
May be more free.

CASSIO. I humbly thank you for 't.

                              [*Exit* IAGO.]

                    I never knew
A Florentin*e* more kind and honest.

*even one of my
own countrymen*

[Enter EMILIA.]

EMILIA. Good morrow, good Lieutenant. I am sorry
or your displeasure, but all will soon be well.   *misfortune*
The General and his wife are talking of it,
And she speaks for you stoutly. The Moor replies
That he you hurt is of great fame in Cyprus
And great affinity, and that in wholesome wisdom   *important kin*
He might not but refuse you. But he protests he loves *could*
        you,
And needs no other suitor but his likings   *affection*
To take the safest occasion by the front   *forelock*
To bring you in again.
    CASSIO.   Yet, I beseech you,
If you think fit or that it may be done,
Give me advantage of some brief discourse
With Desdemona alone.
    EMILIA.   Pray you, come in.
I will bestow you where you shall have time
To speak your bosom freely.   *inner thoughts*
    CASSIO.   I am much bound to you.
                                        [Exeunt.]

SCENE II. *A Room in the Citadel.*

[Enter OTHELLO, IAGO, *and other* GENTLEMEN.]

OTHELLO. These letters give, Iago, to the pilot,
And by him do my duties to the Senate.   *send compli-*
That done, I will be walking on the works.   *ments*
Repair there to me.   *fortifications*
    IAGO.   Well, my good lord, I'll do 't.
    OTHELLO. This fortification, gentlemen, shall we see 't?
    GENTLEMEN. We wait upon your lordship.
                                        [Exeunt.]

SCENE III. *The garden of the Citadel.*

[Enter DESDEMONA, CASSIO, *and* EMILIA.]

DESDEMONA. Be thou assured, good Cassio, I will do
All my abilities in thy behalf.
    EMILIA. Good madam, do. I know it grieves my hus-
        band
As if the case were his.
    DESDEMONA. Oh, that's an honest fellow. Do not
        doubt, Cassio,

But I will have my lord and you again
As friendly as you were.

    CASSIO.   Bounteous madam,
Whatever shall become of Michael Cassio,
He's never anything but your true servant.

    DESDEMONA. Oh, sir, I thank you. You do love my
        lord.
You have known him long, and be you well assured
He shall in strangeness stand no farther off   *aloofness*
Than in a politic distance.   *required by*
                                                policy

    CASSIO.   Ay, but, lady,
That policy may either last so long,
Or feed upon such nice and waterish diet,   *be fed by trifles*
Or breed itself so out of circumstances,   *gain new life*
That, I being absent and my place supplied,   *filled by another*
My general will forget my love and service.

    DESDEMONA. Do not doubt that. Before Emilia here   *fear*
I give thee warrant of thy place. Assure thee,   *position*
If I do vow a friendship, I'll perform it
To the last article. My lord shall never rest,
I'll watch him tame, and talk him out of patience.   *keep him awake,*
                                                  as hawk-taming
His bed shall seem a school, his board a shrift.   *confessional*
I'll intermingle everything he does
With Cassio's suit. Therefore be merry, Cassio,
For thy solicitor shall rather die
Than give thy cause away.

        [Enter OTHELLO *and* IAGO *at a distance.]*

    EMILIA. Madam, here comes my lord.
    CASSIO. Madam, I'll take my leave.
    DESDEMONA. Why, stay, and hear me speak.
    CASSIO. Madam, not now. I am very ill at ease,
Unfit for mine own purposes.   *to plead my case*
    DESDEMONA. Well, do your discretion.

                          [Exit CASSIO.]

    IAGO. Ha! I like not that.
    OTHELLO.   What dost thou say?
    IAGO. Nothing, my lord; or if—I know not what.
    OTHELLO. Was not that Cassio parted from my wife?
    IAGO. Cassio, my lord? No, sure, I cannot think it,
That he would steal away so guilty-like,
Seeing you coming.
    OTHELLO.   I do believe 'twas he.

DESDEMONA. How now, my lord!
I have been talking with a suitor here.
A man that languishes in your displeasure.
OTHELLO. Who is 't you mean?
DESDEMONA. Why, your lieutenant, Cassio. Good my
lord,
If I have any grace or power to move you,
His present reconciliation take.   *accept his apology*
For if he be not one that truly loves you,
That errs in ignorance and not in cunning,   *intentionally*
I have no judgment in an honest face.
I prithee call him back.
OTHELLO.   Went he hence now?
DESDEMONA. Yes, faith, so humbled
That he has left part of his griefs with me.
I suffer with him. Good love, call him back.
OTHELLO. Not now, sweet Desdemon. Some other
time.
DESDEMONA. But shall 't be shortly?
OTHELLO.   The sooner, sweet, for you.
DESDEMONA. Shall 't be tonight at supper?
OTHELLO.   No, not tonight.
DESDEMONA. Tomorrow dinner then?
OTHELLO.   I shall not dine at home.
I meet the captains at the citadel.
DESDEMONA. Why, then, tomorrow night, or Tuesday
morn—
On Tuesday noon, or night, on Wednesday morn.
I prithee name the time, but let it not
Exceed three days. In faith, he's penitent,
And yet his trespass, in our common reason—   *common sense*
Save that they say the wars must make examples
Out of their best—is not almost a fault   *hardly*
To incur a private check. When shall he come?   *rebuke*
Tell me, Othello. I wonder in my soul,
What you could ask me that I should deny
Or stand so mammering on. What! Michael Cassio,   *hesitating*
That came a-wooing with you, and so many a time,
When I have spoke of you dispraisingly,
Hath ta'en your part—to have so much to do
To bring him in! By 'r Lady, I could do much—   *into your favor*
OTHELLO. Prithee, no more! Let him come when he
will.
I will deny thee nothing.
DESDEMONA.   Why, this is not a boon.   *great favor*

'Tis as I should entreat you wear your gloves,
Or feed on nourishing dishes, or keep you warm,
Or sue to you to do a peculia*r* profit   *particular*
To your own person. Nay, when I have a suit
Wherein I mean to touch your love indeed,
It shall be full of poi*s*e and difficulty,   *weight*
And fearfu*l* to be granted.   *hard*
    OTHELLO.   I will deny thee nothing.
Whereon, I do beseech thee, grant me this,
To leave me but a little to myself.
    DESDEMONA.   Shall I deny you? No. Farewell, my
lord.
    OTHELLO.   Farewell, my Desdemona. I'll come to thee
straight.
    DESDEMONA.   Emilia, come. Be it a*s* your fancies   *as you please*
        teach yo*u*.
Whate'er you be, I am obedient.
                    [*Exeunt* DESDEMONA *and* EMILIA.]

    OTHELLO.   Excellent wretch! Perdition catch my soul
But I do love thee! and when I love thee not,
Chao*s* is come agai*n*.   *as before Crea-*
    IAGO.   My noble lord—   *tion*
    OTHELLO.   What dost thou say, Iago?
    IAGO.   Did Michael Cassio, when you wooed my lady,
Know of your love?
    OTHELLO.   He did, from first to last. Why dost thou
ask?
    IAGO.   But for a satisfaction of my thought.
No further harm.
    OTHELLO.   Why of thy thought, Iago?
    IAGO.   I did not think he had been acquainted with her.
    OTHELLO.   Oh yes, and went between us very oft.
    IAGO.   Indeed?
    OTHELLO.   Indeed? Ay, indeed. Discern'st thou aught
        in that?
Is he not honest?
    IAGO.   Honest, my lord?
    OTHELLO.   Honest! Ay, honest.
    IAGO.   My lord, for aught I know.
    OTHELLO.   What dost thou think?
    IAGO.   Think, my lord?
    OTHELLO.   Think, my lord! By Heaven, he echoes me
As if there were some monster in his thought
Too hideous to be shown. Thou didst mean something.

I heard thee say but now, thou lik'st not that
When Cassio left my wife. What didst not like?
And when I told thee he was of my counsel
In my whole course of wooing, thou criedst, 'Indeed?'
And didst contract and purse thy brow together
As if thou then hadst shut up in thy brain
Some horrible conceit. If thou dost love me,   *notion*
Show me thy thought.

IAGO.   My lord, you know I love you.

OTHELLO.   I think thou dost,
And, for I know thou'rt full of love and honesty   *because*
And weigh'st thy words before thou giv'st them breath,
Therefore these stops of thine fright me the more.
For such things in a false disloyal knave
Are tricks of custom, but in a man that's just   *customary*
They are close delations, working from the heart   *secret accusa-*
That passion cannot rule.   *tions*

IAGO.   For Michael Cassio,
I dare be sworn I think that he is honest.

OTHELLO.   I think so too.

IAGO.   Men should be what they seem,
Or those that be not, would they might seem none!   *not honest*

OTHELLO.   Certain, men should be what they seem.

IAGO.   Why then, I think Cassio's an honest man.

OTHELLO.   Nay, yet there's more in this.
I prithee speak to me as to thy thinkings
As thou dost ruminate, and give thy worst of thoughts
The worst of words.

IAGO.   Good my lord, pardon me.
Though I am bound to every act of duty,
I am not bound to that all slaves are free to—   *to do that which*
Utter my thoughts? Why, say they are vile and false,   *. . . to do*
As where's that palace whereinto foul things
Sometimes intrude not? Who has a breast so pure
But some uncleanly apprehensions
Keep leets and law-days, and in session sit   *court days*
With meditations lawful?

OTHELLO.   Thou dost conspire against thy friend, Iago,
If thou but think'st him wronged, and mak'st his ear
A stranger to thy thoughts.

IAGO.   I do beseech you,
Though I perchance am vicious in my guess—   *wrong*
As, I confess, it is my nature's plague
To spy into abuses, and oft my jealousy   *suspicion*
Shapes faults that are not—I entreat you then,

From one that so imperfectly conjects,   *conjectures*
You'd take no notice nor build yourself a trouble
Out of my scattering and unsure observance.   *casual . . .*
It were not for your quiet nor your good,   *observation*
Nor for my manhood, honesty, or wisdom,
To let you know my thoughts.
    OTHELLO.   What dost thou mean?
    IAGO.   Good name in man, and woman, dear my lord,
Is the immediate jewel of our souls.   *most precious*
Who steals my purse steals trash—'tis something, nothing,
'Twas mine, 'tis his, and has been slave to thousands.
But he that filches from me my good name
Robs me of that which not enriches him
And makes me poor indeed.
    OTHELLO. By Heaven, I'll know thy thought.
    IAGO.   You cannot, if my heart were in your hand,
Nor shall not, whilst 'tis in my custody.
    OTHELLO. Ha!
    IAGO.   Oh, beware, my lord, of jealousy!
It is the green-eyed monster which doth mock   *makes sport of*
The meat it feeds on. That cuckold lives in bliss   *i.e., the victim*
Who, certain of his fate, loves not his wronger.   *wronged*
But, oh, what damnèd minutes tells he o'er   *husband*
Who dotes, yet doubts, suspects, yet strongly loves!
    OTHELLO. O misery!
    IAGO.   Poor and content is rich, and rich enough,
But riches fineless is as poor as winter   *limitless*
To him that ever fears he shall be poor.
Good God, the souls of all my tribe defend
From jealousy!
    OTHELLO. Why, why is this?
Think'st thou I'd make a life of jealousy,
To follow still the changes of the moon
With fresh suspicions? No, to be once in doubt
Is once to be resolved. Exchange me for a goat   *at once . . .*
When I shall turn the business of my soul   *determined*
To such exsufflicate and blown surmises,   *inflated*
Matching thy inference. 'Tis not to make me jealous
To say my wife is fair, feeds well, loves company,
Is free of speech, sings, plays, and dances well.
Where virtue is, these are more virtuous.
Nor from mine own weak merits will I draw
The smallest fear or doubt of her revolt,   *faithlessness*
For she had eyes and chose me. No, Iago.
I'll see before I doubt, when I doubt, prove,

And, on the proof, there is no more but this—
Away at once with love or jealousy!

IAGO.   I am glad of this, for now I shall have reason
To show the love and duty that I bear you
With franker spirit.   Therefore, as I am bound,   *duty bound*
Receive it from me.   I speak not yet of proof.
Look to your wife.   Observe her well with Cassio.
Wear your eye thus, not jealous nor secure.   *overconfident*
I would not have your free and noble nature
Out of self-bounty be abused.   Look to 't!   *natural goodness*
I know our country disposition well.
In Venice they do let God see the pranks   *notable for vice*
They dare not show their husbands.   Their best con-
      science
Is not to leave 't undone, but keep 't unknown.

OTHELLO.   Dost thou say so?

IAGO.   She did deceive her father, marrying you.
And when she seemed to shake and fear your looks,
She loved them most.

OTHELLO.   And so she did.

IAGO.   Why, go to, then.
She that so young could give out such a seeming
To seel her father's eyes up close as oak—   *blind*
He thought 'twas witchcraft—but I am much to blame.
I humbly do beseech you of your pardon
For too much loving you.

OTHELLO.   I am bound to thee forever.

IAGO.   I see this hath a little dashed your spirits.

OTHELLO.   Not a jot, not a jot.

IAGO.   I' faith, I fear it has.
I hope you will consider what is spoke
Comes from my love.   But I do see you're moved.
I am to pray you not to strain my speech
To grosser issues nor to larger reach   *conclusions . . .*
Than to suspicion.   *scope*

OTHELLO.   I will not.

IAGO.   Should you do so, my lord,
My speech should fall into such vile success   *result*
As my thoughts aim not at.   Cassio's my trusty friend—
My lord, I see you're moved.

OTHELLO.   No, not much moved.
I do not think but Desdemona's honest.   *chaste*

IAGO.   Long live she so!   And long live you to think so!

OTHELLO.   And, yet, how nature erring from itself—

IAGO.   Ay, there's the point.   As—to be bold with you—

Not to affect many proposèd matches
favor . . .
marriage offers
Of her own clime, complexion, and degree,
Whereto, we see, in all things nature tends—   *desire . . .*
lustful
Foh! one may smell in such a will most rank,
Foul disproportion, thoughts unnatural.
But pardon me, I do not in position   *in affirmation*
Distinctly speak of her, though I may fear   *particularly*
Her will, recoiling to her better judgment,   *desire, adjusting*
May fall to match you with her country forms   *begin comparing*
Venetian types
And happily repent.   *perhaps*
    OTHELLO.   Farewell, farewell.
If more thou dost perceive, let me know more.
Set on thy wife to observe. Leave me, Iago.
    IAGO. My lord, I take my leave.   [*Going.*]

    OTHELLO. Why did I marry? This honest creature,
      doubtless,
Sees and knows more, much more, than he unfolds.

    IAGO [*returning*]. My lord, I would I might entreat
      your honor
To scan this thing no further. Leave it to time.
Though it be fit that Cassio have his place—
For sure he fills it up with great ability—
Yet if you please to hold him off awhile,
You shall by that perceive him and his means.
Note if your lady strain his entertainment   *urges you to re-*
ceive him
With any strong or vehement importunity.
Much will be seen in that. In the meantime,
Let me be thought too busy in my fears—   *too busybody*
As worthy cause I have to fear I am—
And hold her free, I do beseech your Honor.   *guiltless*
    OTHELLO. Fear not my government.   *self-control*
    IAGO. I once more take my leave.
                          [*Exit.*]

    OTHELLO. This fellow's of exceeding honesty,
And knows all qualities, with a learnèd spirit,   *different types*
Of human dealing. If I do prove her haggard,   *From . . . a*
wild hawk
Though that her jesses were my dear heartstrings,   *leg-straps*
I'd whistle her off and let her down the wind   *release, fly away*
To prey at fortune. Haply, for I am black,   *Perhaps*
And have not those soft parts of conversation   *social graces*
That chamberers have, or for I am declined   *court gallants*
Into the vale of years—yet that's not much—
She's gone, I am abused, and my relief   *cheated*

Must be to loathe her. Oh, curse of marriage!
That we can call these delicate creatures ours,
And not their appetites! I had rather be a toad
And live upon the vapor of a dungeon
Than keep a corner in the thing I love
For others' uses. Yet, 'tis the plague of great ones,
Prerogative*d* are they less than the base.　　　　　*privileged*
'Tis destiny unshunnable, like death.
Even then this forkèd plagu*e* is fated to us　　　　*cuckold's horns*
When we do quicke*n*.　　　　　　　　　　　　*as soon as born*
　　　　　　　　Look, where she comes!
If she be false, oh, then Heaven mocks itself.
I'll not believe 't.

　　　[*Enter* DESDEMONA *and* EMILIA.]

DESDEMONA.　How now, my dear Othello?
Your dinner and the generou*s* islanders　　　　　*noble*
By you invited do atten*d* your presence.　　　　　*await*
　　OTHELLO.　I am to blame.
　　DESDEMONA.　　　　　　　Why is your speech so faint?
Are you not well?
　　OTHELLO.　I have a pain upon my forehead here.
　　DESDEMONA.　Faith, that's with watchin*g*, 'twill away　*lack of sleep*
　　　again.
Let me but bind it hard, within this hour
It will be well.
　　OTHELLO.　　Your napki*n* is too little.　　　　*handkerchief*
　　　[*He puts the handkerchief from him, and it drops.*]
Let it alone. Come, I'll go in with you.
　　DESDEMONA.　I am very sorry that you are not well.
　　　　　　　　[*Exeunt* OTHELLO *and* DESDEMONA.]

EMILIA.　I am glad I have found this napkin.
This was her first remembrance from the Moor.
My waywar*d* husband hath a hundred times　　　*unaccountable*
Wooed me to steal it, but she so loves the token,
For he conjure*d* her she should ever keep it,　　　*made her swear*
That she reserves it evermore about her
To kiss and talk to. I'll have the wor*k* ta'en ou*t*　　*pattern copied*
And give 't Iago. What he will do with it
Heaven knows, not I.
I nothing know, but for his fantas*y*—　　　　　*whim*

　　　[*Re-enter* IAGO.]

IAGO.　How now! What do you here alone?

EMILIA.   Do not you chide. I have a thing for you.

IAGO.   A thing for me? It is a common thing—

EMILIA.   Ha?

IAGO.   To have a foolish wife.

EMILIA.   Oh, is that all? What will you give me now
For that same handkerchief?

IAGO.   What handkerchief?

EMILIA.   What handkerchief!
Why, that the Moor first gave to Desdemona,
That which so often you did bid me steal.

IAGO.   Hast stol'n it from her?

EMILIA.   No, faith. She let it drop by negligence,
And, to th' advantage, I being here took 't up.   *opportunely*
Look, here it is.

IAGO.   A good wench! Give it me.

EMILIA.   What will you do with 't, that you have been
    so earnest
To have me filch it?

IAGO [*snatching it*].   Why, what's that to you?

EMILIA.   If it be not for some purpose of import,
Give 't me again. Poor lady, she'll run mad
When she shall lack it.

IAGO.   Be not acknown on 't. I have use for it.   *Know noth-*
Go, leave me.   *ing of it*

                                    [*Exit* EMILIA.]

I will in Cassio's lodging lose this napkin,
And let him find it. Trifles light as air
Are to the jealous confirmations strong
As proofs of Holy Writ. This may do something.
The Moor already changes with my poison.
Dangerous conceits are in their natures poisons,
Which at the first are scarce found to distaste,   *unpleasant*
But, with a little act upon the blood,   *action*
Burn like the mines of sulphur. I did say so.
Look, where he comes!   *Just as I said!*

    [*Enter* OTHELLO.]

                    Not poppy, nor mandragora,   *opium . . .*
Nor all the drowsy syrups of the world   *a drug*
Shall ever medicine thee to that sweet sleep
Which thou ow'dst yesterday.   *owned, possesse*

OTHELLO.   Ha! ha! False to me?

IAGO.   Why, how now, General! No more of that.

OTHELLO.   Avaunt! Be gone! Thou hast set me on   *Be off . . .*
    the rack.   *torture*

I swear 'tis better to be much abused
Than but to know 't a little.

    IAGO. How now, my lord?

    OTHELLO. What sense had I of her stol'n hours of lust?   *idea, feeling*
I saw 't not, thought it not, it harmed not me.
I slept the next night well, was free and merry.
I found not Cassio's kisses on her lips.
He that is robbed, not wanting what is stol'n,   *missing*
Let him not know 't and he's not robbed at all.

    IAGO. I am sorry to hear this.

    OTHELLO. I had been happy if the general camp,
Pioneers and all, had tasted her sweet body,   *trench diggers*
So I had nothing known. Oh, now forever
Farewell the tranquil mind! Farewell content!
Farewell the plumèd troops and the big wars
That make ambition virtue! Oh, farewell!
Farewell the neighing steed and the shrill trump,
The spirit-stirring drum, the ear-piercing fife,
The royal banner, and all quality,   *military rank*
Pride, pomp, and circumstance of glorious war!   *ceremony*
And, O ye mortal engines, whose rude throats   *deadly cannon*
The' immortal Jove's great clamor counterfeit,   *thunder imitate*
Farewell! Othello's occupation's gone!

    IAGO. Is 't possible, my lord?

    OTHELLO. Villain, be sure thou prove my love a whore,
Be sure of it! Give me the ocular proof.
Or by the worth of man's eternal soul,
Thou hadst been better have been born a dog
Than answer my waked wrath.

    IAGO. Is 't come to this?

    OTHELLO. Make me to see 't, or, at the least, so prove it
That the probation bear no hinge nor loop   *proof may have*
To hang a doubt on, or woe upon thy life!

    IAGO. My noble lord—

    OTHELLO. If thou dost slander her and torture me,
Never pray more. Abandon all remorse.   *pity*
On horror's head horrors accumulate,
Do deeds to make Heaven weep, all earth amazed;
For nothing canst thou to damnation add
Greater than that.

    IAGO. O grace! O Heaven defend me!
Are you a man? Have you a soul or sense?
God be wi' you! Take mine office. O wretched fool!
That liv'st to make thine honesty a vice.
O monstrous world! Take note, take note, O world,

To be direct and honest is not safe.
I thank you for this profi*t*, and from hence   *lesson*
I'll love no friend, sit*h* love breeds such offense.   *since*
    OTHELLO.   Nay, stay. Thou shouldst be honest.
    IAGO.   I should be wise, for honesty's a fool
And loses that it works for.
    OTHELLO.   By the world,
I think my wife be honest, and think she is not.
I think that thou art just, and think thou art not.
I'll have some proof. Her name, that was as fresh
As Dian*'s* visage, is now begrimed and black   *goddess of*
As mine own face. If there be cords or knives,   *chastity*
Poison or fire or suffocating streams,
I'll not endure it. Would I were satisfied!
    IAGO.   I see, sir, you are eaten up with passion.
I do repent me that I pu*t* it to you.   *confided in you*
You would be satisfied?
    OTHELLO.   Would? Nay, I will!
    IAGO.   And may—but how? How satisfied, my lord?
Would you, the superviso*r*, grossly gape on,   *over-seer*
Behold her topped?
    OTHELLO.   Death and damnation! Oh!
    IAGO.   It were a tedious difficulty, I think,
To bring them to that prospec*t*. Damn them, then,   *situation*
If ever mortal eyes do see them bolste*r*   *in bed together*
More than their own! What then? how then?
What shall I say? Where's satisfaction?
It is impossible you should see this,
Were they as prim*e* as goats, as hot as monkeys,   *lustful*
As sal*t* as wolves in prid*e*, and fools as gross   *lecherous . . .*
As ignorance made drunk. But yet, I say,   *in heat*
If imputatio*n* and strong circumstances,   *probability*
Which lead directly to the door of truth,
Will give you satisfaction, you may have 't.
    OTHELLO.   Give me a living reason she's disloyal.   *tangible*
    IAGO.   I do not like the office.
But sith I am entered in this cause so far—
Prick*'d* to 't by foolish honesty and love—   *spurred on*
I will go on. I lay with Cassio lately,
And, being troubled with a raging tooth,
I could not sleep.
There are a kind of men so loose of soul
That in their sleeps will mutter their affairs.
One of this kind is Cassio.
In sleep I heard him say, 'Sweet Desdemona,

Let us be wary, let us hide our loves!'
And then, sir, would he grip*e* and wring my hand,   *grip*
Cry out 'Sweet creature!' and then kiss me hard,
As if he plucked up kisses by the roots
That grew upon my lips. Then laid his leg
Over my thigh, and sighed and kissed, and then
Cried, 'Cursèd fate, that gave thee to the Moor!'

OTHELLO. O monstrous! monstrous!

IAGO.   Nay, this was but his dream.

OTHELLO. But this denoted a foregon*e* conclusio*n*.   *earlier experi-*
                                      ence

IAGO. 'Tis a shrew*d* doub*t*, though it be but a dream. *strong suspicion*
And this may help to thicken other proofs
That do demónstrate thinly.

OTHELLO.   I'll tear her all to pieces!

IAGO. Nay, but be wise. Yet we see nothing done.
She may be honest yet. Tell me but this:
Have you not sometimes seen a handkerchief
Spotte*d* with strawberries in your wife's hand?   *embroidered*

OTHELLO. I gave her such a one. 'Twas my first gift.

IAGO. I know not that, but such a handkerchief—
I am sure it was your wife's—did I today
See Cassio wipe his beard with.

OTHELLO.   If 't be that—

IAGO. If it be that, or any that was hers,
It speaks against her with the other proofs.

OTHELLO. Oh, that the slav*e* had forty thousand lives! *e.g., Cassio*
One is too poor, too weak, for my revenge.
Now do I see 'tis true. Look here, Iago,
All my fond love thus do I blow to heaven—
'Tis gone.
Arise, black Vengeance, from thy hollo*w* cell!   *underground*
Yield up, O Love, thy crown and hearte*d* throne   *in my heart*
To tyrannous hate! Swell, bosom, with thy fraug*ht*, *freight, load*
For 'tis of aspics' tongues!   *asp, poison*
                                                 snake

IAGO.   Pray, be conten*t*.   *be calm*

OTHELLO. O blood! Iago, blood!

IAGO. Patience, I say. Your mind, perhaps, may
   change.

OTHELLO. Never Iago. Like to the Ponti*c* sea,   *Black Sea*
Whose icy current and compulsive course
Ne'er feels retiring ebb, but keeps due on
To the Proponti*c* and the Hellespont,   *Sea of Marmora*
Even so my bloody thoughts, with violent pace,
Shall ne'er look back, ne'er ebb to humble love,
Till that a capabl*e* and wide revenge   *comprehensive*

Swallow them up.   [*He kneels.*]
                    Now, by yond marble heaven,   *streaked sky*
In the due reverence of a sacred vow
I here engage my words.
    IAGO.   Do not rise yet. [*Kneels.*]
Witness, you ever-burning lights above,
You elements that clip us round about!   *embrace*
Witness that here Iago doth give up
The execution of his wit, hands, heart,   *actions*
To wronged Othello's service! Let him command,
And to obey shall be in me remorse,   *an obligation*
What bloody work soever.

    [*They rise.*]

    OTHELLO.   I greet thy love,
Not with vain thanks, but with acceptance bounteous,
And will upon the instant put thee to 't.   *to the test*
Within these three days let me hear thee say
That Cassio's not alive.
    IAGO. My friend is dead. 'Tis done as you request.
But let her live.
    OTHELLO. Damn her, lewd minx! Oh, damn her!
Come, go with me apart. I will withdraw
To furnish me with some swift means of death
For the fair devil.—Now art thou my lieutenant.
    IAGO. I am your own forever.
                                        [*Exeunt.*]

SCENE IV. *Before the Citadel.*

[*Enter* DESDEMONA, EMILIA, *and the* CLOWN.]

    DESDEMONA. Do you know, sirrah, where Lieutenant   *lodges*
Cassio lies?
    CLOWN. I dare not say he lies anywhere.
    DESDEMONA. Why, man?
    CLOWN. He is a soldier, and for one to say a soldier
lies is stabbing.
    DESDEMONA. Go to! Where lodges he?
    CLOWN. To tell you where he lodges is to tell you
where I lie.
    DESDEMONA. Can anything be made of this?
    CLOWN. I know not where he lodges, and for me to
devise a lodging, and say he lies here or he lies there,
were to lie in mine own throat.

DESDEMONA. Can you inquire him out, and be edified *so enlightened*
by report?

CLOWN. I will catechize the world for him; that is,
make questions, and by them answer.

DESDEMONA. Seek him. Bid him come hither. Tell
him I have moved my lord in his behalf, and hope all
will be well.

CLOWN. To do this is within the compass of man's wit,
and therefore I will attempt the doing it.

[*Exit* CLOWN.]

DESDEMONA. Where should I lose that handkerchief,
Emilia?

EMILIA. I know not, madam.

DESDEMONA. Believe me, I had rather have lost my
purse
Full of crusadoes. And but my noble Moor *gold coins*
Is true of mind, and made of no such baseness
As jealous creatures are, it were enough
To put him to ill thinking.

EMILIA. Is he not jealous?

DESDEMONA. Who, he? I think the sun where he was
born
Drew all such humors from him. *moods, notions*

EMILIA. Look where he comes!

DESDEMONA. I will not leave him now till Cassio
Be called to him.

[*Enter* OTHELLO.]

How is 't with you, my lord?

OTHELLO. Well, my good lady. [*Aside*] Oh, hardness
to dissemble!—
How do you, Desdemona?

DESDEMONA. Well, my good lord.

OTHELLO. Give me your hand. This hand is moist, *i.e., showing lust*
my lady.

DESDEMONA. It yet has felt no age nor known no
sorrow.

OTHELLO. This argues fruitfulness and liberal heart. *pun: generous,*
Hot, hot, and moist. This hand of yours requires *licentious*
A sequester from liberty, fasting and prayer, *separation*
Much castigation, exercise devout.
For here's a young and sweating devil here
That commonly rebels. 'Tis a good hand,
A frank one.

DESDEMONA. You may, indeed, say so,
For 'twas that hand that gave away my heart.

OTHELLO. A liberal hand! The hearts of old gave
hands,
But our new heraldry is hands not hearts.   *i.e., of marriage*

DESDEMONA. I cannot speak of this. Come now, your
promise.

OTHELLO. What promise, chuck?   *chick, deary*

DESDEMONA. I have sent to bid Cassio come speak with
you.

OTHELLO. I have a salt and sorry rheum offends me.   *miserable cold*
Lend me thy handkerchief.

DESDEMONA.   Here, my lord.

OTHELLO. That which I gave you.

DESDEMONA.   I have it not about me.

OTHELLO. Not?

DESDEMONA. No, 'faith, my lord.

OTHELLO. That is a fault. That handkerchief
Did an Egyptian to my mother give.   *Gipsy*
She was a charmer and could almost read   *prophetess*
The thoughts of people. She told her, while she kept it,
'Twould make her amiable and subdue my father   *lovable*
Entirely to her love, but if she lost it
Or made a gift of it, my father's eye
Should hold her loathly, and his spirits should hunt
After new fancies. She dying gave it me,
And bid me, when my fate would have me wive,
To give it her. I did so. And take heed on 't,
Make it a darling like your precious eye.
To lose 't or give 't away were such perdition
As nothing else could match.

DESDEMONA.   Is 't possible?

OTHELLO. 'Tis true. There's magic in the web of it.   *a female seer*
A sibyl, that had numbered in the world   *200 years old*
The sun to course two hundred compasses,   *inspiration*
In her prophetic fury sewed the work.
The worms were hallowed that did breed the silk,   *dye made from*
And it was dyed in mummy which the skillful   *prepared from*
Conserved of maidens' hearts.

DESDEMONA.   I' faith? Is 't true?

OTHELLO. Most veritable, therefore look to 't well.

DESDEMONA. Then would to God that I had never seen
it!

OTHELLO. Ha! Wherefore?

DESDEMONA. Why do you speak so startingly and rash?

OTHELLO. Is 't lost? is 't gone? Speak! Is it out o'
the way?

DESDEMONA. Heaven bless us!

OTHELLO. Say you?

DESDEMONA. It is not lost, but what an if it were?

OTHELLO. How!

DESDEMONA. I say, it is not lost.

OTHELLO. Fetch 't, let me see it.

DESDEMONA. Why, so I can, sir, but I will not now.
This is a trick to put me from my suit.
Pray you, let Cassio be received again.

OTHELLO. Fetch me that handkerchief. My mind misgives.

DESDEMONA. Come, come,
You'll never meet a more sufficient man.

OTHELLO. The handkerchief!

DESDEMONA. I pray, talk me of Cassio.

OTHELLO. The handkerchief!

DESDEMONA. A man that all his time
Hath founded his good fortunes on your love,
Shared dangers with you—

OTHELLO. The handkerchief!

DESDEMONA. I' faith, you are to blame.

OTHELLO. Zounds!

[*Exit* OTHELLO.]

EMILIA. Is not this man jealous?

DESDEMONA. I ne'er saw this before.
Sure, there's some wonder in this handkerchief.
I am most unhappy in the loss of it.

EMILIA. 'Tis not a year or two shows us a man.   *what a man's like*
They are all but stomachs, and we all but food.
They eat us hungerly, and when they are full
They belch us. Look you! Cassio and my husband.

[*Enter* IAGO *and* CASSIO.]

IAGO. There is no other way—'tis she must do 't.
And, lo, the happiness! Go and impórtune her.   *what luck*

DESDEMONA. How now, good Cassio? What's the news
with you?

CASSIO. Madam, my former suit. I do beseech you
That by your virtuous means I may again   *effective*
Exist, and be a member of his love
Whom I with all the office of my heart   *duty*
Entirely honor. I would not be delayed.

If my offense be of such mortal kind
That nor my service past nor present sorrows   *neither*
Nor purposed merit in futurity   *for the future*
Can ransom me into his love again,
But to know so must be my benefit.   *Merely*
So shall I clothe me in a forced content,
And shut myself up in some other course
To Fortune's alms.   *accept my fate*
    DESDEMONA.   Alas, thrice-gentle Cassio,   *of gentle birth*
My advocation is not now in tune.   *pleading for you*
My lord is not my lord, nor should I know him
Were he in favor as in humor altered.   *face . . . mood*
So help me every spirit sanctified,
As I have spoken for you all my best
And stood within the blank of his displeasure   *aim, bull's-eye*
For my free speech! You must awhile be patient.
What I can do I will, and more I will
Than for myself I dare. Let that suffice you.
    IAGO.   Is my lord angry?
    EMILIA.   He went hence but now,
And certainly in strange unquietness.
    IAGO.   Can he be angry? I have seen the cannon
When it hath blown his ranks into the air
And, like the Devil, from his very arm
Puffed his own brother—and can he be angry?
Something of moment then. I will go meet him;
There's matter in 't indeed, if he be angry.
    DESDEMONA.   I prithee, do so.

                               [Exit IAGO.]

                       Something, sure, of state,
Either from Venice or some unhatched practice   *plot*
Made demonstrable here in Cyprus to him,   *revealed*
Hath puddled his clear spirit. And in such cases   *muddied*
Men's natures wrangle with inferior things,
Though great ones are their object. 'Tis even so,
For let our finger ache, and it endues   *brings*
Our other healthful members even to that sense
Of pain. Nay, we must think men are not gods,
Nor of them look for such observancy   *close attention*
As fits the bridal. Beshrew me much, Emilia,   *honeymoon . . .*
                                          Plague
I was—unhandsome warrior as I am—   *poor soldier*
Arraigning his unkindness with my soul,
But now I find I had suborned the witness,   *corrupted the*
And he's indicted falsely.   *evidence*

EMILIA.   Pray Heaven it be state matters, as you think,
And no conception, nor no jealous toy
Concerning you.

notion . . .
fancy

DESDEMONA.   Alas the day! I never gave him cause.

EMILIA.   But jealous souls will not be answered so.
They are not ever jealous for the cause,
But jealous for they are jealous. 'Tis a monster
Begot upon itself, born on itself.

DESDEMONA.   Heaven keep that monster from Othello's
mind!

EMILIA.   Lady, amen.

DESDEMONA.   I will go seek him. Cassio, walk here-
about.
If I do find him fit, I'll move your suit
And seek to effect it to my uttermost.

CASSIO.   I humbly thank your ladyship.

[*Exeunt* DESDEMONA *and* EMILIA.]

[*Enter* BIANCA.]

BIANCA.   'Save you, friend Cassio!

God preserve
you

CASSIO.   What make you from home?

do . . . away
from

How is it with you, my most fair Bianca?
I' faith, sweet love, I was coming to your house.

BIANCA.   And I was going to your lodging, Cassio.
What! Keep a week away? Seven days and nights?
Eightscore eight hours? and lovers' absent hours,
More tedious than the dial eightscore times?
O weary reckoning!

CASSIO.   Pardon me, Bianca.
I have this while with leaden thoughts been pressed,
But I shall, in a more continuate time,

uninterrupted

Strike off this score of absence. Sweet Bianca,

[*giving her* DESDEMONA's *handkerchief*]
Take me this work out.

copy this
pattern

BIANCA.   O Cassio! whence came this?
This is some token from a newer friend.
To the felt absence now I feel a cause.
Is 't come to this? Well, well.

CASSIO.   Go to, woman!
Throw your vile guesses in the Devil's teeth,
From whence you have them. You are jealous now
That this is from some mistress, some remembrance.
No, by my faith, Bianca.

BIANCA.   Why, whose is it?

CASSIO.   I know not, sweet. I found it in my chamber.

I like the work well. Ere it be demanded—
As like enough it will—I'd have it copied.
Take it and do 't, and leave me for this time.

BIANCA.   Leave you? wherefore?

CASSIO.   I do attend here on the General,   *wait . . . for*
And think it no addition nor my wish   *honor*
To have him see me womaned.   *with a woman*

BIANCA.   Why, I pray you?

CASSIO.   Not that I love you not.

BIANCA.   But that you do not love me.
I pray you bring me on the way a little
And say if I shall see you soon at night.

CASSIO.   'Tis but a little way that I can bring you,
For I attend here, but I'll see you soon.

BIANCA.   'Tis very good. I must be circumstanced.   *yield to circum-*
                                              [Exeunt.]   *stance*

ACT FOUR

Scene I. *Before the Citadel.*

[*Enter* OTHELLO *and* IAGO.]

IAGO.   Will you think so?

OTHELLO.   Think so, Iago!

IAGO.   What!
To kiss in private?

OTHELLO.   An unauthorized kiss.

IAGO.   Or to be naked with her friend in bed
An hour or more, not meaning any harm?

OTHELLO.   Naked in bed, Iago, and not mean harm?
It is hypocrisy against the Devil.   *double-crossing*
They that mean virtuously and yet do so,
The Devil their virtue tempts, and they tempt Heaven.

IAGO.   So they do nothing, 'tis a venial slip.   *So long as . . .*
But if I give my wife a handkerchief—   *pardonable*

OTHELLO.   What then?

IAGO.   Why, then, 'tis hers, my lord, and, being hers,
She may, I think, bestow 't on any man.

OTHELLO.   She is protectress of her honor too.
May she give that?

IAGO.   Her honor is an essence that's not seen.
They have it very oft that have it not.   *are said to have*
But for the handkerchief,—

OTHELLO.   By Heaven, I would most gladly have forgot
   it.

Thou said'st—oh, it comes o'er my memory
As doth the raven o'er the infected house,
Boding to all—he had my handkerchief.

   IAGO. Ay, what of that?

   OTHELLO.   That's not so good now.

   IAGO.   What
If I had said I had seen him do you wrong?
Or heard him say—as knaves be such abroad,
Who having, by their own importunate suit
Or voluntary dotage of some mistress,
Convincèd or supplied them, cannot choose
But they must blab—

   OTHELLO.   Hath he said anything?

   IAGO. He hath, my lord, but be you well assured,
No more than he'll unswear.

   OTHELLO.   What hath he said?

   IAGO. Faith, that he did—I know not what he did.

   OTHELLO. What? what?

   IAGO. Lie—

   OTHELLO. With her?

   IAGO.   With her, on her—what you will.

   OTHELLO. Lie with her! lie on her! We say 'lie on her'
when they belie her. Lie with her? Zounds, that's ful-
some! Handkerchief!—confessions!—handkerchief! To
confess, and be hanged for his labor. First, to be hanged
and then to confess—I tremble at it. Nature would not
invest herself in such shadowing passion without some
instruction. It is not words that shake me thus. Pish!
Noses, ears, and lips. Is 't possible?—Confess!—Handkerchief!—O devil!

                    [Falls in a trance.]

   IAGO. Work on,
My medicine, work! Thus credulous fools are caught,
And many worthy and chaste dames even thus,
All guiltless, meet reproach. What, ho! my lord!
My lord, I say! Othello!

   [Enter CASSIO.*]*

                 How now, Cassio!

   CASSIO. What's the matter?

   IAGO. My lord is fallen into an epilepsy.
This is his second fit, he had one yesterday.

   CASSIO. Rub him about the temples.

Glosses (right margin):
- with death near
- ominous
- infatuation
- overcome them
- satisfied desires
- disgusting
- but to teach me

IAGO.   No, forbear.
The lethargy must have his quiet course.   *fit . . . its*
If not he foams at mouth, and by and by
Breaks out to savage madness. Look, he stirs.
Do you withdraw yourself a little while,
He will recover straight. When he is gone,
I would on great occasion speak with you.

[*Exit* CASSIO.]

How is it, General? Have you not hurt your head?   *pun: cuckold*
    OTHELLO.   Dost thou mock me?   *horns*
    IAGO.   I mock you! No, by Heaven.
Would you would bear your fortunes like a man!
    OTHELLO.   A hornèd man's a monster and a beast.
    IAGO.   There's many a beast then, in a populous city,
And many a civil monster.   *civilized*
    OTHELLO.   Did he confess it?
    IAGO.   Good sir, be a man.
Think every bearded fellow that's but yoked   *married*
May draw with you. There's millions now alive   *be in a like way*
That nightly lie in those unproper beds   *not unshared*
Which they dare swear peculiar. Your case is better.   *are theirs alone*
Oh, 'tis the spite of hell, the fiend's arch-mock,
To lip a wanton in a sécure couch,   *kiss . . . free*
And to suppose her chaste. No, let me know,   *from suspicion*
And knowing what I am, I know what she shall be.   *should be called*
    OTHELLO.   Oh, thou art wise, 'tis certain.
    IAGO.   Stand you awhile apart,
Confine yourself but in a patient list.   *within bounds*
Whilst you were here o'erwhelmèd with your grief—
A passion most unsuiting such a man—
Cassio came hither. I shifted him away,
And laid good 'scuse upon your ecstasy,   *fit*
Bade him anon return and here speak with me,
The which he promised. Do but encave yourself,   *hide*
And mark the fleers, the gibes, and notable scorns   *grins*
That dwell in every region of his face.
For I will make him tell the tale anew,
Where, how, how oft, how long ago, and when
He hath and is again to cope your wife.   *deal with, have*
I say, but mark his gesture. Marry, patience,
Or I shall say you're all in all in spleen   *governed by*
And nothing of a man.   *impulse*
    OTHELLO.   Dost thou hear, Iago?
I will be found most cunning in my patience,

But—dost thou hear?—most bloody.

IAGO.   That's not amiss,
But yet keep time in all. Will you withdraw?   *within measure*
    [OTHELLO *withdraws*.]

Now will I question Cassio of Bianca,
A housewife that by selling her desires   *hussy*
Buys herself bread and clothes. It is a creature
That dotes on Cassio, as 'tis the strumpet's plague
To beguile many and be beguiled by one.
He, when he hears of her, cannot refrain
From the excess of laughter. Here he comes.

    [*Re-enter* CASSIO *from a distance.*]

As he shall smile, Othello shall go mad,   *naive . . .*
And his unbookish jealousy must construe   *interpret*
Poor Cassio's smiles, gestures, and light behavior
Quite in the wrong. [*To him*] How do you now, Lieu-
        tenant?

CASSIO.   The worser that you give me the addition   *the title*
Whose want even kills me.

IAGO.   Ply Desdemona well, and you are sure on 't.   *Urge*
[*Softly*] Now, if this suit lay in Bianca's power,
How quickly should you speed!   *succeed*

CASSIO.   Alas! poor caitiff!   *little wretch!*
    OTHELLO [*aside*]. Look how he laughs already.

IAGO [*loudly*]. I never knew a woman love man so.

CASSIO.   Alas, poor rogue! I think, i' faith, she loves
        me.

    OTHELLO.   Now he denies it faintly, and laughs it
        out.

IAGO.   Do you hear, Cassio?

    OTHELLO.   Now he impórtunes him
To tell it o'er. Go to! well said, well said.

IAGO.   She gives it out that you shall marry her.
Do you intend it?

CASSIO.   Ha, ha, ha!

    OTHELLO.   Do you triumph, Roman? do you tri-   *exult, proud*
        umph?   *man*

CASSIO.   I marry her! What, a customer? I prithee,   *prostitute*
bear some charity to my wit, do not think it so unwhole- *mind . . .*
some. Ha, ha, ha!   *diseased*

    OTHELLO.   So, so, so, so. Laugh that wins!   *Let him laugh!*

IAGO.   Faith, the cry goes you shall marry her.

CASSIO.   Prithee, say true.

IAGO. I am very villain else.

OTHELLO. Have you scored me? Well! *marked, struck*

CASSIO. This is the monkey's own giving out. She is persuaded I will marry her, out of her own love and flattery, not out of my promise. *self-flattery*

OTHELLO. Iago beckons me. Now he begins the story.

CASSIO. She was here even now. She haunts me in every place. I was the other day talking on the sea bank with certain Venetians, and thither comes the bauble, and *plaything* falls me thus about my neck—

OTHELLO. Crying, 'O dear Cassio!' as it were. His gesture imports it.

CASSIO. So hangs and lolls and weeps upon me, so hales *hauls, tugs* and pulls me. Ha, ha, ha!

OTHELLO. Now he tells how she plucked him to my chamber. Oh, I see that nose of yours, but not that dog I shall throw it to.

CASSIO. Well, I must leave her company.

IAGO. Before me! look where she comes! *By my soul!*

CASSIO. 'Tis such another fitchew! Marry, a perfumed *polecat, harlot* one!

[*Enter* BIANCA.]

What do you mean by this haunting of me?

BIANCA. Let the devil and his dam haunt you! What *mother* did you mean by that same handkerchief you gave me even now? I was a fine fool to take it. I must take out the work? A likely piece of work, that you should find it in your chamber and not know who left it there! This is some minx's token, and I must take out the work! There, give it your hobbyhorse, wheresoever you had it, I'll take *harlot* out no work on 't.

CASSIO. How now, my sweet Bianca! How now, how now!

OTHELLO. By Heaven, that should be my handkerchief!

BIANCA. An you'll come to supper tonight, you may. *if* An you will not, come when you are next prepared for.

[*Exit.*]

IAGO. After her, after her!

CASSIO. Faith, I must. She'll rail i' the street else.

IAGO. Will you sup there?

CASSIO. Faith, I intend so.

IAGO. Well, I may chance to see you, for I would very fai*n* speak with you. *gladly*

CASSIO. Prithee, come, will you?

IAGO. Go to! Say no more.

[*Exit* CASSIO.]

OTHELLO [*advancing*]. How shall I murder him, Iago?

IAGO. Did you perceive how he laughed at his vice?

OTHELLO. Oh, Iago!

IAGO. And did you see the handkerchief?

OTHELLO. Was that mine?

IAGO. Yours, by this hand. And to see how he prizes the foolish woman your wife! She gave it him, and he hath given it his whore.

OTHELLO. I would have him nine years a-killing. A fine woman! a fair woman! a sweet woman!

IAGO. Nay, you must forget that.

OTHELLO. Ay, let her rot and perish, and be damned tonight, for she shall not live! No, my heart is turned to stone—I strike it, and it hurts my hand. Oh, the world has not a sweeter creature. She might lie by an emperor's side and command him tasks.

IAGO. Nay, that'*s* not your wa*y*. *i.e., Don't soften.*

OTHELLO. Hang her! I do but say what she is—so delicate with her needle, an admirable musician—oh, she will sing the savageness out of a bear—of so high and plenteous wit and invention!

IAGO. She's the worse for all this.

OTHELLO. Oh, a thousand, a thousand times. And then, of so gentl*e* a conditio*n*! *of good family*

IAGO. Ay, too gentle.

OTHELLO. Nay, that's certain. But yet the pity of it, Iago! O Iago, the pity of it, Iago!

IAGO. If you be so fond ove*r* her iniquity, give her *of* pate*n*t to offend, for, if it touches not you, it comes near *a license* nobody.

OTHELLO. I will chop her into messe*s*. Cuckold me! *little pieces*

IAGO. Oh, 'tis foul in her.

OTHELLO. With mine officer!

IAGO. That's fouler.

OTHELLO. Get me some poison, Iago, this night. I'll not expostulat*e* with her, lest her body and beauty un- *argue* provid*e* my mind again. This night, Iago. *weaken*

IAGO. Do it not with poison, strangle her in her bed, even the bed she hath contaminated.

OTHELLO.   Good, good.   The justice of it pleases.   Very good.

IAGO.   And for Cassio, let me be his undertaker.   *take care of him*
You shall hear more by midnight.

OTHELLO.   Excellent good.

[*A trumpet sounds within.*]

What trumpet is that same?

IAGO.   Something from Venice, sure. 'Tis Lodovico,
Come from the Duke.   And see, your wife is with him.

[*Enter* LODOVICO, DESDEMONA, *and* ATTENDANTS.]

LODOVICO.   God save you, worthy general!

OTHELLO.   With all my heart, sir.

LODOVICO.   The Duke and senators of Venice greet you.

[*Gives him a letter.*]

OTHELLO.   I kiss the instrument of their pleasures.   *document . . . orders*

[*Opens the letter and reads.*]

DESDEMONA.   And what's the news, good cousin Lodovico?

IAGO.   I am very glad to see you, signior.
Welcome to Cyprus.

LODOVICO.   I thank you.   How does Lieutenant Cassio?

IAGO.   Lives, sir.

DESDEMONA.   Cousin, there's fallen between him and
my lord
An unkind breach, but you shall make all well.

OTHELLO.   Are you sure of that?

DESDEMONA.   My lord?

OTHELLO [*reads*].   'This fail you not to do, as you
will'—

LODOVICO.   He did not call.   He's busy in the paper.
Is there division 'twixt thy lord and Cassio?

DESDEMONA.   A most unhappy one.   I would do much   *reconcile*
T' atone them for the love I bear to Cassio.

OTHELLO.   Fire and brimstone!

DESDEMONA.   My lord?

OTHELLO.   Are you wise?

DESDEMONA.   What! is he angry?

LODOVICO.   May be the letter moved him,
For, as I think, they do command him home,   *deputizing . . as governor*
Deputing Cassio in his government.

DESDEMONA.   By my tro*th*, I am glad on 't.   *faith, truly*
OTHELLO.   Indeed!
DESDEMONA.   My lord?
OTHELLO.   I am glad to see you ma*d*.   *insane,* not
                                                 'angry'
DESDEMONA.   How, sweet Othello?
OTHELLO [*striking her*].   Devil!
DESDEMONA.   I have not deserved this.
LODOVICO.   My lord, this would not be believed in
     Venice,
Though I should swear I saw 't. 'Tis ver*y* much.   *going too far!*
Make her amends, she weeps.
     OTHELLO.   O devil, devil!
If that the earth could tee*m* with women's tears,   *reproduce*
Each drop she falls would prove a crocodile.
Out of my sight!
     DESDEMONA [*going*].   I will not stay to offend you.
     LODOVICO.   Truly, an obedient lady!
I do beseech your lordship, call her back.
     OTHELLO.   Mistress!
     DESDEMONA.   My lord?
     OTHELLO.   What would you with her, sir?
     LODOVICO.   Who, I, my lord?
     OTHELLO.   Ay, you did wish that I would make her
     turn.
Sir, she can turn, and turn, and yet go on,
And turn again. And she can weep, sir, weep.
And she's obedient, as you say, obedient,
Very obedient.—Proceed you in your tears.—
Concerning this, sir—O well-painte*d* passion*!*—   *imitated emo-*
                                                            tion
I am commanded home.—Get you away,
I'll send for you anon.—Sir, I obey the mandate,
And will return to Venice.—Hence! avaunt!
                              [*Exit* DESDEMONA.]

Cassio shall have my place. And, sir, tonight,
I do entreat that we may sup together.
You are welcome, sir, to Cyprus.—Goat*s* and monkey*s*!   *lustful animals*
                              [*Exit.*]

     LODOVICO.   Is this the noble Moor whom our full Senate
Call all-in-all sufficient? Is this the nature
Whom passion could not shake? whose solid virtue
The shot of accident nor dart of chance
Could neither graze nor pierce?
     IAGO.   He is much changed.
     LODOVICO.   Are his wits safe? Is he not light of brain?

IAGO.   He's that he is. I may not breathe my censure.   *judgment*
What he might be—if what he might he is not—   *ought to be*
I would to Heaven he were!
LODOVICO.   What! strike his wife!
IAGO.   Faith, that was not so well, yet would I knew
That stroke would prove the worst!
LODOVICO.   Is it his use?   *usual way*
Or did the letters work upon his blood
And new-create this fault?
IAGO.   Alas, alas!
It is not honesty in me to speak
What I have seen and known. You shall observe him,
And his own courses will denote him so   *behavior . . .*
That I may save my speech. Do but go after   *show*
And mark how he continues.
LODOVICO.   I am sorry that I am deceived in him.
                                           [*Exeunt.*]

SCENE II.   *A Room in the Citadel.*

[*Enter* OTHELLO *and* EMILIA.]

OTHELLO.   You have seen nothing, then?
EMILIA.   Nor ever heard, nor ever did suspect.
OTHELLO.   Yes, and you have seen Cassio and she
    together.
EMILIA.   But then I saw no harm, and then I heard
Each syllable that breath made up between them.
OTHELLO.   What! did they never whisper?
EMILIA.   Never, my lord.
OTHELLO.   Nor send you out o' the way?
EMILIA.   Never.
OTHELLO.   To fetch her fan, her gloves, her mask, nor
    nothing?
EMILIA.   Never, my lord.
OTHELLO.   That's strange.
EMILIA.   I durst, my lord, to wager she is honest,
Lay down my soul at stake. If you think other,   *as bet . . .*
Remove your thought, it doth abuse your bosom.   *otherwise*
If any wretch have put this in your head,
Let Heaven requite it with the serpent's curse!   *God's curse on*
For if she be not honest, chaste, and true,   *the serpent*
There's no man happy—the purest of their wives
Is foul as slander.
OTHELLO.   Bid her come hither. Go.
                                        [*Exit* EMILIA.]

She says enough. Yet she's a simple bawd
That cannot say as much. This is a subtle whore,
A closet lock and key of villainous secrets,
And yet she'll kneel and pray. I have seen her do 't.

It would be a
naive madam

a strongbox

[*Enter* DESDEMONA *and* EMILIA.]

DESDEMONA. My lord, what is your will?
OTHELLO.   Pray, chuck, come hither.
DESDEMONA. What is your pleasure?
OTHELLO.   Let me see your eyes.
Look in my face.
DESDEMONA. What horrible fancy's this?
OTHELLO. Some of your function, mistress.
[*To* EMILIA] Leave procreants alone and shut the door.
Cough or cry 'hem' if anbody come.
Your mystery, your mystery. Nay, dispatch.
                                        [*Exit* EMILIA.]

addressing her as
a prostitute

Go about your
work

business . . .
be quick

DESDEMONA. Upon my knees, what does your speech
    import?
I understand a fury in your words
But not the words.
OTHELLO. Why, what art thou?
DESDEMONA. Your wife, my lord, your true and loyal
    wife.
OTHELLO. Come, swear it, damn thyself,
Lest, being like one of Heaven, the devils themselves
Should fear to seize thee. Therefore be double-damned—
Swear thou art honest.
DESDEMONA.   Heaven doth truly know it.
OTHELLO. Heaven truly knows that thou art false as
    hell.
DESDEMONA. To whom, my lord? With whom? How
    am I false?
OTHELLO. Ah, Desdemon! Away, away, away!
DESDEMONA. Alas, the heavy day! Why do you weep?
Am I the motive of these tears, my lord?
If haply you my father do suspect
An instrument of this your calling-back,
Lay not your blame on me. If you have lost him,
Why, I have lost him too.
OTHELLO.   Had it pleased Heaven
To try me with affliction, had they rained
All kinds of sores and shames on my bare head,

looking angelic

chaste

Steeped me in poverty to the very lips,
Given to captivity me and my utmost hopes,
I should have found in some part of my soul
A drop of patience. But, alas, to make me
A fixèd figure for the time of scorn
To point his slow and moving fingers at!   *cf. clock hands*
Yet could I bear that too, well, very well!
But there, where I have garnered up my heart,   *treasured my love*
Where either I must live or bear no life,
The fountain from the which my current runs
Or else dries up—to be discarded thence,
Or keep it as a cistern for foul toads
To knot and gender in! Turn thy complexion there,   *breed . . . blush at that*
Patience, thou young and rose-lipped cherubin.
I here look grim as hell!
 DESDEMONA. I hope my noble lord esteems me honest.
 OTHELLO. Oh, ay, as summer flies are in the shambles,   *slaughterhouse breed . . . egg-laying*
That quicken even with blowing.
O thou black weed, why art so lovely fair?
Thou smell'st so sweet that the sense aches at thee.
Would thou hadst ne'er been born!
 DESDEMONA. Alas, what ignorant sin have I committed?
 OTHELLO. Was this fair paper, this most goodly book,   *her white body*
Made to write 'whore' on? What committed?
Committed! Oh, thou public commoner!   *prostitute*
I should make very forges of my cheeks,
That would to cinders burn up modesty,
Did I but speak thy deeds. What committed?
Heaven stops the nose at it and the moon winks,
The bawdy wind that kisses all it meets
Is hushed within the hollow mine of earth   *cave*
And will not hear 't. What committed?
Impudent strumpet!
 DESDEMONA. By Heaven, you do me wrong.
 OTHELLO. Are not you a strumpet?
 DESDEMONA. No, as I am a Christian.
If to preserve this vessel for my lord
From any other foul unlawful touch
Be not to be a strumpet, I am none.
 OTHELLO. What! not a whore?
 DESDEMONA.   No, as I shall be saved.
 OTHELLO. Is 't possible?
 DESDEMONA. O Heaven, forgiveness!
 OTHELLO.   I cry you mercy, then.   *Pardon me!*

I took you for that cunning whore of Venice
That married with Othello.
   [*Calling out for* EMILIA *as if to the bawd*]
                You, mistress,
That have the office opposite to Saint Peter
And keep the gate of Hell!
   [*Enter* EMILIA.]
                You, you, ay, you!
We have done our course. There's money for your pains.
I pray you, turn the key and keep our counsel.   *let me out . . .*
                    [*Exit.*]   *tell no one*

  EMILIA. Alas! what does this gentleman conceive?   *imagine*
How do you, madam? how do you, my good lady?
  DESDEMONA. Faith, half asleep.
  EMILIA. Good madam, what's the matter with my
    lord?
  DESDEMONA. With who?
  EMILIA.   Why, with my lord, madam.
  DESDEMONA. Who is thy lord?
  EMILIA.   He that is yours, sweet lady.
  DESDEMONA. I have none. Do not talk to me, Emilia.
I cannot weep, nor answer have I none
But what should go by water. Prithee, tonight   *expressed by*
Lay on my bed our wedding sheets. Remember.   *tears*
And call thy husband hither.
  EMILIA.   Here is a change indeed!
                    [*Exit.*]

  DESDEMONA. 'Tis meet I should be used so, very meet.   *proper*
How have I been behaved, that he might stick   *place*
The small'st opinion on my least misuse?   *censure*

   [*Enter* IAGO *and* EMILIA.]

  IAGO. What is your pleasure, madam? How is 't with
    you?
  DESDEMONA. I cannot tell. Those that do teach young
    babes
Do it with gentle means and easy tasks.
He might have chid me so, for, in good faith,
I am a child to chiding.   *react as a child*
  IAGO. What is the matter, lady?
  EMILIA. Alas! Iago, my lord hath so bewhored her,
Thrown such despite and heavy terms upon her
As true hearts cannot bear.

DESDEMONA.   Am I that name, Iago?

IAGO.   What name, fair lady?

DESDEMONA.   Such as she says my lord did say I was.

EMILIA.   He called her whore. A beggar in his drink
Could not have laid such terms upon his calle*t*.   *moll, woman*

IAGO.   Why did he so?

DESDEMONA.   I do not know. I am sure I am none such.

IAGO.   Do not weep, do not weep. Alas the day!

EMILIA.   Hath she forsook so many noble matches,
Her father, and her country, and her friends,
To be called whore? Would it not make one weep?

DESDEMONA.   It is my wretched fortune.

IAGO.   Beshre*w* him for 't!   *Plague take him!*
How comes this tric*k* upon him?   *whim, freak*

DESDEMONA.   Nay, Heaven doth know.

EMILIA.   I will be hanged if some eternal villain,
Some busy and insinuating rogue,
Some cogging, cozening slave, to get some office   *tricky, cheating*
Have not devised this slander. I'll be hanged else.

IAGO.   Fie! There is no such man. It is impossible.

DESDEMONA.   If any such there be, Heaven pardon him!

EMILIA.   A halter pardon him, and Hell gnaw his
bones!
Why should he call her whore? Who keeps her com-
pany?
What place? what time? what form? what likelihood?
The Moor's abused by some villainous knave,
Some base notorious knave, some scurvy fellow.
O Heaven! that such companion*s* Thou'dst unfol*d*,   *rascals . . . reveal*
And put in every honest hand a whip
To las*h* the rascal naked through the world,   *drive with whip*
Even from the east to the west!

IAGO.   Speak within doors.   *quietly*

EMILIA.   Oh, fie upon him! Some such squir*e* he was   *fellow*
That turned your wit the seamy side without,
And made you to suspect me with the Moor.

IAGO.   You are a fool. Go to!

DESDEMONA.   O good Iago,
What shall I do to win my lord again?
Good friend, go to him, for, by this light of Heaven,
I know not how I lost him. Here I kneel.
If e'er my will did trespass 'gainst his love,
Either in discourse of thought or actual deed,
Or that mine eyes, mine ears, or any sense
Delighted them in any other form,

Or that I do not yet, and ever did,
And ever will—though he do shake me off
To beggarly divorcement—love him dearly,
Comfort forswear me! Unkindness may do much,   *forsake*
And his unkindness may defeat my life   *destroy*
But never taint my love. I cannot say 'whore.'
It does abhor me now I speak the word.
To do the act that might th' addition earn   *title*
Not the world's mass of vanity could make me.   *vain riches*
  IAGO. I pray you be content. 'Tis but his humor.
The business of the state does him offense
And he does chide with you.
  DESDEMONA. If 'twere no other—
  IAGO.   'Tis but so, I warr'nt you.

[*Trumpets within*]

Hark how these instruments summon you to supper,
And the great messengers of Venice stay.   *await you*
Go in, and weep not. All things shall be well.
                    [*Exeunt* DESDEMONA *and* EMILIA.]

[*Enter* RODERIGO.]

How now, Roderigo?
  RODERIGO. I do not find that thou deal'st justly with
    me.
  IAGO. What in the contrary?   *to*
  RODERIGO. Every day thou doffest me with some de-   *put me off*
vice, Iago, and rather, as it seems to me, thou keepest
from me all conveniency, than suppliest me with the least   *opportunity*
advantage of hope. I will indeed no longer endure it,   *to further my*
nor am I yet persuaded to put up in peace what already   *put up with*
I have foolishly suffered.
  IAGO. Will you hear me, Roderigo?
  RODERIGO. Faith, I have heard too much, for your
words and performance are no kin together.
  IAGO. You charge me most unjustly.
  RODERIGO. With nought but truth. I have wasted
myself out of my means. The jewels you have had from
me to deliver to Desdemona would half have corrupted
a votarist. You have told me she has received them and   *nun*
returned me expectations and comforts of sudden respect   *notice*
and acquaintance, but I find none.
  IAGO. Well, go to! Very well.

RODERIGO. Very well? go to? I cannot go to, man, nor 'tis not very well. By this hand, I say 'tis very scurvy, and begin to find myself fopped in it. *befooled*

IAGO. Very well.

RODERIGO. I tell you 'tis not very well. I will make myself known to Desdemona. If she will return me my jewels, I will give over my suit and repent my unlawful solicitation. If not, assure yourself I will seek satisfaction of you.

IAGO. You have said now? *are done talking?*

RODERIGO. Ay, and said nothing but what I protest intendment of doing.

IAGO. Why, now I see there's mettle in thee, and even *metal, good stuff*
from this instant do build on thee a better opinion than ever before. Give me thy hand, Roderigo. Thou hast taken against me a most just exception, but yet, I protest, *grievance*
I have dealt most directly in thy affair.

RODERIGO. It hath not appeared.

IAGO. I grant indeed it hath not appeared, and your suspicion is not without wit and judgment. But, Rode- *wisdom*
rigo, if thou hast that within thee indeed, which I have greater reason to believe now than ever—I mean purpose, courage, and valor—this night show it. If thou the next night following enjoyest not Desdemona, take me from *schemes, tor-*
this world with treachery and devise engines for my life. *tures*

RODERIGO. Well, what is it? Is it within reason and compass?

IAGO. Sir, there is especial commission come from Venice to depute Cassio in Othello's place. *appoint*

RODERIGO. Is that true? Why, then Othello and Desdemona return again to Venice.

IAGO. Oh, no! He goes into Mauritania, and takes away with him the fair Desdemona, unless his abode be lingered here by some accident, wherein none can be so determinate as the removing of Cassio. *decisive*

RODERIGO. How do you mean, 'removing' of him?

IAGO. Why, by making him uncapable of Othello's *unable to take*
place, knocking out his brains.

RODERIGO. And that you would have me to do!

IAGO. Ay, if you dare do yourself a profit and a right. He sups tonight with a harlot, and thither will I go to him. He knows not yet of his honorable fortune. If you will watch his going thence, which I will fashion to fall out between twelve and one, you may take him at your pleasure. I will be near to second your attempt, and he

shall fall between us. Come, stand not amazed at it, but
go along with me. I will show you such a necessity in his
death that you shall think yourself bound to put it on
him. It is now high supper time, and the night grows to
waste. About it.

RODERIGO. I will hear further reason for this.

IAGO. And you shall be satisfied.

goes

[*Exeunt.*]

SCENE III. *State Bedroom in the Citadel.*

[*Enter* OTHELLO, LODOVICO, DESDEMONA, EMILIA, *and*
ATTENDANTS.]

LODOVICO. I do beseech you, sir, trouble yourself no
further.

OTHELLO. Oh, pardon me, 'twill do me good to walk.

Not at all!

LODOVICO. Madam, good night. I humbly thank your
ladyship.

DESDEMONA. Your honor is most welcome.

OTHELLO.   Will you walk, sir?—

take a walk

Oh, Desdemona.

DESDEMONA. My lord?

OTHELLO. Get you to bed on th' instant. I will be returned forthwith.

Dismiss your attendant there. Look it be done.

DESDEMONA. I will, my lord.

[*Exit* OTHELLO, *with* LODOVICO *and* ATTENDANTS.]

EMILIA. How goes it now? He looks gentler than he
did.

DESDEMONA. He says he will return incontinent.

immediately

He hath commanded me to go to bed,
And bade me to dismiss you.

EMILIA.   Dismiss me!

DESDEMONA. It was his bidding. Therefore, good
Emilia,

Give me my nightly wearing, and adieu.

dressing-gown

We must not now displease him.

EMILIA. I would you had never seen him.

DESDEMONA. So would not I. My love doth so approve
him

commend

That even his stubbornness, his checks and frowns—
Prithee, unpin me—have grace and favor in them.

EMILIA. I have laid those sheets you bade me on the
bed.

DESDEMONA. All's one. Good faith, how foolish are *No matter!*
our minds!
If I do die before thee, prithee, shroud me
In one of those same sheets.
    EMILIA.   Come, come, you talk!
    DESDEMONA. My mother had a maid called Barbarie.
She was in love, and he she loved proved mad   *wayward*
And did forsake her. She had a song of 'Willow'—   *symbol of lost love*
An old thing 'twas, but it expressed her fortune,   *fate*
And she died singing it. That song tonight
Will not go from my mind. I have much to do
But to go hang my head all at one side   *Not to*
And sing it like poor Barbarie. Prithee, dispatch.
    EMILIA. Shall I go fetch your nightgown?   *dressing-gown*
    DESDEMONA.   No, unpin me here.
This Lodovico is a proper man.   *good-looking*
    EMILIA. A very handsome man.
    DESDEMONA. He speaks well.
    EMILIA. I know a lady in Venice would have walked
barefoot to Palestine for a touch of his nether lip.   *lower*
    DESDEMONA [*singing*].
      The poor soul sat sighing by a sycamore tree—
        Sing all a green willow.
      Her hand on her bosom, her head on her knee—
        Sing willow, willow, willow.
      The fresh streams ran by her, and murmured her
      moans.
        Sing willow, willow, willow.
      Her salt tears fell from her, and softened the stones.
        Sing willow—
Lay by these.—   *put these away*
                willow, willow.
Prithee, hie thee; he'll come anon.   *hurry . . . shortly*
      Sing all a green willow must be my garland.
      Let nobody blame him, his scorn I approve—
Nay, that's not next. Hark! who is it that knocks?
    EMILIA. It is the wind.
    DESDEMONA [*singing on*].
      I called my love false-love, but what said he then?
        Sing willow, willow, willow.
      If I court moe women, you'll couch with moe men.   *more*
Now get thee gone. Good night. Mine eyes do itch.
Does that bode weeping?
    EMILIA.   'Tis neither here nor there.

DESDEMONA. I have heard it said so. Oh, these men,
  these men!
Dost thou in conscience think—tell me, Emilia—
That there be women do abuse their husbands
In such gross kind?   *manner*
  EMILIA.   There be some such, no question.
  DESDEMONA. Wouldst thou do such a deed for all the
    world?
  EMILIA. Why, would not you?
  DESDEMONA.   No, by this Heavenly light!
  EMILIA. Nor I neither by this heavenly light. I might
do 't as well i' th' dark.
  DESDEMONA. Wouldst thou do such a deed for all the
world?
  EMILIA. The world is a huge thing. It is a great price
for a small vice.
  DESDEMONA. Good troth, I think thou wouldst not.
  EMILIA. By my troth, I think I should, and undo 't
when I had done it. Marry, I would not do such a thing
for a joint-ring, nor for measures of lawn, nor for gowns,   *lover's ring*
petticoats, nor caps, nor any petty exhibition. But for the   *fine linen*
                                                              sum of money
whole world. Ud's pity! who would not make her hus-   *God's*
band a cuckold to make him a monarch? I should ven-
ture Purgatory for 't.
  DESDEMONA. Beshrew me, if I would do such a wrong
For the whole world.
  EMILIA. Why, the wrong is but a wrong i' the world,
and having the world for your labor, 'tis a wrong in your
own world, and you might quickly make it right.
  DESDEMONA. I do not think there is any such woman.
  EMILIA. Yes, a dozen, and as many to the vantage as   *more to boot*
    would store the world they played for.   *stock, fill up*
But I do think it is their husbands' faults
If wives do fall. Say that they slack their duties   *as husbands*
And pour our treasures into foreign laps,
Or else break out in peevish jealousies,   *silly*
Throwing restraint upon us. Or say they strike us,   *putting*
Or scant our former having in despite—   *allowance in spite*
Why, we have galls, and though we have some grace,   *resentments*
Yet have we some revenge. Let husbands know
Their wives have sense like them. They see and smell   *sensations*
And have their palates both for sweet and sour
As husbands have. What is it that they do
When they change us for others? Is it sport?   *amorous sport*

I think it is. And doth affection breed it?
I think it doth. Is 't frailty that thus errs?
It is so too. And have not we affections,
Desires for sport, and frailty as men have?
Then, let them use us well, else let them know,
The ills we do, their ills instruct us so.

DESDEMONA. Good night, good night! God me such
    usage send,
Not to pick bad from bad, but by bad mend!

                                [Exeunt.]

desire for pleasure

ways, practices

ACT FIVE

SCENE I. *A Street near* BIANCA's *lodging.*

[*Enter* IAGO *and* RODERIGO.]

IAGO. Here, stand behind this bulk. Straight will he
    come.
Wear thy good rapier bare, and put it home.
Quick, quick. Fear nothing, I'll be at thy elbow.
It makes us, or it mars us. Think of that
And fix most firm thy resolution.

RODERIGO. Be near at hand. I may miscarry in 't.

IAGO. Here, at thy hand. Be bold, and take thy stand.
                                [*Withdraws.*]

RODERIGO. I have no great devotion to the deed,
And yet he has given me satisfying reasons.
'Tis but a man gone. Forth, my sword! He dies.

IAGO. I have rubbed this young quat almost to the
    sense,
And he grows angry. Now, whether he kill Cassio,
Or Cassio him, or each do kill the other,
Every way makes my gain. Live Roderigo,
He calls me to a restitution large
Of gold and jewels that I bobbed from him
As gifts to Desdemona.
It must not be. If Cassio do remain,
He hath a daily beauty in his life
That makes me ugly, and, besides, the Moor
May unfold me to him. There stand I in much peril.
No, he must die. Be 't so! I hear him coming.

[*Enter* CASSIO.]

projection. At once

pimple . . . quick

If R. live . . . complete swindled

by comparison expose

RODERIGO. I know his gait, 'tis he. Villain, thou diest!

[*Makes a pass at* CASSIO.]

CASSIO. That thrust had been my enemy indeed
But that my coa*t* is better than thou think'st.   *with vest of mail*
I will make proof of thine.

[*Draws, and wounds* RODERIGO.]

RODERIGO.   Oh! I am slain!

[IAGO *from behind wounds* CASSIO *in the leg, and
exit.*]

CASSIO. I am maimed forever! Light, ho! Murder!
    murder! [*Falls.*]

[*Enter* OTHELLO.]

OTHELLO. The voice of Cassio. Iago keeps his word.
RODERIGO. Oh, villain that I am!
OTHELLO.   Hark! 'Tis even so.
CASSIO. Oh, help, ho! Light! A surgeon!
OTHELLO. 'Tis he. O brave Iago, honest and just,
That hast such noble sense of thy friend's wrong!
Thou teachest me. Minio*n*, your dea*r* lies dead,   *Hussy, lover*
And your fate hie*s* apace. Strumpet, I come!   *comes quickly*
Forth of my heart those charms, thine eyes, are blotted.
Thy bed, lust-stained, shall with lust's blood be spotted.

[*Exit* OTHELLO.]

[*Enter* LODOVICO *and* GRATIANO.]

CASSIO. What ho! No watc*h*? No passag*e*? Murder!   *watchmen . . .*
    murder!   *passers-by*
GRATIANO. 'Tis some mischance. The cry is very dire-
    ful.
CASSIO. Oh, help!
LODOVICO. Hark!
RODERIGO. O wretched villain!
LODOVICO. Two or three groan. It is a heavy night;   *foggy, dark*
These may be counterfeit*s*. Let's think 't unsafe   *fakes, a trap*
To come in to the cry without more help.
RODERIGO. Nobody come? Then shall I bleed to death.
LODOVICO. Hark!

[*Enter* IAGO, *with a light.*]

GRATIANO. Here's one comes in his shirt, with light
and weapons.

IAGO. Who's there? Whose noise is this that cries on   *out*
    murder?

LODOVICO. We do not know.

IAGO.   Did not you hear a cry?

CASSIO. Here, here! For Heaven's sake, help me.

IAGO.   What's the matter?

GRATIANO. This is Othello's ancient, as I take it.

LODOVICO. The same indeed. A very valiant fellow.

IAGO. What are you here that cry so grievously?

CASSIO. Iago? Oh, I am spoiled, undone by villains!
Give me some help.

IAGO. O me, Lieutenant! What villains have done
    this?

CASSIO. I think that one of them is hereabout
And cannot make away.

IAGO.   O treacherous villains!
[*To* LODOVICO *and* GRATIANO] What are you there?
    Come in, and give some help.

RODERIGO. Oh, help me here!

CASSIO. That's one of them.

IAGO.   O murderous slave! O villain!

[*Stabs* RODERIGO.]

RODERIGO. O damned Iago! O inhuman dog!

IAGO. Kill men i' the dark! Where be those bloody
    thieves?
How silent is this town! Ho! murder! murder!
What may you be? Are you of good or evil?

LODOVICO. As you shall prove us, praise us.   *discover . . .*
                              value

IAGO. Signior Lodovico?

LODOVICO. He, sir.

IAGO. I cry you mercy. Here's Cassio hurt by villains.

GRATIANO. Cassio?

IAGO. How is it, brother?

CASSIO. My leg is cut in two.

IAGO.   Marry, Heaven forbid!
Light, gentlemen. I'll bind it with my shirt.

[*Enter* BIANCA.]

BIANCA. What is the matter, ho? Who is't that cried?

IAGO. Who is 't that cried!

BIANCA. Oh, my dear Cassio! Oh, my sweet Cassio,
Cassio, Cassio!

IAGO. O notable strumpet! Cassio, may you suspect

Who they should be that thus have mangled you?

CASSIO. No.

GRATIANO. I am sorry to find you thus. I have been to
    seek you.

IAGO. Lend me a garter. So. Oh, for a chair,
To bear him easily hence!

BIANCA. Alas, he faints! O Cassio, Cassio, Cassio!

IAGO. Gentlemen all, I do suspect this trash
To be a party in this injury.
Patience awhile, good Cassio. Come, come.
Lend me a light. Know we this face, or no?
Alas, my friend and my dear countryman,
Roderigo? No—yes, sure. O Heaven! Roderigo.

GRATIANO. What? of Venice?

IAGO. Even he, sir. Did you know him?

GRATIANO.   Know him? Ay.

IAGO. Signior Gratiano? I cry you gentle pardon.
These bloody accidents must excuse my manners
That so neglected you.

GRATIANO.   I am glad to see you.

IAGO. How do you, Cassio? Oh, a chair, a chair!

GRATIANO. Roderigo!

IAGO. He, 'tis he. [*A chair is brought in.*] Oh, that's
    well said, the chair.
Some good man bear him carefully from hence.
I'll fetch the General's surgeon. [*To* BIANCA] For you,
    mistress,
Save you your labor. He that lies slain here, Cassio,
Was my dear friend. What malice was betwixt you?

CASSIO. None in the world, nor do I know the man.

IAGO [*To* BIANCA]. What! look you pale? Oh, bear
    him out o' the air.

              [CASSIO *and* RODERIGO *are borne off.*]

Stay you, good gentlemen. Look you pale, mistress?—
Do you perceive the gastness of her eye?   *ghastliness*
Nay, if you stare, we shall hear more anon.
Behold her well, I pray you, look upon her.
Do you see, gentlemen? Nay, guiltiness will speak
Though tongues were out of use.

    [*Enter* EMILIA.]

EMILIA. 'Las! what's the matter? What's the matter,
    husband?

IAGO. Cassio has here been set on in the dark

By Roderigo and fellows that are 'scaped.
He's almost slain, and Roderigo dead

 EMILIA. Alas, good gentleman! Alas, good Cassio!

 IAGO. This is the fruit of whoring. Prithee, Emilia,
Go know of Cassio where he supped tonight.—
What! do you shake at that?

 BIANCA. He supped at my house, but I therefore shake
  not.

 IAGO. Oh, did he so? I charge you, go with me.

 EMILIA. Fie, fie upon thee, strumpet!

 BIANCA. I am no strumpet, but of life as honest
As you that thus abuse me.

 EMILIA.   As I? Foh, fie upon thee!

 IAGO. Kind gentlemen, let's go see poor Cassio dressed. *his wound dressed*
Come, mistress, you must tell 's another tale.
Emilia, run you to the citadel,
And tell my lord and lady what has happed.
Will you go on, I pray. [*Aside*] This is the night *destroys*
That either makes me or fordoes me quite.

           [*Exeunt.*]

SCENE II. *State Bedroom in the Citadel.*

[*Enter* OTHELLO *with a light, and* DESDEMONA *in her
bed.*]

 OTHELLO. It is the cause, it is the cause, my soul. *her infidelity*
Let me not name it to you, you chaste stars!
It is the cause. Yet I'll not shed her blood,
Nor scar that whiter skin of hers than snow
And smooth as monumental alabaster. *translucent stone*
Yet she must die, else she'll betray more men.
Put out the light, and then put out the light. *lamp . . . her life*
If I quench thee, thou flaming minister, *servant*
I can again thy former light restore
Should I repent me. But once put out *thy* light,
Thou cunning'st pattern of excelling nature,
I know not where is that Promethean heat *fire from Heaven*
That can thy light relume. When I have plucked thy *rekindle*
 rose,
I cannot give it vital growth again,
It needs must wither. I'll smell it on the tree.

  [*He kisses her.*]

 O balmy breath, that doth almost persuade

Justice to break her sword! One more, one more.
Be thus when thou art dead, and I will kill thee
And love thee after. Once more, and this the last!
So sweet was ne'er so fatal. I must weep,   *deadly*
But they are cruel tears. This sorrow's heavenly,
It strikes where it doth love. She wakes.

DESDEMONA.   Who's there? Othello?

OTHELLO.   Ay, Desdemona.

DESDEMONA.   Will you come to bed, my lord?

OTHELLO.   Have you prayed tonight, Desdemona?

DESDEMONA.   Ay, my lord.

OTHELLO.   If you bethink yourself of any crime
Unreconciled as yet to Heaven and grace,   *God's mercy*
Solicit for it straight.

DESDEMONA.   Alas, my lord, what may you mean by
    that?

OTHELLO.   Well, do it, and be brief. I will walk by.   *aside*
I would not kill thy unpreparèd spirit.
No, Heaven forfend! I would not kill thy soul.

DESDEMONA.   Talk you of killing?

OTHELLO.   Ay, I do.

DESDEMONA.   Then Heaven
Have mercy on me!

OTHELLO.   Amen, with all my heart!

DESDEMONA.   If you say so, I hope you will not kill me.

OTHELLO.   Hum!

DESDEMONA.   And yet I fear you, for you are fatal then   *deadly*
When your eyes roll so. Why I should fear I know not,
Since guiltiness I know not, but yet I feel I fear.

OTHELLO.   Think on thy sins.

DESDEMONA.   They are loves I bear to you.

OTHELLO.   Ay, and for that thou diest.

DESDEMONA.   That death's unnatural that kills for
    loving.
Alas, why gnaw you so your nether lip?
Some bloody passion shakes your very frame.
These are portents, but yet, I hope, I hope,   *ominous*
They do not point on me.

OTHELLO.   Peace, and be still!

DESDEMONA.   I will so. What's the matter?

OTHELLO.   That handkerchief which I so loved and
    gave thee
Thou gav'st to Cassio.

DESDEMONA.   No, by my life and soul!
Send for the man and ask him.

OTHELLO.   Sweet soul, take heed,
Take heed of perjury, thou art on thy death-bed.

DESDEMONA.   Ay, but not yet to die.

OTHELLO.   Yes, presently.   *immediately*
Therefore confess thee freely of thy sin,
For to deny each article with oath
Cannot remove nor choke the strong conceptio*n*   *thought, purpose*
That I do groan withal. Thou art to die.

DESDEMONA.   Then Lord have mercy on me!

OTHELLO.   I say, amen.

DESDEMONA.   And have you mercy too! I never did
Offend you in my life, never loved Cassio
But with such general warranty of Heaven   *permission*
As I might love. I never gave him token.

OTHELLO.   By Heaven, I saw my handkerchief in his
    hand.
O perjured woman! Thou dost ston*e* my heart,   *turn to stone*
And mak'st me call what I intend to do
A murder, which I thought a sacrifice.
I saw the handkerchief.

DESDEMONA.   He found it then.
I never gave it him. Send for him hither,
Let him confess a truth.

OTHELLO.   He has confessed.

DESDEMONA.   What, my lord?

OTHELLO.   That he hath used thee.

DESDEMONA.   How? unlawfully?

OTHELLO.   Ay.

DESDEMONA.   He will not say so.

OTHELLO.   No, his mouth is stopped.
Honest Iago hath ta'en orde*r* for 't.   *measures*

DESDEMONA.   Oh, my fear interprets! What, is he
    dead?

OTHELLO.   Had all his hairs been lives, my great
    revenge
Had stoma*ch* for them all.   *appetite*

DESDEMONA.   Alas, he is betrayed, and I undone!

OTHELLO.   O strumpet! Weep'st thou for him to my
    face?

DESDEMONA.   Oh, banish me, my lord, but kill me not!

OTHELLO.   Down, strumpet!

DESDEMONA.   Kill me tomorrow, let me live tonight!

OTHELLO.   Nay, if you strive—

DESDEMONA.   But half an hour!

OTHELLO.   Being don*e*, there is no paus*e*.   *settled . . . delay*

DESDEMONA. But while I say one prayer!

OTHELLO.   It is too late.

[He stifles her.]

EMILIA *[calls within]*. My lord, my lord! What, ho!
  My lord, my lord!

OTHELLO. What noise is this? Not dead? not yet
  quite dead?
I that am cruel am yet merciful,
I would not have thee linger in thy pain.
So, so.

EMILIA *[within]*. What, ho! My lord, my lord!

OTHELLO.   Who's there?

EMILIA *[within]*. Oh, good my lord, I would speak a
  word with you.

OTHELLO. Yes, 'tis Emilia.—By and by.—She's dead.   *In a moment*
'Tis like she comes to speak of Cassio's death.
The noise was here. Ha, no more moving?
Still as the grave. Shall she come in? Were 't good?
I think she stirs again. No. What's best to do?
If she come in, she'll sure speak to my wife.
My wife! my wife! What wife? I have no wife.
Oh, insupportable! O heavy hour!
Methinks it should be now a huge eclipse
Of sun *and* moon, and that the affrighted globe   *the fearful*
Should yawn at alteration.   *change*

EMILIA *[within]*.   I do beseech you
That I may speak with you, O good my lord!

OTHELLO. I had forgot thee. Oh, come in, Emilia!—
Soft, by and by.—Let me the curtains draw.—   *wait . . .of*
Where art thou?   *[Unlocks the door.]*   *the bed*

[Enter EMILIA.]

       What's the matter with thee now?

EMILIA. Oh, my good lord, yonder's foul murder
  done.

OTHELLO. What! now?

EMILIA.   But now, my lord.

OTHELLO. It is the very error of the moon.   *just*
She comes more near the earth than she was wont   *aberration*
And makes men mad.

EMILIA. Cassio, my lord, hath killed a young Venetian
Called Roderigo.

OTHELLO.   Roderigo killed!
And Cassio killed!

EMILIA.   No, Cassio is not killed.

OTHELLO.   Not Cassio killed! Then murder's out of
tune,
And sweet revenge grows harsh.

DESDEMONA.   Oh, falsely, falsely murdered!

EMILIA.   O Lord! what cry is that?

OTHELLO.   That? what?

EMILIA.   Out and alas! it is my lady's voice.
Help! Help, ho! help! O lady, speak again!
Sweet Desdemona! O sweet mistress, speak!

DESDEMONA.   A guiltless death I die.

EMILIA.   Oh, who has done this deed?

DESDEMONA.   Nobody. I myself. Farewell!
Commend me to my kind lord. O farewell!
[*She dies.*]

OTHELLO.   Why, how should she be murdered?

EMILIA.   Alas, who knows?

OTHELLO.   You heard her say herself it was not I.

EMILIA.   She said so. I must needs report a truth.

OTHELLO.   She's like a liar gone to burning Hell.
'Twas I that killed her.

EMILIA.   Oh, the more angel she,
And you the blacker devil.

OTHELLO.   She turned to folly, and she was a whore.   *lewdness*

EMILIA.   Thou dost belie her, and thou art a devil.

OTHELLO.   She was false as water.

EMILIA.   Thou art rash as fire to say
That she was false. Oh, she was heavenly true!

OTHELLO.   Cassio did top her. Ask thy husband else.
Oh, I were damned beneath all depth in Hell
But that I did proceed upon just grounds
To this extremity. Thy husband knew it all.

EMILIA.   My husband?

OTHELLO.   Thy husband.

EMILIA.   That she was false to wedlock?

OTHELLO.   Ay, with Cassio. Nay, had she been true,
If Heaven would make me such another world
Of one entire and perfect chrysolite,   *green gem*
I'd not have sold her for it.

EMILIA.   My husband!

OTHELLO.   Ay, 'twas he that told me first.
An honest man he is, and hates the slime
That sticks on filthy deeds.

EMILIA.   My husband!

OTHELLO. What needs this iteration, woman? I say
    thy husband.

EMILIA. O mistress! villainy hath made mocks with *a fool of*
    love.
My husband say that she was false?

OTHELLO.   He, woman.
I say, thy husband. Dost understand the word?
My friend, thy husband, honest, honest Iago.

EMILIA. If he say so, may his pernicious soul
Rot half a grain a day! He lies to the heart.
She was too fond of her most filthy bargain.

OTHELLO. Ha!

EMILIA. Do thy worst.
This deed of thine is no more worthy Heaven
Than thou wast worthy her.

OTHELLO.   Peace! you were best. *best be still*

EMILIA. Thou hast not half the power to do me harm
As I have to be hurt. O gull! O dolt! *dupe, dull ass*
As ignorant as dirt! Thou hast done a deed—
I care not for thy sword—I'll make thee known,
Though I lost twenty lives. Help! help! Ho! help!
The Moor has killed my mistress! Murder! murder!

[*Enter* MONTANO, GRATIANO, IAGO, *and others.*]

MONTANO. What is the matter? How now, General?

EMILIA. Oh, are you come, Iago? You have done well,
That men must lay their murders on your neck.

GRATIANO. What is the matter?

EMILIA. Disprove this villain, if thou be'st a man.
He says thou told'st him that his wife was false.
I know thou didst not, thou'rt not such a villain.
Speak, for my heart is full.

IAGO. I told him what I thought, and told no more
Than what he found himself was apt and true. *likely*

EMILIA. But did you ever tell him she was false?

IAGO. I did.

EMILIA. You told a lie, an odious damnèd lie,
Upon my soul, a lie, a wicked lie!
She false with Cassio! Did you say with Cassio?

IAGO. With Cassio, mistress. Go to, charm your *stop*
    tongue.

EMILIA.　I will not charm my tongue, I am bound to
　　speak.
My mistress here lies murdered in her bed.
ALL.　Oh, Heavens forfend!
EMILIA.　And your reports have set the murder on.
OTHELLO.　Nay, stare not, masters. It is true indeed.
GRATIANO.　'Tis a strange truth.
MONTANO.　O monstrous act!
EMILIA.　　　　　　　　　　Villainy, villainy, villainy!
I think upon 't, I think, I smell 't. O villainy!
I thought so then. I'll kill myself for grief.　　　*earlier*
O villainy, villainy!
IAGO.　What! are you mad? I charge you, get you
　　home.
EMILIA.　Good gentlemen, let me have leave to speak.
'Tis proper I obey him, but not now.
Perchance, Iago, I will ne'er go home.
OTHELLO.　Oh! Oh! Oh!
　　　　　　　　　　　　　　　[*He falls on the bed.*]
EMILIA.　　　　　　　　　　Nay, lay thee down and roar,
For thou hast killed the sweetest innocent
That e'er did lift up eye.
OTHELLO [*rising*].　　Oh, she was foul!
I scarce did know you, uncle. There lies your niece,
Whose breath, indeed, these hands have newly stopped.
I know this act shows terrible and grim.　　　*looks*
GRATIANO.　Poor Desdemon, I am glad thy father's
　　dead.
Thy match was mortal to him, and pure grief　　*killed him*
Shore his old thread in-twain. Did he live now,　*cut . . . life*
This sight would make him do a desperate turn,　*deed*
Yea, curse his better angel from his side,
And fall to reprobation.　　　　　　　　　　*damnation,*
　　　　　　　　　　　　　　　　　　　　　　suicide
OTHELLO.　'Tis pitiful, but yet Iago knows
That she with Cassio hath the act of shame
A thousand times committed. Cassio confessed it.
And she did gratify his amorous works
With the recognizance and pledge of love　　　*token*
Which I first gave her. I saw it in his hand.
It was a handkerchief, an antique token
My father gave my mother.
EMILIA.　O God! O heavenly God!
IAGO.　　　　　　　　　　Zounds! hold your peace.
EMILIA.　'Twill out, 'twill out! I hold my peace, sir?
　　No!

No, I will speak as libera*l* as the nort*h*.   *freely . . .*
                                                        wind
Let Heaven and men and devils, let them all,
All, all, cry shame against me, yet I'll speak.

IAGO.   Be wise, and get you home.

EMILIA.   I will not.

[IAGO *draws and threatens* EMILIA.]

GRATIANO.   Fie!
Your sword upon a woman?

EMILIA.   O thou dull Moor! That handkerchief thou
      speak'st of
I found by fortun*e* and did give my husband,   *chance*
For often with a solemn earnestness,
More than, indeed, belonged to such a trifle,
He begged of me to steal it.

IAGO.   Villainous whore!

EMILIA.   She give it Cassio? No, alas! I found it,
And I did give 't my husband.

IAGO.   Filth, thou liest!

EMILIA.   By Heaven, I do not, I do not, gentlemen.
O murderous coxcom*b*! What should such a fool   *conceited fool*
Do with so good a wife?

OTHELLO.   Are there no stone*s* in Heaven   *thunderbolts*
But what serves for the thunder? Precious villain!

[*The* MOOR *runs at* IAGO. IAGO *kills his wife.*]

GRATIANO.   The woman falls. Sure, he hath killed his
      wife.
                                      [*Exit* IAGO.]

EMILIA.   Ay, ay. Oh, lay me by my mistress' side.

GRATIANO.   He's gone, but his wife's killed.

MONTANO.   'Tis a notorious villain. [*To* GRATIANO]
      Take you this weapon,
Which I have here recovere*d* from the Moor.   *taken, secured*
Come, guard the door without. Let him not pass,
But kill him rather. I'll after that same villain,
For 'tis a damnèd slave.
            [*Exeunt* MONTANO, GRATIANO *and* ATTENDANTS.]

OTHELLO.   I am not valiant neither,
But every puny whipste*r* gets my sword.   *whippersnapper*
But why should honor outlive honesty?
Let it go all.

EMILIA.   What did thy song bode, lady?
Hark, canst thou hear me? I will play the swan,
And die in music. [*Singing*]   *her swan song*
        Willow, willow, willow.
Moor, she was chaste. She loved thee, cruel Moor.
So come my soul to bliss as I speak true.
So speaking as I think, I die, I die.

                                          [*She dies.*]

OTHELLO.   I have another weapon in this chamber.
It is a sword of Spain, the ice brook's tempe*r*.   *tempered steel*
Oh, here it is.—Uncle, I must come forth.
    GRATIANO [*within*].   If thou attempt it, it will cost thee
        dear.
Thou hast no weapon, and perforce must suffer.
    OTHELLO.   Look in upon me then, and speak to me,
Or, nake*d* as I am, I will assault thee.   *unarmed*

    [*Re-enter* GRATIANO]

    GRATIANO.   What is the matter?
    OTHELLO.   Behold! I have a weapon.
A better never did itself sustain
Upon a soldier's thigh. I have seen the day
That with this little arm and this good sword
I have made my way through more impediments
Than twenty times your sto*p*. But—O vain boast!—   *power to stop*
Who can control his fate? 'Tis not so now.   *me*
Be not afraid, though you do see me weaponed.
Here is my journey's end, here is my but*t*   *target, goal*
And very sea-mar*k* of my utmos*t* sai*l*.   *beacon, limit*
Do you go back dismayed? 'Tis a lost fear.   *final voyage*
Ma*n* but a rus*h* against Othello's breast,   *Take . . . reed*
And he retires. Where should Othello go?
Now, how dost thou look now? O ill-starre*d* wench!   *ill-fated*
Pale as thy smock! When we shall meet at comp*t,*   *account,*
This look of thine will hurl my soul from Heaven,   *Judgment*
And fiends will snatch at it. Cold, cold, my girl?
Even like thy chastity.
O cursèd, cursèd slave! Whip me, ye devils,
From the possession of this heavenly sight!
Blow me about in winds! Roast me in sulphur!
Wash me in steep-dow*n* gulf*s* of liquid fire!   *sheer whirlpools*
O Desdemona! Desdemona! dead!
Oh! Oh! Oh!

[*Enter* LODOVICO, MONTANO, IAGO *as a prisoner, and*
OFFICERS, CASSIO *in a chair.*]

LODOVICO. Where is this rash and most unfortunate
    man?
OTHELLO. That's he that was Othello. Here I am.
LODOVICO. Where is that viper? Bring the villain
    forth.
OTHELLO. I look down towards his fee*t*, but that's a   *for cloven hoofs*
    fable.
If that thou be'st a devi*l*, I cannot kill thee.   *i.e., invulnerable*

   [*Wounds* IAGO.]

LODOVICO. Wrench his sword from him.
IAGO.   I bleed, sir, but not killed.
OTHELLO. I am not sorry neither. I'd have thee live,
For in my sen*se* 'tis happiness to die.   *opinion*
LODOVICO. O thou Othello, that wert once so good,
Fallen in the practi*ce* of a damnèd slave,   *by the plotting*
What shall be said to thee?
OTHELLO.   Why, anything.
An honorable murderer, if you will,
For naught did I in hate, but all in honor.
LODOVICO. This wretch hath part confessed his villainy.
Did you and he consent in Cassio's death?
OTHELLO. Ay.
CASSIO. Dear General, I did never give you cause.
OTHELLO. I do believe it, and I ask you pardon.
Will you, I pray, demand that demi-devil
Why he hath thus ensnared my soul and body.
IAGO. Demand me nothing. What you know, you
    know.
From this time forth I never will speak word.
LODOVICO. What! not to pray?
GRATIANO.   Torments will ope your lips.
OTHELLO. Well, thou dost best.
LODOVICO. Sir, you shall understand what hath befall'n,
Which, as I think, you know not. Here is a letter
Found in the pocket of the slain Roderigo,
And here another. The one of them import*s*   *concerns*
The death of Cassio to be undertook
By Roderigo.
OTHELLO. O villain!
CASSIO.   Most heathenish and m*o*st gross!

LODOVICO.   Now here's another discontente*d* paper,   *expressing dis-content*
Found in his pocket too.   And this, it seems,
Roderigo meant t' have sent this damnèd villain,
But tha*t*, belik*e,* Iago in the interim   *doubtless*
Cam*e* in and satisfied him.   *interposed*

OTHELLO.   O the pernicious caiti*ff!*   *wretch*
How came you, Cassio, by that handkerchief
That was my wife's?

CASSIO.   I found it in my chamber;
And he himself confessed it even now
That there he dropped it for a special purpose
Which wrough*t* to his desire.   *worked in with*

OTHELLO.   O fool! fool! fool!

CASSIO.   There is besides in Roderigo's letter
How he upbraids Iago that he made him
Brav*e* me upon the watch, whereon it came   *insult, defy*
That I was cas*t*.   And even but now he spake,   *dismissed*
After long seeming dead.   Iago hur*t* him,   *wounded*
Iago set him on.

LODOVICO [*to* OTHELLO].   You must forsake this room
          and go with us.
Your power and your command is taken off,
And Cassio rules in Cyprus.   For this slave,
If there be any cunning cruelty
That can torment him much and hold him lon*g,*   *long in dying*
It shall be his.   You shall close prisoner rest,
Till that the nature of your fault be known
To the Venetian state.   Come, bring him away.

OTHELLO.   Sof*t* you!   A word or two before you go.   *Wait*
I have done the State some service, and they know 't.
No more of that.   I pray you, in your letters,
When you shall these unlucky deeds relate,
Speak of me as I am.   Nothing extenuate,
Nor set down aught in malice.   Then must you speak
Of one that loved not wisely but too well—
Of one not easily jealous, but, being wrough*t,*   *worked upon*
Perplexe*d* in the extreme—of one whose hand,   *distraught*
Like the base Indian, threw a pearl away
Richer than all his tribe—of one whose subdued eyes,
Albeit unusèd to the meltin*g* mood,   *weeping*
Drops tears as fast as the Arabian trees
Their medicinal gum.   Set you down this,
And say besides, that in Aleppo once,
Where a malignant and a turbaned Turk
Beat a Venetian and traduce*d* the State,   *insulted*

I took by the throat the circumcisèd dog
And smote him thus.

   [He stabs himself.]

LODOVICO.   O bloody period!   *end*
GRATIANO.   All that is spoke is marred.   *spoiled*
OTHELLO.   I kissed thee ere I killed thee. No way but
   this,
Killing myself to die upon a kiss.
                         [Falls on the bed, and dies.]

CASSIO.   This did I fear, but thought he had no weapon;
For he was great of heart.
LODOVICO *[To* IAGO*]*.   O Spartan dog,   *hard-hearted*
More fell than anguish, hunger, or the sea.   *cruel*
Look on the tragic loading of this bed—   *burden*
This is thy work! The object poisons sight,
Let it be hid. Gratiano, keep the house,
And seize upon the fortunes of the Moor,
For they succeed to you. To you, Lord Governor,
Remains the censure of this hellish villain,   *sentencing*
The time, the place, the torture. Oh, enforce it!   *make it hard*
Myself will straight aboard, and to the State   *at once go home*
This heavy act with heavy heart relate.
                         [Exeunt omnes.]

FINIS

Two Critical Commentaries on Shakespeare's *Othello*

Commentary by Thomas Rymer from Chapter VII of *A Short View of
Tragedy* (London, 1692)—modernized in spelling and punctuation.

From all the tragedies acted on our English stage, *Othello* is said to bear
the bell away. The subject is more of a piece, and there is indeed something
like, there is, as it were, some phantom of a fable. The fable is always
accounted the soul of tragedy. And it is the fable which is properly the
poet's part. . . . This fable is drawn from a novel composed in Italian by
Giraldi Cinthio, who also was a writer of tragedies. . . . Shakespeare alters
it from the original in several particulars, but always, unfortunately, for the
worse. . . .

The Fable

*Othello, a blackamoor captain, by talking of his prowess and feats of war,
makes Desdemona, a senator's daughter, to be in love with him and to be
married to him without her parent's knowledge; and, having preferred Cassio*

to be his lieutenant, a place which his ensign Iago sued for, Iago in revenge works the Moor into a jealousy that Cassio cuckolds him—which he effects by stealing and conveying a certain handkerchief which had at the wedding been by the Moor presented to his bride. Hereupon Othello and Iago plot the deaths of Desdemona and Cassio. Othello murders her, and soon after is convinced of her innocence. And as he is about to be carried to prison in order to be punished for the murder, he kills himself.

Whatever rubs or difficulty may stick on the bark, the moral, sure, of this fable is very instructive:

First, this may be a caution to all maidens of quality how, without their parent's consent, they run away with blackamoors. . . .

Secondly, this may be a warning to all good wives that they look well to their linen.

Thirdly, this may be a lesson to husbands that before their jealousy be tragical the proofs may be mathematical. . . .

The *characters* or manners, which are the second part in a tragedy, are not less unnatural and improper than the fable was improbable and absurd.

Othello is made a Venetian general. We see nothing done by him nor related concerning him that comports with the condition of a general, or indeed of a man, unless the killing himself to avoid a death the Law was about to inflict upon him. When his jealousy had wrought him up to a resolution of his taking revenge for the supposed injury, he sets Iago to do the fighting part to kill Cassio, and chooses himself to murder the silly woman his wife, that was like to make no resistance.

His love and his jealousy are no part of a soldier's character, unless for comedy.

But what is most intolerable is Iago. He is no blackamoor soldier, so we may be sure he should be like other soldiers of our acquaintance; yet never in tragedy, nor in comedy, nor in nature, was a soldier with his character. . . .

Nor is our poet more discreet in his Desdemona. He had chosen a soldier for his knave, and a Venetian lady is to be the fool.

This senator's daughter runs away to a carrier's inn, the Sagittary, with a blackamoor, is no sooner wedded to him, but the very night she beds him is importuning and teasing him for a young smock-faced lieutenant, Cassio. And though she perceives the Moor jealous of Cassio, yet will she not forbear, but still rings 'Cassio, Cassio' in both his ears.

Roderigo is the cully of Iago, brought in to be murdered by Iago, that Iago's hands might be the more in blood, and be yet the more abominable villain—who, without that, was too wicked on all conscience, and had more to answer for than any tragedy or Furies could inflict upon him. So there can be nothing in the *characters* either for the profit or to delight an audience.

The third thing to be considered is the *thoughts*. But from such characters we need not expect many that are either true, or fine, or noble.

And without these, that is, without sense or meaning, the fourth part of tragedy, which is the *expression,* can hardly deserve to be treated on distinctly. The verse rumbling in our ears are of good use to help off the action. . . .

So much ado, so much stress, so much passion and repetition about an handkerchief! Why was not this called the Tragedy of the Handkerchief?

What can be more absurd . . . ? Had it been Desdemona's garter, the sagacious Moor might have smelt a rat, but the handkerchief is so remote a trifle, no booby on this side of Mauritania could make any consequence from it. . . .

Rather may we ask here what unnatural crime Desdemona or her parents had committed to bring this judgment down upon her: to wed a blackamoor and, innocent, to be thus cruelly murdered by him. What instruction can we make out of this catastrophe? Or whither must our reflection lead us? Is not this to envenom and sour our spirits, to make us repine and grumble at Providence and the government of the world? If this be our end, what boots it to be virtuous?

Desdemona dropped the handkerchief and missed it that very day after her marriage—it might have been rumpled up with her wedding sheets. And this night that she lay in her wedding sheets, the Fairy Napkin (whilst Othello was stifling her) might have started up to disarm his fury and stop his ungracious mouth. Then might she, in a trance for fear, have lain as dead. Then might he, believing her dead, touched with remorse, have honestly cut his own throat, by the good leave and with the applause of all the spectators—who might thereupon have gone home with a quiet mind, admiring the beauty of Providence, fairly and truly represented on the theater. . . .

But from this scene to the end of the play we meet with nothing but blood and butchery, described much-what to the style of the last speeches and confessions of the persons executed at Tyburn. . . . Desdemona dropped her handkerchief; therefore she must be stifled. Othello, by law to be broken on the wheel, by the poet's cunning escapes with cutting his own throat. Cassio, for I know not what, comes off with a broken shin. Iago murders his benefactor, Roderigo, as this were poetical gratitude. Iago is not yet killed, because there yet never was such a villain alive. . . .

What can remain with the audience to carry home with them from this sort of poetry for their use and edification? How can it work, unless (instead of settling the mind and purging our passions) to delude our senses, disorder our thoughts, addle our brain, pervert our affections, hair our imaginations, corrupt our appetite, and fill our head with vanity, confusion. . . ? Our only hopes for the good of their souls can be that these people go to the playhouse as they do to church, to sit still, look on one another, make no reflection, nor mind the play more than they would a sermon. . . .

Commentary by Harold C. Goddard, from *The Meaning of Shakespeare* (Chicago, University of Chicago Press, 1951).*

The deliberate placing of the highest intellectual gifts and achievements at the service of the lowest human instincts is a phenomenon with which the twentieth century is acquainted on a scale never previously attained. . . . The ideological warfare that precedes and precipitates the physical conflict

* Reprinted from *The Meaning of Shakespeare* by Harold C. Goddard, by permission of The University of Chicago Press. Copyright 1951, The University of Chicago.

(*cold* war as it has significantly come to be called); the propaganda that prepares and unifies public opinion; the conscription, in a dozen spheres, of the nation's brains; the organization of what is revealingly known as the *intelligence* service; but most of all the practical absorption of science into the military effort: these things, apart from the knowledge and skill required for the actual fighting, permit us to define modern war, once it is begun, as an unreserved dedication of the human intellect to death and destruction.

But that is exactly what Iago is—an unreserved dedication of intellect to death and destruction. To the extent that this is true, Iago is an incarnation of the spirit of modern war. . . .   (p. 464)

To those who forget Emerson's wise observation that "perpetual modernness is the measure of merit in any work of art" all this will be an unpardonable digression from the play. To them it will be allegorizing *Othello,* reading into it what could never have entered Shakespeare's head. On the contrary, it is in this case demonstrable from the text that Shakespeare definitely intended precisely this equation between Iago and War, though, naturally, he could not have foreseen how the changes in the conduct of war between his time and ours were to sharpen and point the analogy. . . .   (p. 465)

I doubt whether many people think of *Othello* as a play about war. But it is, even literally. Three of its four main characters are warriors. And the fourth is a warrior's wife, herself referred to by her husband at the climax of his joy as 'my fair warrior.' Even Cassio, whom Iago so despised, was considered worthy by the home government of taking Othello's place in Cyprus. Furthermore, the war between the Venetians and the Turks, which is the background and occasion of the action, is as indispensable to the plot and the 'moral' as the feud between the Capulets and the Montagues is to *Romeo and Juliet.* . . .   (pp. 465-66)

The Turk in this play, until he disappears beneath the waves, is consistently represented as the Enemy. . . . All this at first sight seems of no intrinsic interest. It is mere machinery, mere scenery against which the domestic drama is to be enacted. . . . Reread the play with sharp attention to the parts in which war figures, pondering particularly every allusion to the Turks —there are many of them—and it is inescapable that what Shakespeare is bent on is an insinuation into the underconsciousness of the reader of an analogy between Iago and the Turk. Indeed, in one passage Iago openly makes the identification himself. . . .   (p. 466)

Thus does Shakespeare tie Iago with the Turk—and so with the Enemy, and so with War. The connection is too often reiterated to be coincidence. It is too clearly contrived to be unconscious. It is plainly intentional. . . .   (p. 469)

The secret of social and political strife, of conflict between nations, is only that of individual and domestic strife writ large. War and peace, says *Othello,* . . . are states of the soul. War in the military sense is the outer manifestation of war in the psychological sense pre-existing in the inner worlds of its fomenters and participants. That is not saying that outer conditions have nothing to do with the production of war. But it is only as those conditions first produce a military state of the soul that they secondly produce war in its more generally accepted sense. And, no matter how adverse, they do not necessarily produce a military state of the soul, as Desdemona shows; on the contrary, as Iago shows, that state is a most potent producer of those very conditions. It was to demonstrate this double truth that Dostoevsky wrote *Crime and Punishment*. *Othello* demonstrates it even more compactly.

(p. 492)

III. THE RIDICULOUS PRÉCIEUSES
A Neoclassic Comedy by Molière

Introductory Note to Molière and *Les Précieuses Ridicules*

Unlike Sophocles, who wrote tragedies for festival production in a vast hillside amphitheater, and Shakespeare, who wrote a great variety of dramas for entertainment of the public in playhouses that looked much like innyards open to the sky, Molière wrote farces and comedies for the diversion of the courtly and urbane in what was essentially a modern theater. Though his stage is closer to our own, the fact that he wrote comedy may seem to remove him a bit further from us. For comedy is characteristically time-bound to its period, and it takes a certain consciousness of the social context to enjoy the comedies of yesteryear to the full.

Molière—to use his theatrical name—was born in Paris in 1622, the son of a respectable upholsterer, Jean Poquelin III, who was soon after named official upholsterer to the King. The boy, Jean Baptiste Poquelin, was expected to follow in his father's footsteps. He was given a good education in the humanities at the Jesuit college of Clermont, among sons of the best families of France, including the Prince de Conti and perhaps Cyrano de Bergerac. Then he studied law, was probably admitted to the bar at twenty-one. But he became interested in the theater, perhaps the influence of the red-haired actress Madeleine Béjart, a few years his senior, who lived nearby. He threw in his lot, as Molière, with a little theater group, principally members of the Béjart family. The Illustrious Theater struggled for survival in Paris for a couple of years before failing. Then the troupe took to the road and played in the southern provinces of France for the next thirteen years.

Thereafter, in 1658, under the guidance of Molière and Madeleine, the company returned to Paris with great success. The little farces and comedies that Molière had begun writing, with suitable parts for himself and his fellow actors, amused the young King Louis XIV, and Molière was repeatedly called to perform at Court and to

320

write and stage comedy ballets for sumptuous entertainments at Versailles. With success and financial means, Molière—at the age of forty—married the younger sister (some said daughter) of his long-time intimate friend and early mistress, Madeleine Béjart. Armande was twenty-one years his junior, and he had watched her grow up during the years of family friendship. She was attractive, flirtatious, extravagant. She became a charming actress. Their first child, a son, died; their second, a daughter, lived. Molière, who bore the chief burdens of his theatrical troupe—writing new comedies, directing them, acting the main roles—was apparently ill-suited to domestic life. Whether he was melancholy or jealous, preoccupied with his work or fussy about their elaborate home, marital strain was followed by some years of separation. He was engaged in bitter controversy over certain of his plays; the King made unreasonable demands upon his time and creative energies; he was plagued by growing ill-health. After several years, friends effected a reconciliation between Molière and his wife—they had continued to act together, and he wrote delightful parts for her—and a second son was born to them, only to die within a month. His life-long friend Madeleine had died that winter, and exactly a year after her death, Molière himself died, February 17, 1673, at the age of fifty-one.

Nearly all his thirty-two plays that survive are farces, comedies, or comedy ballets. In them one can see elements of the native French farce (with its domestic slapstick), Spanish comedy of intrigue (with its cape and sword), Italian *commedia dell' arte* (with its stock characters and masks), and Roman comedy (with Plautine story and Terentian style). But Molière was not only a practical actor-dramatist, he was also a respected man of letters, a friend of artists (like Mignard), of poets (like La Fontaine and Boileau), and of the great Prince de Condé and the King himself. With powerful and influential friends, however, he also made important and bitter enemies.

Beginning with *Les Précieuses Ridicules* (1659), a succession of his comedies involved him in sharp controversy. Through this play, for instance, he offended the rival company of actors, certain of the ladies of society, and the brash and overdressed new marquises of the Court. Awaiting their chance, they attacked *L'École des Femmes* ("The School for Wives") in 1662, which was variously said to be indecent, subversive of female education, and dramaturgically improper. He answered his critics in two clever one-act comedies. Then *Tartuffe* (or "The Impostor") created a storm in 1664 that kept the play under a ban for five years—it was said to attack good churchmen and therefore religion itself. *Don Juan* (1665), declared to be impious and atheistical, was withdrawn.

Although he professed that his purpose was simply to make decent people laugh, his comedies and even his hilarious farces shot satirical darts at the inflated, the pretentious, and the false. *Le Misanthrope* ("The Man-hater") laughed critically at the overearnest as well as the superficial in society; *Le Médecin Malgré Lui* ("The Mock Doctor") ridiculed medical quackery; *L'Avare* ("The Miser") satirized the worship of money; *Le Bourgeois Gentilhomme* ("The Would-Be Gentleman") mocked the cultural pretensions of the newly-rich; *Les Femmes Savantes* ("The Learned Ladies") exposed false ideals in education for women; *La Malade Imaginaire* ("The Imaginary Invalid") poked fun at the hypochondriac and at medical pedantry. It was while playing the part of the imaginary invalid—though himself desperately ill—that Molière was taken with his final seizure, to die that evening and (because of enemies still rankling in the Church) to be refused the last rites and decent burial.

Les Précieuses Ridicules is here called "The Ridiculous Précieuses." Other titles given it in English are "The Ridiculous Damosels," "The Romantic Ladies," "The Affected Young Ladies," "The High-Brow Ladies." And something might be said for "The Dizzy Debutantes" or "Two Dames from Dubuque." This comedy, in one rather long act, was probably first performed on November 18, 1659, at the Petit Bourbon theater in Paris. Molière himself played Mascarille to the hilt, with Madeleine, La Grange, Du Croisy, and Jodelet appearing in parts under their own (or rather stage) names. Those struck by its satire were influential enough to prevent its being repeated. But the manuscript was sent to the King, and he approved it, perhaps with some minor changes. On December 2 (at double prices) it was again given, before an enthusiastic and crowded house, and was performed thirty-two times before Easter. Molière, hearing of a bookseller's scheme to publish a pirated version (together with a parody), himself authorized its publication, for which he wrote a graceful preface.

This short play by Molière and his longer works that followed were shortly translated, adapted, or plundered for the English stage. They established themselves as indubitable classics in the repertory of La Comédie Française in Paris and are still played regularly each season. A recording of *Les Précieuses Ridicules* by that company is available in French.

THE RIDICULOUS PRÉCIEUSES
(LES PRÉCIEUSES RIDICULES)

A Comedy In One Act by Jean Baptiste Poquelin Molière

THE CHARACTERS

LA GRANGE ⎫
DU CROISY ⎭ —*worth-while young men of Paris.*

GORGIBUS—*a substantial middle-class citizen.*

MADELON—*his socially-pretentious daughter.*
CATHOS—*her equally pretentious cousin.*

The MARQUIS DE MASCARILLE—*who pays them a call.*
The VISCOUNT JODELET—*who also comes to see them.*

MAROTTE—*the maid to the pretentious young women.*
ALMANZOR, *the footman,* NEIGHBORS, *and* FIDDLERS.

Time: *the mid-seventeenth century in France.*
Place: *the bourgeois home of Gorgibus in Paris.*

SCENE. *The groundfloor great-hall of* GORGIBUS' *house. As the play opens,* LA GRANGE *and* DU CROISY *have just come down from the upstairs drawing room and are on their way to the street door.*

SCENE I. LA GRANGE, DU CROISY

DU CROISY. My worthy La Grange!
LA GRANGE. What now?
DU CROISY. Just look at me without laughing.
LA GRANGE. Well?
DU CROISY. What do you think of our visit? Are you satisfied with it?
LA GRANGE. Do you think either of us has any reason to be?
DU CROISY. Not at all, to tell you the truth.
LA GRANGE.   As for me, I must say that I was quite put out about it. Say now, did ever anybody see a couple of country wenches giving themselves more ridiculous airs, or two men treated with more contempt than we were? They could hardly make up their mind to order chairs for us. I never saw such whispering as went on between them, such yawning, such rubbing of the eyes, and asking so often what time it was. Did they answer anything but "yes," or "no," to what we said to them? In short,

do you not agree with me that if we had been the scum of the earth, we could not have been treated worse?

DU CROISY.   You seem to take it to heart.

LA GRANGE.   No doubt I do, so much so that I am resolved to be revenged on them for their impertinence. I know well enough why they slight us. Affectation has not alone infected Paris, but has also spread into the country, and our ridiculous damsels have sucked in their share of it. In a word, they are a strange medley of preciosity and coquetry. I plainly see what kind of persons will be well received by them. If you will take my advice, we will play them such a trick as shall show them their folly, and teach them to recognize a little better the people they have to deal with.

DU CROISY.   And how can you do this?

LA GRANGE.   I have a certain valet, named Mascarille, who, in the opinion of many people, passes for a kind of wit—for nothing now-a-days is cheaper than wit. He is an extraordinary fellow, who has taken it into his head to ape the man of quality. He usually prides himself on his gallantry and his poetry, and despises so much the other valets that he calls them brutes.

DU CROISY.   Well, what do you mean to do with him?

LA GRANGE.   What do I mean to do with him? He must . . . but first, let's get out of here.

[*They go toward the street door.*]

SCENE II. GORGIBUS, DU CROISY, LA GRANGE.

GORGIBUS [*entering as from his den*].   Well, you have seen my niece and my daughter. How are things going? What's the result of your visit?

LA GRANGE.   They will tell you this better than we. All we can say is: We thank you for the favor you've done us, and remain your most humble servants.

DU CROISY.   Your most humble servants.

[*They leave.*]

GORGIBUS [*alone*].   Hoity-toity! It seems to me they go away dissatisfied. What has upset them? I must find out. [*Calling*] Hi, there!

SCENE III. GORGIBUS, MAROTTE.

MAROTTE [*entering as from upstairs*].   What is it, monsieur?

GORGIBUS.   Where are your mistresses?

MAROTTE.   In their room.

GORGIBUS.   What are they doing?

MAROTTE.   Making lip salve.

GORGIBUS.   There is no end of their pomades. Tell them to come down.

[MAROTTE *exits.*]

These hussies with their ointments have, I think, a mind to ruin me. Everywhere in the house I see nothing but whites of eggs, lac virginal, and a thousand other fooleries I am not acquainted with. Since we have been here they have used up the lard of a dozen hogs at least, and four servants might live on the sheep feet they use every day.

SCENE IV.   MADELON, CATHOS, GORGIBUS.

GORGIBUS [*as the girls come downstairs*].   There's real need, is there, to spend so much money to grease your faces! Tell me, what have you done to those gentlemen that I saw leaving so coldly. Did I not tell you to receive them as persons whom I intended for your husbands?

MADELON.   Dear father, what consideration do you expect us to entertain for the irregular behavior of these people?

CATHOS.   How can a girl of any sense at all, dear uncle, put up with such people?

GORGIBUS.   What fault do you to find with 'em?

MADELON.   Theirs is fine gallantry, indeed. Would you believe it? they began with proposing marriage to us.

GORGIBUS.   With what would you have them begin—with keeping you? Is not their proposal a compliment, to you as well as to me? Can anything be more polite than this? And do they not prove the honesty of their intentions by wishing to enter these holy bonds?

MADELON.   Oh, father! Nothing can be more vulgar than what you have just said. I am ashamed to hear you talk in such a manner. You should cultivate the bel air of things.

GORGIBUS.   I care neither for bel airs nor songs. I tell you marriage is a holy and sacred affair. To begin with that is to act like honest people.

MADELON.   Good Heavens! If everybody was like you a love-story would soon be over. What a fine thing it would have been if Cyrus had immediately espoused Mandane, and if Aronce had been married all at once to Clélie.

GORGIBUS.   What is she jabbering about?

MADELON.   Here is my cousin, father, who will tell you as well as I that matrimony ought never to happen till after other adventures. A lover, to be attractive, must understand how to utter fine sentiments, to breathe soft, tender, and passionate vows—his courtship must be according to the rules. In the first place, he should behold the fair one of whom he becomes enamoured either at a church, or when out walking, or at some public ceremony; or else he should be introduced to her by a relative or a friend, as if by chance, and when he leaves her he should appear pensive and melancholy. For some time he should conceal his passion from the object of his love, but pay her several visits, in every one of which he ought to introduce some gallant subject to exercise the wits of all the company. When the day comes to make his declaration—which generally should be contrived in some shady garden-walk while the company is at a distance—it should be quickly followed by anger, shown by our blushing, which banishes the lover for a time from our presence. Then he finds means to appease us, to accustom us gradually to hear him describe his passion, and to draw from us that confession which causes us so much pain. After that come the adventures, the rivals who thwart mutual inclination, the persecutions of fathers, the jealousies arising without any foundation, complaints, despair, abduction, and its consequences. Thus things are carried on in society, and true gallantry cannot dispense with these forms. But to come out point-blank with a proposal of marriage—to make no love but with a marriage-contract—is to begin a novel at the wrong end! Once more, father, nothing can be more bourgeois, and the mere thought of it makes me sick at heart.

GORGIBUS. What damned jargon is all this? This is hifalutin for sure!

CATHOS. Indeed, uncle, my cousin hits the nail on the head. How can we receive kindly those who are so awkward in gallantry? I could lay a wager they have not even seen a map of the country of *Tenderness,* and that *Love-letters, Trifling attentions, Polite epistles,* and *Sprightly verses* are regions to them unknown. Do you not see that their whole bearing shows it, and that they do not have that air which at a glance gives one a good opinion of people? To come and pay a visit to the object of their love with a leg without any ornaments, a hat without any feathers, a head with its locks inartistically arranged, and a coat that suffers from an insufficiency of ribbons. . . ! Heavens! what lovers are these! what stinginess in dress! what barrenness of conversation! It is unendurable; it is not to be borne. I also observed that their collars were unfashionable and that their breeches were not wide enough by more than half-a-foot.

GORGIBUS. I think they are both mad, nor can I understand anything of this gibberish. Cathos, and you Madelon . . .

MADELON. Pray, father, do not use those strange names, and call us by some other.

GORGIBUS. What do you mean by those strange names? Are they not your Christian names?

MADELON. Good Heavens! how vulgar you are! I confess I wonder how you could possibly be the father of such an intelligent girl as I am. Did ever anybody in genteel style talk of Cathos or of Madelon? And must you not admit that either of these names would be sufficient to disgrace the finest novel in the world?

CATHOS. It is true, uncle, a sensitive ear suffers extremely at hearing these words pronounced, and the name of Polixena, which my cousin has chosen, and that of Amintha, which I have taken, possesses a charm that you must needs acknowledge.

GORGIBUS. Listen—one word will be enough. I do not allow you to take any other names than those that were given you by your godfathers and godmothers; and as for those gentlemen we are speaking about, I know their families and their fortunes, and am determined they shall be your husbands. I am tired of having you upon my hands. Looking after a couple of girls is too heavy a responsibility for a man of my age.

CATHOS. As for me, uncle, all I can say is, that I think marriage a very shocking business. How can one endure the thought of lying beside a man who's actually naked?

MADELON. Give us leave to take the air for a while among the beau-monde of Paris, where we have just arrived. Allow us to sketch at leisure the outline of our novel, and do not hurry on the conclusion too abruptly.

GORGIBUS [aside]. I can no longer doubt it: they are stark mad. [Aloud] Once more, I tell you, I understand nothing of all this gibberish. I will be master, and to cut short all kinds of arguments, either you shall both be married shortly, or, upon my word, you shall be nuns—that I swear.

[He leaves.]

SCENE V. CATHOS, MADELON.

CATHOS. Good Heavens, my dear, how deeply is your father still immersed in material things! how dense his understanding, and what gloom overcasts his soul!

MADELON. What can I do, my dear? I am ashamed of him. I can hardly persuade myself I am indeed his daughter; I believe that, some time or other, it will be discovered that I am of more illustrious descent.

CATHOS. I believe it; really, it is very likely. As for me, when I consider myself . . .

SCENE VI. CATHOS, MADELON, MAROTTE.

MAROTTE [entering]. Here is a footman asks if you are at home, and says his master would like to come to see you.

MADELON. Learn, stupid, to express yourself a little less vulgarly. Say, "Here is an attendant inquiring if it is commodious for you to become visible."

MAROTTE. Bless me! I don't understand Latin, and haven't learned ph'los'phy out of *Cyrus,* like you.

MADELON. Impertinent creature! How can this be borne! And who is this footman's master?

MAROTTE. He told me it was the Marquis de Mascarille.

MADELON. Ah, my dear, a marquis! Well, go and tell him we are visible. This is certainly some wit who has heard of us.

CATHOS. Undoubtedly, my dear.

MADELON. We had better receive him here in this parlor than in our room. Let us at least arrange our hair a little and so maintain our reputation. Come, quickly, and hold for us the Counsellor of the Graces.

MAROTTE. Upon my word, I do not know what sort of a beast that is. You must speak like a Christian if you want me to get your meaning.

CATHOS. Bring us the looking-glass, blockhead! and take care not to soil its surface by the reflection of your image.

[They go upstairs.]

SCENE VII. MASCARILLE, TWO CHAIRMEN.

MASCARILLE *[entering in a sedan chair carried by two porters]*. Stop, chairman, stop. Easy does it! Easy, easy! I think these idiots intend to break me to pieces by jolting me against the walls and the pavement.

FIRST CHAIRMAN. Gad, because the gate is narrow and you would make us bring you in here.

MASCARILLE. To be sure! You rascals, would you have me expose the fulness of my plumes to the inclemency of the rainy season, and let the mud receive the impression of my shoes? Begone, take away your chair.

SECOND CHAIRMAN. Then please to pay us, monsieur.

MASCARILLE. What?

SECOND CHAIRMAN. I say, monsieur, give us our money, if you please.

MASCARILLE *[giving him a box on the ear]*. What, scoundrel, to ask money from a person of my rank!

SECOND CHAIRMAN. Is this the way poor people are to be paid? Will your rank get us a dinner?

MASCARILLE. Ha, ha! I shall teach you to keep your place. These fellows dare to make sport of me!

FIRST CHAIRMAN *[taking up one of the poles of his chair]*. Come, pay us at once.

MASCARILLE. What?

FIRST CHAIRMAN. I say I'll have my money right now.

MASCARILLE. That is sensible.

FIRST CHAIRMAN. Quick, then.

MASCARILLE. Ay, *you* speak properly, but the other is a rascal who does not know what he says. There, are you satisfied?

FIRST CHAIRMAN. No, I am not satisfied. You boxed my friend's ears, and . . . *[holding up his pole]*.

MASCARILLE. Gently. There is something for the box on the ear. People may get anything from me if they go about it in the right way. Go now, but come and fetch me by and by to carry me to the Louvre to the *petit coucher*.

[The CHAIRMEN exeunt.]

Scene VIII. MAROTTE, MASCARILLE.

MAROTTE [*entering*]. Monsieur, my mistresses will come immediately.

MASCARILLE. Let them not hurry themselves. I am very comfortable here, and can wait.

MAROTTE. Here they come.

Scene IX. MADELON, CATHOS, MASCARILLE, ALMANZOR.

MASCARILLE [*after having bowed to them*]. No doubt you will be surprised at the boldness of my visit, mesdames, but your reputation has drawn this disagreeable affair upon you. Merit has for me such potent charms that I run after it everywhere.

MADELON. If you pursue merit you should not hunt upon our estate.

CATHOS. If you find merit amongst us, you must have brought it hither yourself.

MASCARILLE. Ah! I protest against these words. When fame mentioned your deserts it spoke the truth, and you are going to *pic, repic,* and *capot* all that is gallant, taking all the tricks in Paris.

MADELON. Your courtesy goes a little too far in the liberality of its praises. My cousin and I must take care not to give too much credit to your sweet adulation.

CATHOS. My dear, we should call for chairs.

MADELON. Almanzor!

ALMANZOR. [*appearing at a side door*]. Madame.

MADELON. Convey to us hither, instantly, the conveniences of conversation.

MASCARILLE. But, first of all, am I safe here?

[ALMANZOR *proceeds to set forth chairs.*]

CATHOS. What is it you fear?

MASCARILLE. Some grand larceny of my heart, some assassination of liberty. I behold here a pair of eyes that seem to be very naughty boys, that affront liberty, and use a heart most barbarously. Why the deuce do they put themselves on their murderous guard when anyone comes near them? Upon my word, I mistrust them! I must either scamper away, or have some guarantee that they'll do me no mischief.

MADELON. My dear, what a charming facetiousness he has!

CATHOS. I see, indeed, he is an Amilcar.

MADELON. Fear nothing, our eyes have no wicked designs, and your heart may rest in peace, fully assured of their innocence.

CATHOS. But, pray, monsieur, be not inexorable to the easy chair, which, for this last quarter of an hour, has held out its arms towards you. Satisfy its desire to embrace you.

MASCARILLE [*after having combed himself, and adjusted the rolls of his stockings*].   Well, mesdames, and what do you think of Paris?

MADELON.   Alas! what can we think of it?   It would be the very antipodes of reason not to confess that Paris is the grand emporium of marvels, the center of good taste, wit, and gallantry.

MASCARILLE.   As for me, I maintain that, out of Paris, there is no salvation for people of culture.

CATHOS.   Most assuredly.

MASCARILLE.   Paris is somewhat muddy; but then we have sedan chairs.

MADELON.   To be sure; a sedan chair is a wonderful protection against the insults of mud and bad weather.

MASCARILLE.   You receive many visits?   What great wit belongs to your circle?

MADELON.   Alas! we are not yet known, but we are in the way of being so; for a lady of our acquaintance has promised us to bring all the gentlemen who have written for the little magazines.

CATHOS.   And certain others, whom, we have been told, are likewise the sovereign arbiters of all that is cultured and refined.

MASCARILLE.   I can manage this for you better than any one.   They all visit me, and I may say that I never rise without having half-a-dozen wits at my levee.

MADELON.   Good Heavens! you will place us under the greatest obligation if you will do us this kindness, for it is certain we must make the acquaintance of all those gentlemen if we wish to belong to the fashion. They are the persons who can make or unmake one's reputation in Paris. You know that there are some, whose mere visits are sufficient to start the report that you are a *Connaisseuse,* though there should be no other reason for it.   As for me, what I value particularly is, that by means of these ingenious visits, we learn a hundred things which we ought necessarily to know, and which are the quintessence of wit.   Through them we hear the scandal of the day, or whatever niceties are going on in prose or verse.   We know, at the right time, that Monsieur So-and-so has written the finest piece in the world on such a subject; that Madame So-and-so has adapted words to such a tune; that a certain gentleman has written a madrigal upon a favor shown to him; another stanzas upon a fair one who betrayed him; Monsieur Such-a-one wrote a couplet of six lines yesterday evening to Mademoiselle Such-a-one, to which she returned him an answer this morning at eight o'clock; such an author is engaged on such a subject; this writer is busy with the third volume of his novel; that one is putting his works to press.   Those things procure you consideration in every society, and if people are ignorant of them, I would not give one pin for all the wit they may have.

CATHOS.   Indeed, I think it the height of absurdity for anyone who possesses the slightest claim to be called clever not to know even the smallest couplet that is made every day. As for me, I should be very much ashamed if anyone should ask me my opinion about something new, and I had not seen it.

MASCARILLE.   It is really a shame not to know from the very first all that is going on. But do not give yourself any farther trouble, I will establish an Academy of wits at your house, and I give you my word that not a single line of poetry shall be written in Paris, which you shall not know by heart before anybody else. As for me, such as you see me, I amuse myself in that way when I am in the humor, and you may find handed about in the fashionable assemblies of Paris two hundred songs, as many sonnets, four hundred epigrams, and more than a thousand madrigals all made by me, without counting riddles and portraits.

MADELON.   I must acknowledge that I dote upon character portraits. I think there is nothing more charming.

MASCARILLE.   Portraits are difficult, and call for great wit. You shall see some of mine that will not displease you.

CATHOS.   As for me, I am awfully fond of riddles.

MASCARILLE.   They exercise the intelligence. I have already written four of them this morning, which I will give you to guess.

MADELON.   Madrigals are pretty enough when neatly turned.

MASCARILLE.   That is my special talent. I am at present engaged in turning the whole of Roman history into madrigals.

MADELON.   Goodness gracious, that will certainly be the last word! I should like to have at least one copy if you publish it.

MASCARILLE.   I promise you each a copy, in the best binding. It does not become a man of my rank to scribble, but I do it only to serve the publishers, who are always pestering me.

MADELON.   I imagine it must be delightful to see oneself in print.

MASCARILLE.   Undoubtedly. But, by the by, I must recite for you some impromptu verses I made yesterday at the house of a certain duchess, an acquaintance of mine. I am damned clever at extempore verses.

CATHOS.   Extempore verses are certainly the very touchstone of genius.

MASCARILLE.   Listen then.

MADELON.   We are all ears.

MASCARILLE.   *Oh! oh! quite without heed was I,*
         As harmless you I chanced to spy,
              Slily your eyes
              My heart surprise.
         Stop thief! stop thief! stop thief I cry!

CATHOS.   Good Heavens! this is absolutely charming.

MASCARILLE.   Everything I do has the air of a gentleman. There is nothing of the pedant about me.

MADELON.   Two thousand miles from that!

MASCARILLE. Did you observe the beginning, *Oh! oh!?* There is something original in that *oh! oh!* Like a man who all of a sudden thinks about something, *oh! oh!* Taken by surprise as it were, *oh! oh!*

MADELON. Yes, I think that *oh! oh!* admirable.

MASCARILLE. It seems a mere nothing.

CATHOS. Good Heavens! How can you say so? It is one of these things that are priceless.

MADELON. No doubt of it. I would rather have written that *oh! oh!* than an epic poem.

MASCARILLE. Gad, you have good taste.

MADELON. Well, not the worst, anyway.

MASCARILLE. But do you not also admire *quite without heed was I? Quite without heed was I,* that is, I did not pay attention to anything; a natural way of speaking, *quite without heed was I*—of no harm thinking—that is, as I was going along, innocently, without malice, like a poor sheep, *you I chanced to spy,* that is to say, I amuse myself with looking at you, with observing you, with contemplating you. *Slily your eyes. . . .* What do you think of that word *slily*—is it not well chosen?

CATHOS. Perfect.

MASCARILLE. *Slily,* stealthily; just like a cat watching a mouse—*slily.*

MADELON. Nothing can be better.

MASCARILLE. *My heart surprise,* that is, your eyes carry it away from me, rob me of it. *Stop thief! stop thief! stop thief!* Would you not think a man were shouting and running after a thief to catch him? *Stop thief! stop thief! stop thief!*

MADELON. I must admit the turn is witty and sprightly.

MASCARILLE. I will sing you the tune I made to it.

CATHOS. Have you learned music?

MASCARILLE. I? Not at all.

CATHOS. How can you make a tune then?

MASCARILLE. People of rank know everything without ever having learned anything.

MADELON. Of course, my dear.

MASCARILLE. Listen if you like the tune: *Hem, hem. La, la, la, la.* The inclemency of the season has greatly injured the delicacy of my voice; but no matter, it is still gentlemanly. [*He sings*] *Oh! oh! quite without heed was I. . . .*

CATHOS. What a passion breathes in this air! Might one not die with delight?

MADELON. There is something plaintive about it.

MASCARILLE. Don't you think that the air expresses the sentiment perfectly? *Stop thief, stop thief!* And then as if someone cried out very loud, *Stop, stop, stop, stop, stop, stop thief!* Then all at once like a person out of breath, *Stop thief!*

MADELON. Thus it is to understand the perfection of things, the grand perfection, the perfection of perfections. I declare it is altogether wonderful. I am absolutely charmed by the air and the words.

CATHOS. I never yet met with anything so excellent.

MASCARILLE. Everything I do comes naturally, without study.

MADELON. Nature has treated you like a very fond mother, and you are her spoiled child.

MASCARILLE. How do you pass the time, ladies?

CATHOS. With nothing at all.

MADELON. Until now we have endured a terrible fasting from diversion.

MASCARILLE. I am at your service to take you to the theater one of these days, if you will permit me. Indeed, a new comedy is to be acted which I should very much like us to see together.

MADELON. There is no refusing you.

MASCARILLE. But I hope you will applaud it when we go, for I have promised to give the piece a helping hand. The author called upon me this very morning to beg me to do so. It is the custom here for authors to come and read their new plays to people of rank, to induce us to approve of them and give them a reputation. And you may well imagine whether, when we say anything, the pit dares to contradict us. As for me, I am very punctual in these things, and when I have made a promise to a poet, I always cry out "Bravo" before the candles are lighted.

MADELON. Do not say another word—Paris is a wonderful place. A hundred things happen every day which people in the country, however clever, have no idea of.

CATHOS. Since you have told us, we shall make it a point to applaud every word that is said.

MASCARILLE. If I am not mistaken, you look as if you had written a play yourself.

MADELON. Eh! there may be something in what you say.

MASCARILLE. Ah! upon my word, we must see it. Between ourselves, I have written one which I intend to have acted.

CATHOS. Ay! to which company do you mean to give it?

MASCARILLE. What a question! To the great actors of the Hôtel de Bourgogne. They are the only ones who can do it justice. The others are ignorant fellows who recite their parts just as people talk in everyday life. They don't know how to roar out the verses, or how to pause at a beautiful passage. How can you know where the good lines are if the actor doesn't stop at them so as to tell you when to applaud?

CATHOS. Indeed! that is one way of making an audience feel the beauties of any work. Things are only prized when well set off.

MASCARILLE. How do you like my accessories? Do you think they go with my coat?

CATHOS.　Perfectly.

MASCARILLE.　The ribbon is well chosen.

MADELON.　Fabulously. It is real Perdrigeon.

MASCARILLE.　What do you say to my knee ruffles?

MADELON.　They certainly are smart.

MASCARILLE.　I may at least boast that they are a quarter of a yard wider than any that have been made.

MADELON.　I must admit I never saw elegance of dress carried further.

MASCARILLE.　Fasten the reflection of your olfactories upon these gloves.

MADELON.　They smell terribly good.

CATHOS.　I never inhaled a more exquisite perfume.

MASCARILLE.　And this? [*He gives them his powdered wig to smell.*]

MADELON.　It has the most aristocratic odor. It titillates the higher senses most deliciously.

MASCARILLE.　You say nothing of my plumes. How do you like them?

CATHOS.　Frightfully beautiful.

MASCARILLE.　Do you know that every single one of them cost me a Louis-d'or? But it is my hobby to have everything of the very best.

MADELON.　I assure you that you and I are sympathetic. I am furiously particular about everything I wear. I cannot even endure stockings unless they are bought at a fashionable shop.

MASCARILLE [*crying out suddenly*].　Oh! oh! oh! gently. Damme, mesdames, you treat me very badly—I have reason to complain of your behavior—it is not fair.

CATHOS.　What is it? What is the matter?

MASCARILLE.　What! two at once against my heart! To attack me thus right and left. Ha! This is contrary to the law of nations, the combat is too unequal, and I must cry out, "Murder!"

CATHOS.　Well, he does say things in a peculiar way.

MADELON.　He is a consummate wit.

CATHOS.　You are more afraid than hurt, and your heart cries out before it is even wounded.

MASCARILLE.　The devil it does! it is wounded all over from head to foot.

Scene X.　CATHOS, MADELON, MASCARILLE, MAROTTE.

MAROTTE [*entering*].　Madam, somebody asks to see you.

MADELON.　Who!

MAROTTE.　The Viscount de Jodelet.

MASCARILLE.　The Viscount de Jodelet?

MAROTTE.　Yes, sir.

CATHOS.　Do you know him?

MASCARILLE. He is my best friend.

MADELON. Show him in at once.

MASCARILLE. We have not seen each other for some time; I am delighted at this chance.

CATHOS. Here he comes.

SCENE XI. CATHOS, MADELON, JODELET, MASCARILLE, MAROTTE,
ALMANZOR.

MASCARILLE. Ah, Viscount!

JODELET [*as they embrace each other*]. Ah, Marquis!

MASCARILLE. How glad I am to see you!

JODELET. How happy I am to see *you* here.

MASCARILLE. Embrace me once more, I pray you.

MADELON [*to* CATHOS]. My dearest, we begin to be known. People of fashion find the way to our house.

MASCARILLE. Mesdames, allow me to introduce this nobleman to you. Upon my word, he deserves the honor of your acquaintance.

JODELET. It is only right we should come and pay you our respects. Your charms demand their lordly rights from people of all ranks.

MADELON. You carry your civilities to the utmost limits of flattery.

CATHOS. This day ought to be marked in our diary as a red-letter day.

MADELON [*to* ALMANZOR]. Come, boy, must you always be told things over and over again? Do you not observe there must be an additional chair?

MASCARILLE. You must not be astonished to see the Viscount thus. He has but just recovered from an illness, which, as you perceive, has made him so pale.

JODELET. The consequence of continual attendance at Court and the fatigues of war.

MASCARILLE. Do you know, mesdames, that in the Viscount you behold one of the heroes of our age. He is one of the bravest of the brave.

JODELET. Marquis, you are in no way inferior to me. We know what you can do.

MASCARILLE. It is true we have seen one another in action.

JODELET. And in places where it was hot.

MASCARILLE [*looking at* CATHOS *and* MADELON]. Ay, but not so hot as here. Ha, ha, ha!

JODELET. We became acquainted in the army, and the first time we saw each other he commanded a regiment of horse aboard the galleys of Malta.

MASCARILLE. True, but for all that you were in the service before me. I was but a young lieutenant when you commanded two thousand horse.

JODELET. War is a grand thing, but, upon my word, the Court does not reward men of experience like us.

MASCARILLE. That is the reason I intend to hang up my sword.

CATHOS. As for me, I have a tremendous liking for gentlemen of the army.

MADELON. I love them, too, but I like bravery seasoned with wit.

MASCARILLE. Do you remember, Viscount, our taking the half-moon defences from the enemy at the siege of Arras?

JODELET. What do you mean by a half-moon? It was a full moon.

MASCARILLE. I believe you are right.

JODELET. Upon my word, I ought to remember it. I was wounded in the leg by a hand-grenade, of which I still carry the marks. Pray, feel it, and you will see what sort of a wound it was.

CATHOS [putting her hand to the place]. The scar is really large.

MASCARILLE. Give me your hand for a moment, and feel this—there, just at the back of my head. Do you feel it?

MADELON. Ay, I feel something.

MASCARILLE. A musket shot I received in my last campaign.

JODELET [unbuttoning his breast]. Here is a wound that went clear through me at the attack of Gravelines.

MASCARILLE [putting his hand upon the button of his breeches]. I am going to show you a tremendous wound.

MADELON. There is no need to—we believe it without seeing.

MASCARILLE. They are marks of honor that show what a man is made of.

CATHOS. We have no doubt of what you are.

MASCARILLE. Viscount, is your coach in waiting?

JODELET. Why?

MASCARILLE. We shall give these ladies an airing, and give them some refreshments.

MADELON. We cannot go out today.

MASCARILLE. Let us send for the fiddlers then, and have a dance.

JODELET. Upon my word, that is a happy thought.

MADELON. With all our hearts, but we must have some more company.

MASCARILLE. So ho! Champagne, Picard, Bourguignon, Cascaret, Basque, La Verdure, Lorrain, Provençal, La Violette. I wish the devil took all these footmen! I do not think there is a gentleman in France worse served than I am! These rascals are always somewhere else!

MADELON. Almanzor, tell the servants of my lord marquis to go and fetch the musicians, and ask some of the gentlemen and ladies hereabouts to come and people the solitude of our ball.

[Exit ALMANZOR.]

MASCARILLE. Viscount, what do you say of those eyes?

JODELET. Why, Marquis, what do you think of them yourself?

MASCARILLE. I? I say that our freedom will have trouble to get clear of this. At least mine has suffered most violent attacks—my heart hangs by a single thread.

MADELON. How natural is all he says! He gives things a most agreeable turn.

CATHOS. He must expend a tremendous lot of wit.

MASCARILLE. To show you that I am in earnest, I shall make some extempore verses upon my passion. [*Seems to think.*]

CATHOS. Oh! I beseech you by all that I hold sacred, let us hear something made upon us.

JODELET. I should be glad to do so too, but the quantity of blood that I have lost lately has exhausted my poetic vein.

MASCARILLE. Deuce take it! I always make the first verse well, but I find the others more difficult. Upon my word, this is too short a time; but I will make you some extempore verses at my leisure, which you shall think the finest in the world.

JODELET. He is devilish witty.

MADELON. And so gallant and expressive.

MASCARILLE. Viscount, tell me, when did you see the Countess last?

JODELET. I have not paid her a visit for three weeks.

MASCARILLE. You know, the Duke came to see me this morning, and wanted to take me out into the country deer hunting with him?

MADELON. Here come our friends.

SCENE XII. LUCILE, CÉLIMÈNE, CATHOS, MADELON, MASCARILLE, JODELET, MAROTTE, ALMANZOR, *and* FIDDLERS.

MADELON. Well, my dears, we do hope you will pardon us. These gentlemen had a fancy to put life into our heels, and we sent for you to fill up the void of our assembly.

LUCILE. We are certainly much obliged to you.

MASCARILLE. This is a kind of extempore ball, mesdames, but one of these days we shall give you a formal dance. Have the fiddlers come?

ALMANZOR. Yes, monsieur, they are here.

CATHOS. Come then, my dears, take your places.

MASCARILLE [*dancing by himself and singing*]. La, la, la, la, la, la, la, la.

MADELON. What a perfect figure he has.

CATHOS. He looks as if he were a really good dancer.

MASCARILLE [*taking out* MADELON *to dance*]. My freedom will dance a Couranto as well as my feet. Play in time, fiddlers, in time. Oh, what ignorant wretches! There is no dancing to them. The devil take you all, can you not play in time? La, la, la, la, la, la, la, la? Steady, you country-scrapers!

JODELET [*dancing also*]. Hold, do not play so fast. I have just recovered from an illness.

SCENE XIII. DU CROISY, LA GRANGE, CATHOS, MADELON, LUCILE, CÉLIMÈNE, JODELET, MASCARILLE, MAROTTE, *and* FIDDLERS.

LA GRANGE [*entering with a stick in hand*]. Ah! ah! scoundrels, what are you doing here? We have been looking for you three hours. [*He beats* MASCARILLE.]

MASCARILLE. Oh! oh! oh! you did not tell me that blows were part of it.

JODELET [*who is also beaten*]. Oh! oh! oh!

LA GRANGE. It is just like you, rascal, to pretend to be a man of rank.

DU CROISY. This will teach you to know your place.

[LA GRANGE *and* DU CROISY *go out.*]

SCENE XIV. CATHOS, MADELON, LUCILE, CÉLIMÈNE, MASCARILLE, JODELET, MAROTTE, *and* FIDDLERS.

MADELON. What is the meaning of this?

JODELET. It is a wager.

CATHOS. What! allow yourselves to be beaten thus?

MASCARILLE. Gad, I shouldn't take any notice of it, because I am naturally very violent and might lose my temper.

MADELON. To suffer an insult like this in our presence!

MASCARILLE. It is nothing. Let us not leave off. We have known one another for a long time, and among friends one ought not to be so quick to take offense.

SCENE XV. DU CROISY, LA GRANGE, MADELON, CATHOS, LUCILE, CÉLIMÈNE, MASCARILLE, JODELET, MAROTTE, *and* FIDDLERS.

LA GRANGE [*returning*]. Upon my word, rascals, you shall not laugh at us, I promise you. Come in, you there.

[*Three or four men enter.*]

MADELON. What does this mean! to come and disturb us in our own house?

DU CROISY. What, mesdames, shall we allow our footmen to be received better than we are? Shall they come to make love to you at our expense, and even dance with you?

MADELON. Your footmen?

LA GRANGE. Yes, our footmen, and it is neither handsome nor honorable to spoil them for us as you do.

MADELON. O Heaven! what insolence!

LA GRANGE. But they shall not have the advantage of our clothes to dazzle your eyes. If you are determined to love them, it shall be for their handsome looks only. Quick, strip them immediately.

JODELET. Adieu to all our fine clothes.

MASCARILLE. There go the marquisate and viscountship!

DU CROISY. Ah! ah! you knaves, you have the impudence to become our rivals. I assure you, you must borrow elsewhere to make yourselves agreeable to your mistresses.

LA GRANGE. It is too much—to supplant us, and with our own clothes.

MASCARILLE. O Fortune, how fickle you are!

DU CROISY. Quick, strip them to the last rag!

LA GRANGE. Hurry now and take away all these clothes. Now mesdames, in their present condition you may continue your amours with them as long as you please. We leave you perfectly free, and this gentleman and I solemnly declare that we shall not be the least bit jealous.

[LA GRANGE, DU CROISY, *and their men leave.*]

SCENE XVI. MADELON, CATHOS, JODELET, MASCARILLE, *and* FIDDLERS.

CATHOS. Ah, what confusion!

MADELON. I am bursting with vexation.

FIRST FIDDLER [*to* MASCARILLE]. What is the meaning of this? Who is to pay us?

MASCARILLE. Ask monsieur the Viscount.

FIRST FIDDLER [*to* JODELET]. Who is to give us our money?

JODELET. Ask monsieur the Marquis.

SCENE XVII. GORGIBUS, MADELON, CATHOS, JODELET, MASCARILLE, *and* FIDDLERS.

GORGIBUS [*coming in*]. Ah! you hussies, you have us in a nice fix from what I hear! I've been told about your fine goings-on from those two gentlemen who just left.

MADELON. Ah, father! they have played us a cruel trick.

GORGIBUS. Yes, it is a cruel trick, but you may thank your own impertinence for it, you jades. They have revenged themselves for the way you treated them, and yet, unhappy man that I am, I must put up with the affront.

MADELON. Ah! I swear we will be avenged, or I shall die in the attempt. And you, rascals, dare you remain here after your insolence?

MASCARILLE. Do you treat a marquis in this manner? This is the way of the world! The least misfortune causes us to be slighted by those who earlier caressed us. Come along, comrade, let us go and seek our fortune elsewhere. I see clearly that they love naught here but outward show, and have no regard for virtue unadorned.

[They both leave.]

SCENE XVIII. GORGIBUS, MADELON, CATHOS, *and* FIDDLERS.

FIRST FIDDLER. As they have not paid us, monsieur, we expect you to do so, for it was here we played.

GORGIBUS *[beating them as they leave]*. Yes, yes, I shall satisfy you, and this is the coin I will pay you in. As for you, you sluts, I do not know why I should not serve you in the same way. We shall become the common talk and laughing-stock of everybody. This is what you have brought upon yourselves by your foolishness. Go and hide yourselves, you jades, go and hide yourselves forever.

[Alone after they leave.]

And you, that are the cause of their folly, you stupid trash, mischievous amusements for idle minds, you novels, verses, songs, sonnets, and sonatas, the devil take you all.

THE END

Two Critical Commentaries on Molière's *Les Précieuses Ridicules*

Commentary by John Palmer, from *Molière, His Life and Works* (London, Bell, 1930).*

When Molière came to Paris in 1658, the Hôtel de Rambouillet, which had been famous for over thirty years, had already outlived its purpose. It had started as a protest against the bad manners of the time. It had become a conventicle of good taste. Good taste is an excellent critic; but it leads swiftly to impotence and destroys itself by inbreeding. The people who frequented the blue *salon* in Rue St. Thomas, in the fastidious presence of their hostess, refined upon their sentiments and etherealized their wits till nothing was left but affectations of feeling and expression uncorrected by any reference to genuine emotion or common sense. Love itself became a metaphysical abstraction; each separate hair on the head of every possible emotion was numbered; conversation became virtually unintelligible except to the initiated. Wit was the measure of a man, and this seventeenth century wit was little more than the application of a practised verbal dexterity to the simplest matters. Mere refinement speedily gave way to downright affectation. The daughter of the Marquise de Rambouillet, breathing this tenuous atmosphere from childhood is said to have fainted upon hearing a vulgar word, and Monsieur de Montausier, the unfortunate gentleman who married her, was required to spend fourteen years in overcoming one by one the scruples and alarms which were

* Reprinted by permission of G. Bell & Sons, Ltd., and Messrs. Curtis Brown, Ltd.

held to be right and necessary in such cases. . . . Meanwhile, Mademoiselle de Scudéry had also appeared, and her famous Saturdays were spreading the exquisite infection. It was she who invented the Map of the Tender Passion with its Village of Gallant Addresses, its Hamlet of Sweet Letters and Castle of Small Attentions. This was the map which gave the poor Monsieur de Montausier so much trouble. . . . The devotes of the Hôtel de Rambouillet, isolating themselves from the common world, had no standard whereby to correct their own absurdities. No one of any consequence escaped their influence. La Rochefoucauld adored the novels of Mademoiselle de Scudéry and could draw from memory the Map of the Tender Passion. . . .

(pp. 112-13)

Though in 1658 the exquisites had degenerated from leaders of a literary movement to corrupters of form and fashion, there had as yet been not the slightest suggestion that they were in any way ridiculous. All the best people were exquisites. Not to be an exquisite was social obliteration. The wisdom of La Bruyère was wisdom after the event, and the members of the sect who, like Ménage and Segrais, describe the précieuses in their memoirs with a smiling indulgence are saving their faces with posterity by post-dating a discretion which prior to Molière they had not yet attained. No one had effectively mocked the exquisites or troubled their supremacy. Society would no more have dreamed of smiling at the 'enigma' or 'portrait' of the alcove in 1658 than it would dream to-day of smiling at Derby day or the induction of an Archbishop. . . . In 1656 St. Évremond had gently rallied the sect upon its metaphysical affectations and the Abbé de Pure had in the same year published a romance in four volumes in which the camp-followers of the movement were the victims of an irony so gentle, and incidentally so involved, that the author's preciosity was more apparent than his intention to castigate the offense in others. . . .

(p. 115)

These were straws, but the wind had scarce as yet begun to blow. Mademoiselle de Scudéry, with La Rochefoucauld in attendance; Madame de Sévigné with her retinue of precious folk; the solemn Bossuet; the illustrious Corneille, with Ménage, Segrais and the rest, were still untouched. The Map of the Tender Passion was the Michelin Guide to society, and in 1658 it was till as much as one's social life was worth to smile at the exquisites.

Twelve months later everyone of account within twenty leagues of Paris was laughing heartily, and the wisest of the exquisites made merry with the rest. *Les Précieuses Ridicules,* a comedy in one act, destroyed the fashion in single afternoon. There was clearly no appeal against this devastating verict of common sense. Either the exquisites must laugh with the vulgar or e damned for ever in their absurdity. The great lady, who at the height of er fame had snubbed the mighty Richelieu, was equal to this even more angerous crisis. During the early run of the play she invited Molière to erform it on no less than three separate occasions for her own special benefit. et the galled jade wince, our withers are unwrung. Molière met this skillful aneuver by solemnly asserting in his preface that, in portraying his exuisites, he had intended to satirize only a vicious imitation of the excellent iginals. The statement deceived nobody, save certain laborious critics of a later generation. It was an example to the world how a defeat should be accepted and a victory enjoyed by persons of goodwill.

The Marquise was followed by the more discreet of her admirers. . . .

(p. 116)

The general verdict was that of the apocryphal gentleman in the pit who rose in his enthusiasm and cried: *"Courage, courage, Molière, voilà de la bonne comédie"* ["Bravo, bravo, Molière, that's good comedy"]. During the next few months people came from within sixty miles of Paris to see the play.

(p. 117)

Commentary by W. G. Moore, from *Molière, a New Criticism* (Oxford, Clarendon Press, 1949).*

A still earlier play presents an even more intriguing mosaic of social criticism and comic attitude, *Les Précieuses Ridicules*. It has fared so variously at the hands of the critics that it provides a good illustration both of what has been achieved and of what still awaits attention in the field of Molière study. . . .

In the mid-nineteenth century Victor Cousin expounded his theory that *Les Précieuses Ridicules* was an attack, not on the real 'précieuses' but on their pale and artificial imitators. Lanson maintained some fifty years later that the available evidence pointed to the conclusion that Molière was indeed attacking 'la vraie préciosité, celle de l'Hôtel de Rambouillet' ['the genuine preciosity, that of the Hotel de Rambouillet']. He explained the play as the satire of a typical bourgeois against aristocratic elegance: Molière, he wrote, 'nous propose l'idéal le plus bourgeois de la vie paisible d'affections domestiques. Il y a de plus hautes morales.' [Molière . . . 'shows us the most bourgeois ideal of the peaceful life of domestic affections. There are higher moralities.'] Later still came the idea that Molière had not only attacked the 'précieuses' but had defeated them and had killed affectation, or at least had laughed it out of court to such an extent that the final blow of *Les Femmes Savantes* in 1672 brought about what Michaut called 'le discrédit total des précieuses.' All these positions are now either queried or rejected. The most recent theory accounts for the awkward gap of a fortnight between the first two performances by marshalling the arguments for an original version not only more satirical than what we now read, but harsh and gross as well. Adam has at least shown that the social background of the play is much more complicated than either Cousin or Lanson supposed, that social cliques opposed each other in the Paris of 1659 with much of the animosity of the political intrigues of the Fronde, that in particular the circle surrounding Gaston d'Orléans and the Grande Mademoiselle, forming a powerful and licentious coterie, included Molière's friends, d'Aubignac, Boileau, Cotin (not yet an enemy), and that a corresponding group around Fouquet included his enemies, or the enemies of his friends, Ménage, Mlle de Scudéry, Pellisson, Sorel. An actor-manager fresh from the provinces might well show his mettle and court advancement by taking one side against the other and the d'Aubignac party might well demand a satire as indecent as it was merciless. It is plausible again that after an 'alcoviste de qualité' ['nobleman intellectual']

---

* Reprinted by permission of W. G. Moore and The Clarendon Press, Oxford.

obviously in touch with Fouquet, had succeeded in getting the play off the boards after one performance, Molière should make a bold bid to conciliate the party he had been persuaded to lampoon, should not only tone down his play but should perform its new and acceptable version in the house of Mme du Plessis-Guénégaud, as indeed happened. Adam's fascinating study suggests a Molière less dignified and more natural than the official account. It has received some measure of corroboration from an unusual quarter. In a resounding article, which unfortunately appeared only in an out-of-the-way periodical, M. Daniel Mornet has questioned all the accepted ideas on preciosity as a social phenomenon. All too easily in the past, he says, has the mockery of Boileau and Molière been taken as evidence of the actual existence of affectation such as they, and Somaize in their train, describe. Thanks to this confusion 'on a reconstitué une histoire de la préciosité qui n'a à peu près rien à voir avec la réalité' ['a history of preciosity has been reconstructed which has almost no regard for reality']. There is evidence of affectation, in both language and manners, about 1640. There is no evidence that the ladies called 'les précieuses' in 1659 spoke absurdly or indulged in anything more affected than elegant and platonic discussion: 'il n'y en a pas qui aient parlé comme Cathos et Madelon.' ['there were none of them who talked like Cathos and Madelon']. Nor finally is there any evidence that such circles were affected, much less discredited, by Molière's plays. . . .

It would not, I think, be accurate to describe recent work on *Les Précieuses Ridicules* as concerned only with the social background of the play. It concentrates attention on the dramatic nature of Molière's production. We are warned not to look for the wrong things; the plays are not reliable social satire, in the first place, any more than they are (in the first place) dramatized versions of Molière's home life; they are comedies, and until we have discovered what seventeenth-century actors put into their plays we shall not know how distorted is Molière's picture of preciosity, or of medical practice, or of religion in his own day. The positive counterpart to the work of Adam and Mornet on Molière's first Paris play has already been supplied by Ramon Fernandez, who suggests that affectation gave Molière a chance of making dramatic and comic contrast with something vigorous, matter of fact, ebullient, earthy, even coarse, Rabelaisian. . . . (pp. 17-20)

. . . *Les Précieuses Ridicules* was very probably, in its original form, a satire of a quite outspoken kind. Molière seems to have been engaged by the circle of the Grande Mademoiselle to lampoon that of Mlle de Scudéry, which enjoyed the patronage of Fouquet. Certain phrases are strangely similar to those used by Sapho in the *Grand Cyrus* . . . the satiric coupling of absurd speech and 'precious' manners, the suggestion that certain ladies of fashion lived in a quite unreal world of romance and premarital adventures. Their chief sin was to despise all things physical and 'earthy.' In the first version they refer by periphrasis to a commode; they declare the very notion of marriage to be absolutely shocking. One can imagine the *gauloiserie* that actors of farce would put into such a play, the zest with which Mascarille (Molière) would offer to undress in order to show them his wound. The actual undressing of the valets by the masters was in all probability a rough business and the vulgarity of the father may well have been enforced by wink and gesture. (p. 87)

IV. HEDDA GABLER

A Realistic Tragedy by Henrik Ibsen

Introductory Note to Henrik Ibsen and *Hedda Gabler*

IF MOLIÈRE AND French neoclassic drama were most strongly influential in the theater of the later seventeenth and eighteenth centuries, and Shakespeare throughout the nineteenth, certainly Ibsen has exerted the greatest influence thus far upon the twentieth. He has been the "father" of modern drama, as we noted earlier, and *Hedda Gabler* is doubtless his most effective play in the theater and a most provocative drama.

Henrik Ibsen was born in 1828 in Skein, a shipping town on the southeast coast of Norway. His father was of mixed Danish, Scotch, and German descent; his mother, of German. Financial reverses removed the family from the big house in the center of town to poverty in a little broken-down farmhouse. The boy Henrik was given private schooling until he was fifteen; at that time he wanted to become an artist. At sixteen he left home for good, apprenticed to an apothecary at the seaport village of Grimstad, where he lived out his taciturn and lonely adolescence, compounding drugs and verse lampoons upon the customers, seething with private revolt and the revolutionary causes of 1848. By the time he was twenty-two, he had written a blank-verse tragedy, *Cataline,* which one of his two friends took up to Christiania (Oslo) in a vain attempt to find a producer and publisher for him. Ibsen followed, and starved and wrote plays in the capital for a year or so. Then he fortunately secured appointment as "theater poet" of the new National Theater of Bergen, established by the great Norwegian violinist Ole Bull. In Bergen for six years—with a tour for study at the Royal Theater in Copenhagen—Ibsen wrote, translated, adapted, and directed plays, mastering at first hand the problems of theater and dramaturgy. He married at twenty-eight, then accepted an appointment at the second

theater in Christiania in 1857. But this failed shortly and his subsequent years were all struggle and poverty. His own plays—except
for *Love's Comedy,* which was thought scandalous—were poetic
dramas of no great success. His hopes for a government grant were
frustrated. Finally in 1864, aged thirty-six, he abandoned his country
and went to live in Rome. There his genius flourished, and he wrote
two great poetic dramas—*Brand* (1866) and *Peer Gynt* (1867)—that
won him some acceptance and a pension.

He removed to Dresden when he was forty and made his home in
Germany for most of the next twenty-three years. It was here that
he wrote the succession of realistic prose dramas upon which his
fame principally rests. He had already written *The Pillars of Society*—a study of social hypocrisy in the form of a well-made play—
when in 1879 he produced *A Doll's House.* It was Ibsen's first great
success—printed in successive editions, translated within a year into
both English and German, produced in Denmark, Norway, Sweden,
Poland, Germany, and shortly after also in England, France, and
America. Nora's famous declaration of independence was controversial, and the play became (beyond its intention) a rallying cry
of the feminists. There followed *Ghosts* (1881), which dealt frankly
with Mrs. Alving's tragic fight against the life that society thrust
upon her, and her son's final imbecility from the venereal disease of
his father. In *An Enemy of the People* (1882) the idealistic Dr.
Stockmann, who would free his home town from the pollution of its
public baths, is blocked and ousted by the self-interest of his brother
and "the compact majority" of the so-called best people. So on,
writing a new play every second year, Ibsen continued with the
beautiful and symbolic tragedy of misguided idealism, *The Wild
Duck,* and the the somber personal tragedy of *Rosmersholm.* After
the unrealistic and symbolic *Lady from the Sea* came *Hedda Gabler*
(1890), to be followed by *The Master Builder* and but three further
final plays. This sequence of dramas established him as the leading
man of letters of his time.

Throughout the more than twenty years during which he wrote
these plays, his personal life was comparatively detached and un-
eventful, with his wife and son, few friends, and little social life.
His creative imagination seemed to be kindled by casual events or
suggestions, and he made the most of his experiences with people
of his earlier years. He was a painstaking and meticulous craftsman,
wrote out elaborate life-histories of the dramatic characters that he

synthesized. His revolutionary youth once past, he never entered into the movements of social reform so characteristic of his times. He was neither feminist nor socialist. But he did have strong convictions about the importance of personality, the relation of the individual to society, the crushing force of the social majority, the tragic denial of human love. Even in his prose dramas, there is often a poetic quality, the telling use of dramatic symbols, the reassertion of his early mysticism.

In 1891, at the age of sixty-three, he returned to Norway for a visit, was received with great acclaim, and remained to live in Christiania. He was famous now throughout Europe, England, and America. His great dramas were controversially accepted, and he was lionized. Within ten years, however, he suffered a stroke, and his last four lonely years were clouded by aphasia. He died in 1906, at the age of seventy-eight, and the king of Norway attended his public funeral in person.

Hedda Gabler, which was written when he was sixty-two, is one of Ibsen's most mature works. He seems to have been creatively inspired by a summer-resort friendship with a young Viennese girl of eighteen, with whom he then corresponded. Though the full fruit of this inspiration was *The Master Builder,* it seems to have released creative powers that found expression in *Hedda Gabler* written that next year. In June and July, 1890, he was finishing his first draft (which is available for our study), and his revision was completed by the end of November. On December 4, he wrote to his French translator: "The title of the play is *Hedda Gabler*. My intention in giving it this name was to indicate that Hedda, as a personality, is to be regarded rather as her father's daughter than as her husband's wife. It was not my desire to deal in this play with so-called problems. What I principally wanted to do was to depict human beings, human emotions, and human destinies, upon a groundwork of certain of the social conditions and principles of the present day."

The play was published in Copenhagen on December 16, 1890, and almost simultaneously in England (the early Gosse translation) and America. Its first production was in Munich in January, 1891. Other productions of it followed shortly: Berlin, Copenhagen, and Christiania in February; London in April, Paris in August, and New York in a few years. The role of Hedda has challenged the talents of many outstanding actresses: Nance O'Neill, Mrs. Pat Campbell, Mrs. Minnie Maddern Fiske, Eleonora Duse, Alla Nazimova, Katina

Paxinou, and Eva Le Gallienne, of whose interpretation a full-drama recording has been made.

HEDDA GABLER

by Henrik Ibsen

TRANSLATED FROM THE NORWEGIAN BY EDMUND GOSSE
AND WILLIAM ARCHER *

THE CHARACTERS

GEORGE TESMAN—*a scholar, aged 33, recently married.*

HEDDA TESMAN—*his wife, aged 29, daughter of General Gabler.*

EILERT LÖVBORG—*a former admirer of Hedda Gabler.*

MRS. ELVSTED—*Thea, a one-time schoolmate of Hedda.*

JUDGE BRACK—*admirer of Hedda, friend of the family, aged 45.*

MISS TESMAN—*George's Aunt Julia, who helped raise him.*
BERTA—*servant to George and his wife, earlier to Miss Tesman.*

Time: *late nineteenth century, when the play was written.*
Place: *Tesman's villa, in the west end of Christiania.*

ACT ONE

A SPACIOUS, HANDSOME *and tastefully furnished drawing-room, decorated in dark colors. In the back, a wide doorway with curtains drawn back, leading into a smaller room, decorated in the same style as the drawing-room. In the right-hand wall of the front room, a folding door leading out to the hall. In the opposite wall, on the left, a glass door, also with curtains drawn back. Through the panes can be seen part of a veranda outside, and trees covered with autumn foliage. An oval table, with a cover on it, and surrounded by chairs, stands well forward. In front, by the wall on the right, a wide stove of dark porcelain, a high-backed arm-chair, a cushioned foot-rest, and two footstools. A settee, with a small*

---

* Reprinted from *The Collected Works of Henrik Ibsen;* copyright edition—volume X. Copyright 1907 by Charles Scribner's Sons, 1935 by Frank Archer; used by permission of the publishers.

round table in front of it, fills the upper right-hand corner. In front, on the left, a little way from the wall, a sofa. Further back than the glass door, a piano. On either side of the doorway at the back a what-not with terra-cotta and majolica ornaments.—Against the back wall of the inner room a sofa, with a table, and one or two chairs. Over the sofa hangs the portrait of a handsome elderly man in a General's uniform. Over the table a hanging lamp, with an opal glass shade.—A number of bouquets are arranged about the drawing-room, in vases and glasses. Others lie upon the tables. The floors in both rooms are covered with thick carpets.—Morning light. The sun shines in through the glass door.

MISS JULIANA TESMAN, *with her bonnet on and carrying a parasol, comes in from the hall, followed by* BERTA, *who carries a bouquet wrapped in paper.* MISS TESMAN *is a comely and pleasant-looking lady of about sixty-five. She is nicely but simply dressed in a gray walking-costume.* BERTA *is a middle-aged woman of plain and rather countrified appearance.*

MISS TESMAN [*stops close to the door, listens, and says softly*]. Upon my word, I don't believe they are stirring yet!

BERTA [*also softly*]. I told you so, Miss. Remember how late the steamboat got in last night. And then, when they got home!—good Lord, what a lot the young mistress had to unpack before she could get to bed.

MISS TESMAN. Well, well—let them have their sleep out. But let us see that they get a good breath of the fresh morning air when they do appear.

[*She goes to the glass door and throws it open.*]

BERTA [*beside the table, at a loss what to do with the bouquet in her hand*]. I declare there isn't a bit of room left. I think I'll put it down here, Miss. [*She places it on the piano.*]

MISS TESMAN. So you've got a new mistress now, my dear Berta. Heaven knows it was a wrench to me to part with you.

BERTA [*on the point of weeping*]. And do you think it wasn't hard for me, too, Miss? After all the blessed years I've been with you and Miss Rina.

MISS TESMAN. We must make the best of it, Berta. There was nothing else to be done. George can't do without you, you see—he absolutely can't. He has had you to look after him ever since he was a little boy.

BERTA. Ah, but, Miss Julia, I can't help thinking of Miss Rina lying helpless at home there, poor thing. And with only that new girl, too! She'll never learn to take proper care of an invalid.

MISS TESMAN. Oh, I shall manage to train her. And, of course, you know I shall take most of it upon myself. You needn't be uneasy about my poor sister, my dear Berta.

BERTA. Well, but there's another thing, Miss. I'm so mortally afraid I shan't be able to suit the young mistress.

MISS TESMAN. Oh, well—just at first there may be one or two things——

BERTA. Most like she'll be terrible grand in her ways.

MISS TESMAN. Well, you can't wonder at that—General Gabler's daughter! Think of the sort of life she was accustomed to in her father's time. Don't you remember how we used to see her riding down the road along with the General? In that long black habit—and with feathers in her hat?

BERTA. Yes, indeed—I remember well enough!—But, good Lord, I should never have dreamt in those days that she and Master George would make a match of it.

MISS TESMAN. Nor I.—But by the by, Berta—while I think of it: in future you mustn't say Master George. You must say Dr. Tesman.

BERTA. Yes, the young mistress spoke of that, too—last night—the moment they set foot in the house. Is it true then, Miss?

MISS TESMAN. Yes, indeed it is. Only think, Berta—some foreign university has made him a doctor—while he has been abroad, you understand. I hadn't heard a word about it, until he told me himself upon the pier.

BERTA. Well, well, he's clever enough for anything, he is. But I didn't think he'd have gone in for doctoring people, too.

MISS TESMAN. No, no, it's not that sort of doctor he is. [*Nods significantly*] But let me tell you, we may have to call him something still grander before long.

BERTA. You don't say so! What can that be, Miss?

MISS TESMAN [*smiling*]. H'm—wouldn't you like to know! [*With emotion*] Ah, dear, dear—if my poor brother could only look up from his grave now, and see what his little boy has grown into! [*Looks around.*] But bless me, Berta—why have you done this? Taken the chintz covers off all the furniture?

BERTA. The mistress told me to. She can't abide covers on the chairs, she says.

MISS TESMAN. Are they going to make this their everyday sitting-room then?

BERTA. Yes, that's what I understood—from the mistress. Master George—the doctor—he said nothing.

[GEORGE TESMAN *comes from the right into the inner room, humming to himself, and carrying an unstrapped empty portmanteau. He is a middle-sized, young-looking man of thirty-three, rather stout, with a round, open, cheerful face, fair hair and beard. He wears spectacles, and is somewhat carelessly dressed in comfortable indoor clothes.*]

MISS TESMAN. Good morning, good morning, George.

TESMAN [*in the doorway between the rooms*]. Aunt Julia! Dear Aunt Julia! [*Goes up to her and shakes hands warmly.*] Come all this way—so early! Eh?

MISS TESMAN. Why, of course I had to come and see how you were getting on.

TESMAN. In spite of your having had no proper night's rest?

MISS TESMAN. Oh, that makes no difference to me.

TESMAN. Well, I suppose you got home all right from the pier? Eh?

MISS TESMAN. Yes, quite safely, thank goodness. Judge Brack was good enough to see me right to my door.

TESMAN. We were so sorry we couldn't give you a seat in the carriage. But you saw what a pile of boxes Hedda had to bring with her.

MISS TESMAN. Yes, she had certainly plenty of boxes.

BERTA [*to* TESMAN]. Shall I go in and see if there's anything I can do for the mistress?

TESMAN. No thank you, Berta—you needn't. She said she would ring if she wanted anything.

BERTA [*going towards the right*]. Very well.

TESMAN. But look here—take this portmanteau with you.

BERTA [*taking it*]. I'll put it in the attic.

[*She goes out by the hall door.*]

TESMAN. Fancy, Auntie—I had the whole of that portmanteau chock full of copies of documents. You wouldn't believe how much I have picked up from all the archives I have been examining—curious old details that no one has had any idea of——

MISS TESMAN. Yes, you don't seem to have wasted your time on your wedding trip, George.

TESMAN. No, that I haven't. But do take off your bonnet, Auntie. Look here! Let me untie the strings—eh?

MISS TESMAN [*while he does so*]. Well, well—this is just as if you were still at home with us.

TESMAN [*with the bonnet in his hand, looks at it from all sides*]. Why, what a gorgeous bonnet you've been investing in!

MISS TESMAN. I bought it on Hedda's account.

TESMAN. On Hedda's account? Eh?

MISS TESMAN. Yes, so that Hedda needn't be ashamed of me if we happened to go out together.

TESMAN [*patting her cheek*]. You always think of everything, Aunt Julia. [*Lays the bonnet on a chair beside the table.*] And now, look here—suppose we sit comfortably on the sofa and have a little chat, till Hedda comes.

[*They seat themselves. She places her parasol in the corner of the sofa.*]

MISS TESMAN [*takes both his hands and looks at him*]. What a delight it is to have you again, as large as life, before my very eyes, George! My George—my poor brother's own boy!

TESMAN. And it's a delight for me, too, to see you again, Aunt Julia! You, who have been father and mother in one to me.

MISS TESMAN. Oh yes, I know you will always keep a place in your heart for your old aunts.

TESMAN. And what about Aunt Rina? No improvement—eh?

MISS TESMAN. Oh no—we can scarcely look for any improvement in her case, poor thing. There she lies, helpless, as she has lain for all these years. But heaven grant I may not lose her yet awhile. For if I did, I don't know what I should make of my life, George—especially now that I haven't you to look after any more.

TESMAN [*patting her back*]. There, there, there——!

MISS TESMAN [*suddenly changing her tone*]. And to think that here are you a married man, George!—And that you should be the one to carry off Hedda Gabler—the beautiful Hedda Gabler! Only think of it— she, that was so beset with admirers!

TESMAN [*hums a little and smiles complacently*]. Yes, I fancy I have several good friends about town who would like to stand in my shoes— eh?

MISS TESMAN. And then this fine long wedding-tour you have had! More than five—nearly six months——

TESMAN. Well, for me it has been a sort of tour of research as well. I have had to do so much grubbing among old records—and to read no end of books too, Auntie.

MISS TESMAN. Oh yes, I suppose so. [*More confidentially, and lowering her voice a little*] But listen now, George,—have you nothing— nothing special to tell me?

TESMAN. As to our journey?

MISS TESMAN. Yes.

TESMAN. No, I don't know of anything except what I have told you in my letters. I had a doctor's degree conferred on me—but that I told you yesterday.

MISS TESMAN. Yes, yes, you did. But what I mean is—haven't you any—any—expectations——?

TESMAN. Expectations?

MISS TESMAN. Why you know, George—I'm your old auntie!

TESMAN. Why, of course I have expectations.

MISS TESMAN. Ah!

TESMAN. I have every expectation of being a professor one of these days.

MISS TESMAN. Oh yes, a professor——

TESMAN. Indeed, I may say I am certain of it. But my dear Auntie— you know all about that already!

MISS TESMAN [*laughing to herself*]. Yes, of course I do. You are quite right there. [*Changing the subject*] But we were talking about your journey. It must have cost a great deal of money, George?

TESMAN. Well, you see—my handsome traveling-scholarship went a good way.

MISS TESMAN. But I can't understand how you can have made it go far enough for two.

TESMAN. No, that's not so easy to understand—eh?

MISS TESMAN. And especially travelling with a lady—they tell me that makes it ever so much more expensive.

TESMAN. Yes, of course—it makes it a little more expensive. But Hedda had to have this trip, Auntie! She really had to. Nothing else would have done.

MISS TESMAN. No, no, I suppose not. A wedding-tour seems to be quite indispensable nowadays.—But tell me now—have you gone thoroughly over the house yet?

TESMAN. Yes, you may be sure I have. I have been afoot ever since daylight.

MISS TESMAN. And what do you think of it all?

TESMAN. I'm delighted! Quite delighted! Only I can't think what we are to do with the two empty rooms between this inner parlor and Hedda's bedroom.

MISS TESMAN [*laughing*]. Oh my dear George, I daresay you may find some use for them—in the course of time.

TESMAN. Why of course you are quite right, Aunt Julia! You mean as my library increases—eh?

MISS TESMAN. Yes, quite so, my dear boy. It was your library I was thinking of.

TESMAN. I am specially pleased on Hedda's account. Often and often, before we were engaged, she said that she would never care to live anywhere but in Secretary Falk's villa.

MISS TESMAN. Yes, it was lucky that this very house should come into the market, just after you had started.

TESMAN. Yes, Aunt Julia, the luck was on our side, wasn't it—eh?

MISS TESMAN. But the expense, my dear George! You will find it very expensive, all this.

TESMAN [*looks at her, a little cast down*]. Yes, I suppose I shall, Aunt!

MISS TESMAN. Oh, frightfully!

TESMAN. How much do you think? In round numbers?—eh?

MISS TESMAN. Oh, I can't even guess until all the accounts come in.

TESMAN. Well, fortunately, Judge Brack has secured the most favorable terms for me,—so he said in a letter to Hedda.

MISS TESMAN. Yes, don't be uneasy, my dear boy.—Besides, I have given security for the furniture and all the carpets.

TESMAN. Security? You? My dear Aunt Julia—what sort of security could you give?

MISS TESMAN. I have given a mortgage on our annuity.

TESMAN [*jumps up*]. What! On your—and Aunt Rina's annuity!

MISS TESMAN. Yes, I knew of no other plan, you see.

TESMAN [*placing himself before her*]. Have you gone out of your senses, Auntie! Your annuity—it's all that you and Aunt Rina have to live upon.

MISS TESMAN. Well, well—don't get so excited about it. It's only a matter of form you know—Judge Brack assured me of that. It was he that was kind enough to arrange the whole affair for me. A mere matter of form, he said.

TESMAN. Yes, that may be all very well. But nevertheless——

MISS TESMAN. You will have your own salary to depend upon now. And, good heavens, even if we did have to pay up a little——! To eke things out a bit at the start——! Why, it would be nothing but a pleasure to us.

TESMAN. Oh Auntie—will you never be tired of making sacrifices for me!

MISS TESMAN [*rises and lays her hands on his shoulders*]. Have I any other happiness in this world except to smooth your way for you, my dear boy? You, who have had neither father nor mother to depend on. And now we have reached the goal, George! Things have looked black enough for us, sometimes; but, thank heaven, now you have nothing to fear.

TESMAN. Yes, it is really marvelous how everything has turned out for the best.

MISS TESMAN. And the people who opposed you—who wanted to bar the way for you—now you have them at your feet. They have fallen, George. Your most dangerous rival—his fall was the worst.—And now he has to lie on the bed he has made for himself—poor misguided creature.

TESMAN. Have you heard anything of Eilert? Since I went away, I mean.

MISS TESMAN. Only that he is said to have published a new book.

TESMAN. What! Eilert Lövborg! Recently—eh?

MISS TESMAN. Yes, so they say. Heaven knows whether it can be worth anything! Ah, when your new book appears—that will be another story, George! What is it to be about?

TESMAN. It will deal with the domestic industries of Brabant during the Middle Ages.

MISS TESMAN. Fancy—to be able to write on such a subject as that!

TESMAN. However, it may be some time before the book is ready. I have all these collections to arrange first, you see.

MISS TESMAN.   Yes, collecting and arranging—no one can beat you at that. There you are my poor brother's own son.

TESMAN.   I am looking forward eagerly to setting to work at it; especially now that I have my own delightful home to work in.

MISS TESMAN.   And, most of all, now that you have got the wife of your heart, my dear George.

TESMAN [*embracing her*].   Oh yes, yes, Aunt Julia. Hedda—she is the best part of it all! [*Looks towards the doorway*] I believe I hear her coming—eh?

[HEDDA *enters from the left through the inner room. She is a woman of nine-and-twenty. Her face and figure show refinement and distinction. Her complexion is pale and opaque. Her steel-gray eyes express a cold, unruffled repose. Her hair is of an agreeable medium brown, but not particularly abundant. She is dressed in a tasteful, somewhat loose-fitting morning gown.*]

MISS TESMAN [*going to meet* HEDDA].   Good morning, my dear Hedda! Good morning, and a hearty welcome!

HEDDA [*holds out her hand*].   Good morning, dear Miss Tesman! So early a call! That is kind of you.

MISS TESMAN [*with some embarrassment*].   Well—has the bride slept well in her new home?

HEDDA.   Oh yes, thanks. Passably.

TESMAN [*laughing*].   Passably! Come, that's good, Hedda! You were sleeping like a stone when I got up.

HEDDA.   Fortunately. Of course one has always to accustom one's self to new surroundings, Miss Tesman—little by little. [*Looking towards the left*] Oh—there the servant has gone and opened the veranda door, and let in a whole flood of sunshine.

MISS TESMAN [*going towards the door*].   Well, then we will shut it.

HEDDA.   No, no, not that! Tesman, please draw the curtains. That will give a softer light.

TESMAN [*at the door*].   All right—all right.—There now, Hedda, now you have both shade and fresh air.

HEDDA.   Yes, fresh air we certainly must have, with all these stacks of flowers——.   But—won't you sit down, Miss Tesman?

MISS TESMAN.   No, thank you. Now that I have seen that everything is all right here—thank heaven!—I must be getting home again. My sister is lying longing for me, poor thing.

TESMAN.   Give her my very best love, Auntie; and say I shall look in and see her later in the day.

MISS TESMAN.   Yes, yes, I'll be sure to tell her. But by the by, George —[*feeling in her dress pocket*]—I had almost forgotten—I have something for you here.

TESMAN.   What is it, Auntie? Eh?

MISS TESMAN [*produces a flat parcel wrapped in newspaper and hands it to him*]. Look here, my dear boy.

TESMAN [*opening the parcel*]. Well, I declare!—Have you really saved them for me, Aunt Julia! Hedda! isn't this touching—eh?

HEDDA [*beside the whatnot on the right*]. Well, what is it?

TESMAN. My old morning-shoes! My slippers.

HEDDA. Indeed. I remember you often spoke of them while we were abroad.

TESMAN. Yes, I missed them terribly. [*Goes up to her.*] Now you shall see them, Hedda!

HEDDA [*going towards the stove*]. Thanks, I really don't care about it.

TESMAN [*following her*]. Only think—ill as she was, Aunt Rina embroidered these for me. Oh you can't think how many associations cling to them.

HEDDA [*at the table*]. Scarcely for me.

MISS TESMAN. Of course not for Hedda, George.

TESMAN. Well, but now that she belongs to the family, I thought—

HEDDA [*interrupting*]. We shall never get on with this servant, Tesman.

MISS TESMAN. Not get on with Berta?

TESMAN. Why, dear, what puts that in your head? Eh?

HEDDA [*pointing*]. Look there! She has left her old bonnet lying about on a chair.

TESMAN [*in consternation, drops the slippers on the floor*]. Why, Hedda——

HEDDA. Just fancy, if any one should come in and see it!

TESMAN. But Hedda—that's Aunt Julia's bonnet.

HEDDA. Is it!

MISS TESMAN [*taking up the bonnet*]. Yes, indeed it's mine. And, what's more, it's not old, Madam Hedda.

HEDDA. I really did not look closely at it, Miss Tesman.

MISS TESMAN [*trying on the bonnet*]. Let me tell you it's the first time I have worn it—the very first time.

TESMAN. And a very nice bonnet it is too—quite a beauty!

MISS TESMAN. Oh, it's no such great thing, George. [*Looks around her.*] My parasol——? Ah, here. [*Takes it.*] For this is mine too—[*mutters*]—not Berta's.

TESMAN. A new bonnet and a new parasol! Only think, Hedda!

HEDDA. Very handsome indeed.

TESMAN. Yes, isn't it? Eh? But Auntie, take a good look at Hedda before you go! See how handsome she is!

MISS TESMAN. Oh, my dear boy, there's nothing new in that. Hedda was always lovely.

[*She nods and goes towards the right.*]

TESMAN [*following*]. Yes, but have you noticed what splendid condition she is in? How she has filled out on the journey?

HEDDA [*crossing the room*]. Oh, do be quiet——!

MISS TESMAN [*who has stopped and turned*]. Filled out?

TESMAN. Of course you don't notice it so much now that she has that dress on. But I, who can see——

HEDDA [*at the glass door, impatiently*]. Oh, you can't see anything.

TESMAN. It must be the mountain air in the Tyrol——

HEDDA [*curtly, interrupting*]. I am exactly as I was when I started.

TESMAN. So you insist; but I'm quite certain you are not. Don't you agree with me, Auntie?

MISS TESMAN [*who has been gazing at her with folded hands*]. Hedda is lovely—lovely—lovely. [*Goes up to her, takes her head between both hands, draws it downwards, and kisses her hair.*] God bless and preserve Hedda Tesman—for George's sake.

HEDDA [*gently freeing herself*]. Oh—! Let me go.

MISS TESMAN [*in quiet emotion*]. I shall not let a day pass without coming to see you.

TESMAN. No you won't, will you, Auntie? Eh?

MISS TESMAN. Good-bye—good-bye!

[*She goes out by the hall door. TESMAN accompanies her. The door remains half open. TESMAN can be heard repeating his message to AUNT RINA and his thanks for the slippers. In the meantime, HEDDA walks about the room, raising her arms and clenching her hands as if in desperation. Then she flings back the curtains from the glass door, and stands there looking out. Presently TESMAN returns and closes the door behind him.*]

TESMAN [*picks up the slippers from the floor*]. What are you looking at, Hedda?

HEDDA [*once more calm and mistress of herself*]. I am only looking at the leaves. They are so yellow—so withered.

TESMAN [*wraps up the slippers and lays them on the table*]. Well you see, we are well into September now.

HEDDA [*again restless*]. Yes, to think of it!—Already in—in September.

TESMAN. Don't you think Aunt Julia's manner was strange, dear? Almost solemn? Can you imagine what was the matter with her? Eh?

HEDDA. I scarcely know her, you see. Is she not often like that?

TESMAN. No, not as she was to-day.

HEDDA [*leaving the glass door*]. Do you think she was annoyed about the bonnet?

TESMAN. Oh, scarcely at all. Perhaps a little, just at the moment——

HEDDA. But what an idea, to pitch her bonnet about in the drawing-room! No one does that sort of thing.

TESMAN. Well you may be sure Aunt Julia won't do it again.

HEDDA. In any case, I shall manage to make my peace with her.

TESMAN. Yes, my dear, good Hedda, if you only would.

HEDDA. When you call this afternoon, you might invite her to spend the evening here.

TESMAN. Yes, that I will. And there's one thing more you could do that would delight her heart.

HEDDA. What is it?

TESMAN. If you could only prevail on yourself to say *du* to her. For my sake, Hedda? Eh?

HEDDA. No, no, Tesman—you really mustn't ask that of me. I have told you so already. I shall try to call her "Aunt"; and you must be satisfied with that.

TESMAN. Well, well. Only I think now that you belong to the family, you——

HEDDA. H'm—I can't in the least see why——

[*She goes up towards the middle doorway.*]

TESMAN [*after a pause*]. Is there anything the matter with you, Hedda? Eh?

HEDDA. I'm only looking at my old piano. It doesn't go at all well with all the other things.

TESMAN. The first time I draw my salary, we'll see about exchanging it.

HEDDA. No, no—no exchanging. I don't want to part with it. Suppose we put it there in the inner room, and then get another here in its place. When it's convenient, I mean.

TESMAN [*a little taken aback*]. Yes—of course we could do that.

HEDDA [*takes up the bouquet from the piano*]. These flowers were not here last night when we arrived.

TESMAN. Aunt Julia must have brought them for you.

HEDDA [*examining the bouquet*]. A visiting-card. [*Takes it out and reads:*] "Shall return later in the day." Can you guess whose card it is?

TESMAN. No. Whose? Eh?

HEDDA. The name is "Mrs. Elvsted."

TESMAN. Is it really? Sheriff Elvsted's wife? Miss Rysing that was.

HEDDA. Exactly. The girl with the irritating hair, that she was always showing off. An old flame of yours I've been told.

TESMAN [*laughing*]. Oh, that didn't last long; and it was before I knew you, Hedda. But fancy her being in town!

HEDDA. It's odd that she should call upon us. I have scarcely seen her since we left school.

TESMAN. I haven't seen her either for—heaven knows how long. I wonder how she can endure to live in such an out-of-the-way hole—eh?

HEDDA [*after a moment's thought, says suddenly*]. Tell me, Tesman—

isn't it somewhere near there that he—that—Eilert Lövborg is living?

TESMAN.   Yes, he is somewhere in that part of the country.

[BERTA *enters by the hall door.*]

BERTA.   That lady, ma'am, that brought some flowers a little while ago, is here again. [*Pointing*] The flowers you have in your hand, ma'am.

HEDDA.   Ah, is she? Well, please show her in.

[BERTA *opens the door for* MRS. ELVSTED, *and goes out herself.*—MRS. ELVSTED *is a woman of fragile figure, with pretty, soft features. Her eyes are light blue, large, round, and somewhat prominent, with a startled, inquiring expression. Her hair is remarkably light, almost flaxen, and unusually abundant and wavy. She is a couple of years younger than* HEDDA. *She wears a dark visiting dress, tasteful, but not quite in the latest fashion.*]

HEDDA [*receives her warmly*].   How do you do, my dear Mrs. Elvsted? It's delightful to see you again.

MRS. ELVSTED [*nervously, struggling for self-control*].   Yes, it's a very long time since we met.

TESMAN [*gives her his hand*].   And we too—eh?

HEDDA.   Thanks for your lovely flowers——

MRS. ELVSTED.   Oh, not at all—— I would have come straight here yesterday afternoon; but I heard that you were away——

TESMAN.   Have you just come to town? Eh?

MRS. ELVSTED.   I arrived yesterday, about midday. Oh, I was quite in despair when I heard that you were not at home.

HEDDA.   In despair! How so?

TESMAN.   Why, my dear Mrs. Rysing—I mean Mrs. Elvsted——

HEDDA.   I hope that you are not in any trouble?

MRS. ELVSTED.   Yes, I am. And I don't know another living creature here that I can turn to.

HEDDA [*laying the bouquet on the table*].   Come—let us sit here on the sofa——

MRS. ELVSTED.   Oh, I am too restless to sit down.

HEDDA.   Oh no, you're not. Come here.

[*She draws* MRS. ELVSTED *down upon the sofa and sits at her side.*]

TESMAN.   Well? what is it, Mrs. Elvsted——?

HEDDA.   Has anything particular happened to you at home?

MRS. ELVSTED.   Yes—and no. Oh—I am so anxious you should not misunderstand me——

HEDDA.   Then your best plan is to tell us the whole story, Mrs. Elvsted.

TESMAN. I suppose that's what you have come for—eh?

MRS. ELVSTED. Yes, yes—of course it is. Well then, I must tell you—if you don't already know—that Eilert Lövborg is in town, too.

HEDDA. Lövborg——!

TESMAN. What! Has Eilert Lövborg come back? Fancy that, Hedda!

HEDDA. Well, well—I hear it.

MRS. ELVSTED. He has been here a week already. Just fancy—a whole week! In this terrible town, alone! With so many temptations on all sides.

HEDDA. But, my dear Mrs. Elvsted—how does he concern you so much?

MRS. ELVSTED [looks at her with a startled air, and says rapidly]. He was the children's tutor.

HEDDA. Your children's?

MRS. ELVSTED. My husband's. I have none.

HEDDA. Your step-children's, then?

MRS. ELVSTED. Yes.

TESMAN [somewhat hesitatingly]. Then was he—I don't know how to express it—was he—regular enough in his habits to be fit for the post? Eh?

MRS. ELVSTED. For the last two years his conduct has been irreproachable.

TESMAN. Has it indeed? Fancy that, Hedda!

HEDDA. I hear it.

MRS. ELVSTED. Perfectly irreproachable, I assure you! In every respect. But all the same—now that I know he is here—in this great town—and with a large sum of money in his hands—I can't help being in mortal fear for him.

TESMAN. Why did he not remain where he was? With you and your husband? Eh?

MRS. ELVSTED. After his book was published he was too restless and unsettled to remain with us.

TESMAN. Yes, by the by, Aunt Julia told me he had published a new book.

MRS. ELVSTED. Yes, a big book, dealing with the march of civilization—in broad outline, as it were. It came out about a fortnight ago. And since it has sold so well, and been so much read—and made such a sensation——

TESMAN. Has it indeed? It must be something he has had lying by since his better days.

MRS. ELVSTED. Long ago, you mean?

TESMAN. Yes.

MRS. ELVSTED. No, he has written it all since he has been with us—within the last year.

TESMAN. Isn't that good news, Hedda? Think of that.

MRS. ELVSTED. Ah yes, if only it would last!

HEDDA. Have you seen him here in town?

MRS. ELVSTED. No, not yet. I have had the greatest difficulty in finding out his address. But this morning I discovered it at last.

HEDDA [*looks searchingly at her*]. Do you know, it seems to me a little odd of your husband—h'm——

MRS. ELVSTED [*starting nervously*]. Of my husband! What?

HEDDA. That he should send you to town on such an errand—that he does not come himself and look after his friend.

MRS. ELVSTED. Oh no, no—my husband has no time. And besides, I—I had some shopping to do.

HEDDA [*with a slight smile*]. Ah, that is a different matter.

MRS. ELVSTED [*rising quickly and uneasily*]. And now I beg and implore you, Mr. Tesman—receive Eilert Lövborg kindly if he comes to you! And that he is sure to do. You see you were such great friends in the old days. And then you are interested in the same studies—the same branch of science—so far as I can understand.

TESMAN. We used to be, at any rate.

MRS. ELVSTED. That is why I beg so earnestly that you—you too—will keep a sharp eye upon him. Oh, you will promise me that, Mr. Tesman —won't you?

TESMAN. With the greatest of pleasure, Mrs. Rysing——

HEDDA. Elvsted.

TESMAN. I assure you I shall do all I possibly can for Eilert. You may rely upon me.

MRS. ELVSTED. Oh, how very, very kind of you! [*Presses his hands.*] Thanks, thanks, thanks! [*Frightened*] You see, my husband is so very fond of him!

HEDDA [*rising*]. You ought to write to him, Tesman. Perhaps he may not care to come to you of his own accord.

TESMAN. Well, perhaps it would be the right thing to do, Hedda? Eh?

HEDDA. And the sooner the better. Why not at once?

MRS. ELVSTED [*imploringly*]. Oh, if you only would!

TESMAN. I'll write this moment. Have you his address, Mrs.—Mrs. Elvsted.

MRS. ELVSTED. Yes. [*Takes a slip of paper from her pocket, and hands it to him.*] Here it is.

TESMAN. Good, good. Then I'll go in—— [*Looks about him.*] By the by—my slippers? Oh, here.

[*Takes the packet, and is about to go.*]

HEDDA. Be sure you write him a cordial, friendly letter. And a good long one too.

TESMAN. Yes, I will.

MRS. ELVSTED. But please, please don't say a word to show that I have suggested it.

TESMAN. No, how could you think I would? Eh?

[*He goes out to the right, through the inner room.*]

HEDDA [*goes up to* MRS. ELVSTED, *smiles and says in a low voice*] There! We have killed two birds with one stone.

MRS. ELVSTED. What do you mean?

HEDDA. Could you not see that I wanted him to go?

MRS. ELVSTED. Yes, to write the letter——

HEDDA. And that I might speak to you alone.

MRS. ELVSTED [*confused*]. About the same thing?

HEDDA. Precisely.

MRS. ELVSTED [*apprehensively*]. But there is nothing more, Mrs. Tesman! Absolutely nothing!

HEDDA. Oh yes, but there is. There is a great deal more—I can see that. Sit here—and we'll have a cosy, confidential chat.

[*She forces* MRS. ELVSTED *to sit in the easy-chair beside the stove, and seats herself on one of the footstools.*]

MRS. ELVSTED [*anxiously, looking at her watch*]. But, my dear Mrs. Tesman—I was really on the point of going.

HEDDA. Oh, you can't be in such a hurry.—Well? Now tell me something about your life at home.

MRS. ELVSTED. Oh, that is just what I care least to speak about.

HEDDA. But to me, dear——? Why, weren't we schoolfellows?

MRS. ELVSTED. Yes, but you were in the class above me. Oh, how dreadfully afraid of you I was then!

HEDDA. Afraid of me?

MRS. ELVSTED. Yes, dreadfully. For when we met on the stairs you used always to pull my hair.

HEDDA. Did I, really?

MRS. ELVSTED. Yes, and once you said you would burn it off my head.

HEDDA. Oh, that was all nonsense, of course.

MRS. ELVSTED. Yes, but I was so silly in those days.—And since then, too—we have drifted so far—far apart from each other. Our circles have been so entirely different.

HEDDA. Well then, we must try to drift together again. Now listen! At school we said *du* to each other; and we called each other by our Christian names——

MRS. ELVSTED. No, I am sure you must be mistaken.

HEDDA. No, not at all! I can remember quite distinctly. So now we are going to renew our old friendship. [*Draws the footstool closer to*

MRS. ELVSTED.] There now! [*Kisses her cheek.*] You must say *du* to me and call me Hedda. [*Using the "du"—the "thee" and "thou"—of familiar Norwegian discourse.*]

MRS. ELVSTED [*presses and pats her hands*]. Oh, how good and kind you are! I am not used to such kindness.

HEDDA. There, there, there! And I shall say *du* to you, as in the old days, and call you my dear Thora.

MRS. ELVSTED. My name is Thea.

HEDDA. Why, of course! I mean Thea. [*Looks at her compassionately.*] So you are not accustomed to goodness and kindness, Thea? Not in your own home?

MRS. ELVSTED. Oh, if I only had a home! But I haven't any; I have never had a home.

HEDDA [*looks at her for a moment*]. I almost suspected as much.

MRS. ELVSTED [*gazing helplessly before her*]. Yes—yes—yes.

HEDDA. I don't quite remember—was it not as housekeeper that you first went to Mr. Elvsted's?

MRS. ELVSTED. I really went as governess. But his wife—his late wife —was an invalid,—and rarely left her room. So I had to look after the housekeeping as well.

HEDDA. And then—at last—you became mistress of the house.

MRS. ELVSTED [*sadly*]. Yes, I did.

HEDDA. Let me see—about how long ago was that?

MRS. ELVSTED. My marriage?

HEDDA. Yes.

MRS. ELVSTED. Five years ago.

HEDDA. To be sure; it must be that.

MRS. ELVSTED. Oh those five years——! Or at all events the last two or three of them! Oh, if you could only imagine—— [*Lapsing into the use of the formal "De."*]

HEDDA [*giving her a little slap on the hand*]. De? Fie, Thea!

MRS. ELVSTED. Yes, yes, I will try—— Well, if you could only imagine and understand——

HEDDA [*lightly*]. Eilert Lövborg has been in your neighborhood about three years, hasn't he?

MRS. ELVSTED [*looks at her doubtfully*]. Eilert Lövborg— Yes—he has.

HEDDA. Had you known him before, in town here?

MRS. ELVSTED. Scarcely at all. I mean—I knew him by name of course.

HEDDA. But you saw a good deal of him in the country?

MRS. ELVSTED. Yes, he came to us every day. You see, he gave the children lessons; for in a long run I couldn't manage it all myself.

HEDDA. No, that's clear.—And your husband——? I suppose he is often away from home?

MRS. ELVSTED. Yes. Being sheriff, you know, he has to travel about a good deal in his district.

HEDDA [*leaning against the arm of the chair*]. Thea—my poor, sweet Thea—now you must tell me everything—exactly as it stands.

MRS. ELVSTED. Well, then you must question me.

HEDDA. What sort of a man is your husband, Thea? I mean—you know—in everyday life. Is he kind to you?

MRS. ELVSTED [*evasively*]. I am sure he means well in everything.

HEDDA. I should think he must be altogether too old for you. There is at least twenty years' difference between you, is there not?

MRS. ELVSTED [*irritably*]. Yes, that is true, too. Everything about him is repellent to me! We have not a thought in common. We have no single point of sympathy—he and I.

HEDDA. But is he not fond of you all the same? In his own way?

MRS. ELVSTED. Oh I really don't know. I think he regards me simply as a useful property. And then it doesn't cost much to keep me. I am not expensive.

HEDDA. That is stupid of you.

MRS. ELVSTED [*shakes her head*]. It cannot be otherwise—not with him. I don't think he really cares for any one but himself—and perhaps a little for the children.

HEDDA. And for Eilert Lövborg, Thea.

MRS. ELVSTED [*looking at her*]. For Eilert Lövborg? What puts that into your head?

HEDDA. Well, my dear—I should say, when he sends you after him all the way to town—— [*Smiling almost imperceptibly*] And besides, you said so yourself, to Tesman.

MRS. ELVSTED [*with a little nervous twitch*]. Did I? Yes, I suppose I did. [*Vehemently, but not loudly*] No—I may just as well make a clean breast of it at once! For it must all come out in any case.

HEDDA. Why, my dear Thea——?

MRS. ELVSTED. Well, to make a long story short: My husband did not know that I was coming.

HEDDA. What! Your husband didn't know it!

MRS. ELVSTED. No, of course not. For that matter, he was away from home himself—he was traveling. Oh, I could bear it no longer, Hedda! I couldn't indeed—so utterly alone as I should have been in future.

HEDDA. Well? And then?

MRS. ELVSTED. So I put together some of my things—what I needed most—as quietly as possible. And then I left the house.

HEDDA. Without a word?

MRS. ELVSTED. Yes—and took the train straight to town.

HEDDA. Why, my dear, good Thea—to think of you daring to do it!

MRS. ELVSTED [*rises and moves about the room*]. What else could I possibly do?

HEDDA. But what do you think your husband will say when you go home again?

MRS. ELVSTED [*at the table, looks at her*]. Back to him?

HEDDA. Of course.

MRS. ELVSTED. I shall never go back to him again.

HEDDA [*rising and going towards her*]. Then you have left your home—for good and all?

MRS. ELVSTED. Yes. There was nothing else to be done.

HEDDA. But then—to take flight so openly.

MRS. ELVSTED. Oh, it's impossible to keep things of that sort secret.

HEDDA. But what do you think people will say of you, Thea?

MRS. ELVSTED. They may say what they like, for aught *I* care. [*Seats herself wearily and sadly on the sofa.*] I have done nothing but what I had to do.

HEDDA [*after a short silence*]. And what are your plans now? What do you think of doing?

MRS. ELVSTED. I don't know yet. I only know this, that I must live here, where Eilert Lövborg is—if I am to live at all.

HEDDA [*takes a chair from the table, seats herself beside her, and strokes her hands*]. My dear Thea—how did this—this friendship—between you and Eilert Lövborg come about?

MRS. ELVSTED. Oh it grew up gradually. I gained a sort of influence over him.

HEDDA. Indeed?

MRS. ELVSTED. He gave up his old habits. Not because I asked him to, for I never dared do that. But of course he saw how repulsive they were to me; and so he dropped them.

HEDDA [*concealing an involuntary smile of scorn*]. Then you have reclaimed him—as the saying goes—my little Thea.

MRS. ELVSTED. So he says himself, at any rate. And he, on his side, has made a real human being of me—taught me to think, and to understand so many things.

HEDDA. Did he give you lessons too, then?

MRS. ELVSTED. No, not exactly lessons. But he talked to me—talked about such an infinity of things. And then came the lovely, happy time when I began to share in his work—when he allowed me to help him!

HEDDA. Oh he did, did he?

MRS. ELVSTED. Yes! He never wrote anything without my assistance.

HEDDA. You were two good comrades, in fact?

MRS. ELVSTED [*eagerly*]. Comrades! Yes, fancy, Hedda—that is the very word he used!—Oh, I ought to feel perfectly happy; and yet I cannot; for I don't know how long it will last.

HEDDA. Are you no surer of him than that?

MRS. ELVSTED [*gloomily*]. A woman's shadow stands between Eilert Lövborg and me.

HEDDA [*looks at her anxiously*]. Who can that be?

MRS. ELVSTED. I don't know. Some one he knew in his—in his past. Some one he has never been able wholly to forget.

HEDDA. What has he told you—about this?

MRS. ELVSTED. He has only once—quite vaguely—alluded to it.

HEDDA. Well! And what did he say?

MRS. ELVSTED. He said that when they parted, she threatened to shoot him with a pistol.

HEDDA [*with cold composure*]. Oh, nonsense! No one does that sort of thing here.

MRS. ELVSTED. No. And that is why I think it must have been that red-haired singing-woman whom he once——

HEDDA. Yes, very likely.

MRS. ELVSTED. For I remember they used to say of her that she carried loaded firearms.

HEDDA. Oh—then of course it must have been she.

MRS. ELVSTED [*wringing her hands*]. And now just fancy, Hedda—I hear that this singing-woman—that she is in town again! Oh, I don't know what to do——

HEDDA [*glancing towards the inner room*]. Hush! Here comes Tesman. [*Rises and whispers*] Thea—all this must remain between you and me.

MRS. ELVSTED [*springing up*]. Oh yes—yes! For heaven's sake——!

[GEORGE TESMAN, *with a letter in his hand, comes from the right through the inner room.*]

TESMAN. There now—the epistle is finished.

HEDDA. That's right. And now Mrs. Elvsted is just going. Wait a moment—I'll go with you to the garden gate.

TESMAN. Do you think Berta could post the letter, Hedda dear?

HEDDA [*takes it*]. I will tell her to.

[BERTA *enters from the hall.*]

BERTA. Judge Brack wishes to know if Mrs. Tesman will receive him.

HEDDA. Yes, ask Judge Brack to come in. And look here—put this letter in the post.

BERTA [*taking the letter*]. Yes, ma'am.

[*She opens the door for* JUDGE BRACK *and goes out herself.* BRACK *is a man of forty-five; thick-set, but well-built and elastic in his movements. His face is roundish with an aristocratic profile. His hair is short, still almost black, and carefully dressed. His eyes are lively and sparkling. His eyebrows thick. His moustaches are also thick, with short-cut ends. He wears a well-cut walking-suit, a little too youthful for his age. He uses an eyeglass, which he now and then lets drop.*]

JUDGE BRACK [*with his hat in his hand, bowing*]. May one venture to call so early in the day?

HEDDA. Of course one may.

TESMAN [*presses his hand*]. You are welcome at any time. [*Introducing him*] Judge Brack—Miss Rysing——

HEDDA. Oh——!

BRACK [*bowing*]. Ah—delighted——

HEDDA [*looks at him and laughs*]. It's nice to have a look at you by daylight, Judge!

BRACK. Do you find me—altered?

HEDDA. A little younger, I think.

BRACK. Thank you so much.

TESMAN. But what do you think of Hedda—eh? Doesn't she look flourishing? She has actually——

HEDDA. Oh, do leave me alone. You haven't thanked Judge Brack for all the trouble he has taken——

BRACK. Oh, nonsense—it was a pleasure to me——

HEDDA. Yes, you are a friend indeed. But here stands Thea all impatience to be off—so *au revoir*, Judge. I shall be back again presently.

[*Mutual salutations.* MRS. ELVSTED *and* HEDDA *go out by the hall door.*]

BRACK. Well,—is your wife tolerably satisfied——

TESMAN. Yes, we can't thank you sufficiently. Of course she talks of a little rearrangement here and there; and one or two things are still wanting. We shall have to buy some additional trifles.

BRACK. Indeed!

TESMAN. But we won't trouble you about these things. Hedda says she herself will look after what is wanting.—Shan't we sit down? Eh?

BRACK. Thanks, for a moment. [*Seats himself beside the table.*] There is something I wanted to speak to you about, my dear Tesman.

TESMAN. Indeed? Ah, I understand! [*Seating himself*] I suppose it's the serious part of the frolic that is coming now. Eh?

BRACK. Oh, the money question is not so very pressing; though, for that matter, I wish we had gone a little more economically to work.

TESMAN. But that would never have done, you know! Think of Hedda, my dear fellow! You, who know her so well——. I couldn't possibly ask her to put up with a shabby style of living!

BRACK. No, no—that is just the difficulty.

TESMAN. And then—fortunately—it can't be long before I receive my appointment.

BRACK. Well, you see—such things are often apt to hang fire for a time.

TESMAN. Have you heard anything definite? Eh?

BRACK. Nothing exactly definite—— [*Interrupting himself*] But by the by—I have one piece of news for you.

TESMAN. Well?

BRACK. Your old friend, Eilert Lövborg, has returned to town.

TESMAN. I know that already.

BRACK. Indeed! How did you learn it?

TESMAN. From that lady who went out with Hedda.

BRACK. Really? What was her name? I didn't quite catch it.

TESMAN. Mrs. Elvsted.

BRACK. Aha—Sheriff Elvsted's wife? Of course—he has been living up in their regions.

TESMAN. And fancy—I'm delighted to hear that he is quite a reformed character!

BRACK. So they say.

TESMAN. And then he has published a new book—eh?

BRACK. Yes, indeed he has.

TESMAN. And I hear it has made some sensation!

BRACK. Quite an unusual sensation.

TESMAN. Fancy—isn't that good news! A man of such extraordinary talents——. I felt so grieved to think that he had gone irretrievably to ruin.

BRACK. That was what everybody thought.

TESMAN. But I cannot imagine what he will take to now! How in the world will he be able to make his living? Eh?

[*During the last words,* HEDDA *has entered by the hall door.*]

HEDDA [*to* BRACK, *laughing with a touch of scorn*]. Tesman is for ever worrying about how people are to make their living.

TESMAN. Well you see, dear—we were talking about poor Eilert Lövborg.

HEDDA [*glancing at him rapidly*]. Oh, indeed? [*Seats herself in the arm-chair beside the stove and asks indifferently*] What is the matter with him?

TESMAN. Well—no doubt he has run through all his property long ago; and he can scarcely write a new book every year—eh? So I really can't see what is to become of him.

BRACK. Perhaps I can give you some information on that point.

TESMAN. Indeed!

BRACK. You must remember that his relations have a good deal of influence.

TESMAN. Oh, his relations, unfortunately, have entirely washed their hands of him.

BRACK. At one time they called him the hope of the family.

TESMAN. At one time, yes! But he has put an end to all that.

HEDDA. Who knows? [*With a slight smile*] I hear they have reclaimed him up at Sheriff Elvsted's——

BRACK. And then this book that he has published——

TESMAN. Well, well, I hope to goodness they may find something for him to do. I have just written to him. I asked him to come and see us this evening, Hedda dear.

BRACK. But my dear fellow, you are booked for my bachelors' party this evening. You promised on the pier last night.

HEDDA. Had you forgotten, Tesman?

TESMAN. Yes, I had utterly forgotten.

BRACK. But it doesn't matter, for you may be sure he won't come.

TESMAN. What makes you think that? Eh?

BRACK [*with a little hesitation, rising and resting his hands on the back of his chair*]. My dear Tesman—and you too, Mrs. Tesman—I think I ought not to keep you in the dark about something that—that——

TESMAN. That concerns Eilert——?

BRACK. Both you and him.

TESMAN. Well, my dear Judge, out with it.

BRACK. You must be prepared to find your appointment deferred longer than you desired or expected.

TESMAN [*jumping up uneasily*]. Is there some hitch about it? Eh?

BRACK. The nomination may perhaps be made conditional on the result of a competition——

TESMAN. Competition! Think of that, Hedda!

HEDDA [*leans further back in the chair*]. Aha—aha!

TESMAN. But who can my competitor be? Surely not——?

BRACK. Yes, precisely—Eilert Lövborg.

TESMAN [*clasping his hands*]. No, no—it's quite inconceivable! Quite impossible! Eh?

BRACK. H'm—that is what it may come to, all the same.

TESMAN. Well but, Judge Brack—it would show the most incredible lack of consideration for me. [*Gesticulates with his arms.*] For—just think—I'm a married man! We have married on the strength of these prospects, Hedda and I; and run deep into debt; and borrowed money from Aunt Julia too. Good heavens, they had as good as promised me the appointment. Eh?

BRACK. Well, well, well—no doubt you will get it in the end; only after a contest.

HEDDA [*immovable in her arm-chair*]. Fancy, Tesman, there will be a sort of sporting interest in that.

TESMAN. Why, my dearest Hedda, how can you be so indifferent about it?

HEDDA [*as before*]. I am not at all indifferent. I am most eager to see who wins.

BRACK. In any case, Mrs. Tesman, it is best that you should know how matters stand. I mean—before you set about the little purchases I hear you are threatening.

HEDDA. This can make no difference.

BRACK. Indeed! Then I have no more to say. Good-bye! [*To* TESMAN] I shall look in on my way back from my afternoon walk, and take you home with me.

TESMAN. Oh yes, yes—your news has quite upset me.

HEDDA [*reclining, holds out her hand*]. Good-bye, Judge; and be sure you call in the afternoon.

BRACK. Many thanks. Good-bye, good-bye!

TESMAN [*accompanying him to the door*]. Good-bye, my dear Judge! You must really excuse me——

[JUDGE BRACK *goes out by the hall door.*]

TESMAN [*crosses the room*]. Oh Hedda—one should never rush into adventures. Eh?

HEDDA [*looks at him, smiling*]. Do you do that?

TESMAN. Yes, dear—there is no denying—it was adventurous to go and marry and set up house upon mere expectations.

HEDDA. Perhaps you are right there.

TESMAN. Well—at all events, we have our delightful home, Hedda! Fancy, the home we both dreamed of—the home we were in love with, I may almost say. Eh?

HEDDA [*rising slowly and wearily*]. It was part of our compact that we were to go into society—to keep open house.

TESMAN. Yes, if you only knew how I had been looking forward to it! Fancy—to see you as hostess—in a select circle! Eh? Well, well, well—for the present we shall have to get on without society, Hedda—only to invite Aunt Julia now and then.—Oh, I intended you to lead such an utterly different life, dear——!

HEDDA. Of course I cannot have my man in livery just yet.

TESMAN. Oh no, unfortunately. It would be out of the question for us to keep a footman, you know.

HEDDA. And the saddle-horse I was to have had——

TESMAN [*aghast*]. The saddle-horse!

HEDDA. ——I suppose I must not think of that now.

TESMAN. Good heavens, no!—that's as clear as daylight.

HEDDA [*goes up the room*]. Well, I shall have one thing at least to kill time with in the meanwhile.

TESMAN [*beaming*]. Oh thank heaven for that! What is it, Hedda? Eh?

HEDDA [*in the middle doorway, looks at him with covert scorn*]. My pistols, George.

TESMAN [*in alarm*]. Your pistols!

HEDDA [*with cold eyes*]. General Gabler's pistols.

[*She goes out through the inner room, to the left.*]

TESMAN [*rushes up to the middle doorway and calls after her*]. No, for heaven's sake, Hedda darling—don't touch those dangerous things! For my sake, Hedda! Eh?

ACT TWO

THE ROOM AT THE TESMANS' *as in the first act, except that the piano has been removed, and an elegant little writing-table with book-shelves put in its place. A smaller table stands near the sofa on the left. Most of the bouquets have been taken away.* MRS. ELVSTED'S *bouquet is upon the large table in front.—It is afternoon.*

HEDDA, *dressed to receive callers, is alone in the room. She stands by the open glass door, loading a revolver. The fellow to it lies in an open pistol-case on the writing-table.*

HEDDA [*looks down the garden, and calls*]. So you are here again, Judge!

BRACK [*is heard calling from a distance*]. As you see, Mrs. Tesman!

HEDDA [*raises the pistol and points*]. Now I'll shoot you, Judge Brack!

BRACK [*calling unseen*]. No, no, no! Don't stand aiming at me!

HEDDA. This is what comes of sneaking in by the back way. [*She fires.*]

BRACK [*nearer*]. Are you out of your senses!——

HEDDA. Dear me—did I happen to hit you?

BRACK [*still outside*]. I wish you would let these pranks alone!

HEDDA. Come in then, Judge.

[JUDGE BRACK, *dressed as though for a men's party, enters by the glass door. He carries a light overcoat over his arm.*]

BRACK. What the deuce—haven't you tired of that sport, yet? What are you shooting at?

HEDDA. Oh, I am only firing in the air.

BRACK [*gently takes the pistol out of her hand*]. Allow me, Madam! [*Looks at it.*] Ah—I know this pistol well! [*Looks around.*] Where is the case? Ah, here it is. [*Lays the pistol in it, and shuts it.*] Now we won't play at that game any more to-day.

HEDDA. Then what in heaven's name would you have me do with myself?

BRACK. Have you had no visitors?

HEDDA [*closing the glass door*]. Not one. I suppose all our set are still out of town.

BRACK. And is Tesman not at home either?

HEDDA [*at the writing-table, putting the pistol-case in a drawer which she shuts*]. No. He rushed off to his aunt's directly after lunch; he didn't expect you so early.

BRACK. H'm—how stupid of me not to have thought of that!

HEDDA [*turning her head to look at him*]. Why stupid?

BRACK. Because if I had thought of it I should have come a little—earlier.

HEDDA [*crossing the room*]. Then you would have found no one to receive you; for I have been in my room changing my dress ever since lunch.

BRACK. And is there no sort of little chink that we could hold a parley through?

HEDDA. You have forgotten to arrange one.

BRACK. That was another piece of stupidity.

HEDDA. Well, we must just settle down here—and wait. Tesman is not likely to be back for some time yet.

BRACK. Never mind; I shall not be impatient.

[HEDDA *seats herself in the corner of the sofa.* BRACK *lays his overcoat over the back of the nearest chair, and sits down, but keeps his hat in his hand. A short silence. They look at each other.*]

HEDDA. Well?

BRACK [*in the same tone*]. Well?

HEDDA. I spoke first.

BRACK [*bending a little forward*]. Come, let us have a cosy little chat, Mrs. Hedda.

HEDDA [*leaning further back in the sofa*]. Does it not seem like a whole eternity since our last talk? Of course I don't count those few words yesterday evening and this morning.

BRACK. You mean since our last confidential talk? Our last *tête-à-tête*?

HEDDA. Well, yes—since you put it so.

BRACK. Not a day has passed but I have wished that you were home again.

HEDDA. And I have done nothing but wish the same thing.

BRACK. You? Really, Mrs. Hedda? And I thought you had been enjoying your tour so much!

HEDDA. Oh, yes, you may be sure of that!

BRACK. But Tesman's letters spoke of nothing but happiness.

HEDDA. Oh, Tesman! You see, he thinks nothing so delightful as grubbing in libraries and making copies of old parchments, or whatever you call them.

BRACK [*with a spice of malice*]. Well, that is his vocation in life— or part of it at any rate.

HEDDA. Yes, of course; and no doubt when it's your vocation——. But I! Oh, my dear Mr. Brack, how mortally bored I have been.

BRACK [*sympathetically*]. Do you really say so? In downright earnest?

HEDDA. Yes, you can surely understand it——! To go for six whole months without meeting a soul that knew anything of our circle, or could talk about the things we are interested in.

BRACK. Yes, yes—I, too, should feel that a deprivation.

HEDDA. And then, what I found most intolerable of all—

BRACK. Well?

HEDDA. ——was being everlastingly in the company of—one and the same person——

BRACK [*with a nod of assent*]. Morning, noon, and night, yes—at all possible times and seasons.

HEDDA. I said "everlastingly."

BRACK. Just so. But I should have thought, with our excellent Tesman, one could——

HEDDA. Tesman is—a specialist, my dear Judge.

BRACK. Undeniably.

HEDDA. And specialists are not at all amusing to travel with. Not in the long run at any rate.

BRACK. Not even—the specialist one happens to love?

HEDDA. Faugh—don't use that sickening word!

BRACK [*taken aback*]. What do you say, Mrs. Hedda?

HEDDA [*half laughingly, half irritated*]. You should just try it! To hear of nothing but the history of civilization morning, noon, and night——

BRACK. Everlastingly.

HEDDA. Yes, yes, yes! And then all this about the domestic industry of the middle ages——! That's the most disgusting part of it!

BRACK [*looks searchingly at her*]. But tell me—in that case, how am I to understand your——? H'm——

HEDDA. My accepting George Tesman, you mean?

BRACK. Well, let us put it so.

HEDDA. Good heavens, do you see anything so wonderful in that?

BRACK. Yes and no—Mrs. Hedda.

HEDDA. I had positively danced myself tired, my dear Judge. My day was done—— [*With a slight shudder*] Oh, no—I won't say that; nor think it, either!

BRACK. You have assuredly no reason to.

HEDDA. Oh, reasons—— [*Watching him closely*] And George Tesman—after all, you must admit that he is correctness itself.

BRACK. His correctness and respectability are beyond all question.

HEDDA. And I don't see anything absolutely ridiculous about him.—Do you?

BRACK. Ridiculous? N—no—I shouldn't exactly say so——

HEDDA. Well—and his powers of research, at all events, are untiring.—I see no reason why he should not one day come to the front, after all.

BRACK [*looks at her hesitatingly*]. I thought that you, like every one else, expected him to attain the highest distinction.

HEDDA [*with an expression of fatigue*]. Yes, so I did—And then, since he was bent, at all hazards, on being allowed to provide for me—I really don't know why I should not have accepted his offer?

BRACK. No—if you look at it in that light——

HEDDA. It was more than my other adorers were prepared to do for me, my dear Judge.

BRACK [*laughing*]. Well, I can't answer for all the rest; but as for myself, you know quite well that I have always entertained a—a certain respect for the marriage tie—for marriage as an institution, Mrs. Hedda.

HEDDA [*jestingly*]. Oh, I assure you I have never cherished any hopes with respect to you.

BRACK. All I require is a pleasant and intimate interior, where I can make myself useful in every way, and am free to come and go as—as a trusted friend——

HEDDA. Of the master of the house, do you mean?

BRACK [*bowing*]. Frankly—of the mistress first of all; but, of course, of the master, too, in the second place. Such a triangular friendship—if I may call it so—is really a great convenience for all parties, let me tell you.

HEDDA. Yes, I have many a time longed for some one to make a third on our travels. Oh—those railway-carriage *tête-à-têtes*——!

BRACK. Fortunately your wedding journey is over now.

HEDDA [*shaking her head*]. Not by a long—long way. I have only arrived at a station on the line.

BRACK. Well, then the passengers jump out and move about a little, Mrs. Hedda.

HEDDA. I never jump out.

BRACK. Really?

HEDDA. No—because there is always some one standing by to——

BRACK [*laughing*]. To look at your legs, do you mean?

HEDDA. Precisely.

BRACK. Well, but, dear me——

HEDDA [*with a gesture of repulsion*]. I won't have it. I would rather keep my seat where I happen to be—and continue the *tête-à-tête*.

BRACK. But suppose a third person were to jump in and join the couple.

HEDDA. Ah—that is quite another matter!

BRACK. A trusted, sympathetic friend——

HEDDA. ——with a fund of conversation on all sorts of lively topics——

BRACK. ——and not the least bit of a specialist!

HEDDA [*with an audible sigh*]. Yes, that would be a relief, indeed.

BRACK [*hears the front door open, and glances in that direction*]. The triangle is completed.

HEDDA [*half aloud*]. And on goes the train.

[GEORGE TESMAN, *in a gray walking-suit, with a soft felt hat, enters from the hall. He has a number of unbound books under his arm and in his pockets.*]

TESMAN [*goes up to the table beside the corner settee*]. Ouf—what a load for a warm day—all these books. [*Lays them on the table.*] I'm positively perspiring, Hedda. Hallo—are you there already, my dear Judge? Eh? Berta didn't tell me.

BRACK [*rising*]. I came in through the garden.

HEDDA. What books have you got there?

TESMAN [*stands looking them through*]. Some new books on my special subjects—quite indispensable to me.

HEDDA. Your special subjects?

BRACK. Yes, books on his special subjects, Mrs. Tesman.

[BRACK *and* HEDDA *exchange a confidential smile.*]

HEDDA. Do you need still more books on your special subjects?

TESMAN. Yes, my dear Hedda, one can never have too many of them. Of course, one must keep up with all that is written and published.

HEDDA. Yes, I suppose one must.

TESMAN [*searching among his books*]. And look here—I have got hold of Eilert Lövborg's new book, too. [*Offering it to her*] Perhaps you would like to glance through it, Hedda? Eh?

HEDDA. No, thank you. Or rather—afterwards perhaps.

TESMAN. I looked into it a little on the way home.

BRACK. Well, what do you think of it—as a specialist?

TESMAN. I think it shows quite remarkable soundness of judgment. He never wrote like that before. [*Putting the books together*] Now I shall take all these into my study. I'm longing to cut the leaves——! And then I must change my clothes. [*To* BRACK] I suppose we needn't start just yet? Eh?

BRACK. Oh, dear, no—there is not the slightest hurry.

TESMAN. Well, then, I will take my time. [*Is going with his books, but stops in the doorway and turns.*] By the by, Hedda—Aunt Julia is not coming this evening.

HEDDA. Not coming? Is it that affair of the bonnet that keeps her away?

TESMAN. Oh, not at all. How could you think such a thing of Aunt Julia? Just fancy——! The fact is, Aunt Rina is very ill.

HEDDA. She always is.

TESMAN. Yes, but to-day she is much worse than usual, poor dear.

HEDDA. Oh, then it's only natural that her sister should remain with her. I must bear my disappointment.

TESMAN. And you can't imagine, dear, how delighted Aunt Julia seemed to be—because you had come home looking so flourishing!

HEDDA [*half aloud, rising*]. Oh, those everlasting Aunts!

TESMAN. What?

HEDDA [*going to the glass door*]. Nothing.

TESMAN. Oh, all right.

[*He goes through the inner room, out to the right.*]

BRACK. What bonnet were you talking about?

HEDDA. Oh, it was a little episode with Miss Tesman this morning. She had laid down her bonnet on the chair there—[*Looks at him and smiles*]—and I pretended to think it was the servant's.

BRACK [*shaking his head*]. Now, my dear Mrs. Hedda, how could you do such a thing? To that excellent old lady, too!

HEDDA [*nervously crossing the room*]. Well, you see—these impulses come over me all of a sudden; and I cannot resist them. [*Throws herself down in the easy-chair by the stove.*] Oh, I don't know how to explain it.

BRACK [*behind the easy-chair*]. You are not really happy—that is at the bottom of it.

HEDDA [*looking straight before her*]. I know of no reason why I should be—happy. Perhaps you can give me one?

BRACK. Well—amongst other things, because you have got exactly the home you had set your heart on.

HEDDA [*looks up at him and laughs*]. Do you, too, believe in that legend?

BRACK. Is there nothing in it, then?

HEDDA. Oh, yes, there is something in it.

BRACK. Well?

HEDDA. There is this in it, that I made use of Tesman to see me home from evening parties last summer——

BRACK. I, unfortunately, had to go quite a different way.

HEDDA. That's true. I know you were going a different way last summer.

BRACK [*laughing*]. Oh fie, Mrs. Hedda! Well, then—you and Tesman——?

HEDDA. Well, we happened to pass here one evening; Tesman, poor fellow, was writhing in the agony of having to find conversation; so I took pity on the learned man——

BRACK [*smiles doubtfully*]. You took pity? H'm——

HEDDA. Yes, I really did. And so—to help him out of his torment—I happened to say, in pure thoughtlessness, that I should like to live in this villa.

BRACK. No more than that?

HEDDA. Not that evening.

BRACK. But afterwards?

HEDDA. Yes, my thoughtlessness had consequences, my dear Judge.

BRACK. Unfortunately that too often happens, Mrs. Hedda.

HEDDA. Thanks! So you see it was this enthusiasm for Secretary Falk's villa that first constituted a bond of sympathy between George Tesman and me. From that came our engagement and our marriage, and our wedding journey, and all the rest of it. Well, well, my dear Judge—as you make your bed so you must lie, I could almost say.

BRACK. This is exquisite! And you really cared not a rap about it all the time?

HEDDA. No, heaven knows I didn't.

BRACK. But now? Now that we have made it so homelike for you?

HEDDA. Ugh—the rooms all seem to smell of lavender and dried rose-leaves.—But perhaps it's Aunt Julia that has brought that scent with her.

BRACK [*laughing*]. No, I think it must be a legacy from the late Mrs. Secretary Falk.

HEDDA. Yes, there is an odor of mortality about it. It reminds me of a bouquet—the day after the ball. [*Clasps her hands behind her head, leans back in her chair and looks at him.*] Oh, my dear Judge—you cannot imagine how horribly I shall bore myself here.

BRACK. Why should not you, too, find some sort of vocation in life, Mrs. Hedda?

HEDDA. A vocation—that should attract me?

BRACK. If possible, of course.

HEDDA. Heaven knows what sort of a vocation that could be. I often wonder whether—— [*Breaking off*] But that would never do, either.

BRACK. Who can tell? Let me hear what it is.

HEDDA. Whether I might not get Tesman to go into politics, I mean.

BRACK [*laughing*]. Tesman? No, really now, political life is not the thing for him—not at all in his line.

HEDDA. No, I daresay not.—But if I could get him into it all the same?

BRACK. Why—what satisfaction could you find in that? If he is not fitted for that sort of thing, why should you want to drive him into it?

HEDDA. Because I am bored, I tell you! [*After a pause*] So you think it quite out of the question that Tesman should ever get into the ministry?

BRACK. H'm—you see, my dear Mrs. Hedda—to get into the ministry, he would have to be a tolerably rich man.

HEDDA [*rising impatiently*]. Yes, there we have it! It is this genteel poverty I have managed to drop into——! [*Crosses the room.*] That is what makes life so pitiable! So utterly ludicrous!—For that's what it is.

BRACK. Now *I* should say the fault lay elsewhere.

HEDDA. Where, then?

BRACK. You have never gone through any really stimulating experience.

HEDDA. Anything serious, you mean?

BRACK. Yes, you may call it so. But now you may perhaps have one in store.

HEDDA [*tossing her head*]. Oh, you're thinking of the annoyances about this wretched professorship! But that must be Tesman's own affair. I assure you I shall not waste a thought upon it.

BRACK. No, no, I daresay not. But suppose now that what people call —in elegant language—a solemn responsibility were to come upon you? [*Smiling*] A new responsibility, Mrs. Hedda?

HEDDA [*angrily*]. Be quiet! Nothing of that sort will ever happen!

BRACK [*warily*]. We will speak of this again a year hence—at the very outside.

HEDDA [*curtly*]. I have no turn for anything of the sort, Judge Brack. No responsibilities for me!

BRACK. Are you so unlike the generality of women as to have no turn for duties which——?

HEDDA [*beside the glass door*]. Oh, be quiet, I tell you!—I often think there is only one thing in the world I have any turn for.

BRACK [*drawing near to her*]. And what is that, if I may ask?

HEDDA [*stands looking out*]. Boring myself to death. Now you know it. [*Turns, looks towards the inner room and laughs.*] Yes, as I thought! Here comes the Professor.

BRACK [*softly, in a tone of warning*]. Come, come, come, Mrs. Hedda!

[GEORGE TESMAN, *dressed for the party, with his gloves and hat in his hand, enters from the right through the inner room.*]

TESMAN. Hedda, has no message come from Eilert Lövborg? Eh?

HEDDA. No.

TESMAN. Then you'll see he'll be here presently.

BRACK. Do you really think he will come?

TESMAN. Yes, I am almost sure of it. For what you were telling us this morning must have been a mere floating rumor.

BRACK. You think so?

TESMAN. At any rate, Aunt Julia said she did not believe for a moment that he would ever stand in my way again. Fancy that!

BRACK. Well, then, that's all right.

TESMAN [*placing his hat and gloves on a chair on the right*]. Yes, but you must really let me wait for him as long as possible.

BRACK. We have plenty of time yet. None of my guests will arrive before seven or half-past.

TESMAN. Then meanwhile we can keep Hedda company, and see what happens. Eh?

HEDDA [*placing* BRACK's *hat and overcoat upon the corner settee*]. And at the worst Mr. Lövborg can remain here with me.

BRACK [*offering to take his things*]. Oh, allow me, Mrs. Tesman!— What do you mean by "at the worst"?

HEDDA. If he won't go with you and Tesman.

TESMAN [*looks dubiously at her*]. But, Hedda, dear—do you think it would quite do for him to remain with you? Eh? Remember, Aunt Julia can't come.

HEDDA. No, but Mrs. Elvsted is coming. We three can have a cup of tea together.

TESMAN. Oh, yes, that will be all right.

BRACK [*smiling*]. And that would perhaps be the safest plan for him.

HEDDA. Why so?

BRACK. Well, you know, Mrs. Tesman, how you used to gird at my little bachelor parties. You declared they were adapted only for men of the strictest principles.

HEDDA. But no doubt Mr. Lövborg's principles are strict enough now. A converted sinner——

[BERTA *appears at the hall door.*]

BERTA. There's a gentleman asking if you are at home, ma'am——

HEDDA. Well, show him in.

TESMAN [*softly*]. I'm sure it is he! Fancy that!

[EILERT LÖVBORG *enters from the hall. He is slim and lean; of the same age as* TESMAN, *but looks older and somewhat worn-out. His hair and beard are of a blackish brown, his face long and pale, but with patches of color on the cheek-bones. He is dressed in a well-cut black visiting suit, quite new. He has dark gloves and a silk hat. He stops near the door, and makes a rapid bow, seeming somewhat embarrassed.*]

TESMAN [*goes up to him and shakes him warmly by the hand*]. Well, my dear Eilert—so at last we meet again!

EILERT LÖVBORG [*speaks in a subdued voice*]. Thanks for your letter, Tesman. [*Approaching* HEDDA] Will you, too, shake hands with me, Mrs. Tesman?

HEDDA [*taking his hand*]. I am glad to see you, Mr. Lövborg. [*With a motion of her hand*] I don't know whether you two gentlemen——?

LÖVBORG [*bowing slightly*]. Judge Brack, I think.

BRACK [*doing likewise*]. Oh, yes,—in the old days——

TESMAN [*to* LÖVBORG, *with his hands on his shoulders*]. And now you must make yourself entirely at home, Eilert! Mustn't he, Hedda?—For I hear you are going to settle in town again? Eh?

LÖVBORG. Yes, I am.

TESMAN. Quite right, quite right. Let me tell you, I have got hold of your new book; but I haven't had time to read it yet.

LÖVBORG. You may spare yourself the trouble.

TESMAN. Why so?

LÖVBORG. Because there is very little in it.

TESMAN. Just fancy—how can you say so?

BRACK. But it has been very much praised, I hear.

LÖVBORG. That was what I wanted; so I put nothing into the book but what every one would agree with.

BRACK. Very wise of you.

TESMAN. Well, but, my dear Eilert——!

LÖVBORG. For now I mean to win myself a position again—to make a fresh start.

TESMAN [*a little embarrassed*]. Ah, that is what you wish to do? Eh?

LÖVBORG [*smiling, lays down his hat, and draws a packet, wrapped in paper, from his coat pocket*]. But when this one appears, George Tesman, you will have to read it. For this is the real book—the book I have put my true self into.

TESMAN. Indeed? And what is it?

LÖVBORG. It is the continuation.

TESMAN. The continuation? Of what?

LÖVBORG. Of the book.

TESMAN. Of the new book?

LÖVBORG. Of course.

TESMAN. Why, my dear Eilert—does it not come down to our own days?

LÖVBORG. Yes, it does; and this one deals with the future.

TESMAN. With the future! But, good heavens, we know nothing of the future!

LÖVBORG. No; but there is a thing or two to be said about it all the same. [*Opens the packet.*] Look here——

TESMAN. Why, that's not your handwriting.

LÖVBORG. I dictated it. [*Turning over the pages*] It falls into two sections. The first deals with the civilizing forces of the future. And

here is the second—[*Running through the pages towards the end*]—
forecasting the probable line of development.

TESMAN. How odd now! I should never have thought of writing
anything of that sort.

HEDDA [*at the glass door, drumming on the pane*]. H'm—— I daresay not.

LÖVBORG [*replacing the manuscript in its paper and laying the packet
on the table*]. I brought it, thinking I might read you a little of it this
evening.

TESMAN. That was very good of you, Eilert. But this evening——?
[*Looking at* BRACK] I don't quite see how we can manage it——

LÖVBORG. Well, then, some other time. There is no hurry.

BRACK. I must tell you, Mr. Lövborg—there is a little gathering at
my house this evening—mainly in honor of Tesman, you know——

LÖVBORG [*looking for his hat*]. Oh—then I won't detain you——

BRACK. No, but listen—will you not do me the favor of joining us?

LÖVBORG [*curtly and decidedly*]. No, I can't—thank you very much.

BRACK. Oh, nonsense—do! We shall be quite a select little circle.
And I assure you we shall have a "lively time," as Mrs. Hed—as Mrs.
Tesman says.

LÖVBORG. I have no doubt of it. But nevertheless——

BRACK. And then you might bring your manuscript with you, and
read it to Tesman at my house. I could give you a room to yourselves.

TESMAN. Yes, think of that, Eilert,—why shouldn't you? Eh?

HEDDA [*interposing*]. But, Tesman, if Mr. Lövborg would really
rather not! I am sure Mr. Lövborg is much more inclined to remain
here and have supper with me.

LÖVBORG [*looking at her*]. With you, Mrs. Tesman?

HEDDA. And with Mrs. Elvsted.

LÖVBORG. Ah—— [*Lightly*] I saw her for a moment this morning.

HEDDA. Did you? Well, she is coming this evening. So you see you
are almost bound to remain, Mr. Lövborg, or she will have no one to
see her home.

LÖVBORG. That's true. Many thanks, Mrs. Tesman—in that case I
will remain.

HEDDA. Then I have one or two orders to give the servant——

[*She goes to the hall door and rings.* BERTA *enters.* HEDDA *talks to
her in a whisper, and points towards the inner room.* BERTA *nods
and goes out again.*]

TESMAN [*at the same time, to* LÖVBORG]. Tell me, Eilert—is it this
new subject—the future—that you are going to lecture about?

LÖVBORG. Yes.

TESMAN. They told me at the bookseller's that you are going to deliver a course of lectures this autumn.

LÖVBORG.   That is my intention. I hope you won't take it ill, Tesman.

TESMAN.   Oh no, not in the least! But——?

LÖVBORG.   I can quite understand that it must be disagreeable to you.

TESMAN [*cast down*].   Oh, I can't expect you, out of consideration for me, to——

LÖVBORG.   But I shall wait till you have received your appointment.

TESMAN.   Will you wait? Yes, but—yes, but—are you not going to compete with me? Eh?

LÖVBORG.   No; it is only the moral victory I care for.

TESMAN.   Why, bless me—then Aunt Julia was right after all! Oh, yes—I knew it! Hedda! Just fancy—Eilert Lövborg is not going to stand in our way!

HEDDA [*curtly*].   Our way? Pray leave me out of the question.

[*She goes up towards the inner room, where* BERTA *is placing a tray with decanters and glasses on the table.* HEDDA *nods approval, and comes forward again.* BERTA *goes out.*]

TESMAN [*at the same time*].   And you, Judge Brack—what do you say to this? Eh?

BRACK.   Well, I say that a moral victory—h'm—may be all very fine——

TESMAN.   Yes, certainly. But all the same——

HEDDA [*looking at* TESMAN *with a cold smile*].   You stand there looking as if you were thunderstruck——

TESMAN.   Yes—so I am—I almost think——

BRACK.   Don't you see, Mrs. Tesman, a thunderstorm has just passed over?

HEDDA [*pointing towards the inner room*].   Will you not take a glass of cold punch, gentlemen?

BRACK [*looking at his watch*].   A stirrup-cup? Yes, it wouldn't come amiss.

TESMAN.   A capital idea, Hedda! Just the thing! Now that the weight has been taken off my mind——

HEDDA.   Will you not join them, Mr. Lövborg?

LÖVBORG [*with a gesture of refusal*].   No, thank you. Nothing for me.

BRACK.   Why bless me—cold punch is surely not poison.

LÖVBORG.   Perhaps not for every one.

HEDDA.   I will keep Mr. Lövborg company in the meantime.

TESMAN.   Yes, yes, Hedda dear, do.

[*He and* BRACK *go into the inner room, seat themselves, drink punch, smoke cigarettes, and carry on a lively conversation during what follows.* EILERT LÖVBORG *remains standing beside the stove.* HEDDA *goes to the writing-table.*]

HEDDA [*raising her voice a little*]. Do you care to look at some photographs, Mr. Lövborg? You know Tesman and I made a tour in the Tyrol on our way home?

[*She takes up an album, and places it on the table beside the sofa, in the further corner of which she seats herself.* EILERT LÖVBORG *approaches, stops, and looks at her. Then he takes a chair and seats himself to her left, with his back towards the inner room.*]

HEDDA [*opening the album*]. Do you see this range of mountains, Mr. Lövborg? It's the Ortler group. Tesman has written the name underneath. Here it is: "The Ortler group near Meran."

LÖVBORG [*who has never taken his eyes off her, says softly and slowly*]. Hedda—Gabler!

HEDDA [*glancing hastily at him*]. Ah! Hush!

LÖVBORG [*repeats softly*]. Hedda Gabler!

HEDDA [*looking at the album*]. That was my name in the old days —when we two knew each other.

LÖVBORG. And I must teach myself never to say Hedda Gabler again —never, as long as I live.

HEDDA [*still turning over the pages*]. Yes, you must. And I think you ought to practise in time. The sooner the better, I should say.

LÖVBORG [*in a tone of indignation*]. Hedda Gabler married? And married to—George Tesman!

HEDDA. Yes—so the world goes.

LÖVBORG [*using the familiar "du"*]. Oh, Hedda, Hedda—how could you throw yourself away!

HEDDA [*looks sharply at him*]. What? I can't allow this!

LÖVBORG. What do you mean?

[TESMAN *comes into the room and goes towards the sofa.*]

HEDDA [*hears him coming and says in an indifferent tone*]. And this is a view from the Val d'Ampezzo, Mr. Lövborg. Just look at these peaks! [*Looks affectionately up at* TESMAN.] What's the name of these curious peaks, dear?

TESMAN. Let me see. Oh, those are the Dolomites.

HEDDA. Yes, that's it!—Those are the Dolomites, Mr. Lövborg.

TESMAN. Hedda, dear,—I only wanted to ask whether I shouldn't bring you a little punch after all? For yourself, at any rate—eh?

HEDDA. Yes, do, please; and perhaps a few biscuits.

TESMAN. No cigarettes?

HEDDA. No.

TESMAN. Very well.

[*He goes into the inner room and out to the right.* BRACK *sits in the inner room, and keeps an eye from time to time on* HEDDA *and* LÖVBORG.]

LÖVBORG [*softly, as before*].   Answer me, Hedda—how could you go and do this?

HEDDA [*apparently absorbed in the album*].   If you continue to say *du* to me I won't talk to you.

LÖVBORG.   May I not say *du* even when we are alone?

HEDDA.   No. You may think it; but you mustn't say it.

LÖVBORG.   Ah, I understand. It is an offence against George Tesman, whom you love. [*He now returns to using the formal "De."*]

HEDDA [*glances at him and smiles*].   Love? What an idea!

LÖVBORG.   You don't love him then!

HEDDA.   But I won't hear of any sort of unfaithfulness! Remember that.

LÖVBORG.   Hedda—answer me one thing——

HEDDA.   Hush!

[TESMAN *enters with a small tray from the inner room.*]

TESMAN.   Here you are! Isn't this tempting?

[*He puts the tray on the table.*]

HEDDA.   Why do you bring it yourself?

TESMAN [*filling the glasses*].   Because I think it's such fun to wait upon you, Hedda.

HEDDA.   But you have poured out two glasses. Mr. Lövborg said he wouldn't have any——

TESMAN.   No, but Mrs. Elvsted will soon be here, won't she?

HEDDA.   Yes, by the by—Mrs. Elvsted——

TESMAN.   Had you forgotten her? Eh?

HEDDA.   We were so absorbed in these photographs. [*Shows him a picture.*] Do you remember this little village?

TESMAN.   Oh, it's that one just below the Brenner Pass. It was there we passed the night——

HEDDA.   ——and met that lively party of tourists.

TESMAN.   Yes, that was the place. Fancy—if we could only have had you with us, Eilert! Eh?

[*He returns to the inner room and sits beside* BRACK.]

LÖVBORG.   Answer me this one thing, Hedda——

HEDDA.   Well?

LÖVBORG.   Was there no love in your friendship for me, either? Not a spark—not a tinge of love in it?

HEDDA.   I wonder if there was? To me it seems as though we were two good comrades—two thoroughly intimate friends. [*Smilingly*] You especially were frankness itself.

LÖVBORG. It was you that made me so.

HEDDA. As I look back upon it all, I think there was really something beautiful, something fascinating—something daring—in—in that secret intimacy—that comradeship which no living creature so much as dreamed of.

LÖVBORG. Yes, yes, Hedda! Was there not?—When I used to come to your father's in the afternoon—and the General sat over at the window reading his papers—with his back towards us——

HEDDA. And we two on the corner sofa——

LÖVBORG. Always with the same illustrated paper before us——

HEDDA. For want of an album, yes.

LÖVBORG. Yes, Hedda, and when I made my confessions to you—told you about myself, things that at that time no one else knew! There I would sit and tell you of my escapades—my days and nights of devilment. Oh, Hedda—what was the power in you that forced me to confess these things?

HEDDA. Do you think it was any power in me?

LÖVBORG. How else can I explain it? And all those—those round-about questions you used to put to me——

HEDDA. Which you understood so particularly well——

LÖVBORG. How could you sit and question me like that? Question me quite frankly——

HEDDA. In roundabout terms, please observe.

LÖVBORG. Yes, but frankly nevertheless. Cross-question me about—all that sort of thing?

HEDDA. And how could you answer, Mr. Lövborg?

LÖVBORG. Yes, that is just what I can't understand—in looking back upon it. But tell me now, Hedda—was there not love at the bottom of our friendship? On your side, did you not feel as though you might purge my stains away—if I made you my confessor? Was it not so?

HEDDA. No, not quite.

LÖVBORG. What was your motive, then?

HEDDA. Do you think it quite incomprehensible that a young girl—when it can be done—without any one knowing——

LÖVBORG. Well?

HEDDA. ——should be glad to have a peep, now and then, into a world which——

LÖVBORG. Which——?

HEDDA. ——which she is forbidden to know anything about?

LÖVBORG. So that was it?

HEDDA. Partly. Partly—I almost think.

LÖVBORG. Comradeship in the thirst for life. But why should not that, at any rate, have continued?

HEDDA. The fault was yours.

LÖVBORG. It was you that broke with me.

HEDDA. Yes, when our friendship threatened to develop into something more serious. Shame upon you, Eilert Lövborg! How could you think of wronging your—your frank comrade?

LÖVBORG [clenching his hands]. Oh, why did you not carry out your threat? Why did you not shoot me down?

HEDDA. Because I have such a dread of scandal.

LÖVBORG. Yes, Hedda, you are a coward at heart.

HEDDA. A terrible coward. [Changing her tone] But it was a lucky thing for you. And now you have found ample consolation at the Elvsteds'.

LÖVBORG. I know what Thea has confided to you.

HEDDA. And perhaps you have confided to her something about us?

LÖVBORG. Not a word. She is too stupid to understand anything of that sort.

HEDDA. Stupid?

LÖVBORG. She is stupid about matters of that sort.

HEDDA. And I am cowardly. [Bends over towards him, without looking him in the face, and says more softly:] But now I will confide something to you.

LÖVBORG [eagerly]. Well?

HEDDA. The fact that I dared not shoot you down——

LÖVBORG. Yes!

HEDDA. ——that was not my most arrant cowardice—that evening.

LÖVBORG [looks at her a moment, understands, and whispers passionately]. Oh, Hedda! Hedda Gabler! Now I begin to see a hidden reason beneath our comradeship! [Using the familiar pronoun again] You and I——! After all, then, it was your craving for life——

HEDDA [softly, with a sharp glance]. Take care! Believe nothing of the sort!

[Twilight has begun to fall. The hall door is opened from without by BERTA.]

HEDDA [closes the album with a bang and calls smilingly]. Ah, at last! My darling Thea,—come along!

[MRS. ELVSTED enters from the hall. She is in evening dress. The door is closed behind her.]

HEDDA [on the sofa, stretches out her arms towards her]. My sweet Thea—you can't think how I have been longing for you!

[MRS. ELVSTED, in passing, exchanges slight salutations with the gentlemen in the inner room, then goes up to the table and gives HEDDA her hand. EILERT LÖVBORG has risen. He and MRS. ELVSTED greet each other with a silent nod.]

MRS. ELVSTED.　Ought I to go in and talk to your husband for a moment?

HEDDA.　Oh, not at all. Leave those two alone. They will soon be going.

MRS. ELVSTED.　Are they going out?

HEDDA.　Yes, to a supper-party.

MRS. ELVSTED [*quickly, to* LÖVBORG].　Not you?

LÖVBORG.　No.

HEDDA.　Mr. Lövborg remains with us.

MRS. ELVSTED [*takes a chair and is about to seat herself at his side*]. Oh, how nice it is here!

HEDDA.　No, thank you, my little Thea! Not there! You'll be good enough to come over here to me. I will sit between you.

MRS. ELVSTED.　Yes, just as you please.

[*She goes round the table and seats herself on the sofa on* HEDDA's *right.* LÖVBORG *re-seats himself on his chair.*]

LÖVBORG [*after a short pause, to* HEDDA].　Is not she lovely to look at?

HEDDA [*lightly stroking her hair*].　Only to look at?

LÖVBORG.　Yes. For we two—she and I—we are two real comrades. We have absolute faith in each other; so we can sit and talk with perfect frankness——

HEDDA.　Not round about, Mr. Lövborg?

LÖVBORG.　Well——

MRS. ELVSTED [*softly clinging close to* HEDDA].　Oh, how happy I am, Hedda! For, only think, he says I have inspired him, too.

HEDDA [*looks at her with a smile*].　Ah! Does he say that, dear?

LÖVBORG.　And then she is so brave, Mrs. Tesman!

MRS. ELVSTED.　Good heavens—am I brave?

LÖVBORG.　Exceedingly—where your comrade is concerned.

HEDDA.　Ah, yes—courage! If one only had that!

LÖVBORG.　What then? What do you mean?

HEDDA.　Then life would perhaps be livable, after all. [*With a sudden change of tone*] But now, my dearest Thea, you really must have a glass of cold punch.

MRS. ELVSTED.　No, thanks—I never take anything of that kind.

HEDDA.　Well, then, you, Mr. Lövborg.

LÖVBORG.　Nor I, thank you.

MRS. ELVSTED.　No, he doesn't, either.

HEDDA [*looks fixedly at him*].　But if I say you shall?

LÖVBORG.　It would be no use.

HEDDA [*laughing*].　Then I, poor creature, have no sort of power over you?

LÖVBORG.　Not in that respect.

HEDDA. But seriously, I think you ought to—for your own sake.

MRS. ELVSTED. Why, Hedda——!

LÖVBORG. How so?

HEDDA. Or rather on account of other people.

LÖVBORG. Indeed?

HEDDA. Otherwise people might be apt to suspect that—in your heart of hearts—you did not feel quite secure—quite confident in yourself.

MRS. ELVSTED [softly]. Oh, please, Hedda——!

LÖVBORG. People may suspect what they like—for the present.

MRS. ELVSTED [joyfully]. Yes, let them!

HEDDA. I saw it plainly in Judge Brack's face a moment ago.

LÖVBORG. What did you see?

HEDDA. His contemptuous smile, when you dared not go with them into the inner room.

LÖVBORG. Dared not? Of course I preferred to stop here and talk to you.

MRS. ELVSTED. What could be more natural, Hedda?

HEDDA. But the Judge could not guess that. And I saw, too, the way he smiled and glanced at Tesman when you dared not accept his invitation to this wretched little supper-party of his.

LÖVBORG. Dared not! Do you say I dared not?

HEDDA. I don't say so. But that was how Judge Brack understood it.

LÖVBORG. Well, let him.

HEDDA. Then you are not going with them?

LÖVBORG. I will stay here with you and Thea.

MRS. ELVSTED. Yes, Hedda—how can you doubt that?

HEDDA [smiles and nods approvingly to LÖVBORG]. Firm as a rock! Faithful to your principles, now and forever! Ah, that is how a man should be! [Turns to MRS. ELVSTED and caresses her.] Well, now, what did I tell you, when you came to us this morning in such a state of distraction——

LÖVBORG [surprised]. Distraction!

MRS. ELVSTED [terrified]. Hedda—oh, Hedda——!

HEDDA. You can see for yourself! You haven't the slightest reason to be in such mortal terror—— [Interrupting herself] There! Now we can all three enjoy ourselves!

LÖVBORG [who has given a start]. Ah— what is all this, Mrs. Tesman?

MRS. ELVSTED. Oh, my God, Hedda! What are you saying? What are you doing?

HEDDA. Don't get excited! That horrid Judge Brack is sitting watching you.

LÖVBORG. So she was in mortal terror! On my account!

MRS. ELVSTED [softly and piteously]. Oh, Hedda—now you have ruined everything!

LÖVBORG [*looks fixedly at her for a moment. His face is distorted*]. So that was my comrade's frank confidence in me?

MRS. ELVSTED [*imploringly*]. Oh, my dearest friend—only let me tell you——

LÖVBORG [*takes one of the glasses of punch, raises it to his lips, and says in a low, husky voice*]. Your health, Thea!

[*He empties the glass, puts it down, and takes the second.*]

MRS. ELVSTED [*softly*]. Oh, Hedda, Hedda—how could you do this?

HEDDA. *I* do it? *I*? Are you crazy?

LÖVBORG. Here's to your health, too, Mrs. Tesman. Thanks for the truth. Hurrah for the truth!

[*He empties the glass and is about to re-fill it.*]

HEDDA [*lays her hand on his arm*]. Come, come—no more for the present. Remember you are going out to supper.

MRS. ELVSTED. No, no, no!

HEDDA. Hush! They are sitting watching you.

LÖVBORG [*putting down the glass*]. Now, Thea—tell me the truth——

MRS. ELVSTED. Yes.

LÖVBORG. Did your husband know that you had come after me?

MRS. ELVSTED [*wringing her hands*]. Oh, Hedda—do you hear what he is asking?

LÖVBORG. Was it arranged between you and him that you were to come to town and look after me? Perhaps it was the Sheriff himself that urged you to come? Aha, my dear—no doubt he wanted my help in his office. Or was it at the card-table that he missed me?

MRS. ELVSTED [*softly, in agony*]. Oh, Lövborg, Lövborg——!

LÖVBORG [*seizes a glass and is on the point of filling it*]. Here's a glass for the old Sheriff, too!

HEDDA [*preventing him*]. No more just now. Remember, you have to read your manuscript to Tesman.

LÖVBORG [*calmly, putting down the glass*]. It was stupid of me all this, Thea—to take it in this way, I mean. Don't be angry with me, my dear, dear comrade. You shall see—both you and the others—that if I was fallen once—now I have risen again! Thanks to you, Thea.

MRS. ELVSTED [*radiant with joy*]. Oh, heaven be praised——!

[BRACK *has in the meantime looked at his watch. He and* TESMAN *rise and come into the drawing room.*]

BRACK [*takes his hat and overcoat*]. Well, Mrs. Tesman, our time has come.

HEDDA. I suppose it has.

LÖVBORG [*rising*]. Mine too, Judge Brack.

MRS. ELVSTED [*softly and imploringly*]. Oh, Lövborg, don't do it!

HEDDA [*pinching her arm*]. They can hear you!

MRS. ELVSTED [*with a suppressed shriek*]. Ow!

LÖVBORG [*to* BRACK]. You were good enough to invite me.

BRACK. Well, are you coming after all?

LÖVBORG. Yes, many thanks.

BRACK. I'm delighted——

LÖVBORG [*to* TESMAN, *putting the parcel of MS. in his pocket*]. I should like to show you one or two things before I send it to the printers.

TESMAN. Fancy—that will be delightful. But, Hedda dear, how is Mrs. Elvsted to get home? Eh?

HEDDA. Oh, that can be managed somehow.

LÖVBORG [*looking towards the ladies*]. Mrs. Elvsted? Of course, I'll come again and fetch her. [*Approaching*] At ten or thereabouts, Mrs. Tesman? Will that do?

HEDDA. Certainly. That will do capitally.

TESMAN. Well, then, that's all right. But you must not expect me so early, Hedda.

HEDDA. Oh, you may stop as long—as long as ever you please.

MRS. ELVSTED [*trying to conceal her anxiety*]. Well, then, Mr. Lövborg—I shall remain here until you come.

LÖVBORG [*with his hat in his hand*]. Pray do, Mrs. Elvsted.

BRACK. And now off goes the excursion train, gentlemen! I hope we shall have a lively time, as a certain fair lady puts it.

HEDDA. Ah, if only the fair lady could be present unseen——!

BRACK. Why unseen?

HEDDA. In order to hear a little of your liveliness at first hand, Judge Brack.

BRACK [*laughing*]. I should not advise the fair lady to try it.

TESMAN [*also laughing*]. Come, you're a nice one, Hedda! Fancy that!

BRACK. Well, good-bye, good-bye, ladies.

LÖVBORG [*bowing*]. About ten o'clock, then.

[BRACK, LÖVBORG, *and* TESMAN *go out by the hall door. At the same time,* BERTA *enters from the inner room with a lighted lamp, which she places on the drawing-room table; she goes out by the way she came.*]

MRS. ELVSTED [*who has risen and is wandering restlessly about the room*]. Hedda—Hedda—what will come of all this?

HEDDA. At ten o'clock—he will be here. I can see him already—with vine-leaves in his hair—flushed and fearless——

MRS. ELVSTED. Oh, I hope he may.

HEDDA. And then, you see—then he will have regained control over himself. Then he will be a free man for all his days.

MRS. ELVSTED.   Oh, God!—if he would only come as you see him now!

HEDDA.   He will come as I see him—so, and not otherwise! [*Rises and approaches* THEA.] You may doubt him as long as you please; *I* believe in him. And now we will try——

MRS. ELVSTED.   You have some hidden motive in this, Hedda!

HEDDA.   Yes, I have. I want for once in my life to have power to mould a human destiny.

MRS. ELVSTED.   Have you not the power?

HEDDA.   I have not—and have never had it.

MRS. ELVSTED.   Not your husband's?

HEDDA.   Do you think that is worth the trouble? Oh, if you could only understand how poor I am. And fate has made you so rich! [*Clasps her passionately in her arms.*] I think I must burn your hair off, after all.

MRS. ELVSTED.   Let me go! Let me go! I am afraid of you, Hedda!

BERTA [*in the middle doorway*].   Tea is laid in the dining-room, ma'am.

HEDDA.   Very well. We are coming.

MRS. ELVSTED.   No, no, no! I would rather go home alone! At once!

HEDDA.   Nonsense! First you shall have a cup of tea, you little stupid. And then—at ten o'clock—Eilert Lövborg will be here—with vine-leaves in his hair.

[*She drags* MRS. ELVSTED *almost by force towards the middle doorway.*]

ACT THREE

THE ROOM AT THE TESMANS'.   *The curtains are drawn over the middle doorway, and also over the glass door. The lamp, half turned down, and with a shade over it, is burning on the table. In the stove, the door of which stands open, there has been a fire, which is now nearly burnt out.* MRS. ELVSTED, *wrapped in a large shawl, and with her feet upon a footrest, sits close to the stove, sunk back in the armchair.* HEDDA, *fully dressed, lies sleeping upon the sofa, with a sofa-blanket over her.*

MRS. ELVSTED [*after a pause, suddenly sits up in her chair, and listens eagerly. Then she sinks back again wearily, moaning to herself*].   Not yet!—Oh, God—oh, God—not yet!

[BERTA *slips cautiously in by the hall door. She has a letter in her hand.*]

MRS. ELVSTED [*turns and whispers eagerly*].   Well—has any one come?

BERTA [*softly*].   Yes, a girl has just brought this letter.

MRS. ELVSTED [*quickly, holding out her hand*].   A letter! Give it to me!

BERTA.   No, it's for Dr. Tesman, ma'am.

MRS. ELVSTED. Oh, indeed.

BERTA. It was Miss Tesman's servant that brought it. I'll lay it here on the table.

MRS. ELVSTED. Yes, do.

BERTA [*laying down the letter*]. I think I had better put out the lamp. It's smoking.

MRS. ELVSTED. Yes, put it out. It must soon be daylight now.

BERTA [*putting out the lamp*]. It is daylight already, ma'am.

MRS. ELVSTED. Yes, broad day! And no one come back yet——!

BERTA. Lord bless you, ma'am—I guessed how it would be.

MRS. ELVSTED. You guessed?

BERTA. Yes, when I saw that a certain person had come back to town —and that he went off with them. For we've heard enough about that gentleman before now.

MRS. ELVSTED. Don't speak so loud. You will waken Mrs. Tesman.

BERTA [*looks towards the sofa and sighs*]. No, no—let her sleep, poor thing. Shan't I put some wood on the fire?

MRS. ELVSTED. Thanks, not for me.

BERTA. Oh, very well.

[*She goes softly out by the hall door.*]

HEDDA [*is awakened by the shutting of the door, and looks up*]. What's that——?

MRS. ELVSTED. It was only the servant——

HEDDA [*looking about her*]. Oh, we're here——! Yes, now I remember. [*Sits erect upon the sofa, stretches herself, and rubs her eyes.*] What o'clock is it, Thea?

MRS. ELVSTED [*looks at her watch*]. It's past seven.

HEDDA. When did Tesman come home?

MRS. ELVSTED. He has not come.

HEDDA. Not come home yet?

MRS. ELVSTED [*rising*]. No one has come.

HEDDA. Think of our watching and waiting here till four in the morning——

MRS. ELVSTED [*wringing her hands*]. And how I watched and waited for him!

HEDDA [*yawns, and says with her hand before her mouth*]. Well, well —we might have spared ourselves the trouble.

MRS. ELVSTED. Did you get a little sleep?

HEDDA. Oh, yes; I believe I have slept pretty well. Have you not?

MRS. ELVSTED. Not for a moment. I couldn't, Hedda!—not to save my life.

HEDDA [*rises and goes towards her*]. There, there, there! There's nothing to be so alarmed about. I understand quite well what has happened.

MRS. ELVSTED. Well, what do you think? Won't you tell me?

HEDDA. Why, of course, it has been a very late affair at Judge Brack's——

MRS. ELVSTED. Yes, yes—that is clear enough. But all the same——

HEDDA. And then, you see, Tesman hasn't cared to come home and ring us up in the middle of the night. [*Laughing*] Perhaps he wasn't inclined to show himself either—immediately after a jollification.

MRS. ELVSTED. But in that case—where can he have gone?

HEDDA. Of course, he has gone to his aunts' and slept there. They have his old room ready for him.

MRS. ELVSTED. No, he can't be with them; for a letter has just come for him from Miss Tesman. There it lies.

HEDDA. Indeed? [*Looks at the address.*] Why, yes, it's addressed in Aunt Julia's own hand. Well, then, he has remained at Judge Brack's. And as for Eilert Lövborg—he is sitting, with vine-leaves in his hair, reading his manuscript.

MRS. ELVSTED. Oh, Hedda, you are just saying things you don't believe a bit.

HEDDA. You really are a little blockhead, Thea.

MRS. ELVSTED. Oh, yes, I suppose I am.

HEDDA. And how mortally tired you look.

MRS. ELVSTED. Yes, I am mortally tired.

HEDDA. Well, then, you must do as I tell you. You must go into my room and lie down for a little while.

MRS. ELVSTED. Oh, no, no—I shouldn't be able to sleep.

HEDDA. I am sure you would.

MRS. ELVSTED. Well, but your husband is certain to come soon now; and then I want to know at once——

HEDDA. I shall take care to let you know when he comes.

MRS. ELVSTED. Do you promise me, Hedda?

HEDDA. Yes, rely upon me. Just you go in and have a sleep in the meantime.

MRS. ELVSTED. Thanks; then I'll try to.

[*She goes off through the inner room.* HEDDA *goes up to the glass door and draws back the curtains. The broad daylight streams into the room. Then she takes a little hand-glass from the writing-table, looks at herself in it and arranges her hair. Next she goes to the hall door and presses the bell-button.* BERTA *presently appears at the hall door.*]

BERTA. Did you want anything, ma'am?

HEDDA. Yes; you must put some more wood in the stove. I am shivering.

BERTA. Bless me—I'll make up the fire at once. [*She rakes the embers together and lays a piece of wood upon them; then stops and listens.*] That was a ring at the front door, ma'am.

HEDDA. Then go to the door. I will look after the fire.

BERTA. It'll soon burn up.

[*She goes out by the hall door.* HEDDA *kneels on the foot-rest and lays some more pieces of wood in the stove. After a short pause,* GEORGE TESMAN *enters from the hall. He looks tired and rather serious. He steals on tip-toe towards the middle doorway and is about to slip through the curtains.*]

HEDDA [*at the stove, without looking up*]. Good morning.

TESMAN [*turns*]. Hedda! [*Approaching her*] Good heavens—are you up so early? Eh?

HEDDA. Yes, I am up very early this morning.

TESMAN. And I never doubted you were still sound asleep! Fancy that, Hedda!

HEDDA. Don't speak so loud. Mrs. Elvsted is resting in my room.

TESMAN. Has Mrs. Elvsted been here all night?

HEDDA. Yes, since no one came to fetch her.

TESMAN. Ah, to be sure.

HEDDA [*closes the door of the stove and rises*]. Well, did you enjoy yourselves at Judge Brack's?

TESMAN. Have you been anxious about me? Eh?

HEDDA. No, I should never think of being anxious. But I asked if you had enjoyed yourself.

TESMAN. Oh, yes,—for once in a way. Especially the beginning of the evening; for then Eilert read me part of his book. We arrived more than an hour too early—fancy that! And Brack had all sorts of arrangements to make—so Eilert read to me.

HEDDA [*seating herself by the table on the right*]. Well? Tell me, then——

TESMAN [*sitting on a footstool near the stove*]. Oh, Hedda, you can't conceive what a book that is going to be! I believe it is one of the most remarkable things that have ever been written. Fancy that!

HEDDA. Yes, yes; I don't care about that——

TESMAN. I must make a confession to you, Hedda. When he had finished reading—a horrid feeling came over me.

HEDDA. A horrid feeling?

TESMAN. I felt jealous of Eilert for having had it in him to write such a book. Only think, Hedda!

HEDDA. Yes, yes, I am thinking!

TESMAN. And then how pitiful to think that he—with all his gifts—should be irreclaimable, after all.

HEDDA. I suppose you mean that he has more courage than the rest?

TESMAN. No, not at all—I mean that he is incapable of taking his pleasures in moderation.

HEDDA. And what came of it all—in the end?

TESMAN. Well, to tell the truth, I think it might best be described as an orgy, Hedda.

HEDDA. Had he vine-leaves in his hair?

TESMAN. Vine-leaves? No, I saw nothing of the sort. But he made a long, rambling speech in honor of the woman who had inspired him in his work—that was the phrase he used.

HEDDA. Did he name her?

TESMAN. No, he didn't; but I can't help thinking he meant Mrs. Elvsted. You may be sure he did.

HEDDA. Well—where did you part from him?

TESMAN. On the way to town. We broke up—the last of us at any rate—all together; and Brack came with us to get a breath of fresh air. And then, you see, we agreed to take Eilert home; for he had had far more than was good for him.

HEDDA. I daresay.

TESMAN. But now comes the strange part of it, Hedda; or, I should rather say, the melancholy part of it. I declare I am almost ashamed—on Eilert's account—to tell you——

HEDDA. Oh, go on——!

TESMAN. Well, as we were going near town, you see, I happened to drop a little behind the others. Only for a minute or two—fancy that!

HEDDA. Yes, yes, yes, but——?

TESMAN. And then, as I hurried after them—what do you think I found by the wayside? Eh?

HEDDA. Oh, how should I know!

TESMAN. You mustn't speak of it to a soul, Hedda! Do you hear! Promise me, for Eilert's sake. [*Draws a parcel, wrapped in paper, from his coat pocket.*] Fancy, dear—I found this.

HEDDA. Is not that the parcel he had with him yesterday?

TESMAN. Yes, it is the whole of his precious, irreplaceable manuscript! And he had gone and lost it, and knew nothing about it. Only fancy, Hedda! So deplorably——

HEDDA. But why did you not give him back the parcel at once?

TESMAN. I didn't dare to—in the state he was then in——

HEDDA. Did you not tell any of the others that you had found it?

TESMAN. Oh, far from it! You can surely understand that, for Eilert's sake, I wouldn't do that.

HEDDA. So no one knows that Eilert Lövborg's manuscript is in your possession?

TESMAN. No. And no one must know it.

HEDDA. Then what did you say to him afterwards?

TESMAN. I didn't talk to him again at all; for when we got in among the streets, he and two or three of the others gave us the slip and disappeared. Fancy that!

HEDDA. Indeed! They must have taken him home then.

TESMAN. Yes, so it would appear. And Brack, too, left us.

HEDDA And what have you been doing with yourself since?

TESMAN. Well, I and some of the others went home with one of the party, a jolly fellow, and took our morning coffee with him; or perhaps I should rather call it our night coffee—eh? But now, when I have rested a little, and given Eilert, poor fellow, time to have his sleep out, I must take this back to him.

HEDDA [*holds out her hand for the packet*]. No—don't give it to him! Not in such a hurry, I mean. Let me read it first.

TESMAN. No, my dearest Hedda, I mustn't, I really mustn't.

HEDDA. You must not?

TESMAN. No—for you can imagine what a state of despair he will be in when he wakens and misses the manuscript. He has no copy of it, you must know! He told me so.

HEDDA [*looking searchingly at him*]. Can such a thing not be reproduced? Written over again?

TESMAN. No, I don't think that would be possible. For the inspiration, you see——

HEDDA. Yes, yes—I suppose it depends on that—— [*Lightly*] But, by the by—here is a letter for you.

TESMAN. Fancy——!

HEDDA [*handing it to him*]. It came early this morning.

TESMAN. It's from Aunt Julia! What can it be? [*He lays the packet on the other footstool, opens the letter, runs his eye through it, and jumps up.*] Oh, Hedda—she says that poor Aunt Rina is dying!

HEDDA. Well, we were prepared for that.

TESMAN. And that if I want to see her again, I must make haste. I'll run in to them at once.

HEDDA [*suppressing a smile*]. Will you run?

TESMAN. Oh, my dearest Hedda—if you could only make up your mind to come with me! Just think!

HEDDA [*rises and says wearily, repelling the idea*]. No, no, don't ask me. I will not look upon sickness and death. I loathe all sorts of ugliness.

TESMAN. Well, well, then——! [*Bustling around*] My hat——? My overcoat——? Oh, in the hall——. I do hope I mayn't come too late, Hedda! Eh?

HEDDA. Oh, if you run——

[*BERTA appears at the hall door.*]

BERTA. Judge Brack is at the door, and wishes to know if he may come in.

TESMAN. At this time! No, I can't possibly see him.

HEDDA. But I can. [*To* BERTA] Ask Judge Brack to come in.

[BERTA *goes out.*]

HEDDA [*quickly, whispering*]. The parcel, Tesman!

[*She snatches it up from the stool.*]

TESMAN. Yes, give it to me!

HEDDA. No, no, I will keep it till you come back.

[*She goes to the writing-table and places it in the bookcase.* TESMAN *stands in a flurry of haste, and cannot get his gloves on.* JUDGE BRACK *enters from the hall.*]

HEDDA [*nodding to him*]. You are an early bird, I must say.

BRACK. Yes, don't you think so? [*To* TESMAN] Are you on the move, too?

TESMAN. Yes, I must rush off to my aunts'. Fancy—the invalid one is lying at death's door, poor creature.

BRACK. Dear me, is she indeed? Then on no account let me detain you. At such a critical moment——

TESMAN. Yes, I must really rush—— Good-bye! Good-bye!

[*He hastens out by the hall door.*]

HEDDA [*approaching*]. You seem to have made a particularly lively night of it at your rooms, Judge Brack.

BRACK. I assure you I have not had my clothes off, Mrs. Hedda.

HEDDA. Not you, either?

BRACK. No, as you may see. But what has Tesman been telling you of the night's adventures?

HEDDA. Oh, some tiresome story. Only that they went and had coffee somewhere or other.

BRACK. I have heard about that coffee-party already. Eilert Lövborg was not with them, I fancy?

HEDDA. No, they had taken him home before that.

BRACK. Tesman too?

HEDDA. No, but some of the others, he said.

BRACK [*smiling*]. George Tesman is really an ingenuous creature, Mrs. Hedda.

HEDDA. Yes, heaven knows he is. Then is there something behind all this?

BRACK. Yes, perhaps there may be.

HEDDA. Well then, sit down, my dear Judge, and tell your story in comfort.

[*She seats herself to the left of the table.* BRACK *sits near her, at the long side of the table.*]

HEDDA.   Now then?

BRACK.   I had special reasons for keeping track of my guests——or rather of some of my guests—last night.

HEDDA.   Of Eilert Lövborg among the rest, perhaps?

BRACK.   Frankly—yes.

HEDDA.   Now you make me really curious——

BRACK.   Do you know where he and one or two of the others finished the night, Mrs. Hedda?

HEDDA.   If it is not quite unmentionable, tell me.

BRACK.   Oh no, it's not at all unmentionable. Well, they put in an appearance at a particularly animated *soirée.*

HEDDA.   Of the lively kind?

BRACK.   Of the very liveliest——

HEDDA.   Tell me more of this, Judge Brack——

BRACK.   Lövborg, as well as the others, had been invited in advance. I knew all about it. But he had declined the invitation; for now, as you know, he has become a new man.

HEDDA.   Up at the Elvsteds', yes. But he went after all, then?

BRACK.   Well, you see, Mrs. Hedda—unhappily the spirit moved him at my rooms last evening——

HEDDA.   Yes, I hear he found inspiration.

BRACK.   Pretty violent inspiration. Well, I fancy that altered his purpose; for we menfolk are unfortunately not always so firm in our principles as we ought to be.

HEDDA.   Oh, I am sure you are an exception, Judge Brack. But as to Lövborg——?

BRACK.   To make a long story short—he landed at last in Mademoiselle Diana's rooms.

HEDDA.   Mademoiselle Diana's?

BRACK.   It was Mademoiselle Diana that was giving the *soirée,* to a select circle of her admirers and her lady friends.

HEDDA.   Is she a red-haired woman?

BRACK.   Precisely.

HEDDA.   A sort of a—singer?

BRACK.   Oh yes—in her leisure moments. And moreover a mighty huntress—of men—Mrs. Hedda. You have no doubt heard of her. Eilert Lövborg was one of her most enthusiastic protectors—in the days of his glory.

HEDDA.   And how did all this end?

BRACK.   Far from amicably, it appears. After a most tender meeting, they seem to have come to blows——

HEDDA.   Lövborg and she?

BRACK. Yes. He accused her or her friends of having robbed him. He declared that his pocket-book had disappeared—and other things as well. In short, he seems to have made a furious disturbance.

HEDDA. And what came of it all?

BRACK. It came to a general scrimmage, in which the ladies as well as the gentlemen took part. Fortunately the police at last appeared on the scene.

HEDDA. The police too?

BRACK. Yes. I fancy it will prove a costly frolic for Eilert Lövborg, crazy being that he is.

HEDDA. How so?

BRACK. He seems to have made a violent resistance—to have hit one of the constables on the head and torn the coat off his back. So they had to march him off to the police-station with the rest.

HEDDA. How have you learnt all this?

BRACK. From the police themselves.

HEDDA [*gazing straight before her*]. So that is what happened. Then he had no vine-leaves in his hair.

BRACK. Vine-leaves, Mrs. Hedda?

HEDDA [*changing her tone*]. But tell me now, Judge—what is your real reason for tracking out Eilert Lövborg's movements so carefully?

BRACK. In the first place, it could not be entirely indifferent to me if it should appear in the police-court that he came straight from my house.

HEDDA. Will the matter come into court then?

BRACK. Of course. However, I should scarcely have troubled so much about that. But I thought that, as a friend of the family, it was my duty to supply you and Tesman with a full account of his nocturnal exploits.

HEDDA. Why so, Judge Brack?

BRACK. Why, because I have a shrewd suspicion that he intends to use you as a sort of blind.

HEDDA. Oh, how can you think such a thing!

BRACK. Good heavens, Mrs. Hedda—we have eyes in our head. Mark my words! This Mrs. Elvsted will be in no hurry to leave town again.

HEDDA. Well, even if there should be anything between them, I suppose there are plenty of other places where they could meet.

BRACK. Not a single home. Henceforth, as before, every respectable house will be closed against Eilert Lövborg.

HEDDA. And so ought mine to be, you mean?

BRACK. Yes. I confess it would be more than painful to me if this personage were to be made free of your house. How superfluous, how intrusive, he would be, if he were to force his way into——

HEDDA. ——into the triangle?

BRACK. Precisely. It would simply mean that I should find myself homeless.

HEDDA [*looks at him with a smile*]. So you want to be the one cock in the basket—that is your aim.

BRACK [*nods slowly and lowers his voice*]. Yes, that is my aim. And for that I will fight—with every weapon I can command.

HEDDA [*her smile vanishing*]. I see you are a dangerous person—when it comes to the point.

BRACK. Do you think so?

HEDDA. I am beginning to think so. And I am exceedingly glad to think—that you have no sort of hold over me.

BRACK [*laughing equivocally*]. Well, well, Mrs. Hedda—perhaps you are right there. If I had, who knows what I might be capable of?

HEDDA. Come, come now, Judge Brack! That sounds almost like a threat.

BRACK [*rising*]. Oh, not at all! The triangle, you know, ought, if possible, to be spontaneously constructed.

HEDDA. There I agree with you.

BRACK. Well, now I have said all I had to say; and I had better be getting back to town. Good-bye, Mrs. Hedda. [*He goes towards the glass door.*]

HEDDA [*rising*]. Are you going through the garden?

BRACK. Yes, it's a short cut for me.

HEDDA. And then it is a back way, too.

BRACK. Quite so. I have no objection to back ways. They may be piquant enough at times.

HEDDA. When there is shooting practice going on, you mean?

BRACK [*in the doorway, laughing to her*]. Oh, people don't shoot their tame poultry, I fancy.

HEDDA [*also laughing*]. Oh, no, when there is only one cock in the basket——

[*They exchange laughing nods of farewell. He goes. She closes the door behind him.*

HEDDA, *who has become quite serious, stands for a moment looking out. Presently she goes and peeps through the curtain over the middle doorway. Then she goes to the writing-table, takes* LÖV-BORG's *packet out of the bookcase, and is on the point of looking through its contents.* BERTA *is heard speaking loudly in the hall.* HEDDA *turns and listens. Then she hastily locks up the packet in the drawer, and lays the key on the inkstand.*

EILERT LÖVBORG, *with his greatcoat on and his hat in his hand, tears open the hall door. He looks somewhat confused and irritated.*]

LÖVBORG [*looking towards the hall*]. And I tell you I must and will come in! There!

[*He closes the door, turns, sees* HEDDA, *at once regains his self-control, and bows.*]

HEDDA [*at the writing-table*]. Well, Mr. Lövborg, this is rather a late hour to call for Thea.

LÖVBORG. You mean rather an early hour to call on you. Pray pardon me.

HEDDA. How do you know that she is still here?

LÖVBORG. They told me at her lodgings that she had been out all night.

HEDDA [*going to the oval table*]. Did you notice anything about the people of the house when they said that?

LÖVBORG [*looks inquiringly at her*]. Notice anything about them?

HEDDA. I mean, did they seem to think it odd?

LÖVBORG [*suddenly understanding*]. Oh yes, of course! I am dragging her down with me! However, I didn't notice anything.—I suppose Tesman is not up yet?

HEDDA. No—I think not——

LÖVBORG. When did he come home?

HEDDA. Very late.

LÖVBORG. Did he tell you anything?

HEDDA. Yes, I gathered that you had had an exceedingly jolly evening at Judge Brack's.

LÖVBORG. Nothing more?

HEDDA. I don't think so. However, I was so dreadfully sleepy——

[MRS. ELVSTED *enters through the curtains of the middle doorway.*]

MRS. ELVSTED [*going towards him*]. Ah, Lövborg! At last——!

LÖVBORG. Yes, at last. And too late!

MRS. ELVSTED [*looks anxiously at him*]. What is too late?

LÖVBORG. Everything is too late now. It is all over with me.

MRS. ELVSTED. Oh no, no—don't say that!

LÖVBORG. You will say the same when you hear——

MRS. ELVSTED. I won't hear anything!

HEDDA. Perhaps you would prefer to talk to her alone? If so, I will leave you.

LÖVBORG. No, stay—you too. I beg you to stay.

MRS. ELVSTED. Yes, but I won't hear anything, I tell you.

LÖVBORG. It is not last night's adventures that I want to talk about.

MRS. ELVSTED. What is it then——?

LÖVBORG. I want to say that now our ways must part.

MRS. ELVSTED. Part!

HEDDA [*involuntarily*]. I knew it!

LÖVBORG. You can be of no more service to me, Thea.

MRS. ELVSTED. How can you stand there and say that! No more service to you! Am I not to help you now, as before? Are we not to go on working together?

LÖVBORG. Henceforward I shall do no work.

MRS. ELVSTED [*despairingly*]. Then what am I to do with my life?

LÖVBORG. You must try to live your life as if you had never known me.

MRS. ELVSTED. But you know I cannot do that!

LÖVBORG. Try if you cannot, Thea. You must go home again——

MRS. ELVSTED [*in vehement protest*]. Never in this world! Where you are, there will I be also! I will not let myself be driven away like this! I will remain here! I will be with you when the book appears.

HEDDA [*half aloud, in suspense*]. Ah yes—the book!

LÖVBORG [*looks at her*]. My book and Thea's; for that is what it is.

MRS. ELVSTED. Yes, I feel that it is. And that is why I have a right to be with you when it appears! I will see with my own eyes how respect and honor pour in upon you afresh. And the happiness—the happiness —oh, I must share it with you!

LÖVBORG. Thea—our book will never appear.

HEDDA. Ah!

MRS. ELVSTED. Never appear!

LÖVBORG. Can never appear.

MRS. ELVSTED [*in agonized foreboding*]. Lövborg—what have you done with the manuscript?

HEDDA [*looks anxiously at him*]. Yes, the manuscript——?

MRS. ELVSTED. Where is it?

LÖVBORG. Oh Thea—don't ask me about it!

MRS. ELVSTED. Yes, yes, I will know. I demand to be told at once.

LÖVBORG. The manuscript——. Well then—I have torn the manuscript into a thousand pieces.

MRS. ELVSTED [*shrieks*]. Oh no, no——!

HEDDA [*involuntarily*]. But that's not——

LÖVBORG [*looks at her*]. Not true, you think?

HEDDA [*collecting herself*]. Oh well, of course—since you say so. But it sounded so improbable——

LÖVBORG. It is true, all the same.

MRS. ELVSTED [*wringing her hands*]. Oh God—oh God, Hedda—torn his own work to pieces!

LÖVBORG. I have torn my own life to pieces. So why should I not tear my life-work too——?

MRS. ELVSTED. And you did this last night?

LÖVBORG. Yes, I tell you! Tore it into a thousand pieces—and scattered them on the fjord—far out. There there is cool sea-water at any rate—let them drift upon it—drift with the current and the wind. And then presently they will sink—deeper and deeper—as I shall, Thea.

MRS. ELVSTED. Do you know, Lövborg, that what you have done with the book—I shall think of it to my dying day as though you had killed a little child.

LÖVBORG. Yes, you are right. It is a sort of child-murder.

MRS. ELVSTED. How could you, then——! Did not the child belong to me too?

HEDDA [almost inaudibly]. Ah, the child——

MRS. ELVSTED [breathing heavily]. It is all over then. Well, well, now I will go, Hedda.

HEDDA. But you are not going away from town?

MRS. ELVSTED. Oh, I don't know what I shall do. I see nothing but darkness before me.

[She goes out by the hall door.]

HEDDA [stands waiting for a moment]. So you are not going to see her home, Mr. Lövborg?

LÖVBORG. I? Through the streets? Would you have people see her walking with me?

HEDDA. Of course I don't know what else may have happened last night. But is it so utterly irretrievable?

LÖVBORG. It will not end with last night—I know that perfectly well. And the thing is that now I have no taste for that sort of life either. I won't begin it anew. She has broken my courage and my power of braving life out.

HEDDA [looking straight before her]. So that pretty little fool has had her fingers in a man's destiny. [Looks at him.] But all the same, how could you treat her so heartlessly?

LÖVBORG. Oh, don't say that it was heartless!

HEDDA. To go and destroy what has filled her whole soul for months and years! You do not call that heartless!

LÖVBORG. To you I can tell the truth, Hedda.

HEDDA. The truth?

LÖVBORG. First promise me—give me your word—that what I now confide to you Thea shall never know.

HEDDA. I give you my word.

LÖVBORG. Good. Then let me tell you that what I said just now was untrue.

HEDDA. About the manuscript?

LÖVBORG. Yes. I have not torn it to pieces—nor thrown it into the fjord.

HEDDA. No, no——. But—where is it then?

LÖVBORG. I have destroyed it none the less—utterly destroyed it, Hedda!

HEDDA. I don't understand.

LÖVBORG. Thea said that what I had done seemed to her like a child-murder.

HEDDA. Yes, so she said.

LÖVBORG. But to kill his child—that is not the worst thing a father can do to it.

HEDDA. Not the worst?

LÖVBORG. No. I wanted to spare Thea from hearing the worst.

HEDDA. Then what is the worst?

LÖVBORG. Suppose now, Hedda, that a man—in the small hours of the morning—came home to his child's mother after a night of riot and debauchery, and said: "Listen—I have been here and there—in this place and in that. And I have taken our child with me—to this place and to that. And I have lost the child—utterly lost it. The devil knows into what hands it may have fallen—who may have had their clutches on it."

HEDDA. Well—but when all is said and done, you know—this was only a book——

LÖVBORG. Thea's pure soul was in that book.

HEDDA. Yes, so I understand.

LÖVBORG. And you can understand, too, that for her and me together no future is possible.

HEDDA. What path do you mean to take then?

LÖVBORG. None. I will only try to make an end of it all—the sooner the better.

HEDDA [a step nearer him]. Eilert Lövborg—listen to me.—Will you not try to—to do it beautifully?

LÖVBORG. Beautifully? [Smiling] With vine-leaves in my hair, as you used to dream in the old days——?

HEDDA. No, no. I have lost my faith in the vine-leaves. But beautifully nevertheless! For once in a way!—Good-bye! You must go now—and do not come here any more.

LÖVBORG. Good-bye, Mrs. Tesman. And give George Tesman my love. [He is on the point of going.]

HEDDA. No, wait! I must give you a memento to take with you.

[She goes to the writing-table and opens the drawer and the pistol-case; then returns to LÖVBORG with one of the pistols.]

LÖVBORG [looks at her]. This? Is this the memento?

HEDDA [nodding slowly]. Do you recognize it? It was aimed at you once.

LÖVBORG. You should have used it then.

HEDDA. Take it—and do you use it now.

LÖVBORG [puts the pistol in his breast pocket]. Thanks!

HEDDA. And beautifully, Eilert Lövborg. Promise me that!

LÖVBORG. Good-bye, Hedda Gabler.

[*He goes out by the hall door.*]

[HEDDA *listens for a moment at the door. Then she goes up to the writing-table, takes out the packet of manuscript, peeps under the cover, draws a few of the sheets half out, and looks at them. Next she goes over and seats herself in the arm-chair beside the stove, with the packet in her lap. Presently she opens the stove door, and then the packet.*]

HEDDA [*throws one of the quires into the fire and whispers to herself*]. Now I am burning your child, Thea!—Burning it, curly-locks! [*Throwing one or two more quires into the stove*] Your child and Eilert Lövborg's. [*Throws the rest in.*] I am burning—I am burning your child.

ACT FOUR

THE SAME ROOMS *at the* TESMANS'. *It is evening. The drawing-room is in darkness. The back room is lighted by the hanging lamp over the table. The curtains over the glass door are drawn close.*

HEDDA, *dressed in black, walks to and fro in the dark room. Then she goes into the back room and disappears for a moment to the left. She is heard to strike a few chords on the piano. Presently she comes in sight again, and returns to the drawing-room.*

BERTA *enters from the right, through the inner room, with a lighted lamp, which she places on the table in front of the corner settee in the drawing-room. Her eyes are red with weeping, and she has black ribbons in her cap. She goes quietly and circumspectly out to the right* HEDDA *goes up to the glass door, lifts the curtain a little aside, and looks out into the darkness.*

Shortly afterwards, MISS TESMAN, *in mourning, with a bonnet and veil on, comes in from the hall.* HEDDA *goes towards her and holds out her hand.*

MISS TESMAN. Yes, Hedda, here I am, in mourning and forlorn; for now my poor sister has at last found peace.

HEDDA. I have heard the news already, as you see. Tesman sent me a card.

MISS TESMAN. Yes, he promised me he would. But nevertheless thought that to Hedda—here in the house of life—I ought myself to bring the tidings of death.

HEDDA. That was very kind of you.

MISS TESMAN. Ah, Rina ought not to have left us just now. This is not the time for Hedda's house to be a house of mourning.

HEDDA [*changing the subject*]. She died quite peacefully, did she not, Miss Tesman?

MISS TESMAN. Oh, her end was so calm, so beautiful. And then she had the unspeakable happiness of seeing George once more—and bidding him good-bye.—Has he not come home yet?

HEDDA. No. He wrote that he might be detained. But won't you sit down?

MISS TESMAN. No thank you, my dear, dear Hedda. I should like to, but I have so much to do. I must prepare my dear one for her rest as well as I can. She shall go to her grave looking her best.

HEDDA. Can I not help you in any way?

MISS TESMAN. Oh, you must not think of it! Hedda Tesman must have no hand in such mournful work. Nor let her thoughts dwell on it either—not at this time.

HEDDA. One is not always mistress of one's thoughts—

MISS TESMAN [*continuing*]. Ah yes, it is the way of the world. At home we shall be sewing a shroud; and here there will soon be sewing too, I suppose—but of another sort, thank God!

[GEORGE TESMAN *enters by the hall door.*]

HEDDA. Ah, you have come at last!

TESMAN. You here, Aunt Julia? With Hedda? Fancy that!

MISS TESMAN. I was just going, my dear boy. Well, have you done all you promised?

TESMAN. No; I'm really afraid I have forgotten half of it. I must come to you again to-morrow. To-day my brain is all in a whirl. I can't keep my thoughts together.

MISS TESMAN. Why, my dear George, you mustn't take it in this way.

TESMAN. Mustn't——? How do you mean?

MISS TESMAN. Even in your sorrow you must rejoice, as I do—rejoice that she is at rest.

TESMAN. Oh yes, yes—you are thinking of Aunt Rina.

HEDDA. You will feel lonely now, Miss Tesman.

MISS TESMAN. Just at first, yes. But that will not last very long, I hope. I daresay I shall soon find an occupant for poor Rina's little room.

TESMAN. Indeed? Who do you think will take it? Eh?

MISS TESMAN. Oh, there's always some poor invalid or other in want of nursing, unfortunately.

HEDDA. Would you really take such a burden upon you again?

MISS TESMAN. A burden! Heaven forgive you, child—it has been no burden to me.

HEDDA. But suppose you had a total stranger on your hands——

MISS TESMAN. Oh, one soon makes friends with sick folk; and it's such an absolute necessity for me to have some one to live for. Well, heaven be praised, there may soon be something in *this* house, too, to keep an old aunt busy.

HEDDA. Oh, don't trouble about anything here.

TESMAN. Yes, just fancy what a nice time we three might have together, if——?

HEDDA. If——?

TESMAN [*uneasily*]. Oh, nothing. It will all come right. Let us hope so—eh?

MISS TESMAN. Well, well, I daresay you two want to talk to each other. [*Smiling*] And perhaps Hedda may have something to tell you too, George. Good-bye! I must go home to Rina. [*Turning at the door*] How strange it is to think that now Rina is with me and with my poor brother as well!

TESMAN. Yes, fancy that, Aunt Julia! Eh?

[MISS TESMAN *goes out by the hall door.*]

HEDDA [*follows* TESMAN *coldly and searchingly with her eyes*]. I almost believe your Aunt Rina's death affects you more than it does your Aunt Julia.

TESMAN. Oh, it's not that alone. It's Eilert I am so terribly uneasy about.

HEDDA [*quickly*]. Is there anything new about him?

TESMAN. I looked in at his rooms this afternoon, intending to tell him the manuscript was in safe keeping.

HEDDA. Well, did you not find him?

TESMAN. No. He wasn't at home. But afterwards I met Mrs. Elvsted, and she told me that he had been here early this morning.

HEDDA. Yes, directly after you had gone.

TESMAN. And he said that he had torn his manuscript to pieces—eh?

HEDDA. Yes, so he declared.

TESMAN. Why, good heavens, he must have been completely out of his mind! And I suppose you thought it best not to give it back to him, Hedda?

HEDDA. No, he did not get it.

TESMAN. But of course you told him that we had it?

HEDDA. No. [*Quickly*] Did you tell Mrs. Elvsted?

TESMAN. No; I thought I had better not. But you ought to have told him. Fancy, if, in desperation, he should go and do himself some injury! Let me have the manuscript, Hedda! I will take it to him at once. Where is it?

HEDDA [*cold and immovable, leaning on the arm-chair*]. I have not got it.

TESMAN. Have not got it? What in the world do you mean?

HEDDA. I have burnt it—every line of it.

TESMAN [*with a violent movement of terror*]. Burnt! Burnt Eilert's manuscript?

HEDDA. Don't scream so. The servant might hear you.

TESMAN. Burnt! Why, good God——! No, no, no! It's impossible!

HEDDA. It is so, nevertheless.

TESMAN. Do you know what you have done, Hedda? It's unlawful appropriation of lost property. Fancy that! Just ask Judge Brack, and he'll tell you what it is.

HEDDA. I advise you not to speak of it—either to Judge Brack, or to any one else.

TESMAN. But how could you do anything so unheard-of? What put it into your head? What possessed you? Answer me that—eh?

HEDDA [*suppressing an almost imperceptible smile*]. I did it for your sake, George.

TESMAN. For my sake!

HEDDA. This morning, when you told me about what he had read to you——

TESMAN. Yes, yes—what then?

HEDDA. You acknowledged that you envied him his work.

TESMAN. Oh, of course I didn't mean that literally.

HEDDA. No matter—I could not bear the idea that any one should throw you into the shade.

TESMAN [*in an outburst of mingled doubt and joy*]. Hedda! Oh, is this true? But—but—I never knew you show your love like that before. Fancy that!

HEDDA. Well, I may as well tell you that—just at this time—— [*Impatiently, breaking off*] No, no; you can ask Aunt Julia. She will tell you, fast enough.

TESMAN. Oh, I almost think I understand you, Hedda! [*Clasps his hands together.*] Great heavens! do you really mean it? Eh?

HEDDA. Don't shout so. The servant might hear.

TESMAN [*laughing in irrepressible glee*]. The servant! Why, how absurd you are, Hedda. It's only my old Berta! Why, I'll tell Berta myself.

HEDDA [*clenching her hands together in desperation*]. Oh, it is killing me,—it is killing me, all this!

TESMAN. What is, Hedda? Eh?

HEDDA [*coldly, controlling herself*]. All this—absurdity—George.

TESMAN. Absurdity! Do you see anything absurd in my being over-joyed at the news! But after all—perhaps I had better not say anything to Berta.

HEDDA. Oh——why not that too?

TESMAN. No, no, not yet! But I must certainly tell Aunt Julia. And then that you have begun to call me George too! Fancy that! Oh, Aunt Julia will be so happy—so happy!

HEDDA. When she hears that I have burnt Eilert Lövborg's manuscript—for your sake?

TESMAN. No, by the by—that affair of the manuscript—of course nobody must know about that. But that you love me so much, Hedda— Aunt Julia must really share my joy in that! I wonder, now, whether this sort of thing is usual in young wives? Eh?

HEDDA. I think you had better ask Aunt Julia that question too.

TESMAN. I will indeed, some time or other. [*Looks uneasy and downcast again.*] And yet the manuscript—the manuscript! Good God! It is terrible to think what will become of poor Eilert now.

[MRS. ELVSTED, *dressed as in the first act, with hat and cloak, enters by the hall door.*]

MRS. ELVSTED [*greets them hurriedly, and says in evident agitation*]. Oh, dear Hedda, forgive my coming again.

HEDDA. What is the matter with you, Thea?

TESMAN. Something about Eilert Lövborg again—eh?

MRS. ELVSTED. Yes! I am dreadfully afraid some misfortune has happened to him.

HEDDA [*seizes her arm*]. Ah,—do you think so?

TESMAN. Why, good Lord—what makes you think that, Mrs. Elvsted?

MRS. ELVSTED. I heard them talking of him at my boarding-house— just as I came in. Oh, the most incredible rumors are afloat about him to-day.

TESMAN. Yes, fancy, so I heard too! And I can bear witness that he went straight home to bed last night. Fancy that!

HEDDA. Well, what did they say at the boarding-house?

MRS. ELVSTED. Oh, I couldn't make out anything clearly. Either they knew nothing definite, or else——. They stopped talking when they saw me; and I did not dare to ask.

TESMAN [*moving about uneasily*]. We must hope—we must hope that you misunderstood them, Mrs. Elvsted.

MRS. ELVSTED. No, no; I am sure it was of him they were talking. And I heard something about the hospital or——

TESMAN. The hospital?

HEDDA. No—surely that cannot be!

MRS. ELVSTED. Oh, I was in such mortal terror! I went to his lodgings and asked for him there.

HEDDA. You could make up your mind to that, Thea!

MRS. ELVSTED. What else could I do? I really could bear the suspense no longer.

TESMAN. But you didn't find him either—eh?

MRS. ELVSTED. No. And the people knew nothing about him. He hadn't been home since yesterday afternoon, they said.

TESMAN. Yesterday! Fancy, how could they say that?

MRS. ELVSTED. Oh, I am sure something terrible must have happened to him.

TESMAN. Hedda dear—how would it be if I were to go and make inquiries——?

HEDDA. No, no—don't you mix yourself up in this affair.

[JUDGE BRACK, *with his hat in his hand, enters by the hall door, which* BERTA *opens, and closes behind him. He looks grave and bows in silence.*]

TESMAN. Oh, is that you, my dear Judge? Eh?

BRACK. Yes. It was imperative I should see you this evening.

TESMAN. I can see you have heard the news about Aunt Rina?

BRACK. Yes, that among other things.

TESMAN. Isn't it sad—eh?

BRACK. Well, my dear Tesman, that depends on how you look at it.

TESMAN [*looks doubtfully at him*]. Has anything else happened?

BRACK. Yes.

HEDDA [*in suspense*]. Anything sad, Judge Brack?

BRACK. That, too, depends on how you look at it, Mrs. Tesman.

MRS. ELVSTED [*unable to restrain her anxiety*]. Oh! it is something about Eilert Lövborg!

BRACK [*with a glance at her*]. What makes you think that, Madam? Perhaps you have already heard something——?

MRS. ELVSTED [*in confusion*]. No, nothing at all, but——

TESMAN. Oh, for heaven's sake, tell us!

BRACK [*shrugging his shoulders*]. Well, I regret to say Eilert Lövborg has been taken to the hospital. He is lying at the point of death.

MRS. ELVSTED [*shrieks*]. Oh God! oh God——!

TESMAN. To the hospital! And at the point of death!

HEDDA [*involuntarily*]. So soon then——

MRS. ELVSTED [*wailing*]. And we parted in anger, Hedda!

HEDDA [*whispers*]. Thea—Thea—be careful!

MRS. ELVSTED [*not heeding her*]. I must go to him! I must see him alive!

BRACK. It is useless, Madam. No one will be admitted.

MRS. ELVSTED. Oh, at least tell me what has happened to him? What is it?

TESMAN. You don't mean to say that he has himself—— Eh?

HEDDA. Yes, I am sure he has.

TESMAN. Hedda, how can you——?

BRACK [*keeping his eyes fixed upon her*]. Unfortunately you have guessed quite correctly, Mrs. Tesman.

MRS. ELVSTED. Oh, how horrible!

TESMAN. Himself, then! Fancy that!

HEDDA. Shot himself!

BRACK. Rightly guessed again, Mrs. Tesman.

MRS. ELVSTED [*with an effort at self-control*]. When did it happen, Mr. Brack?

BRACK. This afternoon—between three and four.

TESMAN. But, good Lord, where did he do it? Eh?

BRACK [*with some hesitation*]. Where? Well—I suppose at his lodgings.

MRS. ELVSTED. No, that cannot be; for I was there between six and seven.

BRACK. Well then, somewhere else. I don't know exactly. I only know that he was found——. He had shot himself—in the breast.

MRS. ELVSTED. Oh, how terrible! That he should die like that!

HEDDA [*to* BRACK]. Was it in the breast?

BRACK. Yes—as I told you.

HEDDA. Not in the temple?

BRACK. In the breast, Mrs. Tesman.

HEDDA. Well, well—the breast is a good place, too.

BRACK. How do you mean, Mrs. Tesman?

HEDDA [*evasively*]. Oh, nothing—nothing.

TESMAN. And the wound is dangerous, you say—eh?

BRACK. Absolutely mortal. The end has probably come by this time.

MRS. ELVSTED. Yes, yes, I feel it. The end! The end! Oh, Hedda——!

TESMAN. But tell me, how have you learnt all this?

BRACK [*curtly*]. Through one of the police. A man I had some business with.

HEDDA [*in a clear voice*]. At last a deed worth doing!

TESMAN [*terrified*]. Good heavens, Hedda! what are you saying?

HEDDA. I say there is beauty in this.

BRACK. H'm, Mrs. Tesman——

TESMAN. Beauty! Fancy that!

MRS. ELVSTED. Oh, Hedda, how can you talk of beauty in such an act!

HEDDA. Eilert Lövborg has himself made up his account with life. He has had the courage to do—the one right thing.

MRS. ELVSTED. No, you must never think that was how it happened! It must have been in delirium that he did it.

TESMAN. In despair!

HEDDA. That he did not. I am certain of that.

MRS. ELVSTED. Yes, yes! In delirium! Just as when he tore up our manuscript.

BRACK [*starting*]. The manuscript? Has he torn that up?

MRS. ELVSTED. Yes, last night.

TESMAN [*whispers softly*]. Oh, Hedda, we shall never get over this.

BRACK. H'm, very extraordinary.

TESMAN [*moving about the room*]. To think of Eilert going out of the world in this way! And not leaving behind him the book that would have immortalized his name——

MRS. ELVSTED. Oh, if only it could be put together again!

TESMAN. Yes, if it only could! I don't know what I would not give——

MRS. ELVSTED. Perhaps it can, Mr. Tesman.

TESMAN. What do you mean?

MRS. ELVSTED [*searches in the pocket of her dress*]. Look here. I have kept all the loose notes he used to dictate from.

HEDDA [*a step forward*]. Ah——!

TESMAN. You have kept them, Mrs. Elvsted! Eh?

MRS. ELVSTED. Yes, I have them here. I put them in my pocket when I left home. Here they still are——

TESMAN. Oh, do let me see them!

MRS. ELVSTED [*hands him a bundle of papers*]. But they are in such disorder—all mixed up.

TESMAN. Fancy, if we could make something out of them, after all! Perhaps if we two put our heads together——

MRS. ELVSTED. Oh yes, at least let us try——

TESMAN. We will manage it! We must! I will dedicate my life to this task.

HEDDA. You, George? Your life?

TESMAN. Yes, or rather all the time I can spare. My own collections must wait in the meantime. Hedda—you understand, eh? I owe this to Eilert's memory.

HEDDA. Perhaps.

TESMAN. And so, my dear Mrs. Elvsted, we will give our whole minds to it. There is no use in brooding over what can't be undone—eh? We must try to control our grief as much as possible, and——

MRS. ELVSTED. Yes, yes, Mr. Tesman, I will do the best I can.

TESMAN. Well then, come here. I can't rest until we have looked through the notes. Where shall we sit? Here? No, in there, in the back room. Excuse me, my dear Judge. Come with me, Mrs. Elvsted.

MRS. ELVSTED. Oh, if only it were possible!

[TESMAN *and* MRS. ELVSTED *go into the back room. She takes off her hat and cloak. They both sit at the table under the hanging lamp, and are soon deep in an eager examination of the papers.* HEDDA *crosses to the stove and sits in the arm-chair. Presently* BRACK *goes up to her.*]

HEDDA [*in a low voice*]. Oh, what a sense of freedom it gives one, this act of Eilert Lövborg's.

BRACK.   Freedom, Mrs. Hedda? Well, of course, it is a release for him——

HEDDA.   I mean for me. It gives me a sense of freedom to know that a deed of deliberate courage is still possible in this world,—a deed of spontaneous beauty.

BRACK [smiling].   H'm—my dear Mrs. Hedda——

HEDDA.   Oh, I know what you are going to say. For you are a kind of specialist, too, like—you know!

BRACK [looking hard at her].   Eilert Lövborg was more to you than perhaps you are willing to admit to yourself. Am I wrong?

HEDDA.   I don't answer such questions. I only know that Eilert Lövborg has had the courage to live his life after his own fashion. And then —the last great act, with its beauty! Ah! that he should have the will and the strength to turn away from the banquet of life—so early.

BRACK.   I am sorry, Mrs. Hedda,—but I fear I must dispel an amiable illusion.

HEDDA.   Illusion?

BRACK.   Which could not have lasted long in any case.

HEDDA.   What do you mean?

BRACK.   Eilert Lövborg did not shoot himself—voluntarily.

HEDDA.   Not voluntarily!

BRACK.   No. The thing did not happen exactly as I told it.

HEDDA [in suspense].   Have you concealed something? What is it?

BRACK.   For poor Mrs. Elvsted's sake I idealized the facts a little.

HEDDA.   What are the facts?

BRACK.   First, that he is already dead.

HEDDA.   At the hospital?

BRACK.   Yes—without regaining consciousness.

HEDDA.   What more have you concealed?

BRACK.   This—the event did not happen at his lodgings.

HEDDA.   Oh, that can make no difference.

BRACK.   Perhaps it may. For I must tell you—Eilert Lövborg was found shot in—in Mademoiselle Diana's boudoir.

HEDDA [makes a motion as if to rise, but sinks back again].   That is impossible, Judge Brack! He cannot have been there again to-day.

BRACK.   He was there this afternoon. He went there, he said, to demand the return of something which they had taken from him. Talked wildly about a lost child——

HEDDA.   Ah—so that was why——

BRACK.   I thought probably he meant his manuscript; but now I hear he destroyed that himself. So I suppose it must have been his pocket-book.

HEDDA.   Yes, no doubt. And there—there he was found?

BRACK.   Yes, there. With a pistol in his breast-pocket, discharged. The ball had lodged in a vital part.

HEDDA. In the breast—yes.

BRACK. No—in the bowels.

HEDDA [*looks up at him with an expression of loathing*]. That, too! Oh, what curse is it that makes everything I touch turn ludicrous and mean?

BRACK. There is one point more, Mrs. Hedda—another disagreeable feature in the affair.

HEDDA. And what is that?

BRACK. The pistol he carried——

HEDDA [*breathless*]. Well? What of it?

BRACK. He must have stolen it.

HEDDA [*leaps up*]. Stolen it! That is not true! He did not steal it!

BRACK. No other explanation is possible. He must have stolen it—— Hush!

[TESMAN *and* MRS. ELVSTED *have risen from the table in the back room, and come into the drawing-room.*]

TESMAN [*with the papers in both his hands*]. Hedda, dear, it is almost impossible to see under that lamp. Think of that!

HEDDA. Yes, I am thinking.

TESMAN. Would you mind our sitting at your writing-table—eh?

HEDDA. If you like. [*Quickly*] No, wait! Let me clear it first!

TESMAN. Oh, you needn't trouble, Hedda. There is plenty of room.

HEDDA. No, no, let me clear it, I say! I will take these things in and put them on the piano. There!

[*She has drawn out an object, covered with sheet music, from under the bookcase, places several other pieces of music upon it, and carries the whole into the inner room, to the left.* TESMAN *lays the scraps of paper on the writing-table, and moves the lamp there from the corner table. He and* MRS. ELVSTED *sit down and proceed with their work.* HEDDA *returns.*]

HEDDA [*behind* MRS. ELVSTED'S *chair, gently ruffing her hair*]. Well, my sweet Thea,—how goes it with Eilert Lövborg's monument?

MRS. ELVSTED [*looks dispiritedly up at her*]. Oh, it will be terribly hard to put in order.

TESMAN. We must manage it. I am determined. And arranging other people's papers is just the work for me.

[HEDDA *goes over to the stove, and seats herself on one of the footstools.* BRACK *stands over her, leaning on the arm-chair.*]

HEDDA [*whispers*]. What did you say about the pistol?

BRACK [*softly*]. That he must have stolen it.

HEDDA. Why stolen it?

BRACK. Because every other explanation ought to be impossible, Mrs. Hedda.

HEDDA. Indeed?

BRACK [*glances at her*]. Of course, Eilert Lövborg was here this morning. Was he not?

HEDDA. Yes.

BRACK. Were you alone with him?

HEDDA. Part of the time.

BRACK. Did you not leave the room whilst he was here?

HEDDA. No.

BRACK. Try to recollect. Were you not out of the room a moment?

HEDDA. Yes, perhaps just a moment—out in the hall.

BRACK. And where was your pistol-case during that time?

HEDDA. I had it locked up in——

BRACK. Well, Mrs. Hedda?

HEDDA. The case stood there on the writing-table.

BRACK. Have you looked since, to see whether both the pistols are there?

HEDDA. No.

BRACK. Well, you need not. I saw the pistol found in Lövborg's pocket, and I knew it at once as the one I had seen yesterday—and before, too.

HEDDA. Have you it with you?

BRACK. No, the police have it.

HEDDA. What will the police do with it?

BRACK. Search till they find the owner.

HEDDA. Do you think they will succeed?

BRACK [*bends over her and whispers*]. No, Hedda Gabler—not so long as I say nothing.

HEDDA [*looks frightened at him*]. And if you do not say nothing,— what then?

BRACK [*shrugs his shoulders*]. There is always the possibility that the pistol was stolen.

HEDDA [*firmly*]. Death rather than that.

BRACK [*smiling*]. People say such things—but they don't do them.

HEDDA [*without replying*]. And supposing the pistol was not stolen, and the owner is discovered? What then?

BRACK. Well, Hedda—then comes the scandal.

HEDDA. The scandal!

BRACK. Yes, the scandal—of which you are so mortally afraid. You will, of course, be brought before the court—both you and Mademoiselle Diana. She will have to explain how the thing happened—whether it was an accidental shot or murder. Did the pistol go off as he was trying to take it out of his pocket, to threaten her with? Or did she tear the pistol out of his hand, shoot him, and push it back into his pocket?

That would be quite like her; for she is an able-bodied young person, this same Mademoiselle Diana.

HEDDA. But *I* have nothing to do with all this repulsive business.

BRACK. No. But you will have to answer the question: Why did you give Eilert Lövborg the pistol? And what conclusions will people draw from the fact that you did give it to him?

HEDDA [*lets her head sink*]. That is true. I did not think of that.

BRACK. Well, fortunately, there is no danger, so long as I say nothing.

HEDDA [*looks up at him*]. So I am in your power, Judge Brack. You have me at your beck and call, from this time forward.

BRACK [*whispers softly*]. Dearest Hedda—believe me—I shall not abuse my advantage.

HEDDA. I am in your power none the less. Subject to your will and your demands. A slave, a slave then! [*Rises impetuously*] No, I cannot endure the thought of that! Never!

BRACK [*looks half-mockingly at her*]. People generally get used to the inevitable.

HEDDA [*returns his look*]. Yes, perhaps. [*She crosses to the writing-table. Suppressing an involuntary smile, she imitates* TESMAN's *intonations.*] Well? Are you getting on, George? Eh?

TESMAN. Heaven knows, dear. In any case it will be the work of months.

HEDDA [*as before*]. Fancy that! [*Passes her hands softly through* MRS. ELVSTED's *hair.*] Doesn't it seem strange to you, Thea? Here are you sitting with Tesman—just as you used to sit with Eilert Lövborg?

MRS. ELVSTED. Ah, if I could only inspire your husband in the same way!

HEDDA. Oh, that will come, too—in time.

TESMAN. Yes, do you know, Hedda—I really think I begin to feel something of the sort. But won't you go and sit with Brack again?

HEDDA. Is there nothing I can do to help you two?

TESMAN. No, nothing in the world. [*Turning his head*] I trust to you to keep Hedda company, my dear Brack.

BRACK [*with a glance at* HEDDA]. With the very greatest of pleasure.

HEDDA. Thanks. But I am tired this evening. I will go in and lie down a little on the sofa.

TESMAN. Yes, do, dear—eh?

[HEDDA *goes into the back room and draws the curtains. A short pause. Suddenly she is heard playing a wild dance on the piano.*]

MRS. ELVSTED [*starts from her chair*]. Oh—what is that?

TESMAN [*runs to the doorway*]. Why, my dearest Hedda—don't play dance-music tonight! Just think of Aunt Rina! And of Eilert, too!

HEDDA [*puts her head out between the curtains*]. And of Aunt Julia.

And of all the rest of them.—After this, I will be quiet. [*Closes the curtains again.*]

TESMAN [*at the writing-table*]. It's not good for her to see us at this distressing work. I'll tell you what, Mrs. Elvsted,—you shall take the empty room at Aunt Julia's, and then I will come over in the evenings, and we can sit and work there—eh?

HEDDA [*in the inner room*]. I hear what you are saying, Tesman. But how am *I* to get through the evenings out here?

TESMAN [*turning over the papers*]. Oh, I daresay Judge Brack will be so kind as to look in now and then, even though I am out.

BRACK [*in the arm-chair, calls out gaily*]. Every blessed evening, with all the pleasure in life, Mrs. Tesman! We shall get on capitally together, we two!

HEDDA [*speaking loud and clear*]. Yes, don't you flatter yourself we will, Judge Brack? Now that you are the one cock in the basket——

[*A shot is heard within.* TESMAN, MRS. ELVSTED, *and* BRACK *leap to their feet.*]

TESMAN. Oh, now she is playing with those pistols again.

[*He throws back the curtains and runs in, followed by* MRS. ELVSTED. HEDDA *lies stretched on the sofa, lifeless. Confusion and cries.* BERTA *enters in alarm from the right.*]

TESMAN [*shrieks to* BRACK]. Shot herself! Shot herself in the temple! Fancy that!

BRACK [*half-fainting in the arm-chair*]. Good God!—people don't do such things.

Two Critical Commentaries on Ibsen's *Hedda Gabler*

Commentary by Montrose J. Moses, from *Henrik Ibsen, the Man and His Plays* (New York, Mitchell Kennerley, 1908).

Let us say that a canvas was placed before Ibsen upon which certain actual events had traced definite lines. First, there was a Norwegian composer whose wife, blind with jealousy, had burned the manuscript of his symphony. Second, a beautiful woman had married a drunkard who finally succeeded in mastering his weakness. One day, in an ungovernable desire to show her power over him, the wife put a barrel of brandy into his study, and later found him stretched senseless upon the floor. Third, a young man named Holm served as the model for Eilert Lövborg; he was weak in his mind, and in a debauch had lost the manuscript of his book; he had furthermore made Ibsen his legatee in case of his death, and in some indirect way had suggested his association with a lady much on a par with 'Mademoiselle Diana.' These are the few details upon which the dramatist was to build.

Of course one can readily understand the avidity with which people search for the symbol in Ibsen. In a way the pistol does represent the lawlessness in Hedda's nature, the vine leaves are significant of weakness in Lövborg: but never has Ibsen been less with a purpose, other than to paint character realistically—proving nothing through the suggestiveness of poetry, but resting content with the accurate strokes of the painter. Indeed, no more apt comparison has been made than that which likened Ibsen's portrait of Hedda to a canvas of Sargent, where the flesh tints, the sinuous lines, the pose, and the expression all conduce toward suggesting the temperament beneath. Ibsen is not extravagant in color while drawing this figure; everything is concise, unerring, clear-cut, dangerously picturesque. It is not merely that there is exhibited a wonderfully close observation of the feminine nervous framework, but something more; usually an artist looks into the soul of the woman he draws, but few can look out *with* the soul of a woman, can transfer an impersonal sketch to a living, breathing personality. Flinging upon his canvas the common elements of a Norwegian life in the early '60's, Ibsen succeeds in dealing with elemental characteristics acting upon a special type. Hedda Gabler is not the woman every man takes down to dinner, as the critic declared she was; she is not the species, but the variant; she is the composite woman raised to the nth power; she is not the normal type but an aggregate of abnormal types.

Egoism eats into Hedda as acid bites into zinc; she is wholly bad, impelled by a consuming desire to overcome her ennui. She is wicked by virtue of her inherent wickedness. Ibsen has never before so thoroughly depicted feminine decadence. . . . (pp. 428-29)

Hedda is an unscrupulous thirster after life; her temperature slumbers beneath a cold-blooded attitude, until her lust spies an ignoble goal, when she pursues it at feverish heat. She is not a woman, but a vampire; she shuns every quality of womanhood; she desires only to remain unbridled; she abhors any reference to her pregnant state,—a state which might account for her cerebral restlessness, and her neurotic irritability. From the medical standpoint Hedda is an interesting subject; from the criminal standpoint also.

She was a coward in all things that hedged around her independence; she was devoid of heart, to be influenced as Rebecca was influenced; her temptation was to dare, but not to dare bravely; her thirst for beauty was that which is only satisfied with destruction. Her whole attitude toward people was to overcome them; she was a physical beauty, lowly bred, and anxious for social position in order to exercise that physical beauty. Perhaps one might attribute this decadence to her previous education, as some critics are inclined to do; she is vulgar in her tastes, in her strivings, in her associations. She is consumed with curiosity and jealousy; she is productive of only negative qualities; her aristocratic inclination is common; her irresponsibility as to all human ties is coarse. She is wholly bourgeoise. (pp. 430-31)

For subtle, psychological reasoning, Ibsen's portrait of 'Hedda Gabler' remains unequalled; it is the very essence of realism, a replica of viciousness. One regrets that such beauty of workmanship should have been expended upon a figure which has to be rejected after it is fully drawn. There is a certain fascination in bad types, and the attraction of 'Hedda Gabler' is fas-

cination. She is Ibsen's highest point as a feminist; she is Ibsen's lowest point
in the depiction of the feminine.   (pp. 437-38)

Because of his acute vision . . . Ibsen's characters, and most generally his
women, are interesting pathological studies; they carry symptoms which are
to be found in the medical books, and which, though they may not act wholly
in the way science has proved them to act, at least are indicative of neuras-
thenia in its varying degrees. Ibsen blotted out for his purposes any conception of heredity of nobility; his irritation would not allow him to conceive
of such. But in his earlier years he had had just a sufficient amount of medical
training to give him confidence in his ignoring of special diagnosis; he relied
here on his observation.   (p. 516)

Commentary by Theodore Jorgenson, from *Henrik Ibsen, a Study in Art and Personality* (Northfield, Minn., St. Olaf College Press, 1945).*

Hedda Gabler shows frustration resulting from social inhibition and the
want of creative leadership. It issued in disintegration and despair, finally in
self-destruction. . . . Hedda, a supremely gifted young woman, . . . destroyed
herself because she found no satisfaction in her love-life and no outlet for her
creative urge.

She belonged to the highest class in society. It is evident that she is more
German than Norwegian, the name itself indicates that fact. Moreover the
Germans have been inclined to speak of the highest social class in terms of
military position. A general would be of the very highest. . . . General
Gabler had a rich home on a large estate. He had beautiful horses and fine
hunting dogs. He used to take Hedda along horseback riding; and she
enjoyed these little adventures greatly. General Gabler also had a number
of expensive pistols. . . . Beyond a doubt she received the best education
available in the land. Everyone recognized her talent, and she exhibited a
strong desire to dominate others. Aristocratic to the core, she expected others
to serve her. She expected to mold the destinies of men and women. She
liked to feel that she could exercise power; she liked to turn and twist the
wills and the frames of human beings to fit her own interests.

She was strikingly beautiful: tall, athletic, queenly. When she was introduced to the social life of the community, she immediately became the great
star of every gathering. . . .   (pp. 433, 435-36)

In *Hedda Gabler* we find no desire to describe tendencies or movements.
The drama is a play of forces within the personality and in the environment.
It is possible to distinguish three different social groups which appear in more
or less clearly outlined form. The first one may be called the Gabler group.
Hedda is really the only character representative of the noble class, but her
father, General Gabler, is very definitely present in the book even if we do not
see him with the naked eye. The second group may be called the Tesman
people. It includes Jörgen [George] Tesman, his two aunts, who have reared
him, and possibly also the servant Berte. One is inclined to call it the middle
class group. Unquestionably the glamour and the grandeur that is Gabler

---

* Reprinted by permission of The St. Olaf College Press and of Theodore Jorgenson.

will be found lacking in the Tesman group. The people are kind, honest men and women of goodwill, devoted to their loved ones, but they are all mediocre. . . .

The third group in the Gabler tragedy may be called the boheme. In the life of the eighties of the nineteenth century, a high aristocracy was contrasted against smaller groups of city intellectuals. Perhaps the city of Paris was the original breeding place of such organisms. The boheme was made up of radicals; it included drifting individuals, artists and literary men, poverty-stricken failures and impractical geniuses. It was among people from this atmosphere that naturalism grew. . . . They were unconventional both in principle and behavior; they had very few psychological inhibitions . . . they advocated companionate marriages and great freedom in the relations between the sexes. . . . Men like Ejlert Lövborg are in [this] class. . . . He must have come from a cultured background, or he would not have belonged to any group that could make contact with Hedda Gabler. He must have enjoyed years of school, or he would not be a candidate for the professorship. . . . Ejlert Lövborg's dissipation was a moral weakness rather than a social handicap. . . . The boheme group is not altogether made up of men like Ejlert Lövborg. Judge Brack is no doubt a socially gracious figure. . . . To him the liberty of a naturalistic world view is merely a way of taking care of his personal desires. . . . The gutter of boheme existence is seen in the environment of Mademoiselle Diana. . . .

Outside of all these groups, and in possession of a strange purity, stands the figure of Thea Elvsted. She comes from the country. . . .

(pp. 443, 446-47)

When the tragedy of Hedda Gabler was published in the fall of 1890, the immediate reaction to the play was one of bewilderment. The Scandinavian public as well as the critics had been accustomed to look for central ideas and problems in the literature of the seventies and the eighties. Here they found none. A similar bewilderment had been apparent in the days when *The Wild Duck* came out, but even *The Wild Duck* seemed easily under-standable in comparison with the puzzling psychology of General Gabler's daughter. Everyone realized that Ibsen was not trying to teach any moral lesson. Most of the readers were probably acquainted with new tendencies in the art and letters of the day, tendencies that made such a lack of an idea not too surprising. The baffling thing was that Hedda's suicide and some of her previous behavior could not be reconciled with the ordinary thought of what men and women do. The public was inclined to agree with Judge Brack that people simply do not 'do those things.'

It is an indication of Henrik Ibsen's great psychological penetration that approximately forty years had to pass before *Hedda Gabler* as a drama could be appreciated. In the course of the intervening time, psychology had made clear the inner dynamics and the motives of human action to a degree which had not been possible earlier. The frustration of an emotional life and the absence of purpose, in a character born to shape destinies, will not be found very adequate indeed to explain Hedda's final despair.

On the stage the drama has taken its place among the greatest of Henrik Ibsen's achievements. Hedda herself is one of the few great roles an actress may look for. (p. 450)

V. CANDIDA

A Realistic Comedy by Bernard Shaw

Introductory Note to G. Bernard Shaw and *Candida*

To LIVE LONGER THAN Sophocles, to write more plays than Shakespeare, to be as much of a comic in life as Molière was on the stage, to live in the light of Ibsen's new ideas—such it was to be George Bernard Shaw. He died at ninety-four having been an active personality throughout the entire period of modern drama. He wrote more than forty plays. He was the most impudent cut-up and publicized wit of his age. He championed, in his own often perverse way, most of the liberal causes of three generations. Something of this amazing personality can be seen in his *Candida,* his most popular, if not his greatest, comedy.

Bernard Shaw—like most of the writers of English comedy—was an Irishman. He was born in 1856 in Dublin, as was Oscar Wilde. Shaw's father was a poor relation of landed Protestant gentry, unsuccessful in business, an alcoholic with a genial turn for humor. His mother, a singer, was a remarkable woman. Genteel snobbery, coupled with poverty, made his schooling miserable. At fourteen he went to work in a land agent's office, which he disliked. He remained as a junior clerk, but soon with senior responsibilities. Young Shaw, as a Shelleyan, liked to shock his office mates with his professed atheism. By the time he was twenty his mother, leaving her husband in Dublin, had already gone to London to earn her way as a musician. Her son soon joined her there, with some vague notion that he would amount to something. It was ten years before he was earning a living. Meanwhile he was supported by his mother and by small remittances from his father. During his twenties he did odd-jobs in journalism, wrote five unsuccessful novels, developed himself as a public speaker, became interested in the economics of Henry George and the socialism of Karl Marx, the dramas of Ibsen and the music of Wagner. He joined the newly founded Fabian Society, which advocated social evolution rather than Marxian violence, and paved the way for the present Labour

Party in England. He was a tall, angular Irishman, energetic, red-haired and bearded, a clever speaker whether in the dialectic of the platform or of Hyde Park and the Embankment. By chance William Archer got him a place as music critic when he was twenty-nine, and at last he was earning his keep.

During his philandering thirties he was successful, not only as a music and then art critic, but as an active committeeman and popular spellbinder in the social and political movements to which he devoted himself. An unpredictable faddist as the years went on, he was a teetotaling, nonsmoking, sun-bathing vegetarian who preached socialism, advocated sexual freedom, and espoused creative evolution. He championed the New Drama and Ibsen, whom William Archer was introducing to England and translating, and wrote *The Quintessence of Ibsenism* (1890), based upon his Fabian Society lectures. He undertook to write a drama with Archer in 1885, but later finished *Widowers' Houses* alone. His first plays were not suited to the then popular taste. He turned drama critic (1895-98), writing sharp reviews, later reprinted as *Dramatic Opinions and Essays,* idolizing Ibsen's modernity and blasting Shakespearean bard-olatry. In 1898, when he was forty-two, he published his first two volumes of *Plays, Pleasant and Unpleasant* (with the first of his famous Prefaces), also *The Perfect Wagnerite,* and he married his socialist friend, Charlotte Payne-Townshend, with whom he lived until her death in 1943. Success had come to him and stayed with him through the succeeding decades. He was awarded the Nobel Prize (but refused the money) in 1925. He continued to be active as the years went by until he died on November 2, 1950.

Bernard Shaw served no apprenticeship in the theater. He was self-taught as a dramatist, with a native sense of the comic and theatrical. His first "unpleasant" plays were really unsuccessful, even with select audiences: *Widowers' Houses* (1892), based on slum landlordism, was but a provocative adventure at the Independent Theatre; *The Philanderer* (written in 1893) was not produced until much later; *Mrs. Warren's Profession* (1893), on the theme of the economics of prostitution, raised a storm in New York in 1905 and was banned in England until 1924. The "pleasant" plays fared better: *Arms and the Man* (1894)—which later became the musical *The Chocolate Soldier*—was successful, especially in America, dramatizing the paradox that soldiers are the greatest cowards. *You Never Can Tell,* which put parents in their place, was at first a failure, as was *The Man of Destiny,* which cut Napoleon down to size.

Candida (as we shall see) was not successfully produced for ten years!

In 1900 Shaw published *Three Plays for Puritans,* continuing his stream of dramatic paradoxes: *The Devil's Disciple,* contrasting a good renegade with a militant parson, had been successfully produced by Richard Mansfield in New York in 1897; *Caesar and Cleopatra* (1898, 1899) was Shaw's bid to outdo Shakespeare; *Captain Brassbound's Conversion* (1899, 1906) was written for Ellen Terry, whose intimate and readable correspondence with Shaw was later to be published (1931). At least brief mention must be made of further plays: *Man and Superman* (1903, 1905), with its frank discussion of man and woman, and the dream scene of "Don Juan in Hell"; *Major Barbara* (1905), concerning the Salvation Army daughter of a munitions maker; *Androcles and the Lion* (1911), a comedy of the early Christians; *Pygmalion* (1912), in which a phonetics professor re-educates a flower girl; *Saint Joan* (1924), the heroic tragedy of the maid of Lorraine, considered Shaw's masterpiece. But his playwriting continued for fifteen years more after *Saint Joan.*

Candida was written in 1894 as a bid for commercial success. Mansfield undertook to produce it in New York in 1895, but found he could not play Marchbanks and so dropped it. In England it was alternated with Ibsen's *A Doll's House* by the Independent Theatre on its provincial tours in 1897 and 1898. In April 1899 it was given successful "private" performances by a drama teacher in Chicago, with Taylor Holmes as Marchbanks. The Browning Society of Philadelphia staged it in May 1903. This encouraged Arnold Daly to try Marchbanks himself for some matinees in New York later that year—with theatrical success that was great and continuous. After more than 150 performances in New York, Daly took his production on tour in the East and the West, and two other companies were organized to play it in America. Thereafter *Candida* became internationally famous. More recent production of *Candida* in America presented Katharine Cornell (later Peggy Wood) as Candida in 1924 for 143 performances. Miss Cornell revived *Candida* in 1937, again in 1942 (with an all-star cast: Mildred Natwick as Prossy, Raymond Massey as Morell, Dudley Digges as Burgess, and Burgess Meredith as Marchbanks). In her 1946 revival, Burgess was played by Sir Cedric Hardwicke, Marchbanks by Marlon Brando. Olivia de Havilland revived *Candida* for a tour and New York engagement in 1952.

CANDIDA *

A Pleasant Play by George Bernard Shaw

THE CHARACTERS

The REV. JAMES MORELL—*a handsome clergyman and vigorous Socialist.*

CANDIDA—*his wife, aged 33, both youthful and motherly.*

EUGENE MARCHBANKS—*a well-born youth of 18, shy and sensitive, befriended by the Morells.*

MISS PROSERPINE GARNETT—*'Prossy,' aged 30, Morell's secretary.*

The REV. ALEXANDER MILL—*'Lexy,' Morell's young assistant.*

MR. BURGESS—*Candida's unregenerate father, aged 60.*

Time: *in the eighteen-nineties of Victorian England.*
Place: *the sitting room in the parsonage of St. Dominic's, London.*

ACT I

A FINE MORNING *in October 1894 in the north east quarter of London, a vast district miles away from the London of Mayfair and St. James's, and much less narrow, squalid, fetid and airless in its slums. It is strong in unfashionable middle class life: wide-streeted; myriad-populated; well served with ugly iron urinals, Radical clubs, and tram lines carrying a perpetual stream of yellow cars; enjoying in its main thoroughfares the luxury of grass-grown "front gardens" untrodden by the foot of man save as to the path from the gate to the hall door; blighted by a callously endured monotony of miles and miles of unlovely brick houses, black iron railings, stony pavements, slated roofs, and respectably ill dressed or disreputably worse dressed people, quite accustomed to the place, and mostly plodding uninterestedly about somebody else's work. The little energy and eagerness that crop up show themselves in cockney cupidity and business "push." Even the policemen and the chapels are not infrequent enough to break the monotony. The sun is shining cheerfully: there is no fog; and though the smoke effectually prevents anything, whether faces and hands or bricks and mortar, from looking fresh and clean, it is not hanging heavily enough to trouble a Londoner.*

---

* Used by permission of the Public Trustee, the Society of Authors, and Dodd, Mead & Company, Inc.

This desert of unattractiveness has its oasis. Near the outer end of the Hackney Road is a park of 217 acres, fenced in, not by railings, but by a wooden paling, and containing plenty of greensward, trees, a lake for bathers, flower beds which are triumphs of the admired cockney art of carpet gardening, and a sandpit, originally imported from the seaside for the delight of children, but speedily deserted on its becoming a natural vermin preserve for all the petty fauna of Kingsland, Hackney, and Hoxton. A bandstand, an unfurnished forum for religious, anti-religious, and political orators, cricket pitches, a gymnasium, and an old fashioned stone kiosk are among its attractions. Wherever the prospect is bounded by trees or rising green grounds, it is a pleasant place. Where the ground stretches flat to the grey palings, with bricks and mortar, sky signs, crowded chimneys and smoke beyond, the prospect makes it desolate and sordid.

The best view of Victoria Park is commanded by the front window of ST. DOMINIC'S PARSONAGE, *from which not a brick is visible. The parsonage is semi-detached, with a front garden and a porch. Visitors go up the flight of steps to the porch: tradespeople and members of the family go down by a door under the steps to the basement, with a breakfast room, used for all meals, in front, and the kitchen at the back. Upstairs, on the level of the hall door, is the drawing room, with its large plate glass window looking out on the park. In this, the only sitting room that can be spared from the children and the family meals, the parson, the* REVEREND JAMES MAVOR MORELL, *does his work. He is sitting in a strong round backed revolving chair at the end of a long table, which stands across the window, so that he can cheer himself with a view of the park over his left shoulder. At the opposite end of the table, adjoining it, is a little table only half as wide as the other, with a typewriter on it. His typist is sitting at this machine, with her back to the window. The large table is littered with pamphlets, journals, letters, nests of drawers, an office diary, postage scales and the like. A spare chair for visitors having business with the parson is in the middle, turned to his end. Within reach of his hand is a stationery case, and a photograph in a frame. The wall behind him is fitted with bookshelves, on which an adept eye can measure the parson's casuistry and divinity by Maurice's* Theological Essays *and a complete set of Browning's poems, and the reformer's politics by a yellow backed* Progress and Poverty, Fabian Essays, A Dream of John Ball, Marx's *Capital, and half a dozen other literary landmarks in Socialism. Facing him on the other side of the room, near the typewriter, is the door. Further down opposite the fireplace, a bookcase stands on a cellaret, with a sofa near it. There is a generous fire burning; and the hearth, with a comfortable armchair and a black japanned flower-painted coal scuttle at one side, a miniature chair for children on the other, a varnished wooden mantelpiece, with neatly moulded shelves, tiny bits of mirror let into the panels, a travelling clock in a leather case (the inevitable wedding present), and on the wall above a large autotype of the chief figure in Titian's Assumption of the Virgin, is very inviting. Altogether the room is the room of a good housekeeper, vanquished, as far as the table is concerned, by an untidy man, but elsewhere mistress of the situation. The furniture, in its ornamental aspect, betrays the style of the advertized "drawing-room suite" of the pushing suburban furniture dealer; but there is nothing useless or pretentious in the room, money being too scarce in the house of an east end parson to be wasted on snobbish trimmings.*

THE REVEREND JAMES MAVOR MORELL *is a Christian Socialist clergyman of the Church of England, and an active member of the Guild of St. Matthew and the Christian Social Union. A vigorous, genial, popular man of forty, robust and goodlooking, full of energy, with pleasant, hearty, considerate manners, and a sound unaffected voice, which he uses with the clean athletic articulation of a practised orator, and with a wide range and perfect command of expression. He is a first rate clergyman, able to say what he likes to whom he likes, to lecture people without setting himself up against them, to impose his authority on them without humiliating them, and, on occasion, to interfere in their business without impertinence. His well-spring of enthusiasm and sympathetic emotion has never run dry for a moment: he still eats and sleeps heartily enough to win the daily battle between exhaustion and recuperation triumphantly. Withal, a great baby, pardonably vain of his powers and unconsciously pleased with himself. He has a healthy complexion: good forehead, with the brows somewhat blunt, and the eyes bright and eager, mouth resolute but not particularly well cut, and a substantial nose with the mobile spreading nostrils of the dramatic orator, void, like all his features, of subtlety.*

The typist, MISS PROSERPINE GARNETT, *is a brisk little woman of about 30, of the lower middle class, neatly but cheaply dressed in a black merino skirt and a blouse, notably pert and quick of speech, and not very civil in her manner, but sensitive and affectionate. She is clattering away busily at her machine whilst* MORELL *opens the last of his morning's letters. He realizes its contents with a comic groan of despair.*

PROSERPINE. Another lecture?

MORELL. Yes. The Hoxton Freedom Group want me to address them on Sunday morning [*he lays great emphasis on Sunday, this being the unreasonable part of the business*]. What are they?

PROSERPINE. Communist Anarchists, I think.

MORELL. Just like Anarchists not to know that they can't have a parson on Sunday! Tell them to come to church if they want to hear me: it will do them good. Say I can come on Mondays and Thursdays only. Have you the diary there?

PROSERPINE [*taking up the diary*]. Yes.

MORELL. Have I any lecture on for next Monday?

PROSERPINE [*referring to the diary*]. Tower Hamlets Radical Club.

MORELL. Well, Thursday then?

PROSERPINE. English Land Restoration League.

MORELL. What next?

PROSERPINE. Guild of St. Matthew on Monday. Independent Labor Party, Greenwich Branch, on Thursday. Monday, Social-Democratic Federation, Mile End Branch. Thursday, first Confirmation class. [*Impatiently*] Oh, I'd better tell them you can't come. They're only half a dozen ignorant and conceited costermongers without five shillings between them.

MORELL [*amused*]. Ah; but you see they're near relatives of mine.

PROSERPINE [*staring at him*]. Relatives of yours!

MORELL. Yes: we have the same father—in Heaven.

PROSERPINE [*relieved*]. Oh, is that all?

MORELL [*with a sadness which is a luxury to a man whose voice expresses it so finely*]. Ah, you don't believe it. Everybody says it: nobody believes it: nobody. [*Briskly, getting back to business*] Well, well! Come, Miss Proserpine: can't you find a date for the costers? what about the 25th? That was vacant the day before yesterday.

PROSERPINE [*referring to diary*]. Engaged. The Fabian Society.

MORELL. Bother the Fabian Society! Is the 28th gone too?

PROSERPINE. City dinner. You're invited to dine with the Founders' Company.

MORELL. That'll do: I'll go to the Hoxton Group of Freedom instead.

[*She enters the engagement in silence, with implacable disparagement of the Hoxton Anarchists in every line of her face.* MORELL *bursts open the cover of a copy of* The Church Reformer, *which has come by post, and glances through Mr. Stewart Headlam's leader and the Guild of St. Matthew news. These proceedings are presently enlivened by the appearance of* MORELL's *curate, the* REVEREND ALEXANDER MILL, *a young gentleman gathered by* MORELL *from the nearest University settlement, whither he had come from Oxford to give the east end of London the benefit of his university training. He is a conceitedly well intentioned, enthusiastic, immature novice, with nothing positively unbearable about him except a habit of speaking with his lips carefully closed a full half inch from each corner for the sake of a finicking articulation and a set of university vowels, this being his chief means so far of bringing his Oxford refinement (as he calls his habits) to bear on Hackney vulgarity.* MORELL, *whom he has won over by a doglike devotion, looks up indulgently from* The Church Reformer, *and remarks*]

Well, Lexy? Late again, as usual!

LEXY. I'm afraid so. I wish I could get up in the morning.

MORELL [*exulting in his own energy*]. Ha! ha! [*Whimsically*] Watch and pray, Lexy: watch and pray.

LEXY. I know. [*Rising wittily to the occasion*] But how can I watch and pray when I am asleep? Isn't that so, Miss Prossy? [*He makes for the warmth of the fire.*]

PROSERPINE [*sharply*]. Miss Garnett, if you please.

LEXY. I beg your pardon. Miss Garnett.

PROSERPINE. You've got to do all the work today.

LEXY [*on the hearth*]. Why?

PROSERPINE. Never mind why. It will do you good to earn your supper before you eat it, for once in a way, as I do. Come! don't dawdle. You should have been off on your rounds half an hour ago.

LEXY [*perplexed*]. Is she in earnest, Morell?

MORELL [*in the highest spirits, his eyes dancing*]. Yes. I am going to dawdle today.

LEXY. You! You don't know how.

MORELL [*rising*]. Ha! ha! Don't I? I'm going to have this morning all to myself. My wife's coming back: she's due here at 11.45.

LEXY [*surprised*]. Coming back already! with the children? I thought they were to stay to the end of the month.

MORELL. So they are: she's only coming up for two days, to get some flannel things for Jimmy, and to see how we're getting on without her.

LEXY [*anxiously*]. But, my dear Morell, if what Jimmy and Fluffy had was scarlatina, do you think it wise—

MORELL. Scarlatina! Rubbish! it was German measles. I brought it into the house myself from the Pycroft Street school. A parson is like a doctor, my boy: he must face infection as a soldier must face bullets. [*He claps* LEXY *manfully on the shoulders.*] Catch the measles if you can, Lexy: she'll nurse you; and what a piece of luck that will be for you! Eh?

LEXY [*smiling uneasily*]. It's so hard to understand you about Mrs. Morell—

MORELL [*tenderly*]. Ah, my boy, get married: get married to a good woman; and then you'll understand. That's a foretaste of what will be best in the Kingdom of Heaven we are trying to establish on earth. That will cure you of dawdling. An honest man feels that he must pay Heaven for every hour of happiness with a good spell of hard unselfish work to make others happy. We have no more right to consume happiness without producing it than to consume wealth without producing it. Get a wife like my Candida; and you'll always be in arrear with your repayment. [*He pats* LEXY *affectionately and moves to leave the room.*]

LEXY. Oh, wait a bit: I forgot.

[MORELL *halts and turns with the door knob in his hand.*]

Your father-in-law is coming round to see you.

[MORELL, *surprised and not pleased, shuts the door again, with a complete change of manner.*]

MORELL. Mr. Burgess?

LEXY. Yes. I passed him in the park, arguing with somebody. He asked me to let you know that he was coming.

MORELL [*half incredulous*]. But he hasn't called here for three years. Are you sure, Lexy? You're not joking, are you?

LEXY [*earnestly*]. No sir, really.

MORELL [*thoughtfully*]. Hm! Time for him to take another look at Candida before she grows out of his knowledge.

[*He resigns himself to the inevitable, and goes out.*]

[LEXY *looks after him with beaming worship.* MISS GARNETT, *not being able to shake* LEXY, *relieves her feelings by worrying the typewriter.*]

LEXY. What a good man! What a thorough loving soul he is! [*He takes* MORELL's *place at the table, making himself very comfortable as he takes out a cigaret.*]

PROSERPINE [*impatiently, pulling the letter she has been working at off the typewriter and folding it*]. Oh, a man ought to be able to be fond of his wife without making a fool of himself about her.

LEXY [*shocked*]. Oh, Miss Prossy!

PROSERPINE [*snatching at the stationery case for an envelope, in which she encloses the letter as she speaks*]. Candida here, and Candida there, and Candida everywhere! [*She licks the envelope.*] It's enough to drive anyone out of their senses [*thumping the envelope to make it stick*] to hear a woman raved about in that absurd manner merely because she's got good hair and a tolerable figure.

LEXY [*with reproachful gravity*]. I think her extremely beautiful, Miss Garnett. [*He takes the photograph up; looks at it; and adds, with even greater impressiveness*] extremely beautiful. How fine her eyes are!

PROSERPINE. Her eyes are not a bit better than mine: now! [*He puts down the photograph and stares austerely at her.*] And you know very well you think me dowdy and second rate enough.

LEXY [*rising majestically*]. Heaven forbid that I should think of any of God's creatures in such a way! [*He moves stiffly away from her across the room to the neighborhood of the bookcase.*]

PROSERPINE [*sarcastically*]. Thank you. That's very nice and comforting.

LEXY [*saddened by her depravity*]. I had no idea you had any feeling against Mrs. Morell.

PROSERPINE [*indignantly*]. I have no feeling against her. She's very nice, very good-hearted: I'm very fond of her, and can appreciate her real qualities far better than any man can. [*He shakes his head sadly. She rises and comes at him with intense pepperiness.*] You don't believe me? You think I'm jealous? Oh, what a knowledge of the human heart you have, Mr. Lexy Mill! How well you know the weaknesses of Woman, don't you? It must be so nice to be a man and have a fine penetrating intellect instead of mere emotions like us, and to know that the reason we don't share your amorous delusions is that we're all jealous of one another! [*She abandons him with a toss of her shoulders, and crosses to the fire to warm her hands.*]

LEXY. Ah, if you women only had the same clue to Man's strength that you have to his weakness, Miss Prossy, there would be no Woman Question.

PROSERPINE [*over her shoulder, as she stoops, holding her hands to the blaze*]. Where did you hear Morell say that? You didn't invent it yourself: you're not clever enough.

LEXY. That's quite true. I am not ashamed of owing him that, as I owe him so many other spiritual truths. He said it at the annual conference of the Women's Liberal Federation. Allow me to add that though they didn't appreciate it, I, a mere man, did. [*He turns to the bookcase again, hoping that this may leave her crushed.*]

PROSERPINE [*putting her hair straight at a panel of mirror in the mantelpiece*]. Well, when you talk to me, give me your own ideas, such as they are, and not his. You never cut a poorer figure than when you are trying to imitate him.

LEXY [*stung*]. I try to follow his example, not to imitate him.

PROSERPINE [*coming at him again on her way back to her work*]. Yes, you do: you imitate him. Why do you tuck your umbrella under your left arm instead of carrying it in your hand like anyone else? Why do you walk with your chin stuck out before you, hurrying along with that eager look in your eyes? you! who never get up before half past nine in the morning. Why do you say "knoaledge" in church, though you always say "knolledge" in private conversation! Bah! do you think I don't know? [*She goes back to the typewriter.*] Here! come and set about your work: we've wasted enough time for one morning. Here's a copy of the diary for today. [*She hands him a memorandum.*]

LEXY [*deeply offended*]. Thank you. [*He takes it and stands at the table with his back to her, reading it. She begins to transcribe her shorthand notes on the typewriter without troubling herself about his feelings.*]

[*The door opens; and* MR. BURGESS *enters unannounced. He is a man of sixty, made coarse and sordid by the compulsory selfishness of petty commerce, and later on softened into sluggish bumptiousness by overfeeding and commercial success. A vulgar ignorant guzzling man, offensive and contemptuous to people whose labor is cheap, respectful to wealth and rank, and quite sincere and without rancor or envy in both attitudes. The world has offered him no decently paid work except that of a sweater; and he has become, in consequence, somewhat hoggish. But he has no suspicion of this himself, and honestly regards his commercial prosperity as the inevitable and socially wholesome triumph of the ability, industry, shrewdness, and experience in business of a man who in private is easygoing, affectionate, and humorously convivial to a fault. Corporeally he is podgy, with a snoutish nose in the centre of a flat square face, a dust colored beard with a patch of grey in the centre under his chin, and small watery blue eyes with a plaintively sentimental expression, which he transfers easily to his voice by his habit of pompously intoning his sentences.]*

BURGESS [*stopping on the threshold, and looking round*]. They told me Mr. Morell was here.

PROSERPINE [*rising*]. I'll fetch him for you.

BURGESS [*staring disappointedly at her*]. You're not the same young lady as hused to typewrite for him?

PROSERPINE. No.

BURGESS [*grumbling on his way to the hearth-rug*]. No: she was young-er.

[MISS GARNETT *stares at him; then goes out, slamming the door.*]

Startin on your rounds, Mr. Mill?

LEXY [*folding his memorandum and pocketing it*]. Yes; I must be off presently.

BURGESS [*momentously*]. Don't let me detain you, Mr. Mill. What I come about is private between me and Mr. Morell.

LEXY [*huffily*]. I have no intention of intruding, I am sure, Mr. Burgess. Good morning.

BURGESS [*patronizingly*]. Oh, good morning to you.

[MORELL *returns as* LEXY *is making for the door.*]

MORELL [*to* LEXY]. Off to work?

LEXY. Yes, sir.

MORELL. Take my silk handkerchief and wrap your throat up. There's a cold wind. Away with you.

[LEXY, *more than consoled for* BURGESS's *rudeness, brightens up and goes out.*]

BURGESS. Spoilin your korates as usu'l, James. Good mornin. When I pay a man, an' 'is livin depens on me, I keep him in 'is place.

MORELL [*rather shortly*]. I always keep my curates in their places as my helpers and comrades. If you get as much work out of your clerks and warehousemen as I do out of my curates, you must be getting rich pretty fast. Will you take your old chair?

[*He points with curt authority to the armchair beside the fireplace; then takes the spare chair from the table and sits down at an unfamiliar distance from his visitor.*]

BURGESS [*without moving*]. Just the same as hever, James!

MORELL. When you last called—it was about three years ago, I think— you said the same thing a little more frankly. Your exact words then were "Just as big a fool as ever, James!"

BURGESS [*soothingly*]. Well, praps I did; but [*with conciliatory cheerfulness*] I meant no hoffence by it. A clorgyman is privileged to be a bit of a fool, you know: it's ony becomin in 'is profession that he should. Anyhow, I come here, not to rake up hold differences, but to let bygones be bygones. [*Suddenly becoming very solemn, and approaching* MORELL] James: three years ago, you done me a hil turn. You done me hout of a contrac; an when I gev you arsh words in my natural disappointment, you turned my daughrter again me. Well, I've come to hact the part of a Kerischin. [*Offering his hand*] I forgive you, James.

MORELL [*starting up*]. Confound your impudence!

BURGESS [*retreating, with almost lachrymose depreciation of his treatment*]. Is that becomin language for a clorgyman, James? And you so particlar, too!

MORELL [*hotly*]. No, sir: it is not becoming language for a clergyman. I used the wrong word. I should have said damn your impudence: that's what St. Paul or any honest priest would have said to you. Do you think I have forgotten that tender of yours for the contract to supply clothing to the workhouse?

BURGESS [*in a paroxysm of public spirit*]. I hacted in the hinterest of the ratepayers, James. It was the lowest tender: you carn't deny that.

MORELL. Yes, the lowest, because you paid worse wages than any other employer—starvation wages—aye, worse than starvation wages—to the women who made the clothing. Your wages would have driven them to the streets to keep body and soul together. [*Getting angrier and angrier*] Those women were my parishioners. I shamed the Guardians out of accepting your tender. I shamed the ratepayers out of letting them do it: I shamed everybody but you. [*Boiling over*] How dare you, sir, come here and offer to forgive me, and talk about your daughter, and—

BURGESS. Heasy, James! heasy! heasy! Don't git hinto a fluster about nothink. I've howned I was wrong.

MORELL. Have you? I didn't hear you.

BURGESS. Of course I did. I hown it now. Come: I harsk your pardon for the letter I wrote you. Is that enough?

MORELL [*snapping his fingers*]. That's nothing. Have you raised the wages?

BURGESS [*triumphantly*]. Yes.

MORELL. What!

BURGESS [*unctuously*]. I've turned a moddle hemployer. I don't hemploy no women now: they're all sacked; and the work is done by machinery. Not a man 'as less than sixpence a *h*our; and the skilled ands gits the Trade Union rate. [*Proudly*] What ave you to say to me now?

MORELL [*overwhelmed*]. Is it possible! Well, there's more joy in heaven over one sinner that repenteth!—[*Going to* BURGESS *with an explosion of apologetic cordiality*] My dear Burgess: how splendid of you! I most heartily beg your pardon for my hard thoughts. [*Grasping his hand*] And now, don't you feel the better for the change? Come! confess! you're happier. You look happier.

BURGESS [*ruefully*]. Well, praps I do. I spose I must, since you notice it. At all events, I git my contrax assepted by the County Council. [*Savagely*] They dussent ave nothink to do with me unless I paid fair wages: curse em for a parcel o meddlin fools!

MORELL [*dropping his hand, utterly discouraged*]. So that was why you raised the wages! [*He sits down moodily.*]

BURGESS [*severely, in spreading, mounting tones*]. Woy helse should I do it? What does it lead to but drink and huppishness in workin men? [*He seats himself magisterially in the easy chair.*] It's hall very well for you, James: it gits you hinto the papers and makes a great man of you; but you never think of the arm you do, puttin money into the pockets of workin men that they dunno ow to spend, and takin it from people that might be makin a good huse on it.

MORELL [*with a heavy sigh, speaking with cold politeness*]. What is your business with me this morning? I shall not pretend to believe that you are here merely out of family sentiment.

BURGESS [*obstinately*]. Yes I ham: just family sentiment and nothink helse.

MORELL [*with weary calm*]. I don't believe you.

BURGESS [*rising threateningly*]. Don't say that to me again, James Mavor Morell.

MORELL [*unmoved*]. I'll say it just as often as may be necessary to convince you that it's true. I don't believe you.

BURGESS [*collapsing into an abyss of wounded feeling*]. Oh, well, if you're determined to be hunfriendly, I spose I'd better go. [*He moves reluctantly towards the door.* MORELL *makes no sign. He lingers.*] didn't hexpect to find a hunforgivin spirit in you, James. [MORELL *still not responding, he takes a few more reluctant steps doorwards. Then he comes back, whining.*] We huseter git on well enough, spite of our different hopinions. Woy are you so changed to me? I give you my word I come here in peeorr [pure] frenliness, not wishin to be hon bad terms with my hown daughrter's usban. Come, James: be a Kerischin, and shake ands. [*He puts his hand sentimentally on* MORELL's *shoulder.*]

MORELL [*looking up at him thoughtfully*]. Look here, Burgess. Do you want to be as welcome here as you were before you lost that contract?

BURGESS I do, James. I do—honest.

MORELL. Then why don't you behave as you did then?

BURGESS [*cautiously removing his hand*]. Ow d'y'mean?

MORELL. I'll tell you. You thought me a young fool then.

BURGESS [*coaxingly*]. No I didn't, James. I—

MORELL [*cutting him short*]. Yes, you did. And I thought you an old scoundrel.

BURGESS [*most vehemently deprecating this gross self-accusation on* MORELL's *part*]. No you didn't, James. Now you do yourself a hinjustice.

MORELL. Yes I did. Well, that did not prevent our getting on very well together. God made you what I call a scoundrel as He made me what you call a fool.

[*The effect of this observation on* BURGESS *is to remove the keystone of his moral arch. He becomes bodily weak, and, with his eyes fixed on* MORELL *in a helpless stare, puts out his hand apprehensively to balance himself, as if the floor had suddenly sloped under him.* MORELL *proceeds, in the same tone of quiet conviction*]

It was not for me to quarrel with His handiwork in the one case more than in the other. So long as you come here honestly as a self-respecting, thorough, convinced scoundrel, justifying your scoundrelism and proud of it, you are welcome. But [*and now* MORELL's *tone becomes formidable; and he rises and strikes the back of the chair for greater emphasis*] I won't have you here snivelling about being a model employer and a converted man when you're only an apostate with your coat turned for the sake of a County Council contract.

[*He nods at him to enforce the point; then goes to the hearth-rug, where he takes up a comfortably commanding position with his back to the fire, and continues*]

No: I like a man to be true to himself, even in wickedness. Come now: either take your hat and go; or else sit down and give me a good scoundrelly reason for wanting to be friends with me.

[BURGESS, *whose emotions have subsided sufficiently to be expressed by a dazed grin, is relieved by this concrete proposition. He ponders it for a moment, and then, slowly and very modestly, sits down in the chair* MORELL *has just left.*]

That's right. Now out with it.

BURGESS [*chuckling in spite of himself*]. Well, you orr a queer bird, James, and no mistake. But [*almost enthusiastically*] one carn't elp likin you: besides, as I said afore, of course one don't take hall a clorgyman says seriously, or the world couldn't go on. Could it now?

[*He composes himself for graver discourse, and, turning his eyes on* MORELL, *proceeds with dull seriousness*]

Well, I don't mind tellin you, since it's your wish we should be free with one another, that I did think you a bit of a fool once; but I'm beginnin to think that praps I was be'ind the times a bit.

MORELL [*exultant*]. Aha! You're finding that out at last, are you?

BURGESS [*portentously*]. Yes: times 'as changed mor'n I could a believed. Five yorr [year] ago, no sensible man would a thought of takin hup with your hideas. I hused to wonder you was let preach at all. Why, I know a clorgyman what 'as bin kep hout of his job for yorrs by the Bishop o London, although the pore feller's not a bit more religious than you are. But today, if hennyone was to horffer to bet me a thousan poun that you'll hend by bein a bishop yourself, I dussent take the bet. [*Very impressively*] You and your crew are gitting hinfluential: I can see that. They'll ave to give you somethink someday, if it's honly to stop your mouth. You ad the right instinc arter all, James: the line you took is the payin line in the long run for a man o your sort.

MORELL [*offering his hand with thorough decision*]. Shake hands, Burgess. Now you're talking honestly. I don't think they'll make me a bishop; but if they do, I'll introduce you to the biggest jobbers I can get to come to my dinner parties.

BURGESS [*who has risen with a sheepish grin and accepted the hand o friendship*]. You will ave your joke, James. Our quarrel's made up now, ain it?

A WOMAN'S VOICE. Say yes, James.

[*Startled, they turn quickly and find that* CANDIDA *has just come in and is looking at them with an amused maternal indulgence which is her characteristic expression. She is a woman of 33, well built well nourished, likely, one guesses, to become matronly later on, bu now quite at her best, with the double charm of youth and mother hood. Her ways are those of a woman who has found that she ca always manage people by engaging their affection, and who does s frankly and instinctively without the smallest scruple. So far, sh is like any other pretty woman who is just clever enough to mak the most of her sexual attractions for trivially selfish ends; bu* CANDIDA'S *serene brow, courageous eyes, and well set mouth and chi signify largeness of mind and dignity of character to ennoble he cunning in the affections. A wise-hearted observer, looking at he would at once guess that whoever had placed the* Virgin of the A*] sumption *over her hearth did so because he fancied some spiritual resemblance between them, and yet would not suspect either her husband or herself of any such idea, or indeed of any concern with the art of Titian.*

[*Just now she is in bonnet and mantle, carrying a strapped rug with her umbrella stuck through it, a hand-bag, and a supply of illustrated papers.*]

MORELL [*shocked at his remissness*]. Candida! Why—[*he looks at his watch, and is horrified to find it so late*]. My darling! [*Hurrying to her and seizing the rug strap, pouring forth his remorseful regrets all the time*] I intended to meet you at the train. I let the time slip. [*Flinging the rug on the sofa*] I was so engrossed by—[*returning to her*]—I forgot —oh! [*He embraces her with penitent emotion.*]

BURGESS [*a little shamefaced and doubtful of his reception*]. How orr you, Candy? [*She, still in* MORELL's *arms, offers him her cheek, which he kisses.*] James and me is come to an unnerstannin. A honorable unnerstannin. Ain we, James?

MORELL [*impetuously*]. Oh bother your understanding! you've kept me late for Candida. [*With compassionate fervor*] My poor love: how did you manage about the luggage? How—

CANDIDA [*stopping him and disengaging herself*]. There! there! there! I wasn't alone. Eugene has been down with us; and we travelled together.

MORELL [*pleased*]. Eugene!

CANDIDA. Yes: he's struggling with my luggage, poor boy. Go out, dear, at once; or he'll pay for the cab; and I don't want that.

[MORELL *hurries out.* CANDIDA *puts down her handbag; then takes off her mantle and bonnet and puts them on the sofa with the rug, chatting meanwhile.*]

Vell, papa: how are you getting on at home?

BURGESS. The ouse ain't worth livin in since you left it, Candy. I wish you'd come round an give the gurl a talkin to. Who's this Eugene nat's come with you?

CANDIDA. Oh, Eugene's one of James's discoveries. He found him eeping on the Embankment last June. Haven't you noticed our new icture [*pointing to the Virgin*]? He gave us that.

BURGESS [*incredulously*]. Garn! D'you mean to tell me—your hown ather!—that cab touts or such like, orf the Embankment, buys pictures ke that? [*Severely*] Don't deceive me, Candy: it's a 'Igh Church icture; and James chose it hisself.

CANDIDA. Guess again. Eugene isn't a cab tout.

BURGESS. Then what is he? [*Sarcastically*] A nobleman, I spose.

CANDIDA [*nodding delightedly*].   Yes. His uncle's a peer! A real live earl.

BURGESS [*not daring to believe such good news*].   No!

CANDIDA.   Yes. He had a seven day bill for £55 in his pocket when James found him on the Embankment. He thought he couldn't get any money for it until the seven days were up; and he was too shy to ask for credit. Oh, he's a dear boy! We are very fond of him.

BURGESS [*pretending to belittle the aristocracy, but with his eyes gleaming*].   Mm! I thort you wouldn't git a hearl's nevvy visitin in Victawriar Pawrk unless he were a bit of a flat. [*Looking again at the picture*] Of course I don't old with that picture, Candy; but still it's a 'igh class fust rate work of ort: I can see that. Be sure you hintroduce me to im, Candy. [*He looks at his watch anxiously.*] I can ony stay about two minutes.

[MORELL *comes back with* EUGENE, *whom* BURGESS *contemplates moist-eyed with enthusiasm. He is a strange, shy youth of eighteen, slight, effeminate, with a delicate childish voice, and a hunted tormented expression and shrinking manner that show the painful sensitiveness of very swift and acute apprehensiveness in youth, before the character has grown to its full strength. Miserably irresolute, he does not know where to stand or what to do. He is afraid of* BURGESS, *and would run away into solitude if he dared, but the very intensity with which he feels a perfectly commonplace position comes from excessive nervous force; and his nostrils, mouth and eyes betray a fiercely petulant wilfulness, as to the bent of which his brow, already lined with pity, is reassuring. He is so uncommon as to be almost unearthly; and to prosaic people there is something noxious in this unearthliness, just as to poetic people there is something angelic in it. His dress is anarchic. He wears an old blue serge jacket, unbuttoned, over a woolen lawn tennis shirt, with silk handkerchief for a cravat, trousers matching the jacket, an brown canvas shoes. In these garments he has apparently lain in th heather and waded through the waters; and there is no evidence o his having ever brushed them.*

[*As he catches sight of a stranger on entering, he stops, and edge along the wall on the opposite side of the room.*]

MORELL [*as he enters*].   Come along: you can spare us quarter of a hour at all events. This is my father-in-law. Mr. Burgess—Mr. March banks.

MARCHBANKS [*nervously backing against the bookcase*].   Glad to mee you, sir.

BURGESS [*crossing to him with great heartiness, whilst* MORELL joir CANDIDA *at the fire*].   Glad to meet you, I'm shore, Mr. Morchbank

[*Forcing him to shake hands*] Ow do you find yoreself this weather? Ope you ain't lettin James put no foolish ideas into your ed?

MARCHBANKS. Foolish ideas? Oh, you mean Socialism? No.

BURGESS. That's right. [*Again looking at his watch*] Well, I must go now: there's no elp for it. Yore not comin my way, orr you, Mr. Morchbanks?

MARCHBANKS. Which way is that?

BURGESS. Victawriar Pawrk Station. There's a city train at 12.25.

MORELL. Nonsense. Eugene will stay to lunch with us, I expect.

MARCHBANKS [*anxiously excusing himself*]. No—I—I—

BURGESS. Well, well, I shorn't press you: I bet you'd rather lunch with Candy. Some night, I ope, you'll come and dine with me at my club, the Freeman Founders in Nortn Folgit. Come: say you will!

MARCHBANKS. Thank you, Mr. Burgess. Where is Norton Folgate? Down in Surrey, isn't it?

[BURGESS, *inexpressibly tickled, begins to splutter with laughter.*]

CANDIDA [*coming to the rescue*]. You'll lose your train, papa, if you don't go at once. Come back in the afternoon and tell Mr. Marchbanks where to find the club.

BURGESS [*roaring with glee*]. Down in Surrey! Har, har! that's not a bad one. Well, I never met a man as didn't know Nortn Folgit afore. [*Abashed at his own noisiness*] Good-bye, Mr. Morchbanks: I know yore too 'ighbred to take my pleasantry in bad part. [*He again offers his hand.*]

MARCHBANKS [*taking it with a nervous jerk*]. Not at all.

BURGESS. Bye, bye, Candy. I'll look in again later on. So long, James.

MORELL. Must you go?

BURGESS. Don't stir.

[*He goes out with unabated heartiness.*]

MORELL. Oh, I'll see you off.

[*He follows him.*]

[EUGENE *stares after them apprehensively, holding his breath until* BURGESS *disappears.*]

CANDIDA [*laughing*]. Well, Eugene? [*He turns with a start, and comes eagerly towards her, but stops irresolutely as he meets her amused look.*] What do you think of my father?

MARCHBANKS. I—I hardly know him yet. He seems to be a very nice old gentleman.

CANDIDA [*with gentle irony*]. And you'll go to the Freeman Founders to dine with him, won't you?

MARCHBANKS [*miserably, taking it quite seriously*]. Yes, if it will please you.

CANDIDA [*touched*]. Do you know, you are a very nice boy, Eugene, with all your queerness. If you had laughed at my father I shouldn't have minded; but I like you ever so much better for being nice to him.

MARCHBANKS. Ought I to have laughed? I noticed that he said something funny; but I am so ill at ease with strangers; and I never can see a joke. I'm very sorry.

[*He sits down on the sofa, his elbows on his knees and his temples between his fists, with an expression of hopeless suffering.*]

CANDIDA [*bustling him goodnaturedly*]. Oh come! You great baby, you! You are worse than usual this morning. Why were you so melancholy as we came along in the cab?

MARCHBANKS. Oh, that was nothing. I was wondering how much I ought to give the cabman. I know it's utterly silly; but you don't know how dreadful such things are to me—how I shrink from having to deal with strange people. [*Quickly and reassuringly*] But it's all right. He beamed all over and touched his hat when Morell gave him two shillings. I was on the point of offering him ten.

[MORELL *comes back with a few letters and newspapers which have come by the midday post.*]

CANDIDA. Oh, James dear, he was going to give the cabman ten shillings! Ten shillings for a three minutes drive! Oh dear!

MORELL [*at the table, glancing through the letters*]. Never mind her, Marchbanks. The overpaying instinct is a generous one: better than the underpaying instinct, and not so common.

MARCHBANKS [*relapsing into dejection*]. No: cowardice, incompetence. Mrs. Morell's quite right.

CANDIDA. Of course she is. [*She takes up her hand-bag.*] And now I must leave you to James for the present. I suppose you are too much of a poet to know the state a woman finds her house in when she's been away for three weeks. Give me my rug.

[EUGENE *takes the strapped rug from the couch, and gives it to her. She takes it in her left hand, having the bag in her right.*]

Now hang my cloak across my arm. [*He obeys.*] Now my hat. [*He puts it into the hand which has the bag.*] Now open the door for me. [*He hurries before her and opens the door.*] Thanks.

[*She goes out; and* MARCHBANKS *shuts the door.*]

MORELL [*still busy at the table*]. You'll stay to lunch, Marchbanks, of course.

MARCHBANKS [*scared*]. I mustn't. [*He glances quickly at* MORELL *but at once avoids his frank look, and adds, with obvious disingenuousness*] I mean I can't.

MORELL. You mean you won't.

MARCHBANKS [*earnestly*]. No: I should like to, indeed. Thank you very much. But—but—

MORELL. But—but—but—but—Bosh! If you'd like to stay, stay. If you're shy, go and take a turn in the park and write poetry until half past one; and then come in and have a good feed.

MARCHBANKS. Thank you, I should like that very much. But I really mustn't. The truth is, Mrs. Morell told me not to. She said she didn't think you'd ask me to stay to lunch, but that I was to remember, if you did, that you didn't really want me to. [*Plaintively*] She said I'd understand; but I don't. Please don't tell her I told you.

MORELL [*drolly*]. Oh, is that all? Won't my suggestion that you should take a turn in the park meet the difficulty?

MARCHBANKS. How?

MORELL [*exploding good-humoredly*]. Why, you duffer— [*But this boisterousness jars himself as well as* EUGENE. *He checks himself.*] No: I won't put it in that way. [*He comes to* EUGENE *with affectionate seriousness.*] My dear lad: in a happy marriage like ours, there is something very sacred in the return of the wife to her home.

[MARCHBANKS *looks quickly at him, half anticipating his meaning.*]

An old friend or a truly noble and sympathetic soul is not in the way on such occasions; but a chance visitor is.

[*The hunted horror-stricken expression comes out with sudden vividness in* EUGENE's *face as he understands.* MORELL, *occupied with his own thoughts, goes on without noticing this.*]

Candida thought I would rather not have you here; but she was wrong. I'm very fond of you, my boy; and I should like you to see for yourself what a happy thing it is to be married as I am.

MARCHBANKS. Happy! Your marriage! You think that! You believe that!

MORELL [*buoyantly*]. I know it, my lad. La Rochefoucauld said that there are convenient marriages but no delightful ones. You don't know the comfort of seeing through and through a thundering liar and rotten cynic like that fellow. Ha! ha! Now, off with you to the park, and write your poem. Half past one, sharp, mind: we never wait for anybody.

MARCHBANKS [*wildly*]. No: stop: you shan't. I'll force it into the light.

MORELL [*puzzled*]. Eh? Force what?

MARCHBANKS. I must speak to you. There is something that must be settled between us.

MORELL [*with a whimsical glance at his watch*]. Now?

MARCHBANKS [*passionately*]. Now. Before you leave this room. [*He retreats a few steps, and stands as if to bar* MORELL's *way to the door.*]

MORELL [*without moving, and gravely, perceiving now that there is something serious the matter*]. I'm not going to leave it, my dear boy: I thought you were.

[EUGENE, *baffled by his firm tone, turns his back on him, writhing with anger.* MORELL *goes to him and puts his hand on his shoulder strongly and kindly, disregarding his attempt to shake it off.*]

Come: sit down quietly; and tell me what it is. And remember: we are friends, and need not fear that either of us will be anything but patient and kind to the other, whatever we may have to say.

MARCHBANKS [*twisting himself round on him*]. Oh, I am not forgetting myself: I am only [*covering his face desperately with his hands*] full of horror. [*Then, dropping his hands, and thrusting his face forward fiercely at* MORELL, *he goes on threateningly*] You shall see whether this is a time for patience and kindness.

[MORELL, *firm as a rock, looks indulgently at him.*]

Don't look at me in that self-complacent way. You think yourself stronger than I am; but I shall stagger you if you have a heart in your breast.

MORELL [*powerfully confident*]. Stagger me, my boy. Out with it.

MARCHBANKS. First—

MORELL. First?

MARCHBANKS. I love your wife.

[MORELL *recoils, and, after staring at him for a moment in utter amazement, bursts into uncontrollable laughter.* EUGENE *is taken aback, but not disconcerted; and he soon becomes indignant and contemptuous.*]

MORELL [*sitting down to have his laugh out*]. Why, my dear child, of course you do. Everybody loves her: they can't help it. I like it. But [*looking up jocosely at him*] I say, Eugene: do you think yours is a case to be talked about? You're under twenty: she's over thirty. Doesn't it look rather too like a case of calf love?

MARCHBANKS [*vehemently*]. You dare say that of her! You think that way of the love she inspires! It is an insult to her!

MORELL [*rising quickly, in an altered tone*]. To her! Eugene: take care. I have been patient. I hope to remain patient. But there are some things I won't allow. Don't force me to show you the indulgence I should show to a child. Be a man.

MARCHBANKS [*with a gesture as if sweeping something behind him*]. Oh, let us put aside all that cant. It horrifies me when I think of the doses of it she has had to endure in all the weary years during which you have selfishly and blindly sacrificed her to minister to your self-sufficiency: you! [*turning on him*] who have not one thought—one sense—in common with her.

MORELL [*philosophically*]. She seems to bear it pretty well. [*Looking him straight in the face*] Eugene, my boy: you are making a fool of yourself: a very great fool of yourself. There's a piece of wholesome plain speaking for you.

[*He knocks in the lesson with a nod in his old way, and posts himself on the hearthrug, holding his hands behind him to warm them.*]

MARCHBANKS. Oh, do you think I don't know all that? Do you think that the things people make fools of themselves about are any less real and true than the things they behave sensibly about?

[MORELL's *gaze wavers for the first time. He forgets to warm his hands, and stands listening, startled and thoughtful.*]

They are more true: they are the only things that are true. You are very calm and sensible and moderate with me because you can see that I am a fool about your wife; just as no doubt that old man who was here just now is very wise over your Socialism, because he sees that you are a fool about it.

[MORELL's *perplexity deepens markedly.* EUGENE *follows up his advantage, plying him fiercely with questions.*]

Does that prove you wrong? Does your complacent superiority to me prove that *I* am wrong?

MORELL. Marchbanks: some devil is putting these words into your mouth. It is easy—terribly easy—to shake a man's faith in himself. To take advantage of that to break a man's spirit is devil's work. Take care of what you are doing. Take care.

MARCHBANKS [*ruthlessly*]. I know. I'm doing it on purpose. I told you I should stagger you.

[*They confront one another threateningly for a moment. Then* MORELL *recovers his dignity.*]

MORELL [*with noble tenderness*]. Eugene: listen to me. Some day, I hope and trust, you will be a happy man like me.

[EUGENE *chafes intolerantly, repudiating the worth of his happiness.* MORELL, *deeply insulted, controls himself with fine forbearance, and continues steadily with great artistic beauty of delivery*]

You will be married; and you will be working with all your might and valor to make every spot on earth as happy as your own home. You

will be one of the makers of the Kingdom of Heaven on earth; and—
who knows?—you may be a master builder where I am only a humble
journeyman; for don't think, my boy, that I cannot see in you, young
as you are, promise of higher powers than I can ever pretend to. I well
know that it is in the poet that the holy spirit of man—the god within
him—is most godlike. It should make you tremble to think of that—to
think that the heavy burthen and great gift of a poet may be laid upon
you.

MARCHBANKS [*unimpressed and remorseless, his boyish crudity of assertion telling sharply against* MORELL's *oratory*]. It does not make me
tremble. It is the want of it in others that makes me tremble.

MORELL [*redoubling his force of style under the stimulus of his genuine feeling and* EUGENE's *obduracy*]. Then help to kindle it in them—
in me—not to extinguish it. In the future, when you are as happy as
I am, I will be your true brother in the faith. I will help you to believe
that God has given us a world that nothing but our own folly keeps from
being a paradise. I will help you to believe that every stroke of your
work is sowing happiness for the great harvest that all—even the humblest—shall one day reap. And last, but trust me, not least, I will help
you to believe that your wife loves you and is happy in her home. We
need such help, Marchbanks: we need it greatly and always. There are
so many things to make us doubt, if once we let our understanding
be troubled. Even at home, we sit as if in camp, encompassed by a
hostile army of doubts. Will you play the traitor and let them in
on me?

MARCHBANKS [*looking round wildly*]. Is it like this for her here
always? A woman, with a great soul, craving for reality, truth, freedom;
and being fed on metaphors, sermons, stale perorations, mere rhetoric.
Do you think a woman's soul can live on your talent for preaching?

MORELL [*stung*]. Marchbanks: you make it hard for me to control
myself. My talent is like yours insofar as it has any real worth at all.
It is the gift of finding words for divine truth.

MARCHBANKS [*impetuously*]. It's the gift of the gab, nothing more
and nothing less. What has your knack of fine talking to do with the
truth, any more than playing the organ has? I've never been in your
church; but I've been to your political meetings; and I've seen you do
what's called rousing the meeting to enthusiasm: that is, you excited
them until they behaved exactly as if they were drunk. And their wives
looked on and saw what fools they were. Oh, it's an old story; you'll
find it in the Bible. I imagine King David, in his fits of enthusiasm,
was very like you. [*Stabbing him with the words*] "But his wife despised him in her heart."

MORELL [*wrathfully*]. Leave my house. Do you hear?

[*He advances on him threateningly.*]

MARCHBANKS [*shrinking back against the couch*]. Let me alone.
Don't touch me.

> [MORELL *grasps him powerfully by the lapel of his coat: he cowers down on the sofa and screams passionately*]

Stop, Morell: if you strike me, I'll kill myself: I won't bear it. [*Almost in hysterics*] Let me go. Take your hand away.

MORELL [*with slow emphatic scorn*]. You little snivelling cowardly
whelp. [*He releases him.*] Go, before you frighten yourself into a fit.

MARCHBANKS [*on the sofa, gasping, but relieved by the withdrawal of*
MORELL'*s hand*]. I'm not afraid of you: it's you who are afraid of me.

MORELL [*quietly, as he stands over him*]. It looks like it, doesn't it?

MARCHBANKS [*with petulant vehemence*]. Yes, it does.

> [MORELL *turns away contemptuously.* EUGENE *scrambles to his feet and follows him.*]

You think because I shrink from being brutally handled—because [*with tears in his voice*] I can do nothing but cry with rage when I am met with violence—because I can't lift a heavy trunk down from the top of a cab like you—because I can't fight you for your wife as a drunken navvy would: all that makes you think I'm afraid of you. But you're wrong. If I haven't got what you call British pluck, I haven't British cowardice either: I'm not afraid of a clergyman's ideas. I'll fight your ideas. I'll rescue her from her slavery to them. I'll pit my own ideas against them. You are driving me out of the house because you daren't let her choose between your ideas and mine. You are afraid to let me see her again.

> [MORELL, *angered, turns suddenly on him. He flies to the door in involuntary dread.*]

Let me alone, I say. I'm going.

MORELL [*with cold scorn*]. Wait a moment: I am not going to touch you: don't be afraid. When my wife comes back she will want to know why you have gone. And when she finds that you are never going to cross our threshold again, she will want to have that explained too. Now I don't wish to distress her by telling her that you have behaved like a blackguard.

MARCHBANKS [*coming back with renewed vehemence*]. You shall. You must. If you give any explanation but the true one, you are a liar and a coward. Tell her what I said; and how you were strong and manly, and shook me as a terrier shakes a rat; and how I shrank and was terrified; and how you called me a snivelling little whelp and put me out of the house. If you don't tell her, I will: I'll write it to her.

MORELL [*puzzled*]. Why do you want her to know this?

MARCHBANKS [*with lyric rapture*]. Because she will understand me, and know that I understand her. If you keep back one word of it from her—if you are not ready to lay the truth at her feet as I am—then you will know to the end of your days that she really belongs to me and not to you. Good-bye. [*Going.*]

MORELL [*terribly disquieted*]. Stop: I will not tell her.

MARCHBANKS [*turning near the door*]. Either the truth or a lie you must tell her, if I go.

MORELL [*temporizing*]. Marchbanks: it is sometimes justifiable—

MARCHBANKS [*cutting him short*]. I know: to lie. It will be useless. Good-bye, Mr. Clergyman.

[*As he turns to the door, it opens and* CANDIDA *enters in her house-keeping dress.*]

CANDIDA. Are you going, Eugene? [*Looking more observantly at him*] Well, dear me, just look at you, going out into the street in that state! You are a poet, certainly. Look at him, James! [*She takes him by the coat, and brings him forward, showing him to* MORELL.] Look at his collar! look at his tie! look at his hair! One would think some-body had been throttling you.

[EUGENE *instinctively rises to look round at* MORELL; *but she pulls him back.*]

Here! Stand still. [*She buttons his collar; ties his neckerchief in a bow; and arranges his hair.*] There! Now you look so nice that I think you'd better stay to lunch after all, though I told you you mustn't. It will be ready in half an hour. [*She puts a final touch to the bow. He kisses her hand.*] Don't be silly.

MARCHBANKS. I want to stay, of course; unless the reverend gentleman your husband has anything to advance to the contrary.

CANDIDA. Shall he stay, James, if he promises to be a good boy and help me to lay the table?

MORELL [*shortly*]. Oh yes, certainly: he had better.

[*He goes to the table and pretends to busy himself with his papers there.*]

MARCHBANKS [*offering his arm to* CANDIDA]. Come and lay the table.

[*She takes it. They go to the door together. As they pass out he adds*]

I am the happiest of mortals.

MORELL. So was I—an hour ago.

ACT II

THE SAME DAY *later in the afternoon. The same room. The chair for visitors has been replaced at the table.* MARCHBANKS, *alone and idle, is trying to find out how the typewriter works. Hearing someone at the door, he steals guiltily away to the window and pretends to be absorbed in the view.* MISS GARNETT, *carrying the notebook in which she takes down Morell's letters in shorthand from his dictation, sits down at the typewriter and sets to work transcribing them, much too busy to notice* EUGENE. *When she begins the second line she stops and stares at the machine. Something wrong evidently.*

PROSERPINE. Bother! You've been meddling with my typewriter, Mr. Marchbanks; and there's not the least use in your trying to look as if you hadn't.

MARCHBANKS [*timidly*]. I'm very sorry, Miss Garnett. I only tried to make it write. [*Plaintively*] But it wouldn't.

PROSERPINE. Well, you've altered the spacing.

MARCHBANKS [*earnestly*]. I assure you I didn't. I didn't indeed. I only turned a little wheel. It gave a sort of click.

PROSERPINE. Oh, now I understand. [*She restores the spacing, talking volubly all the time.*] I suppose you thought it was a sort of barrel-organ. Nothing to do but turn the handle, and it would write a beautiful love letter for you straight off, eh?

MARCHBANKS [*seriously*]. I suppose a machine could be made to write love letters. They're all the same, aren't they?

PROSERPINE [*somewhat indignantly: any such discussion, except by way of pleasantry, being outside her code of manners*]. How do I know? Why do you ask me?

MARCHBANKS. I beg your pardon. I thought clever people—people who can do business and write letters and that sort of thing—always had to have love affairs to keep them from going mad.

PROSERPINE [*rising, outraged*]. Mr. Marchbanks! [*She looks severely at him, and marches majestically to the bookcase.*]

MARCHBANKS [*approaching her humbly*]. I hope I haven't offended you. Perhaps I shouldn't have alluded to your love affairs.

PROSERPINE [*plucking a blue book from the shelf and turning sharply on him*]. I haven't any love affairs. How dare you say such a thing? The idea!

[*She tucks the book under her arm, and is flouncing back to her machine when he addresses her with awakened interest and sympathy.*]

MARCHBANKS. Really! Oh, then you are shy, like me.

PROSERPINE. Certainly I am not shy. What do you mean?

MARCHBANKS [*secretly*]. You must be: that is the reason there are so few love affairs in the world. We all go about longing for love: it is the first need of our natures, the first prayer of our hearts; but we dare not utter our longing: we are too shy. [*Very earnestly*] Oh, Miss Garnett, what would you not give to be without fear, without shame—

PROSERPINE [*scandalized*]. Well, upon my word!

MARCHBANKS [*with petulant impatience*]. Ah, don't say those stupid things to me: they don't deceive me: what use are they? Why are you afraid to be your real self with me? I am just like you.

PROSERPINE. Like me! Pray are you flattering me or flattering yourself? I don't feel quite sure which. [*She again rises to get back to her work.*]

MARCHBANKS [*stopping her mysteriously*]. Hush! I go about in search of love; and I find it in unmeasured stores in the bosoms of others. But when I try to ask for it, this horrible shyness strangles me; and I stand dumb, or worse than dumb, saying meaningless things: foolish lies. And I see the affection I am longing for given to dogs and cats and pet birds, because they come and ask for it. [*Almost whispering*] It must be asked for: it is like a ghost: it cannot speak unless it is first spoken to. [*At his usual pitch, but with deep melancholy*] All the love in the world is longing to speak; only it dare not, because it is shy! shy! shy! That is the world's tragedy.

[*With a deep sigh he sits in the visitors' chair and buries his face in his hands.*]

PROSERPINE [*amazed, but keeping her wits about her: her point of honor in encounters with strange young men*]. Wicked people get over that shyness occasionally, don't they?

MARCHBANKS [*scrambling up almost fiercely*]. Wicked people means people who have no love: therefore they have no shame. They have the power to ask for love because they don't need it: they have the power to offer it because they have none to give. [*He collapses into his seat, and adds, mournfully*] But we, who have love, and long to mingle it with the love of others: we cannot utter a word. [*Timidly*] You find that, don't you?

PROSERPINE. Look here: if you don't stop talking like this, I'll leave the room, Mr. Marchbanks: I really will. It's not proper.

[*She resumes her seat at the typewriter, opening the blue book and preparing to copy a passage from it.*]

MARCHBANKS [*hopelessly*]. Nothing that's worth saying is proper. [*He rises, and wanders about the room in his lost way.*] I can't understand you, Miss Garnett. What am I to talk about?

PROSERPINE [*snubbing him*]. Talk about indifferent things. Talk about the weather.

MARCHBANKS. Would you talk about indifferent things if a child were by, crying bitterly with hunger?

PROSERPINE. I suppose not.

MARCHBANKS. Well: *I* can't talk about indifferent things with my heart crying out bitterly in its hunger.

PROSERPINE. Then hold your tongue.

MARCHBANKS. Yes: that is what it always comes to. We hold our tongues. Does that stop the cry of your heart? for it does cry: doesn't it? It must, if you have a heart.

PROSERPINE [*suddenly rising with her hand pressed on her heart*]. Oh, it's no use trying to work while you talk like that.

[*She leaves her little table and sits on the sofa. Her feelings are keenly stirred.*]

It's no business of yours whether my heart cries or not; but I have a mind to tell you, for all that.

MARCHBANKS. You needn't. I know already that it must.

PROSERPINE. But mind! if you ever say I said so, I'll deny it.

MARCHBANKS [*compassionately*]. Yes, I know. And so you haven't the courage to tell him?

PROSERPINE [*bouncing up*]. Him! Who?

MARCHBANKS. Whoever he is. The man you love. It might be anybody. The curate, Mr. Mill, perhaps.

PROSERPINE [*with disdain*]. Mr. Mill!!! A fine man to break my heart about, indeed! I'd rather have you than Mr. Mill.

MARCHBANKS [*recoiling*]. No, really: I'm very sorry; but you mustn't think of that. I—

PROSERPINE [*testily, going to the fire-place and standing at it with her back to him*]. Oh, don't be frightened: it's not you. It's not any one particular person.

MARCHBANKS. I know. You feel that you could love anybody that offered—

PROSERPINE [*turning, exasperated*]. Anybody that offered! No, I do not. What do you take me for?

MARCHBANKS [*discouraged*]. No use. You won't make me real answers: only those things that everybody says.

[*He strays to the sofa and sits down disconsolately.*]

PROSERPINE [*nettled at what she takes to be a disparagement of her manners by an aristocrat*]. Oh well, if you want original conversation, you'd better go and talk to yourself.

MARCHBANKS. That is what all poets do: they talk to themselves out loud; and the world overhears them. But it's horribly lonely not to hear someone else talk sometimes.

PROSERPINE. Wait until Mr. Morell comes. He'll talk to you.

[MARCHBANK *shudders.*]

Oh, you needn't make wry faces over him: he can talk better than you. [*With temper*] He'd talk your little head off.

[*She is going back angrily to her place, when he, suddenly enlightened, springs up and stops her.*]

MARCHBANKS. Ah! I understand now.

PROSERPINE [*reddening*]. What do you understand?

MARCHBANKS. Your secret. Tell me: is it really and truly possible for a woman to love him?

PROSERPINE [*as if this were beyond all bounds*]. Well!!

MARCHBANKS [*passionately*]. No: answer me. I want to know: I must know. *I* can't understand it. I can see nothing in him but words, pious resolutions, what people call goodness. You can't love that.

PROSERPINE [*attempting to snub him by an air of cool propriety*]. I simply don't know what you're talking about. I don't understand you.

MARCHBANKS [*vehemently*]. You do. You lie.

PROSERPINE. Oh!

MARCHBANKS. You do understand; and you know. [*Determined to have an answer*] Is it possible for a woman to love him?

PROSERPINE [*looking him straight in the face*]. Yes.

[*He covers his face with his hands.*]

Whatever is the matter with you!

[*He takes down his hands. Frightened at the tragic mask presented to her, she hurries past him at the utmost possible distance, keeping her eyes on his face until he turns from her and goes to the child's chair beside the hearth, where he sits in the deepest dejection. As she approaches the door, it opens and* BURGESS *enters. Seeing him, she ejaculates, "Praise heaven! here's somebody" and feels safe enough to resume her place at her table. She puts a fresh sheet of paper into the typewriter as* BURGESS *crosses to* EUGENE.]

BURGESS [*bent on taking care of the distinguished visitor*]. Well: so this is the way they leave you to yourself, Mr. Morchbanks. I've come to keep you company.

[MARCHBANKS *looks up at him in consternation, which is quite lost on him.*]

James is receivin a deppitation in the dinin room; and Candy is hupstairs heducating of a young stitcher gurl she's hinterested in. [*Con-*

dolingly] You must find it lonesome here with no one but the typist to talk to.

[*He pulls round the easy chair, and sits down.*]

PROSERPINE [*highly incensed*]. He'll be all right now that he has the advantage of your polished conversation: that's one comfort, anyhow.

[*She begins to typewrite with clattering asperity.*]

BURGESS [*amazed at her audacity*]. Hi was not addressin myself to you, young woman, that I'm awerr of.

PROSERPINE. Did you ever see worse manners, Mr. Marchbanks?

BURGESS [*with pompous severity*]. Mr. Morchbanks is a gentleman, and knows his place, which is more than some people do.

PROSERPINE [*fretfully*]. It's well you and I are not ladies and gentlemen: I'd talk to you pretty straight if Mr. Marchbanks wasn't here. [*She pulls the letter out of the machine so crossly that it tears.*] There! now I've spoiled this letter! have to be done all over again! Oh, I can't contain myself: silly old fathead!

BURGESS [*rising, breathless with indignation*]. Ho! I'm a silly ole fat'ead, am I? Ho, indeed [*gasping*]! Hall right, my gurl! Hall right. You just wait till I tell that to yore hemployer. You'll see. I'll teach you: see if I don't.

PROSERPINE [*conscious of having gone too far*]. I—

BURGESS [*cutting her short*]. Ho: you've done it now. No huse a-talkin to me. I'll let you know who I am.

[PROSERPINE *shifts her paper carriage with a defiant bang, and disdainfully goes on with her work.*]

Don't you take no notice of her, Mr. Morchbanks. She's beneath it.

[*He loftily sits down again.*]

MARCHBANKS [*miserably nervous and disconcerted*]. Hadn't we better change the subject? I—I don't think Miss Garnett meant anything.

PROSERPINE [*with intense conviction*]. Oh, didn't I though, just!

BURGESS. I wouldn't demean myself to take notice on her.

[*An electric bell rings twice.*]

PROSERPINE [*gathering up her note-book and papers*]. That's for me.
[*She hurries out.*]

BURGESS [*calling after her*]. Oh, we can spare you.

[*Somewhat relieved by the triumph of having the last word, and yet half inclined to try to improve on it, he looks after her for a mo-*

ment; then subsides into his seat by EUGENE, *and addresses him very confidentially.*]

Now we're alone, Mr. Morchbanks, let me give you a friendly int that I wouldn't give to heverybody. Ow long ave you known my son-in-law James ere?

MARCHBANKS. I don't know. I never can remember dates. A few months, perhaps.

BURGESS. Ever notice hennythink queer about him?

MARCHBANKS. I don't think so.

BURGESS [*impressively*]. No more you wouldn't. That's the danger on it. Well, he's mad.

MARCHBANKS. Mad!

BURGESS. Mad as a Morch 'are. You take notice on him and you'll see.

MARCHBANKS [*uneasily*]. But surely that is only because his opinions—

BURGESS [*touching him on the knee with his forefinger, and pressing it to hold his attention*]. That's the same what I hused to think, Mr. Morchbanks. Hi thought long enough that it was only his opinions; though, mind you, hopinions becomes vurry serious things when people takes to hactin on em as e does. But that's not what I go on. [*He looks round to make sure that they are alone, and bends over to* EUGENE'S *ear.*] What do you think he sez to me this mornin in this very room?

MARCHBANKS. What?

BURGESS. He sez to me—this is as sure as we're settin here now—he sez "I'm a fool," he sez; "and yore a scounderl." Me a scounderl, mind you! And then shook ands with me on it, as if it was to my credit! Do you mean to tell me as that man's sane?

MORELL [*outside, calling to* PROSERPINE *as he opens the door*]. Get all their names and addresses, Miss Garnett.

PROSERPINE [*in the distance*]. Yes, Mr. Morell.

[MORELL *comes in, with the deputation's documents in his hands.*]

BURGESS [*aside to* MARCHBANKS]. Yorr he is. Just you keep your heye on im and see. [*Rising momentously*] I'm sorry, James, to ave to make a complaint to you. I don't want to do it; but I feel I oughter, as a matter o right and dooty.

MORELL. What's the matter?

BURGESS. Mr. Morchbanks will bear me hout: he was a witness. [*Very solemnly*] Yore young woman so far forgot herself as to call me a silly ole fat'ead.

MORELL [*with tremendous heartiness*]. Oh, now, isn't that exactly like Prossy? She's so frank: she can't contain herself! Poor Prossy! Ha! ha!

BURGESS [*trembling with rage*]. And do you hexpec me to put up with it from the like of er?

MORELL. Pooh, nonsense! you can't take any notice of it. Never mind.

[*He goes to the cellaret and puts the papers into one of the drawers.*]

BURGESS. Oh, Hi don't mind. Hi'm above it. But is it right? that's what I want to know. Is it right?

MORELL. That's a question for the Church, not for the laity. Has it done you any harm? that's the question for you, eh? Of course it hasn't. Think no more of it.

[*He dismisses the subject by going to his place at the table and setting to work at his correspondence.*]

BURGESS [*aside to* MARCHBANKS]. What did I tell you? Mad as a atter. [*He goes to the table and asks, with the sickly civility of a hungry man*] When's dinner, James?

MORELL. Not for a couple of hours yet.

BURGESS [*with plaintive resignation*]. Gimme a nice book to read over the fire, will you, James: thur's a good chap.

MORELL. What sort of book? A good one?

BURGESS [*with almost a yell of remonstrance*]. Nah-oo! Summat pleasant, just to pass the time.

[MORELL *takes an illustrated paper from the table and offers it. He accepts it humbly.*]

Thank yer, James.

[*He goes back to the big chair at the fire, and sits there at his ease, reading.*]

MORELL [*as he writes*]. Candida will come to entertain you presently. She has got rid of her pupil. She is filling the lamps.

MARCHBANKS [*starting up in the wildest consternation*]. But that will soil her hands. I can't bear that, Morell: it's a shame. I'll go and fill them. [*He makes for the door.*]

MORELL. You'd better not.

[MARCHBANKS *stops irresolutely.*]

She'd only set you to clean my boots, to save me the trouble of doing it myself in the morning.

BURGESS [*with grave disapproval*]. Don't you keep a servant now, James?

MORELL. Yes: but she isn't a slave; and the house looks as if I kept three. That means that everyone has to lend a hand. It's not a bad plan: Prossy and I can talk business after breakfast while we're washing up. Washing up's no trouble when there are two people to do it.

MARCHBANKS [*tormentedly*]. Do you think every woman is as coarse-grained as Miss Garnett?

BURGESS [*emphatically*]. That's quite right, Mr. Morchbanks: that's quite right. She is coarse-grained.

MORELL [*quietly and significantly*]. Marchbanks!

MARCHBANKS. Yes?

MORELL. How many servants does your father keep?

MARCHBANKS [*pettishly*]. Oh, I don't know.

[*He moves to the sofa, as if to get as far as possible from Morell's questioning, and sits down in great agony of spirit, thinking of the paraffin.*]

MORELL [*very gravely*]. So many that you don't know! [*More aggressively*] When there's anything coarse-grained to be done, you just ring the bell and throw it on to somebody else, eh?

MARCHBANKS. Oh, don't torture me. You don't even ring the bell. But your wife's beautiful fingers are dabbling in paraffin oil while you sit here comfortably preaching about it: everlastingly preaching! preaching! words! words! words!

BURGESS [*intensely appreciating this retort*]. Har, har! Devil a better! [*Radiantly*] Ad you there, James, straight.

[CANDIDA *comes in, well aproned, with a reading lamp trimmed, filled, and ready for lighting. She places it on the table near* MORELL, *ready for use.*]

CANDIDA [*brushing her finger tips together with a slight twitch of her nose*]. If you stay with us, Eugene, I think I will hand over the lamps to you.

MARCHBANKS. I will stay on condition that you hand over all the rough work to me.

CANDIDA. That's very gallant; but I think I should like to see how you do it first. [*Turning to* MORELL] James: you've not been looking after the house properly.

MORELL. What have I done—or not done—my love?

CANDIDA [*with serious vexation*]. My own particular pet scrubbing brush has been used for blackleading.

[*A heartbreaking wail bursts from* MARCHBANKS. BURGESS *looks round, amazed.* CANDIDA *hurries to the sofa.*]

What's the matter? Are you ill, Eugene?

MARCHBANKS. No: not ill. Only horror! horror! horror!

[*He bows his head on his hands.*]

BURGESS [*shocked*]. What! Got the orrors, Mr. Morchbanks! Oh, that's bad, at your age. You must leave it off grajally.

CANDIDA [*reassured*]. Nonsense, papa! It's only poetic horror, isn't it, Eugene [*petting him*]?

BURGESS [*abashed*]. Oh, poetic orror, is it? I beg your pardon, I'm shore.

[*He turns to the fire again, deprecating his hasty conclusion.*]

CANDIDA. What is it, Eugene? the scrubbing brush? [*He shudders.*] Well, there! never mind. [*She sits down beside him.*] Wouldn't you like to present me with a nice new one, with an ivory back inlaid with mother-of-pearl?

MARCHBANKS [*softly and musically, but sadly and longingly*]. No, not a scrubbing brush, but a boat: a tiny shallop to sail away in, far from the world, where the marble floors are washed by the rain and dried by the sun; where the south wind dusts the beautiful green and purple carpets. Or a chariot! to carry us up into the sky, where the lamps are stars, and don't need to be filled with paraffin oil every day.

MORELL [*harshly*]. And where there is nothing to do but to be idle, selfish, and useless.

CANDIDA [*jarred*]. Oh James! how could you spoil it all?

MARCHBANKS [*firing up*]. Yes, to be idle, selfish, and useless: that is, to be beautiful and free and happy: hasn't every man desired that with all his soul for the woman he loves? That's my ideal: what's yours, and that of all the dreadful people who live in these hideous rows of houses? Sermons and scrubbing brushes! With you to preach the sermon and your wife to scrub.

CANDIDA [*quaintly*]. He cleans the boots, Eugene. You will have to clean them to-morrow for saying that about him.

MARCHBANKS. Oh, don't talk about boots! Your feet should be beautiful on the mountains.

CANDIDA. My feet would not be beautiful on the Hackney Road without boots.

BURGESS [*scandalized*]. Come, Candy! don't be vulgar. Mr. Morchbanks ain't accustomed to it. You're givin him the orrors again. I mean the poetic ones.

[MORELL *is silent. Apparently he is busy with his letters: really he is puzzling with misgiving over his new and alarming experience that the surer he is of his moral thrusts, the more swiftly and effectively* EUGENE *parries them. To find himself beginning to fear a man whom he does not respect afflicts him bitterly.*]

[MISS GARNETT *comes in with a telegram.*]

PROSERPINE [*handing the telegram to* MORELL]. Reply paid. The boy's waiting. [*To* CANDIDA, *coming back to her machine and sitting down*] Maria is ready for you now in the kitchen, Mrs. Morell. [CANDIDA *rises*]. The onions have come.

MARCHBANKS [*convulsively*]. Onions!

CANDIDA. Yes, onions. Not even Spanish ones: nasty little red onions. You shall help me to slice them. Come along.

[*She catches him by the wrist and runs out, pulling him after her.* BURGESS *rises in consternation, and stands aghast on the hearth-rug, staring after them.*]

BURGESS. Candy didn't oughter andle a hearl's nevvy like that. It's goin too fur with it. Lookee ere, James: do e often git taken queer like that?

MORELL [*shortly, writing a telegram*]. I don't know.

BURGESS [*sentimentally*]. He talks very pretty. I awlus had a turn for a bit of poetry. Candy takes arter me that-a-way. Huseter make me tell er fairy stories when she was only a little kiddy not that igh [*indicating a stature of two feet or thereabouts*].

MORELL [*preoccupied*]. Ah, indeed.

[*He blots the telegram and goes out.*]

PROSERPINE. Used you to make the fairy stories up out of your own head?

[BURGESS, *not deigning to reply, strikes an attitude of the haughtiest disdain on the hearth-rug.*]

PROSERPINE [*calmly*]. I should never have supposed you had it in you. By the way, I'd better warn you, since you've taken such a fancy to Mr. Marchbanks. He's mad.

BURGESS. Mad! What! Im too!!

PROSERPINE. Mad as a March hare. He did frighten me, I can tell you, just before you came in that time. Haven't you noticed the queer things he says?

BURGESS. So that's what the poetic orrors means. Blame me if it didn't come into my ed once or twyst that he was a bit horff is chump! [*He crosses the room to the door, lifting up his voice as he goes.*] Well, this is a pretty sort of asylum for a man to be in, with no one but you to take care of him!

PROSERPINE [*as he passes her*]. Yes, what a dreadful thing it would be if anything happened to you!

BURGESS [*loftily*]. Don't you haddress no remarks to me. Tell your hemployer that I've gone into the gorden for a smoke.

PROSERPINE [*mocking*]. Oh!

[*Before* BURGESS *can retort,* MORELL *comes back.*]

BURGESS [*sentimentally*]. Going for a turn in the gording to smoke, James.

MORELL [*brusquely*]. Oh, all right, all right.

[BURGESS *goes out pathetically in the character of a weary old man.* MORELL *stands at the table, turning over his papers, and adding, across to* PROSERPINE, *half humorously, half absently*]

Well, Miss Prossy, why have you been calling my father-in-law names?

PROSERPINE [*blushing fiery red, and looking quickly up at him, half scared, half reproachful*]. I— [*She bursts into tears.*]

MORELL [*with tender gaiety, leaning across the table towards her, and consoling her*]. Oh, come! come! come! Never mind, Pross: he *is* a silly old fathead. isn't he?

[*With an explosive sob, she makes a dash at the door, and vanishes, banging it.* MORELL, *shaking his head resignedly, sighs and goes wearily to his chair, where he sits down and sets to work, looking old and careworn.*

[CANDIDA *comes in. She has finished her household work and taken off the apron. She at once notices his dejected appearance, and posts herself quietly at the visitors' chair, looking down at him attentively. She says nothing.*]

MORELL [*looking up, but with his pen raised ready to resume his work*]. Well? Where is Eugene?

CANDIDA. Washing his hands in the scullery under the tap. He will make an excellent cook if he can only get over his dread of Maria.

MORELL [*shortly*]. Ha! No doubt. [*He begins writing again.*]

CANDIDA [*going nearer, and putting her hand down softly on his to stop him as she says*]. Come here. dear. Let me look at you.

[*He drops his pen and yields himself to her disposal. She makes him rise, and brings him a little away from the table, looking at him critically all the time.*]

Turn your face to the light. [*She places him facing the window.*] My boy is not looking well. Has he been overworking?

MORELL. Nothing more than usual.

CANDIDA. He looks very pale, and grey, and wrinkled, and old.

[*His melancholy deepens: and she attacks it with wilful gaiety*]

Here: [*pulling him towards the easy chair*] you've done enough writing for today. Leave Prossy to finish it. Come and talk to me.

MORELL. But—

CANDIDA [*insisting*]. Yes, I must be talked to. [*She makes him sit down and seats herself on the carpet beside his knee.*] Now [*patting his hand*] you're beginning to look better already. Why must you go out every night lecturing and talking? I hardly have one evening a week with you. Of course what you say is all very true; but it does no good: they don't mind what you say to them one little bit. They think they agree with you; but what's the use of their agreeing with you if they go and do just the opposite of what you tell them the moment your back is turned? Look at our congregation at St. Dominic's! Why do they come to hear you talking about Christianity every Sunday? Why, just because they've been so full of business and money-making for six days that they want to forget all about it and have a rest on the seventh; so that they can go back fresh and make money harder than ever! You positively help them at it instead of hindering them.

MORELL [*with energetic seriousness*]. You know very well, Candida, that I often blow them up soundly for that. And if there is nothing in their churchgoing but rest and diversion, why don't they try something more amusing? more self-indulgent? There must be some good in the fact that they prefer St. Dominic's to worse places on Sundays.

CANDIDA. Oh, the worse places aren't open; and even if they were, they daren't be seen going to them. Besides, James dear, you preach so splendidly that it's as good as a play for them. Why do you think the women are so enthusiastic?

MORELL [*shocked*]. Candida!

CANDIDA. Oh, *I* know. You silly boy: you think it's your Socialism and your religion; but if it were that, they'd do what you tell them instead of only coming to look at you. They all have Prossy's complaint.

MORELL. Prossy's complaint! What do you mean, Candida?

CANDIDA. Yes, Prossy, and all the other secretaries you ever had. Why does Prossy condescend to wash up the things, and to peel potatoes and abase herself in all manner of ways for six shillings a week less than she used to get in a city office? She's in love with you, James: that's the reason. They're all in love with you. And you are in love with preaching because you do it so beautifully. And you think it's all enthusiasm for the kingdom of Heaven on earth; and so do they. You dear silly!

MORELL. Candida: what dreadful! what soul-destroying cynicism! Are you jesting? Or—can it be?—are you jealous?

CANDIDA [*with curious thoughtfulness*]. Yes, I feel a little jealous sometimes.

MORELL [*incredulously*]. Of Prossy?

CANDIDA [*laughing*]. No, no, no, no. Not jealous of anybody. Jealous for somebody else, who is not loved as he ought to be.

MORELL. Me?

CANDIDA. You! Why, you're spoiled with love and worship: you get far more than is good for you. No: I mean Eugene.

MORELL [*startled*]. Eugene!

CANDIDA. It seems unfair that all the love should go to you and none to him; although he needs it so much more than you do.

[*A convulsive movement shakes him in spite of himself.*]

What's the matter? Am I worrying you?

MORELL [*hastily*]. Not at all. [*Looking at her with troubled intensity*] You know that I have perfect confidence in you, Candida.

CANDIDA. You vain thing! Are you so sure of your irresistible attractions?

MORELL. Candida: you are shocking me. I never thought of my attractions. I thought of your goodness, of your purity. That is what I confide in.

CANDIDA. What a nasty uncomfortable thing to say to me! Oh, you are a clergyman, James: a thorough clergyman!

MORELL [*turning away from her, heart-stricken*]. So Eugene says.

CANDIDA [*with lively interest, leaning over to him with her arms on his knee*]. Eugene's always right. He's a wonderful boy: I have grown fonder and fonder of him all the time I was away. Do you know, James, that though he has not the least suspicion of it himself, he is ready to fall madly in love with me?

MORELL [*grimly*]. Oh, he has no suspicion of it himself, hasn't he?

CANDIDA. Not a bit.

[*She takes her arms from his knee, and turns thoughtfully, sinking into a more restful attitude with her hands in her lap.*]

Some day he will know: when he is grown up and experienced, like you. And he will know that I must have known. I wonder what he will think of me then.

MORELL. No evil, Candida. I hope and trust, no evil.

CANDIDA [*dubiously*]. That will depend.

MORELL [*bewildered*]. Depend!

CANDIDA [*looking at him*]. Yes: it will depend on what happens to him. [*He looks vacantly at her.*] Don't you see? It will depend on how he comes to learn what love really is. I mean on the sort of woman who will teach it to him.

MORELL [*quite at a loss*]. Yes. No. I don't know what you mean.

CANDIDA [*explaining*]. If he learns it from a good woman, then it will be all right: he will forgive me.

MORELL. Forgive?

CANDIDA. But suppose he learns it from a bad woman, as so many men do, especially poetic men, who imagine all women are angels! Suppose he only discovers the value of love when he has thrown it away and degraded himself in his ignorance! Will he forgive me then, do you think?

MORELL. Forgive you for what?

CANDIDA [*realizing how stupid he is, and a little disappointed, though quite tenderly so*]. Don't you understand?

[*He shakes his head. She turns to him again, so as to explain with the fondest intimacy.*]

I mean, will he forgive me for not teaching him myself? For abandoning him to the bad women for the sake of my goodness, of my purity, as you call it? Ah, James, how little you understand me, to talk of your confidence in my goodness and purity! I would give them both to poor Eugene as willingly as I would give my shawl to a beggar dying of cold, if there were nothing else to restrain me. Put your trust in my love for you, James; for if that went, I should care very little for your sermons: mere phrases that you cheat yourself and others with every day. [*She is about to rise.*]

MORELL. His words!

CANDIDA [*checking herself quickly in the act of getting up*]. Whose words?

MORELL. Eugene's.

CANDIDA [*delighted*]. He is always right. He understands you; he understands me; he understands Prossy; and you, darling, you understand nothing.

[*She laughs, and kisses him to console him. He recoils as if stabbed, and springs up.*]

MORELL. How can you bear to do that when— Oh, Candida [*with anguish in his voice*] I had rather you had plunged a grappling iron into my heart than given me that kiss.

CANDIDA [*amazed*]. My dear: what's the matter?

MORELL [*frantically waving her off*]. Don't touch me.

CANDIDA. James!!!

[*They are interrupted by the entrance of* MARCHBANKS *with* BURGESS, *who stop near the door, staring.*]

MARCHBANKS. Is anything the matter?

MORELL [*deadly white, putting an iron constraint on himself*]. Nothing but this: that either you were right this morning, or Candida is mad.

BURGESS [*in modest protest*]. What! Candy mad too! Oh, come! come! come!

[*He crosses the room to the fireplace, protesting as he goes, and knocks the ashes out of his pipe on the bars.*

[MORELL *sits down at his table desperately, leaning forward to hide his face, and interlacing his fingers rigidly to keep them steady.*]

CANDIDA [*to* MORELL, *relieved and laughing*]. Oh, you're only shocked! Is that all? How conventional all you unconventional people are! [*She sits gaily on the arm of the chair.*]

BURGESS. Come: be'ave yourself, Candy. What'll Mr. Morchbanks think of you?

CANDIDA. This comes of James teaching me to think for myself, and never to hold back out of fear of what other people may think of me. It works beautifully as long as I think the same things as he does. But now! because I have just thought something different! look at him! Just look! [*She points to* MORELL, *greatly amused.*]

[EUGENE *looks, and instantly presses his hand on his heart, as if some pain had shot through it. He sits down on the sofa like a man witnessing a tragedy.*]

BURGESS [*on the hearth-rug*]. Well, James, you certnly haint as himpressive lookin as usu'l.

MORELL [*with a laugh which is half a sob*]. I suppose not. I beg all your pardons: I was not conscious of making a fuss. [*Pulling himself together*] Well, well, well, well, well!

[*He sets to work at his papers again with resolute cheerfulness.*]

CANDIDA [*going to the sofa and sitting beside* MARCHBANKS, *still in a bantering humor*]. Well, Eugene: why are you so sad? Did the onions make you cry?

MARCHBANKS [*aside to her*]. It is your cruelty. I hate cruelty. It is a horrible thing to see one person make another suffer.

CANDIDA [*petting him ironically*]. Poor boy! have I been cruel? Did I make it slice nasty little red onions?

MARCHBANKS [*earnestly*]. Oh, stop, stop: I don't mean myself. You have made him suffer frightfully. I feel his pain in my own heart. I know that it is not your fault: it is something that must happen; but don't make light of it. I shudder when you torture him and laugh.

CANDIDA [*incredulously*]. *I* torture James! Nonsense, Eugene: how you exaggerate! Silly!

[*She rises and goes to the table, a little troubled.*]

Don't work any more, dear. Come and talk to us.

MORELL [*affectionately but bitterly*]. Ah no: *I* can't talk. I can only preach.

CANDIDA [*caressing his hand*]. Well, come and preach.

BURGESS [*strongly remonstrating*]. Aw no, Candy. Ang it all!

[LEXY MILL *comes in, anxious and important.*]

LEXY [*hastening to shake hands with* CANDIDA]. How do you do, Mrs. Morell? So glad to see you back again.

CANDIDA. Thank you, Lexy. You know Eugene, don't you?

LEXY. Oh yes. How do you do, Marchbanks?

MARCHBANKS. Quite well, thanks.

LEXY [*to* MORELL]. I've just come from the Guild of St. Matthew. They are in the greatest consternation about your telegram.

CANDIDA. What did you telegraph about, James?

LEXY [*to* CANDIDA]. He was to have spoken for them tonight. They've taken the large hall in Mare Street and spent a lot of money on posters. Morell's telegram was to say he couldn't come. It came on them like a thunderbolt.

CANDIDA [*surprised, and beginning to suspect something wrong*]. Given up an engagement to speak!

BURGESS. Fust time in his life, I'll bet. Ain't it, Candy?

LEXY [*to* MORELL]. They decided to send an urgent telegram to you asking whether you could not change your mind. Have you received it?

MORELL [*with restrained impatience*]. Yes, yes: I got it.

LEXY. It was reply paid.

MORELL. Yes, I know. I answered it. I can't go.

CANDIDA. But why, James?

MORELL [*almost fiercely*]. Because I don't choose. These people forget that I am a man: they think I am a talking machine to be turned on for their pleasure every evening of my life. May I not have one night at home, with my wife, and my friends?

[*They are all amazed at this outburst, except* EUGENE. *His expression remains unchanged.*]

CANDIDA. Oh, James, you mustn't mind what I said about that. And if you don't go you'll have an attack of bad conscience tomorrow.

LEXY [*intimidated, but urgent*]. I know, of course, that they make the most unreasonable demands on you. But they have been telegraphing all over the place for another speaker; and they can get nobody but the President of the Agnostic League.

MORELL [*promptly*]. Well, an excellent man. What better do they want?

LEXY. But he always insists so powerfully on the divorce of Socialism from Christianity. He will undo all the good we have been doing. Of course you know best; but—[*He shrugs his shoulders and wanders to the hearth beside* BURGESS.]

CANDIDA [*coaxingly*]. Oh, do go, James. We'll all go.

BURGESS [*grumblingly*]. Look ere, Candy! I say! Let's stay at home by the fire, comfortable. He won't need to be mor'n a couple-o-hour away.

CANDIDA. You'll be just as comfortable at the meeting. We'll all sit on the platform and be great people.

EUGENE [*terrified*]. Oh please don't let us go on the platform. No: everyone will stare at us: I couldn't. I'll sit at the back of the room.

CANDIDA. Don't be afraid. They'll be too busy looking at James to notice you.

MORELL. Prossy's complaint, Candida! Eh?

CANDIDA [*gaily*]. Yes: Prossy's complaint.

BURGESS [*mystified*]. Prossy's complaint! What are you talking about, James?

MORELL [*not heeding him, rises; goes to the door; and holds it open, calling in a commanding tone*]. Miss Garnett.

PROSERPINE [*in the distance*]. Yes, Mr. Morell. Coming.

[*They all wait, except* BURGESS, *who turns stealthily to* LEXY.]

BURGESS. Listen ere, Mr. Mill. What's Prossy's complaint? What's wrong with er?

LEXY [*confidentially*]. Well, I don't exactly know; but she spoke very strangely to me this morning. I'm afraid she's a little out of her mind sometimes.

BURGESS [*overwhelmed*]. Why, it must be catchin! Four in the same ouse!

PROSERPINE [*appearing on the threshold*]. What is it, Mr. Morell?

MORELL. Telegraph to the Guild of St. Matthew that I am coming.

PROSERPINE [*surprised*]. Don't they expect you?

MORELL [*peremptorily*]. Do as I tell you.

[PROSERPINE, *frightened, sits down at her typewriter, and obeys.* MORELL, *now unaccountably resolute and forceful, goes across to* BURGESS. CANDIDA *watches his movements with growing wonder and misgiving.*]

MORELL. Burgess: you don't want to come.

BURGESS. Oh, don't put it like that, James. It's ony that it ain't Sunday, you know.

MORELL. I'm sorry. I thought you might like to be introduced to he chairman. He's on the Works Committee of the County Council, nd has some influence in the matter of contracts. [BURGESS *wakes up at nce.*] You'll come?

BURGESS [*with enthusiasm*]. Cawrse I'll come, James. Ain't it awlus a pleasure to ear you!

MORELL [*turning to* PROSSY]. I shall want you to take some notes at he meeting, Miss Garnett, if you have no other engagement. [*She nods, fraid to speak.*] You are coming, Lexy, I suppose?

LEXY. Certainly.

CANDIDA. We're all coming, James.

MORELL. No: you are not coming; and Eugene is not coming. You will stay here and entertain him—to celebrate your return home.

[EUGENE *rises, breathless.*]

CANDIDA. But, James—

MORELL [*authoritatively*]. I insist. You do not want to come; and he does not want to come.

[CANDIDA *is about to protest.*]

Oh, don't concern yourselves: I shall have plenty of people without you: your chairs will be wanted by unconverted people who have never heard me before.

CANDIDA [*troubled*]. Eugene: wouldn't you like to come?

MORELL. I should be afraid to let myself go before Eugene: he is so critical of sermons. [*Looking at him*] He knows I am afraid of him: he told me as much this morning. Well, I shall show him how much afraid I am by leaving him here in your custody, Candida.

MARCHBANKS [*to himself, with vivid feeling*]. That's brave. That's beautiful.

CANDIDA [*with anxious misgiving*]. But—but—Is anything the matter, James? [*Greatly troubled*] I can't understand—

MORELL [*taking her tenderly in his arms and kissing her on the forehead*]. Ah, I thought it was *I* who couldn't understand, dear.

ACT III

PAST TEN *in the evening. The curtains are drawn, and the lamps lighted. The typewriter is in its case: the large table has been cleared and tidied: everything indicates that the day's work is over.*

CANDIDA *and* MARCHBANKS *are sitting by the fire. The reading lamp is on the mantelshelf above* MARCHBANKS, *who is in the small chair, reading aloud. A little pile of manuscripts and a couple of volumes of poetry are on the carpet beside him.* CANDIDA *is in the easy chair. The poker, a light brass one, is upright in her hand. Leaning back and looking intently at the point of it, with her feet stretched towards the blaze, she is in a waking dream, miles away from her surroundings and completely oblivious of* EUGENE.

MARCHBANKS [*breaking off in his recitation*]. Every poet that ever lived has put that thought into a sonnet. He must: he can't help it.

[*He looks to her for assent, and notices her absorption in the poker.*]

Haven't you been listening? [*No response.*] Mrs. Morell!

CANDIDA [*starting*]. Eh?

MARCHBANKS. Haven't you been listening?

CANDIDA [*with a guilty excess of politeness*]. Oh yes. It's very nice. Go on, Eugene. I'm longing to hear what happens to the angel.

MARCHBANKS [*letting the manuscript drop from his hand to the floor*]. I beg your pardon for boring you.

CANDIDA. But you are not boring me, I assure you. Please go on. Do, Eugene.

MARCHBANKS. I finished the poem about the angel quarter of an hour ago. I've read you several things since.

CANDIDA [*remorsefully*]. I'm so sorry, Eugene. I think the poker must have hypnotized me. [*She puts it down.*]

MARCHBANKS. It made me horribly uneasy.

CANDIDA. Why didn't you tell me? I'd have put it down at once.

MARCHBANKS. I was afraid of making you uneasy too. It looked as if it were a weapon. If I were a hero of old I should have laid my drawn sword between us. If Morell had come in he would have thought you had taken up the poker because there was no sword between us.

CANDIDA [*wondering*]. What? [*With a puzzled glance at him*] I can't quite follow that. Those sonnets of yours have perfectly addled me. Why should there be a sword between us?

MARCHBANKS [*evasively*]. Oh, never mind.

[*He stoops to pick up the manuscript.*]

CANDIDA. Put that down again, Eugene. There are limits to my appetite for poetry: even your poetry. You've been reading to me for more than two hours, ever since James went out. I want to talk.

MARCHBANKS [*rising, scared*]. No: I mustn't talk. [*He looks round him in his lost way, and adds, suddenly*] I think I'll go out and take a walk in the park. [*He makes for the door.*]

CANDIDA. Nonsense: it's closed long ago. Come and sit down on the hearth-rug, and talk moonshine as you usually do. I want to be amused. Don't you want to?

MARCHBANKS [*half in terror, half enraptured*]. Yes.

CANDIDA. Then come along.

[*She moves her chair back a little to make room.*

[*He hesitates; then timidly stretches himself on the hearth-rug, face upwards, and throws back his head across her knees, looking up at her.*]

MARCHBANKS. Oh, I've been so miserable all the evening, because I was doing right. Now I'm doing wrong; and I'm happy.

CANDIDA [*tenderly amused at him*]. Yes: I'm sure you feel a great grown-up wicked deceiver. Quite proud of yourself, aren't you?

MARCHBANKS [*raising his hand quickly and turning a little to look round at her*]. Take care. I'm ever so much older than you, if you only knew.

[*He turns quite over on his knees, with his hands clasped and his arms on her lap, and speaks with growing impulse, his blood beginning to stir.*]

May I say some wicked things to you?

CANDIDA [*without the least fear or coldness, and with perfect respect for his passion, but with a touch of her wisehearted maternal humor*]. No. But you may say anything you really and truly feel. Anything at all, no matter what it is. I am not afraid, so long as it is your real self that speaks, and not a mere attitude: a gallant attitude, or a wicked attitude, or even a poetic attitude. I put you on your honor and truth. Now say whatever you want to.

MARCHBANKS [*the eager expression vanishing utterly from his lips and nostrils as his eyes light up with pathetic spirituality*]. Oh, now I can't say anything: all the words I know belong to some attitude or other—all except one.

CANDIDA. What one is that?

MARCHBANKS [*softly, losing himself in the music of the name*]. Candida, Candida, Candida, Candida, Candida. I must say that now, because you have put me on my honor and truth; and I never think or feel Mrs. Morell: it is always Candida.

CANDIDA. Of course. And what have you to say to Candida?

MARCHBANKS. Nothing but to repeat your name a thousand times. Don't you feel that every time is a prayer to you?

CANDIDA. Doesn't it make you happy to be able to pray?

MARCHBANKS. Yes, very happy.

CANDIDA. Well, that happiness is the answer to your prayer. Do you want anything more?

MARCHBANKS. No: I have come into Heaven, where want is unknown.

[MORELL *comes in. He halts on the threshold, and takes in the scene at a glance.*]

MORELL [*grave and self-contained*]. I hope I don't disturb you.

[CANDIDA *starts up violently, but without the smallest embarrassment, laughing at herself.* EUGENE, *capsized by her sudden movement, recovers himself without rising, and sits on the rug hugging his ankles, also quite unembarrassed.*]

CANDIDA. Oh, James, how you startled me! I was so taken up with Eugene that I didn't hear your latchkey. How did the meeting go off? Did you speak well?

MORELL. I have never spoken better in my life.

CANDIDA. That was first rate! How much was the collection?

MORELL. I forgot to ask.

CANDIDA [*to* EUGENE]. He must have spoken splendidly, or he would never have forgotten that. [*To* MORELL] Where are all the others?

MORELL. They left long before I could get away: I thought I should never escape. I believe they are having supper somewhere.

CANDIDA [*in her domestic business tone*]. Oh, in that case, Maria may go to bed. I'll tell her.

[*She goes out to the kitchen.*]

MORELL [*looking sternly down at* MARCHBANKS]. Well?

MARCHBANKS [*squatting grotesquely on the hearth-rug, and actually at ease with* MORELL: *even impishly humorous*]. Well?

MORELL. Have you anything to tell me?

MARCHBANKS. Only that I have been making a fool of myself here in private whilst you have been making a fool of yourself in public.

MORELL. Hardly in the same way, I think.

MARCHBANKS [*eagerly, scrambling up*]. The very, very, very same way. I have been playing the Good Man. Just like you. When you began your heroics about leaving me here with Candida—

MORELL [*involuntarily*]. Candida!

MARCHBANKS. Oh yes: I've got that far. But don't be afraid. Heroics are infectious: I caught the disease from you. I swore not to say a word in your absence that I would not have said a month ago in your presence.

MORELL. Did you keep your oath?

MARCHBANKS [*suddenly perching himself on the back of the easy chair*]. It kept itself somehow until about ten minutes ago. Up to that moment I went on desperately reading to her—reading my own poems—anybody's poems—to stave off a conversation. I was standing outside the gate of Heaven, and refusing to go in. Oh, you can't think how heroic it was, and how uncomfortable! Then—

MORELL [*steadily controlling his suspense*]. Then?

MARCHBANKS [*prosaically slipping down into a quite ordinary attitude on the seat of the chair*]. Then she couldn't bear being read to any longer.

MORELL. And you approached the gate of Heaven at last?

MARCHBANKS. Yes.

MORELL. Well? [*Fiercely*] Speak, man: have you no feeling for me?

MARCHBANKS [*softly and musically*]. Then she became an angel; and there was a flaming sword that turned every way, so that I couldn't go in; for I saw that that gate was really the gate of Hell.

MORELL [*triumphantly*]. She repulsed you!

MARCHBANKS [*rising in wild scorn*]. No, you fool: if she had done that I should never have seen that I was in Heaven already. Repulsed me! You think that would have saved us! virtuous indignation! Oh, you are not worthy to live in the same world with her.

[*He turns away contemptuously to the other side of the room.*]

MORELL [*who has watched him quietly without changing his place*]. Do you think you make yourself more worthy by reviling me, Eugene?

MARCHBANKS. Here endeth the thousand and first lesson. Morell: I don't think much of your preaching after all: I believe I could do it better myself. The man I want to meet is the man that Candida married.

MORELL. The man that—? Do you mean me?

MARCHBANKS. I don't mean the Reverend James Mavor Morell, moralist and windbag. I mean the real man that the Reverend James must have hidden somewhere inside his black coat: the man that Candida loved. You can't make a woman like Candida love you by merely buttoning your collar at the back instead of in front.

MORELL [*boldly and steadily*]. When Candida promised to marry me, I was the same moralist and windbag you now see. I wore my black coat; and my collar was buttoned behind instead of in front. Do you think she would have loved me any the better for being insincere in my profession?

MARCHBANKS [*on the sofa, hugging his ankles*]. Oh, she forgave you, just as she forgives me for being a coward, and a weakling, and what you call a snivelling little whelp and all the rest of it. [*Dreamily*] A woman like that has divine insight: she loves our souls, and not our follies and vanities and illusions, nor our collars and coats, nor any other of the rags and tatters we are rolled up in. [*He reflects on this for an instant: then turns intently to question* MORELL.] What I want to know is how you got past the flaming sword that stopped me.

MORELL. Perhaps because I was not interrupted at the end of ten minutes.

MARCHBANKS [*taken aback*]. What!

MORELL. Man can climb to the highest summits; but he cannot dwell there long.

MARCHBANKS [*springing up*]. It's false: there can he dwell for ever, and there only. It's in the other moments that he can find no rest, no sense of the silent glory of life. Where would you have me spend my moments, if not on the summits?

MORELL. In the scullery, slicing onions and filling lamps.

MARCHBANKS. Or in the pulpit, scrubbing cheap earthenware souls?

MORELL. Yes, that too. It was there that I earned my golden moment, and the right, in that moment, to ask her to love me. *I* did not take the moment on credit; nor did I use it to steal another man's happiness.

MARCHBANKS [*rather disgustedly, trotting back towards the fireplace*].

I have no doubt you conducted the transaction as honestly as if you were buying a pound of cheese. [*He stops on the brink of the hearth-rug, and adds, thoughtfully, to himself, with his back turned to* MORELL] I could only go to her as a beggar.

MORELL [*staring*]. A beggar dying of cold! asking for her shawl!

MARCHBANKS [*turning, surprised*]. Thank you for touching up my poetry. Yes, if you like: a beggar dying of cold, asking for her shawl.

MORELL [*excitedly*]. And she refused. Shall I tell you why she refused? I can tell you, on her own authority. It was because of—

MARCHBANKS. She didn't refuse.

MORELL. Not!

MARCHBANKS. She offered me all I chose to ask for: her shawl, her wings, the wreath of stars on her head, the lilies in her hand, the crescent moon beneath her feet—

MORELL [*seizing him*]. Out with the truth, man: my wife is my wife: I want no more of your poetic fripperies. I know well that if I have lost her love and you have gained it, no law will bind her.

MARCHBANKS [*quaintly, without fear or resistance*]. Catch me by the shirt collar, Morell: she will arrange it for me afterwards as she did this morning. [*With quiet rapture*] I shall feel her hands touch me.

MORELL. You young imp, do you know how dangerous it is to say that to me? Or [*with a sudden misgiving*] has something made you brave?

MARCHBANKS. I'm not afraid now. I disliked you before: that was why I shrank from your touch. But I saw today—when she tortured you—that you love her. Since then I have been your friend: you may strangle me if you like.

MORELL [*releasing him*]. Eugene: if that is not a heartless lie—if you have a spark of human feeling left in you—will you tell me what has happened during my absence?

MARCHBANKS. What happened! Why, the flaming sword—

[MORELL *stamps with impatience.*]

Well, in plain prose, I loved her so exquisitely that I wanted nothing more than the happiness of being in such love. And before I had time to come down from the highest summits, you came in.

MORELL [*suffering deeply*]. So it is still unsettled. Still the misery of doubt.

MARCHBANKS. Misery! I am the happiest of men. I desire nothing now but her happiness. [*In a passion of sentiment*] Oh, Morell, let us both give her up. Why should she have to choose between a wretched little nervous disease like me, and a pig-headed parson like you? Let us go on a pilgrimage, you to the east and I to the west, in search of a worthy lover for her: some beautiful archangel with purple wings—

MORELL. Some fiddlestick! Oh, if she is mad enough to leave me for you, who will protect her? who will help her? who will work for her? who will be a father to her children?

[*He sits down distractedly on the sofa, with his elbows on his knees and his head propped on his clenched fists.*]

MARCHBANKS [*snapping his fingers wildly*]. She does not ask those silly questions. It is she who wants somebody to protect, to help, to work for: somebody to give her children to protect, to help and to work for. Some grown up man who has become as a little child again. Oh, you fool, you fool, you triple fool! I am the man, Morell: I am the man. [*He dances about excitedly, crying*] You don't understand what a woman is. Send for her, Morell: send for her and let her choose between—

[*The door opens and* CANDIDA *enters. He stops as if petrified.*]

CANDIDA [*amazed, on the threshold*]. What on earth are you at, Eugene?

MARCHBANKS [*oddly*]. James and I are having a preaching match; and he is getting the worst of it.

[CANDIDA *looks quickly round at* MORELL. *Seeing that he is distressed, she hurries down to him, greatly vexed.*]

CANDIDA. You have been annoying him. Now I won't have it, Eugene: do you hear? [*She puts her hand on* MORELL's *shoulder, and quite forgets her wifely tact in her anger.*] My boy shall not be worried: I will protect him.

MORELL [*rising proudly*]. Protect!

CANDIDA [*not heeding him: to* EUGENE]. What have you been saying?

MARCHBANKS [*appalled*]. Nothing. I—

CANDIDA. Eugene! Nothing?

MARCHBANKS [*piteously*]. I mean—I—I'm very sorry. I won't do it again: indeed I won't. I'll let him alone.

MORELL [*indignantly, with an aggressive movement towards* EUGENE] Let me alone! You young—

CANDIDA [*stopping him*]. Sh!—no: let me deal with him, James.

MARCHBANKS. Oh, you're not angry with me, are you?

CANDIDA [*severely*]. Yes I am: very angry. I have a good mind to pack you out of the house.

MORELL [*taken aback by* CANDIDA's *vigor, and by no means relishing the position of being rescued by her from another man*]. Gently, Candida gently. I am able to take care of myself.

CANDIDA [*petting him*]. Yes, dear: of course you are. But you mustn't be annoyed and made miserable.

MARCHBANKS [*almost in tears, turning to the door*]. I'll go.

CANDIDA. Oh, you needn't go: I can't turn you out at this time of night. [*Vehemently*] Shame on you! For shame!

MARCHBANKS [*desperately*]. But what have I done?

CANDIDA. I know what you have done: as well as if I had been here all the time. Oh, it was unworthy! You are like a child: you cannot hold your tongue.

MARCHBANKS. I would die ten times over sooner than give you a moment's pain.

CANDIDA [*with infinite contempt for this puerility*]. Much good your dying would do me!

MORELL. Candida, my dear: this altercation is hardly quite seemly. It is a matter between two men; and I am the right person to settle it.

CANDIDA. Two men! Do you call that a man! [*To* EUGENE] You bad boy!

MARCHBANKS [*gathering a whimsically affectionate courage from the scolding*]. If I am to be scolded like a boy, I must make a boy's excuse. He began it. And he's bigger than I am.

CANDIDA [*losing confidence a little as her concern for* MORELL'S *dignity takes the alarm*]. That can't be true. [*To* MORELL] You didn't begin it, James, did you?

MORELL [*contemptuously*]. No.

MARCHBANKS [*indignant*]. Oh!

MORELL [*to* EUGENE]. You began it: this morning.

[CANDIDA, *instantly connecting this with his mysterious allusion in the afternoon to something told him by* EUGENE *in the morning, looks at him with quick suspicion.* MORELL *proceeds, with the emphasis of offended superiority.*]

But your other point is true. I am certainly the bigger of the two, and, I hope, the stronger, Candida. So you had better leave the matter in my hands.

CANDIDA [*again soothing him*]. Yes, dear; but—[*troubled*] I don't understand about this morning.

MORELL [*gently snubbing her*]. You need not understand, my dear.

CANDIDA. But James, I [*the street bell rings*]—Oh bother! Here they all come.

[*She goes out to let them in.*]

MARCHBANKS [*running to* MORELL]. Oh, Morell, isn't it dreadful? She's angry with us: she hates me. What shall I do?

MORELL [*with quaint desperation, walking up and down the middle of the room*]. Eugene: my head is spinning round. I shall begin to laugh presently.

MARCHBANKS [*following him anxiously*]. No, no: she'll think I've thrown you into hysterics. Don't laugh.

[Boisterous voices and laughter are heard approaching. LEXY MILL, *his eyes sparkling, and his bearing denoting unwonted elevation of spirit, enters with* BURGESS, *who is greasy and self-complacent, but has all his wits about him.* MISS GARNETT, *with her smartest hat and jacket on, follows them; but though her eyes are brighter than before, she is evidently a prey to misgiving. She places herself with her back to her typewriting table, with one hand on it to steady herself, passing the other across her forehead as if she were a little tired and giddy.* MARCHBANKS *relapses into shyness and edges away into the corner near the window, where* MORELL's *books are.]*

LEXY *[exhilarated].* Morell: I must congratulate you. *[Grasping his hand]* What a noble, splendid, inspired address you gave us! You surpassed yourself.

BURGESS. So you did, James. It fair kep me awake to the lars' word. Didn't it, Miss Gornett?

PROSERPINE *[worriedly].* Oh, I wasn't minding you: I was trying to make notes.

[She takes out her notebook, and looks at her stenography, which nearly makes her cry.]

MORELL. Did I go too fast, Pross?

PROSERPINE. Much too fast. You know I can't do more than ninety words a minute.

[She relieves her feelings by throwing her notebook angrily beside her machine, ready for use next morning.]

MORELL *[soothingly].* Oh well, well, never mind, never mind, never mind. Have you all had supper?

LEXY. Mr. Burgess has been kind enough to give us a really splendid supper at the Belgrave.

BURGESS *[with effusive magnanimity].* Don't mention it, Mr. Mill *[Modestly]* You're arty welcome to my little treat.

PROSERPINE. We had champagne. I never tasted it before. I fee quite giddy.

MORELL *[surprised].* A champagne supper! That was very hand some. Was it my eloquence that produced all this extravagance?

LEXY *[rhetorically].* Your eloquence, and Mr. Burgess's goodness o heart. *[With a fresh burst of exhilaration]* And what a very fine fellov the chairman is, Morell! He came to supper with us.

MORELL *[with long drawn significance, looking at* BURGESS]. O-o-o-h the chairman. Now I understand.

*[*BURGESS *covers with a deprecatory cough a lively satisfaction wit. his own diplomatic cunning.* LEXY *folds his arms and leans agains.*

the head of the sofa in a high-spirited attitude after nearly losing his balance. CANDIDA *comes in with glasses, lemons, and a jug of hot water on a tray.*]

CANDIDA. Who will have some lemonade? You know our rules: total abstinence.

[*She puts the tray on the table, and takes up the lemon squeezer, looking enquiringly round at them.*]

MORELL. No use, dear. They've all had champagne. Pross has broken her pledge.

CANDIDA [*to* PROSERPINE]. You don't mean to say you've been drinking champagne!

PROSERPINE [*stubbornly*]. Yes I do. I'm only a beer teetotaller, not a champagne teetotaller. I don't like beer. Are there any letters for me to answer, Mr. Morell?

MORELL. No more tonight.

PROSERPINE. Very well. Good night, everybody.

LEXY [*gallantly*]. Had I not better see you home, Miss Garnett?

PROSERPINE. No thank you. I shan't trust myself with anybody tonight. I wish I hadn't taken any of that stuff.

[*She takes uncertain aim at the door; dashes at it; and barely escapes without disaster.*]

BURGESS [*indignantly*]. Stuff indeed! That gurl dunno what champagne is! Pomery and Greeno at twelve and six a bottle. She took two glasses amost straight horff.

MORELL [*anxious about her*]. Go and look after her, Lexy.

LEXY [*alarmed*]. But if she should really be— Suppose she began to sing in the street, or anything of that sort.

MORELL. Just so: she may. That's why you'd better see her safely home.

CANDIDA. Do, Lexy: there's a good fellow.

[*She shakes his hand and pushes him gently to the door.*]

LEXY. It's evidently my duty to go. I hope it may not be necessary. Good night, Mrs. Morell. [*To the rest*] Good night.

[*He goes.* CANDIDA *shuts the door.*]

BURGESS. He was gushin with hextra piety hisself arter two sips. People carn't drink like they useter. [*Bustling across to the hearth*] Well, James: it's time to lock up. Mr. Morchbanks: shall I ave the pleasure of your company for a bit o the way ome?

MARCHBANKS [*affrightedly*]. Yes: I'd better go.

[*He hurries towards the door; but* CANDIDA *places herself before it, barring his way.*]

CANDIDA [*with quiet authority*]. You sit down. You're not going yet.
MARCHBANKS [*quailing*]. No: I—I didn't mean to.

[*He sits down abjectly on the sofa.*]

CANDIDA. Mr. Marchbanks will stay the night with us, papa.
BURGESS. Oh well, I'll say good night. So long, James.

[*He shakes hands with* MORELL, *and goes over to* EUGENE.]

Make em give you a nightlight by your bed, Mr. Morchbanks: it'll comfort you if you wake up in the night with a touch of that complaint of yores. Good night.
MARCHBANKS. Thank you: I will. Good night, Mr. Burgess.

[*They shake hands.* BURGESS *goes to the door.*]

CANDIDA [*intercepting* MORELL, *who is following* BURGESS]. Stay here, dear: I'll put on papa's coat for him.

[*She goes out with* BURGESS.]

MARCHBANKS [*rising and stealing over to* MORELL]. Morell: there's going to be a terrible scene. Aren't you afraid?
MORELL. Not in the least.
MARCHBANKS. I never envied you your courage before.

[*He puts his hand appealingly on* MORELL'S *forearm.*]

Stand by me, won't you?
MORELL [*casting him off resolutely*]. Each for himself, Eugene. She must choose between us now.

[CANDIDA *returns.* EUGENE *creeps back to the sofa like a guilty schoolboy.*]

CANDIDA [*between them, addressing* EUGENE]. Are you sorry?
MARCHBANKS [*earnestly*]. Yes. Heartbroken.
CANDIDA. Well then, you are forgiven. Now go off to bed like a good little boy: I want to talk to James about you.
MARCHBANKS [*rising in great consternation*]. Oh, I can't do that, Morell. I must be here. I'll not go away. Tell her.
CANDIDA [*her suspicions confirmed*]. Tell me what?

[*His eyes avoid hers furtively. She turns and mutely transfers the question to* MORELL.]

MORELL [*bracing himself for the catastrophe*]. I have nothing to tell her, except [*here his voice deepens to a measured and mournful tenderness*] that she is my greatest treasure on earth—if she is really mine.

CANDIDA [*coldly, offended by his yielding to his orator's instinct and treating her as if she were the audience at the Guild of St. Matthew*]. I am sure Eugene can say no less, if that is all.

MARCHBANKS [*discouraged*]. Morell: she's laughing at us.

MORELL [*with a quick touch of temper*]. There is nothing to laugh at. Are you laughing at us, Candida?

CANDIDA [*with quiet anger*]. Eugene is very quick-witted, James. I hope I am going to laugh; but I am not sure that I am not going to be very angry.

[*She goes to the fireplace, and stands there leaning with her arm on the mantelpiece, and her foot on the fender, whilst* EUGENE *steals to* MORELL *and plucks him by the sleeve.*]

MARCHBANKS [*whispering*]. Stop, Morell. Don't let us say anything.

MORELL [*pushing* EUGENE *away without deigning to look at him*]. I hope you don't mean that as a threat, Candida.

CANDIDA [*with emphatic warning*]. Take care, James. Eugene: I asked you to go. Are you going?

MORELL [*putting his foot down*]. He shall not go. I wish him to remain.

MARCHBANKS. I'll go. I'll do whatever you want. [*He turns to the door.*]

CANDIDA. Stop! [*He obeys.*] Didn't you hear James say he wished you to stay? James is master here. Don't you know that?

MARCHBANKS [*flushing with a young poet's rage against tyranny*]. By what right is he master?

CANDIDA [*quietly*]. Tell him, James.

MORELL [*taken aback*]. My dear: I don't know of any right that makes me master. I assert no such right.

CANDIDA [*with infinite reproach*]. You don't know! Oh, James! James! [*To* EUGENE, *musingly*] I wonder do you understand, Eugene!

[*He shakes his head helplessly, not daring to look at her.*]

No: you're too young. Well, I give you leave to stay: to stay and learn.

[*She comes away from the hearth and places herself between them.*]

Now, James! what's the matter? Come: tell me.

MARCHBANKS [*whispering tremulously across to him*]. Don't.

CANDIDA. Come. Out with it!

MORELL [*slowly*]. I meant to prepare your mind carefully, Candida, so as to prevent misunderstanding.

CANDIDA. Yes, dear: I am sure you did. But never mind: I shan't misunderstand.

MORELL. Well—er—[*He hesitates, unable to find the long explanation which he supposed to be available.*]

CANDIDA. Well?

MORELL [*blurting it out badly*]. Eugene declares that you are in love with him.

MARCHBANKS [*frantically*]. No, no, no, no, never. I did not, Mrs. Morell: it's not true. I said I loved you. I said I understood you, and that he couldn't. And it was not after what passed there before the fire that I spoke: it was not, on my word. It was this morning.

CANDIDA [*enlightened*]. This morning!

MARCHBANKS. Yes. [*He looks at her, pleading for credence, and then adds simply*] That was what was the matter with my collar.

CANDIDA. Your collar? [*Suddenly taking in his meaning she turns to* MORELL, *shocked.*] Oh, James: did you—[*she stops*]?

MORELL [*ashamed*]. You know, Candida, that I have a temper to struggle with. And he said [*shuddering*] that you despised me in your heart.

CANDIDA [*turning quickly on* EUGENE]. Did you say that?

MARCHBANKS [*terrified*]. No.

CANDIDA [*almost fiercely*]. Then James has just told me a falsehood. Is that what you mean?

MARCHBANKS. No, no: I—I—[*desperately*] it was David's wife. And it wasn't at home: it was when she saw him dancing before all the people.

MORELL [*taking the cue with a debater's adroitness*]. Dancing before all the people, Candida; and thinking he was moving their hearts by his mission when they were only suffering from—Prossy's complaint.

[*She is about to protest: he raises his hand to silence her.*]

Don't try to look indignant, Candida—

CANDIDA. Try!

MORELL [*continuing*]. Eugene was right. As you told me a few hours after, he is always right. He said nothing that you did not say far better yourself. He is the poet, who sees everything; and I am the poor parson, who understands nothing.

CANDIDA [*remorsefully*]. Do you mind what is said by a foolish boy, because I said something like it in jest?

MORELL. That foolish boy can speak with the inspiration of a child and the cunning of a serpent. He has claimed that you belong to him and not to me; and, rightly or wrongly, I have come to fear that it may be true. I will not go about tortured with doubts and suspicions. I will not live with you and keep a secret from you. I will not suffer the intolerable degradation of jealousy. We have agreed—he and I—that you shall choose between us now. I await your decision.

CANDIDA [*slowly recoiling a step, her heart hardened by his rhetoric in spite of the sincere feeling behind it*]. Oh! I am to choose am I? I suppose it is quite settled that I must belong to one or the other.

MORELL [*firmly*]. Quite. You must choose definitely.

MARCHBANKS [*anxiously*]. Morell: you don't understand. She means that she belongs to herself.

CANDIDA [*turning to him*]. I mean that, and a good deal more, Master Eugene, as you will both find out presently. And pray, my lords and masters, what have you to offer for my choice? I am up for auction, it seems. What do you bid, James?

MORELL [*reproachfully*]. Cand— [*He breaks down: his eyes and throat fill with tears: the orator becomes a wounded animal.*] I can't speak—

CANDIDA [*impulsively going to him*]. Ah, dearest—

MARCHBANKS [*in wild alarm*]. Stop: it's not fair. You musn't show her that you suffer, Morell. I am on the rack too; but I am not crying.

MORELL [*rallying all his forces*]. Yes: you are right. It is not for pity that I am bidding.

[*He disengages himself from* CANDIDA.]

CANDIDA [*retreating, chilled*]. I beg your pardon, James: I did not mean to touch you. I am waiting to hear your bid.

MORELL [*with proud humility*]. I have nothing to offer you but my strength for your defence, my honesty for your surety, my ability and industry for your livelihood, and my authority and position for your dignity. That is all it becomes a man to offer to a woman.

CANDIDA [*quite quietly*]. And you, Eugene? What do you offer?

MARCHBANKS. My weakness. My desolation. My heart's need.

CANDIDA [*impressed*]. That's a good bid, Eugene. Now I know how to make my choice.

[*She pauses and looks curiously from one to the other, as if weighing them.* MORELL, *whose lofty confidence has changed into heartbreaking dread at Eugene's bid, loses all power of concealing his anxiety.* EUGENE, *strung to the highest tension, does not move a muscle.*]

MORELL [*in a suffocated voice: the appeal bursting from the depths of his anguish*]. Candida!

MARCHBANKS [*aside, in a flash of contempt*]. Coward!

CANDIDA [*significantly*]. I give myself to the weaker of the two.

[EUGENE *divines her meaning at once: his face whitens like steel in a furnace.*]

MORELL [*bowing his head with the calm of collapse*].   I accept your sentence, Candida.

CANDIDA.   Do you understand, Eugene?

MARCHBANKS.   Oh, I feel I'm lost.   He cannot bear the burden.

MORELL [*incredulously, raising his head and voice with comic abruptness*].   Do you mean me, Candida?

CANDIDA [*smiling a little*].   Let us sit and talk comfortably over it like three friends.   [*To* MORELL]   Sit down, dear.

[MORELL, *quite lost, takes the chair from the fireside: the children's chair.*]

Bring me that chair, Eugene.

[*She indicates the easy chair.   He fetches it silently, even with something like cold strength, and places it next* MORELL, *a little behind him.   She sits down.   He takes the visitor's chair himself, and sits, inscrutable.   When they are all settled she begins, throwing a spell of quietness on them by her calm, sane, tender tone.*]

You remember what you told me about yourself, Eugene: how nobody has cared for you since your old nurse died: how those clever fashionable sisters and successful brothers of yours were your mother's and father's pets: how miserable you were at Eton: how your father is trying to starve you into returning to Oxford: how you have had to live without comfort or welcome or refuge: always lonely, and nearly always disliked and misunderstood, poor boy!

MARCHBANKS [*faithful to the nobility of his lot*].   I had my books. I had Nature.   And at last I met you.

CANDIDA.   Never mind that just at present.   Now I want you to look at this other boy here! my boy! spoiled from his cradle.   We go once a fortnight to see his parents.   You should come with us, Eugene, to see the pictures of the hero of that household.   James as a baby! the most wonderful of all babies.   James holding his first school prize, won at the ripe age of eight!   James as the captain of his eleven!   James in his first frock coat!   James under all sorts of glorious circumstances!   You know how strong he is (I hope he didn't hurt you): how clever he is: how happy.   [*With deepening gravity*]   Ask James's mother and his three sisters what it cost to save James the trouble of doing anything but be strong and clever and happy.   Ask me what it costs to be James's mother and three sisters and wife and mother to his children all in one.   Ask Prossy and Maria how troublesome the house is even when we have no visitors to help us to slice the onions.   Ask the tradesmen who want to worry James and spoil his beautiful sermons who it is that puts them off. When there is money to give, he gives it: when there is money to refuse,

I refuse it. I build a castle of comfort and indulgence and love for him, and stand sentinel always to keep little vulgar cares out. I make him master here, though he does not know it, and could not tell you a moment ago how it came to be so. [*With sweet irony*] And when he thought I might go away with you, his only anxiety was—what should become of me! And to tempt me to stay he offered me [*leaning forward to stroke his hair caressingly at each phrase*] his strength for my defence! his industry for my livelihood! his dignity for my position! his—[*relenting*] ah, I am mixing up your beautiful cadences and spoiling them, am I not, darling? [*She lays her cheek fondly against his.*]

MORELL [*quite overcome, kneeling beside her chair and embracing her with boyish ingenuousness*]. It's all true, every word. What I am you have made me with the labor of your hands and the love of your heart. You are my wife, my mother, my sisters: you are the sum of all loving care to me.

CANDIDA [*in his arms, smiling, to* EUGENE]. Am I your mother and sisters to you, Eugene?

MARCHBANKS [*rising with a fierce gesture of disgust*]. Ah, never. Out, then, into the night with me!

CANDIDA [*rising quickly*]. You are not going like that, Eugene?

MARCHBANKS [*with the ring of a man's voice—no longer a boy's—in the words*]. I know the hour when it strikes. I am impatient to do what must be done.

MORELL [*who has also risen*]. Candida: don't let him do anything rash.

CANDIDA [*confident, smiling at* EUGENE]. Oh, there is no fear. He has learnt to live without happiness.

MARCHBANKS. I no longer desire happiness: life is nobler than that. Parson James: I give you my happiness with both hands: I love you because you have filled the heart of the woman I loved. Good-bye. [*He goes towards the door.*]

CANDIDA. One last word.

[*He stops, but without turning to her. She goes to him.*]

How old are you, Eugene?

MARCHBANKS. As old as the world now. This morning I was eighteen.

CANDIDA. Eighteen! Will you, for my sake, make a little poem out of the two sentences I am going to say to you? And will you promise to repeat it to yourself whenever you think of me?

MARCHBANKS [*without moving*]. Say the sentences.

CANDIDA. When I am thirty, she will be forty-five. When I am sixty, she will be seventy-five.

MARCHBANKS [*turning to her*]. In a hundred years, we shall be the same age. But I have a better secret than that in my heart. Let me go now. The night outside grows impatient.

CANDIDA. Good-bye.

[*She takes his face in her hands; and as he divines her intention and falls on his knees, she kisses his forehead. Then he flies out into the night. She turns to* MORELL, *holding out her arms to him.*]

Ah, James!

[*They embrace. But they do not know the secret in the poet's heart.*]

Two Critical Commentaries on Bernard Shaw's *Candida*

Commentary by Edward Everett Hale, Jr., from *Dramatists of To-day* (New York, Henry Holt, 1905, 1911).*

Let us get on, however, to *Candida,* for that is, I take it, the best of Mr. Shaw's plays. It was the most successful both on publication and on the stage. It gave most immediate pleasure and comes most readily to mind. It has both ideas and action.

Candida carries the process of eye-opening, so dear to Mr. Shaw, one step farther than *Arms and the Man.* First we have the Rev. James Morell, a Christian Socialist, and therefore at war with the many evils and falsenesses of our social life, and intent in bringing in a good, strong, and honest way of life among people who are too much bent on making money and enjoying themselves to consider carefully the ways in which they do so. Certainly the character is inimitably good, and when we think chiefly of that kind of pleasure that comes from seeing people and things presented in a perfectly natural way and with a perfectly sure touch, aside from what they happen to be, when we answer with a thrill to every certainty of portrayal, and chuckle to ourselves at every small point of human frailty painted for us just as it is, why, the Reverend James appeals to us as few figures upon the modern stage. We have him at his best in the contrast with Mr. Burgess, the "man of sixty, made coarse by the compulsory selfishness of petty commerce"— there we have him at his best, and he makes the right impression, a go-ahead, clear-visioned, plain-speaking man, understanding the world and taking it for what it is. . . . We certainly have here one who sees through the shams of modern life, and by the very clearness of his vision, somehow, has power to make all others feel all their sham pretentiousness. And as he transfixes the ridiculous commercialist who is trying to make friends with the Mammon

---

* Reprinted by permission of Henry Holt and Company, publishers, from Edward Everett Hale, Jr., *Dramatists of To-day.*

of righteousness, we feel that he and we are of those in the front rank of progress, the men who know what is right and so can do it.

And then appears Candida and her poet. He is, to start with, singularly and strangely frank, and strange and singular in other ways. As he and Candida drove from the station he was tormented all the time with wondering what he ought to give the cabman. He is not made to get along well in an everyday world—that is, not as the world considers getting on well.

But it soon appears that the poet is there to show us a range of view above the Reverend James. A poet is a man more sensitive than the rest of the world, and who therefore sees more than most men, and who has more power of expression and therefore says what he sees more exactly. . . . The poet opens up on Morell at once, and comes out of each encounter on top. . . .

I will confess that when "Morell grasps him powerfully by the lapel of his coat, he cowers down on the sofa and screams powerfully," I rather sympathized with the bigger man. And when Morell called him a little snivelling, cowardly whelp, and told him to go before he frightened himself into a fit, I had enough red blood in me to agree with him. But really, of course, it is not anything especially to admire in a man that he is physically so much more powerful than another that he could knock him into a cock-up hat. . . . So clearly the Reverend James is not a finer fellow, with all the breadth of his chest; indeed, he would be the first to discredit the reign of brute force, in spite of the charms of muscular Christianity.

In fact Marchbanks gives us a second eye-opening, and we perceive that the first was, in a measure, deceptive. Mr. Shaw was playing with us. The first was too easy. It is not so much to see through the deceits and shams of society nowadays. . . . Not that Reverend James is absolutely a pretentious gasbag any more than Marchbanks is an inspired prophet. He has a definite, a positive part in the world's work. You cannot reform the world with a few epigrams; most reformers are impracticable persons, which means that they cannot determine details, do not like to take the trouble to make their ideas fit complicated cases. . . . The Rev. James Morell is a typical talker. The original thinker is a dreamer and doesn't like to do anything. The talkers are commonly men of vitality who have neither the imagination to dream nor the patience to think for themselves. They want to do something in this world, but, having no notion of just what they can do, they take it out in talking. They believe absolutely in what they say, while they say it, and they rouse people to a state of excited conviction by the hypnotic power of their language, as Mr. Morell did at the meeting of the Guild of St. Matthew. It is these latter people, those that listen to the talkers, who go ahead and do the world's work in reforming itself; but as they are creatures of the emotions rather than of the intellect, they never follow people like Marchbanks because they do not understand them nor like them, but do follow people like Mr. Morell because they do like them and do not have to understand them.

Of course Mr. Shaw is one of the Marchbankses, but he is not entirely without sympathy for the Morells. (pp. 119-25)

Commentary by Eric Bentley, from *The Playwright as Thinker* (New York, Reynal & Hitchcock, 1946).*

Shaw's *Candida* (1895), one of the best liked of his plays, is about a trite situation. A young man enters the home of a married couple and falls in love with the wife. In the commodity drama of Shaw's day—the Parisian drama of Emile Augier, Dumas *fils,* and Victorien Sardou—there are two ways of dealing with such a situation. The young man can be the hero, the husband can be either a tyrant or a bore or both, and the play can be a protest against bourgeois marriage: an idea for Dumas *fils*. Alternatively the husband can be a genuine pillar of society, the lover a fool or a scoundrel, and the play can end with a vindication of hearth and home and with the discomfiture of the intruder: an idea for Augier.

In the opinion of his audiences Shaw wrote the Augier play. That is why it is so popular. On the surface the titillations of modernity, underneath an utter conventionality: that is what the literati have made out Shaw to be; that is what the public accepts him as. And the Augier play is actually contained within Shaw's. Shaw does show an attractive modern couple upholding the dignity of marriage. The husband of the triangle is such a socialist as everyone can imagine hobnobbing with Shaw himself at meetings of the Fabian society. Against the talented and generous character of this man, the effeminacy of the lover is calculated to excite the contemptuous laughter of any audience. *Candida* audiences go home fairly glowing with the feeling that after all Shaw did the decent thing in the end.

But did he? A moment's thought tells us that the Reverend James Mavor Morell is not what we thought he was. He has been the victim of a life-illusion of Ibsenite proportions: he has thoroughly misunderstand the marriage on which all his boasted confidence and happiness were based. The aesthetic lover, however, whom audiences, congratulating each other on their normality, invariably laugh at, turns out to be stronger than the famous strong man Morell. That, as it proves, is not saying much. Eugene Marchbanks is strong by any standard. He is all the time acquiring that last ability of noble mind, the ability to live without illusions, and at the end he has acquired it. A look through the play will convince the skeptic that Shaw invariably puts the truth in Eugene's mouth and seldom in anybody else's. Even the things that arouse most derision are truths which nobody in the play—or perhaps in the playhouse—shares with Eugene. Shaw, then, pretends to weight the scales in favor of the husband, when actually the lover is the bigger man. Do we then have the Dumas play? Is Eugene the hero, Morell a millstone round his wife's neck? Obviously not. Eugene's superiority leads not to adultery but to his voluntary departure. . .

All this is to judge by the relative weight given to the male rivals in the triangle. It is to reckon without the eponymous heroine. And, since she is

*From *The Playwright as Thinker,* copyright, 1946, by Eric Bentley. Reprinted by permission of Harcourt, Brace and Company, Inc.

indeed an expression of the feminine enigma, she is best left to the last. On the surface Candida seems to be everything to this play: title, leading role, master of the situation. Her charm is so great that no audience would wish to look behind it. . . . Ponder Candida's words and actions, however, for two minutes, and the drama of sentiment falls down like a pack of cards. She is expert at keeping the women away from her husband, yet, aware as she is of her own charms, she does not hesitate to flaunt them before an obviously susceptible young man. She denies all suspicion that he is in love with her long after the fact has become evident. . . . A feline cruelty drives her to taunt her husband by declaring that she would give herself to Eugene if necessary, while taunting Eugene by pointing to him and histrionically demanding: Do you call *that* a man? She caps her cruelty by a fake climax in which she portentously pretends to choose between the two men. Obviously she could not do anything else with Morell but keep him, especially since her own chief pleasure in life is bossing him around; and by this time it is doubtful whether Eugene would take her anyway. He has learned better. . . .

The play is not Augier, for marriage is not vindicated. On the contrary, now that the scales have fallen from Morell's eyes, this marriage can never be the same again. . . . Candida, who is not the heroine that she seems, whose problems are not the main subject of the play as the title of it might suggest, is indeed master of the situation . . . in unintentionally, perhaps inadvisedly, curing both men of their illusions about her and their relation to her. It is by her means that the popular parson is unconverted. It is by her means that the poet learns to live without happiness—that is, without women. The subject of the play is the destiny of the two men. Candida, who alone is unchanged at the end, is the link between them.

Is she, then, the villain of the play? To push the argument so far, simply to invert the more obvious interpretations of the play is to be no nearer to the truth than they. . . . In *Candida* Shaw shows all the truth there is in the Augier philosophy and all the truth there is in the Dumas philosophy. He himself surpasses both . . . by the all-roundness of his vision. . . .

Candida is not simply a bad woman. The sweetness which she pours over the whole play is not the suspect and poisonous sweetness of a she-devil. It is genuine. But it is combined with other, less amiable qualities. . . . *Candida* is the sweeter for not being all sugar. The *Candida* atmosphere—bland yet delicate, graceful yet gay, tender yet ironical—is an emanation of the *Candida* dialectic.   (pp. 165-68)

VI. LIFE WITH FATHER

A Period Comedy by Lindsay and Crouse

Introductory Note to Clarence Day, the playwrights, and *Life with Father*

Comedy, by its very nature, belongs to its own day. But *Life with Father*—which Howard Lindsay and Russel Crouse turned into the most enduring comedy in American theatrical history—really belongs, not only to Clarence Day (happy pun), but to the day and age it depicts, to the day and years when it was written and produced, and to our own and days to come. It pictures New York in the late 1880's; it amused and heartened America during all the years of World War II; and it remains to kindle our laughter and understanding of family life.

Each of the three authors of *Life with Father* contributed significantly to its substance as a period comedy.

Clarence Day, Jr., who wrote the autobiographical and family sketches upon which the play is based, was born in New York in 1874, the son of Father (Clarence, Sr.), a Wall Street broker, and of Mother (Lavinia). He was grandson of a newspaper man, Benjamin H. Day, founder of the New York *Sun,* and nephew of Ben Day, who gave his name to the printing process long in use. Clarence, Jr., went from St. Paul's School to Yale, graduated in 1896, then entered business with his father. A turn in the navy during the Spanish-American War left him with the arthritis that by middle life completely crippled him. He married in 1928, and fathered a daughter. He carried on some business from his bed, but gradually developed himself as a humorous essayist—in prose, verse, and illustration—and ran a book column for the *Metropolitan Magazine.* His first volume, *This Simian World* (1920), was harder on the humans than the apes. His family sketches, written for various journals, were published as *God and My Father* (1932), *Life with Father* (1935), and *Life with Mother* (1937). Father Day, who lived to a ripe age and long enough to read some of the first of these

482

sketches, commented heartily upon their accuracy without any apparent disapproval of their intimate revelation. As a personality, Clarence Day, Jr., was much like the father for whom he was named and for whom he provided a lively immortality. He died from pneumonia at the end of 1935, at age sixty-one.

Howard Lindsay, the actor, chuckled over the Clarence Day sketches as he read them evenings to his wife. He fancied they might make a comedy for them to act in together, and he prevailed upon the author's widow to allow him and his collaborator, Russel Crouse, to proceed with a dramatization.

Lindsay, born in 1889 in Waterford, New York, on the Hudson, was brought up in Atlantic City, went to high school in Boston and to Harvard for one year. He turned from thoughts of the ministry to a decision for the stage, and joined a touring company when he was twenty. After youthful trials—in silent films, vaudeville, burlesque—he got a job with Margaret Anglin as a bit player and assistant manager for five years. After World War I, wherein his special talents were used by the army in France, he returned to the New York stage and married. In 1921 he directed and acted in *Dulcy,* a comedy that not only launched his own successful career but those of George S. Kaufman and Marc Connelly, as playwrights, and of Lynn Fontanne, as actress. His own playwriting began in 1927. In that year his second marriage, to the actress Dorothy Stickney, established a happy partnership that later was to bring them together on the stage as Father and Mother. As such they became the unexpected Day parents of a succession of twenty-eight boys who played and outgrew their roles and their costumes. Howard Lindsay is a thorough-going man of the theater, having survived 45 years as an actor, then director, journeyman playwright, and producer.

Russel Crouse, on the other hand, grew up as a newspaper man. Born in 1893 in Findlay, Ohio, and brought up in Toledo, he missed an Annapolis appointment (failing math) and became a reporter at seventeen. Except for his navy duty in World War I, he continued as a sports writer, journalist, and press agent (for the Theater Guild) until he was forty-four. His interest in Americana led to his book *Mr. Currier and Mr. Ives* (1930). The next year he was in on his first libretto. This led shortly to his collaborating with Howard Lindsay, to scenario work in Hollywood, and to his partnership with Lindsay as theatrical producer—together producing such stage hits as *Arsenic and Old Lace* (1941) and *The Hasty Heart* (1944).

Crouse was widowed after a marriage of twenty years, but happily remarried and has three children.

Howard Lindsay had done a good bit of playwriting and collaborating on librettos before his first work with Russel Crouse in 1934, which was fashioning the book for *Anything Goes,* with music by Cole Porter. Their success together in musical comedy continued. *Life with Father* in 1939 was their first joint effort in the nonmusical form—of which more in a moment. Their next play, *Strip for Action* (1942), was unimportant. Then came their political drama *State of the Union* (1945)—"to stir the conscience of the individual citizen"—which won the Pulitzer Prize in 1946 and ran for two years on Broadway. Their *Life with Mother* (1948) was inevitably less fortunate than *Father,* but played a lively full season, again with Lindsay and his wife in their familiar roles of Father and Mother. With Crouse, Lindsay again did the book for a musical, *Call Me Madam* (1950), this time with music by Irving Berlin. *Remains to be Seen* (1951) was frankly theatrical fare, but good for a year's business.

Life with Father, however, is an American folk comedy of enduring quality. For two years Lindsay (with his special sense of theater) and Crouse (with his gift for comedy) talked over and over the problems of dramatizing the sketches written by Clarence Day. It was no simple matter to provide the necessary, though slight, framework to support the characterizations and nostalgic humor and view of life that emerge from the charming prose pieces originally created for magazine publication. However, once the dramatic structure was set in their minds, scene by scene, they wrote the dialogue of *Life with Father* in seventeen days! Tried out in a summer theater near Skowhegan, Maine, the comedy then opened in New York City, on November 8, 1939, at the old Empire Theater—itself a gracious survival of that earlier time. In the cast were Howard Lindsay (who grew a real beard for the role), Dorothy Stickney, John Drew Devereaux as Clarence, Jr., and Teresa Wright in her stage debut as Mary. *Life with Father* was produced by Oscar Serlin, staged by Bretaigne Windust, designed by Stewart Chaney. It was a triumphant theatrical and critical success and ran for nearly eight years on Broadway (closing on July 12, 1947), finally attaining the all-time record run of 3224 performances! Other companies played *Life with Father* on tour for several seasons, and a film was made in 1947 with William Powell and Irene Dunn as the Day parents.

———

CLARENCE DAY'S

LIFE WITH FATHER

MADE INTO A PLAY *

By Howard Lindsay and Russel Crouse

THE CHARACTERS

FATHER—*Clarence Day, Sr., whom his wife calls "Clare."*

MOTHER—*Mr. Day's wife, whom her husband calls "Vinnie."*

CLARENCE—*Clarence Day, Jr., aged 17, on the verge of Yale.*
  JOHN—*the second Day son, aged 15.*
  WHITNEY—*the third, aged 13.*
  HARLAN—*the fourth, aged 6.*

CORA CARTWRIGHT—*Vinnie's country cousin, aged 30.*

MARY SKINNER—*her pretty, small-town friend, aged 16.*

The Reverend DR. LLOYD—*the Episcopal rector.*
  DR. HUMPHRIES—*the family physician.*
  DR. SOMERS—*a medical consultant.*

MARGARET—*the long-time family cook.*
  ANNIE—*a new maid.*
  DELIA—*a new maid.*
  NORA—*a new maid.*
  MAGGIE—*a new maid.*

Time: *the late eighteen-eighties in New York City.*
Place: *the well-to-do home of Clarence Day, Sr.*

ACT ONE

SCENE I

THE MORNING ROOM *of the Day home at 420 Madison Avenue. In the custom of the Victorian period, this was the room where the family gathered for breakfast, and because it was often the most comfortable room in the house it served also as a living-room for the family and their intimates.*

---

* Reprinted from Clarence Day's *Life with Father* made into a play by Howard Lindsay and Russel Crouse, by permission of Alfred A. Knopf, Inc. Copyright 1939, 1940 by Howard Lindsay, Russel Crouse, and Katharine B. Day.

There is a large arch in the center of the upstage wall of the room, through which we can see the hall and the stairs leading to the second floor, and below them the rail of the stairwell leading to the basement. The room can be closed off from the hall by sliding doors in the archway. The front door of the house, which is stage right, can't be seen, but frequently is heard to slam.

In the Morning Room the sunshine streams through the large window at the right which looks out on Madison Avenue. The room itself is furnished with the somewhat less than comfortable furniture of the period, which is the late 1880's. The general color scheme in drapes and upholstery is green. Below the window is a large comfortable chair where FATHER *generally sits to read his paper. Right of center is the table which serves as a living-room table, with its proper table cover and fruit bowl; but now, expanded by extra leaves, it is doing service as a breakfast table. Against the back wall, either side of the arch, are two console tables which are used by the maid as serving tables. Left of center is a sofa, with a table just above its right end holding a lamp, framed photographs, and other ornaments. In the left wall is a fireplace, its mantel draped with a lambrequin. On the mantel are a clock and other ornaments, and above the mantel is a large mirror in a Victorian frame. The room is cluttered with the minutiæ of the period, including the inevitable rubber plant, and looking down from the walls are the Day ancestors in painted portraits. The room has the warm quality that comes only from having been lived in by a family which enjoys each other's company—a family of considerable means.*

As the curtain rises, ANNIE, *the new maid, a young Irish girl, is finishing setting the table for breakfast. After an uncertain look at the result she crosses over to her tray on the console table.* VINNIE *comes down the stairs and into the room.* VINNIE *is a charming, lovable, and spirited woman of forty. She has a lively mind which darts quickly away from any practical matter. She has red hair.*

ANNIE. Good morning, ma'am.

VINNIE. Good morning, Annie. How are you getting along?

ANNIE. All right, ma'am, I hope.

VINNIE. Now, don't be worried just because this is your first day. Everything's going to be all right—but I do hope nothing goes wrong. [*Goes to the table.*] Now, let's see, is the table all set? [ANNIE *follows her.*] The cream and the sugar go down at this end.

ANNIE [*placing them where* VINNIE *has indicated*]. I thought in the center, ma'am; everyone could reach them easier.

VINNIE. Mr. Day sits here.

ANNIE [*gets a tray of napkins, neatly rolled and in their rings, from the console table*]. I didn't know where to place the napkins, ma'am.

VINNIE. You can tell which go where by the rings.

[*Takes them from the tray and puts them down as she goes around the table.* ANNIE *follows her.*]

This one belongs to Whitney—it has his initial on it, "W"; that one with the little dog on it is Harlan's, of course. He's the baby. This "J" is for John and the "C" is for Clarence. This narrow plain one is mine. And this is Mr. Day's. It's just like mine—except that it got bent one morning. And that reminds me—always be sure Mr. Day's coffee is piping hot.

ANNIE. Ah, your man has coffee instead of tea of a morning?

VINNIE. We all have coffee except the two youngest boys. They have their milk. And, Annie, always speak of my husband as Mr. Day.

ANNIE. I will that.

VINNIE [*correcting her*]. "Yes, ma'am," Annie.

ANNIE. Yes, ma'am.

VINNIE. And if Mr. Day speaks to you, just say: "Yes, sir." Don't be nervous—you'll get used to him.

[CLARENCE, *the eldest son, about seventeen, comes down the stairs and into the room. He is a manly, serious, good-looking boy. Because he is starting in at Yale next year, he thinks he is grown-up. He is red-headed.*]

CLARENCE. Good morning, Mother. [*He kisses her.*]

VINNIE. Good morning, Clarence.

CLARENCE. Did you sleep well, Mother?

VINNIE. Yes, thank you, dear.

[CLARENCE *goes to* FATHER's *chair and picks up the morning paper. To* ANNIE]

We always start with fruit, except the two young boys, who have porridge.

[ANNIE *brings the fruit and porridge to the table.* CLARENCE, *looking at the paper, makes a whistling sound.*]

CLARENCE. Jiminy! Another wreck on the New Haven. That always disturbs the market. Father won't like that.

VINNIE. I do wish that New Haven would stop having wrecks. If they knew how it upset your father— [*Sees that* CLARENCE's *coat has been torn and mended.*] My soul and body, Clarence, what's happened to your coat?

CLARENCE. I tore it. Margaret mended it for me.

VINNIE. It looks terrible. Why don't you wear your blue suit?

CLARENCE. That looks worse than this one. You know, I burnt that hole in it.

VINNIE. Oh, yes—well, you can't go around looking like that. I'll have to speak to your father. Oh, dear!

[JOHN, *who is about fifteen, comes down the stairs and into the room.* JOHN *is gangly and a little overgrown. He is red-headed.*]

JOHN. Good morning, Mother. [*He kisses her.*]

VINNIE. Good morning, John.

JOHN [*to* CLARENCE]. Who won?

CLARENCE. I haven't looked yet.

JOHN. Let me see. [*He tries to take the paper away from* CLARENCE.]

CLARENCE. Be careful!

VINNIE. Boys, don't wrinkle that paper before your father's looked at it.

CLARENCE [*to* JOHN]. Yes!

[VINNIE *turns to* ANNIE.]

VINNIE. You'd better get things started. We want everything ready when Mr. Day comes down.

[ANNIE *exits.*]

Clarence, right after breakfast I want you and John to move the small bureau from my room into yours.

CLARENCE. What for? Is somebody coming to visit us?

JOHN. Who's coming?

VINNIE. I haven't said anyone was coming. And don't you say anything about it. I want it to be a surprise.

CLARENCE. Oh! Father doesn't know yet?

VINNIE. No. And I'd better speak to him about a new suit for you before he finds out he's being surprised by visitors.

[ANNIE *enters with a tray on which are two glasses of milk, which she puts at* HARLAN's *and* WHITNEY's *places at the table.* WHITNEY *comes down the stairs and rushes into the room. He is about thirteen. Suiting his age, he is a lively active boy. He is red-headed.*]

WHITNEY. Morning. [*He kisses his mother quickly, then runs to* CLARENCE *and* JOHN.] Who won?

JOHN. The Giants, 7 to 3. Buck Ewing hit a home run.

WHITNEY. Let me see!

[HARLAN *comes sliding down the banister. He enters the room, runs to his mother, and kisses her.* HARLAN *is a roly-poly, lovable, good-natured youngster of six. He is red-headed.*]

VINNIE. How's your finger, darling?

HARLAN. It itches.

VINNIE [*kissing the finger*]. That's a sign it's getting better. Now don't scratch it. Sit down, boys. Get in your chair, darling.

[*The boys move to the table and take their places.* CLARENCE *puts the newspaper beside his father's plate.* JOHN *stands waiting to place* VINNIE's *chair when she sits.*]

Now, Annie, watch Mr. Day, and as soon as he finishes his fruit—

[*Leaves the admonition hanging in mid-air as the sound of* FATHER's *voice booms from upstairs.*]

FATHER'S VOICE. Vinnie! Vinnie!

[*All eyes turn toward the staircase.* VINNIE *rushes to the foot of the stairs, speaking as she goes.*]

VINNIE. What's the matter, Clare?

FATHER'S VOICE. Where's my necktie?

VINNIE. Which necktie?

FATHER'S VOICE. The one I gave you yesterday.

VINNIE. It isn't pressed yet. I forgot to give it to Margaret.

FATHER'S VOICE. I told you distinctly I wanted to wear that necktie today.

VINNIE. You've got plenty of neckties. Put on another one right away and come down to breakfast.

FATHER'S VOICE. Oh, damn! Damnation!

[VINNIE *goes to her place at the table.* JOHN *places her chair for her, then sits.* WHITNEY *has started eating.*]

CLARENCE. Whitney!

VINNIE. Wait for your father, Whitney.

WHITNEY. Oh, and I'm in a hurry! John, can I borrow your glove today? I'm going to pitch.

JOHN. If I don't play myself.

WHITNEY. Look, if you need it, we're playing in that big field at the corner of Fifty-seventh and Madison.

VINNIE. 'Way up there!

WHITNEY. They're building a house on that vacant lot on Fiftieth Street.

VINNIE. My! My! My! Here we move to Forty-eighth Street just to get out of the city!

WHITNEY. Can't I start breakfast, Mother? I promised to be there by eight o'clock.

VINNIE. After breakfast, Whitney, you have to study your catechism.

WHITNEY. Mother, can't I do that this afternoon?

VINNIE. Whitney, you have to learn five questions every morning before you leave the house.

WHITNEY. Aw, Mother—

VINNIE. You weren't very sure of yourself when I heard you last night.

WHITNEY. I know them now.

VINNIE. Let's see.

[WHITNEY *rises and faces his mother.*]

"What is your name?"

WHITNEY. Whitney Benjamin.

VINNIE. "Who gave you this name?"

WHITNEY. "My sponsors in baptism, wherein I was made a member of Christ, the child of God and an inheritor of the Kingdom of Heaven." Mother, if I hadn't been baptized wouldn't I have a name?

VINNIE. Not in the sight of the Church. "What did your sponsors then for you?"

WHITNEY. "They did promise and vow three things in my name—"

[FATHER *makes his appearance on the stairway and comes down into the room.* FATHER *is in his forties, distinguished in appearance, with great charm and vitality, extremely well dressed in a conservative way. He is red-headed.*]

FATHER [*heartily*]. Good morning, boys. [*They rise and answer him.*] Good morning, Vinnie. [*He goes to her and kisses her.*] Have a good night?

VINNIE. Yes, thank you, Clare.

FATHER. Good! Sit down, boys.

[*The doorbell rings and a postman's whistle is heard.*]

VINNIE. That's the doorbell, Annie.

[ANNIE *exits.*]

Clare, that new suit looks very nice.

FATHER. Too damn tight! [*He sits in his place at the head of the table.*] What's the matter with those fellows over in London? I wrote them a year ago they were making my clothes too tight!

VINNIE. You've put on a little weight, Clare.

FATHER. I weigh just the same as I always have.

[*Attacks his orange. The boys dive into their breakfasts.* ANNIE *enters with the mail, starts to take it to* VINNIE. FATHER *sees her.*]

What's that? The mail? That goes to me.

[ANNIE *gives the mail to* FATHER *and exits with her tray.*]

VINNIE. Well, Clarence has just managed to tear the only decent suit of clothes he has.

FATHER [*looking through the mail*]. Here's one for you, Vinnie. John, hand that to your mother. [*He passes the letter on.*]

VINNIE. Clare dear, I'm sorry, but I'm afraid Clarence is going to have to have a new suit of clothes.

FATHER. Vinnie, Clarence has to learn not to be so hard on his clothes.

CLARENCE. Father, I thought—

FATHER. Clarence, when you start in Yale in the fall, I'm going to set aside a thousand dollars just to outfit you, but you'll get no new clothes this summer.

CLARENCE. Can't I have one of your old suits cut down for me?

FATHER. Every suit I own still has plenty of wear in it. I wear my clothes until they're worn out.

VINNIE. Well, if you want your clothes worn out, Clarence can wear them out much faster than you can.

CLARENCE. Yes, and, Father, you don't get a chance to wear them out. Every time you get a new batch of clothes, Mother sends the old ones to the missionary barrel. I guess I'm just as good as any old missionary.

[ANNIE *returns with a platter of bacon and eggs and a pot of coffee.*]

VINNIE. Clarence, before you compare yourself to a missionary, remember the sacrifices they make.

FATHER [*chuckling*]. I don't know, Vinnie, I think my clothes would look better on Clarence than on some Hottentot. [*To* CLARENCE] Have that black suit of mine cut down to fit you before your mother gets her hands on it.

[ANNIE *clears the fruit.*]

CLARENCE. Thank you, Father. [*To* JOHN] One of Father's suits! Thank you, sir!

FATHER. Whitney, don't eat so fast.

WHITNEY. Well, Father, I'm going to pitch today and I promised to get there early, but before I go I have to study my catechism.

FATHER. What do you bother with that for?

VINNIE [*with spirit*]. Because if he doesn't know his catechism he can't be confirmed!

WHITNEY [*pleading*]. But I'm going to pitch today.

FATHER. Vinnie, Whitney's going to pitch today and he can be confirmed any old time.

VINNIE. Clare, sometimes it seems to me that you don't care whether your children get to Heaven or not.

FATHER. Oh, Whitney'll get to Heaven all right. [*To* WHITNEY] I'll be there before you are, Whitney; I'll see that you get in.

VINNIE. What makes you so sure they'll let you in?

FATHER. Well, if they don't I'll certainly raise a devil of a row.

[ANNIE *is at* FATHER's *side with the platter of bacon and eggs, ready to serve him, and draws back at this astounding declaration, raising the platter.*]

VINNIE [*with shocked awe*]. Clare, I do hope you'll behave when you get to Heaven.

[FATHER *has turned to serve himself from the platter, but* ANNIE, *not yet recovered from the picture of* FATHER *raising a row at the gates of Heaven, is holding it too high for him.*]

FATHER [*storming*]. Vinnie, how many times have I asked you not to engage a maid who doesn't even know how to serve properly?

VINNIE. Clare, can't you see she's new and doing her best?

FATHER. How can I serve myself when she's holding that platter over my head?

VINNIE. Annie, why don't you hold it lower?

[ANNIE *lowers the platter.* FATHER *serves himself, but goes on talking.*]

FATHER. Where'd she come from anyway? What became of the new one we had yesterday? I don't see why you can't keep a maid.

VINNIE. Oh, you don't!

FATHER. All I want is service.

[ANNIE *serves the others nervously. So far as* FATHER *is concerned, however, the storm has passed, and he turns genially to* WHITNEY.]

Whitney, when we get to Heaven we'll organize a baseball team of our own.

[*The boys laugh.*]

VINNIE. It would be just like you to try to run things up there.

FATHER. Well, from all I've heard about Heaven, it seems to be a pretty unbusinesslike place. They could probably use a good man like me.

[*Stamps on the floor three times. It is his traditional signal to summon* MARGARET, *the cook, from the kitchen below.*]

VINNIE. What do you want Margaret for? What's wrong?

[ANNIE *has reached the sideboard and is sniffing audibly.*]

FATHER [*distracted*]. What's that damn noise?

VINNIE. Shhh—it's Annie.

FATHER. Annie? Who's Annie?
VINNIE. The maid.

[ANNIE, *seeing that she has attracted attention, hurries out into the hall where she can't be seen or heard.*]

Clare, aren't you ashamed of yourself?
FATHER [*surprised*]. What have I done now?
VINNIE. You made her cry—speaking to her the way you did.
FATHER. I never said a word to her—I was addressing myself to you.
VINNIE. I do wish you'd be more careful. It's hard enough to keep a maid—and the uniforms just fit this one.

[MARGARET, *the cook, a small Irishwoman of about fifty, hurries into the room.*]

MARGARET. What's wanting?
FATHER. Margaret, this bacon is *good*. [MARGARET *beams and gestures deprecatingly.*] It's *good*. It's done just right!
MARGARET. Yes, sir!

[*She smiles and exits.* ANNIE *returns, recovered, and starts serving the coffee.* VINNIE *has opened her letter and glanced through it.*]

VINNIE. Clare, this letter gives me a good idea. I've decided that next winter I won't give a series of dinners.
FATHER. I should hope not.
VINNIE. I'll give a big musicale instead.
FATHER. You'll give a what?
VINNIE. A musicale.
FATHER [*peremptorily*]. Vinnie, I won't have my peaceful home turned into a Roman arena with a lot of hairy fiddlers prancing about.
VINNIE. I didn't say a word about hairy fiddlers. Mrs. Spiller has written me about this lovely young girl who will come for very little.
FATHER. What instrument does this inexpensive paragon play?
VINNIE. She doesn't play, Clare, she whistles.
FATHER. Whistles? Good God!
VINNIE. She whistles sixteen different pieces. All for twenty-five dollars.
FATHER [*stormily*]. I won't pay twenty-five dollars to any human peanut stand.

[*He tastes his coffee, grimaces, and again stamps three times on the floor.*]

VINNIE. Clare, I can arrange this so it won't cost you a penny. If I invite fifty people and charge them fifty cents apiece, there's the twenty-five dollars right there!

FATHER. You can't invite people to your own house and charge them admission.

VINNIE. I can if the money's for the missionary fund.

FATHER. Then where will you get the twenty-five dollars to pay that poor girl for her whistling?

VINNIE. Now, Clare, let's not cross that bridge until we come to it.

FATHER. And if we do cross it, it will cost me twenty-five dollars. Vinnie, I'm putting my foot down about this musicale, just as I've had to put my foot down about your keeping this house full of visiting relatives. Why can't we live here by ourselves in peace and comfort?

[MARGARET *comes dashing into the room.*]

MARGARET. What's wanting?

FATHER [*sternly*]. Margaret, what is this? [*He holds up his coffee cup and points at it.*]

MARGARET. It's coffee, sir.

FATHER. It is not coffee! You couldn't possibly take water and coffee beans and arrive at that! It's slops, that's what it is—slops! Take it away! Take it away, I tell you!

[MARGARET *takes* FATHER's *cup and dashes out.* ANNIE *starts to take* VINNIE's *cup.*]

VINNIE. Leave my coffee there, Annie! It's perfectly all right!

[ANNIE *leaves the room.*]

FATHER [*angrily*]. It is not! I swear I can't imagine how she concocts such an atrocity. I come down to this table every morning hungry—

VINNIE. Well, if you're hungry, Clare, why aren't you eating your breakfast?

FATHER. What?

VINNIE. If you're hungry, why aren't you eating your breakfast?

FATHER [*thrown out of bounds*]. I am. [*He takes a mouthful of bacon and munches it happily, his eyes falling on* HARLAN.] Harlan, how's that finger? Come over here and let me see it.

[HARLAN *goes to his father's side. He shows his finger.*]

Well, that's healing nicely. Now don't pick that scab or it will leave a scar, and we don't want scars on our fingers, do we? [*He chuckles.*] I guess you'll remember after this that cats don't like to be hugged. It's all right to stroke them, but don't squeeze them. Now go back and finish your oatmeal.

HARLAN. I don't like oatmeal.

FATHER [*kindly*]. It's good for you. Go back and eat it.

HARLAN. But I don't like it.

FATHER [*quietly, but firmly*]. I'll tell you what you like and what you don't like. You're not old enough to know about such things. You've no business not to like oatmeal. It's good.

HARLAN. I hate it.

FATHER [*firmly, but not quietly*]. That's enough! We won't discuss it! Eat that oatmeal at once!

[*In contrast to* HARLAN, WHITNEY *has been eating his oatmeal at a terrific rate of speed. He pauses and puts down his spoon.*]

WHITNEY. I've finished *my* oatmeal. May I be excused?

FATHER. Yes, Whitney, you may go. [WHITNEY *slides off his chair and hurries to the stairs.*] Pitch a good game.

VINNIE. Whitney!

WHITNEY. I'm going upstairs to study my catechism.

VINNIE. Oh, that's all right. Run along.

WHITNEY [*on the way up*]. Harlan, you'd better hurry up and finish your oatmeal if you want to go with me.

[*Throughout breakfast* FATHER *has been opening and glancing through his mail. He has just reached one letter, however, that bewilders him.*]

FATHER. I don't understand why I'm always getting damn fool letters like this!

VINNIE. What is it, Clare?

FATHER. "Dear Friend Day: We are assigning you the exclusive rights for Staten Island for selling the Gem Home Popper for popcorn—"

CLARENCE. I think that's for me, Father.

FATHER. Then why isn't it addressed to Clarence Day, Jr.? [*He looks at the envelope.*] Oh, it is. Well, I'm sorry. I didn't mean to open your mail.

[MARGARET *returns and slips a cup of coffee to the table beside* FATHER.]

VINNIE. I wouldn't get mixed up in that, Clarence. People like popcorn, but they won't go all the way to Staten Island to buy it.

[FATHER *has picked up the paper and is reading it. He drinks his coffee absentmindedly.*]

FATHER. Chauncey Depew's having another birthday.

VINNIE. How nice.

FATHER. He's always having birthdays. Two or three a year. Damn! Another wreck on the New Haven!

VINNIE. Yes. Oh, that reminds me. Mrs. Bailey dropped in yesterday.

FATHER. Was she in the wreck?

VINNIE. No. But she was born in New Haven. Clarence, you're having tea with Edith Bailey Thursday afternoon.

CLARENCE. Oh, Mother, do I have to?

JOHN [singing]. "I like coffee, I like tea. I like the girls and the girls like me."

CLARENCE. Well, the girls don't like me and I don't like them.

VINNIE. Edith Bailey's a very nice girl, isn't she, Clare?

FATHER. Edith Bailey? Don't like her. Don't blame Clarence.

[FATHER goes to his chair by the window and sits down with his newspaper and a cigar. The others rise. HARLAN runs upstairs. ANNIE starts clearing the table and exits with the tray of dishes a little later. VINNIE speaks in a guarded tone to the two boys.]

VINNIE. Clarence, you and John go upstairs and do—what I asked you to.

JOHN. You said the small bureau, Mother?

VINNIE. Shh! Run along.

[The boys go upstairs, somewhat unwillingly. MARGARET enters.]

MARGARET. If you please, ma'am, there's a package been delivered with a dollar due on it. Some kitchen knives.

VINNIE. Oh, yes, those knives from Lewis & Conger's. [She gets her purse from the drawer in the console table and gives MARGARET a dollar.] Here, give this dollar to the man, Margaret.

[MARGARET leaves.]

FATHER. Make a memorandum of that, Vinnie. One dollar and whatever it was for.

VINNIE [looking into purse]. Clare, dear, I'm afraid I'm going to need some more money.

FATHER. What for?

VINNIE. You were complaining of the coffee this morning. Well, that nice French drip coffeepot is broken—and you know how it got broken.

FATHER [taking out his wallet]. Never mind that, Vinnie. As I remember, that coffeepot cost five dollars and something. Here's six dollars. [He gives her six dollars.] And when you get it, enter the exact amount in the ledger downstairs.

VINNIE. Thank you, Clare.

FATHER. We can't go on month after month having the household accounts in such a mess.

VINNIE [she sits on the arm of FATHER's chair]. No, and I've thought of a system that will make my bookkeeping perfect.

FATHER. I'm certainly relieved to hear that. What is it?

VINNIE. Well, Clare dear, you never make half the fuss over how much I've spent as you do over my not being able to remember what I've spent it for.

FATHER. Exactly. This house must be run on a business basis. That's why I insist on your keeping books.

VINNIE. That's the whole point, Clare. All we have to do is open charge accounts everywhere and the stores will do my bookkeeping for me.

FATHER. Wait a minute, Vinnie—

VINNIE. Then when the bills come in you'd know exactly where your money had gone.

FATHER. I certainly would. Vinnie, I get enough bills as it is.

VINNIE. Yes, and those bills always help. They show you just where I spent the money. Now if we had charge accounts everywhere—

FATHER. Now, Vinnie, I don't know about that.

VINNIE. Clare dear, don't you hate those arguments we have every month? I certainly do. Not to have those I should think would be worth something to you.

FATHER. Well, I'll open an account at Lewis & Conger's—and one at McCreery's to start with—we'll see how it works out. [He shakes his head doubtfully. Her victory gained, VINNIE moves away.]

VINNIE. Thank you, Clare. Oh—the rector's coming to tea today.

FATHER. The rector? I'm glad you warned me. I'll go to the club. Don't expect me home until dinner time.

VINNIE. I do wish you'd take a little more interest in the church.

[Goes behind FATHER's chair and looks down at him with concern.]

FATHER. Vinnie, getting me into Heaven's your job. If there's anything wrong with my ticket when I get there, you can fix it up. Everybody loves you so much—I'm sure God must, too.

VINNIE. I'll do my best, Clare. It wouldn't be Heaven without you.

FATHER. If you're there, Vinnie, I'll manage to get in some way, even f I have to climb the fence.

JOHN [from upstairs]. Mother, we've moved it. Is there anything else?

FATHER. What's being moved?

VINNIE. Never mind, Clare. I'll come right up, John. [She goes to he arch, stops. Looks back at FATHER] Oh, Clare, it's eight-thirty. You on't want to be late at the office.

FATHER. Plenty of time.

[VINNIE looks nervously toward the door, then goes upstairs. FATHER returns to his newspaper. VINNIE has barely disappeared when something in the paper arouses FATHER's indignation.]

h, God!

[VINNIE *comes running downstairs.*]

VINNIE.   What's the matter, Clare? What's wrong?
FATHER.   Why did God make so many damn fools and Democrats?
VINNIE [*relieved*].   Oh, politics.

[*She goes upstairs again.*]

FATHER [*shouting after her*].   Yes, but it's taking the bread out of our mouths. It's robbery, that's what it is, highway robbery! Honest Hugh Grant! Honest! Bah! A fine mayor you've turned out to be.

[FATHER *launches into a vigorous denunciation of Mayor Hugh Grant, addressing that gentleman as though he were present in the room, called upon the Day carpet to listen to* FATHER's *opinion of Tammany's latest attack on his pocketbook.*]

If you can't run this city without raising taxes every five minutes, you'd better get out and let someone who can. Let me tell you, sir, that the real-estate owners of New York City are not going to tolerate these conditions any longer. Tell me this—are these increased taxes going into public improvements or are they going into graft—answer me that, honestly, if you can, Mr. Honest Hugh Grant. You can't! I thought so. Bah!

[ANNIE *enters with her tray. Hearing* FATHER *talking, she curtsies and backs into the hall, as if uncertain whether to intrude on* FATHER *and the Mayor.* VINNIE *comes downstairs.*]

If you don't stop your plundering of the pocketbooks of the good citizens of New York, we're going to throw you and your boodle Board of Aldermen out of office.
VINNIE.   Annie, why aren't you clearing the table?
ANNIE.   Mr. Day's got a visitor.
FATHER.   I'm warning you for the last time.
VINNIE.   Oh, nonsense, he's just reading his paper, Annie. Clear the table.

[VINNIE *goes off through the arch.* ANNIE *comes in timidly and starts to clear the table.*]

FATHER [*still lecturing Mayor Grant*].   We pay you a good round sum to watch after our interests, and all we get is inefficiency!

[ANNIE *looks around trying to see the Mayor and, finding the room empty, assumes* FATHER's *remarks are directed at her.*]

I know you're a nincompoop and I strongly suspect you of being a scalawag.

[ANNIE *stands petrified.* WHITNEY *comes downstairs.*]

It's graft—that's what it is—Tammany graft—and if you're not getting it, somebody else is.

WHITNEY [*to* FATHER]. Where's John? Do you know where John is?

FATHER. Dick Croker's running this town and you're just his cat's-paw.

[VINNIE *comes in from downstairs, and* HARLAN *comes down from upstairs.* FATHER *goes on talking. The others carry on their conversation simultaneously, ignoring* FATHER *and his imaginary visitor.*]

HARLAN. Mother, where's John?

VINNIE. He's upstairs, dear.

FATHER. And as for you, Richard Croker—don't think, just because you're hiding behind these minions you've put in public office, that you're going to escape your legal responsibilities.

WHITNEY [*calling upstairs*]. John, I'm going to take your glove!

JOHN [*from upstairs*]. Don't you lose it! And don't let anybody else have it either!

VINNIE. Annie, you should have cleared the table long ago.

[ANNIE *loads her tray feverishly, eager to escape.*]

FATHER [*rising and slamming down the paper in his chair*]. Legal responsibilities—by gad, sir, I mean *criminal* responsibilities.

[*The boys start toward the front door.*]

VINNIE [*starting upstairs*]. Now you watch Harlan, Whitney. Don't let him be anywhere the ball can hit him. Do what Whitney says, Harlan. And don't be late for lunch.

[FATHER *has reached the arch on his way out of the room, where he pauses for a final shot at Mayor Grant.*]

FATHER. Don't forget what happened to William Marcy Tweed—and if you put our taxes up once more, we'll put you in jail!

[*He goes out of the archway to the left. A few seconds later he is seen passing the arch toward the outer door wearing his square derby and carrying his stick and gloves. The door is heard to slam loudly.* ANNIE *seizes her tray of dishes and runs out of the arch to the left toward the basement stairs. A second later there is a scream from* ANNIE *and a tremendous crash.* JOHN *and* CLARENCE *come rushing down and look over the rail of the stairs below.* VINNIE *follows them almost immediately.*]

VINNIE.   What is it? What happened?

CLARENCE.   The maid fell downstairs.

VINNIE.   I don't wonder, with your father getting her so upset. Why couldn't she have finished with the table before she fell downstairs?

JOHN.   I don't think she hurt herself.

VINNIE.   And today of all days! Boys, will you finish the table? And, Clarence, don't leave the house until I talk to you.

[*She goes downstairs.*]

[*During the following scene* CLARENCE *and* JOHN *remove* VINNIE's *best breakfast tablecloth and cram it carelessly into the drawer of the console table, then take out the extra leaves from the table, push it together, and replace the living-room table cover and the bowl of fruit.*]

JOHN.   What do you suppose Mother wants to talk to you about.

CLARENCE.   Oh, probably about Edith Bailey.

JOHN.   What do you talk about when you have tea alone with a girl?

CLARENCE.   We don't talk about anything. I say: "Isn't it a nice day?" and she says: "Yes," and I say: "I think it's a little warmer than yesterday," and she says: "Yes, I like warm weather, don't you?" and I say: "Yes," and then we wait for the tea to come in. And then she says: "How many lumps?" and I say: "Two, thank you," and she says: "You must have a sweet tooth," and I can't say: "Yes" and I can't say: "No," so we just sit there and look at each other for half an hour. Then I say: "Well, it's time I was going," and she says: "Must you?" and I say: "I've enjoyed seeing you very much," and she says: "You must come again," and I say: "I will," and get out.

JOHN [*shaking his head*].   Some fellows like girls.

CLARENCE.   I don't.

JOHN.   And did you ever notice fellows, when they get sweet on a girl—the silly things a girl can make them do? And they don't even seem to know they're acting silly.

CLARENCE.   Well, not for Yours Truly!

[VINNIE *returns from downstairs.*]

VINNIE.   I declare I don't see how anyone could be so clumsy.

CLARENCE.   Did she hurt herself?

VINNIE.   No, she's not hurt—she's just hysterical! She doesn't make sense. Your father may have raised his voice; and if she doesn't know how to hold a platter properly, she deserved it—but I know he didn't threaten to put her in jail. Oh, well! Clarence, I want you to move your things into the front room. You'll have to sleep with the other boys for a night or two.

CLARENCE.   You haven't told us who's coming.

VINNIE [*happily*]. Cousin Cora. Isn't that nice?

CLARENCE. It's not nice for me. I can't get any sleep in there with those children.

JOHN. Wait'll Father finds out she's here! There'll be a rumpus.

VINNIE. John, don't criticize your father. He's very hospitable after he gets used to the idea.

[*The doorbell rings.* JOHN *and* VINNIE *go to the window.*]

JOHN. Yes, it's Cousin Cora. Look, there's somebody with her.

VINNIE [*looking out*]. She wrote me she was bringing a friend of hers. They're both going to stay here.

[*A limping* ANNIE *passes through the hall.*]

Finish with the room, boys.

CLARENCE. Do I have to sleep with the other boys and have tea with Edith Bailey all in the same week?

VINNIE. Yes, and you'd better take your father's suit to the tailor's right away, so it will be ready by Thursday.

[VINNIE *goes down the hall to greet* CORA *and* MARY. CLARENCE *hurries off, carrying the table leaves.*]

VINNIE'S VOICE [*in the hall*]. Cora dear—

CORA'S VOICE. Cousin Vinnie, I'm so glad to see you! This is Mary Skinner.

VINNIE'S VOICE. Ed Skinner's daughter! I'm so glad to see you. Leave your bags in the hall and come right upstairs.

[VINNIE *enters, going toward the stairs.* CORA *follows her, but, seeing* JOHN, *enters the room and goes to him.* MARY *follows* CORA *in timidly.* CORA *is an attractive country cousin of about thirty.* MARY *is a refreshingly pretty small-town girl of sixteen.*]

CORA [*seeing* JOHN]. Well, Clarence, it's so good to see you!

VINNIE [*coming into the room*]. Oh, no, that's John.

CORA. John! Why, how you've grown! You'll be a man before your mother! [*She laughs herself at this time-worn quip.*] John, this is Mary Skinner.

[*They exchange greetings.*]

Vinnie, I have so much to tell you. We wrote you Aunt Carrie broke her hip. That was the night Robert Ingersoll lectured. Of course she couldn't get there; and it was a good thing for Mr. Ingersoll she didn't.

[CLARENCE *enters.*]

And Grandpa Ebbetts hasn't been at all well.

CLARENCE.　How do you do, Cousin Cora? I'm glad to see you.

CORA.　This can't be Clarence!

VINNIE.　Yes, it is.

CORA.　My goodness, every time I see you boys you've grown another foot. Let's see—you're going to St. Paul's now, aren't you?

CLARENCE [*with pained dignity*].　St. Paul's! I was through with St. Paul's long ago. I'm starting in Yale this fall.

MARY.　Yale!

CORA.　Oh, Mary, this is Clarence—Mary Skinner.

[MARY *smiles, and* CLARENCE, *the woman-hater, nods politely and walks away.*]

This is Mary's first trip to New York. She was so excited when she saw a horse car.

VINNIE.　We'll have to show Mary around. I'll tell you—I'll have Mr. Day take us all to Delmonico's for dinner tonight.

MARY.　Delmonico's!

CORA.　Oh, that's marvelous! Think of that, Mary—Delmonico's! And Cousin Clare's such a wonderful host.

VINNIE.　I know you girls want to freshen up. So come upstairs. Clarence, I'll let the girls use your room now, and when they've finished you can move, and bring up their bags. They're out in the hall. [*Starts upstairs with* CORA] I've given you girls Clarence's room, but he didn't know about it until this morning and he hasn't moved out yet.

[VINNIE *and* CORA *disappear upstairs.* MARY *follows more slowly and on the second step stops and looks back.* CLARENCE *has gone into the hall with his back toward* MARY *and stares morosely in the direction of their luggage.*]

CLARENCE.　John, get their old bags.

[JOHN *disappears toward the front door. The voices of* VINNIE *and* CORA *have trailed off into the upper reaches of the house.* CLARENCE *turns to scowl in their direction and finds himself looking full into the face of* MARY.]

MARY.　Cora didn't tell me about you. I never met a Yale man before.

[*She gives him a devastating smile and with an audible whinny of girlish excitement she runs upstairs.* CLARENCE *stares after her a few seconds, then turns toward the audience with a look of "What happened to me just then?" Suddenly, however, his face breaks into a smile which indicates that, whatever has happened, he likes it.*]

CURTAIN

Scene II

THE SAME DAY. *Tea time.*

VINNIE *and the* RECTOR *are having tea.* THE REVEREND DR. LLOYD *is a plump bustling man, very good-hearted and pleasant.* VINNIE *and* DR. LLOYD *have one strong point in common: their devotion to the Church and its rituals.* VINNIE's *devotion comes from her natural piety;* DR. LLOYD's *is a little more professional.*

At rise, DR. LLOYD *is seated with a cup of tea.* VINNIE *is also seated and* WHITNEY *is standing next to her, stiffly erect in the manner of a boy reciting.* HARLAN *is seated next to his mother, watching* WHITNEY's *performance.*

WHITNEY [*reciting*]. "—to worship Him, to give Him thanks; to put my whole trust in Him, to call upon Him—" [*He hesitates.*]

VINNIE [*prompting*]. "—to honor—"

WHITNEY. "—to honor His Holy Name and His word and to serve Him truly all the days of my life."

DR. LLOYD. "What is thy duty toward thy neighbor?"

WHITNEY. Whew! [*He pulls himself together and makes a brave start.*] "My duty toward my neighbor is to love him as myself, and to do to all men as I would they should do unto me; to love, honor, and succor my father and my mother; to honor and obey—"

VINNIE. "—civil authorities."

WHITNEY. "—civil authorities. To—to—to—"

VINNIE [*to* DR. LLOYD]. He really knows it.

WHITNEY. I know most of the others.

DR. LLOYD. Well, he's done very well for so young a boy. I'm sure if he applies himself between now and Sunday I could hear him again—with the others.

VINNIE. There, Whitney, you'll have to study very hard if you want Dr. Lloyd to send your name in to Bishop Potter next Sunday. I must confess to you, Dr. Lloyd, it's really my fault. Instead of hearing Whitney say his catechism this morning I let him play baseball.

WHITNEY. We won, too; 35 to 27.

DR. LLOYD. That's splendid, my child. I'm glad your side won. But winning over your catechism is a richer and fuller victory.

WHITNEY. Can I go now?

VINNIE. Yes, darling. Thank Dr. Lloyd for hearing you and run along.

WHITNEY. Thank you, Dr. Lloyd.

DR. LLOYD. Not at all, my little man.

[WHITNEY *starts out, turns back, takes a piece of cake and runs out.*]

VINNIE. Little Harlan is very apt at learning things by heart.

HARLAN [*scrambling to his feet*]. I can spell Constantinople. Want to hear me?

[DR. LLOYD *smiles his assent.*]

C-o-ennaconny—annaconny—sissaconny—tan-tan-tee—and a nople and a pople and a Constantinople!

DR. LLOYD. Very well done, my child.

VINNIE [*handing him a cake from the tea tray*]. That's nice, darling. This is what you get for saying it so well.

[HARLAN *quickly looks at the cake and back to* DR. LLOYD.]

HARLAN. Want me to say it again for you?

VINNIE. No, darling. One cake is enough. You run along and play with Whitney.

HARLAN. I can spell "huckleberry pie."

VINNIE. Run along, dear.

[HARLAN *goes out, skipping in rhythm to his recitation.*]

HARLAN. *H-a-huckle — b-a-buckle — h-a-huckle-high. H-a-huckle — b-a-*buckle—huckleberry pie!

DR. LLOYD [*amused*]. You and Mr. Day must be very proud of your children.

[VINNIE *beams.*]

I was hoping I'd find Mr. Day at home this afternoon.

VINNIE [*evasively*]. Well, he's usually home from the office by this time.

DR. LLOYD. Perhaps he's gone for a gallop in the park—it's such a fine day. He's very fond of horseback riding, I believe.

VINNIE. Oh, yes.

DR. LLOYD. Tell me—has he ever been thrown from a horse?

VINNIE. Oh, no! No horse would throw Mr. Day.

DR. LLOYD. I've wondered. I thought he might have had an accident. I notice he never kneels in church.

VINNIE. Oh, that's no accident! But I don't want you to think he doesn't pray. He does. Why, sometimes you can hear him pray all over the house. But he never kneels.

DR. LLOYD. Never kneels! Dear me! I was hoping to have the opportunity to tell you and Mr. Day about our plans for the new edifice.

VINNIE. I'm so glad we're going to have a new church.

DR. LLOYD. I'm happy to announce that we're now ready to proceed. The only thing left to do is raise the money.

VINNIE. No one should hesitate about contributing to that.

[*The front door slams.*]

DR. LLOYD. Perhaps that's Mr. Day now.
VINNIE. Oh, no, I hardly think so.

[FATHER *appears in the archway.*]

Why, it is!
FATHER. Oh, damn! I forgot.
VINNIE. Clare, you're just in time. Dr. Lloyd's here for tea.
FATHER. I'll be right in.

[*He disappears the other side of the archway.*]

VINNIE. I'll send for some fresh tea.

[*She goes to the bellpull and rings for the maid.*]

DR. LLOYD. Now we can tell Mr. Day about our plans for the new edifice.
VINNIE [*knowing her man*]. After he's had his tea.

[FATHER *comes back into the room.* DR. LLOYD *rises.*]

FATHER. How are you, Dr. Lloyd?

[CLARENCE *comes down the stairs and eagerly looks around for* MARY.]

CLARENCE. Oh, it was Father.
DR. LLOYD. Very well, thank you.

[*They shake hands.*]

CLARENCE [*to* VINNIE]. They're not back yet?
VINNIE. No! Clarence, no!
　　　　　　　　　[CLARENCE *turns, disappointed, and goes back upstairs.*]

DR. LLOYD. It's a great pleasure to have a visit with you, Mr. Day. Except for a fleeting glimpse on the Sabbath, I don't see much of you.

[FATHER *grunts and sits down.* DELIA, *a new maid, enters.*]

DELIA. Yes, ma'am.
VINNIE. Some fresh tea and a cup for Mr. Day.

[DELIA *exits and* VINNIE *hurries down to the tea table to start the conversation*]

Well, Clare, did you have a busy day at the office?
FATHER. Damn busy.
VINNIE. Clare!

FATHER.　Very busy day.　Tired out.

VINNIE.　I've ordered some fresh tea. [*To* DR. LLOYD] Poor Clare, he must work very hard. He always comes home tired. Although how a man can get tired just sitting at his desk all day, I don't know. I suppose Wall Street is just as much a mystery to you as it is to me, Dr. Lloyd.

DR. LLOYD.　No, no, it's all very clear to me. My mind often goes to the business man. The picture I'm most fond of is when I envision him at the close of the day's work. There he sits—this hard-headed man of affairs—surrounded by the ledgers that he has been studying closely and harshly for hours. I see him pausing in his toil—and by chance he raises his eyes and looks out of the window at the light in God's sky and it comes over him that money and ledgers are dross.

[FATHER *stares at* DR. LLOYD *with some amazement.*]

He realizes that all those figures of profit and loss are without importance or consequence—vanity and dust. And I see this troubled man bow his head and with streaming eyes resolve to devote his life to far higher things.

FATHER.　Well, I'll be damned!

[*At this moment* DELIA *returns with the fresh tea for* FATHER.]

VINNIE.　Here's your tea, Clare.

[FATHER *notices the new maid.*]

FATHER.　Who's this?

VINNIE [*quietly*].　The new maid.

FATHER.　Where's the one we had this morning?

VINNIE.　Never mind, Clare.

FATHER.　The one we had this morning was prettier.

[DELIA, *with a slight resentment, exits.* FATHER *attacks the tea and cakes with relish.*]

Vinnie, these cakes are *good.*

DR. LLOYD.　Delicious!

VINNIE.　Dr. Lloyd wants to tell us about the plans for the new edifice.

FATHER.　The new what?

VINNIE.　The new church—Clare, you knew we were planning to build a new church.

DR. LLOYD.　Of course, we're going to have to raise a large sum of money.

FATHER [*alive to the danger*].　Well, personally I'm against the church hop-skipping-and-jumping all over the town. And it so happens that during the last year I've suffered heavy losses in the market—damned heavy losses—

VINNIE. Clare!

FATHER. —so any contribution I make will have to be a small one.

VINNIE. But, Clare, for so worthy a cause!

FATHER. —and if your Finance Committee thinks it's too small they can blame the rascals that are running the New Haven Railroad!

DR. LLOYD. The amount everyone is to subscribe has already been decided.

FATHER [*bristling*]. Who decided it?

DR. LLOYD. After considerable thought we've found a formula which we believe is fair and equitable. It apportions the burden lightly on those least able to carry it and justly on those whose shoulders we know are stronger. We've voted that our supporting members should each contribute a sum equal to the cost of their pews.

[FATHER's *jaw drops.*]

FATHER. I paid five thousand dollars for my pew!

VINNIE. Yes, Clare. That makes our contribution five thousand dollars.

FATHER. That's robbery. Do you know what that pew is worth today? Three thousand dollars. That's what the last one sold for. I've taken a dead loss of two thousand dollars on that pew already. Frank Baggs sold me that pew when the market was at its peak. He knew when to get out. [*He turns to* VINNIE.] And I'm warning you now that if the market ever goes up I'm going to unload that pew.

VINNIE. Clarence Day! How can you speak of the Lord's temple as though it were something to be bought and sold on Wall Street?

FATHER. Vinnie, this is a matter of dollars and cents, and that's something you don't know anything about!

VINNIE. You talking of religion in terms of dollars and cents seems to me pretty close to blasphemy.

DR. LLOYD [*soothingly*]. Now, Mrs. Day, your husband is a business man and he has a practical approach toward this problem. We've had to be practical about it too—we have all the facts and figures.

FATHER. Oh, really! What's the new piece of property going to cost you?

DR. LLOYD. I think the figure I've heard mentioned is eighty-five thousand dollars—or was it a hundred and eighty-five thousand dollars?

FATHER. What's the property worth where we are now?

DR. LLOYD. Well, there's quite a difference of opinion about that.

FATHER. How much do you have to raise to build the new church?

DR. LLOYD. Now, I've seen those figures—let me see—I know it depends somewhat upon the amount of the mortgage.

FATHER. Mortgage, eh? What are the terms of the amortization?

DR. LLOYD. Amortization? That's not a word I'm familiar with.

FATHER. It all seems pretty vague and unsound to me. I certainly wouldn't let any customer of mine invest on what I've heard.

[*The doorbell rings.*]

DR. LLOYD. We've given it a great deal of thought. I don't see how you can call it vague.

[DELIA *passes along the hall toward the front door.*]

FATHER. Dr. Lloyd, you preach that some day we'll all have to answer to God.
DR. LLOYD. We shall indeed!
FATHER. Well, I hope God doesn't ask you any questions with figures in them.

[CORA'S VOICE *is heard in the hall, thanking* DELIA. VINNIE *goes to the arch just in time to meet* CORA *and* MARY *as they enter, heavily laden with packages, which they put down.* FATHER *and* DR. LLOYD *rise.*]

CORA. Oh. Vinnie, what a day! We've been to every shop in town and— [*She sees* FATHER.] Cousin Clare!
FATHER [*cordially*]. Cora, what are you doing in New York?
CORA. We're just passing through on our way to Springfield.
FATHER. We?

[CLARENCE *comes downstairs into the room with eyes only for* MARY.]

VINNIE. Oh, Dr. Lloyd, this is my favorite cousin, Miss Cartwright, and her friend, Mary Skinner.

[*They exchange mutual how-do-you-do's.*]

DR. LLOYD. This seems to be a family reunion. I'll just run along.
FATHER [*promptly*]. Goodbye, Dr. Lloyd.
DR. LLOYD. Goodbye, Miss Cartwright. Goodbye, Miss—er—
VINNIE. Clarence, you haven't said how-do-you-do to Dr. Lloyd.
CLARENCE. Goodbye, Dr. Lloyd.
VINNIE [*to* DR. LLOYD]. I'll go to the door with you.
[DR. LLOYD *and* VINNIE *go out, talking.*]

FATHER. Cora, you're as welcome as the flowers in May! Have some tea with us. [*To* DELIA] Bring some fresh tea—and some more of those cakes.
CORA. Oh, we've had tea! We were so tired shopping we had tea downtown.

[*With a gesture* FATHER *countermands his order to* DELIA, *who removes the tea table and exits.*]

MARY. At the Fifth Avenue Hotel.

FATHER. At the Fifth Avenue Hotel, eh? Who'd you say this pretty little girl was?

CORA. She's Ed Skinner's daughter. Well, Mary, at last you've met Mr. Day. I've told Mary so much about you, Cousin Clare, that she's just been dying to meet you.

FATHER. Well, sit down! Sit down! Even if you have had tea you can stop and visit for a while. As a matter of fact, why don't you both stay to dinner?

[VINNIE *enters just in time to hear this and cuts in quickly.*]

VINNIE. That's all arranged, Clare. Cora and Mary are going to have dinner with us.

FATHER. That's fine! That's fine!

CORA. Cousin Clare, I don't know how to thank you and Vinnie for your hospitality.

MARY. Yes, Mr. Day.

FATHER. Well, you'll just have to take pot luck.

CORA. No, I mean—

[VINNIE *speaks quickly to postpone the revelation that* FATHER *has house guests.*]

VINNIE. Clare, did you know the girls are going to visit Aunt Judith in Springfield for a whole month?

FATHER. That's fine. How long are you going to be in New York, Cora?

CORA. All week.

FATHER. Splendid. We'll hope to see something of you, eh, Vinnie?

[CORA *looks bewildered and is about to speak.*]

VINNIE. Did you find anything you wanted in the shops?

CORA. Just everything.

VINNIE. I want to see what you got.

CORA. I just can't wait to show you. [*She goes coyly to* FATHER] But I'm afraid some of the packages can't be opened in front of Cousin Clare.

FATHER. Shall I leave the room? [*Laughs at his own joke.*]

CORA. Clarence, do you mind taking the packages up to our room— or should I say your room? [*To* FATHER] Wasn't it nice of Clarence to give up his room to us for a whole week?

FATHER [*with a sudden drop in temperature*]. Vinnie!

VINNIE. Come on, Cora, I just can't wait to see what's in those packages.

[CORA, MARY, *and* VINNIE *start out.* CLARENCE *is gathering up the packages.*]

FATHER [*ominously*]. Vinnie, I wish to speak to you before you go upstairs.

VINNIE. I'll be down in just a minute, Clare.

FATHER. I wish to speak to you now!

[*The girls have disappeared upstairs.*]

VINNIE. I'll be up in just a minute, Cora.

[*We hear a faint* "All right" *from upstairs.*]

FATHER [*his voice is low but stern*]. Are those two women encamped in this house?

VINNIE. Now, Clare!

FATHER [*much louder*]. Answer me, Vinnie!

VINNIE. Just a minute—control yourself, Clare.

[VINNIE, *sensing the coming storm, hurries to the sliding doors.* CLARENCE *has reached the hall with his packages and he, too, has recognized the danger signal and as* VINNIE *closes one door he closes the other, leaving himself out in the hall and* FATHER *and* VINNIE *facing each other in the room.*]

VINNIE [*persuasively*]. Now, Clare, you know you've always liked Cora.

FATHER [*exploding*]. What has that got to do with her planking herself down in my house and bringing hordes of strangers with her?

VINNIE [*reproachfully*]. How can you call that sweet little girl a horde of strangers?

FATHER. Why don't they go to a hotel? New York is full of hotels built for the express purpose of housing such nuisances.

VINNIE. Clare! Two girls alone in a hotel! Who knows what might happen to them?

FATHER. All right. Then put 'em on the next train. If they want to roam—the damned gypsies—lend 'em a hand! Keep 'em roaming!

VINNIE. What have we got a home for if we can't show a little hospitality?

FATHER. I didn't buy this home to show hospitality—I bought it for my own comfort!

VINNIE. Well, how much are they going to interfere with your comfort living in that little room of Clarence's?

FATHER. The trouble is, damn it, they don't live there. They live in the bathroom! Every time I want to take my bath it's full of giggling females—washing their hair. From the time they take, you'd think it was the Seven Sutherland Sisters. I tell you, I won't have it! Send 'em to a hotel. I'll pay the bill gladly, but get them out of here!

[CLARENCE *puts his head through the sliding door.*]

CLARENCE. Father, I'm afraid they can hear you upstairs.
FATHER. Then keep those doors closed!
VINNIE [*with decision*]. Clarence, you open those doors—open them all the way!

[CLARENCE *does so.*]

VINNIE [*to* FATHER, *lowering her voice, but maintaining her spirit*]. Now, Clare, you behave yourself!

[FATHER *glares at her angrily.*]

They're here and they're going to stay here.
FATHER. That's enough, Vinnie! I want no more of this argument. [*He goes to his chair by the window, muttering*] Damnation!
CLARENCE [*to* VINNIE]. Mother, Cousin Cora's waiting for you.
FATHER. What I don't understand is why this swarm of locusts always descends on us without any warning.

[*He sits down.* VINNIE *looks at him; then, convinced of her victory, she goes upstairs.*]

Damn! Damnation! Damn! [*He follows her upstairs with his eyes; he remembers he is very fond of her*] Vinnie! Dear Vinnie! [*He remembers he is very angry at her*] Damn!
CLARENCE. Father, can't I go along with the rest of you to Delmonico's tonight?
FATHER. What's that? Delmonico's?
CLARENCE. You're taking Mother, Cora, and Mary to Delmonico's for dinner.
FATHER [*exploding*]. Oh, God!

[*At this sound from* FATHER, VINNIE *comes flying downstairs again.*]

I won't have it. I won't have it.

[FATHER *stamps angrily across the room.*]

VINNIE [*on the way down*]. Clarence, the doors!
FATHER. I won't stand it, by God! I won't stand it!

[VINNIE *and* CLARENCE *hurriedly close the sliding doors again.*]

VINNIE. Clare! What's the matter now?

FATHER [*with the calm of anger that has turned to ice*].   Do I understand that I can't have dinner in my own home?

VINNIE.   It'll do us both good to get out of this house. You need a little change. It'll make you feel better.

FATHER.   I have a home to have dinner in. Any time I can't have dinner at home this house is for sale!

VINNIE.   Well, you can't have dinner here tonight because it isn't ordered.

FATHER.   Let me tell you I'm ready to sell this place this very minute if I can't live here in peace. And we can all go and sit under a palm tree and live on breadfruit and pickles.

VINNIE.   But, Clare, Cora and Mary want to see something of New York.

FATHER.   Oh, that's it! Well, that's no affair of mine! I am not a guide to Chinatown and the Bowery.

[*Drawing himself up, he stalks out, throwing open the sliding doors. As he reaches the foot of the stairs,* MARY *comes tripping down.*]

MARY.   I love your house, Mr. Day. I could just live here forever.

[FATHER *utters a bark of disgust and continues on upstairs.* MARY *comes into the room a little wide-eyed.*]

Cora's waiting for you, Mrs. Day.

VINNIE.   Oh, yes, I'll run right up.

[*She goes upstairs.*]

CLARENCE.   I'm glad you like our house.

MARY.   Oh, yes, I like it very much. I like green.

CLARENCE.   I like green myself. [*She looks up at his red hair.*]

MARY.   Red's my favorite color.

[*Embarrassed,* CLARENCE *suddenly hears himself talking about something he has never thought about.*]

CLARENCE.   It's an interesting thing about colors. Red's a nice color in a house, too; but outside, too much red would be bad. I mean, for instance, if all the trees and the grass were red. Outside, green is the best color.

MARY [*impressed*].   That's right. I've never thought of it that way—but when you do think of it, it's quite a thought! I'll bet you'll make your mark at Yale.

CLARENCE [*pleased, but modest*].   Oh!

[*The outer door is heard to slam.*]

MARY.   My mother wants me to go to college. Do you believe in girls going to college?

CLARENCE. I guess it's all right if they want to waste that much time
—before they get married, I mean.

[JOHN *comes in bringing* The Youth's Companion.]

JOHN. Oh, hello! Look! A new *Youth's Companion!*

[*They say "Hello" to him.*]

CLARENCE [*from a mature height*]. John enjoys *The Youth's Companion.*

[JOHN *sits right down and starts to read.* CLARENCE *is worried by
this.*]

John!

[JOHN *looks at him non-plussed.* CLARENCE *glances toward* MARY.
JOHN *remembers his manners and stands.* CLARENCE *speaks formally
to* MARY.]

Won't you sit down?

MARY. Oh, thank you!

[*She sits.* JOHN *sits down again quickly and dives back into* The
Youth's Companion. CLARENCE *sits beside* MARY.]

CLARENCE. As I was saying—I think it's all right for a girl to go to
college if she goes to a girls' college.

MARY. Well, Mother wants me to go to Ohio Wesleyan—because it's
Methodist. [*Then almost as a confession*] You see, we're Methodists.

CLARENCE. Oh, that's too bad! I don't mean it's too bad that you're
a Methodist. Anybody's got a right to be anything they want. But
what I mean is—we're Episcopalians.

MARY. Yes, I know. I've known ever since I saw your minister—and
his collar. [*She looks pretty sad for a minute and then her face
brightens.*] Oh, I just remembered—my father was an Episcopalian.
He was baptized an Episcopalian. He was an Episcopalian right up to
the time he married my mother. *She* was the Methodist.

[MARY's *tone would have surprised her mother—and even* MARY,
if she had been listening.]

CLARENCE. I'll bet your father's a nice man.

MARY. Yes, he is. He owns the livery stable.

CLARENCE. He does? Well, then you must like horses.

MARY. Oh, I love horses!

[*They are happily united again in their common love of horses.*]

CLARENCE. They're my favorite animal. Father and I both think there's nothing like a horse!

[FATHER *comes down the stairs and into the room. The children all stand.*]

MARY. Oh, Mr. Day, I'm having such a lovely time here!

FATHER. Clarence is keeping you entertained, eh?

MARY. Oh, yes, sir. We've been talking about everything—colors and horses and religion.

FATHER. Oh! [*To* JOHN] Has the evening paper come yet?

JOHN. No, sir.

FATHER. What are you reading?

JOHN. *The Youth's Companion,* sir.

[WHITNEY *and* HARLAN *enter from the hall,* WHITNEY *carrying a small box.*]

WHITNEY. Look what we've got!

FATHER. What is it?

WHITNEY. Tiddle-dy-winks. We put our money together and bought it.

FATHER. That's a nice game. Do you know how to play it?

WHITNEY. I've played it lots of times.

HARLAN. Show me how to play it.

FATHER. Here, I'll show you.

[*Opens the box and arranges the glass and disks.*]

MARY [*hopefully to* CLARENCE]. Are you going out to dinner with us tonight?

CLARENCE [*looking at* FATHER]. I don't know yet—but it's beginning to look as though I might.

FATHER. It's easy, Harlan. You press down like this and snap the little fellow into the glass. Now watch me—[*He snaps it and it goes off the table.*] The table isn't quite large enough. You boys better play it on the floor.

WHITNEY. Come on, Harlan, I'll take the reds, and you take the yellows.

FATHER. John, have you practiced your piano today?

JOHN. I was going to practice this evening.

FATHER. Better do it now. Music is a delight in the home.

[JOHN *exits, passing* CORA *and* VINNIE *as they enter, coming downstairs.*]

VINNIE. Clare, what do you think Cora just told me? She and Clyde are going to be married this fall!

FATHER. Oh, you finally landed him, eh?

[*Everybody laughs.*]

Well, he's a very lucky man. Cora, being married is the only way to live.

CORA. If we can be half as happy as you and Cousin Vinnie—

VINNIE [*who has gone to the children*]. Boys, shouldn't you be playing that on the table?

WHITNEY. The table isn't big enough. Father told us to play on the floor.

VINNIE. My soul and body! Look at your hands! Delia will have your supper ready in a few minutes. Go wash your hands right away and come back and show Mother they're clean.

[*The boys pick up the tiddle-dy-winks and depart reluctantly. From the next room we hear* JOHN *playing "The Happy Farmer."*]

FATHER [*sitting down on the sofa with* MARY]. Vinnie, this young lady looks about the same age you were when I came out to Pleasantville to rescue you.

VINNIE. Rescue me! You came out there to talk me into marrying you.

FATHER. It worked out just the same. I saved you from spending the rest of your life in that one-horse town.

VINNIE. Cora, the other day I came across a tintype of Clare taken in Pleasantville. I want to show it to you. You'll see who needed rescuing.

[*She goes to the table and starts to rummage around in its drawer.*]

FATHER. There isn't time for that, Vinnie. If we're going to Delmonico's for dinner hadn't we all better be getting ready? It's after six now.

CORA. Gracious! I'll have to start. If I'm going to dine in public with a prominent citizen like you, Cousin Clare—I'll have to look my best.

[*She goes to the arch.*]

MARY. I've changed already.

CORA. Yes, I know, but I'm afraid I'll have to ask you to come along and hook me up, Mary.

MARY. Of course.

CORA. It won't take a minute and then you can come right back.

[FATHER *rises.* MARY *crosses in front of* FATHER *and starts toward the hall, then turns and looks back at him.*]

MARY. Mr. Day, were you always an Episcopalian?

FATHER. What?

MARY. Were you always an Episcopalian?

FATHER. I've always gone to the Episcopal church, yes.

MARY. But you weren't baptized a Methodist or anything, were you? You were baptized an Episcopalian?

FATHER. Come to think of it, I don't believe I was ever baptized at all.

MARY. Oh!

VINNIE. Clare, that's not very funny, joking about a subject like that.

FATHER. I'm not joking—I remember now—I never was baptized.

VINNIE. Clare, that's ridiculous, everyone's baptized.

FATHER [sitting down complacently]. Well, I'm not.

VINNIE. Why, no one would keep a little baby from being baptized.

FATHER. You know Father and Mother—free-thinkers, both of them -believed their children should decide those things for themselves.

VINNIE. But, Clare—

FATHER. I remember when I was ten or twelve years old, Mother said I ought to give some thought to it. I suppose I thought about it, but I never got around to having it done to me.

[The shock to VINNIE is as great as if FATHER had calmly announced himself guilty of murder. She walks to FATHER staring at him in horror. CORA and MARY, sensing the coming battle, withdraw to the neutral shelter of the hall.]

VINNIE. Clare, do you know what you're saying?

FATHER. I'm saying I've never been baptized.

VINNIE [in a sudden panic]. Then something has to be done about it right away.

FATHER [not the least concerned]. Now, Vinnie, don't get excited over nothing.

VINNIE. Nothing! [Then, as only a woman can ask such a question] Clare, why haven't you ever told me?

FATHER. What difference does it make?

VINNIE [the panic returning]. I've never heard of anyone who wasn't baptized. Even the savages in darkest Africa—

FATHER. It's all right for savages and children. But if an oversight was made in my case it's too late to correct it now.

VINNIE. But if you're not baptized you're not a Christian!

FATHER [rising in wrath]. Why, confound it, of course I'm a Christian! A damn good Christian, too!

[FATHER's voice tells CLARENCE a major engagement has begun. He hurriedly springs to the sliding doors and closes them, removing himself, MARY, and CORA from the scene of action.]

A lot better Christian than those psalm-singing donkeys in church!

VINNIE. You can't be if you won't be baptized.

FATHER. I won't be baptized and I will be a Christian! I beg to inform you I'll be a Christian in my own way.

VINNIE. Clare, don't you want to meet us all in Heaven?

FATHER. Of course! And I'm going to!

VINNIE. But you can't go to Heaven if you're not baptized.

FATHER. That's a lot of folderol!

VINNIE. Clarence Day, don't you blaspheme like that! You're coming to church with me before you go to the office in the morning and be baptized then and there!

FATHER. Vinnie, don't be ridiculous! If you think I'm going to stand there and have some minister splash water on me at my age, you're mistaken!

VINNIE. But, Clare—

FATHER. That's enough of this, Vinnie. I'm hungry.

[*Draws himself up and starts for the door. He does not realize that he and* VINNIE *are now engaged in a battle to the death.*]

I'm dressing for dinner.

[*Throws open the doors, revealing* WHITNEY *and* HARLAN, *who obviously have been eavesdropping and have heard the awful revelation of* FATHER's *paganism.* FATHER *stalks past them upstairs. The two boys come down into the room staring at their mother, who has been standing, too shocked at* FATHER's *callous impiety to speak or move.*]

WHITNEY. Mother, if Father hasn't been baptized he hasn't any name. In the sight of the Church he hasn't any name.

VINNIE. That's right! [*To herself*] Maybe we're not even married!

[*This awful thought takes possession of* VINNIE. *Her eyes turn slowly toward the children and she suddenly realizes their doubtful status. Her hand goes to her mouth to cover a quick gasp of horror as the curtain falls.*]

CURTAIN

ACT TWO

Scene I

THE SAME.

The following Sunday. After church.

The stage is empty as the curtain rises. VINNIE *comes into the archway from the street door, dressed in her Sunday best, carrying her prayer book, hymnal, and a cold indignation. As soon as she is in the room,* FATHER *passes across the hall in his Sunday cutaway and silk hat, carrying gloves and cane.* VINNIE *looks over her shoulder at him as he disappears.* CORA, WHITNEY, *and* HARLAN *come into the room,* CORA *glancing after* FATHER *and then toward* VINNIE. *All three walk as though the sound of a footfall might cause an explosion, and speak in subdued tones.*

HARLAN.   Cousin Cora, will you play a game of tiddle-dy-winks with me before you go?

CORA.   I'm going to be busy packing until it's time to leave.

WHITNEY.   We can't play games on Sunday.

[*We hear the door close and* JOHN *enters and looks into the room apprehensively.*]

CORA.   John, where are Clarence and Mary?

JOHN.   They dropped behind—'way behind!

[*He goes upstairs.* WHITNEY *takes* HARLAN'S *hat from him and starts toward the arch.*]

VINNIE.   Whitney, don't hang up your hat. I want you to go over to Sherry's for the ice cream for dinner. Tell Mr. Sherry strawberry—if he has it. And take Harlan with you.

WHITNEY.   All right, Mother.

[*He and* HARLAN, *trained in the good manners of the period, bow and exit.*]

CORA.   Oh, Vinnie, I hate to leave. We've had such a lovely week.

VINNIE [*voice quivers in a tone of scandalized apology*].   Cora, what must you think of Clare, making such a scene on his way out of church today?

CORA.   Cousin Clare probably thinks that you put the rector up to preaching that sermon.

VINNIE [*tone changes from apology to self-defense with overtones of guilt*].   Well, I had to go to see Dr. Lloyd to find out whether we were really married. The sermon on baptism was his own idea. If Clare just hadn't *shouted* so—now the whole congregation knows he's never been baptized! But he's going to be, Cora—you mark my words—he's going to be! I just couldn't go to Heaven without Clare. Why, I get lonesome for him when I go to Ohio.

[FATHER *enters holding his watch. He's also holding his temper. He speaks quietly.*]

FATHER.   Vinnie, I went to the dining-room and the table isn't set for dinner yet.

VINNIE. We're having dinner late today.

FATHER. Why can't I have my meals on time?

VINNIE. The girls' train leaves at one-thirty. Their cab's coming at one o'clock.

FATHER. Cab? The horse cars go right past our door.

VINNIE. They have those heavy bags.

FATHER. Clarence and John could have gone along to carry their bags. Cabs are just a waste of money. Why didn't we have an early dinner?

VINNIE. There wasn't time for an early dinner and church, too.

FATHER. As far as I'm concerned this would have been a good day to miss church.

VINNIE [*spiritedly*]. I wish we had!

FATHER [*flaring*]. I'll bet you put him up to preaching that sermon!

VINNIE. I've never been so mortified in all my life! You stamping up the aisle roaring your head off at the top of your voice!

FATHER. That Lloyd needn't preach at me as though I were some damn criminal! I wanted him to know it, and as far as I'm concerned the whole congregation can know it, too!

VINNIE. They certainly know it now!

FATHER. That suits me!

VINNIE [*pleading*]. Clare, you don't seem to understand what the church is for.

FATHER [*laying down a new Commandment*]. Vinnie, if there's one place the church should leave alone, it's a man's soul!

VINNIE. Clare, dear, don't you believe what it says in the Bible?

FATHER. A man has to use his common sense about the Bible, Vinnie, if he has any. For instance, you'd be in a pretty fix if I gave all my money to the poor.

VINNIE. Well, that's just silly!

FATHER. Speaking of money—where are this month's bills?

VINNIE. Clare, it isn't fair to go over the household accounts while you're hungry.

FATHER. Where are those bills, Vinnie?

VINNIE. They're downstairs on your desk.

[FATHER *exits almost eagerly. Figures are something he understands better than he does women.*]

Of all times! [*To* CORA] It's awfully hard on a woman to love a man like Clare so much.

CORA. Yes, men can be aggravating. Clyde gets me so provoked! We kept company for six years, but the minute he proposed—the moment I said "Yes"—he began to take me for granted.

VINNIE. You have to expect that, Cora. I don't believe Clare has come right out and told me he loves me since we've been married. Of

course I know he does, because I keep reminding him of it. You have
to keep reminding them, Cora.

[*The door slams.*]

CORA.   That must be Mary and Clarence.

[*There's a moment's pause. The two women look toward the hall
—then at each other with a knowing sort of smile.* CORA *rises, goes
up to the arch, peeks out—then faces front and innocently asks*]

Is that you, Mary?

MARY [*dashing in*].   Yes!

[CLARENCE *crosses the arch to hang up his hat.*]

CORA.   We have to change our clothes and finish our packing.
                                                          [*Goes upstairs.*]

[CLARENCE *returns as* MARY *starts up the stairs.*]

MARY [*to* CLARENCE].   It won't take me long.

CLARENCE.   Can I help you pack?

VINNIE [*shocked*].   Clarence!

[MARY *runs upstairs.* CLARENCE *drifts into the living-room somewhat abashed.* VINNIE *collects her hat and gloves, starts out, stops to
look at* CLARENCE, *then comes down to him*]

Clarence, why didn't you kneel in church today?

CLARENCE.   What, Mother?

VINNIE.   Why didn't you kneel in church today?

CLARENCE [*troubled*].   I just couldn't.

VINNIE.   Has it anything to do with Mary? I know she's a Methodist.

CLARENCE.   Oh, no, Mother! Methodists kneel. Mary told me. They
don't get up and down so much, but they stay down longer.

VINNIE.   If it's because your father doesn't kneel—you must remember he wasn't brought up to kneel in church. But you were—you always
have—and, Clarence, you want to, don't you?

CLARENCE.   Oh, yes! I wanted to today! I started to—you saw me
start—but I just couldn't.

VINNIE.   Is that suit of your father's too tight for you?

CLARENCE.   No, it's not too *tight*. It fits fine. But it *is* the suit. Very
peculiar things have happened to me since I started to wear it. I haven't
been myself since I put it on.

VINNIE.   In what way, Clarence? How do you mean?

[CLARENCE *pauses, then blurts out his problem.*]

CLARENCE. Mother, I can't seem to make these clothes do anything Father wouldn't do!

VINNIE. That's nonsense, Clarence—and not to kneel in church is a sacrilege.

CLARENCE. But making Father's trousers kneel seemed more of a sacrilege.

VINNIE. Clarence!

CLARENCE. No! Remember the first time I wore this? It was at Dora Wakefield's party for Mary. Do you know what happened? We were playing musical chairs and Dora Wakefield sat down suddenly right in my lap. I jumped up so fast she almost got hurt.

VINNIE. But it was all perfectly innocent.

CLARENCE. It wasn't that Dora was sitting on my lap—she was sitting on Father's trousers. Mother, I've got to have a suit of my own.

[CLARENCE's *metaphysical problem is one that* VINNIE *can't cope with at this particular minute.*]

VINNIE. My soul and body! Clarence, you have a talk with your father about it. I'm sure if you approach him the right way—you know—tactfully—he'll see—

[MARY *comes downstairs and hesitates at the arch.*]

MARY. Oh, excuse me.

VINNIE. Gracious! Have you finished your packing?

MARY. Practically. I never put my comb and brush in until I'm ready to close my bag.

VINNIE. I must see Margaret about your box lunch for the train. I'll leave you two together. Remember, it's Sunday.

[*She goes downstairs.*]

CLARENCE. I was hoping we could have a few minutes together before you left.

MARY [*not to admit her eagerness*]. Cora had so much to do I wanted to get out of her way.

CLARENCE. Well, didn't you want to see me?

MARY [*self-consciously*]. I did want to tell you how much I've enjoyed our friendship.

CLARENCE. You're going to write me when you get to Springfield, aren't you?

MARY. Of course, if you write me first.

CLARENCE. But you'll have something to write about—your trip—and Aunt Judith—and how things are in Springfield. You write me as soon as you get there.

MARY. Maybe I'll be too busy. Maybe I won't have time.

[*She sits on the sofa.*]

CLARENCE [*with the authority of* FATHER's *trousers*]. You find the time! Let's not have any nonsense about that! You'll write me first—and you'll do it right away, the first day! [*Sits beside her.*]

MARY. How do you know I'll take orders from you?

CLARENCE. I'll show you. [*He takes a quick glance toward the hall.*] Give me your hand!

MARY. Why should I?

CLARENCE. Give me your hand, confound it!

[MARY *gives it to him.*]

MARY. What do you want with my hand?

CLARENCE. I just wanted it.

[*Holding her hand, he melts a little and smiles at her. She melts, too. Their hands, clasped together, are resting on* CLARENCE's *knee and they relax happily.*]

What are you thinking about?

MARY. I was just thinking.

CLARENCE. About what?

MARY. Well, when we were talking about writing each other I was hoping you'd write me first because that would mean you liked me.

CLARENCE [*with the logic of the male*]. What's writing first got to do with my liking you?

MARY. Oh, you *do* like me?

CLARENCE. Of course I do. I like you better than any girl I ever met.

MARY [*with the logic of the female*]. But you don't like me well enough to write first?

CLARENCE. I don't see how one thing's got anything to do with the other.

MARY. But a girl can't write first—because she's a *girl*.

CLARENCE. That doesn't make sense. If a girl has something to write about and a fellow hasn't, there's no reason why she shouldn't write first.

MARY [*starting a flanking movement*]. You know, the first few days I was here you'd do anything for me and then you changed. You used to be a lot of fun—and then all of a sudden you turned into an old sobersides.

CLARENCE. When did I?

MARY. The first time I noticed it was when we walked home from Dora Wakefield's party. My, you were on your dignity! You've been that way ever since. You even dress like an old sober-sides.

[CLARENCE's *face changes as* FATHER's *pants rise to haunt him. Then he notices that their clasped hands are resting on these very pants, and he lifts them off. Agony obviously is setting in.* MARY *sees the expression on his face.*]

What's the matter?

CLARENCE. I just happened to remember something.

MARY. What?

[CLARENCE *doesn't answer, but his face does.*]

Oh, I know. This is the last time we'll be together.

[*She puts her hand on his shoulder. He draws away.*]

CLARENCE. Mary, please!

MARY. But, Clarence! We'll see each other in a month. And we'll be writing each other, too. I hope we will.   [*She gets up.*] Oh, Clarence, please write me first, because it will show me how much you like me. Please! I'll show you how much I like you!

[*She throws herself on his lap and buries her head on his shoulder.* CLARENCE *stiffens in agony.*]

CLARENCE [*hoarsely*]. Get up! Get up!

[*She pulls back her head and looks at him, then springs from his lap and runs away, covering her face and sobbing.* CLARENCE *goes to her.*]

Don't do that, Mary! Please don't do that!

MARY. Now you'll think I'm just a bold and forward girl.

CLARENCE. Oh, no.

MARY. Yes, you will—you'll think I'm bold.

CLARENCE. Oh, no—it's not that.

MARY [*hopefully*]. Was it because it's Sunday?

CLARENCE [*in despair*]. No, it would be the same any day—

[*He is about to explain, but* MARY *flares.*]

MARY. Oh, it's just because you didn't want me sitting on your lap.

CLARENCE. It was nice of you to do it.

MARY. It was nice of me! So you told me to get up! You just couldn't bear to have me sit there. Well, you needn't write me first. You needn't write me any letters at all, because I'll tear them up without opening them!

[FATHER *enters the archway, a sheaf of bills in his hand and his account book under his arm.*]

I guess I know now you don't like me! I never want to see you again. I—I—

[*She breaks and starts to run toward the stairs. At the sight of* FATHER *she stops, but only for a gasp, then continues on upstairs, unable to control her sobs.* CLARENCE, *who has been standing in unhappy indecision, turns to follow her, but stops short at the sight of* FATHER, *who is standing in the arch looking at him with some amazement.* FATHER *looks from* CLARENCE *toward the vanished* MARY, *then back to* CLARENCE.]

FATHER. Clarence, that young girl is crying—she's in tears. What's the meaning of this?

CLARENCE. I'm sorry, Father, it's all my fault.

FATHER. Nonsense! What's that girl trying to do to you?

CLARENCE. What? No, she wasn't—it was—I—how long have you been here?

FATHER. Well, whatever the quarrel was about, Clarence, I'm glad you held your own. Where's your mother?

CLARENCE [*desperately*]. I have to have a new suit of clothes—you've *got* to give me the money for it.

[FATHER's *account book reaches the table with a sharp bang as he stares at* CLARENCE *in astonishment.*]

FATHER. Young man, do you realize you're addressing your father?

[CLARENCE *wilts miserably and sinks into a chair.*]

CLARENCE. I'm sorry, Father—I apologize—but you don't know how important this is to me.

[CLARENCE's *tone of misery gives* FATHER *pause.*]

FATHER. A suit of clothes is so—? Now, why should a—?

[*Something dawns on* FATHER *and he looks up in the direction in which* MARY *has disappeared, then looks back at* CLARENCE.]

Has your need for a suit of clothes anything to do with that young lady?

CLARENCE. Yes, Father.

FATHER. Why, Clarence!

[*Suddenly realizes that women have come into* CLARENCE's *emotional life and there comes a yearning to protect this inexperienced and defenseless member of his own sex.*]

This comes as quite a shock to me.

CLARENCE. What does, Father?

FATHER. Your being so grown up! Still, I might have known that if you're going to college this fall—yes, you're at an age when you'll be meeting girls. Clarence, there are things about women that I think you ought to know!

[*He goes up and closes the doors, then comes down and sits beside* CLARENCE, *hesitating for a moment before he speaks.*]

Yes, I think it's better for you to hear this from me than to have to learn it for yourself. Clarence, women aren't the angels that you think they are! Well, now—first, let me explain this to you. You see, Clarence, we men have to run this world and it's not an easy job. It takes work, and it takes thinking. A man has to be sure of his facts and figures. He has to reason things out. Now, you take a woman—a woman thinks—no I'm wrong right there—a woman doesn't think at all! She gets stirred up! And she gets stirred up over the damnedest things! Now, I love my wife just as much as any man, but that doesn't mean I should stand for a lot of folderol! By God! I won't stand for it!

[*Looks around toward the spot where he had his last clash with* VINNIE.]

CLARENCE. Stand for what, Father?

FATHER [*to himself*]. That's the one thing I will not submit myself to.

[*Has ceased explaining women to* CLARENCE *and is now explaining himself.*]

Clarence, if a man thinks a certain thing is the wrong thing to do he shouldn't do it. If he thinks a thing is right he should do it. Now that has nothing to do with whether he loves his wife or not.

CLARENCE. Who says it has, Father?

FATHER. They do!

CLARENCE. Who, sir?

FATHER. Women! They get stirred up and then they try to get you stirred up, too. If you can keep reason and logic in the argument, a man can hold his own, of course. But if they can *switch* you—pretty soon the argument's about whether you love them or not. I swear I don't know how they do it! Don't you let 'em, Clarence! Don't you let 'em!

CLARENCE. I see what you mean so far, Father. If you don't watch yourself, love can make you do a lot of things you don't want to do.

FATHER. Exactly!

CLARENCE. But if you do watch out and know just how to handle women—

FATHER. Then you'll be all right. All a man has to do is be firm. You know how sometimes I have to be firm with your mother. Just now about this month's household accounts—

CLARENCE. Yes, but what can you do when they cry?

FATHER [*he gives this a moment's thought*]. Well, that's quite a ques. tion. You just have to make them understand that what you're doing is for their good.

CLARENCE. I see.

FATHER [*rising*]. Now, Clarence, you know all about women.

[*Goes to the table and sits down in front of his account book, opening it.* CLARENCE *rises and looks at him.*]

CLARENCE. But, Father—

FATHER. Yes, Clarence.

CLARENCE. I thought you were going to tell me about—

FATHER. About what?

CLARENCE. About women.

[FATHER *realizes with some shock that* CLARENCE *expected him to be more specific.*]

FATHER. Clarence, there are some things gentlemen don't discuss! I've told you all you need to know. The thing for you to remember is— be firm!

[CLARENCE *turns away. There is a knock at the sliding doors.*]

Yes, come in.

[MARY *opens the doors.*]

MARY. Excuse me!

[MARY *enters.* FATHER *turns his attention to the household accounts.* MARY *goes to the couch and picks up her handkerchief and continues around the couch.* CLARENCE *crosses to meet her above the couch, determined to be firm.* MARY *passes him without a glance.* CLARENCE *wilts, then again assuming firmness, turns up into the arch in an attempt to quail* MARY *with a look.* MARY *marches upstairs ignoring him.* CLARENCE *turns back into the room defeated. He looks down at his clothes unhappily, then decides to be firm with his father. He straightens up and steps toward him. At this moment* FATHER, *staring at a bill, emits his cry of rage.*]

FATHER. Oh, God!

[CLARENCE *retreats.* FATHER *rises and holds the bill in question between thumb and forefinger as though it were too repulsive to touch.* VINNIE *comes rushing down the stairs.*]

VINNIE. What's the matter, Clare? What's wrong?

FATHER. I will *not* send this person a check!

[VINNIE *looks at it.*]

VINNIE. Why, Clare, that's the only hat I've bought since March and it was reduced from forty dollars.

FATHER. I don't question your buying the hat or what you paid for it, but the person from whom you bought it—this Mademoiselle Mimi—isn't fit to be in the hat business or any other.

VINNIE. I never went there before, but it's a very nice place and I don't see why you object to it.

FATHER [*exasperated*]. I object to it because this confounded person doesn't put her name on her bills! Mimi what? Mimi O'Brien? Mimi Jones? Mimi Weinstein?

VINNIE. How do I know? It's just Mimi.

FATHER. It isn't just Mimi. She must have some other name, damn it! Now, I wouldn't make out a check payable to Charley or to Jimmy, and I won't make out a check payable to Mimi. Find out what her last name is, and I'll pay her the money.

VINNIE. All right. All right. [*She starts out.*]

FATHER. Just a minute, Vinnie, that isn't all.

VINNIE. But Cora will be leaving any minute, Clare, and it isn't polite for me—

FATHER. Never mind Cora. Sit down.

[CLARENCE *goes into the hall, looks upstairs, wanders up and down the hall restlessly.* VINNIE *reluctantly sits down opposite* FATHER *at the table.*]

Vinnie, you know I like to live well, and I want my family to live well. But this house must be run on a business basis. I must know how much money I'm spending and what for. For instance, if you recall, two weeks ago I gave you six dollars to buy a new coffeepot—

VINNIE. Yes, because you broke the old one. You threw it right on the floor.

FATHER. I'm not talking about that. I'm simply endeavoring—

VINNIE. But it was so silly to break that nice coffeepot, Clare, and there was nothing the matter with the coffee that morning. It was made just the same as always.

FATHER. It was not! It was made in a damned barbaric manner!

VINNIE. I couldn't get another imported one. That little shop has stopped selling them. They said the tariff wouldn't let them. And that's your fault, Clare, because you're always voting to raise the tariff.

FATHER. The tariff protects America against cheap foreign labor. [*He sounds as though he is quoting.*] Now I find that—

VINNIE. The tariff does nothing but put up the prices and that's hard on everybody, especially the farmer.

[She sounds as though she is quoting back.]

FATHER *[annoyed]*. I wish to God you wouldn't talk about matters you don't know a damn thing about!

VINNIE. I do too know about them. Miss Gulick says every intelligent woman should have some opinion—

FATHER. Who, may I ask, is Miss Gulick?

VINNIE. Why, she's that current-events woman I told you about and the tickets are a dollar every Tuesday.

FATHER. Do you mean to tell me that a pack of idle-minded females pay a dollar apiece to hear another female gabble about the events of the day? Listen to me if you want to know anything about the events of the day!

VINNIE. But you get so excited, Clare, and besides, Miss Gulick says that our President, whom you're always belittling, prays to God for guidance and—

FATHER *[having had enough of Miss Gulick]*. Vinnie, what happened to that six dollars?

VINNIE. What six dollars?

FATHER. I gave you six dollars to buy a new coffeepot and now I find that you apparently got one at Lewis & Conger's and charged it. Here's their bill: "One coffeepot—five dollars."

VINNIE. So you owe me a dollar and you can hand it right over.

[She holds out her hand for it.]

FATHER. I'll do nothing of the kind! What did you do with that six dollars?

VINNIE. Why, Clare, I can't tell you now, dear. Why didn't you ask me at the time?

FATHER. Oh, my God!

VINNIE. Wait a moment! I spent four dollars and a half for that new umbrella I told you I wanted and you said I didn't need, but I did, very much.

*[*FATHER *takes his pencil and writes in the account book.]*

FATHER. Now we're getting somewhere. One umbrella—four dollars and a half.

VINNIE. And that must have been the week I paid Mrs. Tobin for two extra days' washing.

FATHER *[entering the item]*. Mrs. Tobin.

VINNIE. So that was two dollars more.

FATHER. Two dollars.

VINNIE. That makes six dollars and fifty cents. And that's another fifty cents you owe me.

FATHER. I don't owe you anything.

[*Stung by* VINNIE'S *tactics into a determination to pin her butterfly mind down.*]

What you owe me is an explanation of where my money's gone! We're going over this account book item by item.

[*Starts to sort the bills for the purposes of cross-examination, but the butterfly takes wing again.*]

VINNIE. I do the very best I can to keep down expenses. And you know yourself that Cousin Phoebe spends twice as much as we do.

FATHER. Damn Cousin Phoebe!—I don't wish to be told how she throws her money around.

VINNIE. Oh, Clare, how can you? And I thought you were so fond of Cousin Phoebe.

FATHER. All right, I am fond of Cousin Phoebe, but I can get along without hearing so much about her.

VINNIE. You talk about your own relatives enough.

FATHER [*hurt*]. That's not fair, Vinnie. When I talk about my relatives I criticize them.

VINNIE. If I can't even speak of Cousin Phoebe—

FATHER. You can speak of her all you want to—but I won't have Cousin Phoebe or anyone else dictating to me how to run my house. Now this month's total—

VINNIE [*righteously*]. I didn't say a word about her dictating, Clare—she isn't that kind!

FATHER [*dazed*]. I don't know what you said. You never stick to the point. I endeavor to show you how to run this house on a business basis and you wind up by jibbering and jabbering about everything under the sun. If you'll just explain to me—

[*Finally cornered,* VINNIE *realizes the time has come for tears. Quietly she turns them on.*]

VINNIE. I don't know what you expect of me. I tire myself out chasing up and down those stairs all day long—trying to look after your comfort—to bring up our children—I do the mending and the marketing and as if that isn't enough, you want me to be an expert bookkeeper, too.

FATHER [*touched where* VINNIE *has hoped to touch him*]. Vinnie, I want to be reasonable; but can't you understand?—I'm doing all this for your own good.

[VINNIE *rises with a moan.* FATHER *sighs with resignation.*]

I suppose I'll have to go ahead just paying the bills and hoping I've got money enough in the bank to meet them. But it's all very discouraging.

VINNIE. I'll try to do better, Clare.

[FATHER *looks up into her tearful face and melts.*]

FATHER. That's all I'm asking.

[*She goes to him and puts her arm around his shoulder.*]

I'll go down and make out the checks and sign them.

[VINNIE *doesn't seem entirely consoled, so he attempts a lighter note to cheer her up.*]

Oh, Vinnie, maybe I haven't any right to sign those checks, since in the sight of the Lord I haven't any name at all. Do you suppose the bank will feel that way about it too—or do you think they'll take a chance?

[*He should not have said this.*]

VINNIE. That's right! Clare, to make those checks good you'll have to be baptized right away.

FATHER [*retreating angrily*]. Vinnie, the bank doesn't care whether I've been baptized or not!

VINNIE. Well, I care! And no matter what Dr. Lloyd says, I'm not sure we're really married.

FATHER. Damn it, Vinnie, we have four children! If we're not married now we never will be!

VINNIE. Oh, Clare, don't you see how serious this is? You've got to do something about it.

FATHER. Well, just now I've got to do something about these damn bills you've run up. [*Sternly*] I'm going downstairs.

VINNIE. Not before you give me that dollar and a half!

FATHER. What dollar and a half?

VINNIE. The dollar and a half you owe me!

FATHER [*thoroughly enraged*]. I don't owe you any dollar and a half! I gave you money to buy a coffeepot for me and somehow it turned into an umbrella for you.

VINNIE. Clarence Day, what kind of a man are you? Quibbling about a dollar and a half when your immortal soul is in danger! And what's more—

FATHER. All right. All right. All right.

[*He takes the dollar and a half from his change purse and gives it to her.*]

VINNIE [*smiling*]. Thank you, Clare.

[VINNIE *turns and leaves the room. Her progress upstairs is a one-woman march of triumph.* FATHER *puts his purse back, gathers up his papers and his dignity, and starts out.* CLARENCE *waylays him in the arch.*]

CLARENCE. Father—you never did tell me—can I have a new suit of clothes?

FATHER. No, Clarence! I'm sorry, but I have to be firm with you, too!

[*He stalks off.* JOHN *comes down the stairs carrying a traveling bag, which he takes out toward the front door. He returns empty-handed and starts up the stairs again.*]

CLARENCE. John, come here a minute.

JOHN [*coming into the room*]. What do you want?

CLARENCE. John, have you got any money you could lend me?

JOHN. With this week's allowance, I'll have about three dollars.

CLARENCE. That's no good. I've got to have enough to buy a new suit of clothes.

JOHN. Why don't you earn some money? That's what I'm going to do. I'm going to buy a bicycle—one of those new low kind, with both wheels the same size—you know, a safety.

CLARENCE. How are you going to earn that much money?

JOHN. I've got a job practically. Look, I found this ad in the paper.

[*He hands* CLARENCE *a clipping from his pocket.*]

CLARENCE [*reading*]. "Wanted, an energetic young man to handle household necessity that sells on sight. Liberal commissions. Apply 312 West Fourteenth Street, Tuesday from eight to twelve." Listen, John, let me have that job.

JOHN. Why should I give you my job? They're hard to get.

CLARENCE. But I've got to have a new suit of clothes.

JOHN. Maybe I could get a job for both of us.

[*The doorbell rings.*]

I'll tell you what I'll do, I'll ask the man.

FATHER [*hurrying to the foot of the stairs*]. Vinnie! Cora! The cab's here. Hurry up!

[*Goes through the arch toward the front door.*]

CLARENCE. John, we've both got to get down there early Tuesday—the first thing.

JOHN. Oh, no you don't—I'm going alone. But I'll put in a good word with the boss about you.

FATHER [*off*]. They'll be right out. Vinnie! Cora!

[*He comes back to the foot of the stairs and calls up.*]

Are you coming? The cab's waiting!

VINNIE [*from upstairs*]. We heard you, Clare. We'll be down in a minute.

[FATHER *comes into the room.*]

FATHER.   John, go upstairs and hurry them down.

[JOHN *goes upstairs.* FATHER *crosses to the window and looks out, then consults his watch.*]

FATHER.   What's the matter with those women? Don't they know cabs cost money? Clarence, go see what's causing this infernal delay!

[CLARENCE *goes out to the hall.*]

CLARENCE.   Here they come, Father.

[MARY *comes sedately downstairs. She passes* CLARENCE *without a glance and goes to* FATHER.]

MARY.   Goodbye, Mr. Day. I can't tell you how much I appreciate your hospitality.

FATHER.   Not at all! Not at all!

[VINNIE *and* CORA *appear at top of stairs and come down.* JOHN *follows with the bags and takes them out.*]

CORA.   Goodbye, Clarence. [*She starts into the room.*]

FATHER.   Cora, we can say goodbye to you on the sidewalk.

VINNIE.   There's no hurry. Their train doesn't go until one-thirty.

FATHER.   Cabs cost money. If they have any waiting to do they ought to do it at the Grand Central Depot. They've got a waiting room there just *for* that.

VINNIE [*to* MARY]. If there's one thing Mr. Day can't stand it's to keep a cab waiting.

CORA.   It's been so nice seeing you again, Clarence.

[*She kisses him.* MARGARET *enters with a box of lunch.*]

MARGARET.   Here's the lunch.

FATHER.   All right. All right. Give it to me. Let's get started.

[MARGARET *gives it to him and exits.*]

CORA.   Where's John?

FATHER.   He's outside. Come on.

[*Leads the way.* CORA *and* VINNIE *follow.* MARY *starts.*]

CLARENCE.   Mary, aren't you going even to shake hands with me?

MARY.   I don't think I'd better. You may remember that when I get too close to you you feel contaminated.

[*Starts out.* CLARENCE *follows her.*]

CLARENCE. Mary!

[*She stops in the arch. He goes to her.*]

You're going to write me, aren't you?

MARY. Are you going to write first?

CLARENCE [*resolutely*]. No, Mary. There are times when a man has to be firm.

[JOHN *enters.*]

JOHN. Mary, Mother says you'd better hurry out before Father starts yelling. It's Sunday.

MARY. Goodbye, John. I'm very happy to have made *your* acquaintance.

[*She walks out. We hear the door close.* JOHN *goes out.* CLARENCE *takes a step toward the door, stops, suffers a moment, then turns to the writing desk, takes paper and pen and ink to the table, and sits down to write a letter.*]

CLARENCE [*writing*]. Dear Mary—

CURTAIN

Scene II

THE SAME.

Two days later. The breakfast table.

HARLAN *and* WHITNEY *are at the table, ready to start breakfast.* CLARENCE *is near the window reading the paper. The places of* JOHN *and* VINNIE *and* FATHER *are empty.* NORA, *a new maid, is serving the fruit and cereal.* NORA *is heavily built and along toward middle age. The doorbell rings and we hear the postman's whistle.* CLARENCE *drops the paper and looks out the window toward the door.* NORA *starts toward the arch.*

CLARENCE. Never mind, Nora. It's the postman. I'll go.

[*He runs out through the arch.*]

WHITNEY [*to* NORA]. You forgot the sugar. It goes here between me and Father.

[CLARENCE *comes back with three or four letters which he sorts eagerly. Then his face falls in utter dejection.* FATHER *comes down the stairs.*]

FATHER. Good morning, boys! John late? [*He shouts*]　John! John! Hurry down to your breakfast.

CLARENCE. John had his breakfast early, Father, and went out to see about something.

FATHER. See about what?

CLARENCE. John and I thought we'd work this summer and earn some money.

FATHER. Good! Sit down boys. [*Goes to his chair.*]

CLARENCE. We saw an ad in the paper and John went down to see about it.

FATHER. Why didn't you go, too?

CLARENCE. I was expecting an answer to a letter I wrote, but it didn't come. Here's the mail. [*He seems depressed.*]

FATHER [*sitting*]. What kind of work is this you're planning to do?

CLARENCE. Sort of salesman, the ad said.

FATHER. Um-hum. Well, work never hurt anybody. It's good for them. But if you're going to work, work hard. King Solomon had the right idea about work. "Whatever thy hand findeth to do," Solomon said, "do thy damnedest!" Where's your mother?

NORA. If you please, sir, Mrs. Day doesn't want any breakfast. She isn't feeling well, so she went back upstairs to lie down again.

FATHER [*uneasily*]. Now, why does your mother do that to me? She knows it just upsets my day when she doesn't come down to breakfast. Clarence, go tell your mother I'll be up to see her before I start for the office.

CLARENCE. Yes, sir.

[*He goes upstairs.*]

HARLAN. What's the matter with Mother?

FATHER. There's nothing the matter with your mother. Perfectly healthy woman. She gets an ache or a twinge and instead of being firm about it, she just gives in to it.

[*The postman whistles. Then the doorbell rings.* NORA *answers it.*]

Boys, after breakfast you find out what your mother wants you to do today. Whitney, you take care of Harlan.

[NORA *comes back with a special delivery letter.*]

NORA. It's a special delivery.

[*She hands it to* FATHER, *who tears it open at once.* CLARENCE *comes rushing down the stairs.*]

CLARENCE. Was that the postman again?

WHITNEY. It was a special delivery.

CLARENCE. Yes? Where is it?

WHITNEY. It was for Father.

CLARENCE [*again disappointed*]. Oh—

[*He sits at the table.* FATHER *has opened the letter and is reading it. Bewildered, he turns it over and looks at the signature.*]

FATHER. I don't understand this at all. Here's a letter from some woman I never even heard of.

[FATHER *tackles the letter again.* CLARENCE *sees the envelope, picks it up, looks at the postmark, worried.*]

CLARENCE. Father!

FATHER. Oh, God!

CLARENCE. What is it, Father?

FATHER. This is the damnedest nonsense I ever read! As far as I can make out this woman claims that she sat on my lap and I didn't like it.

[CLARENCE *begins to turn red.* FATHER *goes on reading a little further and then holds the letter over in front of* CLARENCE.]

Can you make out what that word is?

[CLARENCE *begins feverishly to read as much as possible, but* FATHER *cuts in*]

No, that word right there. [*He points.*]

CLARENCE. It looks like—"curiosity."

[FATHER *withdraws the letter,* CLARENCE'S *eyes following it hungrily.*]

FATHER [*reads*]. "I only opened your letter as a matter of curiosity." [*Breaks off reading aloud as he turns the page.*]

CLARENCE. Yes? Go on.

FATHER. Why, this gets worse and worse! It just turns into a lot of sentimental lovey-dovey mush.

[*Crushes the letter, stalks across the room, and throws it into the fireplace,* CLARENCE *watching him with dismay.*]

Is this someone's idea of a practical joke? Why must I be the butt—

[VINNIE *comes hurrying down the stairs. Her hair is down in two braids over her shoulder. She is wearing a lacy combing jacket over her corset cover, and a striped petticoat.*]

VINNIE. What's the matter, Clare? What's wrong?

FATHER [*going to her*]. Nothing wrong—just a damn fool letter. How are you, Vinnie?

VINNIE [*weakly*]. I don't feel well. I thought you needed me, but if you don't I'll go back to bed.

FATHER. No, now that you're here, sit down with us. [*He moves out her chair.*] Get some food in your stomach. Do you good.

VINNIE [*protesting*]. I don't feel like eating anything, Clare.

[NORA *enters with a tray of bacon and eggs, stops at the serving table.*]

FATHER [*heartily*]. That's all the more reason why you should eat. Build up your strength!

[*He forces* VINNIE *into her chair and turns to speak to* NORA, *who has her back to him.*]

Here— [*Then to* CLARENCE] What's this one's name?

CLARENCE. Nora.

FATHER. Nora! Give Mrs. Day some of the bacon and eggs.

VINNIE. No, Clare!

[NORA, *however, has gone to* VINNIE's *side with the platter.*]

No, take it away, Nora. I don't even want to smell it.

[*The maid retreats, and serves* FATHER; *then* CLARENCE; *then serves coffee and exits.*]

FATHER. Vinnie, it's just weak to give in to an ailment. Any disease can be cured by firmness. What you need is strength of character.

VINNIE. I don't know why you object to my complaining a little. I notice when you have a headache you yell and groan and swear enough.

FATHER. Of course I yell! That's to prove to the headache that I'm stronger than it is. I can usually swear it right out of my system.

VINNIE. This isn't a headache. I think I've caught some kind of a germ. There's a lot of sickness around. Several of my friends have had to send for the doctor. I may have the same thing.

FATHER. I'll bet this is all your imagination, Vinnie. You hear of a lot of other people having some disease and then you get scared and think you have it yourself. So you go to bed and send for the doctor. The doctor—all poppycock!

VINNIE. I didn't say anything about my sending for the doctor.

FATHER. I should hope not. Doctors think they know a damn lot, but they don't.

VINNIE. But Clare, dear, when people are seriously ill you have to do something.

FATHER. Certainly you have to do something! Cheer 'em up—that's the way to cure 'em!

VINNIE [*with slight irony*]. How would you go about cheering them up?

FATHER. I? I'd tell 'em—bah!

[VINNIE, *out of exasperation and weakness, begins to cry.* FATHER *looks at her amazed.*]

What have I done now?

VINNIE. Oh, Clare—hush up!

[*She moves from the table to the sofa, where she tries to control her crying.* HARLAN *slides out of his chair and runs over to her.*]

Harlan dear, keep away from Mother. You might catch what she's got. Whitney, if you've finished your breakfast—

WHITNEY [*rising*]. Yes, Mother.

VINNIE. I promised Mrs. Whitehead to send over Margaret's recipe for floating-island pudding. Margaret has it all written out. And take Harlan with you.

WHITNEY. All right, Mother. I hope you feel better.

[WHITNEY *and* HARLAN *exit.* FATHER *goes over and sits beside* VINNIE *on the sofa.*]

FATHER. Vinnie. [*Contritely*] I didn't mean to upset you. I was just trying to help. [*He pats her hand.*] When you take to your bed I have a damned lonely time around here. So when I see you getting it into your head that you're sick, I want to do something about it. [*He continues to pat her hand vigorously with what he thinks is reassurance.*] Just because some of your friends have given in to this is no reason why you should imagine you're sick, Vinnie.

VINNIE [*snatching her hand away*]. Oh, stop, Clare!—get out of this house and go to your office!

[FATHER *is a little bewildered and somewhat indignant at this rebuff to his tenderness. He gets up and goes out into the hall, comes back with his hat and stick, and marches out of the house, slamming the door.* VINNIE *rises and starts toward the stairs.*]

CLARENCE. I'm sorry you're not feeling well, Mother.

VINNIE. Oh, I'll be all right, Clarence. Remember last fall I had a touch of this and I was all right the next morning.

CLARENCE. Are you sure you don't want the doctor?

VINNIE. Oh, no. I really don't need him—and besides doctors worry your father. I don't want him to be upset.

CLARENCE. Is there anything I can do for you?

VINNIE. Ask Margaret to send me up a cup of tea. I'll try to drink it. I'm going back to bed.

CLARENCE. Do you mind if John and I go out today or will you need us?

VINNIE. You run right along. I just want to be left alone.

[*She exits up the stairs.* CLARENCE *starts for the fireplace eager to retrieve* MARY's *letter.* NORA *enters. He stops.*]

CLARENCE. Oh!—Nora—will you take a cup of tea up to Mrs. Day in her room?

NORA. Yes, sir.

[*Exits.* CLARENCE *hurries around the table, gets the crumpled letter, and starts to read it feverishly. He reads quickly to the end, then draws a deep, happy breath. The door slams. He puts the letter in his pocket.* JOHN *enters, carrying two heavy packages.*]

CLARENCE. Did you get the job?

JOHN. Yes, for both of us. Look, I've got it with me.

CLARENCE. What is it?

JOHN. Medicine.

CLARENCE [*dismayed*]. Medicine! You took a job for us to go out and sell medicine!

JOHN. But it's wonderful medicine.

[*Gets a bottle out of the package and reads from the label*]

"Bartlett's Beneficent Balm—A Boon to Mankind." Look what it cures!

[*He hands the bottle to* CLARENCE.]

CLARENCE [*reading*]. "A sovereign cure for colds, coughs, catarrh, asthma, quinsy, and sore throat; poor digestion, summer complaint, colic, dyspepsia, heartburn, and shortness of breath; lumbago, rheumatism, heart disease, giddiness, and women's complaints; nervous prostration, St. Vitus' dance, jaundice, and la grippe; proud flesh, pink eye, seasickness, and pimples."

[*As* CLARENCE *has read off the list he has become more and more impressed.*]

JOHN. See?

CLARENCE. Say, that sounds all right!

JOHN. It's made "from a secret formula known only to Dr. Bartlett."

CLARENCE. He must be quite a doctor!

JOHN [*enthusiastically*]. It sells for a dollar a bottle and we get twenty-five cents commission on every bottle.

CLARENCE. Well, where does he want us to sell it?

JOHN. He's given us the territory of all Manhattan Island.

CLARENCE. That's bully! Anybody that's sick at all ought to need a bottle of this. Let's start by calling on friends of Father and Mother.

JOHN. That's a good idea. But wait a minute. Suppose they ask us if we use it at our house?

CLARENCE [a little worried]. Oh, yes. It would be better if we could say we did.

JOHN. But we can't because we haven't had it here long enough.

[NORA enters with a tray with a cup of tea. She goes to the table and puts the sugar bowl and cream pitcher on it.]

CLARENCE. Is that the tea for Mrs. Day?

NORA. Yes.

[The suspicion of a good idea dawns on CLARENCE.]

CLARENCE. I'll take it up to her. You needn't bother.

NORA. Thank you. Take it up right away while it's hot.

[She exits. CLARENCE watches her out.]

CLARENCE [eyeing JOHN]. Mother wasn't feeling well this morning.

JOHN. What was the matter with her?

CLARENCE. I don't know—she was just complaining.

JOHN [getting the idea immediately and consulting the bottle]. Well, it says here it's good for women's complaints.

[They look at each other. CLARENCE opens the bottle and smells its contents. JOHN leans over and takes a sniff, too. Then he nods to CLARENCE, who quickly reaches for a spoon and measures out a teaspoonful, which he puts into the tea. JOHN, wanting to be sure MOTHER has enough to cure her, pours still more into the tea from the bottle as

THE CURTAIN FALLS.

[The curtain remains down for a few seconds to denote a lapse of three hours.]

[When the curtain rises again, the breakfast things have been cleared and the room is in order. HARLAN is kneeling on FATHER'S chair looking out the window as if watching for someone. MARGARET comes down from upstairs.]

MARGARET. Has your father come yet?

HARLAN. Not yet.

[NORA enters from downstairs with a steaming teakettle and a towel and meets MARGARET in the hall.]

MARGARET. Hurry that upstairs. The doctor's waiting for it. I've got to go out.

NORA. Where are you going?

MARGARET. I have to go and get the minister.

[NORA *goes upstairs.*]

HARLAN. There's a cab coming up the street.

MARGARET. Well, I hope it's him, poor man—but a cab doesn't sound like your father.

[*She hurries downstairs.* HARLAN *sees something through the window, then rushes to the stairwell and shouts down to* MARGARET.]

HARLAN. Yes, it's Father. Whitney got him all right.

[*Runs back to the window. The front door slams and* FATHER *crosses the arch and hurries upstairs.* WHITNEY *comes into the room.*]

What took you so long?

WHITNEY. Long? I wasn't long. I went right down on the elevated and got Father right away and we came all the way back in a *cab*.

HARLAN. I thought you were never coming.

WHITNEY. Well, the horse didn't go very fast at first. The cabby whipped him and swore at him and still he wouldn't gallop. Then Father spoke to the horse personally— How is Mother?

HARLAN. I don't know. The doctor's up there now.

WHITNEY. Well, she'd better be good and sick or Father may be mad at me for getting him up here—'specially in a cab.

[FATHER *comes down the stairs muttering to himself.*]

FATHER [*indignantly*]. Well, huh!—It seems to me I ought to be shown a little consideration. I guess I've got some feelings, too!

WHITNEY [*hopefully*]. Mother's awfully sick, isn't she?

FATHER. How do I know? I wasn't allowed to stay in the same room with her.

WHITNEY. Did the doctor put you out?

FATHER. No, it was your mother, damn it!

[*He goes out and hangs up his hat and stick, then returns.* FATHER *may be annoyed, but he is also worried.*]

You boys keep quiet around here today.

WHITNEY. She must be pretty sick.

FATHER. She must be, Whitney! I don't know. Nobody ever tells me anything in this house. Not a damn thing!

[DR. HUMPHREYS *comes down the stairs. He's the family-doctor type of the period, with just enough whiskers to make him impressive. He carries his satchel.*]

DR. HUMPHREYS. Mrs. Day is quieter now.

FATHER. How sick is she? What's the matter with her?

DR. HUMPHREYS. She's a pretty sick woman, Mr. Day. I had given her a sedative just before you came—and after you left the room I had to give her another. Have you a telephone?

FATHER. A telephone! No—I don't believe in them. Why?

DR. HUMPHREYS. Well, it would only have saved me a few steps. I'll be back in ten minutes. [*He turns to go.*]

FATHER. Wait a minute—I think I'm entitled to know what's the matter with my wife.

[DR. HUMPHREYS *turns back.*]

DR. HUMPHREYS. What did Mrs. Day have for breakfast this morning?

FATHER. She didn't eat anything—not a thing.

DR. HUMPHREYS. Are you sure?

FATHER. I tried to get her to eat something, but she wouldn't.

DR. HUMPHREYS [*almost to himself*]. I can't understand it.

FATHER. Understand what?

DR. HUMPHREYS. These violent attacks of nausea. It's almost as though she were poisoned.

FATHER. Poisoned!

DR. HUMPHREYS. I'll try not to be gone more than ten or fifteen minutes.

[*He exits.*]

FATHER [*trying to reassure himself*]. Damn doctors! They never know what's the matter with anybody. Well, he'd better get your mother well, and damn soon or he'll hear from me.

WHITNEY. Mother's going to get well, isn't she?

[FATHER *looks at* WHITNEY *sharply as though he is a little angry at anyone even raising the question.*]

FATHER. Of course she's going to get well!

HARLAN [*running to* FATHER]. I hope she gets well soon. When Mamma stays in bed it's lonesome.

FATHER. Yes, it is, Harlan. It's lonesome.

[*He looks around the room and finds it pretty empty.*]

What were you boys supposed to do today?

WHITNEY. I was to learn the rest of my catechism.

FATHER. Well, if that's what your mother wanted you to do, you'd better do it.

WHITNEY. I know it—I think.

FATHER. You'd better be sure.

WHITNEY. I can't be sure unless somebody hears me. Will you hear me?

FATHER [*with sudden willingness to be useful*]. All right. I'll hear you, Whitney.

[WHITNEY *goes to the mantel and gets* VINNIE's *prayer book.* FATHER *sits on the sofa.* HARLAN *climbs up beside him.*]

HARLAN. If Mamma's still sick will you read to me tonight?

FATHER. Of course I'll read to you.

[WHITNEY *opens the prayer book and hands it to* FATHER.]

WHITNEY. Here it is, Father. Just the end of it. Mother knows I know the rest. Look, start here. [*He points.*]

FATHER. All right. [*Reading*]. "How many parts are there in a Sacrament?"

WHITNEY [*reciting*]. "Two; the outward visible sign, and the inward spiritual grace."

[FATHER *nods in approval.*]

FATHER. "What is the outward visible sign or form in Baptism?"

WHITNEY. "Water; wherein the person is baptized, in the name of the Father, and of the Son, and of the Holy Ghost." You haven't been baptized, Father, have you?

FATHER [*ignoring it*]. "What is the inward and spiritual grace?"

WHITNEY. If you don't have to be baptized, why do I have to be confirmed?

FATHER [*ignoring this even more*]. "What is the inward and spiritual grace?"

WHITNEY. "A death unto sin, and a new birth unto righteousness; for being by nature born in sin, and the children of wrath, we are hereby made the children of grace." Is that why you get mad so much, Father— because you're a child of wrath?

FATHER. Whitney, mind your manners! You're not supposed to ask questions of your elders! "What is required of persons to be baptized?"

WHITNEY. "Repentance, whereby—whereby—" [*He pauses.*]

FATHER [*quickly shutting the book and handing it to* WHITNEY]. You don't know it well enough, Whitney. You'd better study it some more.

WHITNEY. Now?

FATHER [*softening*]. No, you don't have to do it now. Let's see, now, what can we do?

WHITNEY. Well, I was working with my tool chest out in the back yard.

[*Edges toward the arch.*]

FATHER. Better not do any hammering with your mother sick upstairs. You'd better stay here.

WHITNEY. I wasn't hammering—I was doing wood-carving.

FATHER. Well, Harlan—how about you? Shall we play some tiddledy-winks?

HARLAN [*edging toward* WHITNEY]. I was helping Whitney.

FATHER. Oh—all right.

[*The boys go out.* FATHER *goes to the stairwell.*]

Boys, don't do any shouting. We all have to be very quiet around here.

[*He stands in the hall and looks up toward* VINNIE, *worried. Then he tiptoes across the room and stares gloomily out of the window. Then he tiptoes back into the hall and goes to the rail of the basement stairs, and calls quietly*]

Margaret!

[*There is no answer and he raises his voice a little*]

Margaret!

[*There is still no answer and he lets loose*]

Margaret! Why don't you answer when you hear me calling?

[*At this moment* MARGARET, *hat on, appears in the arch from the right, having come through the front door.*]

MARGARET. Sh—sh—

[FATHER *turns quickly and sees* MARGARET.]

FATHER. Oh, there you are!

MARGARET [*reprovingly*]. We must all be quiet, Mr. Day—Mrs. Day is very sick.

FATHER [*testily*]. I know she's sick. That's what I wanted you for. You go up and wait outside her door in case she needs anything.

[MARGARET *starts upstairs.*]

And what were you doing out of the house, anyway?

MARGARET. I was sent for the minister.

FATHER [*startled*]. The minister!

MARGARET. Yes, he'll be right in. He's paying off the cab.

[MARGARET *continues upstairs. The door slams.* THE REVEREND DR. LLOYD *appears in the archway and meets* FATHER *in the hall.*]

DR. LLOYD. I was deeply shocked to hear of Mrs. Day's illness. I hope I can be of some service. Will you take me up to her?

FATHER [*with a trace of hostility*]. She's resting now. She can't be disturbed.

DR. LLOYD. But I've been summoned.

FATHER. The doctor will be back in a few minutes and we'll see what he has to say about it. You'd better come in and wait.

DR. LLOYD. Thank you.

[*Comes into the room.* FATHER *follows him reluctantly.*]

Mrs. Day has been a tower of strength in the parish. Everyone liked her so much. Yes, she was a fine woman.

FATHER. I wish to God you wouldn't talk about Mrs. Day as if she were dead.

[NORA *comes down the stairs and looks into the room.*]

NORA. Is the doctor back yet?

FATHER. No. Does she need him?

NORA. She's kinda' restless. She's talking in her sleep and twisting and turning.

[*She goes downstairs.* FATHER *looks up toward* VINNIE'S *room, worried, then looks angrily toward the front door.*]

FATHER. That doctor said he'd be right back. [*He goes to the window.*]

MARGARET [*coming downstairs*]. Here comes the doctor. I was watching for him out the window.

[*She goes to the front door. A moment later* DR. HUMPHREYS *enters.*]

FATHER. Well, doctor—seems to me that was a pretty long ten minutes.

DR. HUMPHREYS [*indignantly*]. See here, Mr. Day, if I'm to be responsible for Mrs. Day's health, I must be allowed to handle this case in my own way.

FATHER. Well, you can't handle it if you're out of the house.

DR. HUMPHREYS [*flaring*]. I left this house because—

[DR. SOMERS, *an imposing medical figure, enters and stops at* DR. HUMPHREYS'S *side*]

This is Dr. Somers.

DR. SOMERS. How do you do?

DR. HUMPHREYS. I felt that Mrs. Day's condition warranted my getting Dr. Somers here as soon as possible for consultation. I hope that meets with your approval.

FATHER [*a little awed*]. Why, yes, of course. Anything that can be done.

DR. HUMPHREYS. Upstairs, doctor!

[*The two doctors go upstairs.* FATHER *turns back into the room, obviously shaken.*]

DR. LLOYD. Mrs. Day is in good hands now, Mr. Day. There's nothing you and I can do at the moment to help.

[*After a moment's consideration* FATHER *decides there is something that can be done to help. He goes to* DR. LLOYD. FATHER *indicates the seat in front of the table to* DR. LLOYD *and they both sit.*]

FATHER. Dr. Lloyd, there's something that's troubling Mrs. Day's mind. I think you know what I refer to.

DR. LLOYD. Yes—you mean the fact that you've never been baptized.

FATHER. I gathered you knew about it from your sermon last Sunday.

[*Looks at him a second with indignant memory.*]

But let's not get angry. I think something had better be done about it.

DR. LLOYD. Yes, Mr. Day.

FATHER. When the doctors get through up there I want you to talk to Mrs. Day. I want you to tell her something.

DR. LLOYD [*eagerly*]. Yes, I'll be glad to.

FATHER. You're just the man to do it! She shouldn't be upset about this—I want you to tell her that my being baptized would just be a lot of damn nonsense.

[*This isn't what* DR. LLOYD *has expected and it is hardly his idea of how to help* MRS. DAY.]

DR. LLOYD. But, Mr. Day!

FATHER. No, she'd take your word on a thing like that—and we've got to do everything we can to help her now.

DR. LLOYD [*rising*]. But baptism is one of the sacraments of the Church—

FATHER [*rising*]. You're her minister and you're supposed to bring her comfort and peace of mind.

DR. LLOYD. But the solution is so simple. It would take only your consent to be baptized.

FATHER. That's out of the question! And I'm surprised that a grown man like you should suggest such a thing.

DR. LLOYD. If you're really concerned about Mrs. Day's peace of mind, don't you think—

FATHER. Now see here—if you're just going to keep her stirred up about this, I'm not going to let you see her at all.

[*He turns away.* DR. LLOYD *follows him.*]

DR. LLOYD. Now, Mr. Day, as you said, we must do everything we can—

[*The doctors come downstairs.* FATHER *sees them.*]

FATHER. Well, doctor, how is she? What have you decided?

DR. HUMPHREYS. We've just left Mrs. Day. Is there a room we could use for our consultation?

FATHER. Of course. [MARGARET *starts downstairs.*] Margaret, you go back upstairs! I don't want Mrs. Day left alone!

MARGARET. I have to do something for the doctor. I'll go back up as soon as I get it started.

FATHER. Well, hurry. And, Margaret, show these gentlemen downstairs to the billiard room.

MARGARET. Yes, sir. This way, doctor—downstairs.

[*Exits, followed by* DR. SOMERS. FATHER *delays* DR. HUMPHREYS.]

FATHER. Dr. Humphreys, you know now, don't you—this isn't serious, is it?

DR. HUMPHREYS. After we've had our consultation we'll talk to you, Mr. Day.

FATHER. But surely you must—

DR. HUMPHREYS. Just rest assured that Dr. Somers will do everything that is humanly possible.

FATHER. Why, you don't mean—

DR. HUMPHREYS. We'll try not to be long.

[*Exits.* FATHER *turns and looks at* DR. LLOYD. *He is obviously frightened.*]

FATHER. This Dr. Somers—I've heard his name often—he's very well thought of, isn't he?

DR. LLOYD. Oh, yes indeed.

FATHER. If Vinnie's really—if anyone could help her, he could—don't you think?

DR. LLOYD. A very fine physician. But there's a greater Help, ever present in the hour of need. Let us turn to Him in prayer. Let us kneel and pray.

[FATHER *looks at him, straightens, then walks to the other side of the room.*]

Let us kneel and pray.

[FATHER *finally bows his head.* DR. LLOYD *looks at him and, not kneeling himself, raises his head and speaks simply in prayer*]

Oh, Lord, look down from Heaven—behold, visit, and relieve this Thy servant who is grieved with sickness, and extend to her Thy accustomed goodness. We know she has sinned against Thee in thought, word, and deed. Have mercy on her, O Lord, have mercy on this miserable sinner. Forgive her—

FATHER. She's not a miserable sinner and you know it!

[*Then* FATHER *speaks directly to the Deity*]

O God! You know Vinnie's not a miserable sinner. She's a damn fine woman! She shouldn't be made to suffer. It's got to stop, I tell you, it's got to stop!

[VINNIE *appears on the stairway in her nightgown.*]

VINNIE. What's the matter, Clare? What's wrong?
FATHER [*not hearing her*]. Have mercy, I say, have mercy, damn it!
VINNIE. What's the matter, Clare? What's wrong?

[FATHER *turns, sees* VINNIE, *and rushes to her.*]

FATHER. Vinnie, what are you doing down here? You shouldn't be out of bed. You get right back upstairs.

[*He now has his arms around her.*]

VINNIE. Oh, Clare, I heard you call. Do you need me?
FATHER [*deeply moved*]. Vinnie—I know now how much I need you. Get well, Vinnie. I'll be baptized. I promise. I'll be baptized.
VINNIE. You will? Oh, Clare!
FATHER. I'll do anything. We'll go to Europe, just we two—you won't have to worry about the children or the household accounts—

[VINNIE *faints against* FATHER's *shoulder*]

Vinnie! [*He stoops to lift her.*]
DR. LLOYD. I'll get the doctor. But don't worry, Mr. Day—she'll be all right now.

[FATHER *lifts* VINNIE *up in his arms.*]

Bless you for what you've done, Mr. Day.
FATHER. What did I do?
DR. LLOYD. You promised to be baptized!
FATHER [*aghast*]. I did?

[*With horror* FATHER *realizes he has been betrayed—and by himself*]

OH, GOD!

CURTAIN

ACT THREE

Scene I

THE SAME.

A month later. Mid-afternoon.

VINNIE *is seated on the sofa embroidering petit point.* MARGARET *enters, as usual uncomfortable at being upstairs.*

MARGARET. You wanted to speak to me, ma'am?

VINNIE. Yes, Margaret, about tomorrow morning's breakfast—we must plan it very carefully.

MARGARET [*puzzled*]. Mr. Day hasn't complained to me about his breakfasts lately. As a matter of fact, I've been blessing my luck!

VINNIE. Oh, no, it's not that. But tomorrow morning I'd like something for his breakfast that would surprise him.

MARGARET [*doubtfully*]. Surprising Mr. Day is always a bit of a risk, ma'am. My motto with him has always been "Let well enough alone."

VINNIE. But if we think of something he especially likes, Margaret—what would you say to kippers?

MARGARET. Well, I've served him kippers, but I don't recall his ever saying he liked them.

VINNIE. He's never said he didn't like them, has he?

MARGARET. They've never got a stamp on the floor out of him one way or the other.

VINNIE. If Mr. Day doesn't say he doesn't like a thing you can assume that he does. Let's take a chance on kippers, Margaret.

MARGARET. Very well, ma'am. [*She starts out.*]

VINNIE [*innocently*]. And, Margaret, you'd better have enough breakfast for two extra places.

MARGARET [*knowingly*]. Oh—so that's it! We're going to have company again.

VINNIE. Yes, my cousin, Miss Cartwright, and her friend are coming back from Springfield. I'm afraid they'll get here just about breakfast time.

MARGARET. Well, in that case I'd better make some of my Sunday morning hot biscuits, too.

VINNIE. Yes. We *know* Mr. Day likes those.

MARGARET. I've been getting him to church with them for the last fifteen years.

[*The door slams.* MARGARET *goes to the arch and looks.*]

Oh, it's Mr. Clarence, ma'am.

[Goes off downstairs and CLARENCE *enters with a large package.]*

CLARENCE. Here it is, Mother. *[He puts it on the table.]*

VINNIE. Oh, it was still in the store! They hadn't sold it! I'm so thrilled. Didn't you admire it, Clarence? *[She hurries over to the table.]*

CLARENCE. Well, it's unusual.

VINNIE *[unwrapping the package].* You know, I saw this down there the day before I got sick. I was walking through the bric-a-brac section and it caught my eye. I was so tempted to buy it! And all the time I lay ill I just couldn't get it out of my head. I can't understand how it could stay in the store all this time without somebody snatching it up.

[She takes it out of the box. It is a large china pug dog.]

Isn't that the darlingest thing you ever saw! It does need a ribbon, though. I've got the very thing somewhere. Oh, yes, I know.

[Goes to the side table and gets a red ribbon out of the drawer.]

CLARENCE. Isn't John home yet?

VINNIE. I haven't seen him. Why?

CLARENCE. Well, you know we've been working, and John went down to collect our money.

VINNIE. That's fine. *[She ties the ribbon around the dog's neck.]* Oh, Clarence, I have a secret for just the two of us; who do you think is coming to visit us tomorrow—Cousin Cora and Mary.

CLARENCE. Yes, I know.

VINNIE. How did you know?

CLARENCE. I happened to get a letter.

*[*JOHN *enters, carrying two packages of medicine.]*

VINNIE. John, did you ever see anything so sweet?

JOHN. What is it?

VINNIE. It's a pug dog. Your father would never let me have a real one, but he can't object to one made of china. This ribbon needs pressing. I'll take it down and have Margaret do it right away.

[Exits with the beribboned pug dog.]

CLARENCE. What did you bring home more medicine for? *[Then with sudden fright]* Dr. Bartlett paid us off, didn't he?

JOHN. Oh, yes!

CLARENCE *[heaving a great sigh of relief].* You had me scared for a minute. When I went down to McCreery's to get that pug dog for Mother, I ordered the daisiest suit you ever saw. Dr. Bartlett owed us sixteen dollars apiece, and the suit was only fifteen. Wasn't that lucky? Come on, give me my money.

JOHN. Clarence, Dr. Bartlett paid us off in medicine.

CLARENCE. You let him pay us off with that old Beneficent Balm!

JOHN. Well, he thanked us, too, for our services to mankind.

CLARENCE [*in agony*]. But my suit!

JOHN. You'll just have to wait for your suit.

CLARENCE. I can't wait! I've got to have it tomorrow—and besides they're making the alterations. I've got to pay for it this afternoon! Fifteen dollars!

JOHN [*helpfully*]. Why don't you offer them fifteen bottles of medicine?

[CLARENCE *gives it a little desperate thought.*]

CLARENCE. They wouldn't take it. McCreery's don't sell medicine.

[JOHN *is by the window and looks out.*]

JOHN. That's too bad. Here comes Father.

CLARENCE. I'll have to brace him for that fifteen dollars. I hate to do it, but I've got to—that's all—I've got to.

JOHN. I'm not going to be here when you do. I'd better hide this somewhere, anyway.

[*Takes the packages and hurries upstairs. The door slams.* FATHER *enters and looks into the room.*]

CLARENCE. Good afternoon, sir.

FATHER. How's your mother, Clarence? Where is she?

CLARENCE. She's all right. She's downstairs with Margaret. Oh, Father—

[FATHER *goes off down the hall and we hear him calling downstairs.*]

FATHER. Vinnie! Vinnie! I'm home.

[*Comes back into the room, carrying his newspaper.*]

CLARENCE. Father, Mother will be well enough to go to church with us next Sunday.

FATHER. That's fine, Clarence. That's fine.

CLARENCE. Father, have you noticed that I haven't been kneeling down in church lately?

FATHER. Clarence, don't let your mother catch you at it.

CLARENCE. Then I've got to have a new suit of clothes right away!

FATHER [*after a puzzled look*]. Clarence, you're not even making sense!

CLARENCE. But a fellow doesn't feel right in cut-down clothes—especially your clothes. That's why I can't kneel down in church—I can't do anything in them you wouldn't do.

FATHER. Well, that's a damn good thing! If my old clothes make you behave yourself I don't think you ought to wear anything else.

CLARENCE [*desperately*]. *Oh, no!* You're you and I'm me! I want to be myself! Besides, you're older and there are things I've got to do that I wouldn't do at your age.

FATHER. Clarence, you should never do anything I wouldn't do.

CLARENCE. Oh, yes,—look, for instance: Suppose I should want to kneel down in front of a girl?

FATHER. Why in Heaven's name should you want to do a thing like that?

CLARENCE. Well, I've got to get married *sometime*. I've got to propose to a girl *sometime*.

FATHER [*exasperated*]. Before you're married, you'll be earning your own clothes, I hope. Don't get the idea into your head I'm going to support you and a wife, too. Besides, at your age, Clarence—

CLARENCE [*hastily*]. Oh, I'm not going to be married right away, but for fifteen dollars I can get a good suit of clothes.

FATHER [*bewildered and irritated*]. Clarence!

[*He stares at him. At this second,* VINNIE *comes through the arch.*]

Why, you're beginning to talk as crazy as your mother. [*He sees her.*] Oh, hello, Vinnie. How're you feeling today?

VINNIE. I'm fine, Clare. [*They kiss.*] You don't have to hurry home from the office every day like this.

[CLARENCE *throws himself in the chair by the window, sick with disappointment.*]

FATHER. Business the way it is, no use going to the office at all.

VINNIE. But you haven't been to your club for weeks.

FATHER. Can't stand the damn place. You do look better, Vinnie. What did you do today?

[*Drops on the sofa.* VINNIE *stands behind the sofa. Her chatter does not succeed in diverting* FATHER *from his newspaper.*]

VINNIE. I took a long walk and dropped in to call on old Mrs. Whitehead.

FATHER. Well, that's fine.

VINNIE. And, Clare, it was the most fortunate thing that ever happened. I've got wonderful news for you! Who do you think was there? Mr. Morley!

FATHER [*not placing him*]. Morley?

VINNIE. You remember—that nice young minister who substituted for Dr. Lloyd one Sunday?

FATHER. Oh, yes! Bright young fellow, preached a good sensible sermon.

VINNIE. It was the only time I ever saw you put five dollars in the plate!

FATHER. Ought to be more ministers like him. I could get along with that young man without any trouble at all.

VINNIE. Well, Clare, his parish is in Audubon—you know, 'way up above Harlem.

FATHER. Is that so?

VINNIE. Isn't that wonderful? Nobody knows you up there. You'll be perfectly safe!

FATHER. Safe? Vinnie, what the devil are you talking about?

VINNIE. I've been all over everything with Mr. Morley and he's agreed to baptize you.

FATHER. Oh, he has—the young whippersnapper! Damn nice of him!

VINNIE. We can go up there any morning, Clare—we don't even have to make an appointment.

FATHER. Vinnie, you're just making a lot of plans for nothing. Who said I was going to be baptized at all?

VINNIE [*aghast*]. Why, Clare! *You* did!

FATHER. Now, Vinnie!—

VINNIE. You gave me your promise—your Sacred Promise. You stood right on that spot and said: "I'll be baptized. I promise—I'll be baptized."

FATHER. What if I did?

VINNIE [*amazed, she comes down and faces him*]. Aren't you a man of your word?

FATHER [*rising*]. Vinnie, that was under entirely different circumstances. We all thought you were dying, so naturally I said that to make you feel better. As a matter of fact, the doctor told me that's what cured you. So it seems to me pretty ungrateful of you to press this matter any further.

VINNIE. Clarence Day, you gave me your Sacred Promise!

FATHER [*getting annoyed*]. Vinnie, you were sick when I said that. Now you're well again.

[MARGARET *enters with the pug dog, which now has the freshly pressed ribbon tied around its neck. She puts it on the table.*]

MARGARET. Is that all right, Mrs. Day?

VINNIE [*dismissingly*]. That's fine, Margaret, thank you.

[MARGARET *exits.*]

My being well has nothing to do with it. You gave me your word! You gave the Lord your word. If you had seen how eager Mr. Morley was to bring you into the fold!

[FATHER, *trying to escape, has been moving toward the arch when suddenly the pug dog catches his eye and he stares at it fascinated.*]

And you're going to march yourself up to his church some morning before you go to the office and be christened. If you think for one minute that I'm going to—

FATHER. What in the name of Heaven is that?

VINNIE. If you think I'm going to let you add the sin of breaking your Solemn and Sacred Promise—

FATHER. I demand to know what that repulsive object is!

VINNIE [*exasperated in her turn*]. It's perfectly plain what it is—it's a pug dog!

FATHER. What's it doing in this house?

VINNIE [*defiantly*]. I wanted it and I bought it.

FATHER. You spent good money for that?

VINNIE. Clare, we're not talking about that! We're talking about you. Don't try to change the subject!

FATHER. How much did you pay for that atrocity?

VINNIE. I don't know. I sent Clarence down for it. Listen to me, Clare—

FATHER. Clarence, what did you pay for that?

CLARENCE. I didn't pay anything. I charged it.

FATHER [*looking at* VINNIE]. Charged it! I might have known. [*To* CLARENCE] How much was it?

CLARENCE. Fifteen dollars.

FATHER. Fifteen dollars for that eyesore?

VINNIE [*to the rescue of the pug dog*]. Don't you call that lovely work of art an eyesore! That will look beautiful sitting on a red cushion by the fireplace in the parlor.

FATHER. If that sits in the parlor, I won't! Furthermore, I don't even want it in the same house with me. Get it out of here!

[*He starts for the stairs.*]

VINNIE. You're just using that for an excuse. You're not going to get out of this room until you set a date for your baptism.

[FATHER *turns at the foot of the stairs.*]

FATHER. I'll tell you one thing! I'll never be baptized while that hideous monstrosity is in this house. [*He stalks upstairs.*]

VINNIE [*calling after him*]. All right! [*She goes to the pug dog.*] All right! It goes back this afternoon and he's christened first thing in the morning.

CLARENCE. But, Mother—

VINNIE. Clarence, you heard him say that he'd be baptized as soon as I got this pug dog out of the house. You hurry right back to McCreery's with it—and be sure they credit us with fifteen dollars.

[*The fifteen dollars rings a bell in* CLARENCE'S *mind.*]

CLARENCE. Oh, say, Mother, while I was at McCreery's, I happened to see a suit I would like very much and the suit was only fifteen dollars.

VINNIE [*regretfully*]. Well, Clarence, I think your suit will have to wait until after I get your father christened.

CLARENCE [*hopefully*]. No. I meant that since the suit cost just the same as the pug dog, if I exchanged the pug dog for the suit—

VINNIE. Why, yes! Then your suit wouldn't cost Father anything! Why, how bright of you, Clarence, to think of that!

CLARENCE [*quickly*]. I'd better start right away before McCreery's closes.

[*They have collected the box, wrapper, and tissue paper.*]

VINNIE. Yes. Let's see. If we're going to take your father all the way up to Audubon— Clarence, you stop at Ryerson & Brown's on your way back and tell them to have a cab here at eight o'clock tomorrow morning.

CLARENCE. Mother, a cab! Do you think you ought to do that?

VINNIE. Well, we can't walk to Audubon.

CLARENCE [*warningly*]. But you know what a cab does to Father!

VINNIE. This is an important occasion.

CLARENCE [*with a shrug*]. All right! A brougham or a Victoria?

VINNIE. Get one of their best cabs—the kind they use at funerals.

CLARENCE. Those cost two dollars an hour! And if Father gets mad—

VINNIE. Well, if your father starts to argue in the morning, you remember—

CLARENCE [*remembering his suit*]. Oh, he agreed to it! We both heard him!

[VINNIE *has removed the ribbon and is about to put the pug dog back in the box.*]

VINNIE [*regretfully*]. I did have my heart set on this. [*An idea comes to her.*] Still—if they didn't sell him in all that time, he might be safe there for a few more weeks

[*She gives the dog a reassuring pat and puts him in the box. She begins to sing "Sweet Marie" happily.* FATHER *comes down the stairs.* CLARENCE *takes his hat and the box and goes happily and quickly out.* FATHER *watches him.*]

I hope you notice that Clarence is returning the pug dog.

FATHER. That's a sign you're getting your faculties back.

[VINNIE *is singing quietly to herself in a satisfied way.*]

Good to hear you singing again, Vinnie. [*Suddenly remembering something*] Oh!—on my way uptown I stopped in at Tiffany's and bought you a little something. Thought you might like it.

[*He takes out of his pocket a small ring-box and holds it out to her. She takes it.*]

VINNIE. Oh, Clare. [*She opens it eagerly.*] What a beautiful ring!

[*She takes the ring out, puts it on her finger, and admires it.*]

FATHER. Glad if it pleases you.

[*He settles down to his newspaper on the sofa.*]

VINNIE. I don't know how to thank you. [*She kisses him.*]
FATHER. It's thanks enough for me to have you up and around again. When you're sick, Vinnie, this house is like a tomb. There's no excitement.
VINNIE [*sitting beside him*]. Clare, this is the loveliest ring you ever bought me. Now that I have this, you needn't buy any more rings.
FATHER. Well, if you don't want any more.
VINNIE. What I'd really like now is a nice diamond necklace.
FATHER [*alarmed*]. Vinnie, do you know how much a diamond necklace costs?
VINNIE. I know, Clare, but don't you see?—your giving me this ring shows that I mean a little something to you. Now, a diamond necklace—
FATHER. Good God, if you don't know by this time how I feel about you! We've been married for twenty years and I've loved you every minute of it.
VINNIE. What did you say?

[*Her eyes well with tears at* FATHER's *definite statement of his love.*]

FATHER. I said we'd been married twenty years and I've loved you every minute of it. But if I have to buy out jewelry stores to prove it— if I haven't shown it to you in my words and actions, I might as well—

[*He turns and sees* VINNIE *dabbing her eyes and speaks with resignation.*]

What have I done now?
VINNIE. It's all right, Clare—I'm just so happy.
FATHER. Happy!
VINNIE. You said you loved me! And this beautiful ring—that's something else I didn't expect. Oh, Clare, I love surprises.

[*She nestles against him.*]

FATHER.   That's another thing I can't understand about you, Vinnie. Now, *I* like to know what to expect. Then I'm prepared to meet it.

VINNIE [*putting her head on his shoulder*].   Yes, I know. But, Clare, life would be pretty dull if we always knew what was coming.

FATHER.   Well, it's certainly not dull around here. In this house you never know what's going to hit you tomorrow.

VINNIE [*to herself*].   Tomorrow!

[*She starts to sing,* FATHER *listening to her happily.*]

> "Every daisy in the dell,
>   Knows my secret, knows it well,
>   And yet I dare not tell,
>   Sweet Marie!"

CURTAIN

Scene II

THE SAME.

The next morning. Breakfast. All the family except JOHN *and* VINNIE *are at the table and in good spirits.*

JOHN [*entering*].   Mother says she'll be right down.

[*He sits at the table.* MAGGIE, *the new maid, enters with a plate of hot biscuits and serves* FATHER. *As* FATHER *takes a biscuit, he glances up at her and shows some little surprise.*]

FATHER.   Who are you? What's your name?
MAGGIE.   Margaret, sir.
FATHER.   Can't be Margaret. We've got one Margaret in the house.
MAGGIE.   At home they call me Maggie, sir.
FATHER [*genially*].   All right, Maggie.

[MAGGIE *continues serving the biscuits.*]

Boys, if her name's Margaret, that's a good sign. Maybe she'll stay awhile. You know, boys, your mother used to be just the same about cooks as she is about maids. Never could keep them for some reason. Well, one day about fifteen years ago—yes, it was right after you were born, John—my, you were a homely baby.

[*They all laugh at* JOHN's *expense.*]

I came home that night all tired out and what did I find?—no dinner, because the cook had left. Well, I decided I'd had just about enough of that, so I just marched over to the employment agency on Sixth Avenue and said to the woman in charge: "Where do you keep the cooks?" She tried to hold me up with a lot of red-tape folderol, but I just walked into the room where the girls were waiting, looked 'em over, saw Margaret, pointed at her, and said: "I'll take that one." I walked her home, she cooked dinner that night, and she's been cooking for us ever since. Damn good cook, too.

[*He stamps on the floor three times.* VINNIE *comes down the stairs dressed in white. Somehow she almost has the appearance of a bride going to her wedding.*]

VINNIE.   Good morning, Clare. Good morning, boys.

[*The boys and* FATHER *rise.* VINNIE *takes her bonnet and gloves and lays them on the chair below the fireplace.* FATHER *goes to* VINNIE's *chair and holds it out for her, glancing at her holiday appearance.* VINNIE *sits.*]

FATHER.   Sit down, boys. [*As* FATHER *returns to his own chair, he notices that all of the boys are dressed in their Sunday best.*] Everyone's dressed up this morning. What's on the program for this fine day?

[VINNIE, *who always postpones crises in the hope some miracle will aid her, postpones this one.*]

VINNIE.   Well, this afternoon May Lewis's mother is giving a party for everyone in May's dancing class. Harlan's going to that.
HARLAN.   I don't want to go, Mamma.
VINNIE.   Why, Harlan, don't you want to go to a party and get ice cream and cake?
HARLAN.   May Lewis always tries to kiss me.

[*This is greeted with family laughter.*]

FATHER [*genially*].   When you get a little older, you won't object to girls' wanting to kiss you, will he, Clarence?

[MARGARET *comes hurrying in.*]

MARGARET.   What's wanting?
FATHER.   Margaret, these kippers are *good*.

[MARGARET *makes her usual deprecatory gesture toward him.*]

Haven't had kippers for a long time. I'm glad you remembered I like them.
MARGARET.   Yes, sir.

[MARGARET *and* VINNIE *exchange knowing looks.* MARGARET *goes out happy.*]

FATHER. What's got into Margaret this morning? Hot biscuits, too!

VINNIE. She knows you're fond of them.

[*The doorbell rings.* MAGGIE *goes to answer it.* VINNIE *stirs nervously in her chair.*]

Who can that be? It can't be the mailman because he's been here.

FATHER [*with sly humor*]. Clarence has been getting a good many special deliveries lately. Is that business deal going through, Clarence?

[*The family has a laugh at* CLARENCE. MAGGIE *comes back into the arch with a suit box.*]

MAGGIE. This is for you, Mr. Day. Where shall I put it?

CLARENCE [*hastily*]. Oh, that's for me, I think. Take it upstairs, Maggie.

FATHER. Wait a minute, Maggie, bring it here. Let's see it.

[CLARENCE *takes the box from* MAGGIE, *who exits. He holds it toward his father.*]

CLARENCE. See, it's for me, Father—Clarence Day, Jr.

FATHER. Let me look. Why, that's from McCreery's and it's marked "Charge." What is it?

VINNIE. It's all right, Clare. It's nothing for you to worry about.

FATHER. Well, at least I think I should know what's being charged to me. What is it?

VINNIE. Now, Clare, stop your fussing. It's a new suit of clothes for Clarence and it's not costing you a penny.

FATHER. It's marked "Charge fifteen dollars"—it's costing me fifteen dollars. And I told Clarence.

VINNIE. Clare, can't you take my word it isn't costing you a penny?

FATHER. I'd like to have you explain why it isn't.

VINNIE [*triumphantly*]. Because Clarence took the pug dog back and got the suit instead.

FATHER. Of course, and they'll charge me fifteen dollars for the suit.

VINNIE. Nonsense, Clare. We gave them the pug dog for the suit. Don't you see?

FATHER. Then they'll charge me fifteen dollars for the pug dog.

VINNIE. But, Clare, they can't! We haven't got the pug dog. We sent that back.

FATHER [*bewildered, but not convinced*]. Now wait a minute, Vinnie. There's something wrong with your reasoning.

VINNIE. I'm surprised, Clare, and you're supposed to be so good at figures. Why, it's perfectly clear to me.

FATHER. Vinnie! They're going to charge me for one thing or the other.

VINNIE.   Don't you let them!

[FATHER *gets up and throws his napkin on the table.*]

FATHER.   Well, McCreery's aren't giving away suits and they aren't giving away pug dogs. [*He walks over to the window in his irritation.*] Can't you get it through your— [*Looking out the window*] Oh, God!

VINNIE.   What is it, Clare? What's wrong?

FATHER.   Don't anybody answer the door.

VINNIE.   Who is it? Who's coming?

FATHER.   Those damn women are back!

WHITNEY.   What women?

FATHER.   Cora and that little idiot.

[CLARENCE *dashes madly up the stairs clutching the box containing his new suit.*]

They're moving in on us again, bag and baggage! [*The doorbell rings.*] Don't let them in!

VINNIE.   Clarence Day, as if we could turn our own relatives away!

FATHER.   Tell them to get back in that cab and drive right on to Ohio. If they're extravagant enough to take cabs when horse cars run right by our door—

[MAGGIE *crosses the hall to answer the doorbell.*]

VINNIE.   Now, Clare—you be quiet and behave yourself. They're here and there's nothing you can do about it. [*She starts toward the hall.*]

FATHER [*shouting after her*].   Well, why do they always pounce on us without warning?—the damn gypsies!

VINNIE [*from the arch*].   Shhh!—Clare! [*Then in her best welcoming tone*] Cora! Mary! It's so nice to have you back again.

CORA.   How are you, Vinnie? We've been so worried about you.

VINNIE.   Oh, I'm fine now!

[CORA *and* MARY *and* VINNIE *enter and* CORA *sweeps right down into the room.*]

CORA.   Hello, Harlan! Whitney! Well, Cousin Clare. Here we are again!

[*Kisses* FATHER *on the cheek. He draws back sternly.* MARY *looks quickly around the room for* CLARENCE, *then greets and is greeted by the other boys.*]

And John! Where's Clarence?

MARY.   Yes, where is Clarence?

VINNIE.   John, go find Clarence and tell him that Cora and Mary are here.

JOHN.   Yes, Mother.

[*Goes upstairs.*]

VINNIE.   You got here just in time to have breakfast with us.

CORA.   We had breakfast at the depot.

VINNIE.   Well, as a matter of fact, we'd just finished.

FATHER [*with cold dignity*].   I haven't finished my breakfast!

VINNIE.   Well, then sit down, Clare. [*To* CORA *and* MARY] Margaret gave us kippers this morning and Clare's so fond of kippers. Why don't we all sit down?

[*Indicates the empty places and the girls sit.* FATHER *resumes his chair and breakfast in stony silence.* MAGGIE *has come into the room to await orders.*]

Maggie, clear those things away.

[*She indicates the dishes in front of the girls, and* MAGGIE *removes them.* FATHER *takes a letter from his stack of morning mail and opens it.*]

Clare, don't let your kippers get cold. [*To* CORA] Now—tell us all about Springfield.

CORA.   We had a wonderful month—but tell us about you, Cousin Vinnie. You must have had a terrible time.

VINNIE.   Yes, I was pretty sick, but I'm all right again now.

CORA.   What was it?

VINNIE.   Well, the doctors don't know exactly, but they did say this —that they'd never seen anything like it before, whatever it was.

CORA.   You certainly look well enough now. Doesn't she, Clare?

[*Whatever is in the letter* FATHER *has been reading comes to him as a shock.*]

FATHER.   Oh, God!

VINNIE.   What's the matter, Clare? What's wrong?

FATHER.   *John! John!*

[JOHN *is seen halfway up the stairs with the girls' bags. He comes running down the stairs, going to* FATHER.]

JOHN.   Yes, Father?

FATHER.   Have you been going around this town selling medicine?

JOHN [*a little frightened*].   Yes, Father.

FATHER.   Dog medicine?

JOHN [*indignantly*].   No, Father, not dog medicine!

FATHER. It must have been dog medicine!

JOHN. It wasn't dog medicine, Father—

FATHER. This letter from Mrs. Sprague says you sold her a bottle of this medicine and that her little boy gave some of it to their dog and it killed him! Now she wants ten dollars from me for a new dog.

JOHN. Well, he shouldn't have given it to a dog! It's for humans! Why, it's Bartlett's Beneficent Balm—"Made from a secret formula"!

FATHER. Have you been going around among our friends and neighbors selling some damned Dr. Munyon patent nostrum?

JOHN. But it's good medicine, Father. I can prove it by Mother.

FATHER. Vinnie, what do you know about this?

VINNIE. Nothing, Clare, but I'm sure that John—

JOHN. No, I mean that day Mother—

FATHER. That's enough! You're going to every house where you sold a bottle of that concoction and buy it all back.

JOHN [dismayed]. But it's a dollar a bottle!

FATHER. I don't care how much it is. How many bottles did you sell?

JOHN. A hundred and twenty-eight.

FATHER [roaring]. A hundred and twenty-eight!

VINNIE. Clare, I always told you John would make a good business man.

FATHER [calmly]. Young man, I'll give you the money to buy it back —a hundred and twenty-eight dollars. And ten more for Mrs. Sprague. That's a hundred and thirty-eight dollars. But it's coming out of your allowance! That means you'll not get another penny until that hundred and thirty-eight dollars is all paid up.

[JOHN starts toward the hall, counting on his fingers, then turns and addresses his father in dismay.]

JOHN. I'll be twenty-one years old!

[FATHER glares at him. JOHN turns and goes on up the stairs, with the bags.]

VINNIE [persuasively]. Clare, you know you've always encouraged the boys to earn their own money.

FATHER. Vinnie, I'll handle this.

[There is a pause. He buries himself in his newspaper.]

CORA [breaking through the constraint]. Of course, Aunt Judith sent her love to all of you—

VINNIE. I haven't seen Judith for years. You'd think living so close to Springfield—maybe I could run up there before the summer's over.

CORA. Oh, she'll be leaving for Pleasantville any day now. Grandpa Ebbetts has been failing very fast and that's why I have to hurry back.

VINNIE. Hurry back? Well, you and Mary can stay with us a few days at least.

CORA. No, I hate to break the news to you, Vinnie, but we can't even stay overnight. We're leaving on the five o'clock train this afternoon.

VINNIE [*disappointed*]. Oh, what a pity!

[FATHER *lowers the paper.*]

FATHER [*heartily*]. Well, Cora, it certainly is good to see you again. [*To* MARY] Young lady, I think you've been enjoying yourself—you look prettier than ever.

[MARY *laughs and blushes.*]

WHITNEY. I'll bet Clarence will think so.

[*The doorbell rings.* MAGGIE *crosses to answer it.*]

FATHER. That can't be another special delivery for Clarence. [*To* MARY, *slyly*] While you were in Springfield our postman was kept pretty busy. Sure you girls don't want any breakfast?

MARY. No, thank you.

[*Rises and goes to the arch and stands looking upstairs, watching for* CLARENCE.]

CORA. Oh, no, thank you, Cousin Clare, we've had our breakfast.

FATHER. At least you ought to have a cup of coffee with us. Vinnie, you might have thought to order some coffee for the girls.

CORA. No, no, thank you, Cousin Clare.

[MAGGIE *appears again in the arch.*]

MAGGIE. It's the cab, ma'am.

[*Exits.*]

FATHER. The cab! What cab?

VINNIE. The cab that's to take us to Audubon.

FATHER. Who's going to Audubon?

VINNIE. We all are. Cora, the most wonderful thing has happened!

CORA. What, Cousin Vinnie?

VINNIE [*happily*]. Clare's going to be baptized this morning.

FATHER [*not believing his ears*]. Vinnie—what are you saying?

VINNIE [*with determination*]. I'm saying you're going to be baptized this morning!

FATHER. I am not going to be baptized this morning or any other morning!

VINNIE. You promised yesterday that as soon as I sent that pug dog back you'd be baptized.

FATHER. I promised no such thing!

VINNIE. You certainly did!

FATHER. I never said anything remotely like that!

VINNIE. Clarence was right here and heard it. You ask him!

FATHER. Clarence be damned! I know what I said! I don't remember exactly, but it wasn't that!

VINNIE. Well, I remember. That's why I ordered the cab!

FATHER [*suddenly remembering*]. The cab! Oh, my God, that cab!

[*He rises and glares out the window at the cab, then turns back and speaks peremptorily.*]

Vinnie! You send that right back!

VINNIE. I'll do nothing of the kind. I'm going to see that you get to Heaven.

FATHER. I can't go to Heaven in a cab!

VINNIE. Well, you can start in a cab! I'm not sure whether they'll ever let you into Heaven or not, but I know they won't unless you're baptized.

FATHER. They can't keep me out of Heaven on a technicality.

VINNIE. Clare, stop quibbling! You might as well face it—you've got to make your peace with God.

FATHER. I never had any trouble with God until you stirred Him up!

[MARY *is tired of waiting for* CLARENCE *and chooses this moment to interrupt.*]

MARY. Mrs. Day?

[VINNIE *answers her quickly, as if expecting* MARY *to supply her with an added argument.*]

VINNIE. Yes, Mary?

MARY. Where do you suppose Clarence is?

FATHER. You keep out of this, young lady! If it hadn't been for you, no one would have known whether I was baptized or not.

[MARY *breaks into tears.*]

Damn! Damnation!

VINNIE Harlan! Whitney! Get your Sunday hats. [*Calls upstairs*] John! Clarence!

[HARLAN *and* WHITNEY *start out, but stop as* FATHER *speaks.*]

FATHER [*blazing with new fire*]. Vinnie, are you mad? Was it your plan that my own children should witness this indignity?

VINNIE. Why, Clare, they'll be proud of you!

FATHER. I suppose Harlan is to be my godfather! [*With determination*] Vinnie, it's no use. I can't go through with this thing and I won't. That's final.

VINNIE. Why, Clare dear, if you feel that way about it—

FATHER. I do!

VINNIE. —the children don't have to go.

[JOHN *enters.*]

JOHN. Yes, Mother?

[FATHER *sees* JOHN *and an avenue of escape opens up.*]

FATHER. Oh, John! Vinnie, I can't do anything like that this morning. I've got to take John down to the office and give him the money to buy back that medicine. [*To* JOHN] When I think of you going around this town selling dog medicine!—

JOHN [*insistently*]. It wasn't dog medicine, Father.

FATHER. John, we're starting downtown this minute!

VINNIE. You're doing no such thing! You gave me your Sacred Promise that day I almost died—

JOHN. Yes, and she would have died if we hadn't given her some of that medicine. That proves it's good medicine!

FATHER [*aghast*]. You gave your mother some of that dog medicine!

VINNIE. Oh, no, John, you didn't! [*Sinks weakly into the chair below the fireplace.*]

JOHN. Yes, we did, Mother. We put some in your tea that morning.

FATHER. You did what? Without her knowing it? Do you realize you might have killed your mother? You did kill Mrs. Sprague's dog.

[*After a solemn pause.*]

John, you've done a very serious thing. I'll have to give considerable thought as to how you're going to be punished for this.

VINNIE. But, Clare—

FATHER. No, Vinnie. When I think of that day—with the house full of doctors—why, Cora, we even sent for the minister. Why, we might have lost you!

[*He goes to* VINNIE, *really moved, and puts his hand on her shoulder.*]

It's all right now, Vinnie, thank God. You're well again. But what I went through that afternoon—the way I felt—I'll never forget it.

VINNIE. Don't talk that way, Clare. You've forgotten it already.

FATHER. What do you mean?

VINNIE. That was the day you gave me your Sacred Promise.

FATHER. But I wouldn't have promised if I hadn't thought you were dying—and you wouldn't have almost died if John hadn't given you that medicine. Don't you see? The whole thing's illegal!

VINNIE. Suppose I had died! It wouldn't make any difference to you. You don't care whether we meet in Heaven or not—you don't care whether you ever see me and the children again.

[*She almost succeeds in crying.* HARLAN *and* WHITNEY *go to her in sympathy, putting their arms around her.*]

FATHER [*distressed*]. Now, Vinnie, you're not being fair to me.

VINNIE. It's all right, Clare. If you don't love us enough there's nothing we can do about it.

[*Hurt,* FATHER *walks away to the other side of the room.*]

FATHER. That's got nothing to do with it! I love my family as much as any man. There's nothing within reason I wouldn't do for you, and you know it! All these years I've struggled and worked just to prove—

[*He has reached the window and looks out.*]

There's that damn cab! Vinnie, you're not well enough to go all the way up to Audubon.

VINNIE [*perkily*]. I'm well enough if we ride.

FATHER. But that trip would take all morning. And those cabs cost a dollar an hour.

VINNIE [*with smug complacence*]. That's one of their best cabs. That costs two dollars an hour.

[FATHER *stares at her a second, horrified—then explodes.*]

FATHER. Then why aren't you ready? Get your hat on! Damn! Damnation! Amen!

[*Exits for his hat and stick.* VINNIE *is stunned for a moment by this sudden surrender, then hastily puts on her bonnet.*]

WHITNEY. Let's watch them start! Come on, Cousin Cora, let's watch them start!

CORA. I wouldn't miss it!

[WHITNEY, HARLAN, *and* CORA *hurry out.* VINNIE *starts, but* JOHN *stops her in the arch.*]

JOHN [*contritely*]. Mother, I didn't mean to almost kill you.

VINNIE. Now, don't you worry about what your father said. [*Tenderly*] It's all right, dear. [*She kisses him.*] It worked out fine!

[*She exits.* JOHN *looks upstairs, then at* MARY, *who has gone to the window.*]

JOHN. Mary! Here comes Clarence!

[JOHN *exits.* MARY *sits in* FATHER'S *chair.* CLARENCE *comes down the stairs in his new suit. He goes into the room and right to* MARY. *Without saying a word he kneels in front of her. They both are starry-eyed.* FATHER, *with hat and stick, comes into the arch on his way out. He sees* CLARENCE *kneeling at* MARY'S *feet.*]

FATHER. *Oh, God!*

[CLARENCE *springs up in embarrassment.* VINNIE *re-enters hurriedly.*]

VINNIE. What's the matter? What's wrong?
CLARENCE. Nothing's wrong, Mother— [*Then, for want of something to say*] Going to the office, Father?
FATHER. No! I'm going to be baptized, damn it!

[*He slams his hat on angrily and stalks out.* VINNIE *gives a triumphant nod and follows him. The curtain starts down, and as it falls,* CLARENCE *again kneels at* MARY'S *feet.*]

CURTAIN

Two Critical Commentaries on Lindsay and Crouse's *Life with Father*

Commentary by Joseph Wood Krutch, "When Men Were Men," from *The Nation*, CXLIX (November 18, 1939), 560.*

"Life with Father" (Empire Theater) is a delightful affair and well calculated to please equally those who do and those who do not know the various reminiscences by Clarence Day upon which it is founded. Russell Crouse and Howard Lindsay, who put it together, have done something considerably more difficult than merely to select and give continuity—they have almost miraculously preserved a flavor which might have been expected to defy translation into another form.

Father was a fine flower of Victorian manhood, and in those days virility didn't mean what D. H. Lawrence means by the word. Manliness was something whose outward expressions were big cigars and high blood pressure, a hearty contempt for women's notions and the sure conviction (wrong of course, since some things are eternal) that *pater familias* was master in his own house. It was also likely to mean, as it certainly did in the case of the elder Day, an egocentric view of the universe so naive that the Master wa

* Reprinted from *The Nation* by permission of Joseph Wood Krutch.

never able to understand why everyone else should not be as anxious for him to have his own way as he was himself.

Considered merely as a case history, Father was an obtuse bully; but Father was loved by his wife and remembered with enormous affection by the son who celebrated both his rages and all those final decisions which mother so quietly revised. The triumph of the play, like the triumph of the sketches upon which it is based, lies in the fact that it makes the paradox understandable, not by explaining it in any rational terms, but by communicating something which portraiture can communicate and case histories cannot. Merely to say that Father meant well would be to add insult to injury; but Father did mean well, and we forgive him as a living person what we could not possibly forgive him as an abstraction. Something is perhaps explained by the fact that in that household which lived in perpetual crisis there were rages and the joy of battle but no rancor and no cruelty, something more perhaps by the fact that Father protected the family against God as well as against anyone else who threatened it, and would no more permit the minister to pray for mother as 'a miserable sinner' when God knew as well as everybody else that she was a good woman than he would consent to the assumption that 'a mere technicality' like his own failure to get himself baptized would keep him out of heaven. But no catalogue of details will really explain the mystery. The family formed a *Gestalt* which meant something other than the sum of its parts, and it is the *Gestalt* which the play captures.

"Life with Father" is enormously funny, but the fun is not based on condescension, and it is sly as often as it is fantastic. There is the highest of high comedy in scenes like that in which Father explains that the reason men so often lose arguments with women is because the subject always gets changed when the man isn't looking and the argument comes somehow to turn, not upon the original question, but upon a new one, namely, whether the man really loves his opponent or not. If the play took its place instantaneously among the biggest of big hits, that is in part because it is certain to please both members of those heterosexual couples which make up the bulk of an audience. While one says to himself, "How like a woman," the other will be saying, "How like a man." And there is no reason why either should tell what he is laughing at.

There are admirable performances by Howard Lindsay and Dorothy Stickney.

Commentary by Henry Seidel Canby, "Clarence and His Father," from
The Saturday Review of Literature, XXI (November 18, 1939), 8.*

"Life with Father," the play based upon Clarence Day's book of that name, and upon other books of his, notably "God and My Father," has been enthusiastically reviewed by the dramatic critics, and is here for a long stay, with the movies to follow; yet I wish the enthusiastic critics had not so often spoken of it as a noble piece of Americana. The play is all that, but it will be unfortunate if playgoers think of it as just a mellow period piece. Like the

---

* Reprinted by permission of Henry S. Canby.

books that preceded it, "Life with Father" recaptured entirely that rare art which flourished so magnificently in the English and American nineteenth centuries, the art of character and personality portrayal. There is no more fully realized and rounded personality in Dickens than Father or than Mother, now given to our American scene.

And yet, everyone should realize that this play and those books could never have been written in the nineteenth century. The art is much the same, but the humor is very different, and the underlying philosophy still more different. Clarence Day was a realist, who knew very well how thoroughly Father and his friends were deluding themselves in thinking that the world of successful business in which they lived was a solid structure reaching down to practical reality, and built by them to endure forever. The reason that Father, in the home, is always defeated by Mother is obvious; in the home, his eminently respectable philosophy of rugged individualism, with the profit motive sacred (presumably) even to God, touches human nature and goes up with an explosion. Not that Mother was a satiric modern! She was simply human reality itself, operating by instinct. The realist was Clarence, who loved them both, and loved them most when they were surest that the conventions they lived by were the Facts of Life.

The authors of the play, Mr. Crouse and Mr. Lindsay, deserve great praise for the skill with which they have turned narrative essays into drama without loss of flavor and with, if possible, a heightening of interest. But credit also should go to the producers, among whom Mrs. Clarence Day must deserve a special hand, for a subtle and perceptive piece of stagecraft. They have realized that "Life with Father" is really a two-generation play, in which we see a family of a past age through the eyes of the second generation. What is more to the point, we see Father through the eyes of a son who is his father over again with the addition of a penetrating and tolerant humor, and the point of view of a century escaped from complacency and deprived of easy confidence.

Those who knew Clarence Day, Jr., well, and I am proud to number myself among them, must have noted with what patient skill Mr. Lindsay, as Father, had been helped to take on the very accent and personality in speech of Clarence himself—the real Clarence. When he said 'damn!' it was Clarence speaking. When he exploded from one mood to another, it was Clarence himself in one of his quick transitions. For in a very real sense, the actual father and son were chips from different sides of the same block, sharing the same essential substance and unmistakable in human likeness. One was nineteenth century, one was twentieth. One was sap wood, one was knot wood of a far more complicated texture, yet (to drop the figure) the book and the play could never have been so good if the son's imagination had not been at home in his father's choleric and positive mind, and loved it none the less because he could see it from the outside as well as from within.

Thus the audience at "Life with Father," thanks to the intuitive skill of directors and actor, are seeing and hearing Clarence Day, Jr., himself, one of the choice spirits of our time, acting the part of the father from whom he got his temperament, though not his philosophy nor his humor nor the range of his mind.

VII. THE GLASS MENAGERIE

A Memory Play by Tennessee Williams

Introductory Note to Tennessee Williams and *The Glass Menagerie*

THE MODERN DRAMA of Ibsen and Shaw and O'Neill—the long period of three generations in which, as we have said, the drama flourished in Europe, in Britain, and in America successively—seemed to have closed with World War II. *Life with Father,* whose comedic scene is laid at the beginning of that sixty-year era, was written and produced at its end. Very different from Clarence Day's family reminiscences were those of the young poet and playwright who wrote *The Glass Menagerie,* ushering in the postwar drama.

Thomas Lanier (Tennessee) Williams was born in 1914 in Columbus, Mississippi, the son of a traveling shoe salesman and an Episcopal clergyman's daughter, of an old Tennessee family. He spent his boyhood in the Mississippi rectory, frail because of diphtheria and eye cataract, with an indulgent mother, a sensitive sister, and a clerical grandfather with literary tastes. When he was thirteen, his father's promotion took the family to St. Louis, where they lived in tenement apartments. He helped his sister Rose whitepaint the walls and furniture of her dingy room and brighten it with her collection of glass animals, which were for him an enduring symbol. After high school he went to the University of Missouri at Columbia. He started well in 1931, but failed R.O.T.C. and slipped badly in his grades after being pledged ATO. It was his fraternity brothers who nicknamed him "Tennessee," which he chose to retain as his name. After two ineffective years, his father insisted that he go to work and got him a job in the shoe factory. He hated his daily work in those Depression years, and spent his nights reading and writing poetry and fiction, sleeping hardly at all. In two years he collapsed, and went to Memphis, where his grandparents now lived, to recuperate for a year. After he returned to St. Louis, his grandmother

569

paid tuition for him to attend Washington University for a year. Helped by his mother, he went up to the State University of Iowa, studying playwriting under E. C. Mabie, and taking his A.B. in 1938.

Then he moved restlessly from place to place, maintaining himself with all manner of odd-jobs—bellhop, elevator boy, theater usher, waiter (giving recitations) in Greenwich Village—and writing continuously. He was twenty-five when a group of one-act plays won him a Group Theater award (1939), and he received a Rockefeller fellowship in playwriting to study with John Gassner at the New School for Social Research. The play he then wrote, *Battle of Angels,* was accepted by the Theater Guild, tried out in Boston in 1940, starring Miriam Hopkins and directed by Margaret Webster. This drama of decadence, sexuality, and violence outraged the audience, was banned by the Boston Watch and Ward, and was withdrawn as a dismal failure.

Tennessee Williams' creative promise warranted further financial grants. From 1940 on his one-act plays, attracting interest in the little theaters, were published annually among the *Best One-Act Plays.* Written with a friend, his full-length drama, *You Touched Me,* based upon a story by D. H. Lawrence, was tried out by the Cleveland and Pasadena Playhouses in 1943. Williams was given a contract to write for M-G-M, but his temperament was hardly congenial to dialogue for Lana Turner and was revolted by assignment to a Margaret O'Brien picture. His services were not required during the remainder of his six months' contract. He lay on the beach at Santa Monica and began turning an original story-idea, that M-G-M had rejected, into a play.

With the unexpected success of *The Glass Menagerie* as a prize play in 1945—of which more presently—Tennessee Williams found himself suddenly the center of unaccustomed attention. Within a year his earlier drama *You Touched Me!* was given a distinguished New York production for a three months' engagement; *27 Wagons Full of Cotton and Other One-Act Plays* was published, and a volume of his short stories was soon promised; he was included in a volume of *Poems of Five Young American Poets;* and the thirty-year-old author was hailed as the white hope of the postwar Drama to come. With success came stifling affluence. After another cataract operation, he went off to Mexico, where he wrote *A Streetcar Named Desire.* It was produced late in 1947, with Jessica Tandy as Blanche and Marlon Brando as Stanley Kowalski, Elia Kazan directing. Its picture of a frustrated Southern belle turned prostitute was both shocking and fascinating. Awarded the Drama Critics' Circle Award and also the Pulitzer Prize, it played for more than two years in New York, was acclaimed both critically and internationally, and was skillfully filmed. *Summer and Smoke,* a further study of Southern decadence and despair, ran for three months in 1948; *The Rose Tatoo,* for the best part of the year 1951; *Camino Real,* for only two months in 1953.

Tennessee Williams, who has devoted himself to "the longings, the futilities, the frustrations at the heart of life," is of less than average height, round-faced, blue-eyed, with an amiable, boyish smile, and disarming honesty and gentleness. He dislikes urban life, enjoys swimming, and is utterly unconcerned about his clothes and appearance. For the most part uninterested in politics, he considers himself a moderate liberal. He is unmarried and footloose. Though he maintains an apartment in the Latin Quarter of New Orleans, he is an inveterate wanderer. He returns occasionally to see his family in St. Louis. His clerical grandfather, well into his nineties, continued a lively interest in his writing. Williams leaves money matters, about which he cares nothing, to his New York agent, Audrey Wood, but made over half the income from *The Glass Menagerie* to his mother.

With Eddie Dowling as coproducer and codirector, *The Glass Menagerie* opened in Chicago on a cold December 26, 1944, with Laurette Taylor (returning to the stage at sixty) as Mrs. Wingfield; Julie Haydon as Laura; Eddie Dowling himself as Tom, the narrator. The enthusiasm of the critics gradually won the play an increasing audience. Then, after thirteen weeks, it was taken to New York, where it received the Drama Critics' Circle Award for 1945. Other awards followed, by a Catholic journal and the Playwrights' Company. Though the critical reviews were mixed, the play was an undoubted success, with 563 performances in New York, a West Coast company with Pauline Lord, and a London company with Helen Hayes. In 1950 a none-too-distinguished film version, abandoning the dream-mood for realism, was made with Gertrude Lawrence, Jane Wyman, and Arthur Kennedy. In *The Glass Menagerie,* so Tennessee Williams is quoted, "I said all the nice things I have to say about people. The future will be harsher." It was.

THE GLASS MENAGERIE *

A Memory Play in Seven Scenes by Tennessee Williams

THE CHARACTERS

AMANDA WINGFIELD—*the mother*
A little woman of great but confused vitality clinging frantically to another time and place. Her characterization must be carefully created, not copied from type. She is not paranoiac, but her life is paranoia. There is much to admire in Amanda, and as much to love and pity as there is to laugh at. Certainly she has endurance and a kind of heroism, and though her foolishness makes her unwittingly cruel at times, there is tenderness in her slight person.

LAURA WINGFIELD—*her daughter*
Amanda, having failed to establish contact with reality, continues to live vitally in her illusions, but Laura's situation is even graver. A childhood illness has left her crippled, one leg slightly shorter than the other, and held in a brace. This defect need not be more than suggested on the stage. Stemming from this, Laura's separation increases till she is like a piece of her own glass collection, too exquisitely fragile to move from the shelf.

TOM WINGFIELD—*her son*
And the narrator of the play. A poet with a job in a warehouse. His nature is not remorseless, but to escape from a trap he has to act without pity.

JIM O'CONNOR—*the gentleman caller*
A nice, ordinary, young man.

Scene: *An Alley in St. Louis*
Time: *Now and the Past*

PART I. *Preparation for a Gentleman Caller*
PART II. *The Gentleman calls*

SCENE 1

THE WINGFIELD APARTMENT *is in the rear of the building, one of those vast hive-like conglomerations of cellular living-units that flower as warty growths in overcrowded urban centers of lower middle-class population and are symptomatic of the impulse of this largest and fundamentally enslaved section of American society to avoid fluidity and differentiation and to exist and function as one interfused mass of automatism.*

The apartment faces an alley and is entered by a fire-escape, a structure whose name is a touch of accidental poetic truth, for all of these huge buildings are always burning with the slow and implacable fires of human desperation. The fire-escape is included in the set—that is, the landing of it and steps descending from it.

The scene is memory and is therefore nonrealistic. Memory takes a lot of poetic license. It omits some details; others are exaggerated, according to the emotional value of the articles it touches, for memory is seated predominantly in the heart. The interior is therefore rather dim and poetic.

At the rise of the curtain, the audience is faced with the dark, grim rear wall of the Wingfield tenement. This building, which runs parallel to the footlights, is flanked on both sides by dark, narrow alleys which run into murky canyons of tangled clotheslines, garbage cans and the sinister lattice-work of neighboring fire-escapes. It is up and down these side alleys that exterior entrances and exits are made, during the play. At the end of TOM's *opening commentary, the dark tenement wall slowly reveals (by means of a transparency) the interior of the ground floor Wingfield apartment.*

Downstage is the living room, which also serves as a sleeping room for LAURA, *the sofa unfolding to make her bed. Upstage, center, and divided by a wide arch or second proscenium with transparent faded portieres (or second curtain), is the dining room. In an old-fashioned what-not in the living room are seen scores of transparent glass animals. A blown-up photograph of the father hangs on the wall of the living room, facing the audience, to the left of the archway. It is the face of a very handsome young man in a doughboy's First World War cap. He is gallantly smiling, ineluctably smiling, as if to say, "I will be smiling forever."*

The audience hears and sees the opening scene in the dining room through both the transparent fourth wall of the building and the transparent gauze portieres of the dining-room arch. It is during this revealing scene that the fourth wall slowly ascends, out of sight. This transparent exterior wall is not brought down again until the very end of the play, during TOM's *final speech.*

The narrator is an undisguised convention of the play. He takes whatever license with dramatic convention as is convenient to his purposes.

TOM *enters dressed as a merchant sailor from alley, stage left, and strolls across the front of the stage to the fire-escape. There he stops and lights a cigarette. He addresses the audience.*

TOM. Yes, I have tricks in my pocket, I have things up my sleeve. But I am the opposite of a stage magician. He gives you illusion that has the appearance of truth. I give you truth in the pleasant disguise of illusion.

To begin with, I turn back time. I reverse it to that quaint period, the thirties, when the huge middle class of America was matriculating in a school for the blind. Their eyes had failed them, or they had failed their eyes, and so they were having their fingers pressed forcibly down on the fiery Braille alphabet of a dissolving economy.

In Spain there was revolution. Here there was only shouting and confusion.

In Spain there was Guernica. Here there were disturbances of labor, sometimes pretty violent, in otherwise peaceful cities such as Chicago, Cleveland, Saint Louis . . .

This is the social background of the play.

[MUSIC.]

The play is memory.

Being a memory play, it is dimly lighted, it is sentimental, it is not realistic.

In memory everything seems to happen to music. That explains the fiddle in the wings.

I am the narrator of the play, and also a character in it.

The other characters are my mother, Amanda, my sister, Laura, and a gentleman caller who appears in the final scenes.

He is the most realistic character in the play, being an emissary from a world of reality that we were somehow set apart from.

But since I have a poet's weakness for symbols, I am using this character also as a symbol; he is the long delayed but always expected something that we live for.

There is a fifth character in the play who doesn't appear except in this larger-than-life-size photograph over the mantel.

This is our father who left us a long time ago.

He was a telephone man who fell in love with long distances; he gave up his job with the telephone company and skipped the light fantastic out of town . . .

The last we heard of him was a picture post-card from Mazatlan, on the Pacific coast of Mexico, containing a message of two words—

"Hello— Good-bye!" and no address.

I think the rest of the play will explain itself. . . .

[AMANDA's *voice becomes audible through the portieres.*

[LEGEND ON SCREEN: "OÙ SONT LES NEIGES."

[*He divides the portieres and enters the upstage area. The interior has lit up softly and through the scrim we see* AMANDA *and* LAURA *seated at a drop-leaf table in the upstage area.* AMANDA *faces the audience.*]

AMANDA [*calling*]. Tom?

TOM. Yes, Mother.

AMANDA. We can't say grace until you come to the table!

TOM. Coming, Mother.

[*He bows slightly and withdraws, reappearing a few moments later in his place at the table.* TOM *and* LAURA *are seated in profile. Eating is indicated by gestures without food or utensils.*]

AMANDA [*to her son*]. Honey, don't *push* with your *fingers*. If you have to push with something, the thing to push with is a crust of bread. And chew—chew! Animals have sections in their stomachs which enable them to digest food without mastication, but human beings are supposed to chew their food before they swallow it down. Eat food leisurely, son, and really enjoy it. A well-cooked meal has lots of delicate flavors that have to be held in the mouth for appreciation. So chew your food and give your salivary glands a chance to function!

[*Tom deliberately lays his imaginary fork down and pushes his chair back from the table.*]

TOM. I haven't enjoyed one bite of this dinner because of your constant directions on how to eat it. It's you that make me rush through meals with your hawk-like attention to every bite I take. Sickening— spoils my appetite—all this discussion of—animal's secretion—salivary glands—mastication!

AMANDA [*lightly*]. Temperament like a Metropolitan star! [*He rises and crosses downstage.*] You're not excused from the table.

TOM. I'm getting a cigarette.

AMANDA. You smoke too much.

[LAURA *rises*.]

LAURA. I'll bring in the blanc mange.

[*He remains standing with his cigarette by the portieres during the following.*]

AMANDA [*rising*]. No, sister, no, sister—you be the lady this time and I'll be the darky.

LAURA. I'm already up.

AMANDA. Resume your seat, little sister—I want you to stay fresh and pretty—for gentlemen callers!

LAURA. I'm not expecting any gentleman callers.

AMANDA [*crossing out to kitchenette. Airily*]. Sometimes they come when they are least expected! Why, I remember one Sunday afternoon in Blue Mountain— [*Enters kitchenette.*]

TOM. I know what's coming!

LAURA. Yes. But let her tell it.

TOM. Again?

LAURA. She loves to tell it.

[AMANDA *returns with bowl of dessert*.]

AMANDA. One Sunday afternoon in Blue Mountain—your mother received—*seventeen!*—gentlemen callers! Why, sometimes there weren't chairs enough to accommodate them all. We had to send the nigger over to bring in folding chairs from the parish house.

TOM [*remaining at portieres*]. How did you entertain those gentlemen callers?

AMANDA. I understood the art of conversation!

TOM. I bet you could talk.

AMANDA. Girls in those days *knew* how to talk, I can tell you.

TOM. Yes?

[IMAGE: AMANDA AS A GIRL ON A PORCH, GREETING CALLERS.]

AMANDA. They knew how to entertain their gentlemen callers. It wasn't enough for a girl to be possessed of a pretty face and a graceful figure—although I wasn't slighted in either respect. She also needed to have a nimble wit and a tongue to meet all occasions.

TOM. What did you talk about?

AMANDA. Things of importance going on in the world! Never anything coarse or common or vulgar.

[*She addresses* TOM *as though he were seated in the vacant chair at the table though he remains by portieres. He plays this scene as though he held the book.*]

My callers were gentlemen—all! Among my callers were some of the most prominent young planters of the Mississippi Delta—planters and sons of planters!

[TOM *motions for music and a spot of light on* AMANDA.
[*Her eyes lift, her face glows, her voice becomes rich and elegiac.*

[SCREEN LEGEND: "OÙ SONT LES NEIGES."]

There was young Champ Laughlin who later became vice-president of the Delta Planters Bank.

Hadley Stevenson who was drowned in Moon Lake and left his widow one hundred and fifty thousand in Government bonds.

There were the Cutrere brothers, Wesley and Bates. Bates was one of my bright particular beaux! He got in a quarrel with that wild Wainwright boy. They shot it out on the floor of Moon Lake Casino. Bates was shot through the stomach. Died in the ambulance on his way to Memphis. His widow was also well-provided for, came into eight or ten thousand acres, that's all. She married him on the rebound—never loved her—carried my picture on him the night he died!

And there was that boy that every girl in the Delta had set her cap for! That beautiful, brilliant young Fitzhugh boy from Greene County!

TOM.   What did he leave his widow?

AMANDA.   He never married! Gracious, you talk as though all of my old admirers had turned up their toes to the daisies!

TOM.   Isn't this the first you've mentioned that still survives?

AMANDA.   That Fitzhugh boy went North and made a fortune—came to be known as the Wolf of Wall Street! He had the Midas touch, whatever he touched turned to gold!

And I could have been Mrs. Duncan J. Fitzhugh, mind you! But—I picked your *father!*

LAURA [*rising*].   Mother, let me clear the table.

AMANDA.   No, dear, you go in front and study your typewriter chart. Or practice your shorthand a little. Stay fresh and pretty!—It's almost time for our gentlemen callers to start arriving.

[*She flounces girlishly toward the kitchenette.*]

How many do you suppose we're going to entertain this afternoon?

[TOM *throws down the paper and jumps up with a groan.*]

LAURA [*alone in the dining room*].   I don't believe we're going to receive any, Mother.

AMANDA [*reappearing, airily*].   What? No one—not one? You must be joking!

[LAURA *nervously echoes her laugh. She slips in a fugitive manner through the half-open portieres and draws them gently behind her. A shaft of very clear light is thrown on her face against the faded tapestry of the curtains.* MUSIC: "THE GLASS MENAGERIE" UNDER FAINTLY. *Lightly*]

Not one gentleman caller? It can't be true! There must be a flood, there must have been a tornado!

LAURA.   It isn't a flood, it's not a tornado, Mother. I'm just not popular like you were in Blue Mountain. . . .

[TOM *utters another groan.* LAURA *glances at him with a faint, apologetic smile. Her voice catching a little*]

Mother's afraid I'm going to be an old maid.

THE SCENE DIMS OUT WITH "GLASS MENAGERIE" MUSIC

SCENE 2

"LAURA, HAVEN'T *You Ever Liked Some Boy?*"

On the dark stage the SCREEN *is lighted with the image of blue roses. Gradually* LAURA's *figure becomes apparent and the screen goes out. The music subsides.*

LAURA *is seated in the delicate ivory chair at the small claw-foot table. She wears a dress of soft violet material for a kimono—her hair tied back from her forehead with a ribbon. She is washing and polishing her collection of glass.*

AMANDA *appears on the fire-escape steps. At the sound of her ascent, LAURA catches her breath, thrusts the bowl of ornaments away and seats herself stiffly before the diagram of the typewriter keyboard as though it held her spellbound. Something has happened to AMANDA. It is written in her face as she climbs to the landing: a look that is grim and hopeless and a little absurd. She has on one of those cheap or imitation velvety-looking cloth coats with imitation fur collar. Her hat is five or six years old, one of those dreadful cloche hats that were worn in the late twenties and she is clasping an enormous black patent-leather pocketbook with nickel clasps and initials. This is her full-dress outfit, the one she usually wears to the D.A.R.*

Before entering she looks through the door. She purses her lips, opens her eyes very wide, rolls them upward and shakes her head. Then she slowly lets herself in the door. Seeing her mother's expression LAURA touches her lips with a nervous gesture.

LAURA. Hello, Mother, I was—

[*She makes a nervous gesture toward the chart on the wall.* AMANDA *leans against the shut door and stares at* LAURA *with a martyred look.*]

AMANDA. Deception? Deception?

[*She slowly removes her hat and gloves, continuing the sweet suffering stare. She lets the hat and gloves fall on the floor—a bit of acting.*]

LAURA [*shakily*]. How was the D.A.R. meeting?

[AMANDA *slowly opens her purse and removes a dainty white handkerchief which she shakes out delicately and delicately touches to her lips and nostrils.*]

Didn't you go to the D.A.R. meeting, Mother?

AMANDA [*faintly, almost inaudibly*]. —No.—No. [*Then more forcibly*] I did not have the strength—to go to the D.A.R. In fact, I did not have the courage! I wanted to find a hole in the ground and hide myself in it forever!

[*She crosses slowly to the wall and removes the diagram of the type-writer keyboard. She holds it in front of her for a second, staring at it sweetly and sorrowfully—then bites her lips and tears it in two pieces.*]

LAURA [*faintly*]. Why did you do that, Mother? [AMANDA *repeats the same procedure with the chart of the Gregg Alphabet.*] Why are you—

AMANDA. Why? Why? How old are you, Laura?

LAURA. Mother, you know my age.

AMANDA. I thought that you were an adult; it seems that I was mistaken. [*She crosses slowly to the sofa and sinks down and stares at* LAURA.]

LAURA. Please don't stare at me, Mother.

[AMANDA *closes her eyes and lowers her head. Count ten.*]

AMANDA. What are we going to do, what is going to become of us, what is the future? [*Count ten.*]

LAURA. Has something happened, Mother?

[AMANDA *draws a long breath and takes out the handkerchief again. Dabbing process.*]

Mother, has—something happened?

AMANDA. I'll be all right in a minute, I'm just bewildered—[*count five*]—by life. . . .

LAURA. Mother, I wish that you would tell me what's happened!

AMANDA. As you know, I was supposed to be inducted into my office at the D.A.R. this afternoon.

[IMAGE: A SWARM OF TYPEWRITERS.]

But I stopped off at Rubicam's Business College to speak to your teachers about your having a cold and ask them what progress they thought you were making down there.

LAURA. Oh. . . .

AMANDA. I went to the typing instructor and introduced myself as your mother. She didn't know who you were. Wingfield, she said. We don't have any such student enrolled at the school!

I assured her she did, that you had been going to classes since early in January.

"I wonder," she said, "if you could be talking about that terribly shy little girl who dropped out of school after only a few days' attendance?"

"No," I said, "Laura, my daughter, has been going to school every day for the past six weeks!"

"Excuse me," she said. She took the attendance book out and there was your name, unmistakably printed, and all the dates you were absent until they decided that you had dropped out of school.

I still said, "No, there must have been some mistake! There must have been some mix-up in the records!"

And she said, "No—I remember her perfectly now. Her hands shook so that she couldn't hit the right keys! The first time we gave a speed-test, she broke down completely—was sick at the stomach and almost had to be carried into the wash-room! After that morning she never showed up any more. We phoned the house but never got any answer"—while I was working at Famous and Barr, I suppose, demonstrating those— Oh!

I felt so weak I could barely keep on my feet!

I had to sit down while they got me a glass of water!

Fifty dollars' tuition, all of our plans—my hopes and ambitions for you—just gone up the spout, just gone up the spout like that.

[LAURA *draws a long breath and gets awkwardly to her feet. She crosses to the victrola and winds it up.*]

What are you doing?

LAURA.   Oh! [*She releases the handle and returns to her seat.*]

AMANDA.   Laura, where have you been going when you've gone out pretending that you were going to business college?

LAURA.   I've just been going out walking.

AMANDA.   That's not true.

LAURA.   It is. I just went walking.

AMANDA.   Walking? Walking? In winter? Deliberately courting pneumonia in that light coat? Where did you walk to, Laura?

LAURA.   All sorts of places—mostly in the park.

AMANDA.   Even after you'd started catching that cold?

LAURA.   It was the lesser of two evils, Mother.

[IMAGE: WINTER SCENE IN PARK.]

I couldn't go back up. I—threw up—on the floor!

AMANDA.   From half past seven till after five every day you mean to tell me you walked around in the park, because you wanted to make me think that you were still going to Rubicam's Business College?

LAURA.   It wasn't as bad as it sounds. I went inside places to get warmed up.

AMANDA.   Inside where?

LAURA.   I went in the art museum and the bird-houses at the Zoo. I visited the penguins every day! Sometimes I did without lunch and

went to the movies. Lately I've been spending most of my afternoons
in the Jewel-box, that big glass house where they raise the tropical flowers.

AMANDA. You did all this to deceive me, just for deception? [LAURA
looks down.] Why?

LAURA. Mother, when you're disappointed, you get that awful suffering look on your face, like the picture of Jesus' mother in the museum!

AMANDA. Hush!

LAURA. I couldn't face it.

[*Pause. A whisper of strings*

[LEGEND: "THE CRUST OF HUMILITY."]

AMANDA [*hopelessly fingering the huge pocketbook*]. So what are we
going to do the rest of our lives? Stay home and watch the parades go
by? Amuse ourselves with the glass menagerie, darling? Eternally play
those worn-out phonograph records your father left as a painful reminder
of him?

We won't have a business career—we've given that up because it gave
us nervous indigestion! [*Laughs wearily*] What is there left but de-
pendency all our lives? I know so well what becomes of unmarried
women who aren't prepared to occupy a position. I've seen such pitiful
cases in the South—barely tolerated spinsters living upon the grudging
patronage of sister's husband or brother's wife!—stuck away in some
little mouse-trap of a room—encouraged by one in-law to visit another—
little birdlike women without any nest—eating the crust of humility all
their life!

Is that the future that we've mapped out for ourselves?

I swear it's the only alternative I can think of!

It isn't a very pleasant alternative, is it?

Of course—some girls *do marry.*

[LAURA *twists her hands nervously.*]

Haven't you ever liked some boy?

LAURA. Yes. I liked one once. [*Rises*] I came across his picture a
while ago.

AMANDA [*with some interest*]. He gave you his picture?

LAURA. No, it's in the year-book.

AMANDA [*disappointed*]. Oh—a high-school boy.

[SCREEN IMAGE: JIM AS HIGH-SCHOOL HERO
BEARING A SILVER CUP.]

LAURA. Yes. His name was Jim. [LAURA *lifts the heavy annual from
the claw-foot table.*] Here he is in *The Pirates of Penzance.*

AMANDA [*absently*]. The what?

LAURA. The operetta the senior class put on. He had a wonderful voice and we sat across the aisle from each other Mondays, Wednesdays and Fridays in the Aud. Here he is with the silver cup for debating. See his grin?

AMANDA [*absently*]. He must have had a jolly disposition.

LAURA. He used to call me—Blue Roses.

[IMAGE: BLUE ROSES.]

AMANDA. Why did he call you such a name as that?

LAURA. When I had that attack of pleurosis—he asked me what was the matter when I came back. I said pleurosis—he thought that I said Blue Roses! So that's what he always called me after that. Whenever he saw me, he'd holler, "Hello, Blue Roses!" I didn't care for the girl that he went out with. Emily Meisenbach. Emily was the best-dressed girl at Soldan. She never struck me, though, as being sincere . . . It says in the Personal Section—they're engaged. That's—six years ago! They must be married by now.

AMANDA. Girls that aren't cut out for business careers usually wind up married to some nice man. [*Gets up with a spark of revival*] Sister, that's what you'll do!

[LAURA *utters a startled, doubtful laugh. She reaches quickly for a piece of glass.*]

LAURA. But, Mother—

AMANDA. Yes? [*Crossing to photograph.*]

LAURA [*in a tone of frightened apology*]. I'm—crippled!

[IMAGE: SCREEN.]

AMANDA. Nonsense! Laura, I've told you never, never to use that word. Why, you're not crippled, you just have a little defect—hardly noticeable, even! When people have some slight disadvantage like that, they cultivate other things to make up for it—develop charm—and vivacity—and—*charm!* That's all you have to do!

[*She turns again to the photograph.*]

One thing your father had *plenty of*—was *charm!*

[TOM *motions to the fiddle in the wings.*]

THE SCENE FADES OUT WITH MUSIC

SCENE 3

LEGEND ON SCREEN: "AFTER THE FIASCO—"

TOM *speaks from the fire-escape landing.*

TOM. After the fiasco at Rubicam's Business College, the idea of getting a gentleman caller for Laura began to play a more and more important part in Mother's calculations.

It became an obsession. Like some archetype of the universal unconscious, the image of the gentleman caller haunted our small apartment. . . .

[IMAGE: YOUNG MAN AT DOOR WITH FLOWERS.]

An evening at home rarely passed without some allusion to this image, this spectre, this hope. . . .

Even when he wasn't mentioned, his presence hung in Mother's preoccupied look and in my sister's frightened, apologetic manner—hung like a sentence passed upon the Wingfields!

Mother was a woman of action as well as words.

She began to take logical steps in the planned direction.

Late that winter and in the early spring—realizing that extra money would be needed to properly feather the nest and plume the bird—she conducted a vigorous campaign on the telephone, roping in subscribers to one of those magazines for matrons called *The Home-maker's Companion,* the type of journal that features the serialized sublimations of ladies of letters who think in terms of delicate cup-like breasts, slim, tapering waists, rich, creamy thighs, eyes like wood-smoke in autumn, fingers that soothe and caress like strains of music, bodies as powerful as Etruscan sculpture.

[SCREEN IMAGE: GLAMOR MAGAZINE COVER

[AMANDA *enters with phone on long extension cord. She is spotted in the dim stage.*]

AMANDA. Ida Scott? This is Amanda Wingfield!

We *missed* you at the D.A.R. last Monday!

I said to myself: She's probably suffering with that sinus condition! How is that sinus condition?

Horrors! Heaven have mercy!—You're a Christian martyr, yes, that's what you are, a Christian martyr!

Well, I just now happened to notice that your subscription to the *Companion's* about to expire! Yes, it expires with the next issue, honey!—just when that wonderful new serial by Bessie Mae Hopper is getting off to such an exciting start. Oh, honey, it's something that you can't miss!

You remember how *Gone With the Wind* took everybody by storm?
You simply couldn't go out if you hadn't read it. All everybody *talked*
was Scarlett O'Hara. Well, this is a book that critics already compare
to *Gone With the Wind*. It's the *Gone With the Wind* of the post-
World War generation!—What?—Burning?—Oh, honey, don't let them
burn, go take a look in the oven and I'll hold the wire! Heavens—I
think she's hung up!

DIM OUT

[LEGEND ON SCREEN: "YOU THINK I'M IN LOVE
WITH CONTINENTAL SHOEMAKERS?"]

[*Before the stage is lighted, the violent voices of* TOM *and* AMANDA
*are heard. They are quarreling behind the portieres. In front of
them stands* LAURA *with clenched hands and panicky expression.
A clear pool of light on her figure throughout this scene.*]

TOM.   What in Christ's name am I—
AMANDA [*shrilly*].   Don't you use that—
TOM.   Supposed to do!
AMANDA.   Expression! Not in my—
TOM.   Ohhh!
AMANDA.   Presence! Have you gone out of your senses?
TOM.   I have, that's true, *driven* out!
AMANDA.   What is the matter with you, you—big—big—IDIOT!
TOM.   Look!—I've got *no thing,* no single thing—
AMANDA.   Lower your voice!
TOM.   In my life here that I can call my OWN! Everything is—
AMANDA.   Stop that shouting!
TOM.   Yesterday you confiscated my books! You had the nerve to—
AMANDA.   I took that horrible novel back to the library—yes! That
hideous book by that insane Mr. Lawrence.

[TOM *laughs wildly.*]

I cannot control the output of diseased minds or people who cater to
them—

[TOM *laughs still more wildly.*]

BUT I WON'T ALLOW SUCH FILTH BROUGHT INTO MY HOUSE! No, no, no,
no, no!
TOM.   House, house! Who pays rent on it, who makes a slave of
himself to—
AMANDA [*fairly screeching*].   Don't you DARE to—
TOM.   No, no, *I* mustn't say things! *I've* got to just—
AMANDA.   Let me tell you—

TOM. I don't want to hear any more!

[*He tears the portieres open. The upstage area is lit with a turgid smoky red glow.*

[AMANDA's *hair is in metal curlers and she wears a very old bathrobe, much too large for her slight figure, a relic of the faithless Mr. Wingfield.*

[*An upright typewriter and a wild disarray of manuscripts is on the drop-leaf table. The quarrel was probably precipitated by* AMANDA's *interruption of his creative labor. A chair lying overthrown on the floor. Their gesticulating shadows are cast on the ceiling by the fiery glow.*]

AMANDA. You *will* hear more, you—

TOM. No, I won't hear more, I'm going out!

AMANDA. You come right back in—

TOM. Out, out, out! Because I'm—

AMANDA. Come back here, Tom Wingfield! I'm not through talking to you!

TOM. Oh, go—

LAURA [*desperately*]. —Tom!

AMANDA. You're going to listen, and no more insolence from you! I'm at the end of my patience!

[*He comes back toward her.*]

TOM. What do you think I'm at? Aren't I supposed to have any patience to reach the end of, Mother? I know, I know. It seems unimportant to you, what I'm *doing*—what I *want* to do—having a little *difference* between them! You don't think that—

AMANDA. I think you've been doing things that you're ashamed of. That's why you act like this. I don't believe that you go every night to the movies. Nobody goes to the movies night after night. Nobody in their right minds goes to the movies as often as you pretend to. People don't go to the movies at nearly midnight, and movies don't let out at two A.M. Come in stumbling. Muttering to yourself like a maniac! You get three hours' sleep and then go to work. Oh, I can picture the way you're doing down there. Moping, doping, because you're in no condition.

TOM [*wildly*]. No, I'm in no condition!

AMANDA. What right have you got to jeopardize your job? Jeopardize the security of us all? How do you think we'd manage if you were—

TOM. Listen! You think I'm crazy *about* the *warehouse*?

[*He bends fiercely toward her slight figure.*]

You think I'm in love with the Continental Shoemakers? You think I want to spend fifty-five *years* down there in that—*celotex interior!* with *fluorescent—tubes!* Look! I'd rather somebody picked up a crowbar and battered out my brains—than go back mornings! I *go!* Every time you come in yelling that God damn *"Rise and Shine!" "Rise and Shine!"* I say to myself, "How *lucky dead* people are!" But I get up. I *go!* For sixty-five dollars a month I give up all that I dream of doing and being *ever!* And you say self—*self's* all I ever think of. Why, listen, if self is what I thought of, Mother, I'd be where he is—GONE! [*Pointing to father's picture*] As far as the system of transportation reaches!

[*He starts past her. She grabs his arm.*]

Don't grab at me, Mother!

AMANDA. Where are you going?

TOM. I'm going to the *movies!*

AMANDA. I don't believe that lie!

TOM [*crouching toward her, overtowering her tiny figure. She backs away, gasping*]. I'm going to opium dens! Yes, opium dens, dens of vice and criminals' hang-outs, Mother. I've joined the Hogan gang, I'm a hired assassin, I carry a tommy-gun in a violin case! I run a string of cat-houses in the Valley! They call me Killer, Killer Wingfield, I'm leading a double-life, a simple, honest warehouse worker by day, by night, a dynamic *czar* of the *underworld, Mother.* I go to gambling casinos, I spin away fortunes on the roulette table! I wear a patch over one eye and a false mustache, sometimes I put on green whiskers. On those occasions they call me—*El Diablo!* Oh, I could tell you things to make you sleepless! My enemies plan to dynamite this place. They're going to blow us all sky-high some night! I'll be glad, very happy, and so will you! You'll go up, up on a broomstick, over Blue Mountain with seventeen gentlemen callers! You ugly—babbling old—*witch.* . . .

[*He goes through a series of violent, clumsy movements, seizing his overcoat, lunging to the door, pulling it fiercely open. The women watch him, aghast. His arm catches in the sleeve of the coat as he struggles to pull it on. For a moment he is pinioned by the bulky garment. With an outraged groan he tears the coat off again, splitting the shoulder of it, and hurls it across the room. It strikes against the shelf of LAURA's glass collection, there is a tinkle of shattering glass. LAURA cries out as if wounded.*]

[MUSIC. LEGEND: "THE GLASS MENAGERIE."]

LAURA [*shrilly*]. My glass!—menagerie. . . . [*She covers her face and turns away.*]

[*But* AMANDA *is still stunned and stupefied by the "ugly witch" so that she barely notices this occurrence. Now she recovers her speech.*]

AMANDA [*in an awful voice*]. I won't speak to you—until you apologize!

[*She crosses through portieres and draws them together behind her.* TOM *is left with* LAURA. LAURA *clings weakly to the mantel with her face averted.* TOM *stares at her stupidly for a moment. Then he crosses to shelf. Drops awkwardly on his knees to collect the fallen glass, glancing at* LAURA *as if he would speak but couldn't.*]

"*The Glass Menagerie*" *steals in as*
THE SCENE DIMS OUT

SCENE 4

THE INTERIOR *is dark. Faint light in the alley.*
A deep-voiced bell in a church is tolling the hour of five as the scene commences.

TOM *appears at the top of the alley. After each solemn boom of the bell in the tower, he shakes a little noise-maker or rattle as if to express the tiny spasm of man in contrast to the sustained power and dignity of the Almighty. This and the unsteadiness of his advance make it evident that he has been drinking.*
As he climbs the few steps to the fire-escape landing light steals up inside. LAURA *appears in night-dress, observing* TOM'S *empty bed in the front room.*

TOM *fishes in his pockets for door-key, removing a motley assortment of articles in the search, including a perfect shower of movie-ticket stubs and an empty bottle. At last he finds the key, but just as he is about to insert it, it slips from his fingers. He strikes a match and crouches below the door.*

TOM [*bitterly*]. One crack—and it falls through!

[LAURA *opens the door.*]

LAURA. Tom! Tom, what are you doing?
TOM. Looking for a door-key.
LAURA. Where have you been all this time?
TOM. I have been to the movies.
LAURA. All this time at the movies?
TOM. There was a very long program. There was a Garbo picture and a Mickey Mouse and a travelogue and a newsreel and a preview of

coming attractions. And there was an organ solo and a collection for the milk-fund—simultaneously—which ended up in a terrible fight between a fat lady and an usher!

LAURA [*innocently*]. Did you have to stay through everything?

TOM. Of course! And, oh, I forgot! There was a big stage show! The headliner on this stage show was Malvolio the Magician. He performed wonderful tricks, many of them, such as pouring water back and forth between pitchers. First it turned to wine and then it turned to beer and then it turned to whiskey. I know it was whiskey it finally turned into because he needed somebody to come up out of the audience to help him, and I came up—both shows! It was Kentucky Straight Bourbon. A very generous fellow, he gave souvenirs.

[*He pulls from his back pocket a shimmering rainbow-colored scarf.*]

He gave me this. This is his magic scarf. You can have it, Laura. You wave it over a canary cage and you get a bowl of gold-fish. You wave it over the gold-fish bowl and they fly away canaries. . . . But the wonderfullest trick of all was the coffin trick. We nailed him into a coffin and he got out of the coffin without removing one nail. [*He has come inside.*] There is a trick that would come in handy for me—get me out of this 2 by 4 situation! [*Flops onto bed and starts removing shoes.*]

LAURA. Tom—Shhh!

TOM. What're you shushing me for?

LAURA. You'll wake up Mother.

TOM. Goody, goody! Pay 'er back for all those "Rise an' Shines." [*Lies down, groaning.*] You know it don't take much intelligence to get yourself into a nailed-up coffin, Laura. But who in hell ever got himself out of one without removing one nail?

[*As if in answer, the father's grinning photograph lights up.*]

SCENE DIMS OUT

[*Immediately following: The church bell is heard striking six. At the sixth stroke the alarm clock goes off in* AMANDA's *room, and after a few moments we hear her calling: "Rise and Shine! Rise and Shine! Laura, go tell your brother to rise and shine!"*]

TOM [*sitting up slowly*]. I'll rise—but I won't shine.

[*The light increases.*]

AMANDA. Laura, tell your brother his coffee is ready.

[LAURA *slips into front room.*]

LAURA. Tom!—It's nearly seven. Don't make Mother nervous. [*He stares at her stupidly. Beseechingly*] Tom, speak to Mother this morning. Make up with her, apologize, speak to her!

TOM. She won't to me. It's her that started not speaking.

LAURA. If you just say you're sorry she'll start speaking.

TOM. Her not speaking—is that such a tragedy?

LAURA. Please—please!

AMANDA [*calling from kitchenette*]. Laura, are you going to do what I asked you to do, or do I have to get dressed and go out myself?

LAURA. Going, going—soon as I get on my coat!

[*She pulls on a shapeless felt hat with nervous, jerky movement, pleadingly glancing at* TOM. *Rushes awkwardly for coat. The coat is one of* AMANDA'S, *inaccurately made-over, the sleeves too short for* LAURA.]

Butter and what else?

AMANDA [*entering upstage*]. Just butter. Tell them to charge it.

LAURA. Mother, they make such faces when I do that.

AMANDA. Sticks and stones can break our bones, but the expression on Mr. Garfinkel's face won't harm us! Tell your brother his coffee is getting cold.

LAURA [*at door*]. Do what I asked you, will you, will you, Tom?

[*He looks sullenly away.*]

AMANDA. Laura, go now or just don't go at all!

LAURA [*rushing out*]. Going—going!

[*A second later she cries out.* TOM *springs up and crosses to door.* AMANDA *rushes anxiously in.* TOM *opens the door.*]

TOM. Laura?

LAURA. I'm all right. I slipped, but I'm all right.

AMANDA [*peering anxiously after her*]. If anyone breaks a leg on those fire-escape steps, the landlord ought to be sued for every cent he possesses!

[*She shuts door. Remembers she isn't speaking and returns to other room.*

[*As* TOM *enters listlessly for his coffee, she turns her back to him and stands rigidly facing the window on the gloomy gray vault of the areaway. Its light on her face with its aged but childish features is cruelly sharp, satirical as a Daumier print.*

[MUSIC UNDER: "AVE MARIA"

[TOM *glances sheepishly but sullenly at her averted figure and slumps at the table. The coffee is scalding hot; he sips it and gasps and spits it back in the cup. At his gasp,* AMANDA *catches her breath and half turns. Then catches herself and turns back to window.*]

[TOM *blows on his coffee, glancing sidewise at his mother. She clears her throat.* TOM *clears his. He starts to rise. Sinks back down again, scratches his head, clears his throat again.* AMANDA *coughs.* TOM *raises his cup in both hands to blow on it, his eyes staring over the rim of it at his mother for several moments. Then he slowly sets the cup down and awkwardly and hesitantly rises from the chair.*]

TOM [*hoarsely*]. Mother. I—I apologize, Mother.

[AMANDA *draws a quick, shuddering breath. Her face works grotesquely. She breaks into childlike tears.*]

I'm sorry for what I said, for everything that I said, I didn't mean it.

AMANDA [*sobbingly*]. My devotion has made me a witch and so I make myself hateful to my children!

TOM. *No,* you *don't.*

AMANDA. I worry so much, don't sleep, it makes me nervous!

TOM [*gently*]. I understand that.

AMANDA. I've had to put up a solitary battle all these years. But you're my right-hand bower! Don't fall down, don't fail!

TOM [*gently*]. I try, Mother.

AMANDA [*with great enthusiasm*]. Try and you will SUCCEED! [*The notion makes her breathless.*] Why, you—you're just *full* of natural endowments! Both of my children—they're *unusual* children! Don't you think I know it? I'm so—*proud!* Happy and—feel I've—so much to be thankful for but— Promise me one thing, Son!

TOM. What, Mother?

AMANDA. Promise, son, you'll—never be a drunkard!

TOM [*turns to her grinning*]. I will never be a drunkard, Mother.

AMANDA. That's what frightened me so, that you'd be drinking! Eat a bowl of Purina!

TOM. Just coffee, Mother.

AMANDA. Shredded wheat biscuit?

TOM. No. No, Mother, just coffee.

AMANDA. You can't put in a day's work on an empty stomach. You've got ten minutes—don't gulp! Drinking too-hot liquids makes cancer of the stomach. . . . Put cream in.

TOM. No, thank you.

AMANDA. To cool it.

TOM. No! No, thank you, I want it black.

AMANDA. I know, but it's not good for you. We have to do all that we can to build ourselves up. In these trying times we live in, all that

we have to cling to is—each other. . . . That's why it's so important to—
Tom, I—I sent out your sister so I could discuss something with you.
If you hadn't spoken I would have spoken to you. [*Sits down.*]

TOM [*gently*]. What is it, Mother, that you want to discuss?

AMANDA. *Laura!*

[TOM *puts his cup down slowly.*]

[LEGEND ON SCREEN: "LAURA."]

[MUSIC: "THE GLASS MENAGERIE."]

TOM. —Oh.—Laura . . .

AMANDA [*touching his sleeve*]. You know how Laura is. So quiet
but—still water runs deep! She notices things and I think she—broods
about them. [TOM *looks up.*] A few days ago I came in and she was
crying.

TOM. What about?

AMANDA. You.

TOM. Me?

AMANDA. She has an idea that you're not happy here.

TOM. What gave her that idea?

AMANDA. What gives her any idea? However, you do act strangely.
I—I'm not criticizing, understand *that!* I know your ambitions do not
lie in the warehouse, that like everybody in the whole wide world—
you've had to—make sacrifices, but—Tom—Tom—life's not easy, it calls
for—Spartan endurance! There's so many things in my heart that I
cannot describe to you! I've never told you but I—*loved* your father. . . .

TOM [*gently*]. I know that, Mother.

AMANDA. And you—when I see you taking after his ways! Staying
out late—and—well, you *had* been drinking the night you were in that—
terrifying condition! Laura says that you hate the apartment and that
you go out nights to get away from it! Is that true, Tom?

TOM. No. You say there's so much in your heart that you can't describe to me. That's true of me, too. There's so much in my heart that
I can't describe to *you!* So let's respect each other's—

AMANDA. But, why—*why,* Tom—are you always so *restless?* Where
do you *go* to, nights?

TOM. I—go to the movies.

AMANDA. Why do you go to the movies so much, Tom?

TOM. I go to the movies because—I like adventure. Adventure is
something I don't have much of at work, so I go to the movies.

AMANDA. But, Tom, you go to the movies *entirely* too *much!*

TOM. I like a lot of adventure.

[AMANDA *looks baffled, then hurt. As the familiar inquisition resumes he becomes hard and impatient again.* AMANDA *slips back into her querulous attitude toward him.*]

[IMAGE ON SCREEN: SAILING VESSEL WITH JOLLY ROGER]

AMANDA.   Most young men find adventure in their careers.

TOM.   Then most young men are not employed in a warehouse.

AMANDA.   The world is full of young men employed in warehouses and offices and factories.

TOM.   Do all of them find adventure in their careers?

AMANDA.   They do or they do without it! Not everybody has a craze for adventure.

TOM.   Man is by instinct a lover, a hunter, a fighter, and none of those instincts are given much play at the warehouse!

AMANDA.   Man is by instinct! Don't quote instinct to me! Instinct is something that people have got away from! It belongs to animals! Christian adults don't want it!

TOM.   What do Christian adults want, then, Mother?

AMANDA.   Superior things! Things of the mind and the spirit! Only animals have to satisfy instincts! Surely your aims are somewhat higher than theirs! Than monkeys—pigs—

TOM.   I reckon they're not.

AMANDA.   You're joking. However, that isn't what I wanted to discuss.

TOM [*rising*].   I haven't much time.

AMANDA [*pushing his shoulders*].   Sit down.

TOM.   You want me to punch in red at the warehouse, Mother?

AMANDA.   You have five minutes. I want to talk about Laura.

[LEGEND: "PLANS AND PROVISIONS."]

TOM.   All right! What about Laura?

AMANDA.   We have to be making some plans and provisions for her. She's older than you, two years, and nothing has happened. She just drifts along doing nothing. It frightens me terribly how she just drifts along.

TOM.   I guess she's the type that people call home girls.

AMANDA.   There's no such type, and if there is, it's a pity! That is unless the home is hers, with a husband!

TOM.   What?

AMANDA.   Oh, I can see the handwriting on the wall as plain as I see the nose in front of my face! It's terrifying!

More and more you remind me of your father! He was out all hours without explanation!—then *left! Good-bye!*

And me with the bag to hold. I saw that letter you got from the
Merchant Marine. I know what you're dreaming of. I'm not standing
here blindfolded.

Very well, then. Then *do* it!

But not till there's somebody to take your place.

TOM. What do you mean?

AMANDA. I mean that as soon as Laura has got somebody to take care
of her, married, a home of her own, independent—why, then you'll be
free to go wherever you please, on land, on sea, whichever way the wind
blows you!

But until that time you've got to look out for your sister. I don't say
me because I'm old and don't matter! I say for your sister because she's
young and dependent.

I put her in business college—a dismal failure! Frightened her so it
made her sick at the stomach.

I took her over to the Young People's League at the church. Another
fiasco. She spoke to nobody, nobody spoke to her. Now all she does is
fool with those pieces of glass and play those worn-out records. What
kind of a life is that for a girl to lead?

TOM. What can I do about it?

AMANDA. Overcome selfishness! Self, self, self is all that you ever
think of!

[TOM *springs up and crosses to get his coat. It is ugly and bulky.
He pulls on a cap with earmuffs.*]

Where is your muffler? Put your wool muffler on!

[*He snatches it angrily from the closet and tosses it around his neck
and pulls both ends tight.*]

Tom! I haven't said what I had in mind to ask you.

TOM. I'm too late to—

AMANDA [*catching his arm—very importunately. Then shyly*]. Down
at the warehouse, aren't there some—nice young men?

TOM. No!

AMANDA. There *must* be—*some* . . .

TOM. Mother— [*Gesture.*]

AMANDA. Find out one that's clean-living—doesn't drink and—ask
him out for sister!

TOM. What?

AMANDA. For *sister!* To *meet!* Get *acquainted!*

TOM [*stamping to door*]. Oh, my go-osh!

AMANDA. Will you? [*He opens door. Imploringly*] Will you?
[*He starts down.*] Will you? *Will* you, dear?

TOM [*calling back*]. Yes!

[AMANDA *closes the door hesitantly and with a troubled but faintly hopeful expression.*

[SCREEN IMAGE: GLAMOR MAGAZINE COVER

[*Spot* AMANDA *at phone.*]

AMANDA. Ella Cartwright? This is Amanda Wingfield! How are you, honey? How is that kidney condition? [*Count five*] Horrors! [*Count five*] You're a Christian martyr, yes, honey, that's what you are, a Christian martyr!

Well, I just now happened to notice in my little red book that your subscription to the *Companion* has just run out! I knew that you wouldn't want to miss out on the wonderful serial starting in this new issue. It's by Bessie Mae Hopper, the first thing she's written since *Honeymoon for Three.*

Wasn't that a strange and interesting story? Well, this one is even lovelier, I believe. It has a sophisticated, society background. It's all about the horsey set on Long Island!

FADE OUT

SCENE 5

LEGEND ON SCREEN: "ANNUNCIATION." *Fade with music.*

It is early dusk of a spring evening. Supper has just been finished in the Wingfield apartment. AMANDA *and* LAURA *in light-colored dresses are removing dishes from the table, in the upstage area, which is shadowy, their movements formalized almost as a dance or ritual, their moving forms as pale and silent as moths.*

TOM, *in white shirt and trousers, rises from the table and crosses toward the fire-escape.*

AMANDA [*as he passes her*]. Son, will you do me a favor?
TOM. What?
AMANDA. Comb your hair! You look so pretty when your hair is combed!

[TOM *slouches on sofa with evening paper. Enormous caption "Franco Triumphs"*]

There is only one respect in which I would like you to emulate your father.
TOM. What respect is that?

AMANDA. The care he always took of his appearance. He never allowed himself to look untidy.

[*He throws down the paper and crosses to fire-escape.*]

Where are you going?

TOM. I'm going out to smoke.

AMANDA. You smoke too much. A pack a day at fifteen cents a pack. How much would that amount to in a month? Thirty times fifteen is how much, Tom? Figure it out and you will be astounded at what you could save. Enough to give you a night-school course in accounting at Washington U! Just think what a wonderful thing that would be for you, Son!

[TOM *is unmoved by the thought.*]

TOM. I'd rather smoke.

[*He steps out on landing, letting the screen door slam.*]

AMANDA [*sharply*]. I know! That's the tragedy of it. . . .

[*Alone, she turns to look at her husband's picture.*

[DANCE MUSIC: "ALL THE WORLD IS WAITING FOR THE SUNRISE!"]

TOM [*to the audience*]. Across the alley from us was the Paradise Dance Hall. On evenings in spring the windows and doors were open and the music came outdoors. Sometimes the lights were turned out except for a large glass sphere that hung from the ceiling. It would turn slowly about and filter the dusk with delicate rainbow colors. Then the orchestra played a waltz or a tango, something that had a slow and sensuous rhythm. Couples would come outside, to the relative privacy of the alley. You could see them kissing behind ash-pits and telephone poles.

This was the compensation for lives that passed like mine, without any change or adventure.

Adventure and change were imminent in this year. They were waiting around the corner for all these kids.

Suspended in the mist over Berchtesgaden, caught in the folds of Chamberlain's umbrella—

In Spain there was Guernica!

But here there was only hot swing music and liquor, dance halls, bars, and movies, and sex that hung in the gloom like a chandelier and flooded the world with brief, deceptive rainbows. . . .

All the world was waiting for bombardments!

[AMANDA *turns from the picture and comes outside.*]

AMANDA [*sighing*].   A fire-escape landing's a poor excuse for a porch. [*She spreads a newspaper on a step and sits down, gracefully and demurely as if she were settling into a swing on a Mississippi veranda.*] What are you looking at?

TOM.   The moon.

AMANDA.   Is there a moon this evening?

TOM.   It's rising over Garfinkel's Delicatessen.

AMANDA.   So it is! A little silver slipper of a moon. Have you made a wish on it yet?

TOM.   Um-hum.

AMANDA.   What did you wish for?

TOM.   That's a secret.

AMANDA.   A secret, huh? Well, I won't tell mine either. I will be just as mysterious as you.

TOM.   I bet I can guess what yours is.

AMANDA.   Is my head so transparent?

TOM.   You're not a sphinx.

AMANDA.   No, I don't have secrets. I'll tell you what I wished for on the moon. Success and happiness for my precious children! I wish for that whenever there's a moon, and when there isn't a moon, I wish for it, too.

TOM.   I thought perhaps you wished for a gentleman caller.

AMANDA.   Why do you say that?

TOM.   Don't you remember asking me to fetch one?

AMANDA.   I remember suggesting that it would be nice for your sister if you brought home some nice young man from the warehouse. I think that I've made that suggestion more than once.

TOM.   Yes, you have made it repeatedly.

AMANDA.   Well?

TOM.   We are going to have one.

AMANDA.   *What?*

TOM.   A gentleman caller!

[THE ANNUNCIATION IS CELEBRATED WITH MUSIC.

[AMANDA *rises.*

[IMAGE ON SCREEN: CALLER WITH BOUQUET.]

AMANDA.   You mean you have asked some nice young man to come over?

TOM.   Yep. I've asked him to dinner.

AMANDA.   You really did?

TOM.   I did!

AMANDA.   You did, and did he—*accept?*

TOM.   He did!

AMANDA. Well, well—well, well! That's—lovely!

TOM. I thought that you would be pleased.

AMANDA. It's definite, then?

TOM. Very definite.

AMANDA. Soon?

TOM. Very soon.

AMANDA. For heaven's sake, stop putting on and tell me some things, will you?

TOM. What things do you want me to tell you?

AMANDA. *Naturally* I would like to know when he's *coming!*

TOM. He's coming tomorrow.

AMANDA. *Tomorrow?*

TOM. Yep. Tomorrow.

AMANDA. But, Tom!

TOM. Yes, Mother?

AMANDA. Tomorrow gives me no time!

TOM. Time for what?

AMANDA. Preparations! Why didn't you phone me at once, as soon as you asked him, the minute that he accepted? Then, don't you see, I could have been getting ready!

TOM. You don't have to make any fuss.

AMANDA. Oh, Tom, Tom, Tom, of course I have to make a fuss! I want things nice, not sloppy! Not thrown together. I'll certainly have to do some fast thinking, won't I?

TOM. I don't see why you have to think at all.

AMANDA. You just don't know. We can't have a gentleman caller in a pig-sty! All my wedding silver has to be polished, the monogrammed table linen ought to be laundered! The windows have to be washed and fresh curtains put up. And how about clothes? We have to *wear* something, don't we?

TOM. Mother, this boy is no one to make a fuss over!

AMANDA. Do you realize he's the first young man we've introduced to your sister? It's terrible, dreadful, disgraceful that poor little sister has never received a single gentleman caller! Tom, come inside!

[*She opens the screen door.*]

TOM. What for?

AMANDA. I want to ask you some things.

TOM. If you're going to make such a fuss, I'll call it off, I'll tell him not to come!

AMANDA. You certainly won't do anything of the kind. Nothing offends people worse than broken engagements. It simply means I'll have to work like a Turk! We won't be brilliant, but we will pass inspection. Come on inside. [TOM *follows, groaning.*] Sit down.

TOM.　Any particular place you would like me to sit?

AMANDA.　Thank heavens I've got that new sofa! I'm also making payments on a floor lamp I'll have sent out! And put the chintz covers on, they'll brighten things up! Of course I'd hoped to have these walls re-papered. . . . What is the young man's name?

TOM.　His name is O'Connor.

AMANDA.　That, of course, means fish—tomorrow is Friday! I'll have that salmon loaf—with Durkee's dressing! What does he do? He works at the warehouse?

TOM.　Of course! How else would I—

AMANDA.　Tom, he—doesn't drink?

TOM.　Why do you ask me that?

AMANDA.　Your father *did!*

TOM.　Don't get started on that!

AMANDA.　He *does* drink, then?

TOM.　Not that I know of!

AMANDA.　Make sure, be certain! The last thing I want for my daughter's a boy who drinks!

TOM.　Aren't you being a little bit premature? Mr. O'Connor has not yet appeared on the scene!

AMANDA.　But will tomorrow. To meet your sister, and what do I know about his character? Nothing! Old maids are better off than wives of drunkards!

TOM.　Oh, my God!

AMANDA.　Be still!

TOM [*leaning forward to whisper*].　Lots of fellows meet girls whom they don't marry!

AMANDA.　Oh, talk sensibly, Tom—and don't be sarcastic!

[*She has gotten a hairbrush.*]

TOM.　What are you doing?

AMANDA.　I'm brushing that cow-lick down! What is this young man's position at the warehouse?

TOM [*submitting grimly to the brush and the interrogation*].　This young man's position is that of a shipping clerk, Mother.

AMANDA.　Sounds to me like a fairly responsible job, the sort of a job *you* would be in if you just had more *get-up*. What is his salary? Have you any idea?

TOM.　I would judge it to be approximately eighty-five dollars a month.

AMANDA.　Well—not princely, but—

TOM.　Twenty more than I make.

AMANDA.　Yes, how well I know! But for a family man, eighty-five dollars a month is not much more than you can just get by on. . . .

TOM.　Yes, but Mr. O'Connor is not a family man.

AMANDA. He might be, mightn't he? Some time in the future?

TOM. I see. Plans and provisions.

AMANDA. You are the only young man that I know of who ignores the fact that the future becomes the present, the present the past, and the past turns into everlasting regret if you don't plan for it!

TOM. I will think that over and see what I can make of it.

AMANDA. Don't be supercilious with your mother! Tell me some more about this—what do you call him?

TOM. James D. O'Connor. The D. is for Delaney.

AMANDA. Irish on *both* sides! *Gracious!* And doesn't drink?

TOM. Shall I call him up and ask him right this minute?

AMANDA. The only way to find out about those things is to make discreet inquiries at the proper moment. When I was a girl in Blue Mountain and it was suspected that a young man drank, the girl whose attentions he had been receiving, if any girl *was,* would sometimes speak to the minister of his church, or rather her father would if her father was living, and sort of feel him out on the young man's character. That is the way such things are discreetly handled to keep a young woman from making a tragic mistake!

TOM. Then how did you happen to make a tragic mistake?

AMANDA. That innocent look of your father's had everyone fooled!

He *smiled*—the world was *enchanted!*

No girl can do worse than put herself at the mercy of a handsome appearance!

I hope that Mr. O'Connor is not too good-looking.

TOM. No, he's not too good-looking. He's covered with freckles and hasn't too much of a nose.

AMANDA. He's not right-down homely, though?

TOM. Not right-down homely. Just medium homely, I'd say.

AMANDA. Character's what to look for in a man.

TOM. That's what I've always said, Mother.

AMANDA. You've never said anything of the kind and I suspect you would never give it a thought.

TOM. Don't be so suspicious of me.

AMANDA. At least I hope he's the type that's up and coming.

TOM. I think he really goes in for self-improvement.

AMANDA. What reason have you to think so?

TOM. He goes to night school.

AMANDA [*beaming*]. Splendid! What does he do, I mean study?

TOM. Radio engineering and public speaking!

AMANDA. Then he has visions of being advanced in the world!

Any young man who studies public speaking is aiming to have an executive job some day!

And radio engineering? A thing for the future!

Both of these facts are very illuminating. Those are the sort of things that a mother should know concerning any young man who comes to call on her daughter. Seriously or—not.

TOM. One little warning. He doesn't know about Laura. I didn't let on that we had dark ulterior motives. I just said, why don't you come and have dinner with us? He said okay and that was the whole conversation.

AMANDA. I bet it was! You're eloquent as an oyster. However, he'll know about Laura when he gets here. When he sees how lovely and sweet and pretty she is, he'll thank his lucky stars he was asked to dinner.

TOM. Mother, you mustn't expect too much of Laura.

AMANDA. What do you mean?

TOM. Laura seems all those things to you and me because she's ours and we love her. We don't even notice she's crippled any more.

AMANDA. Don't say crippled! You know that I never allow that word to be used!

TOM. But face facts, Mother. She is and—that's not all—

AMANDA. What do you mean "not all"?

TOM. Laura is very different from other girls.

AMANDA. I think the difference is all to her advantage.

TOM. Not quite all—in the eyes of others—strangers—she's terribly shy and lives in a world of her own and those things make her seem a little peculiar to people outside the house.

AMANDA. Don't say peculiar.

TOM. Face the facts. She is.

[THE DANCE-HALL MUSIC CHANGES TO A TANGO THAT HAS A MINOR AND SOMEWHAT OMINOUS TONE.]

AMANDA. In what way is she peculiar—may I ask?

TOM [gently]. She lives in a world of her own—a world of—little glass ornaments, Mother. . . .

[Gets up. AMANDA remains holding brush, looking at him, troubled.]

She plays old phonograph records and—that's about all—

[He glances at himself in the mirror and crosses to door.]

AMANDA [sharply]. Where are you going?

TOM. I'm going to the movies. [Out screen door.]

AMANDA. Not to the movies, every night to the movies! [Follows quickly to screen door] I don't believe you always go to the movies!

[He is gone. AMANDA looks worriedly after him for a moment. Then vitality and optimism return and she turns from the door. Crossing to portieres]

Laura! Laura! [LAURA *answers from kitchenette.*]
   LAURA. Yes, Mother.
   AMANDA. Let those dishes go and come in front!

[LAURA *appears with dish towel. Gaily*]

Laura, come here and make a wish on the moon!

[SCREEN IMAGE: MOON]

   LAURA [*entering*]. Moon—moon?
   AMANDA. A little silver slipper of a moon. Look over your left shoulder, Laura, and make a wish!

[LAURA *looks faintly puzzled as if called out of sleep.* AMANDA *seizes her shoulders and turns her at an angle by the door.*]

Now! Now, darling, *wish*!
   LAURA. What shall I wish for, Mother?
   AMANDA [*her voice trembling and her eyes suddenly filling with tears*]. Happiness! Good fortune!

[*The violin rises and the stage dims out.*]

CURTAIN

SCENE 6

IMAGE: HIGH SCHOOL HERO.

[TOM, *narrating.*] And so the following evening I brought Jim home to dinner. I had known Jim slightly in high school. In high school Jim was a hero. He had tremendous Irish good nature and vitality with the scrubbed and polished look of white chinaware. He seemed to move in a continual spotlight. He was a star in basketball, captain of the debating club, president of the senior class and the glee club and he sang the male lead in the annual light operas. He was always running or bounding, never just walking. He seemed always at the point of defeating the law of gravity. He was shooting with such velocity through his adolescence that you would logically expect him to arrive at nothing short of the White House by the time he was thirty. But Jim apparently ran into more interference after his graduation from Soldan. His speed had definitely slowed. Six years after he left high school he was holding a job that wasn't much better than mine.

[IMAGE: CLERK]

He was the only one at the warehouse with whom I was on friendly terms. I was valuable to him as someone who could remember his former glory, who had seen him win basketball games and the silver cup in debating. He knew of my secret practice of retiring to a cabinet of the wash-room to work on poems when business was slack in the warehouse. He called me Shakespeare. And while the other boys in the warehouse regarded me with suspicious hostility, Jim took a humorous attitude toward me. Gradually his attitude affected the others, their hostility wore off and they also began to smile at me as people smile at an oddly fashioned dog who trots across their path at some distance.

I knew that Jim and Laura had known each other at Soldan, and I had heard Laura speak admiringly of his voice. I didn't know if Jim remembered her or not. In high school Laura had been as unobtrusive as Jim had been astonishing. If he did remember Laura, it was not as my sister, for when I asked him to dinner, he grinned and said, "You know, Shakespeare, I never thought of you as having folks!"

He was about to discover that I did. . . .

[LIGHT UP STAGE.

[LEGEND ON SCREEN: "THE ACCENT OF A COMING FOOT."

[*Friday evening. It is about five o'clock of a late spring evening which comes "scattering poems in the sky." A delicate lemony light is in the Wingfield apartment.*

[AMANDA *has worked like a Turk in preparation for the gentleman caller. The results are astonishing. The new floor lamp with its rose-silk shade is in place, a colored paper lantern conceals the broken light fixture in the ceiling, new billowing white curtains are at the windows, chintz covers are on chairs and sofa, a pair of new sofa pillows make their initial appearance. Open boxes and tissue paper are scattered on the floor.*

[LAURA *stands in the middle with lifted arms while* AMANDA *crouches before her, adjusting the hem of the new dress, devout and ritualistic. The dress is colored and designed by memory. The arrangement of* LAURA'S *hair is changed; it is softer and more becoming. A fragile, unearthly prettiness has come out in* LAURA: *she is like a piece of translucent glass touched by light, given a momentary radiance, not actual, not lasting.*]

AMANDA [*impatiently*]. Why are you trembling?
LAURA. Mother, you've made me so nervous!
AMANDA. How have I made you nervous?
LAURA. By all this fuss! You make it seem so important!
AMANDA. I don't understand you, Laura. You couldn't be satisfied with just sitting home, and yet whenever I try to arrange something for

you, you seem to resist it. [*She gets up.*] Now take a look at yourself.
No, wait! Wait just a moment—I have an idea!

LAURA.   What is it now?

[AMANDA *produces two powder puffs which she wraps in handker-chiefs and stuffs in* LAURA'S *bosom.*]

LAURA.   Mother, what are you doing?

AMANDA.   They call them "Gay Deceivers"!

LAURA.   I won't wear them!

AMANDA.   You will!

LAURA.   Why should I?

AMANDA.   Because, to be painfully honest, your chest is flat.

LAURA.   You make it seem like we were setting a trap.

AMANDA.   All pretty girls are a trap, a pretty trap, and men expect
them to be.

[LEGEND: "A PRETTY TRAP"]

Now look at yourself, young lady. This is the prettiest you will ever be!
I've got to fix myself now! You're going to be surprised by your
mother's appearance!

[*She crosses through portieres, humming gaily.*

[LAURA *moves slowly to the long mirror and stares solemnly at her-self. A wind blows the white curtains inward in a slow, graceful motion and with a faint, sorrowful sighing.*]

AMANDA [*off stage*].   It isn't dark enough yet.

[*She turns slowly before the mirror with a troubled look.*

[LEGEND ON SCREEN: "THIS IS MY SISTER:
CELEBRATE HER WITH STRINGS!" MUSIC.]

AMANDA [*laughing, off*].   I'm going to show you something. I'm
going to make a spectacular appearance!

LAURA.   What is it, Mother?

AMANDA.   Possess your soul in patience—you will see! Something I've
resurrected from that old trunk! Styles haven't changed so terribly
much after all. . . . [*She parts the portieres.*] Now just look at your
mother!

[*She wears a girlish frock of yellowed voile with a blue silk sash.
She carries a bunch of jonquils—the legend of her youth is nearly
revived. Feverishly*]

This is the dress in which I led the cotillion. Won the cakewalk twice at Sunset Hill, wore one spring to the Governor's ball in Jackson! See how I sashayed around the ballroom, Laura?

[*She raises her skirt and does a mincing step around the room.*]

I wore it on Sundays for my gentlemen callers! I had it on the day I met your father—

I had malaria fever all that spring. The change of climate from East Tennessee to the Delta—weakened resistance—I had a little temperature all the time—not enough to be serious—just enough to make me restless and giddy!—Invitations poured in—parties all over the Delta!—"Stay in bed," said Mother, "you have fever!"—but I just wouldn't.—I took quinine but kept on going, going!—Evenings, dances!—Afternoons, long, long rides! Picnics—lovely!—So lovely, that country in May.—All lacy with dogwood, literally flooded with jonquils!—That was the spring I had the craze for jonquils. Jonquils became an absolute obsession. Mother said, "Honey, there's no more room for jonquils." And still I kept on bringing in more jonquils. Whenever, wherever I saw them, I'd say, "Stop! Stop! I see jonquils!" I made the young men help me gather the jonquils! It was a joke, Amanda and her jonquils! Finally there were no more vases to hold them, every available space was filled with jonquils. No vases to hold them? All right, I'll hold them myself! And then I—[*She stops in front of the picture.* MUSIC] met your father! Malaria fever and jonquils and then—this—boy. . . .

[*She switches on the rose-colored lamp.*]

I hope they get here before it starts to rain.

[*She crosses upstage and places the jonquils in bowl on table.*]

I gave your brother a little extra change so he and Mr. O'Connor could take the service car home.

LAURA [*with altered look*]. What did you say his name was?
AMANDA. O'Connor.
LAURA. What is his first name?
AMANDA. I don't remember. Oh, yes, I do. It was—Jim!

[LAURA *sways slightly and catches hold of a chair.*

[LEGEND ON SCREEN: "NOT JIM!"]

LAURA [*faintly*]. Not—Jim!
AMANDA. Yes, that was it, it was Jim! I've never known a Jim that wasn't nice!

[MUSIC: OMINOUS]

LAURA. Are you sure his name is Jim O'Connor?

AMANDA. Yes. Why?

LAURA. Is he the one that Tom used to know in high school?

AMANDA. He didn't say so. I think he just got to know him at the warehouse.

LAURA. There was a Jim O'Connor we both knew in high school— [*Then, with effort*] If that is the one that Tom is bringing to dinner— you'll have to excuse me, I won't come to the table.

AMANDA. What sort of nonsense is this?

LAURA. You asked me once if I'd ever liked a boy. Don't you remember I showed you this boy's picture?

AMANDA. You mean the boy you showed me in the year book?

LAURA. Yes, that boy.

AMANDA. Laura, Laura, were you in love with that boy?

LAURA. I don't know, Mother. All I know is I couldn't sit at the table if it was him!

AMANDA. It won't be him! It isn't the least bit likely. But whether it is or not, you will come to the table. You will not be excused.

LAURA. I'll have to be, Mother.

AMANDA. I don't intend to humor your silliness, Laura. I've had too much from you and your brother, both! So just sit down and compose yourself till they come. Tom has forgotten his key so you'll have to let them in, when they arrive.

LAURA [*panicky*]. Oh, Mother—*you* answer the door!

AMANDA [*lightly*]. I'll be in the kitchen—busy!

LAURA. Oh, Mother, please answer the door, don't make me do it!

AMANDA [*crossing into kitchenette*]. I've got to fix the dressing for the salmon. Fuss, fuss—silliness!—over a gentleman caller!

[*Door swings shut.* LAURA *is left alone.*

[LEGEND: "TERROR!"]

[*She utters a low moan and turns off the lamp, sits stiffly on the edge of the sofa, knotting her fingers together.*

[LEGEND ON SCREEN: "THE OPENING OF A DOOR!"]

[TOM *and* JIM *appear on the fire-escape steps and climb to landing. Hearing their approach,* LAURA *rises with a panicky gesture. She retreats to the portieres. The doorbell.* LAURA *catches her breath and touches her throat. Low drums.*]

AMANDA [*calling*]. Laura, sweetheart! The door!

[LAURA *stares at it without moving.*]

JIM.   I think we just beat the rain.

TOM.   Uh-huh.

[*He rings again, nervously.* JIM *whistles and fishes for a cigarette.*]

AMANDA [*very, very gaily*].   Laura, that is your brother and Mr. O'Connor! Will you let them in, darling?

[LAURA *crosses toward kitchenette door.*]

LAURA [*breathlessly*].   Mother—you go to the door!

[AMANDA *steps out of kitchenette and stares furiously at* LAURA. *She points imperiously at the door.*]

LAURA.   Please, please!

AMANDA [*in a fierce whisper*].   What is the matter with you, you silly thing?

LAURA [*desperately*].   Please, you answer it, *please!*

AMANDA.   I told you I wasn't going to humor you, Laura. Why have you chosen this moment to lose your mind?

LAURA.   Please, please, please, you go!

AMANDA.   You'll have to go to the door because I can't!

LAURA [*despairingly*].   I can't either!

AMANDA.   *Why?*

LAURA.   I'm *sick!*

AMANDA.   I'm sick, too—of your nonsense! Why can't you and your brother be normal people? Fantastic whims and behavior!

[TOM *gives a long ring.*]

Preposterous goings on! Can you give me one reason—[*Calls out lyrically*] COMING! JUST ONE SECOND!—why you should be afraid to open a door? Now you answer it, Laura!

LAURA.   Oh, oh, oh . . .

[*She returns through the portieres. Darts to the victrola and winds it frantically and turns it on.*]

AMANDA.   Laura Wingfield, you march right to that door!

LAURA.   Yes—yes, Mother!

[*A faraway, scratchy rendition of "Dardanella" softens the air and gives her strength to move through it. She slips to the door and draws it cautiously open.* TOM *enters with the caller,* JIM O'CONNOR.]

TOM.   Laura, this is Jim. Jim, this is my sister, Laura.

JIM [*stepping inside*].   I didn't know that Shakespeare had a sister!

LAURA [*retreating stiff and trembling from the door*].   How—how do you do?

JIM [*heartily extending his hand*]. Okay!

[LAURA *touches it hesitantly with hers*.]

JIM. Your hand's *cold*, Laura!

LAURA. Yes, well—I've been playing the victrola. . . .

JIM. Must have been playing classical music on it! You ought to play a little hot swing music to warm you up!

LAURA. Excuse me—I haven't finished playing the victrola. . . .

[*She turns awkwardly and hurries into the front room. She pauses a second by the victrola. Then catches her breath and darts through the portieres like a frightened deer*.]

JIM [*grinning*]. What was the matter?

TOM. Oh—with Laura? Laura is—terribly shy.

JIM. Shy, huh? It's unusual to meet a shy girl nowadays. I don't believe you ever mentioned you had a sister.

TOM. Well, now you know. I have one. Here is the *Post Dispatch*. You want a piece of it?

JIM. Uh-huh.

TOM. What piece? The comics?

JIM. Sports! [*Glances at it*] Ole Dizzy Dean is on his bad behavior.

TOM [*disinterest*]. Yeah?

[*Lights cigarette and crosses back to fire-escape door*.]

JIM. Where are *you* going?

TOM. I'm going out on the terrace.

JIM [*goes after him*]. You know, Shakespeare—I'm going to sell you a bill of goods!

TOM. What goods?

JIM. A course I'm taking.

TOM. Huh?

JIM. In public speaking! You and me, we're not the warehouse type.

TOM. Thanks—that's good news. But what has public speaking got to do with it?

JIM. It fits you for—executive positions!

TOM. Awww.

JIM. I tell you it's done a helluva lot for me.

[IMAGE: EXECUTIVE AT DESK.]

TOM. In what respect?

JIM. In every! Ask yourself what is the difference between you an' me and men in the office down front? Brains?—No!—Ability?—No! Then what? Just one little thing—

TOM. What is that one little thing?

JIM.   Primarily it amounts to—social poise! Being able to square up to people and hold your own on any social level!

AMANDA [*off stage*].   Tom?

TOM.   Yes, Mother?

AMANDA.   Is that you and Mr. O'Connor?

TOM.   Yes, Mother.

AMANDA.   Well, you just make yourselves comfortable in there.

TOM.   Yes, Mother.

AMANDA.   Ask Mr. O'Connor if he would like to wash his hands.

JIM.   Aw, no—no—thank you—I took care of that at the warehouse. Tom—

TOM.   Yes?

JIM.   Mr. Mendoza was speaking to me about you.

TOM.   Favorably?

JIM.   What do you think?

TOM.   Well—

JIM.   You're going to be out of a job if you don't wake up.

TOM.   I am waking up—

JIM.   You show no signs.

TOM.   The signs are interior.

[IMAGE ON SCREEN: THE SAILING VESSEL
WITH JOLLY ROGER AGAIN]

TOM.   I'm planning to change.

[*He leans over the rail speaking with quiet exhilaration. The incandescent marquees and signs of the first-run movie houses light his face from across the alley. He looks like a voyager.*]

I'm right at the point of committing myself to a future that doesn't include the warehouse and Mr. Mendoza or even a night-school course in public speaking.

JIM.   What are you gassing about?

TOM.   I'm tired of the movies.

JIM.   Movies!

TOM.   Yes, movies! Look at them— [*A wave toward the marvels of Grand Avenue*] All of those glamorous people—having adventures—hogging it all, gobbling the whole thing up! You know what happens? People go to the *movies* instead of *moving!* Hollywood characters are supposed to have all the adventures for everybody in America, while everybody in America sits in a dark room and watches them have them! Yes, until there's a war. That's when adventure becomes available to the masses! *Everyone's* dish, not only Gable's! Then the people in the dark room come out of the dark room to have some adventures themselves—Goody, goody!—It's our turn now, to go to the South Sea Island

—to make a safari—to be exotic, far-off!—But I'm not patient. I don't want to wait till then. I'm tired of the *movies* and I am *about* to *move!*

JIM [*incredulously*]. Move?

TOM. Yes.

JIM. When?

TOM. Soon!

JIM. Where? Where?

[THEME THREE MUSIC *seems to answer the question, while* TOM *thinks it over. He searches among his pockets.*]

TOM. I'm starting to boil inside. I know I seem dreamy, but inside—well, I'm boiling!—Whenever I pick up a shoe, I shudder a little thinking how short life is and what I am doing!—Whatever that means, I know it doesn't mean shoes—except as something to wear on a traveler's feet! [*Finds paper*] Look—

JIM. What?

TOM. I'm a member.

JIM [*reading*]. The Union of Merchant Seamen.

TOM. I paid my dues this month, instead of the light bill.

JIM. You will regret it when they turn the lights off.

TOM. I won't be here.

JIM. How about your mother?

TOM. I'm like my father. The bastard son of a bastard! See how he grins? And he's been absent going on sixteen years!

JIM. You're just talking, you drip. How does your mother feel about it?

TOM. Shhh!—Here comes Mother! Mother is not acquainted with my plans!

AMANDA [*enters portieres*]. Where are you all?

TOM. On the terrace, Mother.

[*They start inside. She advances to them.* TOM *is distinctly shocked at her appearance. Even* JIM *blinks a little. He is making his first contact with girlish Southern vivacity and in spite of the night-school course in public speaking is somewhat thrown off the beam by the unexpected outlay of social charm. Certain responses are attempted by* JIM *but are swept aside by* AMANDA's *gay laughter and chatter.* TOM *is embarrassed but after the first shock* JIM *reacts very warmly. Grins and chuckles, is altogether won over.*]

[IMAGE: AMANDA AS A GIRL.]

AMANDA [*coyly smiling, shaking her girlish ringlets*]. Well, well, well, so this is Mr. O'Connor. Introductions entirely unnecessary. I've heard so much about you from my boy. I finally said to him, Tom—

good gracious!—why don't you bring this paragon to supper? I'd like to meet this nice young man at the warehouse!—Instead of just hearing him sing your praises so much!

I don't know why my son is so stand-offish—that's not Southern behavior!

Let's sit down and—I think we could stand a little more air in here! Tom, leave the door open. I felt a nice fresh breeze a moment ago. Where has it gone to?

Mmm, so warm already! And not quite summer, even. We're going to burn up when summer really gets started.

However, we're having—we're having a very light supper. I think light things are better fo' this time of year. The same as light clothes are. Light clothes an' light food are what warm weather calls fo'. You know our blood gets so thick during th' winter—it takes a while fo' us to *adjust* ou'selves!—when the season changes . . .

It's come so quick this year. I wasn't prepared. All of a sudden— heavens! Already summer!—I ran to the trunk an' pulled out this light dress— Terribly old! Historical almost! But feels so good—so good an' co-ol, y' know. . . .

TOM. Mother—

AMANDA. Yes, honey?

TOM. How about—supper?

AMANDA. Honey, you go ask Sister if supper is ready! You know that Sister is in full charge of supper! Tell her you hungry boys are waiting for it. [*To* JIM] Have you met Laura?

JIM. She—

AMANDA. Let you in? Oh, good, you've met already! It's rare for a girl as sweet an' pretty as Laura to be domestic! But Laura is, thank heavens, not only pretty but also very domestic. I'm not at all. I never was a bit. I never could make a thing but angel-food cake. Well, in the South we had so many servants. Gone, gone, gone. All vestige of gracious living! Gone completely! I wasn't prepared for what the future brought me. All of my gentlemen callers were sons of planters and so of course I assumed that I would be married to one and raise my family on a large piece of land with plenty of servants. But man proposes—and woman accepts the proposal!—To vary that old, old saying a little bit— I married no planter! I married a man who worked for the telephone company!—That gallantly smiling gentleman over there! [*Points to the picture*] A telephone man who—fell in love with long-distance!—Now he travels and I don't even know where!—But what am I going on for about my—tribulations? Tell me yours—I hope you don't have any! Tom?

TOM [*returning*]. Yes, Mother?

AMANDA. Is supper nearly ready?

TOM. It looks to me like supper is on the table.

AMANDA.   Let me look— [*She rises prettily and looks through portieres.*]   Oh, lovely!—But where is Sister?

TOM.   Laura is not feeling well and she says that she thinks she'd better not come to the table.

AMANDA.   What?—Nonsense!—Laura? Oh, Laura!

LAURA [*off stage, faintly*].   Yes, Mother.

AMANDA.   You really must come to the table. We won't be seated until you come to the table!

Come in, Mr. O'Connor. You sit over there, and I'll—

Laura? Laura Wingfield! You're keeping us waiting, honey! We can't say grace until you come to the table!

[*The back door is pushed weakly open and* LAURA *comes in. She is obviously quite faint, her lips trembling, her eyes wide and staring. She moves unsteadily toward the table.*

[LEGEND: "TERROR!"]

[*Outside a summer storm is coming abruptly. The white curtains billow inward at the windows and there is a sorrowful murmur and deep blue dusk.* LAURA *suddenly stumbles—she catches at a chair with a faint moan.*]

TOM.   Laura!

AMANDA.   Laura!

[*There is a clap of thunder.*

[LEGEND: "AH!"]

[*despairingly*]

Why, Laura, you *are* sick, darling! Tom, help your sister into the living room, dear! Sit in the living room, Laura—rest on the sofa. Well! [*To the gentleman caller*] Standing over the hot stove made her ill!—I told her that it was just too warm this evening, but—

[TOM *comes back in.* LAURA *is on the sofa.*]

Is Laura all right now?

TOM.   Yes.

AMANDA.   What *is* that? Rain? A nice cool rain has come up!

[*She gives the gentleman caller a frightened look.*]

I think we may—have grace—now . . .

[TOM *looks at her stupidly.*]

Tom, honey—you say grace!

TOM. Oh . . . "For these and all thy mercies—"

[*They bow their heads,* AMANDA *stealing a nervous glance at* JIM. *In the living room* LAURA, *stretched on the sofa, clenches her hands to her lips, to hold back a shuddering sob.*]

God's Holy Name be praised—

THE SCENE DIMS OUT

SCENE 7

A SOUVENIR.

Half an hour later. Dinner is just being finished in the upstage area which is concealed by the drawn portieres.

As the curtain rises LAURA *is still huddled upon the sofa, her feet drawn under her, her head resting on a pale blue pillow, her eyes wide and mysteriously watchful. The new floor lamp with its shade of rose-colored silk gives a soft, becoming light to her face, bringing out the fragile, unearthly prettiness which usually escapes attention.. There is a steady murmur of rain, but it is slackening and stops soon after the scene begins; the air outside becomes pale and luminous as the moon breaks out.*

A moment after the curtain rises, the lights in both rooms flicker and go out.

JIM. Hey, there, Mr. Light Bulb!

[AMANDA *laughs nervously.*

[LEGEND: "SUSPENSION OF A PUBLIC SERVICE."]

AMANDA. Where was Moses when the lights went out? Ha-ha. Do you know the answer to that one, Mr. O'Connor?

JIM. No, Ma'am, what's the answer?

AMANDA. In the dark!

[JIM *laughs appreciatively.*]

Everybody sit still. I'll light the candles. Isn't it lucky we have them on the table? Where's a match? Which of you gentlemen can provide a match?

JIM. Here.

AMANDA. Thank you, sir.

JIM. Not at all, Ma'am!

AMANDA. I guess the fuse has burnt out. Mr. O'Connor, can you tell a burnt-out fuse? I know I can't and Tom is a total loss when it comes to mechanics.

[SOUND: *getting up: voices recede a little to kitchenette.*]

Oh, be careful you don't bump into something. We don't want our gentleman caller to break his neck. Now wouldn't that be a fine howdy-do?

JIM. Ha-ha! Where is the fuse-box?

AMANDA. Right here next to the stove. Can you see anything?

JIM. Just a minute.

AMANDA. Isn't electricity a mysterious thing? Wasn't it Benjamin Franklin who tied a key to a kite? We live in such a mysterious universe, don't we? Some people say that science clears up all the mysteries for us. In my opinion it only creates more! Have you found it yet?

JIM. No, Ma'am. All these fuses look okay to me.

AMANDA. Tom!

TOM. Yes, Mother?

AMANDA. That light bill I gave you several days ago. The one I told you we got the notices about?

[LEGEND: "HA!"]

TOM. Oh.—Yeah.

AMANDA. You didn't neglect to pay it by any chance?

TOM. Why, I—

AMANDA. Didn't! I might have known it!

JIM. Shakespeare probably wrote a poem on that light bill, Mrs. Wingfield.

AMANDA. I might have known better than to trust him with it! There's such a high price for negligence in this world!

JIM. Maybe the poem will win a ten-dollar prize.

AMANDA. We'll just have to spend the remainder of the evening in the nineteenth century, before Mr. Edison made the Mazda lamp!

JIM. Candlelight is my favorite kind of light.

AMANDA. That shows you're romantic! But that's no excuse for Tom. Well, we got through dinner. Very considerate of them to let us get through dinner before they plunged us into everlasting darkness, wasn't it, Mr. O'Connor?

JIM. Ha-ha!

AMANDA. Tom, as a penalty for your carelessness you can help me with the dishes.

JIM. Let me give you a hand.

AMANDA. Indeed you will not!

JIM. I ought to be good for something.

AMANDA. Good for something? [*Her tone is rhapsodic*] You? Why, Mr. O'Connor, nobody, *nobody's* given me this much entertainment in years—as you have!

JIM. Aw, now, Mrs. Wingfield!

AMANDA. I'm not exaggerating, not one bit! But Sister is all by her lonesome. You go keep her company in the parlor! I'll give you this lovely old candelabrum that used to be on the altar at the church of the Heavenly Rest. It was melted a little out of shape when the church burnt down. Lightning struck it one spring. Gypsy Jones was holding a revival at the time and he intimated that the church was destroyed because the Episcopalians gave card parties.

JIM. Ha-ha.

AMANDA. And how about you coaxing Sister to drink a little wine? I think it would be good for her! Can you carry both at once?

JIM. Sure. I'm Superman!

AMANDA. Now, Thomas, get into this apron!

[*The door of kitchenette swings closed on* AMANDA's *gay laughter; the flickering light approaches the portieres.*

[LAURA *sits up nervously as he enters. Her speech at first is low and breathless from the almost intolerable strain of being alone with a stranger.*

[THE LEGEND: "I DON'T SUPPOSE YOU REMEMBER ME AT ALL!"

[*In her first speeches in this scene, before* JIM's *warmth overcomes her paralyzing shyness,* LAURA's *voice is thin and breathless as though she has just run up a steep flight of stairs.* JIM's *attitude is gently humorous. In playing this scene it should be stressed that while the incident is apparently unimportant, it is to* LAURA *the climax of her secret life.*]

JIM. Hello, there, Laura.

LAURA [*faintly*]. Hello. [*She clears her throat.*]

JIM. How are you feeling now? Better?

LAURA. Yes. Yes, thank you.

JIM. This is for you. A little dandelion wine.

[*He extends it toward her with extravagant gallantry.*]

LAURA. Thank you.

JIM. Drink it—but don't get drunk!

[*He laughs heartily.* LAURA *takes the glass uncertainly; laughs shyly.*]

Where shall I set the candles?

LAURA. Oh—oh, anywhere . . .

JIM. How about here on the floor? Any objections?

LAURA. No.

JIM. I'll spread a newspaper under to catch the drippings. I like to sit on the floor. Mind if I do?

LAURA. Oh, no.

JIM. Give me a pillow?

LAURA. What?

JIM. A pillow!

LAURA. Oh . . . [*Hands him one quickly.*]

JIM. How about you? Don't you like to sit on the floor?

LAURA. Oh—yes.

JIM. Why don't you, then?

LAURA. I—will.

JIM. Take a pillow!

[LAURA *does. Sits on the other side of the candelabrum.* JIM *crosses his legs and smiles engagingly at her.*]

I can't hardly see you sitting way over there.

LAURA. I can—see you.

JIM. I know, but that's not fair, I'm in the limelight.

[LAURA *moves her pillow closer.*]

Good! Now I can see you! Comfortable?

LAURA. Yes.

JIM. So am I. Comfortable as a cow! Will you have some gum?

LAURA. No, thank you.

JIM. I think that I will indulge, with your permission. [*Musingly unwraps it and holds it up.*] Think of the fortune made by the guy that invented the first piece of chewing gum. Amazing, huh? The Wrigley Building is one of the sights of Chicago.—I saw it summer before last when I went up to the Century of Progress. Did you take in the Century of Progress?

LAURA. No, I didn't.

JIM. Well, it was quite a wonderful exposition. What impressed me most was the Hall of Science. Gives you an idea of what the future will be in America, even more wonderful than the present time is! [*Pause. Smiling at her*] Your brother tells me you're shy. Is that right, Laura?

LAURA. I—don't know.

JIM. I judge you to be an old-fashioned type of girl. Well, I think that's a pretty good type to be. Hope you don't think I'm being too personal—do you?

LAURA [*hastily, out of embarrassment*].   I believe I *will* take a piece of gum, if you—don't mind. [*Clearing her throat*] Mr. O'Connor, have you—kept up with your singing?

JIM.   Singing? Me?

LAURA.   Yes. I remember what a beautiful voice you had.

JIM.   When did you hear me sing?

[VOICE OFF STAGE IN THE PAUSE]

VOICE [*off stage*].

> O blow, ye winds, heigh-ho,
> A-roving I will go!
>   I'm off to my love
>   With a boxing glove—
> Ten thousand miles away!

JIM.   You say you've heard me sing?

LAURA.   Oh, yes! Yes, very often . . . I—don't suppose—you remember me—at all?

JIM [*smiling doubtfully*].   You know I have an idea I've seen you before. I had that idea soon as you opened the door. It seemed almost like I was about to remember your name. But the name that I started to call you—wasn't a name! And so I stopped myself before I said it.

LAURA.   Wasn't it—Blue Roses?

JIM [*springs up. Grinning*].   Blue Roses!—My gosh, yes—Blue Roses!

That's what I had on my tongue when you opened the door!

Isn't it funny what tricks your memory plays? I didn't connect you with high school somehow or other.

But that's where it was; it was high school. I didn't even know you were Shakespeare's sister!

Gosh, I'm sorry.

LAURA.   I didn't expect you to. You—barely knew me!

JIM.   But we did have a speaking acquaintance, huh?

LAURA.   Yes, we—spoke to each other.

JIM.   When did you recognize me?

LAURA.   Oh, right away!

JIM.   Soon as I came in the door?

LAURA.   When I heard your name I thought it was probably you. I knew that Tom used to know you a little in high school. So when you came in the door— Well, then I was—sure.

JIM.   Why didn't you *say* something, then?

LAURA [*breathlessly*].   I didn't know what to say, I was—too surprised!

JIM.   For goodness' sakes! You know, this sure is funny!

LAURA.   Yes! Yes, isn't it, though . . .

JIM. Didn't we have a class in something together?

LAURA. Yes, we did.

JIM. What class was that?

LAURA. It was—singing—Chorus!

JIM. Aw!

LAURA. I sat across the aisle from you in the Aud.

JIM. Aw.

LAURA. Mondays, Wednesdays and Fridays.

JIM. Now I remember—you always came in late.

LAURA. Yes, it was so hard for me, getting upstairs. I had that brace on my leg—it clumped so loud!

JIM. I never heard any clumping.

LAURA [wincing at the recollection]. To me it sounded like—thunder!

JIM. Well, well, well, I never even noticed.

LAURA. And everybody was seated before I came in. I had to walk in front of all those people. My seat was in the back row. I had to go clumping all the way up the aisle with everyone watching!

JIM. You shouldn't have been self-conscious.

LAURA. I know, but I was. It was always such a relief when the singing started.

JIM. Aw, yes, I've placed *you* now! I used to call you Blue Roses. How was it that I got started calling you that?

LAURA. I was out of school a little while with pleurosis. When I came back you asked me what was the matter. I said I had pleurosis— you thought I said Blue Roses. That's what you always called me after that!

JIM. I hope you didn't mind.

LAURA. Oh, no—I liked it. You see, I wasn't acquainted with many— people. . . .

JIM. As I remember you sort of stuck by yourself.

LAURA. I—I—never have had much luck at—making friends.

JIM. I don't see why you wouldn't.

LAURA. Well, I—started out badly.

JIM. You mean being—

LAURA. Yes, it sort of—stood between me—

JIM. You shouldn't have let it!

LAURA. I know, but it did, and—

JIM. You were shy with people!

LAURA. I tried not to be but never could—

JIM. Overcome it?

LAURA. No, I—I never could!

JIM. I guess being shy is something you have to work out of kind of gradually.

LAURA [sorrowfully]. Yes—I guess it—

JIM. Takes time!

LAURA. Yes—

JIM. People are not so dreadful when you know them. That's what you have to remember! And everybody has problems, not just you, but practically everybody has got some problems.

You think of yourself as having the only problems, as being the only one who is disappointed. But just look around you and you will see lots of people as disappointed as you are. For instance, I hoped when I was going to high school that I would be further along at this time, six years later, than I am now— You remember that wonderful write-up I had in *The Torch*?

LAURA. Yes! [*She rises and crosses to table.*]

JIM. It said I was bound to succeed in anything I went into!

[LAURA *returns with the annual.*]

Holy Jeez! *The Torch!*

[*He accepts it reverently. They smile across it with mutual wonder.* LAURA *crouches beside him and they begin to turn through it.* LAURA's *shyness is dissolving in his warmth.*]

LAURA. Here you are in *The Pirates of Penzance!*

JIM [*wistfully*]. I sang the baritone lead in that operetta.

LAURA [*raptly*]. So—*beautifully!*

JIM [*protesting*]. Aw—

LAURA. Yes, yes—beautifully—beautifully!

JIM. You heard me?

LAURA. All three times!

JIM. No!

LAURA. Yes!

JIM. All three performances?

LAURA [*looking down*]. Yes.

JIM. Why?

LAURA. I—wanted to ask you to—autograph my program.

JIM. Why didn't you ask me to?

LAURA. You were always surrounded by your own friends so much that I never had a chance to.

JIM. You should have just—

LAURA. Well, I—thought you might think I was—

JIM. Thought I might think you was—what?

LAURA. Oh—

JIM [*with reflective relish*]. I was beleaguered by females in those days.

LAURA. You were terribly popular!

JIM. Yeah—

LAURA. You had such a—friendly way—

JIM. I was spoiled in high school.
LAURA. Everybody—liked you!
JIM. Including you?
LAURA. I—yes, I—I did, too—

[*She gently closes the book in her lap.*]

JIM. Well, well, well!—Give me that program, Laura.

[*She hands it to him. He signs it with a flourish.*]

There you are—better late than never!
LAURA. Oh, I—what a—surprise!
JIM. My signature isn't worth very much right now.
But some day—maybe—it will increase in value!
Being disappointed is one thing and being discouraged is something
else. I am disappointed but I am not discouraged.
I'm twenty-three years old.
How old are you?
LAURA. I'll be twenty-four in June.
JIM. That's not old age!
LAURA. No, but—
JIM. You finished high school?
LAURA [*with difficulty*]. I didn't go back.
JIM. You mean you dropped out?
LAURA. I made bad grades in my final examinations.

[*She rises and replaces the book and the program. Her voice
strained*]

How is—Emily Meisenbach getting along?
JIM. Oh, that kraut-head!
LAURA. Why do you call her that?
JIM. That's what she was.
LAURA. You're not still—going with her?
JIM. I never see her.
LAURA. It said in the Personal Section that you were—engaged!
JIM. I know, but I wasn't impressed by that—propaganda!
LAURA. It wasn't—the truth?
JIM. Only in Emily's optimistic opinion!
LAURA. Oh—

[LEGEND: "WHAT HAVE YOU DONE SINCE HIGH SCHOOL?"]

[JIM *lights a cigarette and leans indolently back on his elbows smiling at* LAURA *with a warmth and charm which lights her inwardly
with altar candles. She remains by the table and turns in her hands
a piece of glass to cover her tumult.*]

JIM [*after several reflective puffs on a cigarette*]. What have you done since high school? [*She seems not to hear him.*] Huh?

[LAURA *looks up.*]

I said what have you done since high school, Laura?

LAURA. Nothing much.

JIM. You must have been doing something these six long years.

LAURA. Yes.

JIM. Well, then, such as what?

LAURA. I took a business course at business college—

JIM. How did that work out?

LAURA. Well, not very—well—I had to drop out, it gave me—indigestion—

[JIM *laughs gently.*]

JIM. What are you doing now?

LAURA. I don't do anything—much. Oh, please don't think I sit around doing nothing! My glass collection takes up a good deal of time. Glass is something you have to take good care of.

JIM. What did you say—about glass?

LAURA. Collection I said—I have one—

[*She clears her throat and turns away again, acutely shy.*]

JIM [*abruptly*]. You know what I judge to be the trouble with you? Inferiority complex! Know what that is? That's what they call it when someone low-rates himself!

I understand it because I had it, too. Although my case was not so aggravated as yours seems to be. I had it until I took up public speaking, developed my voice, and learned that I had an aptitude for science. Before that time I never thought of myself as being outstanding in any way whatsoever!

Now I've never made a regular study of it, but I have a friend who says I can analyze people better than doctors that make a profession of it. I don't claim that to be necessarily true, but I can sure guess a person's psychology, Laura!

[*Takes out his gum*]

Excuse me, Laura. I always take it out when the flavor is gone. I'll use this scrap of paper to wrap it in. I know how it is to get it stuck on a shoe.

Yep—that's what I judge to be your principal trouble. A lack of confidence in yourself as a person. You don't have the proper amount of faith in yourself. I'm basing that fact on a number of your remarks and also on certain observations I've made. For instance that clumping you thought was so awful in high school. You say that you even dreaded to walk into class. You see what you did? You dropped out of school, you gave up an education because of a clump, which as far as I know was practically nonexistent! A little physical defect is what you have. Hardly noticeable even! Magnified thousands of times by imagination!

You know what my strong advice to you is? Think of yourself as *superior* in some way!

LAURA. In what way would I think?

JIM. Why, man alive, Laura! Just look about you a little. What do you see? A world full of common people! All of 'em born and all of 'em going to die!

Which of them has one-tenth of your good points! Or mine! Or anyone else's, as far as that goes—Gosh!

Everybody excels in some one thing. Some in many!

[*Unconsciously glances at himself in the mirror.*]

All you've got to do is discover in *what!* Take me, for instance.

[*He adjusts his tie at the mirror.*]

My interest happens to lie in electro-dynamics. I'm taking a course in radio engineering at night school, Laura, on top of a fairly responsible job at the warehouse. I'm taking that course and studying public speaking.

LAURA. Ohhhh.

JIM. Because I believe in the future of television!

[*Turning back to her*]

I wish to be ready to go up right along with it. Therefore I'm planning to get in on the ground floor. In fact I've already made the right connections and all that remains is for the industry itself to get under way! Full steam—

[*His eyes are starry.*]

Knowledge—Zzzzzp! Money—Zzzzzzp!—*Power!* That's the cycle democracy is built on!

[*His attitude is convincingly dynamic.* LAURA *stares at him, even her shyness eclipsed in her absolute wonder. He suddenly grins.*]

I guess you think I think a lot of myself!

LAURA. No—o-o-o, I—

JIM. Now how about you? Isn't there something you take more interest in than anything else?

LAURA. Well, I do—as I said—have my—glass collection—

[*A peal of girlish laughter from the kitchen.*]

JIM. I'm not right sure I know what you're talking about. What kind of glass is it?

LAURA. Little articles of it, they're ornaments mostly!

Most of them are little animals made out of glass, the tiniest little animals in the world. Mother calls them a glass menagerie! Here's an example of one, if you'd like to see it! This one is one of the oldest. It's nearly thirteen.

[MUSIC: "THE GLASS MENAGERIE."

[*He stretches out his hand.*]

Oh, be careful—if you breathe, it breaks!

JIM. I'd better not take it. I'm pretty clumsy with things.

LAURA. Go on, I trust you with him!

[*Places it in his palm.*]

There now—you're holding him gently! Hold him over the light, he loves the light! You see how the light shines through him?

JIM. It sure does shine!

LAURA. I shouldn't be partial, but he is my favorite one.

JIM. What kind of a thing is this one supposed to be?

LAURA. Haven't you noticed the single horn on his forehead?

JIM. A unicorn, huh?

LAURA. Mmm-hmmm!

JIM. Unicorns, aren't they extinct in the modern world?

LAURA. I know!

JIM. Poor little fellow, he must feel sort of lonesome.

LAURA [*smiling*]. Well, if he does he doesn't complain about it. He stays on a shelf with some horses that don't have horns and all of them seem to get along nicely together.

JIM. How do you know?

LAURA [*lightly*]. I haven't heard any arguments among them!

JIM [*grinning*]. No arguments, huh? Well, that's a pretty good sign! Where shall I set him?

LAURA. Put him on the table. They all like a change of scenery once in a while!

JIM [*stretching*]. Well, well, well, well—
Look how big my shadow is when I stretch!

LAURA. Oh, oh, yes—it stretches across the ceiling!

JIM [*crossing to door*]. I think it's stopped raining. [*Opens fire-escape door.*] Where does the music come from?

LAURA. From the Paradise Dance Hall across the alley.

JIM. How about cutting the rug a little, Miss Wingfield?

LAURA. Oh, I—

JIM. Or is your program filled up? Let me have a look at it. [*Grasps imaginary card*] Why, every dance is taken! I'll just have to scratch some out.

[WALTZ MUSIC: "LA GOLONDRINA."]

Ahhh, a waltz! [*He executes some sweeping turns by himself then holds his arm toward* LAURA.]

LAURA [*breathlessly*]. I—can't dance!

JIM. There you go, that inferiority stuff!

LAURA. I've never danced in my life!

JIM. Come on, try!

LAURA. Oh, but I'd step on you!

JIM. I'm not made out of glass.

LAURA. How—how—how do we start?

JIM. Just leave it to me. You hold your arms out a little.

LAURA. Like this?

JIM. A little bit higher. Right. Now don't tighten up, that's the main thing about it—relax.

LAURA [*laughing breathlessly*]. It's hard not to.

JIM. Okay.

LAURA. I'm afraid you can't budge me.

JIM. What do you bet I can't?

[*He swings her into motion.*]

LAURA. Goodness, yes, you can!

JIM. Let yourself go, now, Laura, just let yourself go.

LAURA. I'm—

JIM. Come on!

LAURA. Trying!

JIM. Not so stiff— Easy does it!

LAURA. I know but I'm—

JIM. Loosen th' backbone! There now, that's a lot better.

LAURA. Am I?

JIM. Lots, lots better!

[*He moves her about the room in a clumsy waltz.*]

LAURA. Oh, my!

JIM. Ha-ha!

LAURA. Oh, my goodness!

JIM. Ha-ha-ha!

[*They suddenly bump into the table.* JIM *stops.*]

What did we hit on?

LAURA. Table.

JIM. Did something fall off it? I think—

LAURA. Yes.

JIM. I hope that it wasn't the little glass horse with the horn!

LAURA. Yes.

JIM. Aw, aw, aw. Is it broken?

LAURA. Now it is just like all the other horses.

JIM. It's lost its—

LAURA. Horn!

It doesn't matter. Maybe it's a blessing in disguise.

JIM. You'll never forgive me. I bet that that was your favorite piece of glass.

LAURA. I don't have favorites much. It's no tragedy, Freckles. Glass breaks so easily. No matter how careful you are. The traffic jars the shelves and things fall off them.

JIM. Still I'm awfully sorry that I was the cause.

LAURA [*smiling*]. I'll just imagine he had an operation. The horn was removed to make him feel less—freakish!

[*They both laugh.*]

Now he will feel more at home with the other horses, the ones that don't have horns . . .

JIM. Ha-ha, that's very funny! [*Suddenly serious*] I'm glad to see that you have a sense of humor.

You know—you're—well—very different! Surprisingly different from anyone else I know!

[*His voice becomes soft and hesitant with a genuine feeling.*]

Do you mind me telling you that?

[LAURA *is abashed beyond speech.*]

I mean it in a nice way . . .

[LAURA *nods shyly, looking away.*]

You make me feel sort of—I don't know how to put it! I'm usually pretty good at expressing things, but— This is something that I don't know how to say!

[LAURA *touches her throat and clears it—turns the broken unicorn in her hands. Even softer*]

Has anyone ever told you that you were pretty?

[PAUSE: MUSIC.

[LAURA *looks up slowly, with wonder, and shakes her head.*]

Well, you are! In a very different way from anyone else. And all the nicer because of the difference, too.

[*His voice becomes low and husky.* LAURA *turns away, nearly faint with the novelty of her emotions.*]

I wish that you were my sister. I'd teach you to have some confidence in yourself. The different people are not like other people, but being different is nothing to be ashamed of. Because other people are not such wonderful people. They're one hundred times one thousand. You're one times one! They walk all over the earth. You just stay here. They're common as—weeds, but—you—well, you're—*Blue Roses!*

[IMAGE ON SCREEN: BLUE ROSES.

[MUSIC CHANGES.

LAURA. But blue is wrong for—roses . . .
JIM. It's right for you!—You're—pretty!
LAURA. In what respect am I pretty?
JIM. In all respects—believe me! Your eyes—your hair—are pretty! Your hands are pretty!

[*He catches hold of her hand.*]

You think I'm making this up because I'm invited to dinner and have to be nice. Oh, I could do that! I could put on an act for you, Laura, and say lots of things without being very sincere. But this time I am. I'm talking to you sincerely. I happened to notice you had this inferiority complex that keeps you from feeling comfortable with people. Somebody needs to build your confidence up and make you proud instead of shy and turning away and—blushing—
Somebody—ought to—
Ought to—*kiss* you, Laura!

[*His hand slips slowly up her arm to her shoulder.*

[MUSIC SWELLS TUMULTUOUSLY.

[*He suddenly turns her about and kisses her on the lips. When he releases her,* LAURA *sinks on the sofa with a bright, dazed look.* JIM *backs away and fishes in his pocket for a cigarette.*

[LEGEND ON SCREEN: "SOUVENIR."]

Stumble-john!

[*He lights the cigarette, avoiding her look. There is a peal of girlish laughter from* AMANDA *in the kitchen.* LAURA *slowly raises and opens her hand. It still contains the little broken glass animal. She looks at it with a tender, bewildered expression.*]

Stumble-john!
I shouldn't have done that— That was way off the beam.
You don't smoke, do you?

[*She looks up, smiling, not hearing the question. He sits beside her a little gingerly. She looks at him speechlessly—waiting. He coughs decorously and moves a little farther aside as he considers the situation and senses her feelings, dimly, with perturbation. Gently*]

Would you—care for a—mint?

[*She doesn't seem to hear him but her look grows brighter even.*]

Peppermint—Life-Saver? My pocket's a regular drug store—wherever I go . . .

[*He pops a mint in his mouth. Then gulps and decides to make a clean breast of it. He speaks slowly and gingerly.*]

Laura, you know, if I had a sister like you, I'd do the same thing as Tom. I'd bring out fellows and—introduce her to them. The right type of boys of a type to—appreciate her.
Only—well—he made a mistake about me.
Maybe I've got no call to be saying this. That may not have been the idea in having me over. But what if it was?
There's nothing wrong about that. The only trouble is that in my case —I'm not in a situation to—do the right thing.
I can't take down your number and say I'll phone.
I can't call up next week and—ask for a date.
I thought I had better explain the situation in case you—misunderstood it and—hurt your feelings. . . .

[*Pause. Slowly, very slowly,* LAURA's *look changes, her eyes returning slowly from his to the ornament in her palm.* AMANDA *utters another gay laugh in the kitchen.*]

LAURA [*faintly*]. You—won't—call again?
JIM. No, Laura, I can't.

[*He rises from the sofa.*]

As I was just explaining, I've—got strings on me.
Laura, I've—been going steady!
I go out all of the time with a girl named Betty. She's a home-girl like you, and Catholic, and Irish, and in a great many ways we—get along fine.

I met her last summer on a moonlight boat trip up the river to Alton, on the *Majestic*.

Well—right away from the start it was—love!

[LEGEND: LOVE!]

[LAURA *sways slightly forward and grips the arm of the sofa. He fails to notice, now enrapt in his own comfortable being.*]

Being in love has made a new man of me!

[*Leaning stiffly forward, clutching the arm of the sofa,* LAURA *struggles visibly with her storm. But* JIM *is oblivious, she is a long way off.*]

The power of love is really pretty tremendous! Love is something that— changes the whole world, Laura!

[*The storm abates a little and* LAURA *leans back. He notices her again.*]

It happened that Betty's aunt took sick, she got a wire and had to go to Centralia. So Tom—when he asked me to dinner—I naturally just accepted the invitation, not knowing that you—that he—that I—

[*He stops awkwardly.*]

Huh—I'm a stumble-john!

[*He flops back on the sofa. The holy candles in the altar of* LAURA'S *face have been snuffed out. There is a look of almost infinite desolation.* JIM *glances at her uneasily.*]

I wish that you would—say something.

[*She bites her lip which was trembling and then bravely smiles. She opens her hand again on the broken glass ornament. Then she gently takes his hand and raises it level with her own. She carefully places the unicorn in the palm of his hand, then pushes his fingers closed upon it.*]

What are you—doing that for? You want me to have him?—Laura?
[*She nods.*] What for?

LAURA. A—souvenir . . .

[*She rises unsteadily and crouches beside the victrola to wind it up.*

[LEGEND ON SCREEN: "THINGS HAVE A WAY
OF TURNING OUT SO BADLY!"]

[OR IMAGE: "GENTLEMAN CALLER WAVING GOOD-BYE!—GAILY"]

[*At this moment* AMANDA *rushes brightly back in the front room. She bears a pitcher of fruit punch in an old-fashioned cut-glass pitcher and a plate of macaroons. The plate has a gold border and poppies painted on it.*]

AMANDA.   Well, well, well! Isn't the air delightful after the shower? I've made you children a little liquid refreshment.

[*Turns gaily to the gentleman caller*]

Jim, do you know that song about lemonade?

> "Lemonade, lemonade
> Made in the shade and stirred with a spade—
> Good enough for any old maid!"

JIM [*uneasily*].   Ha-ha! No—I never heard it.
AMANDA.   Why, Laura! You look so serious!
JIM.   We were having a serious conversation.
AMANDA.   Good! Now you're better acquainted!
JIM [*uncertainly*].   Ha-ha! Yes.
AMANDA.   You modern young people are much more serious-minded than my generation. I was so gay as a girl!
JIM.   You haven't changed, Mrs. Wingfield.
AMANDA.   Tonight I'm rejuvenated! The gaiety of the occasion, Mr. O'Connor!

[*She tosses her head with a peal of laughter. Spills lemonade*]

Oooo! I'm baptizing myself!
JIM.   Here—let me—
AMANDA [*setting the pitcher down*].   There now. I discovered we had some maraschino cherries. I dumped them in, juice and all!
JIM.   You shouldn't have gone to that trouble, Mrs. Wingfield.
AMANDA.   Trouble, trouble? Why, it was loads of fun!
Didn't you hear me cutting up in the kitchen? I bet your ears were burning! I told Tom how outdone with him I was for keeping you to himself so long a time! He should have brought you over much, much sooner! Well, now that you've found your way, I want you to be a very frequent caller! Not just occasional but all the time.
Oh, we're going to have a lot of gay times together! I see them coming!
Mmm, just breathe that air! So fresh, and the moon's so pretty!
I'll skip back out—I know where my place is when young folks are having a—serious conversation!
JIM.   Oh, don't go out, Mrs. Wingfield. The fact of the matter is I've got to be going.

AMANDA. Going, now? You're joking! Why, it's only the shank of the evening, Mr. O'Connor!

JIM. Well, you know how it is.

AMANDA. You mean you're a young workingman and have to keep workingmen's hours. We'll let you off early tonight. But only on the condition that next time you stay later. What's the best night for you? Isn't Saturday night the best night for you workingmen?

JIM. I have a couple of time-clocks to punch, Mrs. Wingfield. One at morning, another one at night!

AMANDA. My, but you *are* ambitious! You work at night, too?

JIM. No, Ma'am, not work but—Betty!

[*He crosses deliberately to pick up his hat. The band at the Paradise Dance Hall goes into a tender waltz.*]

AMANDA. Betty? Betty? Who's—Betty!

[*There is an ominous cracking sound in the sky.*]

JIM. Oh, just a girl. The girl I go steady with!

[*He smiles charmingly. The sky falls.*

[LEGEND: "THE SKY FALLS."]

AMANDA [*a long-drawn exhalation*]. Ohhhh . . . Is it a serious romance, Mr. O'Connor?

JIM. We're going to be married the second Sunday in June.

AMANDA. Ohhhh—how nice! Tom didn't mention that you were engaged to be married.

JIM. The cat's not out of the bag at the warehouse yet. You know how they are. They call you Romeo and stuff like that.

[*He stops at the oval mirror to put on his hat. He carefully shapes the brim and the crown to give a discreetly dashing effect.*]

It's been a wonderful evening, Mrs. Wingfield. I guess this is what they mean by Southern hospitality.

AMANDA. It really wasn't anything at all.

JIM. I hope it don't seem like I'm rushing off. But I promised Betty I'd pick her up at the Wabash depot, an' by the time I get my jalopy down there her train'll be in. Some women are pretty upset if you keep 'em waiting.

AMANDA. Yes, I know— The tyranny of women!

[*Extends her hand*]

Good-bye, Mr. O'Connor. I wish you luck—and happiness—and success! All three of them, and so does Laura!—Don't you, Laura?

LAURA. Yes!

JIM [*taking her hand*]. Good-bye, Laura. I'm certainly going to treasure that souvenir. And don't you forget the good advice I gave you.

[*Raises his voice to a cheery shout*]

So long, Shakespeare! Thanks again, ladies— Good night!

[*He grins and ducks jauntily out.*

[*Still bravely grimacing,* AMANDA *closes the door on the gentleman caller. Then she turns back to the room with a puzzled expression. She and* LAURA *don't dare to face each other.* LAURA *crouches beside the victrola to wind it.*]

AMANDA [*faintly*]. Things have a way of turning out so badly.
I don't believe that I would play the victrola.
Well, well—well—
Our gentleman caller was engaged to be married!
Tom!

TOM [*from back*]. Yes, Mother?

AMANDA. Come in here a minute. I want to tell you something awfully funny.

TOM [*enters with macaroon and a glass of the lemonade*]. Has the gentleman caller gotten away already?

AMANDA. The gentleman caller has made an early departure.
What a wonderful joke you played on us!

TOM. How do you mean?

AMANDA. You didn't mention that he was engaged to be married.

TOM. Jim? Engaged?

AMANDA. That's what he just informed us.

TOM. I'll be jiggered! I didn't know about that.

AMANDA. That seems very peculiar.

TOM. What's peculiar about it?

AMANDA. Didn't you call him your best friend down at the warehouse?

TOM. He is, but how did I know?

AMANDA. It seems extremely peculiar that you wouldn't know your best friend was going to be married!

TOM. The warehouse is where I work, not where I know things about people!

AMANDA. You don't know things anywhere! You live in a dream; you manufacture illusions!

[*He crosses to door.*]

Where are you going?

TOM. I'm going to the movies.

AMANDA. That's right, now that you've had us make such fools of ourselves. The effort, the preparations, all the expense! The new floor lamp, the rug, the clothes for Laura! All for what? To entertain some other girl's fiancé!

Go to the movies, go! Don't think about us, a mother deserted, an unmarried sister who's crippled and has no job! Don't let anything interfere with your selfish pleasure!

Just go, go, go—to the movies!

TOM. All right, I will! The more you shout about my selfishness to me the quicker I'll go, and I won't go to the movies!

AMANDA. Go, then! Then go to the moon—you selfish dreamer!

[TOM *smashes his glass on the floor. He plunges out on the fire-escape, slamming the door.* LAURA *screams—cut by door. Dance-hall music up.* TOM *goes to the rail and grips it desperately, lifting his face in the chill white moonlight penetrating the narrow abyss of the alley.*

[LEGEND ON SCREEN: "AND SO GOOD-BYE . . ."

[TOM's *closing speech is timed with the interior pantomime. The interior scene is played as though viewed through sound-proof glass.* AMANDA *appears to be making a comforting speech to* LAURA *who is huddled upon the sofa. Now that we cannot hear the mother's speech, her silliness is gone and she has dignity and tragic beauty.* LAURA's *dark hair hides her face until at the end of the speech she lifts it to smile at her mother.* AMANDA's *gestures are slow and graceful, almost dance-like, as she comforts the daughter. At the end of her speech she glances a moment at the father's picture—then withdraws through the portieres. At close of* TOM's *speech,* LAURA *blows out the candles, ending the play.*]

TOM. I didn't go to the moon, I went much further—for time is the longest distance between two places—

Not long after that I was fired for writing a poem on the lid of a shoe-box.

I left Saint Louis. I descended the steps of this fire-escape for a last time and followed, from then on, in my father's footsteps, attempting to find in motion what was lost in space—

I traveled around a great deal. The cities swept about me like dead leaves, leaves that were brightly colored but torn away from the branches. I would have stopped, but I was pursued by something.

It always came upon me unawares, taking me altogether by surprise. Perhaps it was a familiar bit of music. Perhaps it was only a piece of transparent glass—

Perhaps I am walking along a street at night, in some strange city, before I have found companions. I pass the lighted window of a shop where perfume is sold. The window is filled with pieces of colored glass, tiny transparent bottles in delicate colors, like bits of a shattered rainbow.

Then all at once my sister touches my shoulder. I turn around and look into her eyes . . .

Oh, Laura, Laura, I tried to leave you behind me, but I am more faithful than I intended to be!

I reach for a cigarette, I cross the street, I run into the movies or a bar, I buy a drink, I speak to the nearest stranger—anything that can blow your candles out!

[LAURA *bends over the candles.*]

—for nowadays the world is lit by lightning! Blow out your candles, Laura—and so good-bye. . . .

[*She blows the candles out.*]

THE SCENE DISSOLVES

———

Two Critical Commentaries on Tennessee Williams' *The Glass Menagerie*

Commentary by Stark Young, "The Glass Menagerie," from *The New Republic,* CXII (April 16, 1945), 505-6.*

. . . Miss Taylor's role in Mr. Williams' play is that of a frowsy, aging woman who lives with her son and daughter, in a flat off a St. Louis alley. It is a far cry from the Deep South, where her girlhood was spent and her memories dwell, and where she has refused the rich planters' sons because she lost her heart to a man who worked for the telephone company and whose smile misled everybody. The daughter is a cripple, too shy and hurt and vague ever to have got through school. She spends her time playing old phonograph records that her father had left behind when he abandoned her mother and went away for good, and collecting glass animals—hence the title of the play. The son is a failure, discontented with his job in the warehouse, vaguely itching to write poetry, and longing to roam the world. The mother worships, nags, scolds and tries to do her best by her children. Finally, when she thinks it is time her daughter got married, she plagues the son into bringing a man home with him; he brings a friend from the warehouse. The

———

* Reprinted from *Immortal Shadows* by Stark Young; copyright 1948 by Charles Scribner's Sons; used by permission of the publishers.

visitor, impressed though he is with the daughter, turns out to be in love and engaged.

In the end the son follows his father's example and goes off to make his way over the world. . . .

What Miss Laurette Taylor does with these matters can be at least partially imagined if you know the quality of her special gift. This, even after seeing the play, is almost as impossible to convey with anything like the full, wonderful truth. Hers is naturalistic acting of the most profound, spontaneous, unbroken continuity and moving life. . . .

But true as all this may be of Miss Taylor, we must not let that blind us to the case of the play itself and of the whole occasion. The play gives every one of the four characters that it presents a glowing, rich opportunity, genuine emotional motivations, a rhythm of situations that are alive, and speech that is fresh, living, abundant and free of stale theater diction. The author is not awed by the usual sterilities of our playwriting patterns. On the other hand he is too imaginative, genuine, or has too much good taste, to be coy about the free devices on which his play is built.

The Glass Menagerie appears to drag, or go slow, at times, though I am not sure about this and certainly found it less so than a number of people I have heard speak of it. These slow places occur in the Narrator portions and sometimes in the scenes between the mother and son. In my opinion this may be almost entirely due to the fact that Mr. Eddie Dowling does not let himself go enough to make you believe that he is the son of such a mother or such a father, that he longs to wander, to write poetry—I even forgot to remember what he was working at when he sat before the papers on the table, supposed, however, to be bent on a poem. . . .

To say, as Mr. Nichols does in his review in the New York *Times,* that there are such unconnected things with the story as "snatches of talk about the war, bits of psychology, occasional moments of rather florid writing" is mistaken indeed. The part Miss Taylor plays is, quite aside from her rendering of it, the best written role that I have seen in a play for years. All the language and all the motifs are free and true: I recognized them inch by inch, and I should know, for I came from the same part of the country, the same locality and life, in fact, that Mr. Williams does. Such a response and attitude as that Mr. Nichols expresses is the kind of thing that helps to tie our theater down. . . . What we need in the theater is a sense of language, a sense of texture in speech, vibration and impulse in speech. Behind the Southern speech in the mother's part is the echo of great literature, or at least a respect for it. There is the sense in it of her having been born out of a tradition, not out of a box. It has echo and the music of it. The mother's characterization is both appalling and human, cold and loving. No role could be more realistically written than this, but it has the variety, suddenness, passion and freedom, almost unconscious freedom perhaps, of true realism.

Miss Julie Haydon gave one of her translucent performances of a dreaming, wounded, half-out-of-this-world young girl. Mr. Anthony Ross, as the visitor, for whom the author has written a long and excellent scene, original and tender, with the girl, played admirably.

Mr. Jo Mielziner did the complicated setting for *The Glass Menagerie,* streets at the side, a front room, a back room, a wall shutting them off when needed. The scene is effectively ingenious. But even though the story happens in a dream and vagueness may be called for, I see no reason why the color should be so dun. . . .

In the Narrator's opening speech Mr. Williams has provided an excuse for music by saying that the play all happens in the memory and memory always seems to move in music. For *The Glass Menagerie,* therefore, Mr. Paul Bowles has written music that runs in and out of the scenes, sometimes for a long interval, sometimes less. It seems to be a special gift of his, this writing music for a play that becomes a part of the play, strangely beautiful and strangely right.

Commentary by John Gassner, from "Tennessee Williams: Dramatist of Frustration," in *College English,* X (October 1948), 5-6.*

The plays that thrust Tennessee Williams into the limelight have much in common besides their clear focus and economical construction. Both *The Glass Menagerie* and *A Streetcar Named Desire* transmute the base metal of reality into theatrical and, not infrequently, verbal poetry, and both supplement the action with symbolic elements of mood and music. A major theme is southern womanhood helpless in the grip of the presently constituted world, while its old world of social position and financial security is a Paradise Lost. But differences of emphasis and style make the two dramas distinct.

The Glass Menagerie is a memory play evoked in the comments of a narrator, the poet Tom, who is now in the merchant marine, and in crucial episodes from his family life. The form departs from the 'fourth wall' convention of realistic dramaturgy and suggests Japanese Noh-drama, in which story consists mostly of remembered fragments of experience. If Williams had had his way with the Broadway production, *The Glass Menagerie* would have struck its public as even more unconventional, since his text calls for the use of a screen on which pictures and legends are to be projected. Disregarded by the producer-director Eddie Dowling, these stage directions nevertheless appear in the published play. They strike the writer of this article as redundant and rather precious; the young playwright was straining for effect without realizing that his simple tale, so hauntingly self-sufficient, needs no adornment.

As plainly stated by Tom, the background is a crisis in society, for the depression decade is teetering on the brink of the second World War. His tale belongs to a time "when the huge middle-class of America was matriculating in a school for the blind," when "their eyes had failed them, or they had failed their eyes, and so they were having their fingers pressed forcibly down on the fiery Braille alphabet of a dissolving economy," while in Spain there was Guernica. But his memory invokes his home life and the provocations that finally sent him to sea. In episodes softened by the patina of time and

---

* Reprinted by permission of John Gassner and *College English.*

distance he recalls the painful shyness of his lovable crippled sister, Laura, and the tragicomic efforts of his mother, Amanda, to marry her off, as well as his own desperation as an underpaid shoe-company clerk. The climax comes when, nagged by the desperate mother, Tom brings Laura a 'gentleman caller' who turns out to be engaged to another girl.

Without much more story than this, Williams achieved a remarkable synthesis of sympathy and objectivity by making three-dimensional characters out of Tom's family and the gangling beau, who is trying to pull himself out of the rut of a routine position and recover his self-esteem as a schoolboy success. The carping mother could have easily become a caricature, especially when she remembers herself as a southern belle instead of a woman deserted by her husband, a telephone man who 'fell in love with long distances' but who probably found an incitement in his wife's pretensions. She is redeemed for humanity by her solicitude for her children, her laughable but touching effort to sell a magazine subscription over the telephone at dawn, and her admission that the unworldly Laura must get a husband if she is to escape the fate of 'little birdlike women without any nest' Amanda has known in the South. And Laura, too shy even to take a course in typewriting after the first lesson, acquits herself with sweet dignity and becoming stoicism when let down by her first and only gentleman caller; she is an unforgettable bit of Marie Laurencin painting. At the same time, however, Williams knows that pity for the halt and blind must not exclude a sense of reality, that Tom's going out into the world was a necessary and wholesome measure of self-preservation; it is one of humanity's inalienable traits and obligations to try to save itself as best it can. Although Tom will never forget Laura and the candles she blew out, he is now part of the larger world that must find a common salvation in action, "for nowadays the world is lit by lightning."

In *A Streetcar Named Desire,* too, health and disease are at odds with each other, but here the dialectical situation flares up into relentless conflict. The lines are sharply drawn in this more naturalistic drama, whose story, unlike that of *The Glass Menagerie,* is no longer revealed impressionistically through the merciful mist of memory. . . .

VIII. THE CRUCIBLE

An Historical Play by Arthur Miller

Introductory Note to Arthur Miller and *The Crucible*

Two postwar dramatists—Tennessee Williams and Arthur Miller—have written plays that seem likely to endure. Within a year of the same age, both of them experienced the Great Depression. Neither, because of physical disabilities, was engaged in World War II. Both men had training with competent university professors of playwriting. Their prize-winning successes and international fame as new dramatists came within the same few years. Each has written two powerful dramas of highly original dramaturgy. But there the similarity ends, and the short and tall, smooth and rugged contrasts begin: Williams from the South, a wanderer upon the earth; Miller from Brooklyn, at home in Connecticut. One a "dramatist of frustration," the other a playwright of positive protest.

Arthur Miller was born on the upper East side of New York, the Harlem section, the son of Isidore and Augusta (Barnett) Miller. The family moved to Brooklyn, where Arthur went to high school. Then he worked for two years, in an auto-parts warehouse, to save money enough to begin at the University of Michigan. There he made his own way, with an N.Y.A. Depression job and as night editor of the *Michigan Daily,* and wrote plays, studying under Kenneth T. Rowe. He won the Avery Hopwood award for playwriting in 1936 and again in 1937 for $500. In 1938 he took his A.B. degree and won the Theater Guild National Award of $1250. He then went back to New York and began writing for the Federal Theater Project, which was curtailed before his first script was produced. He turned to radio drama and wrote for Columbia Workshop and Cavalcade of America. In 1940 he married his university classmate, Mary Grace Slattery; they have two children. A high-school football injury kept him from active war service, though he worked as a steamfitter at the Brooklyn Navy Yard and wrote radio scripts and one-act plays for civilian morale. In 1942 he was called upon to gather scenario material for Ernie Pyle's *The Story of G. I. Joe.* A by-product of this was the diary of his experiences, *Situation Normal,* published in 1944. The next year appeared his novel, *Focus,* an attack upon antisemitism and racial prejudice.

With an appearance suggesting Lincoln to some, Arthur Miller is 6 ft. 2 in. tall and weighs 170 lbs. He has strong features, dark wavy hair, brown eyes. He is active as a liberal, contributing his creative efforts to labor organizations. He is a plain-living family man, is handy with tools and likes manual work, is neighborly and lives in the country. It is evident that he owes much to the dramaturgy of Ibsen, and he has confessed his debt to O'Neill and Sidney Howard.

His first play to be produced in New York was *The Man Who Had All the Luck* (1944). It closed after four performances, but was said to deserve better. Arthur Miller's second play, *All My Sons,* produced in 1947, dealt with a wartime manufacturer whose defective airplane parts cost the lives of twenty-one pilots. Acclaimed by many reviewers, it was given the Drama Critics' Circle Award and two other prizes, ran for 328 performances, with a European production scheduled at once. It was, however, considered "too liberal" for performance in the occupied countries. A film version, in 1948, featured Edward G. Robinson, Burt Lancaster, and Mady Christians. Arthur Miller's next play was *Death of a Salesman,* produced early in 1949. It depicts the tragic failure of a broken Brooklyn salesman and his two sons who lived by the wrong dreams. Written with ingenious dramaturgy and rare compassion, the play was a triumph both theatrically and critically. It was voted the Critics' Award and then the Pulitzer Prize, was performed 742 times on Broadway (with Lee Cobb). There was an excellent second company (with Thomas Mitchell) and a distinguished filming (with Frederic March). Arthur Miller's next work was an adaptation of Ibsen's *An Enemy of the People;* it ran for only 36 performances in January 1951.

The subject of the Salem witchhunt had been with Arthur Miller since college days, but he did not undertake research for a play upon it until the spring of 1952, when he drove up to study the records and relics at Salem. *The Crucible* opened in New York on January 22, 1953, with Arthur Kennedy and Beatrice Straight in the roles of John Proctor and his wife, and the venerable Walter Hampden as the Deputy-Governor Danforth. It received mixed reviews and qualified acclaim. Though it continued through the season, with 180 or so performances, it was rated a financial failure. The American Bar Association protested that it disparaged lawyers and the legal profession—which the author answered that it did not. *The Crucible* was runner-up for the Critics' Award, but was given the Antoinette Perry Award and shared the Donaldson Award for 1953. In the summer *The Crucible* was redirected by the author himself, with a less distinguished cast, the elimination of heavy scenery, and the insertion of a new scene. It played so prior to opening in Washington, D. C.

When questioned about his play before it opened, Arthur Miller said: "My play is about Salem, but that tells nothing. It's about witch hunts, yes. But that isn't what it's about. I just can't tell briefly what it's about." To another he said that he doesn't pretend to know just what a play means until perhaps a year after he has written it. "A complex play can have many themes, but I don't sit down to write a play with a specific theme worked out in my mind. What I do have in mind is a general sense of the quality I want it to have." Some months later he said of *The Crucible,* "Salem is one of the few dramas in history with a beginning, a middle, and an end. The drama is complete because the people saw the error of their ways quite soon after the tragedy occurred. . . . Today's writers describe man's helplessness and eventual defeat. In Salem you have the story of a defeat because these people were destroyed, and this makes it real today because we believe in defeat. But they understood at the same time what was happening to them. They knew why they struggled . . . they knew how to struggle . . . they did not die helplessly. The moral size of these people drew me . . . they didn't whimper."

He then said, "We should be tired by now of merely documenting the defeat of man. This play is a step toward an assertion of a positive kind of value in contemporary plays."

Miller continued about what he calls "diabolism"—the fear and hatred of opposites. "When tensions exist," he said, "this fear is organized," as it was in Salem whose people "regarded themselves as holders of a light. If this light were extinguished, they believed, the world would end." This "diabolism" has always existed in man, he feels, and we must realize that "conflict is the essence of life."

These thoughts about tension, conflict, struggle, and meaning in life—which might lead us back to the first essay in this volume—should take us directly into Arthur Miller's *The Crucible*.

THE CRUCIBLE *

A Play In Four Acts by Arthur Miller

THE CHARACTERS

JOHN PROCTOR—*a sturdy Salem farmer in his middle 30's.*
ELIZABETH PROCTOR—*his wife, a cold and righteous woman.*

ABIGAIL WILLIAMS—*orphaned niece of the minister, formerly servant girl to the Proctors.*
　MARY WARREN—*a timid girl of 17, now working for them.*
　　SUSANNA WALCOTT—*who, with* BETTY PARRIS *and* MERCY LEWIS, *comprise a group of girl friends.*

REVEREND PARRIS—*the minister of Salem church, father of*
　BETTY PARRIS—*Abigail's cousin, sick in bed, "bewitched."*
REVEREND JOHN HALE—*of nearby Beverly, an expert on witches.*

THOMAS PUTNAM—*a grasping landowner and local politician.*
　MRS. ANN PUTNAM—*his wife, convinced her infants died bewitched.*
　MERCY LEWIS—*their fat, sly servant girl of 18.*

DANFORTH—*deputy governor, in charge of the special court.*
JUDGE HATHORNE—*the Salem judge of the local court.*
CHEEVER—*court clerk;* HERRICK—*town marshal; and* HOPKINS.

REBECCA NURSE—*a respected old woman of 72 and integrity.*
　FRANCIS NURSE—*her old husband, rich in acquired land.*
　GILES COREY—*a powerful and independent old codger of 83.*
　SARAH GOOD—*a disreputable old townswoman.*

TITUBA—*a slave woman and conjurer from the Barbados.*

　Time: *in the American colonial period, 1692.*
　Place: *in and near Salem, Massachusetts.*

A NOTE ON THE HISTORICAL ACCURACY OF THIS PLAY

This play is not history in the sense in which the word is used by the academic historian. Dramatic purposes have sometimes required many characters to be fused into one; the number of girls involved in the "crying-out" has been reduced; Abigail's age has been raised; while there were several judges of almost equal authority, I have symbolized them all in Hathorne and Danforth. However, I believe that the reader will discover here the essential nature of one of the strangest and most awful chapters in human history. The fate of each character is exactly that of his historical model, and there is no one in the drama who did not play a similar—and in some cases exactly the same—role in history.

As for the characters of the persons, little is known about most of them excepting what may be surmised from a few letters, the trial record, certain broadsides written at the time, and references to their conduct in sources of varying reliability. They may therefore be taken as creations of my own, drawn to the best of my ability in conformity with their known behavior, except as indicated in the commentary I have written for this text.

A.M.

ACT ONE
(AN OVERTURE)

A SMALL UPPER BEDROOM *in the home of Reverend Samuel Parris, Salem, Massachusetts, in the spring of the year 1692.*

There is a narrow window at the left. Through its leaded panes the morning sunlight streams. A candle still burns near the bed, which is at the right. A chest, a chair, and a small table are the other furnishings. At the back a door opens on the landing of the stairway to the ground floor. The room gives off an air of clean spareness. The roof rafters are exposed, and the wood colors are raw and unmellowed.

As the curtain rises, REVEREND PARRIS *is discovered kneeling beside the bed, evidently in prayer. His daughter,* BETTY PARRIS, *aged ten, is lying on the bed, inert.*

REVEREND PARRIS *is praying now, and, though we cannot hear his words, a sense of his confusion hangs about him. He mumbles, then seems about to weep; then he weeps, then prays again; but his daughter does not stir on the bed.*

The door opens, and his Negro slave enters. TITUBA *is in her forties.* PARRIS *brought her with him from Barbados, where he spent some years as a merchant before entering the ministry. She enters as one does who can no longer bear to be barred from the sight of her beloved, but she is also very frightened because her slave sense has warned her that, as always, trouble in this house eventually lands on her back.*

TITUBA [*already taking a step backward*]. My Betty be hearty soon?
PARRIS. Out of here!
TITUBA [*backing to the door*]. My Betty not goin' die . . .
PARRIS [*scrambling to his feet in a fury*]. Out of my sight!
[*She is gone.*]

Out of my—[*He is overcome with sobs. He clamps his teeth against them and closes the door and leans against it, exhausted.*] Oh, my God!

God help me! [*Quaking with fear, mumbling to himself through his sobs, he goes to the bed and gently takes* BETTY's *hand.*] Betty. Child. Dear child. Will you wake, will you open up your eyes! Betty, little one . . .

[*He is bending to kneel again when his niece,* ABIGAIL WILLIAMS, *seventeen, enters—a strikingly beautiful girl, an orphan, with an endless capacity for dissembling. Now she is all worry and apprehension and propriety.*]

ABIGAIL. Uncle? [*He looks to her.*] Susanna Walcott's here from Doctor Griggs.

PARRIS. Oh? Let her come, let her come.

ABIGAIL [*leaning out the door to call to* SUSANNA, *who is down the hall a few steps*]. Come in, Susanna.

[SUSANNA WALCOTT, *a little younger than* ABIGAIL, *a nervous, hurried girl, enters.*]

PARRIS [*eagerly*]. What does the doctor say, child?

SUSANNA [*craning around* PARRIS *to get a look at* BETTY]. He bid me come and tell you, reverend sir, that he cannot discover no medicine for it in his books.

PARRIS. Then he must search on.

SUSANNA. Aye, sir, he have been searchin' his books since he left you, sir. But he bid me tell you, that you might look to unnatural things for the cause of it.

PARRIS [*his eyes going wide*]. No—no. There be no unnatural cause here. Tell him I have sent for Reverend Hale of Beverly, and Mr. Hale will surely confirm that. Let him look to medicine and put out all thought of unnatural causes here. There be none.

SUSANNA. Aye, sir. He bid me tell you. [*She turns to go.*]

ABIGAIL. Speak nothin' of it in the village, Susanna.

PARRIS. Go directly home and speak nothing of unnatural causes.

SUSANNA. Aye, sir. I pray for her.

[*She goes out.*]

ABIGAIL. Uncle, the rumor of witchcraft is all about; I think you'd best go down and deny it yourself. The parlor's packed with people, sir. I'll sit with her.

PARRIS [*pressed, turns on her*]. And what shall I say to them? That my daughter and my niece I discovered dancing like heathen in the forest?

ABIGAIL. Uncle, we did dance; let you tell them I confessed it—and I'll be whipped if I must be. But they're speakin' of witchcraft. Betty's not witched.

PARRIS. Abigail, I cannot go before the congregation when I know you have not opened with me. What did you do with her in the forest?

ABIGAIL. We did dance, uncle, and when you leaped out of the bush so suddenly, Betty was frightened and then she fainted. And there's the whole of it.

PARRIS. Child. Sit you down.

ABIGAIL [*quavering, as she sits*]. I would never hurt Betty. I love her dearly.

PARRIS. Now look you, child, your punishment will come in its time. But if you trafficked with spirits in the forest I must know it now, for surely my enemies will, and they will ruin me with it.

ABIGAIL. But we never conjured spirits.

PARRIS. Then why can she not move herself since midnight? This child is desperate! [ABIGAIL *lowers her eyes.*] It must come out—my enemies will bring it out. Let me know what you done there. Abigail, do you understand that I have many enemies?

ABIGAIL. I have heard of it, uncle.

PARRIS. There is a faction that is sworn to drive me from my pulpit. Do you understand that?

ABIGAIL. I think so, sir.

PARRIS. Now then, in the midst of such disruption, my own household is discovered to be the very center of some obscene practice. Abominations are done in the forest—

ABIGAIL. It were sport, uncle!

PARRIS [*pointing at* BETTY]. You call this sport? [*She lowers her eyes. He pleads*] Abigail, if you know something that may help the doctor, for God's sake tell it to me. [*She is silent.*] I saw Tituba waving her arms over the fire when I came on you. Why was she doing that? And I heard a screeching and gibberish coming from her mouth. She were swaying like a dumb beast over that fire!

ABIGAIL. She always sings her Barbados songs, and we dance.

PARRIS. I cannot blink what I saw, Abigail, for my enemies will not blink it. I saw a dress lying on the grass.

ABIGAIL [*innocently*]. A dress?

PARRIS [*it is very hard to say*]. Aye, a dress. And I thought I saw—someone naked running through the trees!

ABIGAIL [*in terror*]. No one was naked! You mistake yourself, uncle!

PARRIS [*with anger*]. I saw it! [*He moves from her. Then, resolved*] Now tell me true, Abigail. And I pray you feel the weight of truth upon you, for now my ministry's at stake, my ministry and perhaps your cousin's life. Whatever abomination you have done, give me all of it now, for I dare not be taken unaware when I go before them down there.

ABIGAIL. There is nothin' more. I swear it, uncle.

PARRIS [*studies her, then nods, half convinced*]. Abigail, I have fought here three long years to bend these stiff-necked people to me, and now, just when some good respect is rising for me in the parish, you compromise my very character. I have given you a home, child, I have put clothes upon your back—now give me upright answer. Your name in the town—it is entirely white, is it not?

ABIGAIL [*with an edge of resentment*]. Why, I am sure it is, sir. There be no blush about my name.

PARRIS [*to the point*]. Abigail, is there any other cause than you have told me, for your being discharged from Goody Proctor's service? I have heard it said, and I tell you as I heard it, that she comes so rarely to the church this year for she will not sit so close to something soiled. What signified that remark?

ABIGAIL. She hates me, uncle, she must, for I would not be her slave. It's a bitter woman, a lying, cold, sniveling woman, and I will not work for such a woman!

PARRIS. She may be. And yet it has troubled me that you are now seven month out of their house, and in all this time no other family has ever called for your service.

ABIGAIL. They want slaves, not such as I. Let them send to Barbados for that. I will not black my face for any of them! [*With ill-concealed resentment at him*] Do you begrudge my bed, uncle?

PARRIS. No—no.

ABIGAIL [*in a temper*]. My name is good in the village! I will not have it said my name is soiled! Goody Proctor is a gossiping liar!

[*Enter* MRS. ANN PUTNAM. *She is a twisted soul of forty-five, a death-ridden woman, haunted by dreams.*]

PARRIS [*as soon as the door begins to open*]. No—no, I cannot have anyone. [*He sees her, and a certain deference springs into him, although his worry remains.*] Why, Goody Putnam, come in.

MRS. PUTNAM [*full of breath, shiny-eyed*]. It is a marvel. It is surely a stroke of hell upon you.

PARRIS. No, Goody Putnam, it is—

MRS. PUTNAM [*glancing at* BETTY]. How high did she fly, how high?

PARRIS. No, no, she never flew—

MRS. PUTNAM [*very pleased with it*]. Why, it's sure she did. Mr. Collins saw her goin' over Ingersoll's barn, and come down light as bird, he says!

PARRIS. Now, look you, Goody Putnam, she never—

[*Enter* THOMAS PUTNAM, *a well-to-do, hard-handed landowner, near fifty.*]

Oh, good morning, Mr. Putnam.

PUTNAM. It is a providence the thing is out now! It is a providence.

[*He goes directly to the bed.*]

PARRIS. What's out, sir, what's—?

[MRS. PUTNAM *goes to the bed.*]

PUTNAM [*looking down at* BETTY]. Why, *her* eyes is closed! Look you, Ann.

MRS. PUTNAM. Why, that's strange. [*To* PARRIS] Ours is open.

PARRIS [*shocked*]. Your Ruth is sick?

MRS. PUTNAM [*with vicious certainty*]. I'd not call it sick; the Devil's touch is heavier than sick. It's death, y'know, it's death drivin' into them, forked and hoofed.

PARRIS. Oh, pray not! Why, how does Ruth ail?

MRS. PUTNAM. She ails as she must—she never waked this morning, but her eyes open and she walks, and hears naught, sees naught, and cannot eat. Her soul is taken, surely.

[PARRIS *is struck.*]

PUTNAM [*as though for further details*]. They say you've sent for Reverend Hale of Beverly?

PARRIS [*with dwindling conviction now*]. A precaution only. He has much experience in all demonic arts, and I—

MRS. PUTNAM. He has indeed; and found a witch in Beverly last year, and let you remember that.

PARRIS. Now, Goody Ann, they only thought that were a witch, and I am certain there be no element of witchcraft here.

PUTNAM. No witchcraft! Now look you, Mr. Parris—

PARRIS. Thomas, Thomas, I pray you, leap not to witchcraft. I know that you—you least of all, Thomas, would ever wish so disastrous a charge laid upon me. We cannot leap to witchcraft. They will howl me out of Salem for such corruption in my house.

PUTNAM [*at the moment he is intent upon getting* PARRIS, *for whom he has only contempt, to move toward the abyss*]. Mr. Parris, I have taken your part in all contention here, and I would continue; but I cannot if you hold back in this. There are hurtful, vengeful spirits layin' hands on these children.

PARRIS. But, Thomas, you cannot—

PUTNAM. Ann! Tell Mr. Parris what you have done.

MRS. PUTNAM. Reverend Parris, I have laid seven babies unbaptized in the earth. Believe me, sir, you never saw more hearty babies born. And yet, each would wither in my arms the very night of their birth. I have spoke nothin', but my heart has clamored intimations. And now, this year, my Ruth, my only—I see her turning strange. A secret child she has become this year, and shrivels like a sucking mouth were pullin' on her life too. And so I thought to send her to your Tituba—

PARRIS. To Tituba! What may Tituba—?

MRS. PUTNAM. Tituba knows how to speak to the dead, Mr. Parris.

PARRIS. Goody Ann, it is a formidable sin to conjure up the dead!

MRS. PUTNAM. I take it on my soul, but who else may surely tell us what person murdered my babies?

PARRIS [*horrified*]. Woman!

MRS. PUTNAM. They were murdered, Mr. Parris! And mark this proof! Mark it! Last night my Ruth were ever so close to their little spirits; I know it, sir. For how else is she struck dumb now except some power of darkness would stop her mouth? It is a marvelous sign, Mr. Parris!

PUTNAM. Don't you understand it, sir? There is a murdering witch among us, bound to keep herself in the dark.

[PARRIS *turns to* BETTY, *a frantic terror rising in him.*]

Let your enemies make of it what they will, you cannot blink it more.

PARRIS [*to* ABIGAIL]. Then you were conjuring spirits last night.

ABIGAIL [*whispering*]. Not I, sir—Tituba and Ruth.

PARRIS [*turns now, with new fear, and goes to* BETTY, *looks down at her, and then, gazing off*]. Oh, Abigail, what proper payment for my charity! Now I am undone.

PUTNAM. You are not undone! Let you take hold here. Wait for no one to charge you—declare it yourself. You have discovered witchcraft—

PARRIS. In my house? In my house, Thomas? They will topple me with this! They will make of it a—

[*Enter* MERCY LEWIS, *the Putnams' servant, a fat, sly, merciless girl of eighteen.*]

MERCY. Your pardons. I only thought to see how Betty is.

PUTNAM. Why aren't you home? Who's with Ruth?

MERCY. Her grandma come. She's improved a little, I think—she give a powerful sneeze before.

MRS. PUTNAM. Ah, there's a sign of life!

MERCY. I'd fear no more, Goody Putnam. It were a grand sneeze; another like it will shake her wits together, I'm sure.

[*She goes to the bed to look.*]

PARRIS. Will you leave me now, Thomas? I would pray a while alone.

ABIGAIL. Uncle, you've prayed since midnight. Why do you not go down and—

PARRIS. No—no. [*To* PUTNAM] I have no answer for that crowd. I'll wait till Mr. Hale arrives. [*To get* MRS. PUTNAM *to leave*] If you will, Goody Ann . . .

PUTNAM. Now look you, sir. Let you strike out against the Devil, and the village will bless you for it! Come down, speak to them—pray with them. They're thirsting for your word, Mister! Surely you'll pray with them.

PARRIS [*swayed*]. I'll lead them in a psalm, but let you say nothing of witchcraft yet. I will not discuss it. The cause is yet unknown. I have had enough contention since I came; I want no more.

MRS. PUTNAM. Mercy, you go home to Ruth, d'y'hear?

MERCY. Aye, mum.

[MRS. PUTNAM *goes out.*]

PARRIS [*to* ABIGAIL]. If she starts for the window, cry for me at once.

ABIGAIL. I will, uncle.

PARRIS [*to* PUTNAM]. There is a terrible power in her arms today.

[*He goes out with* PUTNAM.]

ABIGAIL [*with hushed trepidation*]. How is Ruth sick?

MERCY. It's weirdish, I know not—she seems to walk like a dead one since last night.

ABIGAIL [*turns at once and goes to* BETTY, *and now, with fear in her voice*]. Betty? [BETTY *doesn't move. She shakes her.*] Now stop this! Betty! Sit up now!

[BETTY *doesn't stir.* MERCY *comes over.*]

MERCY. Have you tried beatin' her? I gave Ruth a good one and it waked her for a minute. Here, let me have her.

ABIGAIL [*holding* MERCY *back*]. No, he'll be comin' up. Listen, now; if they be questioning us, tell them we danced—I told him as much already.

MERCY. Aye. And what more?

ABIGAIL. He knows Tituba conjured Ruth's sisters to come out of the grave.

MERCY. And what more?

ABIGAIL. He saw you naked.

MERCY [*clapping her hands together with a frightened laugh*]. Oh, Jesus!

[*Enter* MARY WARREN, *breathless. She is seventeen, a subservient, naive, lonely girl.*]

MARY WARREN. What'll we do? The village is out! I just come from the farm; the whole country's talkin' witchcraft! They'll be callin' us witches, Abby!

MERCY [*pointing and looking at* MARY WARREN]. She means to tell, I know it.

MARY WARREN. Abby, we've got to tell. Witchery's a hangin' error, a hangin' like they done in Boston two year ago! We must tell the truth, Abby! You'll only be whipped for dancin', and the other things!

ABIGAIL. Oh, *we'll* be whipped!

MARY WARREN. I never done none of it, Abby. I only looked!

MERCY [*moving menacingly toward* MARY]. Oh, you're a great one for lookin', aren't you, Mary Warren? What a grand peeping courage you have!

[BETTY, *on the bed, whimpers.* ABIGAIL *turns to her at once.*]

ABIGAIL. Betty? [*She goes to* BETTY.] Now, Betty, dear, wake up now. It's Abigail. [*She sits* BETTY *up and furiously shakes her.*] I'll beat you, Betty! [BETTY *whimpers.*] My, you seem improving. I talked to your papa and I told him everything. So there's nothing to—

BETTY [*darts off the bed, frightened of* ABIGAIL, *and flattens herself against the wall*]. I want my mama!

ABIGAIL [*with alarm, as she cautiously approaches* BETTY]. What ails you, Betty? Your mama's dead and buried.

BETTY. I'll fly to Mama. Let me fly!

[*She raises her arms as though to fly, and streaks for the window, gets one leg out.*]

ABIGAIL [*pulling her away from the window*]. I told him everything; he knows now, he knows everything we—

BETTY. You drank blood, Abby! You didn't tell him that!

ABIGAIL. Betty, you never say that again! You will never—

BETTY. You did, you did! You drank a charm to kill John Proctor's wife! You drank a charm to kill Goody Proctor!

ABIGAIL [*smashes her across the face*]. Shut it! Now shut it!

BETTY [*collapsing on the bed*]. Mama, Mama! [*She dissolves into sobs.*]

ABIGAIL. Now look you. All of you. We danced. And Tituba conjured Ruth Putnam's dead sisters. And that is all. And mark this. Let either of you breathe a word, or the edge of a word, about the other things, and I will come to you in the black of some terrible night and I will bring a pointy reckoning that will shudder you. And you know I can do it; I saw Indians smash my dear parents' heads on the pillow next to mine, and I have seen some reddish work done at night, and I can make you wish you had never seen the sun go down! [*She goes to* BETTY *and roughly sits her up.*] Now, you—sit up and stop this!

[*But* BETTY *collapses in her hands and lies inert on the bed.*]

MARY WARREN [*with hysterical fright*]. What's got her?

[ABIGAIL *stares in fright at* BETTY.]

Abby, she's going to die! It's a sin to conjure, and we—
ABIGAIL [*starting for* MARY]. I say shut it, Mary Warren!

[*Enter* JOHN PROCTOR . . . *a farmer in his middle thirties—powerful of body, even-tempered, and not easily led. . . . On seeing him,* MARY WARREN *leaps in fright.*]

MARY WARREN. Oh! I'm just going home, Mr. Proctor.
PROCTOR. Be you foolish, Mary Warren? Be you deaf? I forbid you leave the house, did I not? Why shall I pay you? I am looking for you more often than my cows!
MARY WARREN. I only come to see the great doings in the world.
PROCTOR. I'll show you a great doin' on your arse one of these days. Now get you home; my wife is waitin' with your work!

[*Trying to retain a shred of dignity, she goes slowly out.*]

MERCY LEWIS [*both afraid of him and strangely titillated*]. I'd best be off. I have my Ruth to watch. Good morning, Mr. Proctor.

[MERCY *sidles out. Since* PROCTOR's *entrance,* ABIGAIL *has stood as though on tiptoe, absorbing his presence, wide-eyed. He glances at her, then goes to* BETTY *on the bed.*]

ABIGAIL. Gah! I'd almost forgot how strong you are, John Proctor!
PROCTOR [*looking at* ABIGAIL *now, the faintest suggestion of a knowing smile on his face*]. What's this mischief here?
ABIGAIL [*with a nervous laugh*]. Oh, she's only gone silly somehow.
PROCTOR. The road past my house is a pilgrimage to Salem all morning. The town's mumbling witchcraft.
ABIGAIL. Oh, posh! [*Winningly she comes a little closer, with a confidential, wicked air.*] We were dancin' in the woods last night, and my uncle leaped in on us. She took fright, is all.
PROCTOR [*his smile widening*]. Ah, you're wicked yet, aren't y'!

[*A trill of expectant laughter escapes her, and she dares come closer, feverishly looking into his eyes.*]

You'll be clapped in the stocks before you're twenty.

[*He takes a step to go, and she springs into his path.*]

. ABIGAIL. Give me a word, John. A soft word.

[*Her concentrated desire destroys his smile.*]

PROCTOR. No, no, Abby. That's done with.

ABIGAIL [*tauntingly*]. You come five mile to see a silly girl fly? I know you better.

PROCTOR [*setting her firmly out of his path*]. I come to see what mischief your uncle's brewin' now. [*With final emphasis*] Put it out of mind, Abby.

ABIGAIL [*grasping his hand before he can release her*]. John—I am waitin' for you every night.

PROCTOR. Abby, I never give you hope to wait for me.

ABIGAIL [*now beginning to anger—she can't believe it*]. I have something better than hope, I think!

PROCTOR. Abby, you'll put it out of mind. I'll not be comin' for you more.

ABIGAIL. You're surely sportin' with me.

PROCTOR. You know me better.

ABIGAIL. I know how you clutched my back behind your house and sweated like a stallion whenever I come near! Or did I dream that? It's she put me out, you cannot pretend it were you. I saw your face when she put me out, and you loved me then and you do now!

PROCTOR. Abby, that's a wild thing to say—

ABIGAIL. A wild thing may say wild things. But not so wild, I think. I have seen you since she put me out; I have seen you nights.

PROCTOR. I have hardly stepped off my farm this sevenmonth.

ABIGAIL. I have a sense for heat, John, and yours has drawn me to my window, and I have seen you looking up, burning in your loneliness. Do you tell me you've never looked up at my window?

PROCTOR. I may have looked up.

ABIGAIL [*now softening*]. And you must. You are no wintry man. I know you, John. I *know* you. [*She is weeping.*] I cannot sleep for dreamin'; I cannot dream but I wake and walk about the house as though I'd find you comin' through some door.

[*She clutches him desperately.*]

PROCTOR [*gently pressing her from him, with great sympathy but firmly*]. Child—

ABIGAIL [*with a flash of anger*]. How do you call me child!

PROCTOR. Abby, I may think of you softly from time to time. But I will cut off my hand before I'll ever reach for you again. Wipe it out of mind. We never touched, Abby.

ABIGAIL. Aye, but we did.

PROCTOR. Aye, but we did not.

ABIGAIL [*with a bitter anger*]. Oh, I marvel how such a strong man may let such a sickly wife be—

PROCTOR [*angered—at himself as well*]. You'll speak nothin' of Elizabeth!

ABIGAIL. She is blackening my name in the village! She is telling lies about me! She is a cold, sniveling woman, and you bend to her! Let her turn you like a—

PROCTOR [*shaking her*]. Do you look for whippin'?

[*A psalm is heard being sung below.*]

ABIGAIL [*in tears*]. I look for John Proctor that took me from my sleep and put knowledge in my heart! I never knew what pretense Salem was, I never knew the lying lessons I was taught by all these Christian women and their covenanted men! And now you bid me tear the light out of my eyes? I will not, I cannot! You loved me, John Proctor, and whatever sin it is, you love me yet!

[*He turns abruptly to go out. She rushes to him.*]

John, pity me, pity me!

[*The words "going up to Jesus" are heard in the psalm, and* BETTY *claps her ears suddenly and whines loudly.*]

ABIGAIL. Betty?

[*She hurries to* BETTY, *who is now sitting up and screaming.* PROCTOR *goes to* BETTY *as* ABIGAIL *is trying to pull her hands down, calling "Betty!"*]

PROCTOR [*growing unnerved*]. What's she doing? Girl, what ails you? Stop that wailing!

[*The singing has stopped in the midst of this, and now* PARRIS *rushes in.*]

PARRIS. What happened? What are you doing to her? Betty!

[*He rushes to the bed, crying, "Betty, Betty!"* MRS. PUTNAM *enters, feverish with curiosity, and with her* THOMAS PUTNAM *and* MERCY LEWIS. PARRIS, *at the bed, keeps lightly slapping* BETTY'S *face, while she moans and tries to get up.*]

ABIGAIL. She heard you singin' and suddenly she's up and screamin'.

MRS. PUTNAM. The psalm! The psalm! She cannot bear to hear the Lord's name!

PARRIS. No, God forbid. Mercy, run to the doctor! Tell him what's happened here!

[MERCY LEWIS *rushes out.*]

MRS. PUTNAM. Mark it for a sign, mark it!

[REBECCA NURSE, *seventy-two, enters. She is white-haired, leaning upon her walking-stick.*]

PUTNAM [*pointing at the whimpering* BETTY]. That is a notorious sign of witchcraft afoot, Goody Nurse, a prodigious sign!

MRS. PUTNAM. My mother told me that! When they cannot bear to hear the name of—

PARRIS [*trembling*]. Rebecca, Rebecca, go to her, we're lost. She suddenly cannot bear to hear the Lord's—

[GILES COREY, *eighty-three, enters. He is knotted with muscle, canny, inquisitive, and still powerful.*]

REBECCA. There is hard sickness here, Giles Corey, so please to keep the quiet.

GILES. I've not said a word. No one here can testify I've said a word. Is she going to fly again? I hear she flies.

PUTNAM. Man, be quiet now!

[*Everything is quiet.* REBECCA *walks across the room to the bed. Gentleness exudes from her.* BETTY *is quietly whimpering, eyes shut.* REBECCA *simply stands over the child, who gradually quiets.*]

MRS. PUTNAM [*astonished*]. What have you done?

[REBECCA, *in thought, now leaves the bedside and sits.*]

PARRIS [*wondrous and relieved*]. What do you make of it, Rebecca?

PUTNAM [*eagerly*]. Goody Nurse, will you go to my Ruth and see if you can wake her?

REBECCA [*sitting*]. I think she'll wake in time. Pray calm yourselves. I have eleven children, and I am twenty-six times a grandma, and I have seen them all through their silly seasons, and when it come on them they will run the Devil bowlegged keeping up with their mischief. I think she'll wake when she tires of it. A child's spirit is like a child, you can never catch it by running after it; you must stand still, and, for love, it will soon itself come back.

PROCTOR. Aye, that's the truth of it, Rebecca.

MRS. PUTNAM. This is no silly season, Rebecca. My Ruth is bewildered, Rebecca; she cannot eat.

REBECCA. Perhaps she is not hungered yet. [*To* PARRIS] I hope you are not decided to go in search of loose spirits, Mr. Parris. I've heard promise of that outside.

PARRIS. A wide opinion's running in the parish that the Devil may be among us, and I would satisfy them that they are wrong.

PROCTOR. Then let you come out and call them wrong. Did you consult the wardens before you called this minister to look for devils?

PARRIS. He is not coming to look for devils!

PROCTOR. Then what's he coming for?

PUTNAM. There be children dyin' in the village, Mister!

PROCTOR. I seen none dyin'. This society will not be a bag to swing around your head, Mr. Putnam. [*To* PARRIS] Did you call a meeting before you—?

PUTNAM. I am sick of meetings; cannot the man turn his head without he have a meeting?

PROCTOR. He may turn his head, but not to Hell!

REBECCA. Pray, John, be calm. [*Pause. He defers to her.*] Mr. Parris, I think you'd best send Reverend Hale back as soon as he come. This will set us all to arguin' again in the society, and we thought to have peace this year. I think we ought rely on the doctor now, and good prayer.

MRS. PUTNAM. Rebecca, the doctor's baffled!

REBECCA. If so he is, then let us go to God for the cause of it. There is prodigious danger in the seeking of loose spirits. I fear it, I fear it. Let us rather blame ourselves and—

PUTNAM. How may we blame ourselves? I am one of nine sons; the Putnam seed have peopled this province. And yet I have but one child left of eight—and now she shrivels!

REBECCA. I cannot fathom that.

MRS. PUTNAM [*with a growing edge of sarcasm*]. But I must! You think it God's work you should never lose a child, nor grandchild either, and I bury all but one? There are wheels within wheels in this village, and fires within fires!

PUTNAM [*to* PARRIS]. When Reverend Hale comes, you will proceed to look for signs of witchcraft here.

PROCTOR [*to* PUTNAM]. You cannot command Mr. Parris. We vote by name in this society, not by acreage.

PUTNAM. I never heard you worried so on this society, Mr. Proctor. I do not think I saw you at Sabbath meeting since snow flew.

PROCTOR. I have trouble enough without I come five mile to hear him preach only hellfire and bloody damnation. Take it to heart, Mr. Parris. There are many others who stay away from church these days because you hardly ever mention God any more.

PARRIS [*now aroused*]. Why, that's a drastic charge!

REBECCA. It's somewhat true; there are many that quail to bring their children—

PARRIS. I do not preach for children, Rebecca. It is not the children who are unmindful of their obligations toward this ministry.

REBECCA. Are there really those unmindful?

PARRIS. I should say the better half of Salem village—

PUTNAM. And more than that!

PARRIS. Where is my wood? My contract provides I be supplied with all my firewood. I am waiting since November for a stick, and even in November I had to show my frostbitten hands like some London beggar!

GILES. You are allowed six pound a year to buy your wood, Mr. Parris.

PARRIS. I regard that six pound as part of my salary. I am paid little enough without I spend six pound on firewood.

PROCTOR. Sixty, plus six for firewood—

PARRIS. The salary is sixty-six pound, Mr. Proctor! I am not some preaching farmer with a book under my arm; I am a graduate of Harvard College.

GILES. Aye, and well instructed in arithmetic!

PARRIS. Mr. Corey, you will look far for a man of my kind at sixty pound a year! I am not used to this poverty; I left a thrifty business in the Barbados to serve the Lord. I do not fathom it, why am I persecuted here? I cannot offer one proposition but there be a howling riot of argument. I have often wondered if the Devil be in it somewhere; I cannot understand you people otherwise.

PROCTOR. Mr. Parris, you are the first minister ever did demand the deed to this house—

PARRIS. Man! Don't a minister deserve a house to live in?

PROCTOR. To live in, yes. But to ask ownership is like you shall own the meeting house itself; the last meeting I were at you spoke so long on deeds and mortgages I thought it were an auction.

PARRIS. I want a mark of confidence, is all! I am your third preacher in seven years. I do not wish to be put out like the cat whenever some majority feels the whim. You people seem not to comprehend that a minister is the Lord's man in the parish; a minister is not to be so lightly crossed and contradicted—

PUTNAM. Aye!

PARRIS. There is either obedience or the church will burn like Hell is burning!

PROCTOR. Can you speak one minute without we land in Hell again? I am sick of Hell!

PARRIS. It is not for you to say what is good for you to hear!

PROCTOR. I may speak my heart, I think!

PARRIS [in a fury]. What, are we Quakers? We are not Quakers here yet, Mr. Proctor. And you may tell that to your followers!

PROCTOR. My followers!

PARRIS [now he's out with it]. There is a party in this church. I am not blind; there is a faction and a party.

PROCTOR. Against you?

PUTNAM. Against him and all authority!

PROCTOR. Why, then I must find it and join it.

[There is shock among the others.]

REBECCA. He does not mean that.

PUTNAM. He confessed it now!

PROCTOR. I mean it solemnly, Rebecca; I like not the smell of this "authority."

REBECCA. No, you cannot break charity with your minister. You are another kind, John. Clasp his hand, make your peace.

PROCTOR. I have a crop to sow and lumber to drag home.

[*He goes angrily to the door and turns to* COREY *with a smile.*]

What say you, Giles, let's find the party. He says there's a party.

GILES. I've changed my opinion of this man, John. Mr. Parris, I beg your pardon. I never thought you had so much iron in you.

PARRIS [*surprised*]. Why, thank you, Giles!

GILES. It suggests to the mind what the trouble be among us all these years. [*To all*] Think on it. Wherefore is everybody suing everybody else? Think on it now, it's a deep thing, and dark as a pit. I have been six time in court this year—

PROCTOR [*familiarly, with warmth, although he knows he is approaching the edge of* GILES' *tolerance with this*]. Is it the Devil's fault that a man cannot say you good morning without you clap him for defamation? You're old, Giles, and you're not hearin' so well as you did.

GILES [*he cannot be crossed*]. John Proctor, I have only last month collected four pound damages for you publicly sayin' I burned the roof off your house, and I—

PROCTOR [*laughing*]. I never said no such thing, but I've paid you for it, so I hope I can call you deaf without charge. Now come along, Giles, and help me drag my lumber home.

PUTNAM. A moment, Mr. Proctor. What lumber is that you're draggin', if I may ask you?

PROCTOR. My lumber. From out my forest by the riverside.

PUTNAM. Why, we are surely gone wild this year. What anarchy is this? That tract is in my bounds, it's in my bounds, Mr. Proctor.

PROCTOR. In your bounds! [*Indicating* REBECCA] I bought that tract from Goody Nurse's husband five months ago.

PUTNAM. He had no right to sell it. It stands clear in my grand-father's will that all the land between the river and—

PROCTOR. Your grandfather had a habit of willing land that never belonged to him, if I may say it plain.

GILES. That's God's truth; he nearly willed away my north pasture but he knew I'd break his fingers before he'd set his name to it. Let's get your lumber home, John. I feel a sudden will to work coming on.

PUTNAM. You load one oak of mine and you'll fight to drag it home.

GILES. Aye, and we'll win too, Putnam—this fool and I. Come on!

[*He turns to* PROCTOR *and starts out.*]

PUTNAM. I'll have my men on you, Corey! I'll clap a writ on you!

[*Enter* REVEREND JOHN HALE *of Beverly.* MR. HALE *is nearing forty, a tight-skinned, eager-eyed intellectual. This is a beloved errand for him; on being called here to ascertain witchcraft he felt the pride of the specialist whose unique knowledge has at last been publicly called for. . . . Coming into Salem now,* REVEREND HALE *conceives of himself much as a young doctor on his first call. His painfully acquired armory of symptoms, catchwords, and diagnostic procedures are now to be put to use at last. . . . He appears loaded down with half a dozen heavy books.*]

HALE. Pray you, someone take these!

PARRIS [*delighted*]. Mr. Hale! Oh! it's good to see you again! [*Taking some books*] My, they're heavy!

HALE [*setting down his books*]. They must be; they are weighted with authority.

PARRIS [*a little scared*]. Well, you do come prepared!

HALE. We shall need hard study if it comes to tracking down the Old Boy. [*Noticing* REBECCA] You cannot be Rebecca Nurse?

REBECCA. I am, sir. Do you know me?

HALE. It's strange how I knew you, but I suppose you look as such a good soul should. We have all heard of your great charities in Beverly.

PARRIS. Do you know this gentleman? Mr. Thomas Putnam. And his good wife Ann.

HALE. Putnam! I had not expected such distinguished company, sir.

PUTNAM [*pleased*]. It does not seem to help us today, Mr. Hale. We look to you to come to our house and save our child.

HALE. Your child ails too?

MRS. PUTNAM. Her soul, her soul seems flown away. She sleeps and yet she walks . . .

PUTNAM. She cannot eat.

HALE. Cannot eat! [*Thinks on it. Then, to* PROCTOR *and* GILES COREY] Do you men have afflicted children?

PARRIS. No, no, these are farmers. John Proctor—

GILES COREY. He don't believe in witches.

PROCTOR [*to* HALE]. I never spoke on witches one way or the other. Will you come, Giles?

GILES. No—no, John, I think not. I have some few queer questions of my own to ask this fellow.

PROCTOR. I've heard you to be a sensible man, Mr. Hale. I hope you'll leave some of it in Salem.

[PROCTOR *goes.* HALE *stands embarrassed for an instant.*]

PARRIS [*quickly*]. Will you look at my daughter, sir? [*Leads* HALE *to the bed.*] She has tried to leap out the window; we discovered her this morning on the highroad, waving her arms as though she'd fly.

HALE [*narrowing his eyes*]. Tries to fly.

PUTNAM. She cannot bear to hear the Lord's name, Mr. Hale; that's a sure sign of witchcraft afloat.

HALE [*holding up his hands*]. No, no. Now let me instruct you. We cannot look to superstition in this. The Devil is precise; the marks of his presence are definite as stone, and I must tell you all that I shall not proceed unless you are prepared to believe me if I should find no bruise of hell upon her.

PARRIS. It is agreed, sir—it is agreed—we will abide by your judgment.

HALE. Good then. [*He goes to the bed, looks down at* BETTY. *To* PARRIS] Now, sir, what were your first warning of this strangeness?

PARRIS. Why, sir—I discovered her—[*indicating* ABIGAIL] and my niece and ten or twelve of the other girls, dancing in the forest last night.

HALE [*surprised*]. You permit dancing?

PARRIS. No, no, it were secret—

MRS. PUTNAM [*unable to wait*]. Mr. Parris's slave has knowledge of conjurin', sir.

PARRIS [*to* MRS. PUTNAM]. We cannot be sure of that, Goody Ann—

MRS. PUTNAM [*frightened, very softly*]. I know it, sir. I sent my child—she should learn from Tituba who murdered her sisters.

REBECCA [*horrified*]. Goody Ann! You sent a child to conjure up the dead?

MRS. PUTNAM. Let God blame me, not you, not you, Rebecca! I'll not have you judging me any more! [*To* HALE] Is it a natural work to lose seven children before they live a day?

PARRIS. Sssh!

[REBECCA, *with great pain, turns her face away. There is a pause.*]

HALE. Seven dead in childbirth.

MRS. PUTNAM [*softly*]. Aye.

[*Her voice breaks; she looks up at him. Silence.* HALE *is impressed.* PARRIS *looks to him. He goes to his books, opens one, turns pages, then reads. All wait, avidly.*]

PARRIS [*hushed*]. What book is that?

MRS. PUTNAM. What's there, sir?

HALE [*with a tasty love of intellectual pursuit*]. Here is all the invisible world, caught, defined, and calculated. In these books the Devil stands stripped of all his brute disguises. Here are all your familiar spirits—your incubi and succubi; your witches that go by land, by air, and by sea; your wizards of the night and of the day. Have no fear now —we shall find him out if he has come among us, and I mean to crush him utterly if he has shown his face!

[*He starts for the bed.*]

REBECCA. Will it hurt the child, sir?

HALE. I cannot tell. If she is truly in the Devil's grip we may have to rip and tear to get her free.

REBECCA. I think I'll go, then. I am too old for this. [*She rises.*]

PARRIS [*striving for conviction*]. Why, Rebecca, we may open up the boil of all our troubles today!

REBECCA. Let us hope for that. I go to God for you, sir.

PARRIS [*with trepidation—and resentment*]. I hope you do not mean we go to Satan here! [*Slight pause.*]

REBECCA. I wish I knew.

[*She goes out; they feel resentful of her note of moral superiority.*]

PUTNAM [*abruptly*]. Come, Mr. Hale, let's get on. Sit you here.

GILES. Mr. Hale, I have always wanted to ask a learned man—what signifies the readin' of strange books?

HALE. What books?

GILES. I cannot tell; she hides them.

HALE. Who does this?

GILES. Martha, my wife. I have waked at night many a time and found her in a corner, readin' of a book. Now what do you make of that?

HALE. Why, that's not necessarily—

GILES. It discomfits me! Last night—mark this—I tried and tried and could not say my prayers. And then she close her book and walks out of the house, and suddenly—mark this—I could pray again!

HALE. Ah! The stoppage of prayer—that is strange. I'll speak further on that with you.

GILES. I'm not sayin' she's touched the Devil, now, but I'd admire to know what books she reads and why she hides them. She'll not answer me, y' see.

HALE. Aye, we'll discuss it. [*To all*] Now mark me, if the Devil is in her you will witness some frightful wonders in this room, so please to keep your wits about you. Mr. Putnam, stand close in case she flies. Now, Betty, dear, will you sit up?

[PUTNAM *comes in closer, ready-handed.* HALE *sits* BETTY *up, but she hangs limp in his hands.*]

Hmmm. [*He observes her carefully. The others watch breathlessly.*] Can you hear me? I am John Hale, minister of Beverly. I have come to help you, dear. Do you remember my two little girls in Beverly?

[*She does not stir in his hands.*]

PARRIS [*in fright*]. How can it be the Devil? Why would he choose my house to strike? We have all manner of licentious people in the village!

HALE. What victory would the Devil have to win a soul already bad? It is the best the Devil wants, and who is better than the minister?

GILES. That's deep, Mr. Parris, deep, deep!

PARRIS [*with resolution now*]. Betty! Answer Mr. Hale! Betty!

HALE. Does someone afflict you, child? It need not be a woman, mind you, or a man. Perhaps some bird invisible to others comes to you—perhaps a pig, a mouse, or any beast at all. Is there some figure bids you fly?

[*The child remains limp in his hands. In silence he lays her back on the pillow. Now, holding out his hands toward her, he intones*]

In nomine Domini Sabaoth sui filiique ite ad infernos.

[*She does not stir. He turns to* ABIGAIL, *his eyes narrowing.*]

Abigail, what sort of dancing were you doing with her in the forest?

ABIGAIL. Why—common dancing is all.

PARRIS. I think I ought to say that I—I saw a kettle in the grass where they were dancing.

ABIGAIL. That were only soup.

HALE. What sort of soup were in this kettle, Abigail?

ABIGAIL. Why, it were beans—and lentils, I think, and—

HALE. Mr. Parris, you did not notice, did you, any living thing in the kettle? A mouse, perhaps, a spider, a frog—?

PARRIS [*fearfully*]. I—do believe there were some movement—in the soup.

ABIGAIL. That jumped in, we never put it in!

HALE [*quickly*]. What jumped in?

ABIGAIL. Why, a very little frog jumped—

PARRIS. A frog, Abby!

HALE [*grasping* ABIGAIL]. Abigail, it may be your cousin is dying. Did you call the Devil last night?

ABIGAIL. I never called him! Tituba, Tituba . . .

PARRIS [*blanched*]. She called the Devil?

HALE. I should like to speak with Tituba.

PARRIS. Goody Ann, will you bring her up?

[MRS. PUTNAM *exits.*]

HALE. How did she call him?

ABIGAIL. I know not—she spoke Barbados.

HALE. Did you feel any strangeness when she called him? A sudden cold wind, perhaps? A trembling below the ground?

ABIGAIL. I didn't see no Devil! [*Shaking* BETTY] Betty, wake up. Betty! Betty!

HALE. You cannot evade me, Abigail. Did your cousin drink any of the brew in that kettle?

ABIGAIL. She never drank it!

HALE. Did you drink it?

ABIGAIL. No, sir!

HALE. Did Tituba ask you to drink it?

ABIGAIL. She tried, but I refused.

HALE. Why are you concealing? Have you sold yourself to Lucifer?

ABIGAIL. I never sold myself! I'm a good girl! I'm a proper girl!

[MRS. PUTNAM *enters with* TITUBA, *and instantly* ABIGAIL *points at* TITUBA.]

ABIGAIL. She made me do it! She made Betty do it!

TITUBA [*shocked and angry*]. Abby!

ABIGAIL. She makes me drink blood!

PARRIS. Blood!!

MRS. PUTNAM. My baby's blood?

TITUBA. No, no, chicken blood. I give she chicken blood!

HALE. Woman, have you enlisted these children for the Devil?

TITUBA. No, no, sir, I don't truck with no Devil!

HALE. Why can she not wake? Are you silencing this child?

TITUBA. I love me Betty!

HALE. You have sent your spirit out upon this child, have you not? Are you gathering souls for the Devil?

ABIGAIL. She sends her spirit on me in church; she makes me laugh at prayer!

PARRIS. She have often laughed at prayer!

ABIGAIL. She comes to me every night to go and drink blood!

TITUBA. You beg *me* to conjure! She beg *me* make charm—

ABIGAIL. Don't lie! [*To* HALE] She comes to me while I sleep; she's always making me dream corruptions!

TITUBA. Why you say that, Abby?

ABIGAIL. Sometimes I wake and find myself standing in the open doorway and not a stitch on my body! I always hear her laughing in my sleep. I hear her singing her Barbados songs and tempting me with—

TITUBA. Mister Reverend, I never—

HALE. [*resolved now*]. Tituba, I want you to wake this child.

TITUBA. I have no power on this child, sir.

HALE. You most certainly do, and you will free her from it now! When did you compact with the Devil?

TITUBA. I don't compact with no Devil!

PARRIS. You will confess yourself or I will take you out and whip you to your death, Tituba!

PUTNAM.   This woman must be hanged! She must be taken and hanged!

TITUBA [*terrified, falls to her knees*].   No, no, don't hang Tituba! I tell him I don't desire to work for him, sir.

PARRIS.   The Devil?

HALE.   Then you saw him! [TITUBA *weeps.*] Now Tituba, I know that when we bind ourselves to Hell it is very hard to break with it. We are going to help you tear yourself free—

TITUBA [*frightened by the coming process*].   Mister Reverend, I do believe somebody else be witchin' these children.

HALE.   Who?

TITUBA.   I don't know, sir, but the Devil got him numerous witches.

HALE.   Does he! [*It is a clue.*] Tituba, look into my eyes. Come, look into me. [*She raises her eyes to his fearfully.*] You would be a good Christian woman, would you not, Tituba?

TITUBA.   Aye, sir, a good Christian woman.

HALE.   And you love these little children?

TITUBA.   Oh, yes, sir, I don't desire to hurt little children.

HALE.   And you love God, Tituba?

TITUBA.   I love God with all my bein'.

HALE.   Now, in God's holy name—

TITUBA.   Bless Him. Bless Him.

[*She is rocking on her knees, sobbing in terror.*]

HALE.   And to His glory—

TITUBA.   Eternal glory. Bless Him—bless God . . .

HALE.   Open yourself, Tituba—open yourself and let God's holy light shine on you.

TITUBA.   Oh, bless the Lord.

HALE.   When the Devil comes to you does he ever come—with another person? [*She stares up into his face.*] Perhaps another person in the village? Someone you know.

PARRIS.   Who came with him?

PUTNAM.   Sarah Good? Did you ever see Sarah Good with him? Or Osburn?

PARRIS.   Was it man or woman came with him?

TITUBA.   Man or woman. Was—was woman.

PARRIS.   What woman? A woman, you said. What woman?

TITUBA.   It was black dark, and I—

PARRIS.   You could see him, why could you not see her?

TITUBA.   Well, they was always talking; they was always runnin' round and carryin' on—

PARRIS.   You mean out of Salem? Salem witches?

TITUBA.   I believe so, yes, sir.

[*Now* HALE *takes her hand. She is surprised.*]

HALE. Tituba. You must have no fear to tell us who they are, do you understand? We will protect you. The Devil can never overcome a minister. You know that, do you not?

TITUBA [*kisses* HALE's *hand*]. Aye, sir, oh, I do.

HALE. You have confessed yourself to witchcraft, and that speaks a wish to come to Heaven's side. And we will bless you, Tituba.

TITUBA [*deeply relieved*]. Oh, God bless you, Mr. Hale!

HALE [*with rising exaltation*]. You are God's instrument put in our hands to discover the Devil's agents among us. You are selected, Tituba, you are chosen to help us cleanse our village. So speak utterly, Tituba, turn your back on him and face God—face God, Tituba, and God will protect you.

TITUBA [*joining with him*]. Oh, God, protect Tituba!

HALE [*kindly*]. Who came to you with the Devil? Two? Three? Four? How many?

[TITUBA *pants, and begins rocking back and forth again, staring ahead.*]

TITUBA. There was four. There was four.

PARRIS [*pressing in on her*]. Who? Who? Their names, their names!

TITUBA [*suddenly bursting out*]. Oh, how many times he bid me kill you, Mr. Parris!

PARRIS. Kill me!

TITUBA [*in a fury*]. He say Mr. Parris must be kill! Mr. Parris no goodly man, Mr. Parris mean man and no gentle man, and he bid me rise out of my bed and cut your throat! [*They gasp.*] But I tell him "No! I don't hate that man. I don't want kill that man." But he say, "You work for me, Tituba, and I make you free! I give you pretty dress to wear, and put you way high up in the air, and you gone fly back to Barbados!" And I say, "You lie, Devil, you lie!" And then he come one stormy night to me, and he say, "Look! I have *white* people belong to me." And I look—and there was Goody Good.

PARRIS. Sarah Good!

TITUBA [*rocking and weeping*]. Aye, sir, and Goody Osburn.

MRS. PUTNAM. I knew it! Goody Osburn were midwife to me three times. I begged you, Thomas, did I not? I begged him not to call Osburn because I feared her. My babies always shriveled in her hands!

HALE. Take courage, you must give us all their names. How can you bear to see this child suffering? Look at her, Tituba. [*He is indicating* BETTY *on the bed.*] Look at her God-given innocence; her soul is so tender; we must protect her, Tituba; the Devil is out and preying on her like a beast upon the flesh of the pure lamb. God will bless you for your help.

[ABIGAIL *rises, staring as though inspired, and cries out.*]

ABIGAIL.   I want to open myself!

[*They turn to her, startled. She is enraptured, as though in a pearly light.*]

I want the light of God, I want the sweet love of Jesus! I danced for the Devil; I saw him; I wrote in his book; I go back to Jesus; I kiss His hand. I saw Sarah Good with the Devil! I saw Goody Osburn with the Devil! I saw Bridget Bishop with the Devil!

[*As she is speaking,* BETTY *is rising from the bed, a fever in her eyes, and picks up the chant.*]

BETTY [*staring too*].   I saw George Jacobs with the Devil! I saw Goody Howe with the Devil!

PARRIS.   She speaks! [*He rushes to embrace* BETTY.] She speaks!

HALE.   Glory to God! It is broken, they are free!

BETTY [*calling out hysterically and with great relief*].   I saw Martha Bellows with the Devil!

ABIGAIL.   I saw Goody Sibber with the Devil!

[*It is rising to a great glee.*]

PUTNAM.   The marshal, I'll call the marshal!

[PARRIS *is shouting a prayer of thanksgiving.*]

BETTY.   I saw Alice Barrow with the Devil!

[*The curtain begins to fall.*]

HALE [*as* PUTNAM *goes out*].   Let the marshal bring irons!

ABIGAIL.   I saw Goody Hawkins with the Devil!

BETTY.   I saw Goody Bibber with the Devil!

ABIGAIL.   I saw Goody Booth with the Devil!

[*On their ecstatic cries

THE CURTAIN FALLS

ACT TWO

THE COMMON ROOM *of Proctor's house, eight days later.*

At the right is a door opening on the fields outside. A fireplace is at the left, and behind it a stairway leading upstairs. It is the low, dark, and rather long living room of the time. As the curtain rises, the room is empty. From above, ELIZABETH *is heard softly singing to the children. Presently the door opens and* JOHN PROCTOR *enters, carrying his gun. He glances about the room as he comes toward the fireplace, then halts for an instant as he hears her singing. He continues on to the fireplace, leans the gun against the wall as he swings a pot out of the fire and smells it. Then he lifts out the ladle and tastes. He is not quite pleased. He reaches to a cupboard, takes a pinch of salt, and drops it into the pot. As he is tasting again, her footsteps are heard on the stair. He swings the pot into the fireplace and goes to a basin and washes his hands and face.* ELIZABETH *enters.*

ELIZABETH. What keeps you so late? It's almost dark.

PROCTOR. I were planting far out to the forest edge.

ELIZABETH. Oh, you're done then.

PROCTOR. Aye, the farm is seeded. The boys asleep?

ELIZABETH. They will be soon. [*And she goes to the fireplace, proceeds to ladle up stew in a dish.*]

PROCTOR. Pray now for a fair summer.

ELIZABETH. Aye.

PROCTOR. Are you well today?

ELIZABETH. I am. [*She brings the plate to the table, and, indicating the food*] It is a rabbit.

PROCTOR [*going to the table*]. Oh, is it! In Jonathan's trap?

ELIZABETH. No, she walked into the house this afternoon; I found her sittin' in the corner like she come to visit.

PROCTOR. Oh, that's a good sign walkin' in.

ELIZABETH. Pray God. It hurt my heart to strip her, poor rabbit.

[*She sits and watches him taste it.*]

PROCTOR. It's well seasoned.

ELIZABETH [*blushing with pleasure*]. I took great care. She's tender?

PROCTOR. Aye. [*He eats. She watches him.*] I think we'll see green fields soon. It's warm as blood beneath the clods.

ELIZABETH. That's well.

[PROCTOR *eats, then looks up.*]

PROCTOR. If the crop is good I'll buy George Jacob's heifer. How would that please you?

ELIZABETH. Aye, it would.

PROCTOR [*with a grin*]. I mean to please you, Elizabeth.

ELIZABETH [*it is hard to say*]. I know it, John.

[*He gets up, goes to her, kisses her. She receives it. With a certain disappointment, he returns to the table.*]

PROCTOR [*as gently as he can*]. Cider?

ELIZABETH [*with a sense of reprimanding herself for having forgot*]. Aye! [*She gets up and goes and pours a glass for him. He now arches his back.*]

PROCTOR. This farm's a continent when you go foot by foot droppin' seeds in it.

ELIZABETH [*coming with the cider*]. It must be.

PROCTOR [*drinks a long draught, then, putting the glass down*]. You ought to bring some flowers in the house.

ELIZABETH. Oh! I forgot! I will tomorrow.

PROCTOR. It's winter in here yet. On Sunday let you come with me, and we'll walk the farm together; I never see such a load of flowers on the earth. [*With good feeling he goes and looks up at the sky through the open doorway.*] Lilacs have a purple smell. Lilac is the smell of nightfall, I think. Massachusetts is a beauty in the spring!

ELIZABETH. Aye, it is.

[*There is a pause. She is watching him from the table as he stands there absorbing the night. It is as though she would speak but cannot. Instead, now, she takes up his plate and glass and fork and goes with them to the basin. Her back is turned to him. He turns to her and watches her. A sense of their separation rises.*]

PROCTOR. I think you're sad again. Are you?

ELIZABETH [*she doesn't want friction, and yet she must*]. You come so late I thought you'd gone to Salem this afternoon.

PROCTOR. Why? I have no business in Salem.

ELIZABETH. You did speak of going, earlier this week.

PROCTOR [*he knows what she means*]. I thought better of it since.

ELIZABETH. Mary Warren's there today.

PROCTOR. Why'd you let her? You heard me forbid her go to Salem any more!

ELIZABETH. I couldn't stop her.

PROCTOR [*holding back a full condemnation of her*]. It is a fault, it is a fault, Elizabeth—you're the mistress here, not Mary Warren.

ELIZABETH. She frightened all my strength away.

PROCTOR. How may that mouse frighten you, Elizabeth? You—

ELIZABETH. It is a mouse no more. I forbid her go, and she raises up her chin like the daughter of a prince and says to me, "I must go to Salem, Goody Proctor; I am an official of the court!"

PROCTOR. Court! What court?

ELIZABETH. Aye, it is a proper court they have now. They've sent four judges out of Boston, she says, weighty magistrates of the General Court, and at the head sits the Deputy Governor of the Province.

PROCTOR [*astonished*]. Why, she's mad.

ELIZABETH. I would to God she were. There be fourteen people in the jail now, she says.

[PROCTOR *simply looks at her, unable to grasp it.*]

And they'll be tried, and the court have power to hang them too, she says.

PROCTOR [*scoffing, but without conviction*]. Ah, they'd never hang—

ELIZABETH. The Deputy Governor promise hangin' if they'll not confess, John. The town's gone wild, I think. She speak of Abigail, and I thought she were a saint, to hear her. Abigail brings the other girls into the court, and where she walks the crowd will part like the sea for Israel. And folks are brought before them, and if they scream and howl and fall to the floor—the person's clapped in the jail for bewitchin' them.

PROCTOR [*wide-eyed*]. Oh, it is a black mischief.

ELIZABETH. I think you must go to Salem, John. [*He turns to her.*] I think so. You must tell them it is a fraud.

PROCTOR [*thinking beyond this*]. Aye, it is, it is surely.

ELIZABETH. Let you go to Ezekiel Cheever—he knows you well. And tell him what she said to you last week in her uncle's house. She said it had naught to do with witchcraft, did she not?

PROCTOR [*in thought*]. Aye, she did, she did. [*Now, a pause.*]

ELIZABETH [*quietly, fearing to anger him by prodding*]. God forbid you keep that from the court, John. I think they must be told.

PROCTOR [*quietly, struggling with his thought*]. Aye, they must, they must. It is a wonder they do believe her.

ELIZABETH. I would go to Salem now, John—let you go tonight.

PROCTOR. I'll think on it.

ELIZABETH [*with her courage now*]. You cannot keep it, John.

PROCTOR [*angering*]. I know I cannot keep it. I say I will think on it!

ELIZABETH [*hurt, and very coldly*]. Good, then, let you think on it.

[*She stands and starts to walk out of the room.*]

PROCTOR. I am only wondering how I may prove what she told me, Elizabeth. If the girl's a saint now, I think it is not easy to prove she's fraud, and the town gone so silly. She told it to me in a room alone—I have no proof for it.

ELIZABETH. You were alone with her?

PROCTOR [*stubbornly*]. For a moment alone, aye.

ELIZABETH. Why, then, it is not as you told me.

PROCTOR [*his anger rising*]. For a moment, I say. The others come in soon after.

ELIZABETH [*quietly—she has suddenly lost all faith in him*]. Do as you wish, then. [*She starts to turn.*]

PROCTOR. Woman. [*She turns to him.*] I'll not have your suspicion any more.

ELIZABETH [*a little loftily*]. I have no—

PROCTOR. I'll not have it!

ELIZABETH. Then let you not earn it.

PROCTOR [*with a violent undertone*]. You doubt me yet?

ELIZABETH [*with a smile, to keep her dignity*]. John, if it were not Abigail that you must go to hurt, would you falter now? I think not.

PROCTOR. Now look you—

ELIZABETH. I see what I see, John.

PROCTOR [*with solemn warning*]. You will not judge me more, Elizabeth. I have good reason to think before I charge fraud on Abigail, and I will think on it. Let you look to your own improvement before you go to judge your husband any more. I have forgot Abigail, and—

ELIZABETH. And I.

PROCTOR. Spare me! You forget nothin' and forgive nothin'. Learn charity, woman. I have gone tiptoe in this house all seven month since she is gone. I have not moved from there to there without I think to please you, and still an everlasting funeral marches round your heart. I cannot speak but I am doubted, every moment judged for lies, as though I come into a court when I come into this house!

ELIZABETH. John, you are not open with me. You saw her with a crowd, you said. Now you—

PROCTOR. I'll plead my honesty no more, Elizabeth.

ELIZABETH [*now she would justify herself*]. John, I am only—

PROCTOR. No more! I should have roared you down when first you told me your suspicion. But I wilted, and, like a Christian, I confessed. Confessed! Some dream I had must have mistaken you for God that day. But you're not, you're not, and let you remember it! Let you look sometimes for the goodness in me, and judge me not.

ELIZABETH. I do not judge you. The magistrate sits in your heart that judges you. I never thought you but a good man, John—[*with a smile*] only somewhat bewildered.

PROCTOR [*laughing bitterly*]. Oh, Elizabeth, your justice would freeze beer!

[*He turns suddenly toward a sound outside. He starts for the door as* MARY WARREN *enters. As soon as he sees her, he goes directly to her and grabs her by her cloak, furious.*]

How do you go to Salem when I forbid it? Do you mock me? [*Shaking her.*] I'll whip you if you dare leave this house again!

[*Strangely, she doesn't resist him, but hangs limply by his grip.*]

MARY WARREN. I am sick, I am sick, Mr. Proctor. Pray, pray, hurt me not.

[*Her strangeness throws him off, and her evident pallor and weakness. He frees her.*]

My insides are all shuddery; I am in the proceedings all day, sir.

PROCTOR [*with draining anger—his curiosity is draining it*]. And what of these proceedings here? When will you proceed to keep this house, as you are paid nine pound a year to do—and my wife not wholly well?

[*As though to compensate,* MARY WARREN *goes to* ELIZABETH *with a small rag doll.*]

MARY WARREN. I made a gift for you today, Goody Proctor. I had to sit long hours in a chair, and passed the time with sewing.

ELIZABETH [*perplexed, looking at the doll*]. Why, thank you, it's a fair poppet.

MARY WARREN [*with a trembling, decayed voice*]. We must all love each other now, Goody Proctor.

ELIZABETH [*amazed at her strangeness*]. Aye, indeed we must.

MARY WARREN [*glancing at the room*]. I'll get up early in the morning and clean the house. I must sleep now. [*She turns and starts off.*]

PROCTOR. Mary. [*She halts.*] Is it true? There be fourteen women arrested?

MARY WARREN. No, sir. There be thirty-nine now—

[*She suddenly breaks off and sobs and sits down, exhausted.*]

ELIZABETH. Why, she's weepin'! What ails you, child?

MARY WARREN. Goody Osburn—will hang!

[*There is a shocked pause, while she sobs.*]

PROCTOR. Hang! [*He calls into her face.*] Hang, y'say?

MARY WARREN [*through her weeping*]. Aye.

PROCTOR. The Deputy Governor will permit it?

MARY WARREN. He sentenced her. He must. [*To ameliorate it*] But not Sarah Good. For Sarah Good confessed, y'see.

PROCTOR. Confessed! To what?

MARY WARREN. That she—[*in horror at the memory*] she sometimes made a compact with Lucifer, and wrote her name in his black book—

with her blood—and bound herself to torment Christians till God's thrown down—and we all must worship Hell forevermore.

[*Pause.*]

PROCTOR. But—surely you know what a jabberer she is. Did you tell them that?

MARY WARREN. Mr. Proctor, in open court she near to choked us all to death.

PROCTOR. How, choked you?

MARY WARREN. She sent her spirit out.

ELIZABETH. Oh, Mary, Mary, surely you—

MARY WARREN [*with an indignant edge*]. She tried to kill me many times, Goody Proctor!

ELIZABETH. Why, I never heard you mention that before.

MARY WARREN. I never knew it before. I never knew anything before. When she come into the court I say to myself, I must not accuse this woman, for she sleep in ditches, and so very old and poor. But then—then she sit there, denying and denying, and I feel a misty coldness climbin' up my back, and the skin on my skull begin to creep, and I feel a clamp around my neck and I cannot breathe air; and then [*entranced*] I hear a voice, a screamin' voice, and it were my voice—and all at once I remembered everything she done to me!

PROCTOR. Why? What did she do to you?

MARY WARREN [*like one awakened to a marvelous secret insight*]. So many time, Mr. Proctor, she come to this very door, beggin' bread and a cup of cider—and mark this: whenever I turned her away empty, she *mumbled*.

ELIZABETH. Mumbled! She may mumble if she's hungry.

MARY WARREN. But *what* does she mumble? You must remember, Goody Proctor. Last month—a Monday, I think—she walked away, and I thought my guts would burst for two days after. Do you remember it?

ELIZABETH. Why—I do, I think, but—

MARY WARREN. And so I told that to Judge Hathorne, and he asks her so. "Goody Osburn," says he, "what curse do you mumble that this girl must fall sick after turning you away?" And then she replies [*mimicking an old crone*] "Why, your excellence, no curse at all. I only say my commandments; I hope I may say my commandments," says she!

ELIZABETH. And that's an upright answer.

MARY WARREN. Aye, but then Judge Hathorne say, "Recite for us your commandments!"—[*leaning avidly toward them*] and of all the ten she could not say a single one. She never knew no commandments, and they had her in a flat lie!

PROCTOR. And so condemned her?

MARY WARREN [*now a little strained, seeing his stubborn doubt*]. Why, they must when she condemned herself.

PROCTOR. But the proof, the proof!

MARY WARREN [*with greater impatience with him*]. I told you the proof. It's hard proof, hard as rock, the judges said.

PROCTOR [*pauses an instant, then*]. You will not go to court again, Mary Warren.

MARY WARREN. I must tell you, sir, I will be gone every day now. I am amazed you do not see what weighty work we do.

PROCTOR. What work you do! It's strange work for a Christian girl to hang old women!

MARY WARREN. But, Mr. Proctor, they will not hang them if they confess. Sarah Good will only sit in jail some time—[*recalling*] and here's a wonder for you; think on this. Goody Good is pregnant!

ELIZABETH. Pregnant! Are they mad? The woman's near to sixty!

MARY WARREN. They had Doctor Griggs examine her, and she's full to the brim. And smokin' a pipe all these years, and no husband either! But she's safe, thank God, for they'll not hurt the innocent child. But be that not a marvel? You must see it, sir, it's God's work we do. So I'll be gone every day for some time. I'm—I am an official of the court, they say, and I—

[*She has been edging toward offstage.*]

PROCTOR. I'll official you!

[*He strides to the mantel, takes down the whip hanging there.*]

MARY WARREN [*terrified, but coming erect, striving for her authority*]. I'll not stand whipping any more!

ELIZABETH [*hurriedly, as* PROCTOR *approaches*]. Mary, promise now you'll stay at home—

MARY WARREN [*backing from him, but keeping her erect posture, striving, striving for her way*]. The Devil's loose in Salem, Mr. Proctor; we must discover where he's hiding!

PROCTOR. I'll whip the Devil out of you!

[*With whip raised he reaches out for her, and she streaks away and yells.*]

MARY WARREN [*pointing at* ELIZABETH]. I saved her life today!

[*Silence. His whip comes down.*]

ELIZABETH [*softly*]. I am accused?

MARY WARREN [*quaking*]. Somewhat mentioned. But I said I never see no sign you ever sent your spirit out to hurt no one, and seeing I do live so closely with you, they dismissed it.

ELIZABETH. Who accused me?

MARY WARREN. I am bound by law, I cannot tell it. [*To* PROCTOR]
I only hope you'll not be so sarcastical no more. Four judges and the
King's deputy sat to dinner with us but an hour ago. I—I would have
you speak civilly to me, from this out.

PROCTOR [*in horror, muttering in disgust at her*]. Go to bed.

MARY WARREN [*with a stamp of her foot*]. I'll not be ordered to bed
no more, Mr. Proctor! I am eighteen and a woman, however single!

PROCTOR. Do you wish to sit up? Then sit up.

MARY WARREN. I wish to go to bed!

PROCTOR [*in anger*]. Good night, then!

MARY WARREN. Good night.

[*Dissatisfied, uncertain of herself, she goes out. Wide-eyed, both,*
PROCTOR *and* ELIZABETH *stand staring.*]

ELIZABETH [*quietly*]. Oh, the noose, the noose is up!

PROCTOR. There'll be no noose.

ELIZABETH. She wants me dead. I knew all week it would come to
this!

PROCTOR [*without conviction*]. They dismissed it. You heard her
say—

ELIZABETH. And what of tomorrow? She will cry me out until they
take me!

PROCTOR. Sit you down.

ELIZABETH. She wants me dead, John, you know it!

PROCTOR. I say sit down!

[*She sits, trembling. He speaks quietly, trying to keep his wits.*]

Now we must be wise, Elizabeth.

ELIZABETH [*with sarcasm, and a sense of being lost*]. Oh, indeed,
indeed!

PROCTOR. Fear nothing. I'll find Ezekiel Cheever. I'll tell him she
said it were all sport.

ELIZABETH. John, with so many in the jail, more than Cheever's help
is needed now, I think. Would you favor me with this? Go to Abigail.

PROCTOR [*his soul hardening as he senses . . .*]. What have I to say
to Abigail?

ELIZABETH [*delicately*]. John—grant me this. You have a faulty understanding of young girls. There is a promise made in any bed—

PROCTOR [*striving against his anger*]. What promise!

ELIZABETH. Spoke or silent, a promise is surely made. And she may
dote on it now—I am sure she does—and thinks to kill me, then to take
my place.

[PROCTOR'S *anger is rising; he cannot speak.*]

ELIZABETH. It is her dearest hope, John, I know it. There be a thousand names; why does she call mine? There be a certain danger in calling such a name—I am no Goody Good that sleeps in ditches, nor Osburn, drunk and half-witted. She'd dare not call out such a farmer's wife but there be monstrous profit in it. She thinks to take my place, John.

PROCTOR. She cannot think it! [*He knows it is true.*]

ELIZABETH [*"reasonably"*]. John, have you ever shown her somewhat of contempt? She cannot pass you in the church but you will blush—

PROCTOR. I may blush for my sin.

ELIZABETH. I think she sees another meaning in that blush.

PROCTOR. And what see you? What see you, Elizabeth?

ELIZABETH [*"conceding"*]. I think you be somewhat ashamed, for I am there, and she so close.

PROCTOR. When will you know me, woman? Were I stone I would have cracked for shame this seven month!

ELIZABETH. Then go and tell her she's a whore. Whatever promise she may sense—break it, John, break it.

PROCTOR [*between his teeth*]. Good, then. I'll go.

[*He starts for his rifle.*]

ELIZABETH [*trembling, fearfully*]. Oh, how unwillingly!

PROCTOR [*turning on her, rifle in hand*]. I will curse her hotter than the oldest cinder in hell. But pray, begrudge me not my anger!

ELIZABETH. Your anger! I only ask you—

PROCTOR. Woman, am I so base? Do you truly think me base?

ELIZABETH. I never called you base.

PROCTOR. Then how do you charge me with such a promise? The promise that a stallion gives a mare I gave that girl!

ELIZABETH. Then why do you anger with me when I bid you break it?

PROCTOR. Because it speaks deceit, and I am honest! But I'll plead no more! I see now your spirit twists around the single error of my life, and I will never tear it free!

ELIZABETH [*crying out*]. You'll tear it free—when you come to know that I will be your only wife, or no wife at all! She has an arrow in you yet, John Proctor, and you know it well!

[*Quite suddenly, as though from the air, a figure appears in the doorway. They start slightly. It is MR. HALE. He is different now—drawn a little, and there is a quality of deference, even of guilt, about his manner now.*]

HALE. Good evening.

PROCTOR [*still in his shock*]. Why, Mr. Hale! Good evening to you, sir. Come in, come in.

HALE [*to* ELIZABETH]. I hope I do not startle you.

ELIZABETH. No, no, it's only that I heard no horse—

HALE. You are Goodwife Proctor.

PROCTOR. Aye; Elizabeth.

HALE [*nods, then*]. I hope you're not off to bed yet.

PROCTOR [*setting down his gun*]. No, no.

[HALE *comes further into the room. And* PROCTOR, *to explain his nervousness*]

We are not used to visitors after dark, but you're welcome here. Will you sit you down, sir?

HALE. I will. [*He sits.*] Let you sit, Goodwife Proctor.

[*She does, never letting him out of her sight. There is a pause as* HALE *looks about the room.*]

PROCTOR [*to break the silence*]. Will you drink cider, Mr. Hale?

HALE. No, it rebels my stomach; I have some further traveling yet tonight. Sit you down, sir. [PROCTOR *sits.*] I will not keep you long, but I have some business with you.

PROCTOR. Business of the court?

HALE. No—no, I come of my own, without the court's authority. Hear me. [*He wets his lips.*] I know not if you are aware, but your wife's name is—mentioned in the court.

PROCTOR. We know it, sir. Our Mary Warren told us. We are entirely amazed.

HALE. I am a stranger here, as you know. And in my ignorance I find it hard to draw a clear opinion of them that come accused before the court. And so this afternoon, and now tonight, I go from house to house—I come now from Rebecca Nurse's house and—

ELIZABETH [*shocked*]. Rebecca's charged!

HALE. God forbid such a one be charged. She is, however—mentioned somewhat.

ELIZABETH [*with an attempt at a laugh*]. You will never believe, I hope, that Rebecca trafficked with the Devil.

HALE. Woman, it is possible.

PROCTOR [*taken aback*]. Surely you cannot think so.

HALE. This is a strange time, Mister. No man may longer doubt the powers of the dark are gathered in monstrous attack upon this village. There is too much evidence now to deny it. You will agree, sir?

PROCTOR [*evading*]. I—have no knowledge in that line. But it's hard to think so pious a woman be secretly a Devil's bitch after seventy year of such good prayer.

HALE. Aye. But the Devil is a wily one, you cannot deny it. However, she is far from accused, and I know she will not be. [*Pause.*] I thought, sir, to put some questions as to the Christian character of this house, if you'll permit me.

PROCTOR [*coldly, resentful*]. Why, we—have no fear of questions, sir.

HALE. Good, then. [*He makes himself more comfortable.*] In the book of record that Mr. Parris keeps, I note that you are rarely in the church on Sabbath Day.

PROCTOR. No, sir, you are mistaken.

HALE. Twenty-six time in seventeen month, sir. I must call that rare. Will you tell me why you are so absent?

PROCTOR. Mr. Hale, I never knew I must account to that man for I come to church or stay at home. My wife were sick this winter.

HALE. So I am told. But you, Mister, why could you not come alone?

PROCTOR. I surely did come when I could, and when I could not I prayed in this house.

HALE. Mr. Proctor, your house is not a church; your theology must tell you that.

PROCTOR. It does, sir, it does; and it tells me that a minister may pray to God without he have golden candlesticks upon the altar.

HALE. What golden candlesticks?

PROCTOR. Since we built the church there were pewter candlesticks upon the altar; Francis Nurse made them, y'know, and a sweeter hand never touched the metal. But Parris came, and for twenty week he preach nothin' but golden candlesticks until he had them. I labor the earth from dawn of day to blink of night, and I tell you true, when I look to heaven and see my money glaring at his elbows—it hurt my prayer, sir, it hurt my prayer. I think, sometimes, the man dreams cathedrals, not clapboard meetin' houses.

HALE [*thinks, then*]. And yet, Mister, a Christian on Sabbath Day must be in church. [*Pause.*] Tell me—you have three children?

PROCTOR. Aye. Boys.

HALE. How comes it that only two are baptized?

PROCTOR [*starts to speak, then stops, then, as though unable to restrain this*]. I like it not that Mr. Parris should lay his hand upon my baby. I see no light of God in that man. I'll not conceal it.

HALE. I must say it, Mr. Proctor; that is not for you to decide. The man's ordained, therefore the light of God is in him.

PROCTOR [*flushed with resentment but trying to smile*]. What's your suspicion, Mr. Hale?

HALE. No, no, I have no—

PROCTOR. I nailed the roof upon the church, I hung the door—

HALE. Oh, did you! That's a good sign, then.

PROCTOR. It may be I have been too quick to bring the man to book, but you cannot think we ever desired the destruction of religion. I think that's in your mind, is it not?

HALE [*not altogether giving way*]. I—have—there is a softness in your record, sir, a softness.

ELIZABETH. I think, maybe, we have been too hard with Mr. Parris. I think so. But sure we never loved the Devil here.

HALE [*nods, deliberating this. Then, with the voice of one administering a secret test*]. Do you know your commandments, Elizabeth?

ELIZABETH [*without hesitation, even eagerly*]. I surely do. There be no mark of blame upon my life, Mr. Hale. I am a covenanted Christian woman.

HALE. And you, Mister?

PROCTOR [*a trifle unsteadily*]. I—am sure I do, sir.

HALE [*glances at her open face, then at* JOHN, *then*]. Let you repeat them, if you will.

PROCTOR. The Commandments.

HALE. Aye.

PROCTOR [*looking off, beginning to sweat*]. Thou shalt not kill.

HALE. Aye.

PROCTOR [*counting on his fingers*]. Thou shalt not steal. Thou shalt not covet thy neighbor's goods, nor make unto thee any graven image. Thou shalt not take the name of the Lord in vain; thou shalt have no other gods before me. [*With some hesitation*] Thou shalt remember the Sabbath Day and keep it holy. [*Pause. Then*] Thou shalt honor thy father and mother. Thou shalt not bear false witness.

[*He is stuck. He counts back on his fingers, knowing one is missing.*]

Thou shalt not make unto thee any graven image.

HALE. You have said that twice, sir.

PROCTOR [*lost*]. Aye. [*He is flailing for it.*]

ELIZABETH [*delicately*]. Adultery, John.

PROCTOR [*as though a secret arrow had pained his heart*]. Aye. [*Trying to grin it away—to* HALE] You see, sir, between the two of us we do know them all.

[HALE *only looks at* PROCTOR, *deep in his attempt to define this man.* PROCTOR *grows more uneasy.*]

I think it be a small fault.

HALE. Theology, sir, is a fortress; no crack in a fortress may be accounted small.

[*He rises; he seems worried now. He paces a little, in deep thought.*]

PROCTOR. There be no love for Satan in this house, Mister.

HALE. I pray it, I pray it dearly. [*He looks to both of them, an attempt at a smile on his face, but his misgivings are clear.*] Well, then—I'll bid you good night.

ELIZABETH [*unable to restrain herself*]. Mr. Hale. [*He turns.*] I do think you are suspecting me somewhat? Are you not?

HALE [*obviously disturbed—and evasive*]. Goody Proctor, I do not judge you. My duty is to add what I may to the godly wisdom of the court. I pray you both good health and good fortune. [*To* JOHN] Good night, sir. [*He starts out.*]

ELIZABETH [*with a note of desperation*]. I think you must tell him, John.

HALE. What's that?

ELIZABETH [*restraining a call*]. Will you tell him?

[*Slight pause.* HALE *looks questioningly at* JOHN.]

PROCTOR [*with difficulty*]. I—I have no witness and cannot prove it, except my word be taken. But I know the children's sickness had naught to do with witchcraft.

HALE [*stopped, struck*]. Naught to do—?

PROCTOR. Mr. Parris discovered them sportin' in the woods. They were startled and took sick.

[*Pause.*]

HALE. Who told you this?

PROCTOR [*hesitates, then*]. Abigail Williams.

HALE. Abigail!

PROCTOR. Aye.

HALE [*his eyes wide*]. Abigail Williams told you it had naught to do with witchcraft!

PROCTOR. She told me the day you came, sir.

HALE [*suspiciously*]. Why—why did you keep this?

PROCTOR. I never knew until tonight that the world is gone daft with this nonsense.

HALE. Nonsense! Mister, I have myself examined Tituba, Sarah Good, and numerous others that have confessed to dealing with the Devil. They have *confessed* it.

PROCTOR. And why not, if they must hang for denyin' it? There are them that will swear to anything before they'll hang; have you never thought of that?

HALE. I have. I—I have indeed. [*It is his own suspicion, but he resists it. He glances at* ELIZABETH, *then at* JOHN.] And you—would you testify to this in court?

PROCTOR. I—had not reckoned with goin' into court. But if I must I will.

HALE. Do you falter here?

PROCTOR. I falter nothing, but I may wonder if my story will be credited in such a court. I do wonder on it, when such a steady-minded minister as you will suspicion such a woman that never lied, and cannot, and the world knows she cannot! I may falter somewhat, Mister; I am no fool.

HALE [*quietly—it has impressed him*]. Proctor, let you open with me now, for I have a rumor that troubles me. It's said you hold no belief that there may even be witches in the world. Is that true, sir?

PROCTOR [*he knows this is critical, and is striving against his disgust with* HALE *and with himself for even answering*]. I know not what I have said, I may have said it. I have wondered if there be witches in the world—although I cannot believe they come among us now.

HALE. Then you do not believe—

PROCTOR. I have no knowledge of it; the Bible speaks of witches, and I will not deny them.

HALE. And you, woman?

ELIZABETH. I—I cannot believe it.

HALE [*shocked*]. You cannot!

PROCTOR. Elizabeth, you bewilder him!

ELIZABETH [*to* HALE]. I cannot think the Devil may own a woman's soul, Mr. Hale, when she keeps an upright way, as I have. I am a good woman, I know it; and if you believe I may do only good work in the world, and yet be secretly bound to Satan, then I must tell you, sir, I do not believe it.

HALE. But, woman, you do believe there are witches in—

ELIZABETH. If you think that I am one, then I say there are none.

HALE. You surely do not fly against the Gospel, the Gospel—

PROCTOR. She believe in the Gospel, every word!

ELIZABETH. Question Abigail Williams about the Gospel, not myself!

[HALE *stares at her.*]

PROCTOR. She do not mean to doubt the Gospel, sir, you cannot think it. This be a Christian house, sir, a Christian house.

HALE. God keep you both; let the third child be quickly baptized, and go you without fail each Sunday in to Sabbath prayer; and keep a solemn, quiet way among you. I think—

[GILES COREY *appears in doorway.*]

GILES. John!

PROCTOR. Giles! What's the matter?

GILES. They take my wife.

[FRANCIS NURSE *enters.*]

GILES. And his Rebecca!

PROCTOR [*to* FRANCIS]. Rebecca's in the *jail!*

FRANCIS. Aye, Cheever come and take her in his wagon. We've only now come from the jail, and they'll not even let us in to see them.

ELIZABETH. They've surely gone wild now, Mr. Hale!

FRANCIS [*going to* HALE]. Reverend Hale! Can you not speak to the Deputy Governor? I'm sure he mistakes these people—

HALE. Pray calm yourself, Mr. Nurse.

FRANCIS. My wife is the very brick and mortar of the church, Mr. Hale—[*indicating* GILES] and Martha Corey, there cannot be a woman closer yet to God than Martha.

HALE. How is Rebecca charged, Mr. Nurse?

FRANCIS [*with a mocking, half-hearted laugh*]. For murder, she's charged! [*Mockingly quoting the warrant*] "For the marvelous and supernatural murder of Goody Putnam's babies." What am I to do, Mr. Hale?

HALE [*turns from* FRANCIS, *deeply troubled, then*]. Believe me, Mr. Nurse, if Rebecca Nurse be tainted, then nothing's left to stop the whole green world from burning. Let you rest upon the justice of the court; the court will send her home, I know it.

FRANCIS. You cannot mean she will be tried in court!

HALE [*pleading*]. Nurse, though our hearts break, we cannot flinch; these are new times, sir. There is a misty plot afoot so subtle we should be criminal to cling to old respects and ancient friendships. I have seen too many frightful proofs in court—the Devil is alive in Salem, and we dare not quail to follow wherever the accusing finger points!

PROCTOR [*angered*]. How may such a woman murder children?

HALE [*in great pain*]. Man, remember, until an hour before the Devil fell, God thought him beautiful in Heaven.

GILES. I never said my wife were a witch, Mr. Hale; I only said she were reading books!

HALE. Mr. Corey, exactly what complaint were made on your wife?

GILES. That bloody mongrel Walcott charge her. Y'see, he buy a pig of my wife four or five year ago, and the pig died soon after. So he come dancin' in for his money back. So my Martha, she says to him, "Walcott, if you haven't the wit to feed a pig properly, you'll not live to own many," she says. Now he goes to court and claims that from that day to this he cannot keep a pig alive for more than four weeks because my Martha bewitch them with her books!

[*Enter* EZEKIEL CHEEVER. *A shocked silence.*]

CHEEVER. Good evening to you, Proctor.

PROCTOR. Why, Mr. Cheever. Good evening.

CHEEVER. Good evening, all. Good evening, Mr. Hale.

PROCTOR. I hope you come not on business of the court.

CHEEVER. I do, Proctor, aye. I am clerk of the court now, y'know.

[*Enter* MARSHAL HERRICK, *a man in his early thirties, who is some-what shamefaced at the moment.*]

GILES. It's a pity, Ezekiel, that an honest tailor might have gone to Heaven must burn in Hell. You'll burn for this, do you know it?

CHEEVER. You know yourself I must do as I'm told. You surely know that, Giles. And I'd as lief you'd not be sending me to Hell. I like not the sound of it, I tell you; I like not the sound of it.

[*He fears* PROCTOR, *but starts to reach inside his coat.*]

Now believe me, Proctor, how heavy be the law, all its tonnage I do carry on my back tonight. [*He takes out a warrant.*] I have a warrant for your wife.

PROCTOR [*to* HALE]. You said she were not charged!

HALE. I know nothin' of it. [*To* CHEEVER] When were she charged?

CHEEVER. I am given sixteen warrant tonight, sir, and she is one.

PROCTOR. Who charged her?

CHEEVER. Why, Abigail Williams charge her.

PROCTOR. On what proof, what proof?

CHEEVER [*looking about the room*]. Mr. Proctor, I have little time. The court bid me search your house, but I like not to search a house. So will you hand me any poppets that your wife may keep here?

PROCTOR. Poppets?

ELIZABETH. I never kept no poppets, not since I were a girl.

CHEEVER [*embarrassed, glancing toward the mantel where sits Mary Warren's poppet*]. I spy a poppet, Goody Proctor.

ELIZABETH. Oh! [*Going for it*] Why, this is Mary's.

CHEEVER [*shyly*]. Would you please to give it to me?

ELIZABETH [*handing it to him, asks* HALE]. Has the court discovered a text in poppets now?

CHEEVER [*carefully holding the poppet*]. Do you keep any others in this house?

PROCTOR. No, nor this one either till tonight. What signifies a poppet?

CHEEVER. Why, a poppet—[*he gingerly turns the poppet over*] a poppet may signify— Now, woman, will you please to come with me?

PROCTOR. She will not! [*To* ELIZABETH] Fetch Mary here.

CHEEVER [*ineptly reaching toward* ELIZABETH]. No, no, I am forbid to leave her from my sight.

PROCTOR [*pushing his arm away*]. You'll leave her out of sight and out of mind, Mister. Fetch Mary, Elizabeth.

[ELIZABETH *goes upstairs.*]

HALE. What signifies a poppet, Mr. Cheever?

CHEEVER [*turning the poppet over in his hands*]. Why, they say it may signify that she—[*He has lifted the poppet's skirt, and his eyes widen in astonished fear.*] Why, this, this—

PROCTOR [*reaching for the poppet*]. What's there?

CHEEVER. Why—[*He draws out a long needle from the poppet*]— it is a needle! Herrick, Herrick, it is a needle!

[HERRICK *comes toward him.*]

PROCTOR [*angrily, bewildered*]. And what signifies a needle!

CHEEVER [*his hands shaking*]. Why, this go hard with her, Proctor, this—I had my doubts, Proctor, I had my doubts, but here's calamity. [*To* HALE, *showing the needle*] You see it, sir, it is a needle!

HALE. Why? What meanin' has it?

CHEEVER [*wide-eyed, trembling*]. The girl, the Williams girl, Abigail Williams, sir. She sat to dinner in Reverend Parris's house tonight, and without word nor warnin' she falls to the floor. Like a struck beast, he says, and screamed a scream that a bull would weep to hear. And he goes to save her, and, stuck two inches in the flesh of her belly, he draw a needle out. And demandin' of her how she come to be so stabbed, she [*to* PROCTOR *now*] testify it were your wife's familiar spirit pushed it in.

PROCTOR. Why, she done it herself! [*To* HALE] I hope you're not takin' this for proof, Mister!

[HALE, *struck by the proof, is silent.*]

CHEEVER. 'Tis hard proof! [*To* HALE] I find here a poppet Goody Proctor keeps. I have found it, sir. And in the belly of the poppet a needle's stuck. I tell you true, Proctor, I never warranted to see such proof of Hell, and I bid you obstruct me not, for I—

[*Enter* ELIZABETH *with* MARY WARREN. PROCTOR, *seeing* MARY WARREN, *draws her by the arm to* HALE.]

PROCTOR. Here now! Mary, how did this poppet come into my house?

MARY WARREN [*frightened for herself, her voice very small*]. What poppet's that, sir?

PROCTOR [*impatiently, pointing at the doll in* CHEEVER's *hand*]. This poppet, this poppet.

MARY WARREN [*evasively, looking at it*]. Why, I—I think it is mine.

PROCTOR. It is your poppet, is it not?

MARY WARREN [*not understanding the direction of this*]. It—is, sir.

PROCTOR. And how did it come into this house?

MARY WARREN [*glancing about at the avid faces*]. Why—I made it in the court, sir, and—give it to Goody Proctor tonight.

PROCTOR [*to* HALE]. Now, sir—do you have it?

HALE. Mary Warren, a needle have been found inside this poppet.

MARY WARREN [*bewildered*]. Why, I meant no harm by it, sir.

PROCTOR [*quickly*]. You stuck that needle in yourself?

MARY WARREN. I—I believe I did, sir, I—

PROCTOR [*to* HALE]. What say you now?

HALE [*watching* MARY WARREN *closely*]. Child, you are certain this be your natural memory? May it be, perhaps, that someone conjures you even now to say this?

MARY WARREN. Conjures me? Why, no, sir, I am entirely myself, I think. Let you ask Susanna Walcott—she saw me sewin' it in court. [*Or better still*] Ask Abby, Abby sat beside me when I made it.

PROCTOR [*to* HALE, *of* CHEEVER]. Bid him begone. Your mind is surely settled now. Bid him out, Mr. Hale.

ELIZABETH. What signifies a needle?

HALE. Mary—you charge a cold and cruel murder on Abigail.

MARY WARREN. Murder! I charge no—

HALE. Abigail were stabbed tonight; a needle were found stuck into her belly—

ELIZABETH. And she charges me?

HALE. Aye.

ELIZABETH [*her breath knocked out*]. Why—! The girl is murder! She must be ripped out of the world!

CHEEVER [*pointing at* ELIZABETH]. You've heard that, sir! Ripped out of the world! Herrick, you heard it!

PROCTOR [*suddenly snatching the warrant out of* CHEEVER's *hands*]. Out with you.

CHEEVER. Proctor, you dare not touch the warrant.

PROCTOR [*ripping the warrant*]. Out with you!

CHEEVER. You've ripped the Deputy Governor's warrant, man!

PROCTOR. Damn the Deputy Governor! Out of my house!

HALE. Now, Proctor, Proctor!

PROCTOR. Get y'gone with them! You are a broken minister.

HALE. Proctor, if she is innocent, the court—

PROCTOR. If *she* is innocent! Why do you never wonder if Parris be innocent, or Abigail? Is the accuser always holy now? Were they born this morning as clean as God's fingers? I'll tell you what's walking Salem—vengeance is walking Salem. We are what we always were in Salem, but now the little crazy children are jangling the keys of the kingdom, and common vengeance writes the law! This warrant's vengeance! I'll not give my wife to vengeance!

ELIZABETH. I'll go, John—

PROCTOR. You will not go!

HERRICK. I have nine men outside. You cannot keep her. The law binds me, John, I cannot budge.

PROCTOR [to HALE, *ready to break him*]. Will you see her taken?

HALE. Proctor, the court is just—

PROCTOR. Pontius Pilate! God will not let you wash your hands of this!

ELIZABETH. John—I think I must go with them.

[*He cannot bear to look at her.*]

Mary, there is bread enough for the morning; you will bake, in the afternoon. Help Mr. Proctor as you were his daughter—you owe me that, and much more. [*She is fighting her weeping. To* PROCTOR] When the children wake, speak nothing of witchcraft—it will frighten them. [*She cannot go on.*]

PROCTOR. I will bring you home. I will bring you soon.

ELIZABETH. Oh, John, bring me soon!

PROCTOR. I will fall like an ocean on that court! Fear nothing, Elizabeth.

ELIZABETH [*with great fear*]. I will fear nothing.

[*She looks about the room, as though to fix it in her mind.*]

Tell the children I have gone to visit someone sick.

[*She walks out the door,* HERRICK *and* CHEEVER *behind her. For a moment,* PROCTOR *watches from the doorway. The clank of chain is heard.*]

PROCTOR. Herrick! Herrick, don't chain her!

[*He rushes out the door. From outside*]

Damn you, man, you will not chain her! Off with them! I'll not have it! I will not have her chained!

[*There are other men's voices against his.* HALE, *in a fever of guilt and uncertainty, turns from the door to avoid the sight;* MARY WARREN *bursts into tears and sits weeping.* GILES COREY *calls to* HALE.]

GILES. And yet silent, minister? It is fraud, you know it is fraud! What keeps you, man?

[PROCTOR *is half braced, half pushed into the room by* TWO DEPUTIES *and* HERRICK.]

PROCTOR. I'll pay you, Herrick, I will surely pay you!

HERRICK [*panting*]. In God's name, John, I cannot help myself. I must chain them all. Now let you keep inside this house till I am gone!

[*He goes out with his deputies.*]

[PROCTOR *stands there, gulping air. Horses and a wagon creaking are heard.*]

HALE [*in great uncertainty*]. Mr. Proctor—

PROCTOR. Out of my sight!

HALE. Charity, Proctor, charity. What I have heard in her favor, I will not fear to testify in court. God help me, I cannot judge her guilty or innocent—I know not. Only this consider: the world goes mad, and it profit nothing you should lay the cause to the vengeance of a little girl.

PROCTOR. You are a coward! Though you be ordained in God's own tears, you are a coward now!

HALE. Proctor, I cannot think God be provoked so grandly by such a petty cause. The jails are packed—our greatest judges sit in Salem now—and hangin's promised. Man, we must look to cause proportionate. Were there murder done, perhaps, and never brought to light? Abomination? Some secret blasphemy that stinks to Heaven? Think on cause, man, and let you help me to discover it. For there's your way, believe it, there is your only way, when such confusion strikes upon the world. [*He goes to* GILES *and* FRANCIS.] Let you counsel among yourselves; think on your village and what may have drawn from heaven such thundering wrath upon you all. I shall pray God open up our eyes.

[HALE *goes out.*]

FRANCIS [*struck by* HALE's *mood*]. I never heard no murder done in Salem.

PROCTOR [*he has been reached by* HALE's *words*]. Leave me, Francis, leave me.

GILES [*shaken*]. John—tell me, are we lost?

PROCTOR. Go home now, Giles. We'll speak on it tomorrow.

GILES. Let you think on it. We'll come early, eh?

PROCTOR. Aye. Go now, Giles.

GILES. Good night, then.

[GILES COREY *goes out. After a moment*]

MARY WARREN [*in a fearful squeak of a voice*]. Mr. Proctor, very likely they'll let her come home once they're given proper evidence.

PROCTOR. You're coming to the court with me, Mary. You will tell it in the court.

MARY WARREN. I cannot charge murder on Abigail.

PROCTOR [*moving menacingly toward her*]. You will tell the court how that poppet come here and who stuck the needle in.

MARY WARREN. She'll kill me for sayin' that! [PROCTOR *continues toward her.*] Abby'll charge lechery on you, Mr. Proctor!

PROCTOR [*halting*]. She's told you!

MARY WARREN. I have known it, sir. She'll ruin you with it, I know she will.

PROCTOR [*hesitating, and with deep hatred of himself*]. Good. Then her saintliness is done with. [MARY *backs from him.*] We will slide together into our pit; you will tell the court what you know.

MARY WARREN [*in terror*]. I cannot, they'll turn on me—

[PROCTOR *strides and catches her, and she is repeating, "I cannot, I cannot!"*]

PROCTOR. My wife will never die for me! I will bring your guts into your mouth but that goodness will not die for me!

MARY WARREN [*struggling to escape him*]. I cannot do it, I cannot!

PROCTOR [*grasping her by the throat as though he would strangle her*]. Make your peace with it! Now Hell and Heaven grapple on our backs, and all our old pretense is ripped away—make your peace!

[*He throws her to the floor, where she sobs, "I cannot, I cannot . . ." And now, half to himself, staring, and turning to the open door*]

Peace. It is a providence, and no great change; we are only what we always were, but naked now. [*He walks as though toward a great horror, facing the open sky.*] Aye, naked! And the wind, God's icy wind, will blow!

[*And she is over and over again sobbing, "I cannot, I cannot, I cannot," as*

THE CURTAIN FALLS

ACT THREE

THE VESTRY ROOM *of the Salem meeting house, now serving as the ante-room of the General Court.*

As the curtain rises, the room is empty, but for sunlight pouring through two high windows in the back wall. The room is solemn, even forbidding. Heavy beams jut out, boards of random widths make up the walls. At the right are two doors leading into the meeting house proper, where the court is being held. At the left another door leads outside.

There is a plain bench at the left, and another at the right. In the center a rather long meeting table, with stools and a considerable arm-chair snugged up to it.

Through the partitioning wall at the right we hear a prosecutor's voice, JUDGE HATHORNE'S, asking a question; then a woman's voice, MARTHA COREY'S, replying.

HATHORNE'S VOICE. Now, Martha Corey, there is abundant evidence in our hands to show that you have given yourself to the reading of fortunes. Do you deny it?

MARTHA COREY'S VOICE. I am innocent to a witch. I know not what a witch is.

HATHORNE'S VOICE. How do you know, then, that you are not a witch?

MARTHA COREY'S VOICE. If I were, I would know it.

HATHORNE'S VOICE. Why do you hurt these children?

MARTHA COREY'S VOICE. I do not hurt them. I scorn it!

GILES' VOICE [roaring]. I have evidence for the court!

[Voices of townspeople rise in excitement.]

DANFORTH'S VOICE. You will keep your seat!

GILES' VOICE. Thomas Putnam is reaching out for land!

DANFORTH'S VOICE. Remove that man, Marshal!

GILES' VOICE. You're hearing lies, lies!

[A roaring goes up from the people.]

HATHORNE'S VOICE. Arrest him, Excellency!

GILES' VOICE. I have evidence. Why will you not hear my evidence?

[The door opens and GILES is half carried into the vestry room by HERRICK.]

GILES. Hands off, damn you, let me go!

HERRICK. Giles, Giles!

GILES. Out of my way, Herrick! I bring evidence—

HERRICK. You cannot go in there, Giles; it's a court!

[Enter HALE from the court.]

HALE. Pray be calm a moment.

GILES. You, Mr. Hale, go in there and demand I speak.

HALE. A moment, sir, a moment.

GILES. They'll be hangin' my wife!

[JUDGE HATHORNE enters. He is in his sixties, a bitter, remorseless Salem judge.]

HATHORNE. How do you dare come roarin' into this court! Are you gone daft, Corey?

GILES. You're not a Boston judge yet, Hathorne. You'll not call me daft!

[Enter DEPUTY GOVERNOR DANFORTH and, behind him, EZEKIEL CHEEVER and PARRIS. On his appearance, silence falls. DANFORTH is a grave man in his sixties, of some humor and sophistication that *does not, however, interfere with an exact loyalty to his position and his cause. He comes down to* GILES, *who awaits his wrath.*]

DANFORTH [*looking directly at* GILES]. Who is this man?

PARRIS. Giles Corey, sir, and a more contentious—

GILES [*to* PARRIS]. I am asked the question, and I am old enough to answer it! [*To* DANFORTH, *who impresses him and to whom he smiles through his strain*] My name is Corey, sir, Giles Corey. I have six hundred acres, and timber in addition. It is my wife you be condemning now. [*He indicates the courtroom.*]

DANFORTH. And how do you imagine to help her cause with such contemptuous riot? Now be gone. Your old age alone keeps you out of jail for this.

GILES [*beginning to plead*]. They be tellin' lies about my wife, sir, I—

DANFORTH. Do you take it upon yourself to determine what this court shall believe and what it shall set aside?

GILES. Your Excellency, we mean no disrespect for—

DANFORTH. Disrespect indeed! It is disruption, Mister. This is the highest court of the supreme government of this province, do you know it?

GILES [*beginning to weep*]. Your Excellency, I only said she were readin' books, sir, and they come and take her out of my house for—

DANFORTH [*mystified*]. Books! What books?

GILES [*through helpless sobs*]. It is my third wife, sir; I never had no wife that be so taken with books, and I thought to find the cause of it, d'y'see, but it were no witch I blamed her for. [*He is openly weeping.*] I have broke charity with the woman, I have broke charity with her.

[*He covers his face, ashamed.* DANFORTH *is respectfully silent.*]

HALE. Excellency, he claims hard evidence for his wife's defense. I think that in all justice you must—

DANFORTH. Then let him submit his evidence in proper affidavit. You are certainly aware of our procedure here, Mr. Hale. [*To* HERRICK] Clear this room.

HERRICK. Come now, Giles.

[*He gently pushes* COREY *out.*]

FRANCIS. We are desperate, sir; we come here three days now and cannot be heard.

DANFORTH. Who is this man?

FRANCIS. Francis Nurse, Your Excellency.

HALE. His wife's Rebecca that were condemned this morning.

DANFORTH. Indeed! I am amazed to find you in such uproar. I have only good report of your character, Mr. Nurse.

HATHORNE. I think they must both be arrested in contempt, sir.

DANFORTH [*to* FRANCIS]. Let you write your plea, and in due time I will—

FRANCIS. Excellency, we have proof for your eyes; God forbid you shut them to it. The girls, sir, the girls are frauds.

DANFORTH. What's that?

FRANCIS. We have proof of it, sir. They are all deceiving you.

[DANFORTH *is shocked, but studying* FRANCIS.]

HATHORNE. This is contempt, sir, contempt!

DANFORTH. Peace, Judge Hathorne. Do you know who I am, Mr. Nurse?

FRANCIS. I surely do, sir, and I think you must be a wise judge to be what you are.

DANFORTH. And do you know that near to four hundred are in the jails from Marblehead to Lynn, and upon my signature?

FRANCIS. I—

DANFORTH. And seventy-two condemned to hang by that signature?

FRANCIS. Excellency, I never thought to say it to such a weighty judge, but you are deceived.

[*Enter* GILES COREY *from left. All turn to see as he beckons in* MARY WARREN *with* PROCTOR. MARY *is keeping her eyes to the ground;* PROCTOR *has her elbow as though she were near collapse.*]

PARRIS [*on seeing her, in shock*]. Mary Warren! [*He goes directly to bend close to her face.*] What are you about here?

PROCTOR [*pressing* PARRIS *away from her with a gentle but firm motion of protectiveness*]. She would speak with the Deputy Governor.

DANFORTH [*shocked by this, turns to* HERRICK]. Did you not tell me Mary Warren were sick in bed?

HERRICK. She were, Your Honor. When I go to fetch her to the court last week, she said she were sick.

GILES. She has been strivin' with her soul all week, Your Honor; she comes now to tell the truth of this to you.

DANFORTH. Who is this?

PROCTOR. John Proctor, sir. Elizabeth Proctor is my wife.

PARRIS. Beware this man, Your Excellency, this man is mischief.

HALE [*excitedly*]. I think you must hear the girl, sir, she—

DANFORTH [*who has become very interested in* MARY WARREN *and only raises a hand toward* HALE]. Peace. What would you tell us, Mary Warren?

[PROCTOR *looks at her, but she cannot speak.*]

PROCTOR. She never saw no spirits, sir.

DANFORTH [*with great alarm and surprise, to* MARY]. Never saw no spirits!

GILES [*eagerly*]. Never.

PROCTOR [*reaching into his jacket*]. She has signed a deposition, sir—

DANFORTH [*instantly*]. No, no, I accept no depositions. [*He is rapidly calculating this; he turns from her to* PROCTOR.] Tell me, Mr. Proctor, have you given out this story in the village?

PROCTOR. We have not.

PARRIS. They've come to overthrow the court, sir! This man is—

DANFORTH. I pray you, Mr. Parris. Do you know, Mr. Proctor, that the entire contention of the state in these trials is that the voice of Heaven is speaking through the children?

PROCTOR. I know that, sir.

DANFORTH [*thinks, staring at* PROCTOR, *then turns to* MARY WARREN]. And you, Mary Warren, how came you to cry out people for sending their spirits against you?

MARY WARREN. It were pretense, sir.

DANFORTH. I cannot hear you.

PROCTOR. It were pretense, she says.

DANFORTH. Ah? And the other girls? Susanna Walcott, and—the others? They are also pretending?

MARY WARREN. Aye, sir.

DANFORTH [*wide-eyed*]. Indeed.

[*Pause. He is baffled by this. He turns to study* PROCTOR's *face.*]

PARRIS [*in a sweat*]. Excellency, you surely cannot think to let so vile a lie be spread in open court!

DANFORTH. Indeed not, but it strike hard upon me that she will dare come here with such a tale. Now, Mr. Proctor, before I decide whether I shall hear you or not, it is my duty to tell you this. We burn a hot fire here; it melts down all concealment.

PROCTOR. I know that, sir.

DANFORTH. Let me continue. I understand well, a husband's tenderness may drive him to extravagance in defense of a wife. Are you certain in your conscience, Mister, that your evidence is the truth?

PROCTOR. It is. And you will surely know it.

DANFORTH. And you thought to declare this revelation in the open court before the public?

PROCTOR. I thought I would, aye—with your permission.

DANFORTH [*his eyes narrowing*]. Now, sir, what is your purpose in so doing?

PROCTOR. Why, I—I would free my wife, sir.

DANFORTH. There lurks nowhere in your heart, nor hidden in your spirit, any desire to undermine this court?

PROCTOR [*with the faintest faltering*]. Why, no, sir.

CHEEVER [*clears his throat, awakening*]. I— Your Excellency.

DANFORTH. Mr. Cheever.

CHEEVER. I think it be my duty, sir— [*Kindly, to* PROCTOR.] You'll not deny it, John. [*To* DANFORTH] When we come to take his wife, he damned the court and ripped your warrant.

PARRIS. Now you have it!

DANFORTH. He did that, Mr. Hale?

HALE [*takes a breath*]. Aye, he did.

PROCTOR. It were a temper, sir. I knew not what I did.

DANFORTH [*studying him*]. Mr. Proctor.

PROCTOR. Aye, sir.

DANFORTH [*straight into his eyes*]. Have you ever seen the Devil?

PROCTOR. No, sir.

DANFORTH. You are in all respects a Gospel Christian?

PROCTOR. I am, sir.

PARRIS. Such a Christian that will not come to church but once in a month!

DANFORTH [*restrained—he is curious*]. Not come to church?

PROCTOR. I—I have no love for Mr. Parris. It is no secret. But God I surely love.

CHEEVER. He plow on Sunday, sir.

DANFORTH. Plow on Sunday!

CHEEVER [*apologetically*]. I think it be evidence, John. I am an official of the court, I cannot keep it.

PROCTOR. I—I have once or twice plowed on Sunday. I have three children, sir, and until last year my land give little.

GILES. You'll find other Christians that do plow on Sunday if the truth be known.

HALE. Your Honor, I cannot think you may judge the man on such evidence.

DANFORTH. I judge nothing.

[*Pause. He keeps watching* PROCTOR, *who tries to meet his gaze.*]

I tell you straight, Mister—I have seen marvels in this court. I have seen people choked before my eyes by spirits; I have seen them stuck by pins and slashed by daggers. I have until this moment not the slightest reason to suspect that the children may be deceiving me. Do you understand my meaning?

PROCTOR. Excellency, does it not strike upon you that so many of these women have lived so long with such upright reputation, and—

PARRIS. Do you read the Gospel, Mr. Proctor?

PROCTOR. I read the Gospel.

PARRIS. I think not, or you should surely know that Cain were an upright man, and yet he did kill Abel.

PROCTOR. Aye, God tells us that. [*To* DANFORTH] But who tells us Rebecca Nurse murdered seven babies by sending out her spirit on them? It is the children only, and this one will swear she lied to you.

[DANFORTH *considers, then beckons* HATHORNE *to him.* HATHORNE *leans in, and he speaks in his ear.* HATHORNE *nods.*]

HATHORNE. Aye, she's the one.

DANFORTH. Mr. Proctor, this morning, your wife send me a claim in which she states that she is pregnant now.

PROCTOR. My wife pregnant!

DANFORTH. There be no sign of it—we have examined her body.

PROCTOR. But if she says she is pregnant, then she must be! That woman will never lie, Mr. Danforth.

DANFORTH. She will not?

PROCTOR. Never, sir, never.

DANFORTH. We have thought it too convenient to be credited. However, if I should tell you now that I will let her be kept another month; and if she begin to show her natural signs, you shall have her living yet another year until she is delivered—what say you to that?

[JOHN PROCTOR *is struck silent.*]

Come now. You say your only purpose is to save your wife. Good, then, she is saved at least this year, and a year is long. What say you, sir? It is done now.

[*In conflict,* PROCTOR *glances at* FRANCIS *and* GILES.]

Will you drop this charge?

PROCTOR. I—I think I cannot.

DANFORTH [*now an almost imperceptible hardness in his voice*]. Then your purpose is somewhat larger.

PARRIS. He's come to overthrow this court, Your Honor!

PROCTOR. These are my friends. Their wives are also accused—

DANFORTH [*with a sudden briskness of manner*]. I judge you not, sir. I am ready to hear your evidence.

PROCTOR. I come not to hurt the court; I only—

DANFORTH [*cutting him off*]. Marshal, go into the court and bid Judge Stoughton and Judge Sewall declare recess for one hour. And let them go to the tavern, if they will. All witnesses and prisoners are to be kept in the building.

HERRICK. Aye, sir. [*Very deferentially*] If I may say it, sir, I know this man all my life. It is a good man, sir.

DANFORTH [*it is the reflection on himself he resents*]. I am sure of it, Marshal.

[HERRICK *nods, then goes out.*]

Now, what deposition do you have for us, Mr. Proctor? And I beg you be clear, open as the sky, and honest.

PROCTOR [*as he takes out several papers*]. I am no lawyer, so I'll—

DANFORTH. The pure in heart need no lawyers. Proceed as you will.

PROCTOR [*handing* DANFORTH *a paper*]. Will you read this first, sir? It's a sort of testament. The people signing it declare their good opinion of Rebecca, and my wife, and Martha Corey.

[DANFORTH *looks down at the paper.*]

PARRIS [*to enlist* DANFORTH's *sarcasm*]. Their good opinion!

[*But* DANFORTH *goes on reading, and* PROCTOR *is heartened.*]

PROCTOR. These are all landholding farmers, members of the church. [*Delicately, trying to point out a paragraph*] If you'll notice, sir— they've known the women many years and never saw no sign they had dealings with the Devil.

[PARRIS *nervously moves over and reads over* DANFORTH's *shoulder.*]

DANFORTH [*glancing down a long list*]. How many names are here?

FRANCIS. Ninety-one, Your Excellency.

PARRIS [*sweating*]. These people should be summoned.

[DANFORTH *looks up at him questioningly.*]

For questioning.

FRANCIS [*trembling with anger*]. Mr. Danforth, I gave them all my word no harm would come to them for signing this.

PARRIS. This is a clear attack upon the court!

HALE [*to* PARRIS, *trying to contain himself*]. Is every defense an attack upon the court? Can no one—?

PARRIS. All innocent and Christian people are happy for the courts in Salem! These people are gloomy for it. [*To* DANFORTH *directly*] And I think you will want to know, from each and every one of them, what discontents them with you!

HATHORNE. I think they ought to be examined, sir.

DANFORTH. It is not necessarily an attack, I think. Yet—

FRANCIS. These are all covenanted Christians, sir.

DANFORTH. Then I am sure they may have nothing to fear. [*Hands* CHEEVER *the paper.*] Mr. Cheever, have warrants drawn for all of these —arrest for examination. [*To* PROCTOR] Now, Mister, what other information do you have for us?

[FRANCIS *is still standing, horrified.*]

You may sit, Mr. Nurse.

FRANCIS. I have brought trouble on these people; I have—

DANFORTH. No, old man, you have not hurt these people if they are of good conscience. But you must understand, sir, that a person is either with this court or he must be counted against it, there be no road between. This is a sharp time, now, a precise time—we live no longer in the dusky afternoon when evil mixed itself with good and befuddled the world. Now, by God's grace, the shining sun is up, and them that fear not light will surely praise it. I hope you will be one of those.

[MARY WARREN *suddenly sobs.*]

She's not hearty, I see.

PROCTOR. No, she's not, sir. [*To* MARY, *bending to her, holding her hand, quietly*] Now remember what the angel Raphael said to the boy Tobias. Remember it.

MARY WARREN [*hardly audible*]. Aye.

PROCTOR. "Do that which is good, and no harm shall come to thee."

MARY WARREN. Aye.

DANFORTH. Come, man, we wait you.

[MARSHAL HERRICK *returns, and takes his post at the door.*]

GILES. John, my deposition, give him mine.

PROCTOR. Aye. [*He hands* DANFORTH *another paper.*] This is Mr. Corey's deposition.

DANFORTH. Oh? [*He looks down at it. Now* HATHORNE *comes behind him and reads with him.*]

HATHORNE [*suspiciously*]. What lawyer drew this, Corey?

GILES. You know I never hired a lawyer in my life, Hathorne.

DANFORTH [*finishing the reading*]. It is very well phrased. My compliments. Mr. Parris, if Mr. Putnam is in the court, will you bring him in?

[HATHORNE *takes the deposition, and walks to the window with it.* PARRIS *goes into the court.*]

You have no legal training, Mr. Corey?

GILES [*very pleased*]. I have the best, sir—I am thirty-three time in court in my life. And always plaintiff, too.

DANFORTH. Oh, then you're much put-upon.

GILES. I am never put-upon; I know my rights, sir, and I will have them. You know, your father tried a case of mine—might be thirty-five year ago, I think.

DANFORTH. Indeed.

GILES. He never spoke to you of it?

DANFORTH. No, I cannot recall it.

GILES. That's strange, he give me nine pound damages. He were a fair judge, your father. Y'see, I had a white mare that time, and this fellow come to borrow the mare—

[*Enter* PARRIS *with* THOMAS PUTNAM. *When he sees* PUTNAM, GILES' *ease goes; he is hard.*]

Aye, there he is.

DANFORTH. Mr. Putnam, I have here an accusation by Mr. Corey against you. He states that you coldly prompted your daughter to cry witchery upon George Jacobs that is now in jail.

PUTNAM. It is a lie.

DANFORTH [*turning to* GILES]. Mr. Putnam states your charge is a lie. What say you to that?

GILES [*furious, his fists clenched*]. A fart on Thomas Putnam, that is what I say to that!

DANFORTH. What proof do you submit for your charge, sir?

GILES. My proof is there! [*Pointing to the paper*] If Jacobs hangs for a witch he forfeit up his property—that's law! And there is none but Putnam with the coin to buy so great a piece. This man is killing his neighbors for their land!

DANFORTH. But proof, sir, proof.

GILES [*pointing at his deposition*]. The proof is there! I have it from an honest man who heard Putnam say it! The day his daughter cried out on Jacobs, he said she'd given him a fair gift of land.

HATHORNE. And the name of this man?

GILES [*taken aback*]. What name?

HATHORNE. The man that give you this information.

GILES [*hesitates, then*]. Why, I—I cannot give you his name.

HATHORNE. And why not?

GILES [*hesitates, then bursts out*]. You know well why not! He'll lay in jail if I give his name!

HATHORNE. This is contempt of the court, Mr. Danforth!

DANFORTH [*to avoid that*]. You will surely tell us the name.

GILES. I will not give you no name. I mentioned my wife's name once and I'll burn in hell long enough for that. I stand mute.

DANFORTH. In that case, I have no choice but to arrest you for contempt of this court, do you know that?

GILES. This is a hearing; you cannot clap me for contempt of a hearing.

DANFORTH. Oh, it is a proper lawyer! Do you wish me to declare the court in full session here? Or will you give me good reply?

GILES [*faltering*]. I cannot give you no name, sir, I cannot.

DANFORTH. You are a foolish old man. Mr. Cheever, begin the record. The court is now in session. I ask you, Mr. Corey—

PROCTOR [*breaking in*]. Your Honor—he has the story in confidence, sir, and he—

PARRIS. The Devil lives on such confidences! [*To* DANFORTH] Without confidences there could be no conspiracy, Your Honor!

HATHORNE. I think it must be broken, sir.

DANFORTH [*to* GILES]. Old man, if your informant tells the truth let him come here openly like a decent man. But if he hide in anonymity I must know why. Now sir, the government and central church demand of you the name of him who reported Mr. Thomas Putnam a common murderer.

HALE. Excellency—

DANFORTH. Mr. Hale.

HALE. We cannot blink it more. There is a prodigious fear of this court in the country—

DANFORTH. Then there is a prodigious guilt in the country. Are *you* afraid to be questioned here?

HALE. I may only fear the Lord, sir, but there is fear in the country nevertheless.

DANFORTH [*angered now*]. Reproach me not with the fear in the country; there is fear in the country because there is a moving plot to topple Christ in the country!

HALE. But it does not follow that everyone accused is part of it.

DANFORTH. No uncorrupted man may fear this court, Mr. Hale! None! [*To* GILES] You are under arrest in contempt of this court. Now sit you down and take counsel with yourself, or you will be set in the jail until you decide to answer all questions.

[GILES COREY *makes a rush for* PUTNAM. PROCTOR *lunges and holds him.*]

PROCTOR. No, Giles!

GILES [*over* PROCTOR's *shoulder at* PUTNAM]. I'll cut your throat, Putnam, I'll kill you yet!

PROCTOR [*forcing him into a chair*]. Peace, Giles, peace. [*Releasing him.*] We'll prove ourselves. Now we will.

[*He starts to turn to* DANFORTH.]

GILES. Say nothin' more, John. [*Pointing at* DANFORTH.] He's only playin' you! He means to hang us all!

[MARY WARREN *bursts into sobs.*]

DANFORTH. This is a court of law, Mister. I'll have no effrontery here!

PROCTOR. Forgive him, sir, for his old age. Peace, Giles, we'll prove it all now. [*He lifts up* MARY's *chin.*] You cannot weep, Mary. Remember the angel, what he say to the boy. Hold to it, now; there is your rock.

[MARY *quiets. He takes out a paper, and turns to* DANFORTH.]

This is Mary Warren's deposition. I—I would ask you remember, sir, while you read it, that until two week ago she were no different than the other children are today. [*He is speaking reasonably, restraining all his fears, his anger, his anxiety.*] You saw her scream, she howled, she swore familiar spirits choked her; she even testified that Satan, in the form of women now in jail, tried to win her soul away, and then when she refused—

DANFORTH. We know all this.

PROCTOR. Aye, sir. She swears now that she never saw Satan; nor any spirit, vague or clear, that Satan may have sent to hurt her. And she declares her friends are lying now.

[PROCTOR *starts to hand* DANFORTH *the deposition, and* HALE *comes up to* DANFORTH *in a trembling state.*]

HALE. Excellency, a moment. I think this goes to the heart of the matter.

DANFORTH [*with deep misgivings*]. It surely does.

HALE. I cannot say he is an honest man; I know him little. But in all justice, sir, a claim so weighty cannot be argued by a farmer. In God's name, sir, stop here; send him home and let him come again with a lawyer—

DANFORTH [*patiently*]. Now look you, Mr. Hale—

HALE. Excellency, I have signed seventy-two death warrants; I am a minister of the Lord, and I dare not take a life without there be a proof so immaculate no slightest qualm of conscience may doubt it.

DANFORTH. Mr. Hale, you surely do not doubt my justice.

HALE. I have this morning signed away the soul of Rebecca Nurse, Your Honor. I'll not conceal it, my hand shakes yet as with a wound! I pray you, sir, *this* argument let lawyers present to you.

DANFORTH. Mr. Hale, believe me; for a man of such terrible learning you are most bewildered—I hope you will forgive me. I have been thirty-two year at the bar, sir, and I should be confounded were I called upon to defend these people. Let you consider, now— [*To* PROCTOR *and the others*] And I bid you all do likewise. In an ordinary crime, how does one defend the accused? One calls up witnesses to prove his innocence. But witchcraft is *ipso facto,* on its face and by its nature, an invisible crime, is it not? Therefore, who may possibly be witness to it? The witch and the victim. None other. Now we cannot hope the witch will accuse herself; granted? Therefore, we must rely upon her victims —and they do testify, the children certainly do testify. As for the witches, none will deny that we are most eager for all their confessions. Therefore, what is left for a lawyer to bring out? I think I have made my point. Have I not?

HALE. But this child claims the girls are not truthful, and if they are not—

DANFORTH. That is precisely what I am about to consider, sir. What more may you ask of me? Unless you doubt my probity?

HALE [*defeated*]. I surely do not, sir. Let you consider it, then.

DANFORTH. And let you put your heart to rest. Her deposition, Mr. Proctor.

[PROCTOR *hands it to him.* HATHORNE *rises, goes beside* DANFORTH, *and starts reading.* PARRIS *comes to his other side.* DANFORTH *looks at* JOHN PROCTOR, *then proceeds to read.* HALE *gets up, finds position near the judge, reads too.* PROCTOR *glances at* GILES. FRANCIS *prays silently, hands pressed together.* CHEEVER *waits placidly, the sublime official, dutiful.* MARY WARREN *sobs once.* JOHN PROCTOR *touches her head reassuringly.* Presently DANFORTH *lifts his eyes, stands up, takes out a kerchief and blows his nose. The others stand aside as he moves in thought toward the window.*]

PARRIS [*hardly able to contain his anger and fear*]. I should like to question—

DANFORTH [*his first real outburst, in which his contempt for* PARRIS *is clear*]. Mr. Parris, I bid you be silent!

[*He stands in silence, looking out the window. Now, having established that he will set the gait*]

Mr. Cheever, will you go into the court and bring the children here?

[CHEEVER *gets up and goes out upstage.* DANFORTH *now turns to* MARY.]

Mary Warren, how came you to this turnabout? Has Mr. Proctor threatened you for this deposition?

MARY WARREN. No, sir.

DANFORTH. Has he ever threatened you?

MARY WARREN [*weaker*]. No, sir.

DANFORTH [*sensing a weakening*]. Has he threatened you?

MARY WARREN. No, sir.

DANFORTH. Then you tell me that you sat in my court, callously lying, when you knew that people would hang by your evidence? [*She does not answer.*] Answer me!

MARY WARREN [*almost inaudibly*]. I did, sir.

DANFORTH. How were you instructed in your life? Do you not know that God damns all liars? [*She cannot speak.*] Or is it now that you lie?

MARY WARREN. No, sir—I am with God now.

DANFORTH. You are with God now.

MARY WARREN. Aye, sir.

DANFORTH [*containing himself*]. I will tell you this—you are either lying now, or you were lying in the court, and in either case you have committed perjury and you will go to jail for it. You cannot lightly say you lied, Mary. Do you know that?

MARY WARREN. I cannot lie no more. I am with God, I am with God.

[*But she breaks into sobs at the thought of it, and the right door opens, and enter* SUSANNA WALCOTT, MERCY LEWIS, BETTY PARRIS, *and finally* ABIGAIL. CHEEVER *comes to* DANFORTH.]

CHEEVER. Ruth Putnam's not in the court, sir, nor the other children.

DANFORTH. These will be sufficient. Sit you down, children.

[*Silently they sit.*]

Your friend, Mary Warren, has given us a deposition. In which she swears that she never saw familiar spirits, apparitions, nor any manifest of the Devil. She claims as well that none of you have seen these things either. [*Slight pause.*] Now, children, this is a court of law. The law, based upon the Bible, and the Bible, writ by Almighty God, forbid the practice of witchcraft, and describe death as the penalty thereof. But likewise, children, the law and Bible damn all bearers of false witness. [*Slight pause.*] Now then. It does not escape me that this deposition may be devised to blind us; it may well be that Mary Warren has been conquered by Satan, who sends her here to distract our sacred purpose. If so, her neck will break for it. But if she speak true, I bid you now drop your guile and confess your pretense, for a quick confession will go easier with you. [*Pause.*] Abigail Williams, rise.

[ABIGAIL *slowly rises.*]

Is there any truth in this?

ABIGAIL. No, sir.

DANFORTH [*thinks, glances at* MARY, *then back to* ABIGAIL]. Children, a very augur bit will now be turned into your souls until your honesty is proved. Will either of you change your positions now, or do you force me to hard questioning?

ABIGAIL. I have naught to change, sir. She lies.

DANFORTH [*to* MARY]. You would still go on with this?

MARY WARREN [*faintly*]. Aye, sir.

DANFORTH [*turning to* ABIGAIL]. A poppet were discovered in Mr. Proctor's house, stabbed by a needle. Mary Warren claims that you sat beside her in the court when she made it, and that you saw her make it and witnessed how she herself stuck her needle into it for safe-keeping. What say you to that?

ABIGAIL [*with a slight note of indignation*]. It is a lie, sir.

DANFORTH [*after a slight pause*]. While you worked for Mr. Proctor, did you see poppets in that house?

ABIGAIL. Goody Proctor always kept poppets.

PROCTOR. Your Honor, my wife never kept no poppets. Mary Warren confesses it was her poppet.

CHEEVER. Your Excellency.

DANFORTH. Mr. Cheever.

CHEEVER. When I spoke with Goody Proctor in that house, she said she never kept no poppets. But she said she did keep poppets when she were a girl.

PROCTOR. She has not been a girl these fifteen years, Your Honor.

HATHORNE. But a poppet will keep fifteen years, will it not?

PROCTOR. It will keep if it is kept, but Mary Warren swears she never saw no poppets in my house, nor anyone else.

PARRIS. Why could there not have been poppets hid where no one ever saw them?

PROCTOR [*furious*]. There might also be a dragon with five legs in my house, but no one has ever seen it.

PARRIS. We are here, Your Honor, precisely to discover what no one has ever seen.

PROCTOR. Mr. Danforth, what profit this girl to turn herself about? What may Mary Warren gain but hard questioning and worse?

DANFORTH. You are charging Abigail Williams with a marvelous cool plot to murder, do you understand that?

PROCTOR. I do, sir. I believe she means to murder.

DANFORTH [*pointing at* ABIGAIL, *incredulously*]. This child would murder your wife?

PROCTOR. It is not a child. Now hear me, sir. In the sight of the congregation she were twice this year put out of this meetin' house for laughter during prayer.

DANFORTH [*shocked, turning to* ABIGAIL]. What's this? Laughter during—!

PARRIS. Excellency, she were under Tituba's power at that time, but she is solemn now.

GILES. Aye, now she is solemn and goes to hang people!

DANFORTH. Quiet, man.

HATHORNE. Surely it have no bearing on the question, sir. He charges contemplation of murder.

DANFORTH. Aye. [*He studies* ABIGAIL *for a moment, then*] Continue, Mr. Proctor.

PROCTOR. Mary. Now tell the Governor how you danced in the woods.

PARRIS [*instantly*]. Excellency, since I come to Salem this man is blackening my name. He—

DANFORTH In a moment, sir. [*To* MARY WARREN, *sternly, and surprised*] What is this dancing?

MARY WARREN. I— [*She glances at* ABIGAIL, *who is staring down at her remorselessly. Then appealing to* PROCTOR] Mr. Proctor—

PROCTOR [*taking it right up*]. Abigail leads the girls to the woods, Your Honor, and they have danced there naked—

PARRIS. Your Honor, this—

PROCTOR [*at once*]. Mr. Parris discovered them himself in the dead of night! There's the "child" she is!

DANFORTH [*it is growing into a nightmare, and he turns, astonished, to* PARRIS]. Mr. Parris—

PARRIS. I can only say, sir, that I never found any of them naked, and this man is—

DANFORTH. But you discovered them dancing in the woods? [*Eyes on* PARRIS, *he points at* ABIGAIL.] Abigail?

HALE. Excellency, when I first arrived from Beverly, Mr. Parris told me that.

DANFORTH. Do you deny it, Mr. Parris?

PARRIS. I do not, sir, but I never saw any of them naked.

DANFORTH. But she have *danced*?

PARRIS [*unwillingly*]. Aye, sir.

[DANFORTH, *as though with new eyes, looks at* ABIGAIL.]

HATHORNE. Excellency, will you permit me? [*He points at* MARY WARREN.]

DANFORTH [*with great worry*]. Pray, proceed.

HATHORNE. You say you never saw no spirits, Mary, were never threatened or afflicted by any manifest of the Devil or the Devil's agents.

MARY WARREN [*very faintly*]. No, sir.

HATHORNE [*with a gleam of victory*]. And yet, when people accused of witchery confronted you in court, you would faint, saying their spirits came out of their bodies and choked you—

MARY WARREN. That were pretense, sir.

DANFORTH. I cannot hear you.

MARY WARREN. Pretense, sir.

PARRIS. But you did turn cold, did you not? I myself picked you up many times, and your skin were icy. Mr. Danforth, you—

DANFORTH. I saw that many times.

PROCTOR. She only pretended to faint, Your Excellency. They're all marvelous pretenders.

HATHORNE. Then can she pretend to faint now?

PROCTOR. Now?

PARRIS. Why not? Now there are no spirits attacking her, for none in this room is accused of witchcraft. So let her turn herself cold now, let her pretend she is attacked now, let her faint. [*He turns to* MARY WARREN.] Faint!

MARY WARREN. Faint?

PARRIS. Aye, faint. Prove to us how you pretended in the court so many times.

MARY WARREN [*looking to* PROCTOR]. I—cannot faint now, sir.

PROCTOR [*alarmed, quietly*]. Can you not pretend it?

MARY WARREN. I— [*She looks about as though searching for the passion to faint.*] I—have no *sense* of it now, I—

DANFORTH. Why? What is lacking now?

MARY WARREN. I—cannot tell, sir, I—

DANFORTH. Might it be that here we have no afflicting spirit loose, but in the court there were some?

MARY WARREN. I never saw no spirits.

PARRIS. Then see no spirits now, and prove to us that you can faint by your own will, as you claim.

MARY WARREN [*stares, searching for the emotion of it, and then shakes her head*]. I—cannot do it.

PARRIS. Then you will confess, will you not? It were attacking spirits made you faint!

MARY WARREN. No, sir, I—

PARRIS. Your Excellency, this is a trick to blind the court!

MARY WARREN. It's not a trick! [*She stands.*] I—I used to faint because I—I thought I saw spirits.

DANFORTH. *Thought* you saw them!

MARY WARREN. But I did not, Your Honor.

HATHORNE. How could you think you saw them unless you saw them?

MARY WARREN. I—I cannot tell how, but I did. I—I heard the other girls screaming, and you, Your Honor, you seemed to believe them, and I— It were only sport in the beginning, sir, but then the whole world cried spirits, spirits, and I—I promise you, Mr. Danforth, I only thought I saw them but I did not.

[DANFORTH *peers at her.*]

PARRIS [*smiling, but nervous because* DANFORTH *seems to be struck by* MARY WARREN's *story*]. Surely Your Excellency is not taken by this simple lie.

DANFORTH [*turning worriedly to* ABIGAIL]. Abigail. I bid you now search your heart and tell me this—and beware of it, child, to God every soul is precious and His vengeance is terrible on them that take life without cause. Is it possible, child, that the spirits you have seen are illusion only, some deception that may cross your mind when—

ABIGAIL. Why, this—this—is a base question, sir.

DANFORTH. Child, I would have you consider it—

ABIGAIL. I have been hurt, Mr. Danforth; I have seen my blood runnin' out! I have been near to murdered every day because I done my duty pointing out the Devil's people—and this is my reward? To be mistrusted, denied, questioned like a—

DANFORTH [*weakening*]. Child, I do not mistrust you—

ABIGAIL [*in an open threat*]. Let *you* beware, Mr. Danforth. Think you to be so mighty that the power of Hell may not turn *your* wits? Beware of it! There is—

[*Suddenly, from an accusatory attitude, her face turns, looking into the air above—it is truly frightened.*]

DANFORTH [*apprehensively*]. What is it, child?

ABIGAIL [*looking about in the air, clasping her arms about her as though cold*]. I—I know not. A wind, a cold wind, has come.

[*Her eyes fall on* MARY WARREN.]

MARY WARREN [*terrified, pleading*]. Abby!

MERCY LEWIS [*shivering*]. Your Honor, I freeze!

PROCTOR. They're pretending!

HATHORNE [*touching* ABIGAIL'S *hand*]. She is cold, your Honor, touch her!

MERCY LEWIS [*through chattering teeth*]. Mary, do you send this shadow on me?

MARY WARREN. Lord, save me!

SUSANNA WALCOTT. I freeze, I freeze!

ABIGAIL [*shivering visibly*]. It is a wind, a wind!

MARY WARREN. Abby, don't do that!

DANFORTH [*himself engaged and entered by* ABIGAIL]. Mary Warren, do you witch her? I say to you, do you send your spirit out?

[*With a hysterical cry* MARY WARREN *starts to run.* PROCTOR *catches her.*]

MARY WARREN [*almost collapsing*]. Let me go, Mr. Proctor, I cannot, I cannot—

ABIGAIL [*crying to Heaven*]. Oh, Heavenly Father, take away this shadow!

[*Without warning or hesitation,* PROCTOR *leaps at* ABIGAIL *and, grabbing her by the hair, pulls her to her feet. She screams in pain.*

DANFORTH, *astonished, cries,* "What are you about?" *and* HATHORNE *and* PARRIS *call,* "Take your hands off her!" *and out of it all comes* PROCTOR's *roaring voice.*]

PROCTOR.   How do you call Heaven! Whore! Whore!

[HERRICK *breaks* PROCTOR *from her.*]

HERRICK.   John!
DANFORTH.   Man! Man, what do you—
PROCTOR [*breathless and in agony*].   It is a whore!
DANFORTH [*dumfounded*].   You charge—?
ABIGAIL.   Mr. Danforth, he is lying!
PROCTOR.   Mark her! Now she'll suck a scream to stab me with, but—
DANFORTH.   You will prove this! This will not pass!
PROCTOR [*trembling, his life collapsing about him*].   I have known her, sir. I have known her.
DANFORTH.   You—you are a lecher?
FRANCIS [*horrified*].   John, you cannot say such a—
PROCTOR.   Oh, Francis, I wish you had some evil in you that you might know me! [*To* DANFORTH] A man will not cast away his good name. You surely know that.
DANFORTH [*dumfounded*].   In—in what time? In what place?
PROCTOR [*his voice about to break, and his shame great*].   In the proper place—where my beasts are bedded. On the last night of my joy, some eight months past. She used to serve me in my house, sir

[*He has to clamp his jaw to keep from weeping.*]

A man may think God sleeps, but God sees everything, I know it now. I beg you, sir, I beg you—see her what she is. My wife, my dear good wife, took this girl soon after, sir, and put her out on the highroad. And being what she is, a lump of vanity, sir— [*He is being overcome.*] Excellency, forgive me, forgive me.

[*Angrily against himself he turns away from the* GOVERNOR *for a moment. Then, as though to cry out is his only means of speech left*]

She thinks to dance with me on my wife's grave! And well she might, for I thought of her softly. God help me, I lusted, and there *is* a promise in such sweat. But it is a whore's vengeance, and you must see it; I set myself entirely in your hands. I know you must see it now.
DANFORTH [*blanched, in horror, turning to* ABIGAIL].   You deny every scrap and tittle of this?
ABIGAIL.   If I must answer that, I will leave and I will not come back again!

[DANFORTH *seems unsteady.*]

PROCTOR. I have made a bell of my honor! I have rung the doom of my good name—you will believe me, Mr. Danforth! My wife is innocent, except she knew a whore when she saw one!

ABIGAIL [*stepping up to* DANFORTH]. What look do you give me? [DANFORTH *cannot speak.*] I'll not have such looks! [*She turns and starts for the door.*]

DANFORTH. You will remain where you are!

[HERRICK *steps into her path. She comes up short, fire in her eyes.*]

Mr. Parris, go into the court and bring Goodwife Proctor out.

PARRIS [*objecting*]. Your Honor, this is all a—

DANFORTH [*sharply to* PARRIS]. Bring her out! And tell her not one word of what's been spoken here. And let you knock before you enter.

[PARRIS *goes out.*]

Now we shall touch the bottom of this swamp. [*To* PROCTOR] Your wife, you say, is an honest woman.

PROCTOR. In her life, sir, she have never lied. There are them that cannot sing, and them that cannot weep—my wife cannot lie. I have paid much to learn it, sir.

DANFORTH. And when she put this girl out of your house, she put her out for a harlot?

PROCTOR. Aye, sir.

DANFORTH. And knew her for a harlot?

PROCTOR. Aye, sir, she knew her for a harlot.

DANFORTH. Good then. [*To* ABIGAIL] And if she tell me, child, it were for harlotry, may God spread His mercy on you!

[*There is a knock. He calls to the door.*]

Hold! [*To* ABIGAIL] Turn your back. Turn your back. [*To* PROCTOR] Do likewise. [*Both turn their backs—*ABIGAIL *with indignant slowness.*] Now let neither of you turn to face Goody Proctor. No one in this room is to speak one word, or raise a gesture aye or nay. [*He turns toward the door, calls*] Enter!

[*The door opens.* ELIZABETH *enters with* PARRIS. PARRIS *leaves her. She stands alone, her eyes looking for* PROCTOR.]

Mr. Cheever, report this testimony in all exactness. Are you ready?

CHEEVER. Ready, sir.

DANFORTH. Come here, woman.

[ELIZABETH *comes to him, glancing at* PROCTOR's *back.*]

Look at me only, not at your husband. In my eyes only.

ELIZABETH [*faintly*]. Good, sir.

DANFORTH. We are given to understand that at one time you dismissed your servant, Abigail Williams.

ELIZABETH. That is true, sir.

DANFORTH. For what cause did you dismiss her?

[*Slight pause. Then* ELIZABETH *tries to glance at* PROCTOR.]

You will look in my eyes only and not at your husband. The answer is in your memory and you need no help to give it to me. Why did you dismiss Abigail Williams?

ELIZABETH [*not knowing what to say, sensing a situation, wetting her lips to stall for time*]. She—dissatisfied me. [*Pause.*] And my husband.

DANFORTH. In what way dissatisfied you?

ELIZABETH. She were—[*She glances at* PROCTOR *for a cue.*]

DANFORTH. Woman, look at me! [ELIZABETH *does.*] Were she slovenly? Lazy? What disturbance did she cause?

ELIZABETH. Your Honor, I—in that time I were sick. And I— My husband is a good and righteous man. He is never drunk as some are, nor wastin' his time at the shovelboard, but always at his work. But in my sickness—you see, sir, I were a long time sick after my last baby, and I thought I saw my husband somewhat turning from me. And this girl—[*She turns to* ABIGAIL.]

DANFORTH. Look at me.

ELIZABETH. Aye, sir. Abigail Williams—[*She breaks off.*]

DANFORTH. What of Abigail Williams?

ELIZABETH. I came to think he fancied her. And so one night I lost my wits, I think, and put her out on the highroad.

DANFORTH. Your husband—did he indeed turn from you?

ELIZABETH [*in agony*]. My husband—is a goodly man, sir.

DANFORTH. Then he did not turn from you.

ELIZABETH [*starting to glance at* PROCTOR]. He—

DANFORTH [*reaches out and holds her face, then*]. Look at me! To your own knowledge, has John Proctor ever committed the crime of lechery?

[*In a crisis of indecision she cannot speak.*]

Answer my question! Is your husband a lecher!

ELIZABETH [*faintly*]. No, sir.

DANFORTH. Remove her, Marshal.

PROCTOR. Elizabeth, tell the truth!

DANFORTH. She has spoken. Remove her!

PROCTOR [*crying out*]. Elizabeth, I have confessed it!

ELIZABETH. Oh, God!

[*The door closes behind her.*]

PROCTOR. She only thought to save my name!

HALE. Excellency, it is a natural lie to tell; I beg you, stop now before another is condemned! I may shut my conscience to it no more—private vengeance is working through this testimony! From the beginning this man has struck me true. By my oath to Heaven, I believe him now, and I pray you call back his wife before we—

DANFORTH. She spoke nothing of lechery, and this man has lied!

HALE. I believe him! [*Pointing at* ABIGAIL] This girl has always struck me false! She has—

[ABIGAIL, *with a weird, wild, chilling cry, screams up to the ceiling.*]

ABIGAIL. You will not! Begone! Begone, I say!

DANFORTH. What is it, child?

[*But* ABIGAIL, *pointing with fear, is now raising up her frightened eyes, her awed face, toward the ceiling—the girls are doing the same—and now* HATHORNE, HALE, PUTNAM, CHEEVER, HERRICK, *and* DANFORTH *do the same.*]

What's there? [*He lowers his eyes from the ceiling, and now he is frightened; there is real tension in his voice.*] Child!

[*She is transfixed—with all the girls, she is whimpering open-mouthed, agape at the ceiling.*]

Girls! Why do you—?

MERCY LEWIS [*pointing*]. It's on the beam! Behind the rafter!

DANFORTH [*looking up*]. Where!

ABIGAIL. Why—? [*She gulps.*] Why do you come, yellow bird?

PROCTOR. Where's a bird? I see no bird!

ABIGAIL [*to the ceiling*]. My face? My face?

PROCTOR. Mr. Hale—

DANFORTH. Be quiet!

PROCTOR [*to* HALE]. Do you see a bird?

DANFORTH. Be quiet!!

ABIGAIL [*to the ceiling, in a genuine conversation with the "bird," as though trying to talk it out of attacking her*]. But God made my face; you cannot want to tear my face. Envy is a deadly sin, Mary.

MARY WARREN [*on her feet with a spring, and horrified, pleading*]. Abby!

ABIGAIL [*unperturbed, continuing to the "bird"*]. Oh, Mary, this is a black art to change your shape. No, I cannot, I cannot stop my mouth; it's God's work I do.

MARY WARREN. Abby, I'm *here!*

PROCTOR [*frantically*]. They're pretending, Mr. Danforth!

ABIGAIL [*now she takes a backward step, as though in fear the bird will swoop down momentarily*]. Oh, please, Mary! Don't come down.

SUSANNA WALCOTT. Her claws, she's stretching her claws!

PROCTOR. Lies, lies.

ABIGAIL [*backing further, eyes still fixed above*]. Mary, please don't hurt me!

MARY WARREN [*to* DANFORTH]. I'm not hurting her!

DANFORTH [*to* MARY WARREN]. Why does she see this vision?

MARY WARREN. She sees nothin'!

ABIGAIL [*now staring full front as though hypnotized, and mimicking the exact tone of* MARY WARREN'S *cry*]. She sees nothin'!

MARY WARREN [*pleading*]. Abby, you mustn't!

ABIGAIL AND ALL THE GIRLS [*all transfixed*]. Abby, you mustn't!

MARY WARREN [*to all the girls*]. I'm here, I'm here!

GIRLS. I'm here, I'm here!

DANFORTH [*horrified*]. Mary Warren! Draw back your spirit out of them!

MARY WARREN. Mr. Danforth!

GIRLS [*cutting her off*]. Mr. Danforth!

DANFORTH. Have you compacted with the Devil? Have you?

MARY WARREN. Never, never!

GIRLS. Never, never!

DANFORTH [*growing hysterical*]. Why can they only repeat you?

PROCTOR. Give me a whip—I'll stop it!

MARY WARREN. They're sporting. They—!

GIRLS. They're sporting!

MARY WARREN [*turning on them all hysterically and stamping her feet*]. Abby, stop it!

GIRLS [*stamping their feet*]. Abby, stop it!

MARY WARREN. Stop it!

GIRLS. Stop it!

MARY WARREN [*screaming it out at the top of her lungs, and raising her fists*]. Stop it!!

GIRLS [*raising their fists*]. Stop it!!

[MARY WARREN, *utterly confounded, and becoming overwhelmed by* ABIGAIL'S—*and the* GIRLS'—*utter conviction, starts to whimper, hands half raised, powerless, and* ALL THE GIRLS *begin whimpering exactly as she does.*]

DANFORTH. A little while ago you were afflicted. Now it seems you afflict others; where did you find this power?

MARY WARREN [*staring at* ABIGAIL]. I—have no power.

GIRLS. I have no power.

PROCTOR. They're gulling you, Mister!

DANFORTH. Why did you turn about this past two weeks? You have seen the Devil, have you not?

HALE [*indicating* ABIGAIL *and the* GIRLS]. You cannot believe them!

MARY WARREN. I—

PROCTOR [*sensing her weakening*]. Mary, God damns all liars!

DANFORTH [*pounding it into her*]. You have seen the Devil, you have made compact with Lucifer, have you not?

PROCTOR. God damns liars, Mary!

[MARY *utters something unintelligible, staring at* ABIGAIL, *who keeps watching the "bird" above.*]

DANFORTH. I cannot hear you. What do you say?

[MARY *utters again unintelligibly.*]

You will confess yourself or you will hang! [*He turns her roughly to face him.*] Do you know who I am? I say you will hang if you do not open with me!

PROCTOR. Mary, remember the angel Raphael—do that which is good and—

ABIGAIL [*pointing upward*]. The wings! Her wings are spreading! Mary, please, don't, don't—!

HALE. I see nothing, Your Honor!

DANFORTH. Do you confess this power! [*He is an inch from her face.*] Speak!

ABIGAIL. She's going to come down! She's walking the beam!

DANFORTH. Will you speak!

MARY WARREN [*staring in horror*]. I cannot!

GIRLS. I cannot!

PARRIS. Cast the Devil out! Look him in the face! Trample him! We'll save you, Mary, only stand fast against him and—

ABIGAIL [*looking up*]. Look out! She's coming down!

[*She and* ALL THE GIRLS *run to one wall, shielding their eyes. And now, as though cornered, they let out a gigantic scream, and* MARY, *as though infected, opens her mouth and screams with them. Gradually* ABIGAIL *and the* GIRLS *leave off, until only* MARY *is left there, staring up at the "bird," screaming madly. All watch her, horrified by this evident fit.* PROCTOR *strides to her.*]

PROCTOR. Mary, tell the Governor what they—[*He has hardly got a word out, when, seeing him coming for her, she rushes out of his reach, screaming in horror.*]

MARY WARREN. Don't touch me—don't touch me! [*At which the* GIRLS *halt at the door.*]

PROCTOR [*astonished*]. Mary!

MARY WARREN [*pointing at* PROCTOR].   You're the Devil's man!

[*He is stopped in his tracks.*]

PARRIS.   Praise God!

GIRLS.   Praise God!

PROCTOR [*numbed*].   Mary, how—?

MARY WARREN.   I'll not hang with you! I love God, I love God.

DANFORTH [*to* MARY].   He bid you do the Devil's work?

MARY WARREN [*hysterically, indicating* PROCTOR].   He come at me by night and every day to sign, to sign, to—

DANFORTH.   Sign what?

PARRIS.   The Devil's book? He come with a book?

MARY WARREN [*hysterically, pointing at* PROCTOR, *fearful of him*].   My name, he want my name. "I'll murder you," he says, "if my wife hangs! We must go and overthrow the court," he says!

[DANFORTH's *head jerks toward* PROCTOR, *shock and horror in his face.*]

PROCTOR [*turning, appealing to* HALE].   Mr. Hale!

MARY WARREN [*her sobs beginning*].   He wake me every night, his eyes were like coals and his fingers claw my neck, and I sign, I sign . . .

HALE.   Excellency, this child's gone wild!

PROCTOR [*as* DANFORTH's *wide eyes pore on him*].   Mary, Mary!

MARY WARREN [*screaming at him*].   No, I love God; I go your way no more. I love God, I bless God. [*Sobbing, she rushes to* ABIGAIL.] Abby, Abby, I'll never hurt you more!

[*They all watch, as* ABIGAIL, *out of her infinite charity, reaches out and draws the sobbing* MARY *to her, and then looks up to* DANFORTH.]

DANFORTH [*to* PROCTOR].   What are you?

[PROCTOR *is beyond speech in his anger.*]

You are combined with anti-Christ, are you not? I have seen your power; you will not deny it! What say you, Mister?

HALE.   Excellency—

DANFORTH.   I will have nothing from you, Mr. Hale! [*To* PROCTOR] Will you confess yourself befouled with Hell, or do you keep that black allegiance yet? What say you?

PROCTOR [*his mind wild, breathless*].   I say—I say—God is dead!

PARRIS.   Hear it, hear it!

PROCTOR [*laughs insanely, then*].   A fire, a fire is burning! I hear the boot of Lucifer, I see his filthy face! And it is my face, and yours, Danforth! For them that quail to bring men out of ignorance, as I have quailed, and as you quail now when you know in all your black hearts that this be fraud—God damns our kind especially, and we will burn, we will burn together!

DANFORTH. Marshal! Take him and Corey with him to the jail!

HALE [*starting across to the door*]. I denounce these proceedings!

PROCTOR. You are pulling Heaven down and raising up a whore!

HALE. I denounce these proceedings, I quit this court!

[*He slams the door to the outside behind him.*]

DANFORTH [*calling to him in a fury*]. Mr. Hale! Mr. Hale!

THE CURTAIN FALLS

ACT FOUR

A CELL IN SALEM JAIL, *that fall.*

At the back is a high barred window; near it, a great, heavy door. Along the walls are two benches.

The place is in darkness but for the moonlight seeping through the bars. It appears empty. Presently footsteps are heard coming down a corridor beyond the wall, keys rattle, and the door swings open. MAR-SHAL HERRICK *enters with a lantern.*

He is nearly drunk, and heavy-footed. He goes to a bench and nudges a bundle of rags lying on it.

HERRICK. Sarah, wake up! Sarah Good!

[*He then crosses to the other bench.*]

SARAH GOOD [*rising in her rags*]. Oh, Majesty! Comin', comin'! Tituba, he's here, His Majesty's come!

HERRICK. Go to the north cell; this place is wanted now.

[*He hangs his lantern on the wall.* TITUBA *sits up.*]

TITUBA. That don't look to me like His Majesty; look to me like the marshal.

HERRICK [*taking out a flask*]. Get along with you now, clear this place.

[*He drinks, and* SARAH GOOD *comes and peers up into his face.*]

SARAH GOOD. Oh, is it you, Marshal! I thought sure you be the devil comin' for us. Could I have a sip of cider for me goin'-away?

HERRICK [*handing her the flask*]. And where are you off to, Sarah?

TITUBA [*as* SARAH *drinks*]. We goin' to Barbados, soon the Devil gits here with the feathers and the wings.

HERRICK. Oh? A happy voyage to you.

SARAH GOOD. A pair of bluebirds wingin' southerly, the two of us! Oh, it be a grand transformation, Marshal! [*She raises the flask to drink again.*]

HERRICK [*taking the flask from her lips*]. You'd best give me that or you'll never rise off the ground. Come along now.

TITUBA. I'll speak to him for you, if you desires to come along, Marshal.

HERRICK. I'd not refuse it, Tituba; it's the proper morning to fly into Hell.

TITUBA. Oh, it be no Hell in Barbados. Devil, him be pleasure-man in Barbados, him be singin' and dancin' in Barbados. It's you folks— you riles him up 'round here; it be too cold 'round here for that Old Boy. He freeze his soul in Massachusetts, but in Barbados he just as sweet and—

[*A bellowing cow is heard, and* TITUBA *leaps up and calls to the window.*]

Aye, sir! That's him, Sarah!

SARAH GOOD. I'm here, Majesty!

[*They hurriedly pick up their rags as* HOPKINS, *a guard, enters.*]

HOPKINS. The Deputy Governor's arrived.

HERRICK [*grabbing* TITUBA]. Come along, come along.

TITUBA [*resisting him*]. No, he comin' for me. I goin' home!

HERRICK [*pulling her to the door*]. That's not Satan, just a poor old cow with a hatful of milk. Come along now, out with you!

TITUBA [*calling to the window*]. Take me home, Devil! Take me home!

SARAH GOOD [*following the shouting* TITUBA *out*]. Tell him I'm goin', Tituba! Now you tell him Sarah Good is goin' too!

[*In the corridor outside* TITUBA *calls on—*"Take me home, Devil; Devil take me home!" *and* HOPKINS' *voice orders her to move on.* HERRICK *returns and begins to push old rags and straw into a corner. Hearing footsteps, he turns, and enter* DANFORTH *and* JUDGE HATHORNE. *They are in greatcoats and wear hats against the bitter cold. They are followed in by* CHEEVER, *who carries a dispatch case and a flat wooden box containing his writing materials.*]

HERRICK. Good morning, Excellency.

DANFORTH. Where is Mr. Parris?

HERRICK. I'll fetch him. [*He starts for the door.*]

DANFORTH. Marshal. [HERRICK *stops.*] When did Reverend Hale arrive?

HERRICK. It were toward midnight, I think.

DANFORTH [*suspiciously*]. What is he about here?

HERRICK. He goes among them that will hang, sir. And he prays with them. He sits with Goody Nurse now. And Mr. Parris with him.

DANFORTH. Indeed. That man have no authority to enter here, Marshal. Why have you let him in?

HERRICK. Why, Mr. Parris command me, sir. I cannot deny him.

DANFORTH. Are you drunk, Marshal?

HERRICK. No, sir; it is a bitter night, and I have no fire here.

DANFORTH [*containing his anger*]. Fetch Mr. Parris.

HERRICK. Aye, sir.

DANFORTH. There is a prodigious stench in this place.

HERRICK. I have only now cleared the people out for you.

DANFORTH. Beware hard drink, Marshal.

HERRICK. Aye, sir.

[*He waits an instant for further orders. But* DANFORTH, *in dissatisfaction, turns his back on him, and* HERRICK *goes out. There is a pause.* DANFORTH *stands in thought.*]

HATHORNE. Let you question Hale, Excellency; I should not be surprised he have been preaching in Andover lately.

DANFORTH. We'll come to that; speak nothing of Andover. Parris prays with him. That's strange.

[*He blows on his hands, moves toward the window, and looks out.*]

HATHORNE. Excellency, I wonder if it be wise to let Mr. Parris so continuously with the prisoners.

[DANFORTH *turns to him, interested.*]

I think, sometimes, the man has a mad look these days.

DANFORTH. Mad?

HATHORNE. I met him yesterday coming out of his house, and I bid him good morning—and he wept and went his way. I think it is not well the village sees him so unsteady.

DANFORTH. Perhaps he have some sorrow.

CHEEVER [*stamping his feet against the cold*]. I think it be the cows, sir.

DANFORTH. Cows?

CHEEVER. There be so many cows wanderin' the highroads, now their masters are in the jails, and much disagreement who they will belong to now. I know Mr. Parris be arguin' with farmers all yesterday—there is great contention, sir, about the cows. Contention make him weep, sir; it were always a man that weep for contention.

[*He turns, as do* HATHORNE *and* DANFORTH, *hearing someone coming up the corridor.* DANFORTH *raises his head as* PARRIS *enters. He is gaunt, frightened, and sweating in his greatcoat.*]

PARRIS [*to* DANFORTH, *instantly*].   Oh, good morning, sir, thank you for coming, I beg your pardon wakin' you so early. Good morning, Judge Hathorne.

DANFORTH.   Reverend Hale have no right to enter this—

PARRIS.   Excellency, a moment.

[*He hurries back and shuts the door.*]

HATHORNE.   Do you leave him alone with the prisoners?

DANFORTH.   What's his business here?

PARRIS [*prayerfully holding up his hands*].   Excellency, hear me. It is a providence. Reverend Hale has returned to bring Rebecca Nurse to God.

DANFORTH [*surprised*].   He bids her confess?

PARRIS [*sitting*].   Hear me. Rebecca have not given me a word this three month since she came. Now she sits with him, and her sister and Martha Corey and two or three others, and he pleads with them, confess their crimes and save their lives.

DANFORTH.   Why—this is indeed a providence. And they soften, they soften?

PARRIS.   Not yet, not yet. But I thought to summon you, sir, that we might think on whether it be not wise, to—[*He dares not say it.*] I had thought to put a question, sir, and I hope you will not—

DANFORTH.   Mr. Parris, be plain, what troubles you?

PARRIS.   There is news, sir, that the court—the court must reckon with. My niece, sir, my niece—I believe she has vanished.

DANFORTH.   Vanished!

PARRIS.   I had thought to advise you of it earlier in the week, but—

DANFORTH.   Why? How long is she gone?

PARRIS.   This be the third night. You see, sir, she told me she would stay a night with Mercy Lewis. And next day, when she does not return, I send to Mr. Lewis to inquire. Mercy told him she would sleep in *my* house for a night.

DANFORTH.   They are both gone?!

PARRIS [*in fear of him*].   They are, sir.

DANFORTH [*alarmed*].   I will send a party for them. Where may they be?

PARRIS.   Excellency, I think they be aboard a ship.

[DANFORTH *stands agape.*]

My daughter tells me how she heard them speaking of ships last week, and tonight I discover my—my strongbox is broke into.

[*He presses his fingers against his eyes to keep back tears.*]

HATHORNE [*astonished*]. She have robbed you?
PARRIS. Thirty-one pound is gone. I am penniless.

[*He covers his face and sobs.*]

DANFORTH. Mr. Parris, you are a brainless man!

[*He walks in thought, deeply worried.*]

PARRIS. Excellency, it profit nothing you should blame me. I cannot think they would run off except they fear to keep in Salem any more. [*He is pleading.*] Mark it, sir, Abigail had close knowledge of the town, and since the news of Andover has broken here—
DANFORTH. Andover is remedied. The court returns there on Friday, and will resume examinations.
PARRIS. I am sure of it, sir. But the rumor here speaks rebellion in Andover, and it—
DANFORTH. There is no rebellion in Andover!
PARRIS. I tell you what is said here, sir. Andover have thrown out the court, they say, and will have no part of witchcraft. There be a faction here, feeding on that news, and I tell you true, sir, I fear there will be riot here.
HATHORNE. Riot! Why at every execution I have seen naught but high satisfaction in the town.
PARRIS. Judge Hathorne—it were another sort that hanged till now. Rebecca Nurse is no Bridget that lived three year with Bishop before she married him. John Proctor is not Isaac Ward that drank his family to ruin. [*To* DANFORTH] I would to God it were not so, Excellency, but these people have great weight yet in the town. Let Rebecca stand upon the gibbet and send up some righteous prayer, and I fear she'll wake a vengeance on you.
HATHORNE. Excellency, she is condemned a witch. The court have—
DANFORTH [*in deep concern, raising a hand to* HATHORNE]. Pray you. [*To* PARRIS] How do you propose, then?
PARRIS. Excellency, I would postpone these hangin's for a time.
DANFORTH. There will be no postponement.
PARRIS. Now Mr. Hale's returned, there is hope, I think—for if he bring even one of these to God, that confession surely damns the others in the public eye, and none may doubt more that they are all linked to Hell. This way, unconfessed and claiming innocence, doubts are multiplied, many honest people will weep for them, and our good purpose is lost in their tears.
DANFORTH [*after thinking a moment, then going to* CHEEVER]. Give me the list.

[CHEEVER *opens the dispatch case, searches.*]

PARRIS. It cannot be forgot, sir, that when I summoned the congregation for John Proctor's excommunication there were hardly thirty people come to hear it. That speak a discontent, I think, and—

DANFORTH [*studying the list*]. There will be no postponement.

PARRIS. Excellency—

DANFORTH. Now, sir—which of these in your opinion may be brought to God? I will myself strive with him till dawn.

[*He hands the list to* PARRIS, *who merely glances at it.*]

PARRIS. There is not sufficient time till dawn.

DANFORTH. I shall do my utmost. Which of them do you have hope for?

PARRIS [*not even glancing at the list now, and in a quavering voice, quietly*]. Excellency—a dagger—[*He chokes up.*]

DANFORTH. What do you say?

PARRIS. Tonight, when I open my door to leave my house—a dagger clattered to the ground.

[*Silence.* DANFORTH *absorbs this. Now* PARRIS *cries out.*]

You cannot hang this sort. There is danger for me. I dare not step outside at night!

[*REVEREND HALE enters. They look at him for an instant in silence. He is steeped in sorrow, exhausted, and more direct than he ever was.*]

DANFORTH. Accept my congratulations, Reverend Hale; we are gladdened to see you returned to your good work.

HALE [*coming to* DANFORTH *now*]. You must pardon them. They will not budge.

[*HERRICK enters, waits.*]

DANFORTH [*conciliatory*]. You misunderstand, sir; I cannot pardon these when twelve are already hanged for the same crime. It is not just.

PARRIS [*with failing heart*]. Rebecca will not confess?

HALE. The sun will rise in a few minutes. Excellency, I must have more time.

DANFORTH. Now hear me, and beguile yourselves no more. I will not receive a single plea for pardon or postponement. Them that will not confess will hang. Twelve are already executed; the names of these seven are given out, and the village expects to see them die this morning. Postponement now speaks a floundering on my part; reprieve or pardon must cast doubt upon the guilt of them that died till now. While I speak God's law, I will not crack its voice with whimpering. If retaliation is your fear, know this—I should hang ten thousand that dared to rise against the law, and an ocean of salt tears could not melt the resolution of the statutes. Now draw yourselves up like men and help me, as you are bound by Heaven to do. Have you spoken with them all, Mr. Hale?

HALE.　All but Proctor. He is in the dungeon.

DANFORTH [to HERRICK]. What's Proctor's way now?

HERRICK.　He sits like some great bird; you'd not know he lived except he will take food from time to time.

DANFORTH [after thinking a moment]. His wife—his wife must be well on with child now.

HERRICK.　She is, sir.

DANFORTH.　What think you, Mr. Parris? You have closer knowledge of this man; might her presence soften him?

PARRIS.　It is possible, sir. He have not laid eyes on her these three months. I should summon her.

DANFORTH [to HERRICK]. Is he yet adamant? Has he struck at you again?

HERRICK.　He cannot, sir, he is chained to the wall now.

DANFORTH [after thinking on it]. Fetch Goody Proctor to me. Then let you bring him up.

HERRICK.　Aye, sir.

[HERRICK goes. There is silence.]

HALE.　Excellency, if you postpone a week and publish to the town that you are striving for their confessions, that speak mercy on your part, not faltering.

DANFORTH.　Mr. Hale, as God have not empowered me like Joshua to stop this sun from rising, so I cannot withhold from them the perfection of their punishment.

HALE [harder now]. If you think God wills you to raise rebellion, Mr. Danforth, you are mistaken!

DANFORTH [instantly]. You have heard rebellion spoken in the town?

HALE.　Excellency, there are orphans wandering from house to house; abandoned cattle bellow on the highroads, the stink of rotting crops hangs everywhere, and no man knows when the harlots' cry will end his life—and you wonder yet if rebellion's spoke? Better you should marvel how they do not burn your province!

DANFORTH.　Mr. Hale, have you preached in Andover this month?

HALE.　Thank God they have no need of me in Andover.

DANFORTH.　You baffle me, sir. Why have you returned here?

HALE.　Why, it is all simple. I come to do the Devil's work. I come to counsel Christians they should belie themselves. [His sarcasm col-

lapses.] There is blood on my head! Can you not see the blood on my head!!

PARRIS.   Hush!

[*For he has heard footsteps. They all face the door.* HERRICK *enters with* ELIZABETH. *Her wrists are linked by heavy chain, which* HERRICK *now removes. Her clothes are dirty; her face is pale and gaunt.* HERRICK *goes out.*]

DANFORTH [*very politely*].   Goody Proctor. [*She is silent.*] I hope you are hearty?

ELIZABETH [*as a warning reminder*].   I am yet six month before my time.

DANFORTH.   Pray be at your ease, we come not for your life. We—[*uncertain how to plead, for he is not accustomed to it*] Mr. Hale, will you speak with the woman?

HALE.   Goody Proctor, your husband is marked to hang this morning.

[*Pause.*]

ELIZABETH [*quietly*].   I have heard it.

HALE.   You know, do you not, that I have no connection with the court? [*She seems to doubt it.*] I come of my own, Goody Proctor. I would save your husband's life, for if he is taken I count myself his murderer. Do you understand me?

ELIZABETH.   What do you want of me?

HALE.   Goody Proctor, I have gone this three month like our Lord into the wilderness. I have sought a Christian way, for damnation's doubled on a minister who counsels men to lie.

HATHORNE.   It is no lie, you cannot speak of lies.

HALE.   It is a lie! They are innocent!

DANFORTH.   I'll hear no more of that!

HALE [*continuing to* ELIZABETH].   Let you not mistake your duty as I mistook my own. I came into this village like a bridegroom to his beloved, bearing gifts of high religion; the very crowns of holy law I brought, and what I touched with my bright confidence, it died; and where I turned the eye of my great faith, blood flowed up. Beware, Goody Proctor—cleave to no faith when faith brings blood. It is mistaken law that leads you to sacrifice. Life, woman, life is God's most precious gift; no principle, however glorious, may justify the taking of it. I beg you, woman, prevail upon your husband to confess. Let him give his lie. Quail not before God's judgment in this, for it may well be God damns a liar less than he that throws his life away for pride. Will you plead with him? I cannot think he will listen to another.

ELIZABETH [*quietly*].   I think that be the Devil's argument.

HALE [*with a climactic desperation*]. Woman, before the laws of God we are as swine! We cannot read His will!

ELIZABETH. I cannot dispute with you, sir; I lack learning for it.

DANFORTH [*going to her*]. Goody Proctor, you are not summoned here for disputation. Be there no wifely tenderness within you? He will die with the sunrise. Your husband. Do you understand it?

[*She only looks at him.*]

What say you? Will you contend with him? [*She is silent.*] Are you stone? I tell you true, woman, had I no other proof of your unnatural life, your dry eyes now would be sufficient evidence that you delivered up your soul to Hell! A very ape would weep at such calamity! Have the devil dried up any tear of pity in you? [*She is silent.*] Take her out. It profit nothing she should speak to him!

ELIZABETH [*quietly*]. Let me speak with him, Excellency.

PARRIS [*with hope*]. You'll strive with him? [*She hesitates.*]

DANFORTH. Will you plead for his confession or will you not?

ELIZABETH. I promise nothing. Let me speak with him.

[*A sound—the sibilance of dragging feet on stone. They turn. A pause.* HERRICK *enters with* JOHN PROCTOR. *His wrists are chained. He is another man, bearded, filthy, his eyes misty as though webs had overgrown them. He halts inside the doorway, his eye caught by the sight of* ELIZABETH. *The emotion flowing between them prevents anyone from speaking for an instant. Now* HALE, *visibly affected, goes to* DANFORTH *and speaks quietly.*]

HALE. Pray, leave them, Excellency.

DANFORTH [*pressing* HALE *impatiently aside*]. Mr. Proctor, you have been notified, have you not?

[PROCTOR *is silent, staring at* ELIZABETH.]

I see light in the sky, Mister; let you counsel with your wife, and may God help you turn your back on Hell.

[PROCTOR *is silent, staring at* ELIZABETH.]

HALE [*quietly*]. Excellency, let—

[DANFORTH *brushes past* HALE *and walks out.* HALE *follows.* CHEEVER *stands and follows,* HATHORNE *behind.* HERRICK *goes.* PARRIS, *from a safe distance, offers*]

PARRIS. If you desire a cup of cider, Mr. Proctor, I am sure I—

[PROCTOR *turns an icy stare at him, and he breaks off.* PARRIS *raises his palms toward* PROCTOR.]

God lead you now.

[PARRIS *goes out.*]

[*Alone.* PROCTOR *walks to her, halts. It is as though they stood in a spinning world. It is beyond sorrow, above it. He reaches out his hand as though toward an embodiment not quite real, and as he touches her, a strange soft sound, half laughter, half amazement, comes from his throat. He pats her hand. She covers his hand with hers. And then, weak, he sits. Then she sits, facing him.*]

PROCTOR.   The child?
ELIZABETH.   It grows.
PROCTOR.   There is no word of the boys?
ELIZABETH.   They're well. Rebecca's Samuel keeps them.
PROCTOR.   You have not seen them?
ELIZABETH.   I have not.

[*She catches a weakening in herself and downs it.*]

PROCTOR.   You are a—marvel, Elizabeth.
ELIZABETH.   You—have been tortured?
PROCTOR.   Aye. [*Pause.*]

[*She will not let herself be drowned in the sea that threatens her.*]

They come for my life now.
ELIZABETH.   I know it.

[*Pause.*]

PROCTOR.   None—have yet confessed?
ELIZABETH.   There be many confessed.
PROCTOR.   Who are they?
ELIZABETH.   There be a hundred or more, they say. Goody Ballard is one; Isaiah Goodkind is one. There be many.
PROCTOR.   Rebecca?
ELIZABETH.   Not Rebecca. She is one foot in Heaven now; naught may hurt her more.
PROCTOR.   And Giles?
ELIZABETH.   You have not heard of it?
PROCTOR.   I hear nothin', where I am kept.
ELIZABETH.   Giles is dead.

[*He looks at her incredulously.*]

PROCTOR.   When were he hanged?

ELIZABETH [*quietly, factually*]. He were not hanged. He would not answer aye or nay to his indictment; for if he denied the charge they'd hang him surely, and auction out his property. So he stand mute, and died Christian under the law. And so his sons will have his farm. It is the law, for he could not be condemned a wizard without he answer the indictment, aye or nay.

PROCTOR. Then how does he die?

ELIZABETH [*gently*]. They press him, John.

PROCTOR. Press?

ELIZABETH. Great stones they lay upon his chest until he plead aye or nay. [*With a tender smile for the old man*] They say he gave them but two words. "More weight," he says. And died.

PROCTOR [*numbed—a thread to weave into his agony*]. "More weight."

ELIZABETH. Aye. It were a fearsome man, Giles Corey.

[*Pause.*]

PROCTOR [*with great force of will, but not quite looking at her*]. I have been thinking I would confess to them, Elizabeth.

[*She shows nothing.*]

What say you? If I give them that?

ELIZABETH. I cannot judge you, John.

[*Pause.*]

PROCTOR [*simply—a pure question*]. What would you have me do?

ELIZABETH. As you will, I would have it. [*Slight pause.*] I want you living, John. That's sure.

PROCTOR [*pauses, then with a flailing of hope*]. Giles' wife? Have she confessed?

ELIZABETH. She will not.

[*Pause.*]

PROCTOR. It is a pretense, Elizabeth.

ELIZABETH. What is?

PROCTOR. I cannot mount the gibbet like a saint. It is a fraud. I am not that man.

[*She is silent.*]

My honesty is broke, Elizabeth; I am no good man. Nothing's spoiled by giving them this lie that were not rotten long before.

ELIZABETH. And yet you've not confessed till now. That speak goodness in you.

PROCTOR. Spite only keeps me silent. It is hard to give a lie to dogs. [*Pause, for the first time he turns directly to her.*] I would have your forgiveness, Elizabeth.

ELIZABETH. It is not for me to give, John, I am—

PROCTOR. I'd have you see some honesty in it. Let them that never lied die now to keep their souls. It is pretense for me, a vanity that will not blind God nor keep my children out of the wind. [*Pause.*] What say you?

ELIZABETH [*upon a heaving sob that always threatens*]. John, it come to naught that I should forgive you, if you'll not forgive yourself.

[*Now he turns away a little, in great agony.*]

It is not my soul, John, it is yours.

[*He stands, as though in physical pain, slowly rising to his feet with a great immortal longing to find his answer. It is difficult to say, and she is on the verge of tears.*]

Only be sure of this, for I know it now: Whatever you will do, it is a good man does it.

[*He turns his doubting, searching gaze upon her.*]

I have read my heart this three month, John. [*Pause.*] I have sins of my own to count. It needs a cold wife to prompt lechery.

PROCTOR [*in great pain*]. Enough, enough—

ELIZABETH [*now pouring out her heart*]. Better you should know me!

PROCTOR. I will not hear it! I know you!

ELIZABETH. You take my sins upon you, John—

PROCTOR [*in agony*]. No, I take my own, my own!

ELIZABETH. John, I counted myself so plain, so poorly made, no honest love could come to me! Suspicion kissed you when I did; I never knew how I should say my love. It were a cold house I kept!

[*In fright, she swerves, as* HATHORNE *enters.*]

HATHORNE. What say you, Proctor? The sun is soon up.

[PROCTOR, *his chest heaving, stares, turns to* ELIZABETH. *She comes to him as though to plead, her voice quaking.*]

ELIZABETH. Do what you will. But let none be your judge. There be no higher judge under Heaven than Proctor is! Forgive me, forgive me, John—I never knew such goodness in the world!

[*She covers her face, weeping.*]
[PROCTOR *turns from her to* HATHORNE; *he is off the earth, his voice hollow.*]

PROCTOR. I want my life.

HATHORNE [*electrified, surprised*]. You'll confess yourself?

PROCTOR. I will have my life.

HATHORNE [*with a mystical tone*]. God be praised! It is a providence!

[*He rushes out the door, and his voice is heard calling down the corridor.*]

He will confess! Proctor will confess!

PROCTOR [*with a cry, as he strides to the door*]. Why do you cry it? [*In great pain he turns back to her.*] It is evil, is it not? It is evil.

ELIZABETH [*in terror, weeping*]. I cannot judge you, John, I cannot!

PROCTOR. Then who will judge me? [*Suddenly clasping his hands*] God in Heaven, what is John Proctor, what is John Proctor? [*He moves as an animal, and a fury is riding in him, a tantalized search.*] I think it is honest, I think so; I am no saint.

[*As though she had denied this he calls angrily at her.*]

Let Rebecca go like a saint; for me it is fraud!

[*Voices are heard in the hall, speaking together in suppressed excitement.*]

ELIZABETH. I am not your judge, I cannot be. [*As though giving him release*] Do as you will, do as you will!

PROCTOR. Would you give them such a lie? Say it. Would you ever give them this?

[*She cannot answer.*]

You would not; if tongs of fire were singeing you you would not! It is evil. Good, then—it is evil, and I do it!

[HATHORNE *enters with* DANFORTH, *and, with them,* CHEEVER, PARRIS, *and* HALE. *It is a businesslike, rapid entrance, as though the ice had been broken.*]

DANFORTH [*with great relief and gratitude*]. Praise to God, man, praise to God; you shall be blessed in Heaven for this.

[CHEEVER *has hurried to the bench with pen, ink, and paper.* PROCTOR *watches him.*]

Now then, let us have it. Are you ready, Mr. Cheever?

PROCTOR [*with a cold, cold horror at their efficiency*]. Why must it be written?

DANFORTH. Why, for the good instruction of the village, Mister; this we shall post upon the church door! [*To* PARRIS, *urgently*] Where is the marshal?

PARRIS [*runs to the door and calls down the corridor*]. Marshal! Hurry!

DANFORTH. Now, then, Mister, will you speak slowly, and directly to the point, for Mr. Cheever's sake.

[*He is on record now, and is really dictating to* CHEEVER, *who writes.*]

Mr. Proctor, have you seen the Devil in your life?

[PROCTOR's *jaws lock.*]

Come, man, there is light in the sky; the town waits at the scaffold; I would give out this news. Did you see the Devil?

PROCTOR. I did.

PARRIS. Praise God!

DANFORTH. And when he come to you, what were his demand?

[PROCTOR *is silent.* DANFORTH *helps.*]

Did he bid you to do his work upon the earth?

PROCTOR. He did.

DANFORTH. And you bound yourself to his service?

[DANFORTH *turns, as* REBECCA NURSE *enters, with* HERRICK *helping to support her. She is barely able to walk.*]

Come in, come in, woman!

REBECCA [*brightening as she sees* PROCTOR]. Ah, John! You are well, then, eh?

[PROCTOR *turns his face to the wall.*]

DANFORTH. Courage, man, courage—let her witness your good example that she may come to God herself. Now hear it, Goody Nurse! Say on, Mr. Proctor. Did you bind yourself to the Devil's service?

REBECCA [*astonished*]. Why, John!

PROCTOR [*through his teeth, his face turned from* REBECCA]. I did.

DANFORTH. Now, woman, you surely see it profit nothin' to keep this conspiracy any further. Will you confess yourself with him?

REBECCA. Oh, John—God send his mercy on you!

DANFORTH. I say, will you confess yourself, Goody Nurse?

REBECCA. Why, it is a lie, it is a lie; how may I damn myself? I cannot, I cannot.

DANFORTH. Mr. Proctor. When the Devil came to you did you see Rebecca Nurse in his company?

[PROCTOR *is silent.*]

Come, man, take courage—did you ever see her with the Devil?
PROCTOR [*almost inaudibly*]. No.

[DANFORTH, *now sensing trouble, glances at* JOHN *and goes to the table, and picks up a sheet—the list of condemned.*]

DANFORTH. Did you ever see her sister, Mary Easty, with the Devil?
PROCTOR. No, I did not.
DANFORTH [*his eyes narrow on* PROCTOR]. Did you ever see Martha Corey with the Devil?
PROCTOR. I did not.
DANFORTH [*realizing, slowly putting the sheet down*]. Did you ever see anyone with the Devil?
PROCTOR. I did not.
DANFORTH. Proctor, you mistake me. I am not empowered to trade your life for a lie. You have most certainly seen some person with the Devil.

[PROCTOR *is silent.*]

Mr. Proctor, a score of people have already testified they saw this woman with the Devil.
PROCTOR. Then it is proved. Why must I say it?
DANFORTH. Why "must" you say it! Why, you should rejoice to say it if your soul is truly purged of any love for Hell!
PROCTOR. They think to go like saints. I like not to spoil their names.
DANFORTH [*inquiring, incredulous*]. Mr. Proctor, do you think they go like saints?
PROCTOR [*evading*]. This woman never thought she done the Devil's work.
DANFORTH. Look you, sir. I think you mistake your duty here. It matters nothing what she thought—she is convicted of the unnatural murder of children, and you for sending your spirit out upon Mary Warren. Your soul alone is the issue here, Mister, and you will prove its whiteness or you cannot live in a Christian country. Will you tell me now what persons conspired with you in the Devil's company?

[PROCTOR *is silent.*]

To your knowledge was Rebecca Nurse ever—
PROCTOR. I speak my own sins; I cannot judge another. [*Crying out, with hatred*] I have no tongue for it.
HALE [*quickly to* DANFORTH]. Excellency, it is enough he confess himself. Let him sign it, let him sign it.

PARRIS [*feverishly*].   It is a great service, sir. It is a weighty name; it will strike the village that Proctor confess. I beg you, let him sign it. The sun is up, Excellency!

DANFORTH [*considers; then with dissatisfaction*].   Come, then, sign your testimony. [*To* CHEEVER] Give it to him.

[CHEEVER *goes to* PROCTOR, *the confession and a pen in hand*. PROCTOR *does not look at it*.]

Come, man, sign it.

PROCTOR [*after glancing at the confession*].   You have all witnessed it— it is enough.

DANFORTH.   You will not sign it?

PROCTOR.   You have all witnessed it; what more is needed?

DANFORTH.   Do you sport with me? You will sign your name or it is no confession, Mister!

[*His breast heaving with agonized breathing*, PROCTOR *now lays the paper down and signs his name*.]

PARRIS.   Praise be to the Lord!

[PROCTOR *has just finished signing when* DANFORTH *reaches for the paper. But* PROCTOR *snatches it up, and now a wild terror is rising in him, and a boundless anger*.]

DANFORTH [*perplexed, but politely extending his hand*].   If you please, sir.

PROCTOR.   No.

DANFORTH [*as though* PROCTOR *did not understand*].   Mr. Proctor, I must have—

PROCTOR.   No, no. I have signed it. You have seen me. It is done! You have no need for this.

PARRIS.   Proctor, the village must have proof that—

PROCTOR.   Damn the village! I confess to God, and God has seen my name on this! It is enough!

DANFORTH.   No, sir, it is—

PROCTOR.   You came to save my soul, did you not? Here! I have confessed myself; it is enough!

DANFORTH.   You have not con—

PROCTOR.   I have confessed myself! Is there no good penitence but it be public? God does not need my name nailed upon the church! God sees my name; God knows how black my sins are! It is enough!

DANFORTH.   Mr. Proctor—

PROCTOR.   You will not use me! I am no Sarah Good or Tituba, I am John Proctor! You will not use me! It is no part of salvation that you should use me!

DANFORTH. I do not wish to—

PROCTOR. I have three children—how may I teach them to walk like men in the world, and I sold my friends?

DANFORTH. You have not sold your friends—

PROCTOR. Beguile me not! I blacken all of them when this is nailed to the church the very day they hang for silence!

DANFORTH. Mr. Proctor, I must have good and legal proof that you—

PROCTOR. You are the high court, your word is good enough! Tell them I confessed myself; say Proctor broke his knees and wept like a woman; say what you will, but my name cannot—

DANFORTH [*with suspicion*]. It is the same, is it not? If I report it or you sign to it?

PROCTOR [*he knows it is insane*]. No, it is not the same! What others say and what I sign to is not the same!

DANFORTH. Why? Do you mean to deny this confession when you are free?

PROCTOR. I mean to deny nothing!

DANFORTH. Then explain to me, Mr. Proctor, why you will not let—

PROCTOR [*with a cry of his whole soul*]. Because it is my name! Because I cannot have another in my life! Because I lie and sign myself to lies! Because I am not worth the dust on the feet of them that hang! How may I live without my name? I have given you my soul; leave me my name!

DANFORTH [*pointing at the confession in* PROCTOR's *hand*]. Is that document a lie? If it is a lie I will not accept it! What say you? I will not deal in lies, Mister!

[PROCTOR *is motionless.*]

You will give me your honest confession in my hand, or I cannot keep you from the rope.

[PROCTOR *does not reply.*]

Which way do you go, Mister?

[*His breast heaving, his eyes staring,* PROCTOR *tears the paper and crumples it, and he is weeping in fury, but erect.*]

DANFORTH. Marshal!

PARRIS [*hysterically, as though the tearing paper were his life*]. Proctor, Proctor!

HALE. Man, you will hang! You cannot!

PROCTOR [*his eyes full of tears*]. I can. And there's your first marvel, that I can. You have made your magic now, for now I do think I see some shred of goodness in John Proctor. Not enough to weave a banner with, but white enough to keep it from such dogs.

[ELIZABETH, *in a burst of terror, rushes to him and weeps against his hand.*]

Give them no tear! Tears pleasure them! Show honor now, show a stony heart and sink them with it!

[*He has lifted her, and kisses her now with great passion.*]

REBECCA. Let you fear nothing! Another judgment waits us all!
DANFORTH. Hang them high over the town! Who weeps for these, weeps for corruption!

[*He sweeps out past them.* HERRICK *starts to lead* REBECCA, *who almost collapses, but* PROCTOR *catches her, and she glances up at him apologetically.*]

REBECCA. I've had no breakfast.
HERRICK. Come, man.

[HERRICK *escorts them out,* HATHORNE *and* CHEEVER *behind them.* ELIZABETH *stands staring at the empty doorway.*]

PARRIS [*in deadly fear, to* ELIZABETH]. Go to him, Goody Proctor! There is yet time!

[*From outside a drumroll strikes the air.* PARRIS *is startled.* ELIZABETH *jerks about toward the window.*]

PARRIS. Go to him! [*He rushes out the door, as though to hold back his fate*]. Proctor! Proctor!

[*Again, a short burst of drums.*]

HALE. Woman, plead with him! [*He starts to rush out the door, and then goes back to her.*] Woman! It is pride, it is vanity.

[*She avoids his eyes, and moves to the window.. He drops to his knees.*]

Be his helper!—What profit him to bleed? Shall the dust praise him? Shall the worms declare his truth? Go to him, take his shame away!
ELIZABETH [*supporting herself against collapse, grips the bars of the window, and with a cry*]. He have his goodness now. God forbid I take it from him!

[*The final drumroll crashes, then heightens violently.* HALE *weeps in frantic prayer, and the new sun is pouring in upon her face, and the drums rattle like bones in the morning air.*]

THE CURTAIN FALLS

Not long after the fever died, Parris was voted from office, walked out on the highroad, and was never heard of again.

The legend has it that Abigail turned up later as a prostitute in Boston.

Twenty years after the last execution, the government awarded compensation to the victims still living, and to the families of the dead. However, it is evident that some people still were unwilling to admit their total guilt, and also that the factionalism was still alive, for some beneficiaries were actually not victims at all, but informers.

Elizabeth Proctor married again, four years after Proctor's death.

In solemn meeting, the congregation rescinded the excommunications—this in March 1712. But they did so upon orders of the government. The jury, however, wrote a statement praying forgiveness of all who had suffered.

Certain farms which had belonged to the victims were left to ruin, and for more than a century no one would buy them or live on them.

To all intents and purposes, the power of theocracy in Massachusetts was broken.

A. M.

Two Critical Commentaries on Arthur Miller's historical play, *The Crucible*

Commentary by George Jean Nathan, "Henrik Miller," in *Theatre Arts*, XXXVII (April, 1953), 24–26.*

As Strindberg was the most positive influence on O'Neill so Ibsen is the most positive on Arthur Miller. O'Neill as a consequence was primarily interested in analyzing the grinding emotions of man and woman that often lie below the calmer surface emotions. Miller as a consequence is primarily interested in man's sociological aspects. Above all, O'Neill as a dramatist was concerned with character, whereas Miller seems in large part to be concerned with theme and with character only incidentally. Though in his worthy *Death of a Salesman* he achieved character, it still and nevertheless occasionally had the effect of being inserted into his theme rather than emerging naturally and easily out of it; and in *The Crucible,* his latest play, we find all theme and no character. His people are spokesmen for him, not for themselves. They possess humanity, when they possess it at all, only in the distant sense that a phonograph recording of it does. They speak and act at an obvious turning of his crank. And the result is a play of large thematic force whose warmth, even heat, remains on the other side of the footlights and is not communicated, save in cold, intellectual terms, to its audience. It is impressive, as a lecture may be impressive, but for the major part it is equally remote from the listener's heart and feeling.

---

* Reprinted by permission of George Jean Nathan.

As heretofore, Miller shows himself to be a thoroughly honest and thoroughly sincere dramatist who, unlike the great majority of our present American playwrights, has nothing of the box-office toady in his composition, and all credit to him on that score. But he also and at the same time here shows himself as one whose conscious indifference to the box-office seems to be accompanied by an unconscious indifference to any kind of theatrical audience, even one of the higher grade. It may be, of course, that he thought he had worked out his theme in terms of character and so would insinuate it into such an audience's emotion. That I can not tell. But if he did, he has failed. And if, on the other hand, he believed that the sheer vitality of his theme would satisfactorily infiltrate itself in his audience, independent of any recognizable and pulsing character to assist it, he has not yet sufficiently educated himself in dramatic eccentricity.

That theme, centered on the historical Salem witch hunts and witch trials in the last years of the seventeenth century, is the mass hysteria born of superstition, ignorance, fear and bigotry and the tragedy it can bear for the guiltless. The play, which unfortunately veers toward extended documentation, seeks to crystallize the thesis in the persons of a man and wife who fall victims to the witch hunt but they too unfortunately are more mere documentary mouthpieces of the author than human beings with any real life, and their tragedy accordingly has the distant air of a dramatic recitation rather than of any personal suffering. Though Miller has written some scenes with his customary energetic pen, though there is a certain eloquence in them and though here and there contagious drama threatens to issue forth, it is this lack of character convincingly and warmly to project the whole into an audience's emotions that enfeebles the play. There is, in addition, such a repetitive flavor to it—it seems at times that the author is saying exactly the same thing over and over again—that the whole gives the effect of being on a treadmill and that, while there is an appearance of motion, it is really static.

The scene in the second act wherein the young women in the grip of hysteria proclaim again their certainty of the operation of evil spirits and overwhelm another of their number who has been cozened into denial is the play's closest approach to infectious drama. The prologue, in which the seeds of the witch mania are sown, also has promise but, except for the subsequent scene noted, the promise is never realized and what we get is largely only discourse, sometimes interesting in itself, that does not succeed in ridding itself of its dialectic chill and in resolving itself, for all its fury, into even the mild fever of affecting drama.

That Miller had contemporary parallels in mind is obvious. He has, indeed, had them so closely in mind that he has not been able to put them out of it when a momentary forgetfulness of them would have profited his play. Though he does not at any point emphasize them and in this respect remains the dramatic artist, they somehow persist in indicating their hold upon him, and a wayward sense of propaganda, that enemy of dramatic art, forces its way into his auditor's consciousness. There is, let it be repeated, power in this play and not only power but intellectual purpose. Yet the power is that of an impersonal machine and the intellectual purpose that of an historical analyst, with a dramatist late in arriving on the scene and, when he does arrive, too deeply impressed and overcome by his materials to guide them into dramatic life. . . .

The Crucible, in sum, is an honorable sermon on a vital theme that misses because the sting implicit in it has been disinfected with an editorial tincture and because, though it contains the potential deep vibrations of life, it reduces them to mere superficial tremors.

Commentary by Brooks Atkinson, " 'The Crucible,' Arthur Miller's Dramatization of the Salem Witch Trial in 1692," in the *New York Times,* February 1, 1953, Sec. 2, p. 1.*

Although opinions vary about details of the workmanship, Arthur Miller's new play, *The Crucible,* has made a deep impression on the town. Put it down as the most notable new play by an American so far this season, for Mr. Miller has an independent mind, professional skill and personal courage. *The Crucible* is the story of the hysterical persecution of people accused of witchcraft in Salem in 1692 when fear paralyzed the judicial faculties of men in authority. Probably Mr. Miller has had to alter some of the details of the record to make a tidy play out of a big historical subject; and he has also made a few remarks in passing that apply specifically to the public intolerance of today. But fundamentally, *The Crucible* is a portrait of the terror and ferocity with which a few Americans, mostly God-fearing men, once accused each other of allegiance to the devil.

Terrible as this story may seem today, it is founded on fact. Things like this did happen in America in the seventeenth century. The time was ripe for an explosion. After about seventy years of religious and civil omnipotence, the Puritan theocracy was breaking up, for two new generations of colonial Americans had come to maturity and new settlers had come in. The mood was fanatical. The nearer the theocracy came to an end, the more desperately it insisted on conformity.

Thirty years before the Salem trial the Puritans had hanged four Quakers in Boston for heresy. And at the time of the Salem trial even educated men like Cotton Mather accepted 'satanic molestations,' as he called them, as facts of nature. Everything was ready for the cruel frenzy that swept the town and came to a climax in the year of Mr. Miller's play.

As a matter of historical record, the community quickly recovered. The next year the Governor released from jail everyone accused of witchcraft. And five years later the jurors who had condemned their neighbors publicly confessed that they had been deluded. But that did not restore the lives of twenty innocent people who had been put to death for not confessing to something they knew to be a lie.

Since *The Crucible* is a play about bigotry, it has certain current significance. . . . But Mr. Miller is not delivering a polemic or offering *The Crucible* as a deadly parallel. For the difference between the Salem trial and

---

* Reprinted from the *New York Times* by permission of Brooks Atkinson.

the current hysteria is a fundamental one. There never were any witches. But there have been spies and traitors in recent days. All the Salem witches were victims of public fear. . . . [But] some of the people accused of treason and disloyalty today have been guilty.

In *The Crucible* the parallels are minor to the central horror of the witch-hunt in Salem; and they involve the irresponsibility and maliciousness of the accusers, the avidity with which most people accept the accusations as proof of guilt and the bias against anyone who defends the accused people. Obviously, Mr. Miller has these things in mind, for no one can write about bigotry today in a historical vacuum. But they are incidental to the play as a whole, which dramatizes a unique episode in American history long before the time of representative government and the constitutional judicial system. . . .

In *The Crucible* Mr. Miller is more interested in his theme than in his people. Using the realistic form of *All My Sons,* he tells the sweeping, tragic story of a momentous historical event that has left a scar on our history. Most of his characters are instruments of the action first and human beings with private lives and thoughts at second hand. John Proctor and his wife, Elizabeth, are the only people who really interest Mr. Miller. After a frenetic prologue, Mr. Miller finds a quiet interlude in which to present them at home and listen to their hopes and misgivings; and in the last act he brings them together again and searches their hearts for a word of civilized comfort in a barbaric storm.

But he is so generally absorbed in the headlong rush of the story that he has difficulty in finding room for his chief characters. Perhaps that explains why *The Crucible* is a gripping and exciting play without much human warmth. It is swift and shrill but emotionally external. . . .

The acting is passionately alive. As the deputy governor who presides over the trial, Walter Hampden plays with a towering fanaticism that is enormously effective, since it conveys the vengeful self-righteousness of the true theocrat.

In the central parts of John Proctor and his wife, Arthur Kennedy and Beatrice Straight give superb performances. These parts have true perspective in the writing because Mr. Miller admires these people. Through the understanding and skill of the acting, Mr. Kennedy and Miss Straight have created two admirable characters who set a moral standard.

Out of a dark episode in American history Mr. Miller has written a fiery play.

APPENDIX

An APPENDIX is the out-behind-the-barn of a book—or in-the-woodshed or down-in-the-basement, depending upon the society in which you were nurtured. It is the place to stow used lumber and almost discarded oddments. It is also the place to which the family tyrant repairs to discipline recalcitrant or errant youth, whether with strap or assignment of punitive duty. It is also the place for acknowledgment of stolen trifles and revelation of secret sources of information; whispered questions and answers on the nature and meaning of things; suggestions of places to go, things to do, books to read in the fuller experiencing of life—and occasional mischief too, of course, and trial flights of the more serious kind!

Out of sight is not always out of mind. The various materials hidden away here in the Appendix—once you have prowled around amongst them—will be remembered as occasion requires.

First of all, there are NOTES here for each of the five essays and short plays in Part One and for each of the plays with commentaries in Part Two. These are not the usual source notes, the centipedarian notes of the term paper or article of scholarship. They do indicate sources, of course, but are keyed to the essay sections rather than to the pages or the precise point of reference, and are intended to serve the larger purpose of suggesting the pertinent literature.

Second, in the appendix material for each essay and play comes a set of QUERIES. These are by no means exhaustive. They may be useful as the basis for some reflective thought following the reading of the play. Framing answers to them may serve to pattern the characters and action and meaning more clearly, and to fix the drama in mind. Or these queries may prove to be a springboard for group discussion.

Third is a series of SUGGESTIONS FOR STUDY for each essay and play. From these the instructor may wish to make class or individual assignments for written or oral reports, or they may well suggest yet other and more original undertakings to enlarge the scope of the course and put into effect the understandings of drama and life that are being developed.

AND FURTHER READING is suggested, in the fourth place, as appendix material for each essay and play. From the reading suggestions the instructor, again, may choose to make individual or class assignments. Without detailed notes and formal bibliography, then, this Appendix will nevertheless serve as a guide and an introduction to the wide and diverse literature of the theater and drama.

Finally, for each of the five essays of Part One, there is a pair of OUTLINE WORKSHEETS that may be useful for some instructors and students, whether as the basis for compact written reports, or as the basis for disciplined discussion.

Part One

I. PRELIMINARY—ORIENTATION TO DRAMA—
"A GOOD LESSON!"

NOTES. The headquote for Essay I is from SHELDON CHENEY, The Theatre: Three Thousand Years of Drama, Acting, and Stagecraft (New York, Longmans, Green, 1929), p. 1. [§ 1.] MORDECAI GORELIK, New Theatres for Old (New York, Samuel French, 1940), p. 4, speaks of the stage as one of the ways truth can be revealed to people. [§ 2.] GEORGE FREEDLEY and JOHN REEVES, A History of the Theater (New York, Crown, 1941) gives a readable account of the beginnings of Drama. Another recent general history is ALLARDYCE NICOLL, World Drama (New York, Harcourt, Brace, 1950). [§ 4.] On the relation of Theater to Literature, see THOMAS MUNRO, The Arts and Their Interrelations (New York, Liberal Arts Press, 1949), pp. 497-500; for a different approach see CHARLES W. COOPER, The Arts and Humanity (New York, Philosophical Library, 1952). In the American study of theater and drama, the way was led by CLAYTON HAMILTON, The Theory of the Theater (rev. ed.; New York, Holt, 1939) and the older BRANDER MATTHEWS, A Study of the Drama (Boston, Houghton Mifflin, 1910). In literary study, see THOMAS C. POLLOCK, The Nature of Literature (Princeton, N. J., Princeton University Press, 1942) and, of greatest significance, I. A. RICHARDS, Principles of Literary Criticism (New York, Harcourt, Brace, 1928). [§ 5.] The definition of 'a stageplay' is taken from CHAS. W. COOPER and PAUL A. CAMP, Designing the Play (New York, Appleton-Century-Crofts, 1942), but in substance goes back to Aristotle.

LAURENCE HOUSMAN, The Unexpected Years (Indianapolis, Bobbs-Merrill, 1936) provides interesting autobiographical material, with references to the Victoria playlets. Production data for Victoria Regina will be found in BURNS MANTLE, The Best Plays of 1935-1936 (New York, Dodd, Mead, 1936) and succeeding volumes.

QUERIES. In the opening of "A Good Lesson!" whose anxiety is reflected by the Queen's Gentleman? What does Anson's "studied nonchalance" cover?

Why is Richards concerned? Had recent British princes, the Queen's uncles, been distinguished for their domestic stability and fidelity?

What are Prince Albert's characteristics as shown in the scene with Anson? What evidence of his German origin? of his interest in public affairs? of his devotion to duty? of his stubborn independence?

What are Queen Victoria's characteristics as shown in this play? What evidence is there that she is self-willed? obstinate? imperious? passionate? little? What evidence that she is both suspicious and affectionate? impatient and devoted? scatterbrained and practical?

Why does Albert remain seated when the Queen comes in? When do you feel that he would rise? Why does he insist that she sit down? call her "Weibchen" [little wife]? appeal to her thrift? save her self-esteem?

What is the good lesson that the servants at Windsor learned? that Victoria learned? that Albert learned? What is the general meaning or theme of "A Good Lesson!" as you interpret it?

As you consider the playbook and then imagine the stageplay created from it, what are the auditory values that would be added to the script by the theater? the visual values?

What different senses of the word "drama" would be useful in your discussion of "A Good Lesson!"?

SUGGESTIONS FOR STUDY.

A. DRAMA GLOSSARY. Using 3" x 5" cards or slips of paper, begin to make a glossary of the terms useful in considering the Drama. Print the term at the top of the card; then define it as used in the essay. Certain of the dramaturgic terms have several senses, which should be numbered and listed. When appropriate or helpful, add an illustration or specific instance from your own experience. Page references, if you wish to add them, may be useful. The cards may handily be alphabetized.

B. LIBRARY EXPLORATION. Books about the Drama are to be found in many different sections of your college or university library. Use the card catalogue as a guide to discovering the library classification and general call numbers of drama books of these several sorts—American, British, and French plays; history of dramatic literature, of the theater; play production, acting, directing, scene design, costume, make-up, lighting; playwriting, dramatic theory, dramatic criticism. Then, if you have access to the stacks, find out where such books are shelved. Take a few minutes to browse in each section, spotting books that you may care to come back to later on.

C. YOUR PERSONAL INVENTORY. Use the accompanying form to make a study of your personal experience and taste in the field of drama.

D. LOCAL DRAMA SURVEY. Use the second of these forms in making a study of the drama available in your present community.

AND FURTHER READING.

A. HISTORY. Undertake some reading on the beginnings of the Drama in one of the general histories cited in the Notes above: CHENEY, FREEDLEY and REEVES, or NICOLL; or in GLENN HUGHES, *The Story of the Theater* (New York, Samuel French, 1928).

B. THEORY. Undertake some reading on the theory of Drama or literature in one of the following, as noted above: HAMILTON, MATTHEWS, RICHARDS, or

PERSONAL INVENTORY OF DRAMA EXPERIENCES

Use this outline as a tool and guide in making an inventory of all your various experiences in theater art and dramatic literature. Your future understanding, appreciation, and enjoyment of drama will develop from your present knowledge, experience, and taste. This self-analysis will help you to Know Thyself.

Crease your paper down the center to mark off double columns. Write or type single-spaced and use both sides of a sheet of paper in order to keep this inventory compact in form.

1. *Your name,* last name first—your age—your college class.
   Your home town and state—your high school.
   Extent of travel—New York City, other theater centers, abroad.

2. *Dramas you have read*—estimate the total number.
   List titles (but no more than 10) in double column.
   Star or asterisk those you studied in class.
   Generalize upon your playreading in one brief sentence.

3. *Stageplays you have seen*—estimate the total number.
   List titles (up to 10) again in double column.
   Star or asterisk those seen in professional theaters.
   Generalize upon your playgoing in a single statement.

4. *Cinema, radio, and TV drama*—estimate your experience.
   List up to 10 titles, underline movies, quote TV plays.
   Star the dramatic and theater classics you have thus seen.
   Again generalize in a brief comment.

5. *Dramatic and theatrical experience*—estimate total.
   List the plays (up to 10) you have acted or worked in.
   Star if you played lead; double star if you directed.
   Generalize upon the range of your theater experience.

6. *Courses in drama*—estimate the number of college units.
   List courses in Dramatic Literature (left column).
   List courses in Theater Art (right column).
   Generalize upon the nature of this course work.

7. *Reading about drama*—estimate the total amount.
   In what newspapers have you read play reviews? (left column)
   In what magazines have you read play reviews? (right column)
   What biographies of dramatists, actors, etc., have you read?
   What books of dramatic history, criticism, etc.?

8. *Taste in drama*—evaluate your own taste in one sentence.
   What are your favorite three or four modern dramas?
   Whom do you consider the best modern dramatist?
   What earlier dramas have you particularly enjoyed?
   What types of plays do you strongly prefer?
   What, in brief, do you consider the qualities of a good drama?

Use this outline as a tool and guide in making a survey of the drama in its local dimension, and thus becoming more fully aware of the theater art and dramatic literature near at hand.

Crease your paper down the center to mark off double columns. Write or type single-spaced and use both sides of a sheet of paper in order to keep this survey compact.

1. *Area*—city, town, or boundaries—covered by this survey.
   Sources of information used in making this study.

2. *Theaters and stageplays*—number of each in current season.
   List theaters by name—with titles of current plays.
   List other theaters (dark)—titles of plays (coming).
   List the auditoriums, opera houses, etc.,—their shows.
   Generalize in regard to professional theater in the area.

3. *Nonprofessional theaters and plays*—give the number current.
   List community and art theaters—with current plays.
   List also plays at present announced for the season.
   Generalize in regard to the nonprofessional theater.

4. *College and university theaters*—give number in the area.
   List the college groups—with titles of current plays.
   List also plays at present announced for the season.
   Generalize about the educational theater in the area.

5. *Cinema, radio, and TV drama*—number of theaters and stations.
   List theaters for first-run, old, art, and foreign films—with any out-standing current or coming attractions.
   List radio and TV stations broadcasting drama in the area—with current and coming programs of stage classics and with current and coming programs of screen classics.
   Generalize about the cinema, radio, and TV drama available.

6. *Courses in drama*—total number available in your institution.
   List courses currently given in theater art (left column).
   List courses currently given in dramatic literature (right).
   Generalize about the drama course offerings available.

7. *Library resources*—following survey suggested in SUGGESTION B above.
   General estimate of drama resources of your college library.
   What other drama collections are available: departmental? city library? county? nearby colleges and universities?

8. *News and reviews*—number of useful papers and magazines.
   List newspapers that run local play reviews (left column).
   List available journals that carry New York reviews (right).
   List drama magazines available in the college library (left).
   List drama journals carried on local newsstands (right).

POLLOCK, or in the quite different FRANK M. WHITING, *An Introduction to the Theater* (New York, Harper, 1954).

C. HOUSMAN MINOR. Read further about the life and work of Laurence Housman. For a concise account see STANLEY J. KUNITZ and HOWARD HAYCRAFT, *Twentieth Century Authors* (New York, H. W. Wilson, 1942) and *Who's Who*. For his trials as a playwright, his troubles with the censor, his late success in the theater, you will find pleasant reading in *The Unexpected Years* (*op. cit.*).

D. VICTORIA REGENERATA. For a general account of the Queen turn to one of the standard encyclopedias or to the *Dictionary of National Biography*. Then select one or two other short plays from Housman's extended dramatic biography of the Queen—*Victoria Regina, The Golden Sovereign,* or *Gracious Majesty* (New York, Scribner, 1935, 1937, 1942)—for pleasant reading. Helen Hayes has recorded two of the scenes ("Album of Stars," Decca DL 9002 [1950]). Many of these same episodes in her life are treated brilliantly by LYTTON STRACHEY in the critical biography, *Queen Victoria* (New York, Harcourt, Brace, 1921); you will find them also in the official biography, Sir SIDNEY LEE, *Queen Victoria* (New York, Macmillan, 1903), and in Queen Victoria's own numerous journals and letters that have been published. As you read further, compare different treatments of the same episode.

II. THE PLAYSCRIPT—CREATION BY THE PLAYWRIGHT— *FUMED OAK*

NOTES. The headquote for Essay II is from JOHN VAN DRUTEN, *Playwright at Work* (New York, Harper, 1953), p. 17, a very readable account by a skillful dramatist. [§ 1.] MORDECAI GORELIK (*op. cit.*), pp. 21-22, holds that a stageplay is first a "show" and secondly a "story." The word "poet," it is interesting to note, derives from the Greek for "maker." [§ 2.] GEORGE R. STEWART, *Storm* (New York, Random House, 1949) comes to mind as a story about an inanimate thing. The definition of "story" is from COOPER and CAMP, *Designing the Play* (*op. cit.*), p. 1. [§ 4.] The quotation is from BRANDER MATTHEWS, *A Study of the Drama* (*op. cit.*), pp. 161-62. FERDINAND BRUNETIÈRE, *The Law of the Drama* (1894) is to be found translated in BARRETT H. CLARK (ed.), *European Theories of the Drama* (New York, Crown, 1947). See CLAYTON HAMILTON (*op. cit.*), pp. 77-78, on the theater's method of storytelling. See SAMUEL SELDEN, *An Introduction to Playwriting* (New York, Appleton-Century-Crofts, 1946), pp. 41 ff. For ARISTOTLE, *Poetics* in a readable form, see LANE COOPER, *Aristotle on the Art of Poetry* (New York, Harcourt, Brace, 1913). GUSTAV FREYTAG, *Technique of the Drama* (1863), tr. Elias MacEwan (4th ed.; Chicago, Scott, Foresman, 1904), pp. 126, 186. Yet another sense of "scene" is frequent: any particularly dramatic incident in life or drama.

For biographical data on Noel Coward see KUNITZ and HAYCRAFT, *Twentieth Century Authors* (*op. cit.*), *Current Biography* (1941), and NOEL COWARD, *Present Indicative* (New York, Doubleday, 1937) and *Future Indefinite* (New York, Doubleday, 1954). See BURNS MANTLE, *Best Plays of 1936-37* (New York, Dodd, Mead, 1937) and the successive volumes for the theatrical data. The quotations are from NOEL COWARD, *Present Indicative* (*op. cit.*), p. 287, and from the Foreword to *Tonight at 8:30* (New York, Doubleday, 1936).

QUERIES. Wouldn't it be easy to overlook the importance of Mrs. Rockett in this unpleasant comedy, *Fumed Oak?* How old do you judge her to be? What are we told of her husband? Of her sister or sister-in-law, Aunt Daisy? Of her three daughters? What of seventeen years ago when Nora was married and Phyllis engaged? What was her part in trapping Henry? What is her present place in his home? What of her financial position? her health? her friends? her relation to Doris? to Elsie? to Henry? Why, after all, does the playwright give such a full case history of Mrs. Rockett?

What is Doris's goal in life? What are indicated as the chief symbols of her suburban respectability? What in the setting and stage props? What in her way of life? At what points can we see the reality beneath the surface? What is the significance of the title *Fumed Oak?* At what two places in the play is this pointed out? Would an audience understand it the first time?

From what, during these past fifteen years, has Henry plotted to escape? Does he dislike his vocation? What is wrong with his home life? When did he realize he had been tricked into marriage? What did he give up when he married Doris? What had he planned to do? How did he keep his dream alive? What did he do in his steps toward escape and self-realization? How does he rationalize his desertion? Is there any hope for Elsie? What?

John Gassner writes of Coward as "savage when he cast a scornful glance at middle-class respectability in . . . *Fumed Oak,* in which a harassed white-collar slave casts off wife, mother-in-law and child, all of them equally impossible" (*Masters of the Drama,* p. 624). What do you think of this interpretation and evaluation? Is Henry blameless? Is there nothing to be said for Doris?

How would you phrase the over-all meaning, the theme, or the moral of *Fumed Oak* as you understand it?

SUGGESTIONS FOR STUDY.

A. MORE GLOSSARY. Continue making a glossary as suggested above for Essay I. You may wish to look up some of these terms in your own college dictionary or in an unabridged dictionary or in the *New English Dictionary* (the O. E. D.) in the library, and then note down the somewhat different definitions for their dramaturgic senses.

B. FUNCTIONAL ANALYSIS. In the final paragraphs of § 5 of the essay, eight different dramaturgic functions of dialogue are specified: (1) to reveal character, (2) to suggest scene and mood, (3) to accompany action, (4) to serve as action, (5) to narrate or evaluate past or off-stage action, (6) to clarify the plot structure, (7) to state or suggest the theme, (8) to provide verbal delight. Now turn to *Fumed Oak*—perhaps about the middle of Scene II—and consider the function or functions of each speech for two or three pages. You may wish to pencil the above numbers lightly in the margins as a means of noting the data of your analysis.

C. WHAT HAPPENS WHEN. You have already noted that *Fumed Oak,* unusual as a one-act play, includes two scenes. (1) Now divide it up into its *basic scenes.* Draw a *line* across the margin to mark the beginning of each such scene; list above it the *characters* who are already on stage and under it the characters who enter at this point; designate the basic scene with a *letter:* A, B, C, D, etc. (2) There are six rather short basic scenes in Scene I. What happens in each of them? Phrase a sentence for each basic scene summarizing its *action,* the incidents that comprise it. (3) You have already noted that Scene II is made up of one long basic scene. Yet, with a little thought, you can divide it up into what you consider its component *incidents.* Put a dotted line across the margin wherever you believe that an important new incident begins; number these 1, 2, 3, etc., for your reference. Summarize each of these incidents in a sentence.

D. ANATOMY OF PLOT. Use the Plot Analysis outline worksheet as a guide in making a study of *Fumed Oak* or of some other one-act or full-length play as may be suggested to you.

In one sentence of 50 to 150 words, summarize and structuralize the principal action of the drama. The following formula may be helpful: name of *protagonist* (chief *traits*) who *wants* something, is *opposed* by certain forces, which he meets in *incidents of conflict,* complications, and crises, culminating with the end of the story.

E. PERSONALITIES. Use the second of these forms as a guide in making a Character Analysis of Doris or Henry Gow, or of some character from another drama as suggested.

In about 50 to 150 words summarize the events in the life of the character as revealed in the drama. (*Note.* This will probably not be the same as the whole action of the drama, which begins not with birth but with the inciting incident.)

AND FURTHER READING.

A. DRAMATIC THEORY. Carry further your reading in CLAYTON HAMILTON or BRANDER MATTHEWS (see Notes for Essay I), or undertake reading in FRED B. MILLET and GERALD E. BENTLEY, *The Art of the Drama* (New York, Appleton-Century-Crofts, 1935) or in ALAN REYNOLDS THOMPSON, *The Anatomy of Drama* (Berkeley, University of California Press, 1942).

B. DRAMATURGY. For reading in dramatic theory with special reference to playwriting, look up the time-honored WILLIAM ARCHER, *Play-Making* (Boston, Small-Maynard, 1912) or GEORGE PIERCE BAKER, *Dramatic Technique* (Boston, Houghton Mifflin, 1919). Recent and shorter works, in addition to JOHN VAN DRUTEN (*op. cit.*) and SAMUEL SELDON (*op. cit.*), are LAJOS EGRI, *The Art of Dramatic Writing* (New York, Simon & Schuster, 1946) and KENNETH MACGOWAN, *A Primer of Playwriting* (New York, Random House, 1951).

C. COWARD FOR FUN. Among the other one-act plays that comprise *Tonight at 8:30,* there are a number that may be read with interest: *Still Life, The Astonished Heart, Red Peppers.* In NOEL COWARD, *Play Parade* (New York, Doubleday, 1934) will be found Coward's early plays, including *Hay Fever, Private Lives, Design for Living,* and *Cavalcade.* His *Blithe Spirit* (New York, Doubleday, 1941) is a most hilarious farce comedy.

D. COMPARATIVE READING. As a means of discovering how differently the same story is treated in the different media of prose fiction and drama, study comparatively any one of the following pairs: the SOMERSET MAUGHAM story "Miss Thompson" (called "Rain" in his collection *East and West*) and JOHN COLTON and CLEMENCE RANDOLPH, *Rain* (New York. Boni & Liveright, 1923);

Use this outline as a tool and guide in giving close attention to your experience of the assigned drama. The careful analysis of a few dramas will greatly increase your ability in structuralizing the plays you see and read, increasing your understanding, appreciation, and enjoyment of them.

Write or type your answers single-spaced, using both sides of the sheet as needed in order to keep your analysis compact.

1. *Type of plot*—classification or general description.
   Is the action of this drama clearly plotted or unplotted?
   Is the pattern that of a conflict plot? If not, describe the design of its action, adjusting your answers below accordingly.

2. *Plot forces*—the pattern of the action.
   a. *Protagonist.* Who is the chief character as regards plot?
      What are his principal character traits?
      What is his strongest desire, will, or goal?
   b. *Opposing force.* Who or what is the chief antagonist?
      What are his or its principal characteristics?
      What other forces are aligned against the protagonist?
   c. *Deciding factor.* Who or what is the deciding factor?
      How does it operate to decide the dramatic conflict?

3. *Components of the whole action*—happenings from the very start.
   a. *Inciting incident.* What started the chain of events?
      What, prior to this, was the initial situation?
   b. *Dramatic question.* What question then suggests itself?
      What other dramatic questions maintain suspense?
   c. *Conflict, complications, crises.* What in succession are the chief incidents of conflict, complication, crisis?
   d. *Climax.* What is the climactic crisis in the story?
      Is it nearer the middle or the end of the whole action?
   e. *The end.* What is the final incident? the final situation?
      Would you describe it as catastrophe? denouement? or what?

4. *Structure of the enacted drama*—within the framework of the play.
   a. *Structure.* Chronological? dramatic? fifth-act? flashback?
   b. *Situation at rise.* What characters are revealed? where?
      At what point in the whole action does the curtain rise?
   c. *Exposition.* What important relationships are made clear?
      What important antecedent events are narrated?
      By what dramatic means is the exposition given?
      What proportion of the enacted drama is expository?
      What expository material is given later in the play?
   d. *Off-stage action.* What important events occur off-stage?
      What important incidents occur between scenes or acts?
      How are these happenings communicated to the audience?
   e. *Larger units of dramatic construction.* How many acts? scenes?
      What is the time (period) and place (geographic)?
      What is the time (date, hour) and place of each scene?

```
┌─────────────────────────────────────────────────────────────┐
│                                                             │
│     CHARACTER ANALYSIS OF  [name of character]              │
│                                                             │
└─────────────────────────────────────────────────────────────┘
```

Use this outline as a tool and guide in giving close attention to your experiencing of a particular character in a drama. The full and thoughtful consideration of a few dramatic characters will increase your skill in interpreting and understanding the persons you meet in life as well as in other plays.

Write or type your answers single-spaced, using both sides of the sheet as needed in order to keep your analysis compact.

1. *Identification*—name of play, playwright, and period.
   To what general type and style does the play belong?

2. *Personality traits of the character*—abstracted from the play.
   a. *Physical.* What sex, age, face, stature, vitality, voice?
      What individualizes him as regards physical traits?
      What mannerisms in posture, walk, gesture, action?
   b. *Mental.* What I.Q.? mental type? education? creativity?
      What fixed ideas? life views? interests? skills?
      What are his mannerisms of thought and speech?
   c. *Emotional.* Is he extrovert, introvert? objective, egocentric?
      What strength, depth, and control of emotions?
      What emotional attitudes, loves, hates, weaknesses?
   d. *Social.* What are his sociability? dominance? security?
      What marital, social, economic, religious adjustments?
      What mannerisms distinguish his social behavior?

3. *Behavior of the character*—his relation to the story.
   a. *Relationships.* What is his kinship to other characters?
      What is his relationship to the dramatic scene?
   b. *Actions and motivation*—what the character does and why.
      What part did he have in the antecedent events?
      What does he do in the enacted drama? (List in left column.)
      Why does he do these things? (List motives in right column.)
   c. *Plot.* What place does he occupy in the plot structure?
      What other functions does he serve in the drama?
   d. *Theme.* What is his relation to the theme of the drama?
      Does he give expression to the general meaning?

4. *Characterization*—the playwright's creation of the character.
   a. *Factors.* What factors seem to have shaped the character?
      Is there an historical person back of the character?
      How far is he determined by dramatic necessity?
      Is he highly individualized or a type character?
      Does he reflect the playwright's view of life?
   b. *Devices.* What devices are used in his characterization?
      What traits are stated in the stage directions?
      What traits are described by other characters?
      What traits are revealed by the character's own words?
      What traits are shown by what the character does?
      What traits are suggested by the environment?

the THOMAS LODGE romance *Rosalynde* and SHAKESPEARE, *As You Like It;*
the JOHN STEINBECK novelette *Of Mice and Men* and his own dramatization
under the same title (both New York, Covici, Friede, 1937); the SINCLAIR
LEWIS novel *Dodsworth* (New York, Harcourt, Brace, 1929) and the SIDNEY
HOWARD drama *Dodsworth* (New York, Harcourt, Brace, 1934); the
HENRY JAMES novel *Washington Square* (London, Macmillan, 1881) and
the RUTH and AUGUSTUS GOETZ drama *The Heiress* (New York, Dramatists
Play Service, 1948).

III. THE STAGEPLAY—PLAY PRODUCTION— *THE LONG VOYAGE HOME*

NOTES. The headquote for Essay III is from ELIZABETH DREW, *Discovering
Drama* (New York, Norton, 1937), p. 13. [§ 1.] See COOPER, *The Arts and
Humanity* (*op. cit.*), chap. vi, for a fuller discussion of interpretative creative
activity. [§ 2.] With regard to the art of acting, see SAMUEL SELDEN, *The
Stage in Action* (New York, Appleton-Century-Crofts, 1940), and CONSTANTIN
STANISLAVSKI, *An Actor Prepares* (New York, Theatre Arts, 1936). All
modern study of semantic interpretation owes a debt to C. K. OGDEN and I. A.
RICHARDS, *The Meaning of Meaning* (New York, Harcourt, Brace, 1923).
[§ 3.] On the art of scene design, see HAROLD BURRIS-MEYER and EDWARD C.
COLE, *Scenery for the Theater* (Boston, Little, Brown, 1938) and SAMUEL
SELDEN and HUNTON D. SELLMAN, *Stage Scenery and Lighting* (New York,
Appleton-Century-Crofts, 1936), also JOHN GASSNER and others, *Producing the
Play* (New York, Dryden Press, 1941). [§ 4.] For costuming see FAIRFAX P.
WALKUP, *Dressing the Part* (2d ed.; New York, Appleton-Century-Crofts,
1950) and LUCY BARTON, *Historic Costume for the Stage* (Boston, Walter H.
Baker, 1935); for technical production, WILLIAM P. HALSTEAD, *Stage Manage-
ment for the Amateur Theater* (New York, Appleton-Century-Crofts, 1937)
and COOPER and CAMP, *Designing the Play* (*op. cit.*). [§ 5.] On directing,
see ALEXANDER DEAN, *Fundamentals of Play Direction* (New York, Farrar &
Rinehart, 1941), HUBERT C. HEFFNER in *Modern Theater Practice* (3d ed.;
New York, Appleton-Century-Crofts, 1946), and essays by WORTHINGTON
MINER and HAROLD CLURMAN in GASSNER, *Producing the Play* (*op. cit.*). For
the emergence of the director, see TOBY COLE and HELEN KRICH CHINOY, *Directing the Play* (Indianapolis, Bobbs-Merrill, 1953), pp. 13-67.

JOHN GASSNER, *Masters of the Drama* (New York, Random House, 1940,
p. 648) also considers the *S. S. Glencairn* plays as a first masterpiece of modern
American drama. See BARRETT H. CLARK, *Eugene O'Neill, the Man and His
Plays* (rev. ed.; New York, Dover Publications, 1947), and RALPH SANBORN
and BARRETT H. CLARK, *A Bibliography of the Works of Eugene O'Neill* (New
York, Random House, 1931).

QUERIES. What are some of the problems that actors would have to face
as interpretative creative artists in developing the principal roles in *The Long
Voyage Home?*
    Should Olson be the center of attention when the seamen enter? Why not?
(Brooks Atkinson remembered for more than a dozen years the lumbering,
beautiful, masterful performance Walter Abel gave of Olson in the 1924

production.) What will distinguish him from Driscoll, Cocky, and Ivan? Is Olson essentially a stock character, "a dumb Swede"? How might the actor individualize him? How broad should his dialect be? How can Olson's refusals to drink be played for best effect? In what tone should his dream of family, farm, and future home be spoken? Is there any significant business for the actor? or will his performance be almost entirely speech? Why has the playwright given him so little action?

How can the actor of Driscoll keep his role from overpowering Olson's? If Driscoll, as Olson's companion, does not come to his rescue, what purpose does he serve in the play? In this play is Driscoll merely the type "ebullient Irishman"? Should his dialect, gestures, and business be restrained (so as to keep the role in focus) or broad (for comic effect)? In what different ways should he be contrasted with Olson?

How can the actors of Fat Joe and Nick and Freda keep their parts from becoming merely melodramatic? In what way is each of them somewhat individualized? What are the bits of significant stage business that each of them must execute clearly enough for the audience to see and note? Why are they—in contrast to Olson—given so much action throughout the play?

SUGGESTIONS FOR STUDY.

A. THEATER OBSERVED. (a) With others of your class arrange to be given a guided tour of your college or university theater—its stage and flies, workshop and scene dock, switchboard and lighting equipment, wardrobe and prop storage, etc.—for the purpose of furthering your understanding of the theater as a workshop and machine. (b) With others of your class, again, arrange with the director of your college theater to attend a blocking-out or business rehearsal, whether on stage or in a rehearsal room—for the purpose of observing the actors and director as they develop the pattern of pantomime and speech for a stageplay.

B. CONTINUING GLOSSARY. Add to your glossary such theatrical terms as you encounter. If you wish to enrich your glosses, turn to the excellent glossary in MORDECAI GORELIK, *New Theatres for Old* (*op. cit.*), to BERNARD SOBEL, *The Theatre Handbook* (New York, Crown, 1940) or, for technical terms only, to JOHN GASSNER, *Producing the Play* (*op. cit.*).

C. SCENE DESIGN. Use the form below as a guide in designing a stage setting, floor plan and (if you wish) elevation, for *The Long Voyage Home*.

D. DESIGNING MOVEMENT. Using the floor plan developed above—and the second of the forms below—design the stage movement for three or four pages of the play, including the first entrance of the seamen, or the climax of the play, or as assigned.

E. READING REHEARSAL. Sitting about in a semicircle with others, cast the play and read the dialogue, taking the parts. (One person may read the business directions, but not of course the speech headings and directions, in a flat or subdued tone.) These hints may be helpful: (1) Try to read your part "in character," suggesting the personality as well as the dialect. (2) Pick up your cues, don't pause between speeches unless there is some reason to do so; but don't rush the actual reading of your lines. (3) Communicate as much of the full meaning as you can—the tone, the feeling, and the intention of the line as well as the sense of it, as you understand them. (4) Let your vivid imagination and feeling for the dramatic scene guide your reading, and

```
┌─────────────────────────────────────────────────────────┐
│                                                         │
│        SCENE DESIGN FOR  [name of play]                 │
│                                                         │
└─────────────────────────────────────────────────────────┘
```

Use this outline as a guide in designing the stage setting or settings for a particular play. Though you may protest that you "can't draw a line," the thoughtful analysis of the scenes of a few plays and the careful development of at least floor plans for them will greatly increase your realization of three-dimensional space relations and your capacity to control and enjoy your visual imagery of scene in reading.

Write or type your answers single-spaced on the top half of a sheet of unruled paper; then work out your floor plan in the space below it.

1. *Identification*—general description of the stage setting.
   What is the geographic place (country, city)? and period?
   What particular place is specified? at what time? season?

2. *Scenic requisites*—elements necessary to acting out the story.
   What entrances (doors, etc.) are called for? leading where?
   What other openings (windows, etc.)? with what seen beyond?
   What special items (stairs, fireplace, alcove, etc.)? where?
   What stage props (chairs, tables, other furniture)? where?
   Is there any requisite relationship of these one to another?

3. *Scenic relations*—the setting and the other story elements.
   What relation has the scene to the characters? to their lives?
   What relation to the action? to the plot? to construction?
   What relation has it to the mood? to the over-all meaning?
   What relation to period and place? to type of play and style?

4. *Floor plan*—a diagram of the stage setting as seen from above.

   [Work first on scratch paper, sketching freely, keeping proportions as best you can.

   [The usual width of a stage opening (the proscenium) is about 30', but the setting itself is usually no more than 24' wide at the front, tormentors (masking curtains) filling the spaces to the left and right.
      As the sides of the conventional box set are raked (angled in so that the spectators on the sides of the auditorium can see), the back wall of the set will usually be no more than 20' in width, often less.

   [Re-draw your floor plan to scale on the bottom half of the sheet used to answer the above sets of questions.
      Use a ruler. A convenient scale is either $\frac{3}{16}'' = 1'$ or 5 mm = 1'. In either case 1″ on your floor plan will be about 5' on the actual stage.
      Draw a solid line near the bottom of the page to represent the front edge of the stage. Then work back from that.]

5. *Elevation*—a sketch of the stage setting as seen from out front.
   Wouldn't you like to sketch the stage picture? and try color?

DESIGNING STAGE MOVEMENT FOR [name of play]

Use this outline in designing the stage movement for several pages of a particular play. Deciding exactly where the actors may well stand or sit and move in relation to each other within the stage setting is an exacting consideration. It calls for close and creative reading. Designing the stage movement for a number of scenes will increase your skill in realizing the potential action as you read dramas.

Crease your paper down the center to mark off double columns. With your floor plan already worked out to scale, draw ten or twelve half-scale floor plans on a sheet of typing paper, five or six to a column. To do this most easily, draw a reduced scale floor plan and then trace, stencil, or copy it freely and swiftly—it need not be exact for this purpose.

[Use initial letters as symbols for the characters: D for Driscoll, O for Olson, etc.

[Mark the first little floor plan to show the relative stage positions of the characters at the beginning of the basic scene for which you are designing the stage movement.

[Draw small arrows—curved or straight, long or short—to indicate where each actor moves to or comes from.

[Number these arrows in the order in which the stage movements take place, and put the same numbers in the margin of your playbook to indicate at what point in the dialogue the action takes place.

[One or two diagrams per page will be enough, unless there is an unusual amount of stage movement.

[Give each diagram a page number to key it to your playbook for ready reference.]

Note. Many directors make diagrams of stage movement as part of their study and preparation for rehearsing a play, but they draw them, sometimes very informally, in the margins of their scripts. Of course they do not make them on a separate sheet of paper as above suggested for this exercise.

allow yourself such bodily expression and gestures as come without effort. This sort of group reading will increase your realization of the dramatic potential of the dialogue.

F. WALKING REHEARSAL. Clear enough space in a room to mark off the floor plan lightly with chalk, approximately to scale. Then arrange chairs so as to simulate the larger stage props. With others of your class, cast the play, take turns at directing, and block out the stage movement of at least parts of the play in a reading-and-business rehearsal. Bear in mind that a stageplay is a story directly acted out. Try not only to follow the stage directions but to act out the business implicit in the lines themselves. This sort of exercise should increase your appreciation of pantomime.

AND FURTHER READING.

A. THE ART OF THE THEATER. Undertake some further reading in one of the books on theater art cited in the Notes above, or in one of the following: TOBY COLE, *Actors on Acting* (New York, Crown, 1949), MORTON C. EUSTIS, *Players at Work* (New York, Theatre Arts, 1937), JOHN DOLMAN, JR., *The Art of Acting* (New York, Harper, 1949), MILTON K. SMITH, *Play Production* (rev. ed.; New York, Appleton-Century-Crofts, 1948), LEE SIMONSON, *The Art of Scenic Design* (New York, Harper, 1950), THEODORE FUCHS, *Stage Lighting* (Boston, Little, Brown, 1929).

B. THEATER LORE. There is much reading of interest on famous theatrical personalities: ELEANOR RUGGLES, *Prince of Players, Edwin Booth* (New York, Norton, 1953), JOSEPH JEFFERSON, *Rip Van Winkle, autobiography* (New York, Appleton-Century-Crofts, 1950), CRAIG TIMBERLAKE, *David Belasco, the Bishop of Broadway* (New York, Library Publishers, 1954), GENE FOWLER, *Goodnight, Sweet Prince* (New York, Viking, 1944), EVA LE GALLIENNE, *With a Quiet Heart* (New York, Viking, 1953), CONSTANTIN STANISLAVSKI, *My Life in Art* (Boston, Little, Brown, 1924).

C. MORE O'NEILL. Read the other three plays in the *S.S. Glencairn* group in EUGENE O'NEILL, *Moon of the Caribbees, and Six Other Plays of the Sea* (New York, Modern Library, 1923); or *Anna Christie,* in a volume with *The Emperor Jones* and *The Hairy Ape* (New York, Modern Library, 1937); or *Desire Under the Elms* in *Nine Plays by Eugene O'Neill* (New York, Modern Library, 1941).

IV. THE PLAY—SPECTATOR OR READER— *THE HAPPY JOURNEY*

NOTES. The headquote for Essay IV is from JOHN MASON BROWN, *The Art of Playgoing* (New York, Norton, 1936), p. 36. [§ 1.] See COOPER, *The Arts and Humanity* (*op. cit.*), pp. 210-16 on the arts as fulfilling human needs. HORACE, *The Art of Poetry* is in CLARK, *European Theories of the Drama* (*op. cit.*), p. 35. [§ 2.] This analysis owes much to RICHARDS, *Principles of Literary Criticism* (*op. cit.*). NICHOLAS VARDAC, *Stage and Screen* (Cambridge, Harvard University Press, 1949), p. 93, indicates that for Sir Henry Irving the play was primarily spectacle. For a fuller account of the playgoer's sensory perception, see COOPER (*op. cit.*), pp. 219-31. [§ 3.] For a further discussion of naïve and critical responses, see *ibid.,* chaps. viii, ix. The James-Lange theory of emotion is readily available in the psychological literature. See also PAUL T. YOUNG, *Emotion in Man and Animal* (New York, Wiley, 1943) and M. FELDENKRAIS, *Body and Mature Behavior* (London, Routledge, 1949). On group response in the theater, see BROWN (*op. cit.*), pp. 38 ff., and CLAYTON HAMILTON (cited for Essay I), pp. 19 ff. For "the willing suspension of disbelief," see SAMUEL T. COLERIDGE, *Biographia Literaria* (London, 1817), chap. xiv. An amazing study of panic and fear response in a radio audience is reported in HADLEY CANTRIL, *The Invasion from Mars* (Princeton, N. J., Princeton University Press, 1947). [§ 4.] Bottom the Weaver in SHAKESPEARE, *A Midsummer-Night's Dream* (I, ii) saw himself in each of the roles of "Pyramus and Thisbe." See, again, RICHARDS (*op. cit.*), and POLLOCK, *The Nature of Literature* (*op. cit.*), pp. 55-56, 81, etc. For a more detailed treatment of the six aspects of the reading experience, see CHARLES W. COOPER, *Preface to Poetry* (New York, Harcourt, Brace, 1946), chap. iv-ix. Here and elsewhere the author is indebted to ALBERT W. UPTON, *Design for Thinking* (Whittier, Calif., Whittier College, 1949). The "spire of meaning" is from JOHN GALSWORTHY, "Some Platitudes Concerning Drama" in *The Inn of Tranquility* (New York, Scribner, 1912).

See *Current Biography* (1943) for an account of Thornton Wilder. For "Some Thoughts on Playwriting," see AUGUSTO CENTENO (ed.), *The Intent of the Artist* (Princeton, N. J., Princeton University Press, 1941); the quotation is from pp. 94-95. The correspondence: THORNTON WILDER and SOL LESSER, "Our Town—From Stage to Screen," in *Theatre Arts,* XXIV (November, 1940), 815-24.

QUERIES. Is there really no plot to *The Happy Journey?* Are the incidents really strung along at random? or are they patterned? Could this be a plot without conflict?

Who is the protagonist? Isn't it warm-hearted Mrs. Kirby? Is this simply the story of the family journey to Camden to see Beulah? If so, what was the inciting incident? Was it Pa's getting his vacation early? or Beulah's losing her baby? What is it, then, that Mrs. Kirby desires? Is it simply to go and comfort Beulah? What does she want in life for Arthur and Caroline? for herself and Elmer?

Is there an antagonist, an opposing force, anything that stands in the way, blocks, frustrates Mrs. Kirby? What is the significance of the passing funeral? of Ma's tiff with Arthur? of her plan to send Elmer and Arthur over to the Y? What, then, is the deciding factor in her life? Does Ma Kirby succeed? or is she beaten down in her conflicts with life?

Is there some danger that the reader or spectator may overlook Wilder's meaning in his delight with the homey characterization, the true-to-life incidents, the amusing pantomime, the novelty of treatment, the colloquial dialogue and local color? In what way is it a "happy" journey? in what ways is it not? Are the play titles *The Happy Journey* and *The Long Voyage Home* similar in their symbolic significance? What is the difference in their dramatic irony? How would you phrase the over-all meaning of Wilder's play? What lines and incidents especially suggest the theme?

SUGGESTIONS FOR STUDY.

A. Creative Playreading. Review the first two or three of the fourfold suggestions made in section five of the essay. Then try to make use of them in rereading *The Happy Journey*. Such a conscious effort, applied in several instances, will increase your skill and enjoyment in reading drama.

B. Taking the Journey. As suggested after the third essay, (*a*) join with others in a reading rehearsal of *The Happy Journey* or, if scripts are available, of scenes from *Our Town*. Then (*b*), with someone serving as director or at least coordinator, experiment with a walking rehearsal of the same scenes, as a further experience in realizing the dramatic and theatrical potential of the play.

C. Audience Observed. Find or make an opportunity to observe closely a theater audience. If possible, study the script carefully before you go to the play, and try to anticipate what the various responses will be, penciling them in the margins. Try to get a seat over to the side so that by turning a bit you can watch the spectators as well as the play, and note their various individual and group reactions. By observing outward evidences of their responses, you will come to understand more fully your own experiences as a playgoer.

D. Playgoer's Report. As a device for guiding your comments upon a stageplay you have just seen, the outline worksheet below may be useful.

E. Reader's Remarks. The second of these two forms may be helpful at times in commenting upon a drama you have read.

AND FURTHER READING.

A. The Playgoer's Experience. Undertake some reading in john mason brown (*op. cit.*) or clayton hamilton (*op. cit.*), or in collected reviews of a dramatic critic such as g. bernard shaw, *Dramatic Opinions and Essays* [1895-98] (New York, Brentano's, 1906), george jean nathan, *Passing Judgment* (New York, Knopf, 1935), or stark young, *Immortal Shadows* (New York, Scribner, 1948). Or delve into the psychological literature on audience responses, group panic and fear (see cantril, *op. cit.*), vicarious sexual experience, laughter, tears, applause, etc.

B. The Reader's Experience. Undertake some reading in richards (*op. cit.*). Or read some book specifically on the reading of poetry—cooper, *Preface to Poetry* (*op. cit.*), cleanth brooks and robert penn warren, *Understanding Poetry* (New York, Holt, 1938), or some other—as the basis for comparing the poem-reading and the play-reading experiences.

C. Wilder and Wilder. Read further in thornton wilder: *The Long Christmas Dinner and Other Plays in One Act* (New York, Coward-McCann, 1931), or *Our Town* (New York, Coward-McCann, 1938), or *The Skin of Our Teeth* (New York, Harper, 1942). Or you may wish to read one of his novels, *The Bridge of San Luis Rey* (New York, Boni, 1927) or *The Ides of March* (New York, Harper, 1948). Or you may be interested in "Some Thoughts on Playwriting" and the *Our Town* correspondence.

Use these questions (a) merely as a suggestive guide in the reporting of a particular stageplay, or (b) as a formal outline to be followed in detail. They may in either case help you to focus your attention upon the various components of your complex theater experience. Doing this on two or three occasions may enrich your enjoyment of plays and give substance to your discussion of them.

(a) Write or type double-spaced, answering each group of questions informally in one paragraph. Or, (b), if you are directed to do so, write or type single-spaced, answering the questions briefly in a formal outline.

1. *Factual data*—identifying the production of the stageplay.
   What is the playwright's name? the play? number of acts?
   What is the type of play? the subtype? the style?
   Who produced the play? at what theater? When did you see it?
   Who are the principal actors (with names of characters)?
   Who directed the stageplay? designed the sets? costumes?

2. *Story of the stageplay*—summarizing certain of the story elements.
   Who are the chief characters? what relation to the others?
   What is the geographic place and the period of the action?
   What are the component acts and scenes, with time and place?
   What, in a 50 to 150 word synopsis, is the whole action?

3. *Naïve response*—commenting on your affective responses to it.
   What visual free images do you recall of off-stage scenes?
   What free images of other sorts (if any) did you experience?
   Were you conscious of any empathic responses to the action?
   What emotions (if any) did you yourself feel? at what points?
   What outward responses do you recall making to the stageplay?
   What other sorts of response: mood, formal feelings, beauty?

4. *Critical interpretation*—commenting on your thoughtful response.
   Had you any difficulty interpreting dialogue and pantomime?
   What are the chief traits of the protagonist? will or desire?
   What are the opposing forces and deciding factor (if any)?
   What is the inciting incident? the climax? the conclusion?
   What is the structure of the enacted drama? situation at rise?
   What for you is the theme? its relation to plot and character?

5. *Evaluation*—commenting on the value of your experience.
   What is your evaluation of the playscript as a drama?
       Did you really enjoy the story of the stageplay?
       Did the playwright succeed in doing what he intended?
       How would you compare the script with others of the sort?
   What is your evaluation of the enacting and production of it?
       How were the actors in impersonation, pantomime, speech?
       How were the direction, design, and technical production?
       What is your over-all judgment of the value of this play?

748

Use these questions (a) merely as a suggestive guide in commenting upon a particular drama that you have just read, or (b) as a formal outline to be followed in detail. In either case, make this an instrument for sharpening your consideration of the component parts of your reading experience. Commenting upon a few dramas in some such way as this should enlarge the scope of your enjoyment of plays and give substance to your discussion of them.

(a) Write or type double-spaced, composing paragraphs informally upon the five general topics. Or (b), if you are asked to do so, write or type single-spaced, answering the questions briefly in outline form.

1. *Factual data*—identifying the drama that you have read.
   What is the dramatist's name? the drama? the number of acts?
   What is the type of drama? the subtype? the style?
   What was its first publication? place, publisher, date?
   What, if different, is the book from which you read it?

2. *Story of the drama*—summarizing certain of the story elements.
   Who are the chief characters? what relations to each other?
   What is the geographic place and the period of the action?
   What are the component acts and scenes, with time and place?
   What, in a 50 to 150 word synopsis, is the whole action?

3. *Naïve response*—commenting on your affective responses to it.
   What settings and characters can you still "see" clearly?
   What dramatic situations and incidents can you now picture?
   What characters' voices or actual speeches can you "hear"?
   Were you conscious at any points of empathized responses?
   What emotions (if any) did you yourself feel as you read?
   What other sorts of response: mood, formal feelings, beauty?

4. *Critical interpretation*—commenting on your thoughtful response.
   Had you any difficulty interpreting dialogue and directions?
   What are the chief traits of the protagonist? will or desire?
   What are the opposing forces and deciding factor (if any)?
   What are the inciting incident? the climax? the conclusion?
   What is the structure of the enacted drama? situation at rise?
   What for you is the theme? its relation to plot and character?

5. *Evaluation*—commenting on the value of your experience.
   Was your reading enjoyable? Did you really like the play?
   Did the dramatist succeed in doing what he intended to do?
   How does the drama compare with others that you have read?
   How does it measure up to your ideal of "a good drama"?
   What is your over-all judgment of the worth of this drama?

V. THE DRAMA—HISTORY, TYPES, STYLES—
H.M.S. PINAFORE

NOTES. The headquote for Essay V is from ERIC BENTLEY, *The Playwright as Thinker* (New York, Reynal & Hitchcock, 1946), p. 56. [§ 2.] On the Greek theater see ALLARDYCE NICOLL, *The Development of the Theater* (rev. ed.; New York, Harcourt, Brace, 1937), also ROY C. FLICKINGER, *The Greek Theater and Its Drama* (Chicago, University of Chicago Press, 1926) and JAMES T. ALLEN, *Stage Antiquities of the Greeks and Romans* (New York, Longmans, Green, 1927). General accounts of all the periods are to be found in CHENEY, *The Theatre,* FREEDLEY and REEVES, *History of the Theater,* and NICOLL, *World Drama* (all cited for Essay I) and in other such works. For the Elizabethan theater see JOHN CRANFORD ADAMS, *The Globe Playhouse* (Cambridge, Harvard University Press, 1942); for the Elizabethan drama, see THOMAS M. PARROTT and R. M. BALL, *A Short View of Elizabethan Drama* (New York, Scribner, 1943). For the Spanish corral, see HUGO A. RENNERT, *The Spanish Stage in the Time of Lope de Vega* (New York, Hispanic Society of America, 1909). For the neoclassic theater—indeed for all periods—see KARL MANTZIUS, *History of Theatrical Art* (6 vols.; New York, Peter Smith, 1905, 1937), and A. M. NAGLER, *Sources of Theatrical History* (New York, Theatre Annual, 1952). Of special interest for the romantic and modern periods are NICHOLAS VARDAC, *Stage and Screen* (*op. cit.*), and MORDECAI GORELIK, *New Theatres for Old* (*op. cit.*), *and* BARRETT H. CLARK and GEORGE FREEDLEY, *A History of Modern Drama* (New York, Appleton-Century-Crofts, 1947). [§ 3.] See ASHLEY THORNDIKE, *Tragedy* (New York, Macmillan, 1916). There is a good essay "On the Enjoyment of Tragedy" by HERBERT F. ALLEN in *The Play's the Thing* (Cedar Rapids, Iowa, Torch Press, 1927). Many of the works on tragedy are excerpted in BARRETT H. CLARK, *European Theories of the Drama* (*op. cit.*). For Aristotle, see LANE COOPER, *Aristotle* (*op. cit.*). In considering comedy, see ASHLEY THORNDIKE, *Comedy* (New York, Macmillan, 1929); LANE COOPER, *An Aristotelian Theory of Comedy* (New York, Harcourt, Brace, 1922); GEORGE MEREDITH, *An Essay on Comedy* (London, 1897); WILLARD SMITH, *The Nature of Comedy* (Boston, Badger, 1930). [§ 4.] For a well-known chapter on the historic styles, see WILLIAM A. NEILSON, *The Essentials of Poetry* (Boston, Houghton Mifflin, 1921). Useful brief discussions of the styles: WILLIAM THRALL and ADDISON HIBBARD, *Handbook to Literature* (New York, Doubleday, 1936) and JOSEPH T. SHIPLEY, *Dictionary of World Literature* (rev. ed.; New York, Philosophical Library, 1953). For nineteenth and twentieth century styles, see VARDAC, BENTLEY, and GORELIK (all cited above).

For Gilbert and Sullivan see, among others, W. A. DARLINGTON, *The World of Gilbert and Sullivan* (New York, Crowell, 1950), HESKETH PEARSON, *Gilbert and Sullivan* (New York, Harper, 1935).

QUERIES. What do you think of Allardyce Nicoll's comment on W. S. Gilbert? "A concealed sadness gives distinction to his most humorous scenes. . . . The fever and fret of mankind weigh heavily on his senses. . . . On the surface *H.M.S. Pinafore* . . . is a carefree extravaganza replete with all the most orthodox patriotic sentiments of Victorian England. . . . Underneath, however, [it has] an ironic tang. . . . Whereas outwardly his scenes appear to be invested merely with easy laughter and the delicate play of a punning wit, in reality they are informed by a kind of world-weariness." (*World Drama,* pp. 464-65).

Where specifically can you detect evidence of this "concealed sadness" in the libretto? of "the fever and fret of mankind"? of its "ironic tang"? of its "world-weariness"? Through what characters does Gilbert reflect these sentiments?

Where do you find instances of "carefree extravaganza"? of "easy laughter"? of "punning wit"? Through what devices does Gilbert achieve his risible effects?

What are some of the contemporary butts of Gilbert's satire? What about the Navy ruling against swearing? What about middle-class [Sir] Joseph Porter rising through politics to become the First Lord of the Queen's Navee? You will find an interesting comment upon this topsy-turvy social situation in W. A. DARLINGTON (*op. cit.*), pp. 53-59.

SUGGESTIONS FOR STUDY.

A. THE LAST GLOSS. Add to your glossary the names of the dramatic types and subtypes and styles. You may wish to enrich certain of your entries by referring to THRALL and HIBBARD and to JOSEPH SHIPLEY (both cited above).

B. MUSICAL COMEDY. Gather the material from standard reference works for a short history of musical comedy (dramatic burlesque, comedy ballet, ballad opera, comic opera, operetta, etc.) from Aristophanes through Molière, Gay, Sheridan, and Gilbert, to Victor Herbert, Kaufman, and Hammerstein.

C. OFF THE RECORD. Find a recording of *H.M.S. Pinafore* in your record library, also a copy of the music, the vocal score. With others from your class, enjoy a performance of this operetta, following the libretto and/or score. It will be hard *not* to hum or sing along—nor should you refrain, but rather yield—and join in with the chorus!

D. THEATRICAL HISTORY. The following outline worksheet may be of use in making a study of the theatrical history of a particular play.

E. DRAMATIC HISTORY. The second of the two worksheets may be useful when you study the literary history of a particular drama.

AND FURTHER READING.

A. HISTORIC PERIOD. In one of the general histories of the theater and drama—CHENEY, FREEDLEY and REEVES (both cited above), NICOLL, *World Drama* (*op. cit.*), GLENN HUGHES, *Story of the Theater* (*op. cit.*)—read the chapter on one of the past periods. Then skim the comparable chapter in another book of similar scope and note the differences in treatment and emphasis.

B. CONTEMPORARY. Read about one of the notable New York plays of the past season or so. You will doubtless find the playbook (in condensed form) in *The Best Plays* series, edited by BURNS MANTLE and others in later years, with the statistical data indexed. Use *The New York Theater Critics' Reviews* for reading the newspaper reviews of the play. Through *Readers' Guide* find and read a number of the magazine reviews. *Book Review Digest* will give an evaluation of the playbook as drama, quoting from dramatic criticism.

Use these questions and outline as a guide in making a study of the theatrical history of a drama. Begin your research by using the bibliography in a standard reference work on the theater and drama. Proceed from that to appropriate histories and annals of the theater of the period, and then go to biographical and critical studies of the playwright. Diligent search may uncover interesting data that will make the drama itself more meaningful. But you will be frustrated at certain points, for answers to all your questions simply will not be forthcoming.

(a) Write or type double-spaced, composing informal but informative paragraphs upon the five general topics, with footnotes as for a term paper. Or (b), if so directed, write or type single-spaced, answering the questions compactly in outline form, adding a list of the books from which you have drawn your information.

1. *Factual data*—the stageplay and its historical background.
What is the name of the playwright? the play? style and type?
In what country was it produced? in what period? what year?
Under what government? political conditions? international?
What were the economic, social, intellectual characteristics?

2. *The playwright*—his personality and composition of the script.
What is the playwright's full name? dates of birth and death?
What were his personality traits? his appearance?
What previous plays did he write? types? styles? success?
When did he write this playscript? at what age? where?
What specific sources of material? theatrical circumstances?

3. *The playscript*—descriptive analysis of the playbook itself.
What are the chief characters? other memorable characters?
What, in a single brief sentence, is the action of the story?
What is the theme? what is its relation to the plot?
To what type and subtype of drama does it belong? How does it evidence this in structure, audience effect, etc.?
In what dramatic style is it written? How does it evidence this in dialogue, characterization, structure, conventions?

4. *The production*—theatrical data on the original production.
What organization or individual produced it? opening date?
At what theater? of what sort? (pictures?) in what city?
Who were the chief actors? cast in what roles? (pictures?)
Who directed the play? what relation to playwright? script?
Who designed the stage setting? the costumes? (pictures?)

5. *Appraisal*—the popular and critical success of the stageplay.
How long did the play run? road? provinces? other productions?
Was it revived? translated? produced in other countries?
How was it received by the reviewers and dramatic critics?
Where, by whom, and when was it published? acting edition?
What place does it hold in the histories of the theater?

Use these questions and outline as a guide in preparing a study of the literary history of a drama. Begin your research by using the bibliography in a standard reference work on literature and drama. Proceed from that to appropriate histories of the literature and drama of the period, and then go to biographical and critical works on the playwright. Although you will certainly not find answers to all of these questions or others that you may ask, your search may lead you to the discovery of pertinent items of yet greater interest.

(a) Write or type double-spaced, composing informal but informative paragraphs upon the five general topics, with footnotes as for a term paper. Or (b), if so directed, write or type single-spaced, answering the questions compactly in outline form, adding a list of the books or articles from which you have drawn your material.

1. *Factual data*—production, publication, and period of the drama.
What is the name of the dramatist? the drama? style and type?
In what country was it produced? in what period? what year?
What organization produced it? in what city? in what theater?
Where, by whom, and when was it first published? pages? price?

2. *The dramatist*—his personality and composition of the drama.
What is the dramatist's full name? dates of birth and death?
What were his personality traits and his appearance?
What previous plays did he write? type? style? success?
What nondramatic works did he write? in what literary forms?
When did he write this playscript? under what circumstances?

3. *The drama*—descriptive analysis of the playbook itself.
Who are the chief characters? other memorable characters?
What, in a single sentence, is the action of the story?
What is the theme? what is its relation to the plot?
To what type and subtype of drama does it belong? How does it evidence this in structure, intended effects, etc.?
In what dramatic style is it written? How does it evidence this in dialogue, characterization, structure, conventions?

4. *Literary history*—the drama as an expression of its times.
Does it reveal the dramatist's personality? life? thought?
What are the sources of the dramatist's story and material?
What literary and theatrical influences helped to shape it?
How does it reveal the social, economic, political conditions?
How does it reflect the cultural and intellectual currents?

5. *Critical appraisal*—place of this drama in literary history.
What editions? reprints? in collected works? anthologies?
What influence upon the works of other dramatists?
What reputation as a man of letters did the dramatist have?
What has been the judgment of this drama by literary critics?
What place does it hold in histories of literature and drama?

From these various sources, arrive at some judgment yourself as to the place of the work in contemporary theater and drama.

C. BOOK AND SCORE. Some musical comedies are readily available—librettos, vocal score, recordings. Perhaps you will want to look up GILBERT and SULLIVAN, *The Complete Plays* (New York, Modern Library, 1936) and enjoy reading another libretto along with score and records. Or you may find the book for GEORGE S. KAUFMAN and MORRIE RYSKIND, *Of Thee I Sing* (New York, Knopf, 1932) or KAUFMAN and MOSS HART, *I'd Rather Be Right* (New York, Random House, 1937), both of which are rich in comedy, satire, and catchy lyrics. Or your library may have the vocal score for OSCAR HAMMERSTEIN II and RICHARD ROGERS, *Oklahoma!* (New York, Williamson Music, 1943) or for their *South Pacific* (New York, Williamson Music, 1949).

Part Two

I. *ANTIGONE*—BY SOPHOCLES

NOTES. The biographical data on Sophocles are drawn from CEDRIC H. WHITMAN, *Sophocles, a Study of Heroic Humanism* (cited in the commentary), SIR PAUL HARVEY, *Oxford Companion to Classical Literature,* and standard reference works. For the modern versions, see CLARK and FREEDLEY (*op. cit.*) and the BURNS MANTLE, *Best Plays* series (*op. cit.*). Summaries of the Thebes story are to be found in EDITH HAMILTON, *Mythology* (Boston, Little, Brown, 1942) and E. F. WATLING, *Sophocles, the Theban Plays* (Baltimore, Penguin Books, 1947).

Certain references in *Antigone* may be made clear by the family tree of the Theban kings: Cadmus, brother of Europa, slew the dragon and planted its teeth, from which sprang up warriors, some of whom helped him to found Thebes. His great-grandson Laius was the father of Oedipus. Semele, the daughter of Cadmus, was attractive to Zeus, and by him was the mother of Dionysus—the god, variously called Bacchus and Iacchus, of wine and fertility and the theater. Niobe, of whom Antigone speaks in Scene IV, was the daughter of Tantalus, and had seven sons and seven daughters of whom she boasted; when they were put to death by the gods, she wept, whereupon she was turned into a stone column, from which tears still flowed. In Ode IV, the Chorus sings of three children of kings each of whom was entombed: Danae, who by Zeus begot Perseus; Dryas' son, Lycurgus, who persecuted Dionysus and was entombed for it; and Cleopatra, the daughter of Boreas, the North Wind, entombed by her husband to suffer watching the blinding of her sons by his second wife. Eurydice's eldest son, Megareus, was one of the seven Theban leaders who died defending the City.

DUDLEY FITTS and ROBERT FITZGERALD in the new version of *Antigone* have made some minor cuts, simplified the mythology, and omitted sixteen lines (considered spurious) from Antigone's long speech in Scene IV. They have used less usual spelling for a number of the names, and have used terms from Greek dramaturgy for the parts of the play and of the choral odes.

QUERIES. What do you consider the central conflict in the play *Antigone*? Is it between Antigone and Creon? between two views of the State? or two kinds of Law? or two sorts of loyalty?

What is Creon's theory of the family? of the relation of father to son? man to wife? What is Creon's theory of the State? of the relation of King to State? to elders and to citizens? Why does Creon accuse Ismene too and press the charge against Antigone?

What is the relation of Ismene to Antigone? What is her line of reasoning? what is Antigone's? What are the various forces that bear upon Antigone? the prophecies, misfortunes, curses? the personal bonds and family ties?

What is the character of Teiresias? the dramatic function?

What portions of the whole story (*a*) precede the prologue and (*b*) occur off-stage during the course of the enacted drama? How much time elapses from prologue through exodos? How much time elapses between the several scenes? What is the relation of each ode to what precedes and to what follows? to the character of the Chorus?

How would you double the parts so as to have the play performed by no more than three actors plus the Chorus?

What facts in the life of Sophocles seem to you of special relevance to an understanding of *Antigone*? What details of the Thebes story and character relationships are necessary to an understanding of the drama?

Why would *Antigone* have been of special interest during World Wars I and II? Why its special appeal to Parisians in 1943? What does it have to say to us today?

SUGGESTIONS FOR STUDY.

A. FITTS-FITZGERALD AND JEBB. Find a copy of the *Antigone* in Jebb's prose translation. It is included in RICHARD C. JEBB, *The Tragedies of Sophocles* (London, Cambridge University Press, 1904); in WHITNEY J. OATES and EUGENE O'NEILL, JR., *The Complete Greek Drama* (New York, Random House, 1938); and in various anthologies. Read it through rapidly; then compare the two versions and list their characteristic differences.

B. ANTIGONE OR CREON. Give some thought to one or the other, using the Character Analysis worksheet as a guide. Refer back to the text of *Antigone* and note the sources of the characterizing data. Then refer once more to the Oates and the Whitman commentaries, reconsidering their character interpretations.

C. IN THE GREEK THEATER. Make a brief study of the Greek theater and its art, using reference works cited above (in Notes to Essay V). See, also, MARGARETE BIEBER, *The History of the Greek and Roman Theater* (Princeton, N. J., Princeton University Press, 1939). Now consider how *Antigone* was produced in fifth-century Greece.

D. IN OUR THEATER TODAY. Give some thought to the problem of producing *Antigone* in various theatrical styles today. In their commentary to *Antigone*, FITTS and FITZGERALD make the following suggestions:

. . . In a version designed for the modern stage certain changes are inevitable. It cannot be urged too strongly that the words of the Odes must be intelligible to the audience; and they are almost certain not to be intelligible if they are chanted in unison by so large a group, with or without musical accompani-

*ment. It is suggested, then, that in producing this play no attempt be made
to follow the ancient choric method. There should be no dancing. The
Párodos, for example, should be a solemn but almost unnoticeable evolution
of moving or still patterns accompanied by a drum-beat whose rhythm may
be derived from the cadence of the Ode itself. The lines given to the Chorus
in the Odes should probably be spoken by single voices. The only accompani-
ment should be percussion: we follow Allan Sly's score of the* Alcestis *in suggesting a large side drum from which the snares have been removed, to be
struck with two felt-headed tympani sticks, one hard, one soft.*

*A careful production might make successful use of masks. They should be
of the Benda type used in the production of O'Neill's* The Great God Brown:
*lifelike, closely fitting the contours of the face, and valuable only as they give
the effect of immobility to character. On no account should there be any
attempt to reproduce the Greek mask, which was larger than life size and
served a function non-existent on the modern stage—the amplification of
voice and mood for projection to the distant seats of the outdoor theatre.*

*If masks are used at all, they might well be allotted only to those characters
who are somewhat depersonalized by official position or discipline: Creon,
Teiresias, the Chorus and Choragos, possibly the Messenger. By this rule,
Antigonê has no mask; neither has Ismenê, Haimon, nor Eurydicê. If Creon
is masked, we see no objection, in art or feeling, to the symbolic removal of
his mask before he returns with the dead body of his son.*

AND FURTHER READING.

A. Œdipus. The other two Theban plays may well be read in DUDLEY
FITTS (ed.), *Greek Plays in Modern Translation* (New York, Dial Press, 1953)
—the *King Œdipus* by WILLIAM BUTLER YEATS, and *Oedipus at Colonus* by
ROBERT FITZGERALD; or in E. F. WATLING (trans.), *Sophocles, the Theban Plays*
(*op. cit.*).

B. Electra. *Electra* is, perhaps, the most inviting one of the other plays
by Sophocles. A verse translation by FRANCIS FERGUSON is in FITTS (ed.), (*op.
cit.*); another is by E. F. WATLING, *Electra* (Baltimore, Penguin Books, 1953);
the standard prose version is by JEBB (*op. cit.*). Sophocles' *Electra* may well
be compared with AESCHYLUS, *Choephoroe* and with EURIPIDES, *Electra,* which
are available in various translations.

C. French Versions. Very readable is the World War II play, JEAN
ANOUILH, *Antigone,* adapted by Lewis Galantiere (New York, Random House,
1946). An earlier modern version is by JEAN COCTEAU (1922), trans. by
CARL WILDMAN, in ERIC BENTLEY, *The Play, an Anthology* (New York, Prentice-Hall, 1951).

II. *OTHELLO*—BY WILLIAM SHAKESPEARE

NOTES. Biographical data on Shakespeare are readily available in such
handy works as G. B. HARRISON, *Introducing Shakespeare* (rev. ed.; Baltimore,
Penguin Books, 1947), TUCKER BROOKE, *Shakespeare of Stratford* (New Haven,
Yale University Press, 1926), and the older WILLIAM A. NEILSON and ASHLEY
H. THORNDIKE, *The Facts About Shakespeare* (rev. ed.; New York, Macmillan,

1931). The most readable recent biography is MARCHETTE CHUTE, *Shakespeare of London* (New York, Dutton, 1949); an older one, JOSEPH Q. ADAMS, *A Life of William Shakespeare* (Boston, Houghton Mifflin, 1923). Shakespeare's source for *Othello* is Novella VII by GIRALDI CINTHIO, *Hecatommithi* [hundred tales] (1565), translated in HORACE H. FURNESS (ed.), *Othello* (New Variorum Ed.; Philadelphia, Lippincott, 1886) and in W. C. HAZLITT (ed.), *Shakespeare's Library*, vol. 4 (London, 1875). The Folio text of *Othello*, with the Quarto variants and modern emendations noted marginally, is in the 1929 Nonesuch text, HERBERT FARJEON (ed.), *The Complete Works of William Shakespeare*, vol. 3 (New York, Random House, 1953); the FURNESS (ed.), *Othello* (*op. cit.*), also reprinting the Folio text, gives the Quarto and emended readings, and all the older interpretations. The commentary on *Othello* by THOMAS RYMER (cited in commentary) is reprinted in J. E. SPINGARN, *Critical Essays of the Seventeenth Century*, vol. 2 (London, Oxford University Press, 1908). Selections from earlier commentaries are reprinted in FURNESS (*op. cit.*); the more recent critics cited are A. C. BRADLEY, *Shakespearean Tragedy* (London, Macmillan, 1904); LILY B. CAMPBELL, *Shakespeare's Tragic Heroes, Slaves of Passion* (London, Cambridge University Press, 1930); G. WILSON KNIGHT, *The Wheel of Fire* (new ed.; New York, Oxford University Press, 1949). For Charles Hart, see the *Dictionary of National Biography* (D. N. B.); for Edwin Booth, see ELEANOR RUGGLES, *Prince of Players* (*op. cit.*). For modern productions in America, see BURNS MANTLE, *Best Plays of 1943-1944*, etc. The recording of Margaret Webster's production of *Othello* is Columbia Masterworks (SL 153). The most complete notes on *Othello* are those of GEORGE L. KITTREDGE, *Sixteen Plays of Shakespeare* (Boston, Ginn, 1946), also published separately.

QUERIES. Is Othello the protagonist of the play or is Iago? With which of the two are your sympathies? Which of the two is the more fully portrayed and characterized? Which is the leading role in the cast? Which is the central figure from the standpoint of plot?

How many different reasons does Iago have for plotting Othello's downfall? Why isn't he content with Cassio's undoing? Does he want Desdemona for himself? Then why does he egg on Othello to kill her? Why does he encourage Roderigo? Why kill him? What life scheme has he for himself? Wherein is his attraction as a personality?

Is it important to the story that Othello is a Moor? Might he as well have been a Basque or a Briton? Does his race make any difference to the Venetian State? to Brabantio? to Iago? to Desdemona? What use does Iago make of this factor in his plotting to undo Othello?

Why in Act IV, scene ii, does Othello treat Emilia as though she were a bawdyhouse keeper or procuress? What had her relation to him been (if Iago's gossip is true)? What function does she now perhaps serve (if Cassio is seeing Desdemona secretively)? What does the scene tell us about Othello's past and about his present tortured mind?

What, for you, are the principal and minor themes of *Othello*? What is the relation of these themes to the story and its incidents? to the chief and minor characters? to the important speeches and to the diction and imagery generally? Does *Othello* have a "moral"—whether of the sort Rymer read into it or not—that you would call its lesson? Does *Othello* have an over-all meaning—whether of the sort Goddard proposes or some other—that you would call its value for our times?

SUGGESTIONS FOR STUDY.

A. COMMENTS ON COMMENTARY. After a careful study of the critical selections by Rymer and by Goddard—or other critics as suggested—reread *Othello* thoughtfully so as to see upon what evidence the critics based their views. Also note the evidence that the critics seem to have overlooked. Write, then, a short critique of the commentaries so studied.

B. PLOTTING THE PLOT. Make use of the Plot Analysis worksheet in studying *Othello* more closely. First structuralize the drama with Othello as the protagonist; then see how differently it is patterned if Iago is viewed as the protagonist. WORTHINGTON MINER once wrote, "A play is a preamble to a climax, and that climax must be the consummate statement of the play's intention" (in GASSNER, *Producing the Play* [*op. cit.*], p. 221).

C. ELIZABETHAN PRODUCTION. Make a brief study of the Elizabethan theater, using JOHN C. ADAMS, *The Globe Playhouse* (*op. cit.*) or his article "That Virtuous Fabrick" in *Shakespeare Quarterly*, II (January, 1951), 2-11. Then consider where upon the multiple stage you would play each of the scenes of *Othello*. Note particularly the problem of clearing the stage at the end of Act V, scene i, and the closing of the play, Act V, scene ii.

D. THE OTHELLO ROLE. Something of the great actors' interpretations of Othello can be studied in ARTHUR COLBY SPRAGUE, *Shakespeare and the Actors* (Cambridge, Harvard University Press, 1944). An interpretation of much of *Othello* was worked out by the great director of the Moscow Art Theater, KONSTANTIN STANISLAVSKY, *Stanislavsky Produces Othello,* tr. Helen Nowak (London, Geoffrey Bles, 1948), a selection of which is reprinted in COLE and CHINOY, *Directing the Play* (*op. cit.*), pp. 221-41.

AND FURTHER READING.

A. SHAKESPEARE THE MAN. Undertake the reading of a biographical or general study of Shakespeare—CHUTE, *Shakespeare of London* (*op. cit.*), HAZELTON SPENCER, *The Art and Life of Shakespeare* (New York, Harcourt, Brace, 1940), JOSEPH QUINCY ADAMS, *Life of William Shakespeare* (*op. cit.*), or H. B. HARRISON, *Introducing Shakespeare* (*op. cit.*).

B. THE SOURCE TRANSMUTED. Read a translation of Shakespeare's source for *Othello*—CINTHIO, novella VII from *Hecatommithi* (*op. cit.*)—for a fuller appreciation of Shakespeare's creative gift.

C. COMPARATIVE CRITICISM. Read two substantial commentaries on *Othello* —by BRADLEY, CAMPBELL, or KNIGHT (all cited above) or by others as suggested—with the idea of coming to a fuller understanding of the drama by the critical comparison of differing interpretations of it.

D. CURRENT READING. Become acquainted with the *Shakespeare Quarterly* (New York, Shakespeare Association of America). Use its annual Index as a guide to surveying the *Othello* scholarship for a recent year. *The Shakespeare Newsletter* (Pembroke, N. C., Louis Marder) is filled with current items of interest on Shakespearean scholarship and theatrical production.

III. *LES PRÉCIEUSES RIDICULES*—BY MOLIÈRE

NOTES. A most readable biography is JOHN PALMER, *Molière, His Life and Works* (cited in commentary); the same author's very complete article is in *The Encyclopædia Britannica,* 14th ed. (1929). An excellent short biography is H. ASHTON, *Molière* (New York, Dutton, 1930). Older studies are BRANDER MATTHEWS, *Molière, His Life and Works* (New York, Scribner, 1910); H. C. CHATFIELD-TAYLOR, *Molière* (New York, Duffield, 1906); KARL MANTZIUS, *Molière and His Times* (vol. 4 in his *History of Theatrical Art* [*op. cit.*]). See also HENRY C. LANCASTER, *The Period of Molière* (2 vol.; Part III of his *History of French Dramatic Literature in the Seventeenth Century* [Baltimore, Johns Hopkins Press, 1936]; or Part V, *Recapitulation* [1942]). For an excellent but incomplete interpretation, see PERCY A. CHAPMAN, *The Spirit of Molière* (Princeton, N. J., Princeton University Press, 1940). For recent views, see W. G. MOORE, *Molière, A New Criticism* (cited in commentary).

The standard edition in French is EUGÈNE DEPOIS and PAUL MESNARD (eds.), *Oeuvres de Molière* (14 vol. in Les Grands Ecrivains series; Paris, Hachette, 1873–95). A convenient edition is A. W. WALLER (trans.), *The Plays of Molière in French with an English* [prose] *Translation* (Edinburgh, John Grant, 1926). For a reprint of eighteenth century translations of twenty plays, see MOLIÈRE, *Comedies* (2 vols.; New York, Dutton, 1929). Six of the comedies are in MOLIÈRE, *Plays* (New York, Modern Library, 1924). A new translation is JOHN WOOD (trans.), *Molière, Five Plays* (Baltimore, Penguin Books, 1953).

QUERIES. Who is the protagonist of *Les Précieuses Ridicules*? La Grange? (Is it not his will and desire that sets in motion the incidents of the play, which culminates in his triumph?) Or Madelon? (Is it not her pretensions to preciosity that give the comedy its name and cause her and Cathos to reject worthy suitors and fall for obvious pretenders to gentility?) Or Mascarille? (Is not his, after all, the leading role, the central figure, and is not his playing the part of a *nouveau-riche* marquis the central business of the play?) What, very briefly, *is* the plot line as considered from each of these three points of view?

What are the principal sources of comic effect in this play? At what points do you think an audience would enjoy a good belly laugh? How much of the fun would be dependent upon the lines? the characterization? the incidents themselves? the comic stage business of the actors?

Molière, who hurried his comedy to the printer so as to forestall a pirated edition, wrote in his Preface:

. . . I am appearing in print without leisure to collect my thoughts, and I have time for no more than a few words to explain my intentions in the matter of this comedy. I should have liked to show that, at all points, it remains within the bounds of honest and permissible satire; that the finest of things are likely to be copied by fools who deserve to be 'tossed in a blanket'; that these vicious imitations of the most perfect things have always been the subject matter of comedy; and that, for the same reason that real scholars and true heroes have not taken it upon themselves to be offended by the Learned Doctor of comedy and by the Captain—any more than judges, princes, and

*kings upon seeing Trivelin or some other stage valet or comic, as a burlesque
Judge, Prince, or King—so the true précieuses would be wrong to take offense
when one portrays the ridiculous women who imitate them so badly. . . .*

How do you interpret this statement of the playwright's intention in relation
to the commentaries by Palmer and by Moore? What do you yourself feel
to be the butt of the satire?

To what extent is the play "time-bound to its period," dependent for enjoyment upon a knowledge of its social background? What bearing might it
have upon our own society? What is the present value of its satire?

SUGGESTIONS FOR STUDY.

A. The Role of Mascarille—or of Madelon or other character as suggested. Study the role with some care, analyzing and interpreting the characterizing data and building up a conception of the whole personality. Then
decide how you might project this character to an audience. (By the way, in
playing Mascarille, Molière used a "little mask," as the character's name
implies. Cf. moore, *op. cit.,* p. 33.) Practice now in reading the lines in an
effort to achieve the character and comic effects that you think Molière
intended. Following such individual preparation, you may enjoy a group
reading.

B. Designing. Undertake the designing, either of a setting appropriate
to *Les Précieuses Ridicules,* or of the costume for one or more of the characters. (See the works mentioned on page 741.) Carry on some study in the
household architecture or in the urban and courtly attire of the period of
young Louis XIV as the basis for your design.

C. Social Background. Make a study of the social history of the period,
the social structure and the customs and manners, as the basis for a fuller
understanding and enjoyment of the comedy. Useful for this study: H. ashton, *Preface to Molière* (Toronto, Longmans, Green, 1927); carl friedrich,
The Age of the Baroque (New York, Harper, 1952); w. h. lewis, *The Splendid Century* (New York, Sloane, 1954).

AND FURTHER READING.

A. Molière Himself. Read one of the biographies or general studies—
the ashton, palmer, chapman, matthews, or chatfield-taylor (all cited
above)—or arthur tilley, *Molière* (London, Cambridge University Press,
1921).

B. Baroque Theater. For further reading on the theater of Molière and
that of his ridiculous rivals, see mantzius (*op. cit.*). For an imaginative portrayal of Molière's rival theater, read Act I of edmond rostand, *Cyrano de
Bergerac* (New York, Modern Library, 1929). Supplement with other reading
in the theater of the period.

C. More Molière. Read any one of the longer comedies of Molière—*The
School for Wives, Tartuffe, The Misanthrope,* or some other as suggested.
In addition to the translations and editions in the Notes above, see morris
bishop (trans.), *The Would-Be Invalid* (New York, Appleton-Century-Crofts,
1950). Older translations are by henri van laun, by curtis hidden page,
and by lady (Isabella Augusta) gregory.

IV. *HEDDA GABLER*—BY HENRIK IBSEN

NOTES. An early biography is EDMUND GOSSE, *Henrik Ibsen* (New York, Scribner, 1908); more recent is HALVDAN KOHT, *The Life of Ibsen* (2 vols.; New York, Norton, 1931). An informative article by R. E. ROBERTS, author of a life of Ibsen, is in the *Encyclopædia Britannica* (14th ed.). Other biographical and critical studies include MONTROSE J. MOSES, *Henrik Ibsen, the Man and His Plays* (New York, Kennerley, 1908); OTTO HELLER, *Henrik Ibsen, Plays and Problems* (Boston, Houghton Mifflin, 1912), and THEODORE JORGENSON, *Henrik Ibsen, a Study in Art and Personality* (Northfield, Minn., St. Olaf College Press, 1945). See also, BERNARD SHAW, *The Quintessence of Ibsenism* (Boston, B. R. Tucker, 1891; New York, Brentano's, 1909, 1913)—reprinted in SHAW, *Selected Prose* (New York, Dodd, Mead, 1952), and ERIC BENTLEY, *The Playwright as Thinker* (*op. cit.*). The quotation from Ibsen's letter is in WILLIAM ARCHER, Introduction to *Hedda Gabler* (1907) in *Collected Works of Henrik Ibsen* (New York, Scribner, 1906–12). For theatrical data on American productions see *Index to the Best Plays Series, 1899–1950* (New York, Dodd, Mead, 1950) and the volumes in the BURNS MANTLE, *Best Plays* series. The standard edition of Ibsen is WILLIAM ARCHER and others (trans. and ed.), HENRIK IBSEN, *Collected Works* (*op. cit.*).

Difficulty in translation is posed by the second person singular *de* and *du* (corresponding to our archaic *thee* and *thou*), the Norwegian use of which, instead of the plural form (as in our *you*), is a sign of intimacy and familiarity. It is dramatically important to the relationship of Hedda to Thea in Act I and of Hedda to Lövborg in Act II.

It would be a mistake to overlook the Dionysian symbolism in Hedda's hope that Eilert will return with "vine leaves in his hair." Some versions translate Hedda's Norwegian phrase "cock of the basket" (referring to Judge Brack) with the English idiom "cock of the walk."

QUERIES. Why did Hedda Gabler marry at all? Why didn't she marry Judge Brack? or Eilert Lövborg? Why did she marry George Tesman? What had her relation been to Judge Brack before her marriage? What had been her relation to Eilert? to George? What is her relation to him as her husband?

What influence did General Gabler have upon his daughter? How long has he been dead? What glimpses does Ibsen give of Hedda's girlhood? upbringing and schooling? the influences upon her young womanhood?

What do you think is "wrong" with Hedda? What do you think are the "causes" of her psychopathy? What have been her purposes in life? Why can't she enter into the interests and purposes of her husband? Why doesn't her pregnancy promise a fulfilling purpose?

What symbols does Ibsen develop as the drama unfolds? What do they mean? and upon what evidence in the text of the play do you hypothesize such interpretations?

What was Ibsen's intention as an artist in writing *Hedda Gabler*? Do you feel that his statement, quoted in the Introductory Note, suggests that he had no clear purpose in writing the play other than the portrayal of certain characters, with their emotions and interrelationships, and what happens to them?

If, as Ibsen says, the play deals with no problem, is it necessarily without theme? without over-all meaning and significance? What are its values for you?

What are the principal differences in point of view and interpretation between MONTROSE J. MOSES and THEODORE JORGENSON as evidenced in their commentaries? Which seems to have been more successful in placing Hedda "upon a groundwork of certain of the social conditions and principles" of Ibsen's times?

SUGGESTIONS FOR STUDY.

A. EVOLUTION OF HEDDA. Published as vol. 12 in IBSEN, *Collected Works* (*op. cit.*), *From Ibsen's Workshop* (1911) includes translations of notes, scenarios, and drafts of the modern plays, among them *Hedda Gabler*. On the basis of this material, study the evolution of the drama, the characters, plot, dialogue and symbols.

B. HEDDA'S PERSONALITY PROBLEM. First make use of the Character Analysis worksheet as a guide in gathering the characterizing data on Hedda Gabler from the drama and synthesizing her personality. Then, as a background for understanding Hedda's neurosis, make use of readings in psychology and mental health, among which the following may prove helpful: LYNDE C. STECKLE, *Problems of Human Adjustment* (rev. ed.; New York, Harper, 1954); LAWRENCE I. O'KELLY, *Introduction to Psychopathology* (New York, Prentice-Hall, 1949); KARL A. MENNINGER, *Man Against Himself* (New York, Harcourt, Brace, 1938), a study of suicide.

C. THE HEDDA RECORDS. Under the direction of Margaret Webster, Ibsen's complete drama, *Hedda Gabler,* has been recorded, with Eva Le Gallienne as Hedda, by Theater Masterworks. With book and pencil in hand, study the interpretation and also note any really different phrases in the translation.

AND FURTHER READING.

A. IBSEN THE MAN. Undertake the reading of one of the available studies of Ibsen and his work, such as GOSSE, MOSES, HELLER, KOHT, or JORGENSON (cited above)—or some other as suggested.

B. POETIC DRAMA. Read either IBSEN, *Peer Gynt* or *Brand* (vol. 3 or 4 in the *Collected Works*), together with the introduction to it by William Archer or C. H. Herford. The incidental music composed by Edward Grieg, for a production of *Peer Gynt* in 1886, is now more widely known than the poetic drama itself.

C. SOCIAL DRAMA. Read one of the following: Ibsen, *A Doll's House, Ghosts, An Enemy of the People, The Wild Duck,* or *Rosmersholm.* Inexpensive editions are available of the older translations: IBSEN, *Eleven Plays* (New York, Modern Library, 1935); *Ghosts, The Wild Duck, An Enemy of the People* (New York, Rinehart, 1948); and a new translation by UNA ELLIS-FERMOR, *Pillars of Society, The Wild Duck, Hedda Gabler* (Baltimore, Penguin Books, 1950).

D. SHAW ON IBSEN. Beginning in 1890, the year of *Hedda Gabler,* Bernard Shaw helped to popularize Ibsen in England and America. You may read with interest BERNARD SHAW, *The Quintessence of Ibsenism* (*op. cit.*), also the reviews of current Ibsen productions (1895–98) in BERNARD SHAW, *Dramatic Opinions and Essays* (2 vols.; New York, Brentano's, 1906).

V. *CANDIDA*—BY BERNARD SHAW

NOTES. Other English writers of comedy, who are Irish in one way or another, are William Congreve, George Farquhar, and Richard B. Sheridan. The authorized Shaw biography is ARCHIBALD HENDERSON, *Bernard Shaw, Playboy and Prophet* (New York, Appleton-Century-Crofts, 1932), which carries a heavy load of data. A highly personal and injudicious account is FRANK HARRIS, *Bernard Shaw, an unauthorized biography* (New York, Simon & Schuster, 1931), which was touched up and toned down by Shaw himself. Very readable and revealing is BERNARD SHAW, *Sixteen Self Sketches* (New York, Dodd, Mead, 1949). There is, of course, a vast critical literature: In addition to ERIC BENTLEY, *The Playwright as Thinker* (*op. cit.*) and the same author's *Bernard Shaw* (New York, New Directions, 1947), there are G. K. CHESTERTON, *George Bernard Shaw* (New York, John Lane, 1909), JAMES HUNEKER, *Iconoclasts* (rev. ed.; New York, Scribner, 1922), GASSNER, *Masters of the Drama* (*op. cit.*), CLARK and FREEDLEY, *History of Modern Drama* (*op. cit.*), and EDMUND FULLER, *George Bernard Shaw, Critic of Western Morale* (New York, Scribner, 1950). The plays are readily available: BERNARD SHAW, *Nine Plays* (New York, Dodd, Mead, 1935) and *Six* [different] *Plays* (Dodd, Mead, 1941); and *The Complete Plays* [up to that time!] (London, Constable, 1931). Inexpensive editions of individual plays, with the Prefaces: BERNARD SHAW, *Pygmalion, Caesar and Cleopatra, Major Barbara,* and *Saint Joan* (all Baltimore, Penguin Books, 1951). For theatrical data on American productions see, in addition to HENDERSON (*op. cit.*), the *Index to the Best Plays Series* (*op. cit.*) and the successive volumes of that invaluable record.

QUERIES. How do you account for the continued popularity of *Candida*? Is it a play with a burning social message? or a formula comedy merely warmed by good characterization and adorned by witty lines? What do you consider to be its comic values? What are the best acting roles? the best dramatic and theatrical scenes (incidents)? the best speeches and bits of dialogue?

How would you account for the fact that the play was at first considered by actors with an especial interest in Marchbanks, whereas today it is always considered to be Candida's play? Is there anything of interest in the fact that the first English performances were as an alternating play with Ibsen's *A Doll's House*?

When Hale says in his commentary: "Of course Mr. Shaw is one of the Marchbankses, but he is not entirely without sympathy for the Morells," what do you interpret him as meaning? What *is* the relation of Marchbanks to Shaw's personality and life experience as you understand and know them? What of their economic and social and personal adjustments, their literary enthusiasms, their vocations, their philosophies? On the other hand, what of Shaw's life do you find in Morell? What of their economic and social and personal adjustments, etc.? In calling Morell "a typical talker"—as distinct from "the original thinker"—is Hale implying that Shaw, too, is unoriginal in his ideas, one of those who "having no notion of just what they can do, they take it out in talking"? Was Shaw, through the years, one of those, like Morell, whom people heeded and followed "because they do like them and do not have to understand them"?

What are the two dramatic patterns in which Eric Bentley says the story of Candida might have been written? What is the Augier play? the Dumas play? What does Bentley mean when he says: "In *Candida* Shaw shows all the truth there is in the Augier philosophy and all the truth there is in the Dumas philosophy"? What is each of these? What, in Bentley's view as here excerpted, is Shaw's dramatic pattern and philosophy for *Candida*?

What does Bentley mean in saying, "Candida is not simply a bad woman"? What might Beatrice Webb (wife of Sidney Webb, socialist friends of Shaw) have meant in saying that Candida was "a sentimental prostitute"? (Quoted in HENDERSON, *op. cit.*, p. 478n.) What is your own judgment of how she behaves toward both Morell and Marchbanks?

What in Hale's commentary "dates" it as contemporary with *Candida's* production in America? What in Bentley's commentary "dates" it as contemporary with us today?

SUGGESTIONS FOR STUDY.

A. THE POET'S SECRET. The closing stage direction ends: "But they do not know the secret in the poet's heart." Is this merely a literary gesture? (After all, no audience ever sees the directions in the playscript.) Could the actor of Marchbanks in any way convey such an idea to the audience? For the reader of *Candida* as a drama this sentence may be important. What *is* the secret in the poet's heart as he leaves? (*a*) Study the Marchbanks and Candida lines in the closing scene very closely, and then hypothesize an answer. (*b*) Search out a number of interpretations of this formerly much-discussed question—not the least interesting of which is Shaw's.

B. CRITICAL NOTIONS. Read JAMES HUNEKER, "The Truth about Shaw," *Metropolitan Magazine,* XX (1904), 635, or JAMES HUNEKER, *Iconoclasts* (*op. cit.*), pp. 233-268, for one critic's views of the play. Shaw's letter to Huneker about *Candida* is quoted in BENTLEY, *The Playwright as Thinker* (*op. cit.*), pp. 349-50. Read also the critical views of EDMUND FULLER, *George Bernard Shaw* (*op. cit.*), pp. 25-29. Compare these with the two commentaries reprinted in this book as the basis for your own fuller understanding of the characters and the play.

C. COMPARING PLAYS. To sharpen your study of Shaw as a dramatist, read two plays for comparison: SHAW, *Caesar and Cleopatra* (*op. cit.*) and SHAKESPEARE, *Antony and Cleopatra* or JOHN DRYDEN, *All for Love,* and compare and contrast them from a variety of standpoints. Or read SHAW, *Saint Joan* (*op. cit.*) and MAXWELL ANDERSON, *Joan of Lorraine* (Washington, Anderson House, 1946) as the basis for making a similar study of Shaw's dramaturgy and thought. Or read IBSEN, *A Doll's House* (*op. cit.*) and compare it with *Candida*.

AND FURTHER READING.

A. SHAW THE MAN. Read BERNARD SHAW, *Sixteen Self Sketches* (*op. cit.*) or, with caution, FRANK HARRIS, *Bernard Shaw* (*op. cit.*) with a view to catching something of the spirit of the Shaw personality. Or, using earlier volumes of *Readers' Guide* find half a dozen magazine articles about Shaw, interviews with pictures, etc. Or read HESKETH PEARSON, *G. B. S.: a Full-length Portrait* (New York, Harper, 1942).

B. SHAVIAN DRAMA. Read further among Shaw's early comedies: *Arms and the Man, The Devil's Disciple, Major Barbara, Pygmalion,* or *Androcles and the Lion.* Or read *Man and Superman*—the dream interlude, "Don Juan in Hell," has been recorded as read by the First Drama Quartet: Charles Boyer, Charles Laughton, Sir Cedric Hardwicke, and Agnes Moorhead (Columbia Masterworks SL 166, ML 4611)—and "The Revolutionist's Handbook" at the end of the volume.

C. SHAVIAN PROSE. Read further in the nondramatic works of BERNARD SHAW, *Selected Prose,* ed. Diarmuid Russell (New York, Dodd, Mead, 1952), or *Dramatic Opinions and Essays* (*op. cit.*), or Prefaces to various volumes of his plays, or ELLEN TERRY and BERNARD SHAW, *A Correspondence,* ed. [Miss] Christopher St. John (New York, Putnam, 1931), or BERNARD SHAW and MRS. PATRICK CAMPBELL, *Their Correspondence* (New York, Knopf, 1952).

VI. *LIFE WITH FATHER*—BY LINDSAY AND CROUSE

NOTES. The year *Life with Father* was produced was notable in the American theater, with such different and successful comedies as KAUFMAN and HART, *The Man Who Came to Dinner,* and THURBER and NUGENT, *The Male Animal,* with the promising WILLIAM SAROYAN, *The Time of Your Life* (winning both the prizes), and with dramas reflecting the opening of World War II: ROBERT E. SHERWOOD, *There Shall Be No Night,* and CLARE BOOTHE [Luce], *Margin for Error.*

For biographical data on Clarence Day, Jr., see KUNITZ and HAYCRAFT, *Twentieth Century Authors* (*op. cit.*), and the collected autobiographical sketches, CLARENCE DAY, *Life with Father and Mother, including God and My Father* (New York, Knopf, 1943). For Howard Lindsay and Russel Crouse, see *Current Biography* (1942 and 1941), also *Who's Who in America* (1954-1955) and *Life* magazine, XXI (Nov. 11, 1946), 116-18. The theatrical data are, again, to be found in BURNS MANTLE, *Best Plays of 1939-1940* (*op. cit.*) and the following volumes. For brief critical excerpts, see *Book Review Digest* (1940); for a further listing of reviews and dramatic criticism, see *Readers' Guide to Periodical Literature;* for the moving picture listing, see *Catalog of Copyright Entries, Motion Pictures, 1940-1949;* for a listing of cinema reviews, see *Readers' Guide* under "moving picture plays"; for newspaper reviews, reprinted, see the *New York Theater Critics' Reviews,* I (1940), 457-59.

The playbook, HOWARD LINDSAY and RUSSEL CROUSE, *Clarence Day's Life with Father, made into a play* . . . with an Introduction by Brooks Atkinson (New York, Knopf, 1940). In CLARK and FREEDLEY, *A History of Modern Drama* (*op. cit.*), p. 738, Clark writes of *Life with Father* as "one of the few plays that may be thought of as an American theater classic."

QUERIES. What is it in *Life with Father* that "belongs" to the late 1880's or, say, 1891, when Clarence Jr. was seventeen? Does the period seem the same as that of *Hedda Gabler* (1890) and of *Candida* (1894)? In what ways is Mother comparable to and different from Candida? and Nora in *A Doll's*

House (if you have read it)? What are some of the "period" items in the setting and costumes? in the characters and family pattern? in the situations and incidents? in the dialogue and diction?

Why does Henry S. Canby say that "this play . . . could never have been written in the nineteenth century"? What in the humor and the underlying philosophy show it to be an expression of the 1930's? In what ways does the portrayal of Father "belong" to the Depression decade? What are specific touches in *Life with Father* that date it as an expression of the late 1930's?

What sorts of things in this comedy are apparently timeless, as true today as in 1939 or 1891?

What are the sure-fire comic effects, certain to make an audience laugh or a reader smile? Which comic effects result from wit or humor in the lines as such? Which are dependent upon situations and incidents? Which come from character traits and characterization?

Is Father the protagonist? Does he evoke our sympathetic interest? As *Life with Father* is obviously a comedy, would you not expect the protagonist to win out in the conflicts in which he is engaged? But does Father finally triumph? What are some of "these final decisions," as Krutch calls them, "which mother so quietly revised"? If "Father, in the home, is always defeated by Mother," as Canby points out, what keeps the play from being a sort of comic tragedy, chronicling the losing struggle of a strong (if imperfect) personality opposed by overwhelming forces arrayed against him?

SUGGESTIONS FOR STUDY.

A. THE PLOT LINE. Review the discussion of action, plot, and dramatic construction (see page 32). Then make use of the Plot Analysis outline worksheet as an aid in patterning the action of *Life with Father*. Granted that this comedy is one of character and of incident rather than one of plot, yet the play will be held together in the experience of most people by a story framework. The question of protagonist and antagonist, then, is not merely an academic one here. As in *Othello,* it is crucial as regards the pattern of the play for you. Is Father, dynamic as he is, an almost powerless protagonist? Or is it Mother who, in her irrational round-about way, shapes the course of the action? And what of Clarence? Is the little love story thrown in for mere theatrical effect? Or is it an integral part of the whole action? Work out, finally, a narrative summary that will serve to give form and structure to your experience of the play as a whole.

B. THE COMEDY LINE. Review the remarks on comedy (pages 135-38) and do some additional reading in such a book as WILLARD SMITH, *The Nature of Comedy* (*op. cit.*). Then proceed to a close analysis of some one scene from *Life with Father*. Mark the places where you think an audience would be amused, and indicate (by some system of symbols) the degree of laughter response you think would be evoked. Consider now what would cause the laughter in each case. Your discussion of these judgments with another person who has studied the same scene independently may be illuminating.

C. REVIEW OF REVIEWS. Use the *New York Theater Critics' Reviews* (*op. cit.*), reading the newspaper reviews of *Life with Father*. Then, through *Readers' Guide,* find a number of the magazine reviews of the play. What generalizations can you make? Is the critical quality of the reviews in newspapers different from that of the weekly journals?

AND FURTHER READING.

A. God and Father. The Clarence Day sketches, first to appear as a book, were called *God and My Father* (1932). Read this slim volume, or the section so called in the collected edition, with an eye to seeing what Lindsay and Crouse did with their material. It would be a more ambitious undertaking to make a comprehensive study of the relation of the comedy to its source.

B. Mother, Too. You might like to read LINDSAY and CROUSE, *Life with Mother* (New York, Knopf, 1949), and to consider some of the special problems posed by the writing of a sequel to a popular work. Why do you think that it is less successful than *Father*? What did the dramatic critics have to say about it?

C. The Union. In many ways, LINDSAY and CROUSE, *State of the Union* (New York, Random House, 1946) is their most ambitious work. You may wish to make a study of its themes and meaning as you read it carefully. Does it seem to you to have any significant relation to *Life with Father*?

VII. *THE GLASS MENAGERIE*—BY TENNESSEE WILLIAMS

NOTES. MORDECAI GORELIK, *New Theaters for Old* (*op. cit.*, p. 27) wrote in 1940: "If . . . the production method of today is illusory [realistic or naturalistic, see page 140, above], it may be that the production method of tomorrow will be non-illusory. It may be that dramatic form right now is starting on one of its historic transitions toward a new goal, leaving the era of Maxwell Anderson and Noel Coward behind it as a memory." See also the paragraph on contemporary drama on page 132, above.

Biographical data on Tennessee Williams are found in *Current Biography* (1946) and in *Who's Who in America* (1954-1955). PAUL MOOR, "A Mississippian Named Tennessee," *Harper's*, CXXXVII (July, 1948), 63-71, writes on the basis of personal acquaintance. See also JOHN GASSNER, Introduction to *The Glass Menagerie* in *Treasury of the Theater* (rev. ed.; New York, Simon & Schuster, 1950) and "Tennessee Williams: Dramatist of Frustration," *College English*, X (October 1948), 1-7; and NORRIS HOUGHTON, "Tomorrow Arrives Today," *Theatre Arts*, XXX (February 1946), 85-86.

A few references in *The Glass Menagerie* may call for notes. *Guernica:* a Basque town in northern Spain which, bombed by Franco with German planes during the Civil War, became a symbol among liberals of fascist ruthlessness. *Berchtesgaden:* the mountain-top retreat of Hitler, where he dreamed destruction of democracy. *Chamberlain's umbrella:* always carried by Neville Chamberlain, the elderly Conservative prime minister of England before World War II, a symbol of appeasement. *Ole Dizzy Dean:* brilliant pitcher for the St. Louis Cardinals, who suffered a shoulder injury. *Century of Progress;* Chicago World's Fair, 1933.

PRODUCTION NOTES by TENNESSEE WILLIAMS

Being a "memory play," The Glass Menagerie can be presented with unusual freedom of convention. Because of its considerably delicate or tenuous material, atmospheric touches and subtleties of direction play a particularly im-

portant part. Expressionism and all other unconventional techniques in drama have only one valid aim, and that is a closer approach to truth. When a play employs unconventional techniques, it is not, or certainly shouldn't be, trying to escape its responsibility of dealing with reality, or interpreting experience, but is actually or should be attempting to find a closer approach, a more penetrating and vivid expression of things as they are. The straight realistic play with its genuine frigidaire and authentic ice-cubes, its characters that speak exactly as its audience speaks, corresponds to the academic landscape and has the same virtue of a photographic likeness. Everyone should know nowadays the unimportance of the photographic in art: that truth, life, or reality is an organic thing which the poetic imagination can represent or suggest, in essence, only through transformation, through changing into other forms than those which were merely present in appearance.

These remarks are not meant as a preface only to this particular play. They have to do with a conception of a new, plastic theatre which must take the place of the exhausted theatre of realistic conventions if the theatre is to resume vitality as a part of our culture.

THE SCREEN DEVICE. *There is* only one important difference between the original and acting version of the play *and that is the* omission *in the latter of the device which I tentatively included in my* original *script. This device was the use of a screen on which were projected magic-lantern slides bearing images or titles. I do not regret the omission of this device from the present Broadway production. The extraordinary power of Miss Taylor's performance made it suitable to have the utmost simplicity in the physical production. But I think it may be interesting to some readers to see how this device was conceived. So I am putting it into the published manuscript. These images and legends, projected from behind, were cast on a section of wall between the front-room and dining-room areas, which should be indistinguishable from the rest when not in use.*

The purpose of this will probably be apparent. It is to give accent to certain values in each scene. Each scene contains a particular point (or several) which is structurally the most important. In an episodic play, such as this, the basic structure or narrative line may be obscured from the audience; the effect may seem fragmentary rather than architectural. This may not be the fault of the play so much as a lack of attention in the audience. The legend or image upon the screen will strengthen the effect of what is merely allusion in the writing and allow the primary point to be made more simply and lightly than if the entire responsibility were on the spoken lines. Aside from this structural value, I think the screen will have a definite emotional appeal, less definable but just as important. An imaginative producer or director may invent many other uses for this device than those indicated in the present script. In fact the possibilities of the device seem much larger to me than the instance of this play can possibly utilize.

THE MUSIC. *Another extra-literary accent in this play is provided by the use of music.. A single recurring tune, "The Glass Menagerie," is used to give emotional emphasis to suitable passages. This tune is like circus music, not when you are on the grounds or in the immediate vicinity of the parade, but when you are at some distance and very likely thinking of something else.*

It seems under those circumstances to continue almost interminably and it weaves in and out of your preoccupied consciousness; then it is the lightest, most delicate music in the world and perhaps the saddest. It expresses the surface vivacity of life with the underlying strain of immutable and inexpressible sorrow. When you look at a piece of delicately spun glass you think of two things: how beautiful it is and how easily it can be broken. Both of those ideas should be woven into the recurring tune, which dips in and out of the play as if it were carried on a wind that changes. It serves as a thread of connection and allusion between the narrator with his separate point in time and space and the subject of his story. Between each episode it returns as reference to the emotion, nostalgia, which is the first condition of the play. It is primarily Laura's music and therefore comes out most clearly when the play focuses upon her and the lovely fragility of glass which is her image.

THE LIGHTING. *The lighting in the play is not realistic. In keeping with the atmosphere of memory, the stage is dim. Shafts of light are focused on selected areas or actors, sometimes in contradistinction to what is the apparent center. For instance, in the quarrel scene between Tom and Amanda, in which Laura has no active part, the clearest pool of light is on her figure. This is also true of the supper scene, when her silent figure on the sofa should remain the visual center. The light upon Laura should be distinct from the others, having a peculiar pristine clarity such as light used in early religious portraits of female saints or madonnas. A certain correspondence to light in religious paintings, such as El Greco's, where the figures are radiant in atmosphere that is relatively dusky, could be effectively used throughout the play. (It will also permit a more effective use of the screen.) A free, imaginative use of light can be of enormous value in giving a mobile, plastic quality to plays of a more or less static nature.*

T. W.

QUERIES. What are the autobiographical elements in *The Glass Menagerie?* In the character and life experiences of Tom? in the environment? in the family? Is a drama any more "true" simply because (in your knowledge) it has grown out of the playwright's personal experience?

What is the difference between Williams' use of the narrator and Thornton Wilder's in *The Happy Journey?* in *Our Town* (if you have read it)? Do you know of any other uses of the device?

What other nonrealistic devices are part of Williams' dramaturgy in this play? Which ones seem to you to be merely theatrical tricks? Which ones do you think most effective in giving the drama its unique quality?

Which do you consider the more important symbols in the drama? Laura's limp, the father's picture, the movies, the victrola, the typewriter, the glass animals (especially the unicorn, the horn, and the result of its being broken off), Jim, the storm, the candles? What different meanings do these symbols have for Laura, for Tom, and for Amanda?

SUGGESTIONS FOR STUDY.

A. THE PRODUCTION NOTES. Make a close study of the above Notes by TENNESSEE WILLIAMS, which he printed with *The Glass Menagerie.* Take into account the quotation of MORDECAI GORELIK (above) and also the commentary of JOHN GASSNER following the text of the play.

B. VARIETY OF OPINIONS. Read the newspaper reviews of *The Glass Menagerie* in the *New York Theater Critics' Reviews,* VI (1945), 234-37. Then search out other dramatic criticism, using *Readers' Guide.* Generalize upon the audience response to the production as revealed by these various opinions.

C. SYMBOLISM. In line with the Queries above, make a systematic study of Tennessee Williams' use of symbols in *The Glass Menagerie.*

AND FURTHER READING.

A. THE WILLIAMS PERSONALITY. Use the biographical references cited above in the Notes as the basis for further study of Tennessee Williams. Other items: WILLIAMS, "The Catastrophe of Success," in *The Glass Menagerie* (New Classics ed.; New York, New Directions, 1949) and ALAN S. DOWNER, "Mr. Williams and Mr. Miller," in *Furioso* (summer, 1949). Find more recent items through *Readers' Guide.*

B. STREETCAR AND SUMMER. Read another drama: TENNESSEE WILLIAMS, *A Streetcar Named Desire* (New York, New Directions, 1947), or *Summer and Smoke* (New York, New Directions, 1948). Both are also available in JOHN GASSNER (ed.), *Best American Plays, Third Series, 1945-1951* (New York, Crown, 1952).

C. OTHER WILLIAMS. Read further in TENNESSEE WILLIAMS, finding some of his one-act plays, his short stories, his poetry mentioned in the Introductory Note.

VIII. *THE CRUCIBLE*—BY ARTHUR MILLER

NOTES. Biographical material on Arthur Miller—as usual with contemporary figures—is found scattered in *Current Biography* (1947), *Who's Who in America* (1954-1955), brief paragraphs in volumes of *The Best Plays* series, various introductions to his plays, magazine articles, and newspaper stories. Miller wrote an interesting article for the New York *Times* (February 8, 1953) on his research trip to Salem. The controversy with the Bar Association is reported in the *Times* (March 9, 1953); Miller's reply followed and letters about the play by various persons (see New York *Times* Index). Of special interest regarding *The Crucible* is the interview with Miller and the director, Jed Harris, prior to the play's out-of-town opening: LEWIS FUNKE, "Thoughts on a Train Bound for Wilmington," New York *Times,* January 18, 1953, Sec. 2, pp. 1, 3, from which comes the first of the three quotations from Miller in the Introductory Note. Another interview with Miller about *The Crucible:* HENRY HEWES, "Arthur Miller and How He Went to the Devil," *Saturday Review,* XXXVI (January 31, 1953), 24-26, whence the second Miller quotation. A later interview: JOHN and ALICE GRIFFIN, "Arthur Miller Discusses *The Crucible,*" *Theatre Arts,* XXXVII (October, 1953), 33-34, from which the third Miller quotation. The publication of the play: ARTHUR MILLER, *The Crucible* (New York, Viking, 1953). The new scene he wrote for it is included in the version printed in *Theatre Arts,* XXXVII (October, 1953). In addition to the BROOKS ATKINSON commentary (New York *Times,* February 1, 1953) reprinted in part in this book, he wrote an earlier review of *The Crucible* (New York *Times,* January 23/24, 1954) and a later review

(New York *Times,* July 2, 1953). Again, for the theatrical data, see *The Best Plays* series.

DOCUMENTATION AND DISCUSSION by ARTHUR MILLER, two selections
from the prose commentary published as part of *The Crucible.*

. . . But the people of Salem in 1692 were not quite the dedicated folk that arrived on the Mayflower. *A vast differentiation had taken place, and in their own time a revolution had unseated the royal government and substituted a junta which was at this moment in power. The times, to their eyes, must have been out of joint, and to the common folk must have seemed as insoluble and complicated as do ours today. It is not hard to see how easily many could have been led to believe that the time of confusion had been brought upon them by deep and darkling forces. No hint of such speculation appears on the court record, but social disorder in any age breeds such mystical suspicions, and when, as in Salem, wonders are brought forth from below the social surface, it is too much to expect people to hold back very long from laying on the victims with all the force of their frustrations.*

The Salem tragedy, which is about to begin in these pages, developed from a paradox. It is a paradox in whose grip we still live, and there is no prospect yet that we will discover its resolution. Simply, it was this: for good purposes, even high purposes, the people of Salem developed a theocracy, a combine of state and religious power whose function was to keep the community together, and to prevent any kind of disunity that might open it to destruction by material or ideological enemies. It was forged for a necessary purpose and accomplished that purpose. But all organization is and must be grounded on the idea of exclusion and prohibition, just as two objects cannot occupy the same space. Evidently the time came in New England when the repressions of order were heavier than seemed warranted by the dangers against which the order was organized. The witch-hunt was a perverse manifestation of the panic which set in among all classes when the balance began to turn toward greater individual freedom.

When one rises above the individual villainy displayed, one can only pity them all, just as we shall be pitied someday. It is still impossible for man to organize his social life without repressions, and the balance has yet to be struck between order and freedom.

The witch-hunt was not, however, a mere repression. It was also, and as importantly, a long overdue opportunity for everyone so inclined to express publicly his guilt and sins, under the cover of accusations against the victims. It suddenly became possible—and patriotic and holy—for a man to say that Martha Corey had come into his bedroom at night, and that, while his wife was sleeping at his side, Martha laid herself down on his chest and "nearly suffocated him." Of course it was her spirit only, but his satisfaction at confessing himself was no lighter than if it had been Martha herself. One could not ordinarily speak such things in public.

Long-held hatreds of neighbors could now be openly expressed, and vengeance taken, despite the Bible's charitable injunctions. Land-lust which had been expressed before by constant bickering over boundaries and deeds, could now be elevated to the arena of morality; one could cry witch against one's neighbor and feel perfectly justified in the bargain. Old scores could be

settled on a plane of heavenly combat between Lucifer and the Lord; sus-
picions and the envy of the miserable toward the happy could and did burst
out in the general revenge. . . . (pp. 6-8)

. . . Like Reverend Hale and the others on this stage, we conceive the Devil
as a necessary part of a respectable view of cosmology. Ours is a divided
empire in which certain ideas and emotions and actions are of God, and their
opposites are of Lucifer. It is as impossible for most men to conceive of a
morality without sin as of an earth without "sky." Since 1692 a great but
superficial change has wiped out God's beard and the Devil's horns, but the
world is still gripped between two diametrically opposed absolutes. The con-
cept of unity, in which positive and negative are attributes of the same force,
in which good and evil are relative, ever-changing, and always joined to the
same phenomenon—such a concept is still reserved to the physical sciences
and to the few who have grasped the history of ideas. When it is recalled that
until the Christian era the underworld was never regarded as a hostile area,
that all gods were useful and essentially friendly to man despite occasional
lapses; when we see the steady and methodical inculcation into humanity of
the idea of man's worthlessness—until redeemed—the necessity of the Devil
may become evident as a weapon, a weapon designed and used time and time
again in every age to whip men into a surrender to a particular church or
church-state.

Our difficulty in believing the—for want of a better word—political inspira-
tion of the Devil is due in great part to the fact that he is called up and
damned not only by our social antagonists but by our own side, whatever it
may be. The Catholic Church, through its Inquisition, is famous for cultivat-
ing Lucifer as the arch-fiend, but the Church's enemies relied no less upon the
Old Boy to keep the human mind enthralled. Luther was himself accused of
alliance with Hell, and he in turn accused his enemies. To complicate matters
further, he believed that he had had contact with the Devil and had argued
theology with him. I am not surprised at this, for at my own university a
professor of history—a Lutheran, by the way—used to assemble his graduate
students, draw the shades, and commune in the classroom with Erasmus.
He was never, to my knowledge, officially scoffed at for this, the reason being
that the university officials, like most of us, are the children of a history which
still sucks at the Devil's teats. At this writing, only England has held back
before the temptations of contemporary diabolism. In the countries of the
Communist ideology, all resistance of any import is linked to the totally
malign capitalist succubi, and in America any man who is not reactionary in
his views is open to the charge of alliance with the Red hell. Political opposi-
tion, thereby, is given an inhumane overlay which then justifies the abrogation
of all normally applied customs of civilized intercourse. A political policy is
equated with moral right, and opposition to it with diabolical malevolence.
Once such an equation is effectively made, society becomes a congeries of plots
and counterplots, and the main role of government changes from that of the
arbiter to that of the scourge of God. . . . (pp. 33-34)

QUERIES. In which one of the historic styles (see page 138) is *The
Crucible* conceived and written? What are the specific evidences of this in
the plot? in the characters? in the dialogue?

What, for you, are the various themes of the play? What does the title mean? Might you have overlooked what Atkinson speaks of (New York *Times,* July 2, 1953) as the "drama about a man and woman whose devotion to each other is haunted by the memory of an infidelity"?

What seems to be the difference in view between George Jean Nathan (as expressed in the commentary) and Arthur Miller (as quoted in the Introductory Note) in regard to the theme of the drama?

What are the contemporary parallels that Miller had in mind? Can you cite parallels from other periods of history? from other contemporary instances? Is the drama meaningful only as a social and political document? What are the human and dramatic values above or beyond the question of its immediacy?

SUGGESTIONS FOR STUDY.

A. SALEM AND HISTORY. Undertake some historical study of the Salem witch-hunts. A recent work: MARION L. STARKEY, *The Devil in Massachusetts* (New York, Knopf, 1949). Look up Salem in two or three standard histories. Read the complete prose documentation and discussion by ARTHUR MILLER in the published playbook (*op. cit.*), also reprinted in *Theatre Arts,* XXXVII (October, 1953). Consider now the historicity of *The Crucible.* For an adverse comment see *School and Society,* LXXVII (March, 1953), 185-86.

B. CRUCIBLE AND CRITICS. Using the *New York Theater Critics' Reviews,* the *Book Review Digest,* and dramatic criticism listed in *Readers' Guide,* study the fate of *The Crucible* at the hands of the critics.

C. MILLER'S VIEWS. Using the sources cited above in the Notes and the prose commentary published with the play, study Miller's intent as a playwright in writing *The Crucible.*

AND FURTHER READING.

A. MILLER THE MAN. Using the sources cited above in the Notes, and further as listed in *Readers' Guide,* read further about Arthur Miller, his life and personality.

B. SONS AND SALESMAN. Read ARTHUR MILLER, *All My Sons* (New York, Reynal & Hitchcock, 1947) or his *Death of a Salesman* (New York, Viking, 1949; a special edition, Bantam, 1951). Consider, then, the relation of the play to *The Crucible.*

C. NONDRAMATIC MILLER. Read ARTHUR MILLER, *Situation Normal* (New York, Reynal & Hitchcock, 1944) or *Focus* (New York, Reynal & Hitchcock, 1945). What relation does the work bear to *The Crucible?*

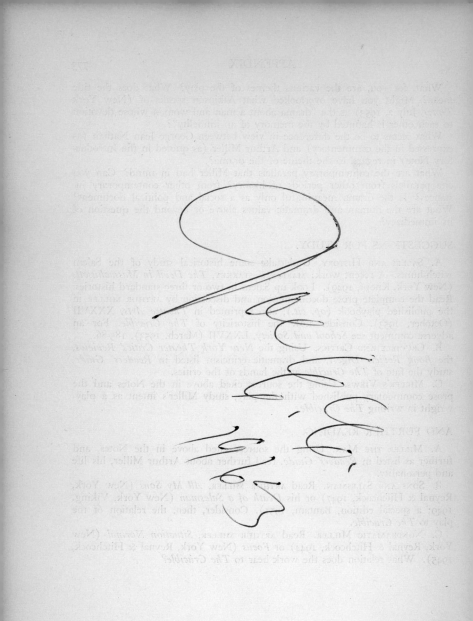

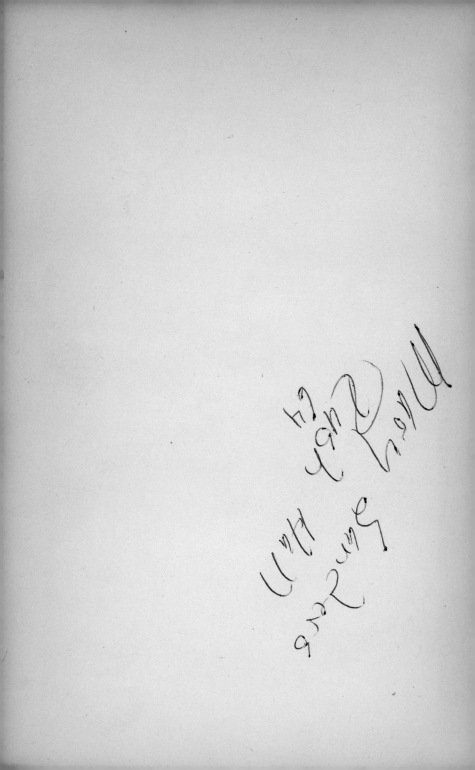